Aggression in Global Perspective
(PGPS-115)

Pergamon Titles of Related Interest

Alexander/Gleason BEHAVIORAL AND QUANTITATIVE
PERSPECTIVES ON TERRORISM
Center for Research on Aggression PREVENTION AND CONTROL
OF AGGRESSION
Goldstein/Carr/Davidson/Wehr IN RESPONSE TO AGGRESSION
Miron/Goldstein HOSTAGE
Rapoport/Alexander THE MORALITY OF TERRORISM

Related Journals*

INTERNATIONAL JOURNAL OF INTERCULTURAL RELATIONS
INTERNATIONAL JOURNAL OF LAW AND PSYCHIATRY
JOURNAL OF CRIMINAL JUSTICE

*Free specimen copies available upon request.

PERGAMON GENERAL PSYCHOLOGY SERIES
EDITORS
Arnold P. Goldstein, *Syracuse University*
Leonard Krasner, *SUNY at Stony Brook*

Aggression in Global Perspective

edited by

Arnold P. Goldstein
Marshall H. Segall

Center for Research on Aggression
Syracuse University

PERGAMON PRESS
New York   Oxford   Toronto   Sydney   Paris   Frankfurt

Pergamon Press Offices:

U.S.A.   Pergamon Press Inc., Maxwell House, Fairview Park,
                     Elmsford, New York 10523, U.S.A.

U.K.   Pergamon Press Ltd., Headington Hill Hall,
                     Oxford OX3 0BW, England

CANADA   Pergamon Press Canada Ltd., Suite 104, 150 Consumers Road,
                     Willowdale, Ontario M2J 1P9, Canada

AUSTRALIA   Pergamon Press (Aust.) Pty. Ltd., P.O. Box 544,
                     Potts Point, NSW 2011, Australia

FRANCE   Pergamon Press SARL, 24 rue des Ecoles,
                     75240 Paris, Cedex 05, France

FEDERAL REPUBLIC Pergamon Press GmbH, Hammerweg 6,
OF GERMANY   D-6242 Kronberg-Taunus, Federal Republic of Germany

Library of Congress Cataloging in Publication Data
Main entry under title:

Aggression in global perspective.

   (Pergamon general psychology series ; 115)
   Includes index.
   1. Aggressiveness (Psychology)--Cross-cultural
studies. I. Goldstein, Arnold P. II. Segall,
Marshall H. III. Series.
BF575.A3A52   1982   302.5′4   82-10131
ISBN 0-08-026346-1   AACR2

Printed in the United States of America

Contents

v

Preface

Aggression in its diverse individuals and collective forms has long been, and remains, a world-wide problem of the first magnitude. When viewed in global perspective, contemporary aggression takes many guises—violence and vandalism by juveniles in schools and in their communities; child and spouse abuse and other forms of domestic or familial violence; assaults, muggings, and homicides; rape and other sex-related crimes; politically-motivated terrorism; racially- or economically-motivated mob violence; and aggression in many forms directly or indirectly initiated by the state. As the chapters which follow will make clear, this is far from an exhaustive list. We could add athletic mayhem, clan blood feuds, ritual torture, police brutality, organized warfare, and much, much more. The variety, intensity, frequency, and overall prevalence of overt aggressive behavior throughout the world is starkly and appallingly high.

This book was initiated, organized, and written in direct response to this state of affairs, to this unremittingly high level of global aggression. Our specific purposes are several. The chapters which follow describe contemporary manifestations of aggression in a large number of nations representing almost the entire world. These descriptions are placed in a cultural context, thus helping us understand why, for the given country or region, aggression currently assumes particular forms, rates, and intensities. Such contextual information is also utilized in most of the ensuing chapter to aid in understanding how aggression "fits in" or is conceptualized in each nation's stream of daily living. Each chapter author was also charged by us to deal similarly with his or her society's efforts to control aggression, and to promote prosocial alternatives to aggression. How is it done? When and why does it succeed or fail? What additional controls and alternatives might lie ahead for each nation or region?

Topics such as these, addressed by most of this volume's contributors, enabled us to devote our introductory chapter to comparative cross-cultural efforts. Here we seek to draw upon these individual cultural perspectives on aggression, aggression control, and aggression alternatives to offer a more unified, global perspective. We compare, contrast, distill differences and similarities, put forth what we feel we may optimally learn from one another, and suggest specific directions for future research and applied efforts at better understanding of aggression, more effectively controlling it, and more successfully enhancing its prosocial counterparts.

A prefatory comment seems appropriate from us regarding our bases for selecting the nations represented in this book, as well as the particular social or behavioral scientists who wrote its chapters. Our goal in country selection, as this book's title makes clear, was truly global representation. All major areas of the world were to be included. Our efforts toward this end were especially energetic and persistent and, while we were largely successful, two important areas are not represented in this book. We feel this absence keenly, as our goal was truly total and comprehensive representation, and our diverse efforts toward this end were protracted and very considerable. It is, perhaps, a significant cross-cultural statement itself that, in spite of these diverse efforts, no Soviet or Arab social or behavioral scientist felt able or willing to join us. We are both saddened and chagrined at this state of affairs, and can only hope that the future will bring more open international scientific communication, especially about such volatile topics as aggression, its control, and its alternatives.

The chapter authors are noted scientists and authors on the topic of aggression. They were recommended to us via their writings, their involvement in such organizations as the International Society for Research on Aggression, and their high standing in the global community of scientists. Collectively, they constitute a distinguished, expert panel of knowledgeable scientists. We are delighted with their participation.

Our goal has been to organize and offer a book which presents both an elucidating and a utilitarian picture of aggression in global perspective: elucidating, in that it serves to help deepen our understanding of the meaning and nature of aggression throughout the world; utilitarian, in that its companion focus on aggression controls and alternatives in global perspective actually functions to aid the constructive, prosocial, anti-aggression efforts which do exist, or might exist, to more readily and more fully succeed.

Arnold P. Goldstein
Marshall H. Segall

Aggression in Global Perspective
(PGPS-115)

1

Aggression in Global Perspective:
A Research Strategy

Marshall H. Segall

INTRODUCTION: THE RESEARCH OBJECTIVE
AND STRATEGY

The thrust of the research to be described in this volume is to understand why humans behave aggressively and violently. That they do is beyond doubt. That they do so to different degrees, in different manners, and for a variety of different reasons is also clear, as all of the contributions to this volume illustrate. At the same time, there are doubtless some universal features of human aggression, as these same contributions also show. The pancultural similarities *and* the cross-cultural differences in aggressive behavior together comprise the puzzle on which we and our international collaborators are working.

The chapters which they have contributed, plus our own account of aggression in the United States, are, in a sense, the puzzle pieces. Assembling them into a more or less coherent picture is the ultimate objective of the research effort in which we are all engaged. The picture we are aiming for in this book cannot possibly be the definitive picture of human aggression in global perspective. That, obviously, must await more information than is presently available to us. But, as the eighteen chapters which follow this one show, there is more than enough to prompt us to make a first pass at the picture. We do so with the hope that the sketch which results will reflect reality at least in broad outline.

As the reader will discover, it is not easy to digest and merge all the information contained in the accounts of aggression in the 18 different settings covered in this volume. While each is a case that is interesting in its own right, case accounts are raw data in the context of our real objective. They need to be compared and contrasted and examined as a collectivity in an effort to glean whatever generalizations, however tentative, they might support.

They must also be compared with the works of those earlier students of aggression who share our ultimate goal and who have assembled their own tentative pictures. Especially noteworthy, in this regard, are the social scientists, including anthropologists, political scientists, and cross-cultural psychologists whose research orientation, like ours, is comparative. What they have learned must be set down here next to what we have learned and all of it must be viewed as a whole. Their pieces and our pieces are all part of the same puzzle. We will, therefore, gather in as many pieces that seem to be a part of the puzzle before we attempt our tentative solutions.

A Methodological Preamble

But first, a word about our general strategy for a continuing research program in which the present volume comprises a first step. What we will try to do is identify as many as possible of the various factors in the natural and man-made environments of humans which might influence, in reliable ways, their behaviors relating to conflict, aggression, and violence. These ecocultural factors we consider to comprise the context in which such behaviors occur. We recognize that these factors are distributed in a dazzling variety of ways across human habitats and that they include features of the habitats themselves (e.g., climate and terrain) plus many other factors (e.g., economic systems, political structures, and socialization practices), some correlated with environmental features and some which cut across them. In our overall research strategy, this large set of ecocultural, contextual factors, singly, in combination, and very likely in interaction with each other, comprise our independent variables.

But which ones of the seemingly endless list of independent variables deserve our attention? How do we choose them; how do we even commence the search? We find compelling, and we accept, the advice of Robert LeVine, a psychological anthropologist.

> Research into causal relations can begin with dependent or independent variables. . . . Starting with independent variables entails the risk that their effects will turn out to be trivial, irrelevant, or otherwise uninteresting according to the criteria by which the scientist evaluates his research. . . . Beginning with dependent variables guarantees the scientist that his efforts will be directed toward explaining a phenomenon he considers important or interesting. This could be thought of as the etiological approach, in which a well documented variation of definite interest to the investigator and perhaps broader social significance poses an explanatory problem for research, that is, a search of causes. [LeVine, 1970, pp. 565–566]

The enterprise we are engaged in is an etiological approach, a search for causes of aggression. But to make that search worth commencing, we must have differences in aggressive behavior that require explanation. Unless we have differences in the ways human beings who happen to be scattered around the world react when confronted by a situation that might make some frustrated, some angry, or some pugnacious, then we don't have a problem in the sense that LeVine, and we following him, understand *problem*. By the same token, whenever such a difference has been documented, our work has just begun; then must commence the search for the operative independent variables.

To begin, then, we need differences. Yet, the real goal of the enterprise is to emerge with universals. There is no paradox here, since the differences we refer to are *behavioral* differences, while the universals we seek are *principles,* or laws, that explain that behavior whenever it occurs. In other words, we are not seeking behavioral differences in aggression merely to demonstrate them, nor to proclaim gleefully their existence because we prize human variety. In the case of aggression, there is, as we shall argue below, some good reason to call attention to the simple fact of behavioral differences, but the essence of our work is to seek those differences in order then to determine the variables which produce them, anywhere and everywhere. It is, of course, epistemologically obvious that the establishment of universal generalizations about behavior requires variation in both that behavior and in the numerous factors which co-vary with it. This is true of all science; it is certainly true of cross-cultural psychology, the research strategy that characterizes our present effort to understand human aggression.

To say that we are engaged in cross-cultural psychology is not to say, however, that we shall use *culture* to explain aggression. Culture is, undoubtedly, conceptually unclear (Jahoda, 1980). It just won't do as an independent variable, not for aggression, not for any behavior that interests us. Whatever culture is (and we settle for the appropriately broad and loose definition of Moore and Lewis (1952): ". . . anything one person can learn from all other persons"), it is too gross, too diffuse, too multifactored to qualify as a variable. It is a valuable concept because the term, especially as Moore and Lewis and we use it, calls attention to the simple fact that the stuff of culture is learnable and indeed learned; and that, via learning, it is transmitted over time, usually through interpersonal contacts. So, the process of cultural transmission concerns us; nonetheless, we resist the temptation to explain differences in aggression as "caused by culture." Such a statement is empty.

Following the suggestions of the anthropologist/psychologist team, Robert L. and Ruth Munroe (Munroe & Munroe, 1980) we think of culture as dissected into numerous, separable (albeit often correlated) contextual factors, including basic institutions, subsistence patterns, social and political organizations, languages, social rules governing interpersonal relations, divisions of labor by sex, age or other dimensions, population density, dwelling styles, and more, so many more that an exhaustive list of such potential independent variables is impossible.

All those anthropologists and cross-cultural psychologists who pursue hologeistic research in the tradition of Murdock (1957, 1967) and Naroll (1973), among others, employing either coded ethnographies like the Standard Cross-Cultural Sample or the Human Relations Area Files or systematically coordinated multiple-site field work in order to test universal hypotheses about human behavior, employ variables like those enumerated above. In all such work, behavioral differences across cultural groups are related to one or more (and it is almost always more) variables as presence or absence of, or degree of presence of, some specific contextual factor. And so it is in our work on aggression.

A Conceptual Framework

Assuming that we are confronted with facts about aggression that reveal reliable behavioral differences between human groups and that our objective is to relate them to the kinds or variables listed here, it is useful also to have an overarching conceptual framework about how human behavior changes over time and, by implication, comes to differ over space. We find that framework most cogently expressed in Donald Campbell's evolutionary epistemology (1977). Campbell's view of behavioral development at the individual level (and of change at the social level as well) is a model *based on* (but not identical with) contemporary theories of biological evolution. It is a model which emphasizes random variation and selective retention, tending toward adaptiveness in a circuitous manner and only in the long run. The behavioral variations are nonprescient; environmental selection for adaptiveness occurs only after the fact of behavioral change. Analogous to physiological natural selection, which operates effectively at the species level, is trial and error learning at the individual level (and through social influence of one kind or another, at various group levels). Thus, the learning of each organism and the dynamics of all cultures tend toward adaptiveness, again in a nonprescient way, with environmental response to the trial variations determining their viability. In a virtual paraphrase of the Campbellian position, and in equally cogent language, B. F. Skinner (1981) asserted, "Selection by consequences is a causal mode found only in living things or in machines made by living things. It was first recognized in natural selection, but it also accounts for the shaping and maintenance of the behavior of the individual and the evolution of cultures [p. 501]."

It should, of course, be obvious that neither Campbell nor Skinner, by referring to natural selection, were suggesting genetic determination for aggression, or for any other complex human action, or for cultural change. Rather, they were simply pointing out that biological evolution and human learning (and hence cultural change, since human learning is what culture is all about) are parallel processes both tending toward the same end—survival—through non-prescient selection.

So, if we have reason to believe that some behavior related to aggression is culturally influenced, we still have to ask, "In what way might this particular behavior, which we find in this/these particular place(s) be adaptive?" In this formal respect, we must think as biologists and ask, "What do we know about the ecocultural contexts of the groups for which behavior A prevails and those of the groups for which behavior *A-prime* prevails that makes each of those behaviors fit the contexts in which they are found?"

This conceptual framework which we have adopted is in tune with a growing ecocultural emphasis in cross-cultural psychology, as is found, for example, in Berry's (1975) perspective wherein most complex human behaviors and the cultural recipes for them are cumulatively selected for their adaptive character and are transmitted intergenerationally by social processes, including socialization and enculturation, rather than by genetic adaptation.

The Nature-Nurture Controversy

Because *aggression* is our topic, it may be necessary to be very explicit about where we stand on the question of genetic determination, particularly since we have just emphasized our interest in processes that parallel natural selection. As is well known, human aggression is widely thought to have a genetic basis. It may well be that this is the single most popular view. It certainly is among laypersons. And over the past few decades, many scientists have written works which have restored respectability to it. However, in accord with most students of aggression, we do not find the aggression-instinct arguments, in any of the several versions which have appeared in recent years (e.g., Ardrey, 1966; Lorenz, 1963; Lumsden & Wilson, 1981; Morris, 1967; Storr, 1968; Wilson, 1975), at all compelling.

While we share with Lumsden and Wilson their notion that social learning can stimulate Mendelian transmission, we reject their notion of "epigenetic rules" whereby genetically-based neurobiological constraints channel behavior in particular directions. We do not believe that complex social behaviors are determined by natural selection; we know of no evidence for the existence of a heritable genetic bias in the development of complex social behavior.

As for the Lorenzian insistence on an aggressive instinct, the compelling reasons for rejecting it are almost too familiar to bear restatement. Berkowitz (1969) and Kim (1976), among others, have documented many of the errors of fact and reasoning which mark Lorenz's work. As Kim so aptly put it,

> the Lorenzian theory of aggression and war is seriously flawed on conceptual, methodological, and substantive grounds. The cavalier use of operationally ill-defined terms and concepts, the almost exclusive reliance on causal anecdotes, the disregard of empirical studies contradicting the monocausal paradigm, the inductive/extrapolative leaps to solve the level-of-analysis problem, the cross-species generalizations based on the recurrent tendency to advance argument in finalistic terms with little supporting evidence—all these weaknesses warrant scientific disapproval of the Lorenzian theory. [pp. 270-271]

The mere fact of differences across societies in degree, form, and concomitants of aggressive behavior is, in our view, an overwhelming problem for instinct theorists and sociobiologists. We doubt that they are equipped to solve it by remaining within their theoretical frameworks. And we will not try to do it for them.

The behavioral differences with which we are here confronted are, of course, also a problem for us, who work within *our* theoretical framework—social learning theory—buttressed by Campbellian evolutionary epistemology and Skinnerian selection-by-consequences. But, as we have tried to make clear in the foregoing discussion, differences are precisely what our theoretical predilections have primed us to expect. It may not be easy to make sense out of them, but we welcome them, indeed require them, as the raw material to be entered into our search for explanations of human aggression. For us, the differences are a problem only in the happiest sense of that term, a scientific puzzle, one for which we believe the solution resides in a social learning approach.

And, one more preliminary word on the nature vs. nurture controversy as regards human aggression. As we have noted, genetic hypotheses and learning hypotheses, as competing alternatives, both must ultimately be assessed in the light of their competence in pointing to systemic fit. While we find learning more plausible than biological evolution as the mechanism that provides that fit for aggression, we nonetheless acknowledge that only when the adaptiveness of the aggressive behavior is accounted for can that behavior be said to be understood. So, in the end, our criterion for success is the same as the sociobiologist's or the instinct theorist's. Like them, we have to explain aggression wherever it occurs, in whatever form. We have to show how it fits its setting. But, unlike some instinct theorists, we do not ever have to claim that aggression is "good." Functional, yes, in the sense that a given degree of aggression fits other features of a particular ecocultural setting, but good for the aggressors or further victims? Absolutely not! Only instinct theories or other frameworks which employ hydraulic system metaphors force their adherents into that morally repugnant and scientifically indefensible stance.

ANTHROPOLOGICAL LESSONS ON AGGRESSION

The anthropological literature on aggression and violence is both ethnographic and nomothetic. The ethnographic portion is descriptive of particular societies, intensively studied, one at a time, usually by a particular anthropologist who specializes in that society. (The case studies of the large-scale contemporary societies included in this volume are like ethnographies in most of these respects.) The nomothetic portion of the anthropological literature is composed of what are often called hologeistic studies (see Schaefer, 1977, for a history and contemporary description of the field), which are comparative, across many societies, extensively examined, usually via secondary analyses of previously published ethnographies. Scholars engaged in hologeistic research seek to test cross-cultural, universal hypotheses about human behavior, usually employing quantitative techniques that reveal patterns of associations. The long-range objectives of the research program of which the present book marks a start are clearly akin to those of the hologeistic scholars.

We believe that many non-anthropologist students of aggression are unfamiliar with the anthropological literature on aggression, particularly several recent works of the hologeistic variety. We have consulted many of these works and will describe or summarize those which we believe offer intriguing hypotheses, with supporting data, about ecocultural and socialization correlates of aggression. Our review of the literature will not be exhaustive; it is too large and varied. And, given the objectives of this chapter, we shall pay less attention to the purely ethnographic works that deal with aggression, which are very numerous indeed, than we shall to the less numerous comparative studies.

The Ethnographic Evidence

First, however, we shall say a few words about the ethnographic literature, for it offers students of aggression some important preliminary lessons. To begin with, that literature shows clearly that there are societies in which adults, in their dealings with each other, with their children, and sometimes even with outsiders, seldom behave aggressively. As Ashley Montagu (1978) stated, in his introduction to a collection of ethnographic reports dealing with several widely dispersed, non-literate societies:

> Many human societies cannot be characterized as aggressive. . . . There are societies in which both inter- and intragroup aggression is low, as among the Toda of Southern Indi and there are societies in which both inter- and intragroup aggression are nonexistent, as among the Tasady of Mindanao,* in the Philippines. . . . [Other] societies that are notable for their unaggressiveness . . . are the Punan of Borneo, the Hadza of Tanzania, the Birhor of Southern India, the Veddahs of Ceylon, the Arapesh of New Guinea, the Australian aborigines, the Yamis of Orchid Island off Taiwan, the Semai of Malaya, the Tikopia of the Western Pacific, the Land Dayaks of Sarawak, the Lepchas of Sikkim, the Papago Indians, the Hopi, the Zuni, and the Pueblo peoples generally, the Tahitians, and the Ifaluk of the Pacific. [pp. 3-5].

This long, recently compiled list is not exhaustive. Far from that. Ethnographers have documented other cases of societies, mostly small, and mostly nonliterate ones, where the frequent acts of aggression and violence which seem so "natural" in large, complex, usually technologically advanced societies, like nearly all of those discussed in later chapters of the present volume, are, rather than frequent, virtually absent.

However, a review of the ethnographic literature would also show that some forms of aggression occur in nearly every society, including most of these societies in Montagu's list. Moreover, there are good reasons to be skeptical about assertions that aggression is "nonexistent" in *any* society, if only because no observer can ever be sure to have detected every behavior that takes place nor to have appropriately and fully interpreted every act that was observed. So, this first lesson from ethnography regarding societal differences in aggression is that such differences exist and do indeed span a wide range of magnitudes but that aggression is at the same time quite likely a universal phenomenon. Its universality *coupled with* its wide-ranging variation is what makes it such an intriguing scientific puzzle.

The second lesson concerns the level of complexity that must be expected in any satisfactory solution to that puzzle. The ethnographic literature, in addition to pointing to many cases of small, nonliterate societies that display very low levels of aggression, contains cases of similar societies, also small and nonliterate, that are *highly* aggressive, such as the somewhat notorious Yanomamo of Southern Venezuela, whose frequent warfare has been described as ferocious, an adjective that seems appropriate, given the ethnographic details provided by Chagnon (1968). So, the puzzle cannot be solved simply by appealing to societal size, simplicity, or level of technological development.

The variability in human aggression, the range and diversity of aggressive behaviors, and their distribution over numerous other variables—geographic, cultural, economic, political— are what convince us that research that focuses on ecocultural, social, and experiential antecedents of aggression is both necessary and promising. That aggression's antecedents are many and complex and probably intertwined, interactive, and confounded as well, further convinces us that research that has any hope at all of understanding aggression must be multidisciplinary, multimethod, and very open-minded.

There is a third lesson to be gleaned from ethnographic research. since that research suggests that aggression's antecedents are many and complex, there must be some sets of condi-

---

*Ed. Note. The Tasaday are a special case. Comprising only 26 individuals, 13 of them children, when discovered in 1966, they have not been well studied. As noted below in this chapter, skepticism regarding the "nonexistence" of aggression in such societies is clearly in order.

tions that only are found to exist in some societies, but also are encouraged to take root and flourish in other societies, if human aggression is to be controlled and reduced. An optimistic hope, then, which can be derived from what the ethnographies tell us about the nonstereotypy of human aggression, is that competent research can reveal potentially pragmatic approaches to the inculcation and enculturation of nonaggressive behavioral alternatives to situations where aggression is presently the norm. If aggressiveness varies in some as yet undetermined but systematic fashion, and if the conditions which contribute to lesser aggressiveness, wherever they prevail, can confidently be ascertained, then those conditions might be encouraged anywhere.

However, to realize these promises—both the scientific one of understanding and the pragmatic one of controlling human aggression—we must go beyond ethnography per se. Digesting available ethnographic descriptions or compiling additional ones would serve merely to underscore the lessons just reviewed and to reiterate the promises just enunciated. The ethnographic facts alone do not provide the generalizations we seek, either to understand human aggression or to intervene in efforts to control, reduce, or minimize it. For that task to be undertaken properly, we must adopt the kind of hypothesis-testing stance that is characteristic of hologeistic research.

Hologeistic Studies of Aggression

Using ethnographies as data sources, hologeistic research aims for generalizations about human behavior. Exploiting the many kinds of variations that exist across the many hundreds of societies in the world, hologeistic researchers seek regularities in association and covariations in diverse characteristics that might serve as the basis for plausible inferences regarding causality. The causal statements about human behavior that emerge from hologeistic studies are, of course, no more than inferences since the forms of analysis available in such studies are no better than correlational. The hologeistic research must take the ethnographic facts as they are (or, more properly stated, as they have been described in the first instance by others) and examine their covariates. But whatever limitations regarding the establishment of causality that this fact implies, and however numerous and serious the threats to validity inherent in having to employ secondary data sources of varying quality (for discussion of these problems and ways to solve them, see Naroll, 1962, 1973; and Naroll, Michik, & Naroll, 1980), hologeistic research is an unparalleled research strategy for discovering what goes with what on the broadest possible canvass—the many and diverse habitats in which the human animal survives.

To employ this method, one samples from the many hundreds of human societies for which ethnographic descriptions have already been compiled. These exist in several convenient sets and in highly usable formats, with very large numbers of characteristics extracted, coded, stored in accessible form, and very much subject to quantitative analysis. The best known and most convenient of these sets are the Human Relations Area Files (see Barry, 1980 for a thorough description), the Standard Cross-Cultural Sample (Murdock & White, 1969) and the Ethnographic Atlas (Murdock, 1967). Sets of coded variables from one or another of these data sets can conveniently be found in Barry and Schlegel (1980) and Textor (1967). Examples of hypothesis testing employing such coded variables can also be found in those two sources, among many others. And the topics covered are wide ranging, many of which, of course, have little to do with aggression.

However, among the coded variables available in these and similar sources are many that do relate to aggression and many more that describe social structures, economic systems, socialization practices, and other societal characteristics that plausibly might be expected to relate to aggression. Not surprisingly, then, considerable research that seeks cross-cultural generalizations about human aggression has already been accomplished. Equally not surprisingly, the goal of such research—truly to understand why aggression varies the way it does—remains elusive. In an effort to determine how far hologeistic research has carried us toward that goal, we turn now to some selected examples of studies that at least have asked some of the questions that need to be asked. We shall see that many of the tentative answers raise still other questions. We shall also see that many such questions remain to be raised. And we shall see, as was suggested in our cursory review of the relevant ethnographic literature, that the story of the antecedents of aggression is indeed a complex one.

We shall begin our digest of that story by considering some cross-cultural studies relating to socialization emphases.

Inculcation of Aggressiveness During Childhood

Considerable cross-cultural evidence exists to support the general proposition that many traits which are functional for adult activities in particular societies are, in part at least, inculcated during childhood. Thus, Barry, Child, and Bacon (1959) found relations between adult subsistence economic activities and various socialization emphases during childhood, in such domains as training to be nurturant, to be independent, to be obedient, and other such traits. If aggressiveness may be thought of as a trait, it is reasonable to ask (1) whether societies differ in the degree to which it is inculcated during childhood and (2) whether such differences relate to other trait-inculcations or other aspects of culture, especially economic activities.

To pursue this question, Barry, Josephson, Lauer, and Marshall (1976, 1980) scored nearly 150 societies drawn from the Standard Cross-Cultural Sample (Murdock & White, 1969, 1980) on inculcation of aggressiveness among children beween the ages of approximately four and twelve years of age (both early and later during that age span), for both boys and girls, and along with a number of other variables. They found considerable variation across societies in inculcation of aggressiveness, defined as:

> aggressive behavior toward people (including peers) or animals, which may be implicitly inculcated or condoned by adults, e.g., parental urging to stand up for oneself or retaliate against aggression. Exhortations or frequent retelling of heroic myths may also instill aggressiveness; overt and covert inculcation are both included. [Barry et al., 1976, 1980, p. 215]

Using a 5-point scale (subdivided with plus and minus for finer discrimination) with 3 indicating "moderately strong inculcation," 5 "extremely strong inculcation," and 1 "no inculcation of the trait or strong inculcation of its opposite," they were able to make confident judgments for 148 societies on, for example, aggressiveness among boys during later childhood. Regarding this trait, the judgments were distributed as follows:

- 92 societies (62%) were judged to employ moderately strong inculcation of aggressiveness, i.e., were scored from 3⁻ to 3⁺
- 24 (16%) were scored 4⁻ or 4
- 8 (5%) were scored 4⁺ or 5
- 24 (16%) were scored from 2⁻ to 2⁺
- No societies scored lower than 2⁻

As this distribution of scores shows, the modal tendency in this sample, to employ moderately strong inculcation of aggressiveness in boys, was characteristic of nearly two thirds of the societies, which indicates considerable worldwide pervasiveness of aggression-inculcation. In addition, another fifth of the societies appeared to inculcate aggressiveness to an even higher than modal degree. Just under a fifth scored low.

Societies scoring both high and low were found in all regions of the world; regional differences across the high and low scoring societies were minor, with a slightly disproportionate number of high aggression-inculcation societies in Africa and a slightly disproportionate number of low aggression-inculcation societies in East Asia.

So, the first finding in this study is that there are cross-cultural differences in the degree to which aggression is inculcated in boys during later childhood. Similar differences were found also for boys during early childhood, so similar that there is no need here to describe those differences in any detail.

For girls, at both stages of childhood, there were again similar patterns of differences among the societies. However, a sex difference was found; in most societies, and on the average over all societies, there was more inculcation of aggressiveness for boys than for girls, with the sex difference more marked during the later period than during early childhood. Also, for both boys and girls, the mean rating of degree of aggression-inculcation was higher in the later childhood stage than in the earlier one (Barry et al., 1976, 1980, p. 219). Despite these mean differences involving gender and stage, plus the interaction between gender and stage, the following generalization clearly holds: Societies vary in aggression-inculcation during all of childhood and for both sexes, with the variation across societies following the pattern described above in detail for boys during later childhood.

With what does this cross-cultural variation in aggression-inculcation correlate? It correlates with other socialization variables. For example, it correlates positively with inculcation of "fortitude" (training to suppress pain and fear reactions) and with inculcation of "competitiveness" (encouragement to achieve superiority over others). The correlations among all three of these inculcation variables was high enough (Pearson Rs between .38 and .45 for all possible pairs) that Barry and his colleagues could justifiably combine them into a single cluster which they labeled "toughness." This cluster was independent of four other inculcation clusters included in this study (maturity, sociability, dutifulness, and submission). However, aggression-inculcation by itself was found to be negatively correlated with two measures of the inculcation of sociability cluster, namely inculcation of honesty and inculcation of trust. So, training to be aggressive is stressed where training to be honest and trusting of others is not stressed. And, training to be aggressive tends to be a part of a general toughness-inculcation syndrome.

The toughness-inculcation syndrome (which, as we have just seen, includes aggression-inculcation) is in turn related to certain structural characteristics of the societies. One of these, which involves marriage systems, lineage, and residence patterns, can be characterized as "availability of contact with another during infancy." High contact with mother during infancy was found to be associated with high inculcation of aggressiveness during later childhood, for both boys and girls, but more strongly for boys.

In addition, one part of the toughness-inculcation syndrome, inculcation of competitiveness, was associated with importance of animal husbandry, a subsistence economy variable. (However, aggression-inculcation per se was not, nor was the over all toughness-inculcation syndrome.)

So, the best, albeit tentative generalization to be gleaned from the Barry, Josephson, Lauer, and Marshall (1976, 1980) study is that, despite considerable worldwide inculcation of aggressiveness during childhood (with the mode characterizable as moderately high), there are variations in degree, with more of it likely in societies where infants have much contact with mothers, and with one of its correlates, inculcation of competitiveness, more likely to occur in societies where animal husbandry is an important feature of the economy.

With regard to this last point, it may be instructive to consider the Masai, the society which in this study earned the highest aggression-inculcation score. The Masai are well-known East African pastoralists who, during infancy, rely exclusively on female caretakers. Later in childhood, following genital maturation (and perhaps as late as 18 years of age), both boys and girls are subjected to relatively severe initiation ceremonies. These involve genital operations (circumcision and clitorodectemy) and are judged anthropologically (e.g., by Schlegel & Barry, 1979, 1980) to stress same-sex bonding and, especially for males, valor (rather than wisdom or responsibility, which are the foci of many other initiation ceremonies). Thus, the Masai serve well to illustrate the kinds of societies which inculcate aggression more than most, and to underscore the kinds of cultural variables which reinforce that socialization emphasis.

For contrast, consider the case of the Tahitians. Not included in the Barry et al. (1976, 1980) study, they have been described recently by Levy (1978) as gentle, affectionate, tender, and living in harmony in an easy, nonfrustrating environment. Relevant to our present concern with inculcation of aggressiveness and its correlates, it is clear from Levy's account that the Tahitians score low in this regard. Moreover, Levy reports, "Young infants are the center of attention, cherished, fussed over, gratified, protected and a sense of basic trust is instilled [p. 227]." "Also communicated, are the notions that masculinity, striving and aggression are dangerous, but cooperation with nature will be successful [p. 228]." "And childcare, from infancy onward, is the responsibility of many, not only mothers, with more than half the homes in the community having adopted children [p. 228]."

As the reader of this volume encounters the various descriptions of aggression in 18 contemporary nation-states, he might profitably read them with an eye toward hints regarding the magnitude of aggression inculcation present therein. Do economic variables and degree of contact with mothers operate in such societies as they do in the smaller, nonliterate societies covered by the Barry et al. (1976, 1980) study?

The Socialization of Aggressive Behavior by Children

When children behave aggressively, caretakers and others react. Those reactions, whatever they may be, presumably have consequences for strengthening or weakening of the behaviors. This notion, widely shared by most social learning theorists, was a feature of a classic cross-cultural study of mothers and children in six selected societies (Minturn & Lambert, 1964; Whiting, 1963; Whiting & Whiting, 1975). While not a hologeistic study, strictly speaking, since it involved only six societies, it is certainly in the hypothesis-testing tradition of such studies and, in certain respects, possesses some methodological advantages over them, e.g., the use of standard observations for all cases in the sample. The six-cultures-study ranged widely over a series of questions, but a portion of the study dealt with aggression and related matters. It is that portion to which we now turn.

Observations were made by anthropologist/psychologist teams of mothers and of children of both sexes in two age groups (3-6 years and 7-11 years) in Okinawa, India, the Philippines, Mexico, Kenya, and New England in the United States. Among the children, two forms of aggressive behavior were observed, termed by the authors "opportunity aggression" and "retaliatory aggression" (roughly speaking, unprovoked and provoked). Interviews with mothers provided information regarding their ways of coping with such behavior when displayed by their children. Numerous cultural differences were found in this study. Among those most relevant to our present concerns are the following.

Mothers in these six societies varied in their reactions to aggression directed to themselves by their children. The African sample (Nyansongo, a Gusii community in Kenya) was the most punitive in this regard, the Indian mothers (the Rajputs of Khalapur) least. An interesting correlate was the degree to which mothers make independent economic contributions (maximal in Nyansongo, minimal in Khalapur).

Regarding aggression directed by children against other children, Mexican mothers (Mixtecans of Juxtlahuaca) were most punitive and mothers in the United States ("Orchard Town" in New England) sample were least punitive, even encouraging retaliation by their children to aggression stemming from their peers. The most interesting correlate here was the degree of structural relationship with neighbors. The less close the relationship, the less concern mothers showed over the peer-directed aggression of their children. As one Mexican mother put it, ". . . if our children don't get along, then my brother and I may come to a parting of the ways [Lambert, 1971, p. 51]."

What impact did these and other socialization tendencies have on the behavior of the children? No simple answer is possible. The facts regarding aggressive behavior by children cannot be understood out of context. And that context included numerous other kinds of behaviors. However, these were reduced to 12 behavioral categories: seeks help, seeks attention, seeks dominance, suggests responsibility, offers support, offers help, acts sociably, touches, reprimands, "assaults" sociably, assaults, and symbolically aggresses, plus a separately treated category of compliance. These behavioral categories were multidimensionally scaled and two dimensions emerged, one defined as "dependent and dominant versus nurturant and responsible" and the other, "sociable versus generally aggressive." The first was found to be related primarily to cultural complexity, with less complexity paired with nurturance and responsibility. The second related mostly to household structure (most notably whether families were nuclear or not), with children in nonnuclear families more aggressive. But, more important, the two behavioral dimensions and the two societal characteristics were interrelated; both sets of characteristics have to be taken into account to understand the different patterns of the two behavioral dimensions. In other words, socioeconomic complexity and household structure combine to influence the combination of behaviors characteristic of each society. Consider two concrete examples.

The children from the New England town, whose setting involved a nuclear household structure and a complex socioeconomic system, were alone in scoring both on the nonnurturant-nonresponsible side of the first behavioral dimension and on the sociable side of the second behavioral dimension. The children in the Kenyan village, whose setting involved a nonnuclear household structure and a relatively simple socioeconomic system, were alone in scoring on both the nurturant-responsible side of the first dimension and toward the authoritarian-aggressive side of the second one. To complicate the picture further, mothers' workload was implicated in the cross-cultural differences. But, if one were, in spite of these complexities, to venture a "simple" hypothesis regarding both (a) the socialization of aggression and (b) manifest aggression, it would be as follows. It comes in several parts.

- Aggression against caretakers is punished most where children's obedience is necessarily valued by mothers who contribute economically and need help from their children, especially in households where other adults are present.
- Aggression against other children is punished most where economics demand good relations with close neighbors.
- Whatever the sanctions against aggression, it is most likely to occur in cultures with patrilineal extended families, combined with simple economic systems.

In short, the socialization of aggression, whether severe or lax, does not by itself predict the manifestation of aggression. Severe socialization of aggression does not reduce it. Indeed, it may enhance it. Or, it may coexist with it because high manifestation of aggression by children may elicit stronger sanctions against it from their caretakers. So, while we have simplified the picture regarding aggression and its socialization that emerges from the six-cultures study, it is a picture that is not, in an absolute sense, simple at all.

But we do have a sense of what variables deserve further research: socioeconomic complexity, household structure, and the workload of mothers. Recent work by members of the six-cultures-research team (e.g., Lambert & Tan, 1979) on three different aggressive styles of children (self-instigated, retaliatory, and "surprise" aggression) showed again that such variables are implicated both in mothers' behavior and that of their children.

From another large-scale, on-going hologeistic research project, one that focuses on correlates of parental acceptance and rejection (Rohner, 1975; 1980; Rohner & Nielson, 1978; Rohner & Rohner, 1979), evidence has consistently accumulated to support the view that rejected children throughout the world are more hostile or passively aggressive than are accepted children, particularly when caretakers behave hostilely toward them, thereby providing aggressive models to emulate (Rohner, 1980, p. 6). And, of course, it is usually the case that a given generation's hostile children grow up to be the next generation's hostile adults (as shown in Rohner, 1975, with a sample of 101 societies), so that conditions for intergenerational transmission of a syndrome of hostility, mistrust, and rejection seem easily established and very difficult to remove.

In both the Rohner project and the work done by Lambert and his associates within the framework of the six cultures study, there is concern with maternal warmth as a variable influencing tendencies to aggress in children. Warm mothers are, in Rohner's terminology, accepting mothers. Lambert's (1971) analysis of maternal warmth (showing little hostility in dealings with children, rarely using physical punishment) showed that it is more likely to be the characteristic mode of behavior of mothers when there are other adults in the household who can share tasks (especially child-rearing), when there are fewer siblings around to function as competitors, and when fewer "courtyard cousins" are present to serve as potential targets for mothers to respond with severe sanctions.

To summarize, the several studies that deal with socialization of aggression in children show that caretakers' (particularly mothers') reactions to children impact in nonsurprising ways on children's tendencies to aggress. In addition, the relevant behaviors of the caretakers are a complex product of socioeconomic and household structural variables. These notions now appear to be panculturally valid. Do they apply, then, to technologically developed societies such as those described in this volume?

Sex Differences in Aggression

A recent review of 130 studies done on sex differences in North America from the 1930s through the mid-1970s (Rohner, 1976) confirmed the well-known fact that American males, both men and boys, are more aggressive than females. Rarely did a study show the reverse; most supported the generalization of more male aggressiveness, while a few studies showed no significant sex difference. The sex differences were not as large among adults as among children, but the proportion of studies that found males more aggressive was almost as high for adults as for children. In all these respects, the cross-cultural evidence leads to the same conclusion. Using the same sample of 101 societies in the parental acceptance and rejection study, Rohner (1976) found that, while aggression by males and females was positively correlated (in societies in which males were more aggressive than in other societies, so were females), males tended to be more aggressive than females in most societies. And while that sex difference was less marked during adulthood, it does not totally disappear, even as women become more aggressive and men less aggressive. Thus, the North American findings that males from early in life are more aggressive than females can now, in Rohner's words, "be raised to the level of a panspecies generalization [p. 69]."

This generalization, Rohner noted, is subject to diverse explanations. One would attribute the sex difference to differential socialization pressures; but, while evidence for such differential socialization can indeed be adduced, the best available cross-cultural evidence on inculcation of aggression (Barry et al., 1976) showed the sex difference in this regard to be small, albeit consistent. Indeed, in many societies in that study, the pressures on boys and girls to be aggressive are about the same. So, this simple hypothesis seems wanting.

Another attributes the sex difference to the sexual division of labor, which in turn leads to different socialization pressures on boys and girls because the adult roles they will have to play call for different adult traits, with the male roles requiring more aggressiveness. Again, support for this view can be found; and, though Rohner rejects it, we find it rather compelling. Rohner's objection is based on the fact that differentiation between the sexes during childhood, as found, for example, by Barry, Bacon, and Child (1957), is so consistent across cultures that one must suspect that the differentiation reflects a "phylogenetically acquired, species predisposition" [Rohner, 1976, p. 70]. Rohner suggests that, even if males and females are assigned different tasks during adulthood and it is preparation for these tasks that calls for differential socialization, one still must explain, for example, "why boys around the world are assigned tasks that lead to greater aggression than girls [p. 70]." But, in our view, Barry et al. (1957) satisfactorily answered that question by noting that the sexual division of labor known to most subsistence-level societies is one that derives primarily from the simple fact that females are child-bearers and that close-to-home activities being assigned to females would be an adaptive response, at least in many kinds of ecologies, as has also been argued persuasively by Van Leeuwen (1978). And, in one of the reports to emerge from the six cultures study (Whiting & Edwards, 1973), there is at least one important finding that supports this argument. In two of the societies—in Kenya where some child-care and other domestic tasks are assigned to boys, and in New England where tasks assigned to girls are not stereotypically feminine ones—sex differences in behavior (including responding aggressively) were smaller or less frequent than in the other societies.

Furthermore, the Whiting and Edwards paper has become a center of controversy involving Maccoby and Jacklin (1980) and Tieger (1980). The former two psychologists had argued earlier (1966) that the cross-cultural evidence, particularly that from the six cultures study, supported their contention that males are biologically predisposed toward aggressive behavior. Tieger, on the other hand, found their argument wanting, and emphasized the same finding from Whiting and Edwards (1973) that we cite here, namely that, as Tieger (1980) puts it, "the greatest variation . . . is found in societies where children's work roles differ from traditional patterns most strongly [p. 945]." In their 1980 rejoinder, Maccoby and Jacklin emphasized a measure, based on data pooled over societies, which does support an early sex difference. It is impossible to resolve the dispute here. Accordingly, some attention must be given to Rohner's third and preferred explanation for sex differences in aggression, which posits a genetic predisposition which is subject to interaction with enculturative pressures. He thereby places himself in the Maccoby and Jacklin camp. Whatever the explanation, sex differences in aggressiveness do seem to be very wide spread and a continuing search for the contributing factors is likely to be a feature of cross-cultural research on aggression. Perhaps in the chapters solicited for this volume, some such factors may be discerned.

Organized Violent Conflict

A kind of aggression that is well known in the more industrialized societies described in detail in this volume is intergroup hostility, one form of which, warfare, is both a feature of their recent histories and a continuing possibility for which many such nations remain vigilant. Organized feuding and warfare are not unknown among the kinds of societies that anthropologists study, either. The anthropological literature on organized, sanctioned violence deals with both feuding and war. As noted earlier, the anthropological literature (in this respect among others) is both ethnographic (idiographic) and hologeistic (nomothetic), and it is a very large literature. As such, it can not exhaustively be reviewed here. But we will present a summary of some of it, especially recent works of the hologeistic variety, since these offer some intriguing hypotheses about why groups engage in feuding and warfare.

Since the early 1960s, a number of studies have been completed which illustrate the complexity of influences that seem to impinge on various forms of organized combativeness, including feuding and both internal and external warfare. These three, while they share certain characteristics, need to be distinguished from each other, as will become clear when we review the findings from a few studies. The distinctions among them relate to the anthropological concepts of *political community* and *cultural unit,* with the former defined as "a group of people whose membership is defined in terms of occupancy of a common territory and who have an official with the specific function of announcing group decisions [Naroll, 1964, p. 286]" and with cultural units composed of contiguous political communities that speak a common language and in other respects are culturally similar. The three forms of organized combativeness relate to these social group distinctions as follows: Feuding occurs within a political community, internal warfare occurs between political communities that are parts of the same cultural unit, and external warfare occurs between cultural units.

Feuding. Feuding is usually characterized (e.g., Otterbein, 1968) as an ambush by an organized band on a member of their own political community, usually to avenge an act of homicide. The victim is often a relative of the earlier killer, and he is usually killed in turn. At least two studies have revealed that the frequency of feuding, so defined, relates to the presence or absence of fraternal interest groups—localized groups of related males, a form of social organization which is found in societies that have patrilocal residence patterns. The first study (Van Velzen & Van Wetering, 1960) compared patrilocal with matrilocal societies on five different indices of intrasocietal conflict and found the patrilocal societies to be less peaceful than the matrilocal ones on all five. The second study (Otterbein & Otterbein, 1965) concentrated on feuding per se and indexed the importance of fraternal interest groups by two factors—patrilocal residence and polygyny. In this study, it was shown that feuding was more likely to occur in societies with fraternal interest groups.

Internal Warfare. Keith Otterbein later reasoned (1968) that the existence of fraternal interest should "also produce warfare between political communities [p. 281]." But, in this study, only one of two indices of fraternal interest groups (i.e., polygyny) was significantly related to internal warfare ($X^2 = 3.93$, N = 42 societies, p < .05); patrilocal residence was not. A complication, then, that needs to be kept in mind is that polygyny and patrilocality, while both indices of fraternal interest groups, are different variables in their own right. In one set of 50 societies examined by Otterbein, of 33 patrilocal ones, only 18 were polygynous; among the 17 nonpatrilocal ones, 3 were polygynous. Thus, the notion that fraternal interest groups "produce" internal warfare might better read "polygynous societies are groups in which internal warfare is more likely." We shall return to this point later.

Putting aside for the moment the questionable relationship of fraternal interest groups and internal warfare, we can extract from Otterbein's (1968) study another interesting (but essentially unconfirmed) hypothesis. It concerns the degree of political centralization that characterizes a society. Centralized political systems have authority patterns that usually limit the initiation of warfare to one designated individual or agency (as in modern industrialized states and in many traditional societies as well); in uncentralized political systems, warfare can usually be initiated by anyone. This fact, demonstrated empirically for 42 societies (16 centralized, 26 not) in Otterbein's own study, led him to predict that centralized societies would be more likely to engage in frequent internal warfare. In fact, they are not. There was no significant relationship found and the trend was even in the opposite direction. This forced him, and us, to push the analysis a step further.

When Otterbein broke down his sample into polygynous and nonpolygynous societies, he found that it was primarily in the former that political centralization was related to internal warfare; in patrilocal societies, the politically centralized ones were those most likely to inhibit internal warfare, while in nonpatrilocal societies, no such relationship prevailed. Similarly, political centralization and war inhibition were related in polygynous societies, but not in nonpolygynous societies. So, it is tempting once again to suggest that fraternal interest groups (presence or absence) is a relevant variable, since, as noted above, patrilocality and polygyny are both indices of that variable. Accordingly, Otterbein reasoned as follows: Since anyone can initiate warfare in uncentralized political systems, especially if patrilocal and/or polygynous, then in such societies, internal war should be more frequent. He did find the expected significant interaction: in uncentralized political systems, those with fraternal interest groups were more prone to internal war, while in centralized political systems, those without fraternal interest groups were more prone. It was, however, not possible to determine whether the interest group variable or the ability to initiate war variable was the better predictor of internal warfare proneness. Despite this ambiguity, Otterbein (1968) asserted that "societies with fraternal interest groups are more likely to have both feuding and internal war than societies without fraternal interest groups [p. 287]." In our opinion, this often cited assertion must be qualified by stating that fraternal interest groups *possibly* increase the frequency of internal warfare only in uncentralized political systems, where it can be initiated by nearly anyone.

External War as an Independent Variable. In both the study of feuding (Otterbein & Otterbein, 1965) and the study of internal warfare (Otterbein, 1968), the frequency of external war was employed as an independent variable. Arguing, as many students of aggression might, that intergroup conflict, such as was between different cultural units, creates cohesion within such units, it can be predicted that external war would be negatively correlated with both feuding and internal warfare. However, in the case of feuding, the centralized/uncentralized political system variable intervened to affect that predicted relationship; in centralized societies, feuding and war were negatively correlated but, in uncentralized societies, they were actually positively related. On the other hand, no such interaction prevailed with regard to internal warfare. So, to summarize the picture to this point: External war seems not to reduce internal warfare in either kind of society (centralized or not). And warfare per se, whether internal or external, is accompanied by diminished feuding only in centralized societies where, presumably, leaders can suppress feuding when necessary.

External War as a Dependent Variable. We have just considered some evidence that external warfare has a dampening effect on feuding, but only in centralized societies, and no such effect on internal warfare, regardless of degree of political centralization. We saw earlier that feuding was more common in patrilocal and polygynous societies (which, as we have noted more than once may or may not best be explained in terms of the presence of fraternal interest groups) and that internal warfare was more common in polygynous societies but not in patrilocal ones. Polygyny thus related to both feuding and internal warfare. Does it relate to external war, too? Is the presence of polygyny a factor in the frequency of external war? Can some of the variation in the frequency of external war be attributed to this widespread form of marriage? And, since polygyny is one index of fraternal interest groups, is the existence of such groups also implicated in the external war story?

To approach answers to these questions, we must once again weave through a complex set of hologeistic studies. The first in this set, interestingly, did not ask whether polygyny contributes to war, but whether war contributes to polygyny. Melvin Ember (1974) sought to explain the existence of polygyny, noting the availability of alternative, but not necessarily competing, hypotheses: (1) Long post-partum sex taboos, shown by John Whiting (1964) to be more frequent in protein-poor subsistence level societies, led men to acquire multiple wives as sex objects; and (2) Sex-ratios favoring women would set the stage for polygyny. Ember's (1975) study found more support for the sex-ratio hypothesis. Moreover, and importantly for our present concerns, he found an explanation for gender imbalances favoring women in the fact of warfare mortality. When Ember controlled statistically for male mortality in warfare, Whiting's (1964) relationship between a long post-partum sex taboo and polygyny disappeared. In more warlike societies that suffered high male mortality, polygyny was more common. Ember interpreted this to mean that polygyny was an adaptive response to warfare mortality, since polygyny served as a device for maximation of reproductive rates that could lead to a replenishing of a regularly depleted pool of potential warriors.

Keeping in mind that the relationship found by Ember, like those in all hologeistic studies, is correlational, its directionality is a matter of conjecture. One could propose that polygyny sets the stage for warfare, rather than vice versa. Plausibly, one could argue that in polygynous societies, where males are shared by females, males are relatively dispensable and hence war and the male mortality which results from it would be relatively affordable. What Ember (1974) found was that warfare, mortality, sex ratios, and polygyny were interrelated. His suggested causal chain ran from warfare mortality to polygyny; we are offering, as a plausible alternative, one running from polygyny to warfare.

Our hypothesis would be challenged by a well-known paper by Divale and Harris (1976) which argued that warfare is fought in order to remedy shortages of women, a notion that contradicts ours, and one that requires that warfare be more frequent in societies with sex ratios favoring males. While Divale and Harris presented some data showing that to be the case on a cross-cultural sample, a recent reanalysis of their data by Ember (1981) cast serious doubt on their conclusion. And when Ember in his 1981 paper compared 7 high warfare frequency societies with 8 low frequency ones as to their sex ratios, he clearly found female surplus significantly more often in the high warfare frequency societies.

So, the best available evidence at present is that polygyny and warfare are positively related. Nevertheless, Ember (1981) does not point to polygyny as a "cause" of warfare; he merely used the sex ratio finding as a basis for rejecting the Divale and Harris (1976) hypothesis that fighting for women is a "cause" of warfare.

If shortage of women is not a cause of war, struggle over other resources that might be in short supply could well be. This notion was recently challenged by Sillitoe (1977) who alleged to have demonstrated that among 26 small societies in New Guinea there was no relationship between warfare and population pressures. But a reanalysis by Ember (1981) of Sillitoe's own data showed that warfare was indeed more common in parts of New Guinea where population pressures were higher. This led Ember to argue that "people . . . go to war to try to gain access to scarce resources [p. 2]." This he dubbed an ecological explanation of warfare. Using another ecological variable—famine or severe food shortage—Ember found this also related to frequency of warfare in New Guinea. So, land and food pressures may be contributing factors.

Another popular line of argument regarding warfare has been that proneness to war is rooted in childhood socialization, with excessive punishment during childhood leading to an abundance of warlike personalities. Several studies support this line, including Russell (1972), Eckhardt (1973), and Prescott (1975). Some of the correlations reported in Textor (1967) also point in this direction. But, as Ember (1981) notes, if one employs societies for which Rohner (1975) provides ratings of parental acceptance/rejection and for which Ember has warfare frequency scores (18 societies), warfare is found to be more common among the "accepting" societies. Thus, this particular psychological explanation of warfare remains on shaky ground.

Some support for it, however, is found in another recent cross-cultural study; but, again, its findings are very complex and the one concerning socialization, on which we are presently focusing, has to be viewed in context. Marc Ross (1980) contrasted two broad explanations for external warfare (and also for internal conflict). One of these was structural in nature, dealing with such variables as the existence of cross-cutting ties created by local exogamy (preference for marriage outside local communities), and by matrilocality (which disperses males following marriage), and patrilocality and polygyny which imply a lack of cross-cutting ties. The other was dispositional in nature and deals with such variables as severity of socialization, fostering of affection and warmth, and closeness/distance of father-child ties. He investigated these two classes of variables (structural and dispositional) in a sample of 90 societies from the Standard Cross-Cultural Sample (Murdock & White, 1969, 1980). A general finding was that dispositional variables were more important (accounted for more than structural variables). More specifically, lack of affection during childhood and harshness of socialization were both related to overt conflict, and independently of structure. Lack of affection was associated more with external conflict, and harshness of socialization (which includes aggression inculcation) was associated more with internal conflict, but these two socialization variables contributed to both kinds of conflict in both politically centralized and uncentralized societies.

On the other hand, some structural variables also related to overt conflict, but in more complex ways. In uncentralized societies, polygyny and animal husbandry combined with the dispositional variables to account for internal conflict; but, in such societies, there was no effect of these variables on external warfare. In centralized societies, lack of checks on political authority and socioeconomic complexity combine with dispositional variables to account for internal conflict; for external conflict, polygyny and socioeconomic complexity are important.

These findings can be better comprehended, perhaps, if reordered as follows: When Ross (1980) divided his sample into centralized and uncentralized societies, he found that in uncentralized societies,

1. child-rearing patterns that de-emphasize affection and warmth *and* training styles which are severe and aggressive correlate with conflict, both internal and external, and
2. the existence of cross-cutting ties limit internal conflict.

In centralized societies, he found that

1. the differences between internal and external conflict are greater,
2. internal conflict relates to severe socialization and to unchecked political authority, and
3. external warfare is associated with an early end to childhood and weak father-child ties, to greater socioeconomic complexity, and to polygyny.

For our present purposes, the most important fact to be gleaned from this very thorough study is that "societies using harsher and less affectionate socialization practices have higher levels of both internal and external conflict [p. 13]." This finding derived from an analysis in which both types of societies, centralized and uncentralized, were merged.

In a subsequent analysis, the two kinds of societies were treated separately, and the harshness of the socialization variable was broken down into its several component variables (degree of corporal punishment, degree of pain infliction on infants, and degree to which fortitude and aggression are inculcated during childhood). For uncentralized societies, aggression inculcation (which we learn from Barry, Josephson, Lauer, and Marshall, 1976, 1980 relates to mother-child contact during infancy, degree of father absence, and importance of animal husbandry) is a very good predictor of external warfare. Along with lack of affection toward children, aggression inculcation accounted for nearly all of the variance in external warfare among the uncentralized societies in Ross's sample. Fortitude inculcation (but not aggression inculcation per se) was an important predictor of internal conflict. Combined once again with lack of affection toward children, it predicted nearly all of the variance in internal conflict among uncentralized societies. In centralized societies, as we have already noted, these socialization variables did better in accounting for internal conflict than for external warfare. But other socialization variables were, as already noted, associated with external warfare in centralized societies (e.g., an early end to childhood and weak father-child ties).

Since none of the structural hypotheses mentioned earlier found consistent support across the two types of societies and across the two forms of conflict, while the dispositional hypotheses did, a tentative conclusion derivable from Ross's efforts is that future research on feuding and warfare which focuses on socialization emphases and consequent individual dispositions may well be fruitful. While structural variables surely can't be ignored either, they may best be treated as setting the stage for certain socialization emphases. For example, we know from Berry, Josephson, Lauer, and Marshall (1976, 1980) that importance of animal husbandry (a structural variable which Ross found to relate to internal conflict in uncentralized societies) predicts, and may set the stage for competitiveness, a component in the Barry et al. "toughness training," a variable which overlaps considerably with Ross's "aggression and toughness in socialization."

So it does appear that a useful model is one in which structural variables are treated as eco-cultural settings affecting the probability that certain socialization practices, emphases, and styles will prevail; and that these, in turn, affect the dispositions of adults to engage in overt conflict. Of course, one cannot preclude the possibility of direct effects of certain structural variables, such as polygyny, for example, which we have seen above relates to warfare frequency. But even where such relationships exist, it might be reasonable to expect complementary socialization effects. At least, Ross's work underscores the need to look for them.

Crime

Universally, some forms of aggression are defined as criminal. At least under certain conditions, assaults on persons or transgressions against their property are subject to negative sanctions. Industrialized societies, such as those described in this book, have elaborate criminal justice systems that are ostensibly designed to control crime. Debates continue in many of these nations regarding these systems and their effectiveness, or lack thereof. The attention paid to crime by our colleagues who prepared the chapters in this volume probably reflects the attention paid to it by the media and the public in all of the countries represented here.

In smaller, subsistence-level and near subsistence-level societies, crimes are also recognized and dealt with, equally ineffectively, by various means. Clearly, then, those aggressive acts defined as crimes occur universally, to a lesser or greater extent. It matters little that the nature of the acts defined as criminal may vary somewhat from society to society. Most striking is that, everywhere, some aggressive acts are perceived as unacceptable and dealt with by some institutionalized practices meant to keep them at some minimal level of occurrence.

Thus, not only do sociologists in industrialized societies devote considerable attention to criminal behavior, so do anthropologists. While the anthropological literature on crime is not very large, it contains considerable material, both empirical findings and theoretical notions, that students of aggression in global perspective can ill afford to ignore. We shall here consider two studies, one employing ethnographic data from the Human Relations Area Files, the other a part of the six cultures study. From these we shall see (1) criminal behavior is mostly a male phenomenon, (2) it relates to both structural and socialization variables, and (3) sex-role identity may provide an explanation for criminal aggression.

Despite some recent reports, mostly journalistic, of a narrowing of the gap between male and female crime statistics, it remains strikingly true that most crimes are committed by males. This sex difference is well documented in industrialized societies (in the United States, for example, in the 1970s, more than nine out of every ten crimes were committed by males), and anthropologists and cross-cultural psychologists who have studied crime hologeistically (e.g., Bacon, Child, & Barry, 1963) "have no doubt that this sex difference characterizes most societies [p. 292]."

So, cross-cultural research that seeks childhood antecedents of criminal behavior has tended to focus on the childhood experiences of boys. This was so for Bacon, Child, and Barry (1963) who found 48 societies among a sample of 110 in the Human Relations Area Files for which comparative ratings on criminal behavior, socialization practices, and family structure could confidently be made. Their study yielded several findings of considerable interest.

For example, and of primary importance, the 48 societies varied in frequency of crime of two types, theft and personal crime. These two types correlated with each other (R = .46) but, when examined separately, had different antecedent correlates, which we shall examine a bit later. For the moment, it should be stressed that the kinds of aggressive behavior which qualify as criminal, both stealing property and harming persons, occur to varying degrees in various nonliterate societies.

Secondly, variation relates systematically to a feature of family structure and household composition in a way that suggests that an important antecedent to criminal behavior among males is a lack of opportunity for young boys to form an identification with the father. In monogomous nuclear family societies, which provide maximal presence of fathers during infancy and childhood, frequency of theft and of personal crime is relatively low. In polygynous mother-child household societies, characterized by maximal father absence, the frequencies are relatively high. Indeed, the frequency of both types of crime increase steadily over four forms of household characterized by decreasing degree of father presence, of which the two mentioned above are the extremes. This finding fits with data collected some years ago in the United States on juvenile delinquents (e.g., Glueck & Glueck, 1950), on lower-class culture (Miller, 1958) and with cross-cultural data on male initiation rites (Whiting, Kluckhohn, & Anthony, 1958) all of which point to an overcompensatory effort on the part of males who lacked early opportunity to identify as such to assert their masculinity in an aggressive way. Thus, while this finding provided by Bacon and his colleagues (1963) concerns a structural variable (household structure), a plausible psychological hypothesis (which might be dubbed *compensatory machoism*) can be adduced to account for it.

The third finding to be noted from the Bacon et al. (1963) study is that, while both forms of crime relate to father absence, as was just detailed above, theft and personal crime have different patterns of socialization correlates. *Theft* is negatively correlated with childhood indulgence and positively correlated with socialization anxiety (or the degree to which punishment is employed and anxiety provoked during socialization). This finding may also be related to the U.S. data on delinquents (Glueck & Glueck, 1950) with both sets of findings suggesting that parenting styles that do not instill feelings of being loved lead to impulses to steal. As Bacon and his colleagues note, this hypothesis is similar to the psychoanalytic view of the motivation underlying kleptomania.

Of more direct relevance to our concerns is a fourth finding, this one concerning personal crime, which involves attempts to injure or kill persons, assaults, rapes, and other forms of aggression and violence. The pattern of child-training factors which correlate positively with personal crime include dependence socialization anxiety (which is composed of abrupt transition to independence training, severity and frequency of punishment for dependency, and evidence of emotional disturbance in children surrounding independence training) plus prolonged and exclusive mother-child sleeping arrangements. Bacon et al. (1963) suggest that these experiences produce persistent attitudes of rivalry, distrust, and hostility (p. 298), a suggestion which finds support in another finding from their study that frequency of personal crime is negatively correlated with a measure of general trustfulness and positively correlated with hostility in folk tales, an index of adult suspiciousness about the social environment.

This complex of findings from the Bacon et al. (1963) cross-cultural study provides the basis for an hypothesis about the sociopsychological conditions that might predispose males in any society to acts of personal aggression. The key conditions include any childhood experiences that set the stage for compensatory machismo, doubts concerning one's ability to function independently, and a view of the social environment as threatening, hostile, and not to be trusted. In the kinds of small societies that were included in the Bacon et al. study, the childhood experiences were perhaps not the sort that one finds readily in the kinds of societies featured in this book (e.g., exclusive mother-child sleeping arrangements), but there may well be some functionally identical or at least similar ones that exist, to varying degrees, in industrialized societies. For example, father absence, independence training, teachings regarding the nature of the social environment, and the instilling of trust are all variables that might be expected anywhere to produce the psychological states, including motives and attitudes, that Bacon and his colleagues have suggested contribute to aggression.

Following on the Bacon, Child and Barry (1963) study, Beatrice Whiting (1965) pursued the masculine protest (or, as we have termed it, compensatory machismo) notion, adding to it the concept of status envy (identifying with adult males who are perceived as controlling valued resources). Reasoning that males reared during early childhood primarily by females will be most susceptible to this kind of status envy, she examined field notes collected in the six cultures study and found that the two societies in which physical assault and homicide were at high levels (Khalapur in India and Nyansongo in Kenya) were characterized by lower father salience and higher adult male prestige. More specifically, in both of these societies, husbands and wives do not regularly eat, sleep, work, or relax together. Infants seldom see their fathers. Fathers and all adult males enjoy many prerogatives. Both societies also have a tradition of extolling warriors and cattle-raiders. Note, for example, the following ethnographic observation about the Kenyan society:

> The initiation rites that every adolescent boy in Nyansongo experiences stress the value of manliness—especially toughness and bravery. In the old days after initiation, a boy joined other warriors in the cattle villages and spent his time defending the herds and raiding other groups, stealing their cattle and sexually assaulting their women. [Whiting, 1965, p. 131]

And, she concludes, it would seem as if there were a never-ending cycle. The separation of the sexes leads to a conflict of identity in the boy children, to unconscious fear of being feminine; which leads to "protest masculinity," exaggeration of the difference between men and women, antagonism against and fear of women, male solidarity and hence to isolation of women and very young children [Whiting, 1965, p. 137]

This brief consideration of Whiting's findings marks the end of our effort in this chapter to extract some generalizations about human aggression from the anthropological literature. We have by no means finished the job. We have, instead, simply brought it to a temporary halt. We have halted in this abrupt fashion because we cannot complete this very substantial task in space available to us, nor is it our purpose in this chapter to do so. We are willing to stop here because we believe we have gone far enough to suggest the major aggression-relevant ideas which we believe reside in the anthropological literature. The reader will by now recognize that we believe that literature teaches us to take a functional, ecocultural perspective on aggression, to focus on both structural variables and socialization variables, to expect that parenting matters mightily, and to very much be concerned with relations between the sexes, if we expect ever to understand why human aggression is, on the one hand, as pervasive as it is and, on the other, so varied across human societies. Rather than overwhelm the reader with further details, we turn now to a presentation of a conceptual framework which we believe is compatible with the lessons from the anthropological research, one that can guide us and our colleagues in the necessarily continuing effort we must all make to study aggression in global perspective.

TOWARD CONCEPTUAL CLARITY; SOME DEFINITIONS

The literature on aggression employs terms whose meaning is often imprecise. Communication among students of aggression suffers as a consequence. If we are to attempt a conceptual framework for future research, an effort to clarify the terminology used in that framework is useful.

Following Strauss (1979), we suggest that some firm distinctions need to be made among such terms as *conflict, hostility, aggression,* and *violence*. While we cannot expect that our own definitions will erase the conceptual confusion that is present in the literature, or supersede the diverse, often competing conceptual schemes of others (e.g., Coser, 1956, and Dahrendorf, 1959, who interpret the same term—*conflict*—in very different ways), we hope at least to make clear what *we* mean by the various aggression-related terms that we use. And, by so doing, some theoretical implications of our framework may become more obvious. Further, it may assist the reader as he moves through the 18 case studies which comprise the largest part of this book.

Conflict. We shall use conflict in the Dahrendorf (1959) and Strauss (1979) sense, i.e., to refer to conflict of interest, a bona fide disagreement between two or more persons or groups about allocation of resources of whatever kind. Thus, conflict is a situational matter, a state of affairs, a characteristic of an interaction involving persons and some feature(s) of their environment. Conflict in this sense is similar to a competition; the term says nothing about how the persons involved in it will behave. It merely notes the existence of a situation in which two or more persons want different outcomes, or want the same outcome when not all can have it. Any situation, then, in which A's anticipated gain is potentially at B's expense, or in which one's winning presupposes the other's losing, is what we mean by conflict. The only behavioral component in this concept is a cognitive one; we assume that the participants in a conflict will be aware, to at least some minimal degree, of its existence and their involvement in it. That awareness, of course, can only be assumed or inferred from some behavior that appears to be a consequence of the conflict, especially some apparent effort to resolve it.

Conflict Resolution. Whenever a conflict exists, we assume the parties involved in it will attempt to resolve it in one way or another. Often, perhaps most often, they will each try to resolve it in their own favor, at least in the early stages of the attempted resolution. Whatever means are employed, these are, in our opinion, best thought of as strategies, tactics, and management procedures. They are behaviors, acts by the participants in the conflict that make the situation dynamic, moving it toward one kind or another of resolution. These acts are, for all participants, probably multiply determined; the determinants include such variables as the nature of the conflict, cultural or subcultural norms for conflict resolution, personality variables of the participants, and their short-term "states" including emotional levels. One such state could be, of course, anger. But more of that, later.

Frustration. By frustration, we prefer to indicate a feature of environmental states of affairs, rather than a state of the organism. However, it is that feature of situations, including and especially conflicts, which impinge directly on any person involved in them, which comprises a block to need or want satisfaction. It can lead to anger or to hostility and, usually whenever it does, it makes likely forms of behavior we call aggression.

Anger. By anger, we refer to a hypothetical construct, in the sense that it is a presumed-to-exist state of the organism, inferred from some observed behavior, that denotes a feeling or an emotion often experienced by persons involved in conflicts or in other circumstances in which they find their needs or wants frustrated. We reserve the term for a relatively short-lived feeling, usually provoked by the behavior of other actors in the conflict, who serve as the source of frustration. Anger is usually directed toward those persons, although it may sometimes be transferred (displaced) to others.

Hostility. We prefer to employ hostility for another presumed-to-exist state of the organism that resembles anger in all respects except that hostility is longer lasting. If anger is an acute state, hostility tends to be chronic, existing long after its original instigation, and often directed rather diffusely, as in the case (for example) of enduring ethnic hostility. We conceive it as usually less intense than anger and often not as readily detected.

Aggression. Obviously, aggression is the key term in our conceptual framework; it is also the one that presents the most difficulties. In contrast with much popular use of the word, we use it to refer to any behavior by one person that inflicts harm on another. We would stretch that definition somewhat to allow aggression to include behavior which, by a consensus of observers, appears to have harm infliction as its intent. Thus, we would score as an aggressive act, pulling the trigger of a gun pointed at another person, even when the gun misfires and no visible harm results. But we are uneasy about the subjectivity of *intent* judgments and, for this reason, do not define aggression as behavior that stems from the intent to harm, as some students do. Better, we think, to define aggression as behavior that has harm infliction as its *consequence,* but allow consensual inference of harm infliction as intent. In any case, it is highly desirable to emphasize that aggression is a class label for *behaviors,* thereby avoiding any necessary connotations of underlying motives, intentions, or feelings, even though all such states of the organism performing the behaviors might be reasonable inferences. In our conceptual scheme, we will theorize about such states, but prefer to keep aggression as a relatively pure behavioral term, albeit one defined in terms of its primary consequence, harm infliction. By so doing, we avoid some unnecessary problems: for example, Aronson (1972) distinguished between *instrumental aggression* (responding in a harm-inflicting way in order to get what one wants without wanting to hurt anyone) and *intentional aggression* (responses for which harm infliction is the desired end); Aronson urged reserving the label aggression for the latter. As we use the term, *aggression* covers both. While we see merits in Aronson's suggested distinction, we see it relating to matters of substance rather than of definition. We do, however, offer our own distinction centering around the concept of aggression and it involves our own term, *protoaggression*.

Protoaggression. By protoaggression, we refer to any behavior which has the following characteristics: intense, gross, diffuse efforts to satisfy needs, with those efforts sometimes directed against others. The feature of aggression which it *lacks* is any intent whatsoever to harm. Thus, it is different from Aronson's instrumental aggression, where, although harm infliction is not the desired end, it is nonetheless part of the presumed intentional state of the aggressor. Protoaggression includes no such intent. We will use the term primarily in reference to the behavior of human infants, who, we shall argue, often behave in "protoaggressive" ways, struggling diffusely and intently to get what they want without meaning to inflict harm, even in instances in which they (inadvertently) do. This concept will be discussed at some length later.

Violence. Like aggression, violence is behavior that inflicts harm. We distinguish it from aggression in only a few ways. We think of it as often (but not always) more intense than aggression, often having multiple perpetrators and victims. The violent actors often act in concert, sometimes in sanctioned, authorized, or agitator-led ways. Examples of violence include gang attacks, riots, large-scale vandalism, and, as a special case having many characteristics peculiar to it, warfare.

A CONCEPTUAL FRAMEWORK FOR THE STUDY OF AGGRESSION IN GLOBAL PERSPECTIVE

The few terms defined above—conflict, conflict resolution, frustration, anger, hostility, aggression, protoaggression, and violence—are the cornerstones of our conceptual framework, which will now be set out. A few additional terms will be introduced when appropriate, but those (e.g., culture, socialization) are general concepts that pertain to much more than aggression. But to reveal our framework in the most meaningful fashion, we must begin with one of those more general concepts, culture.

The Ecocultural Context

Segall (1981) recently asserted that the overarching problem of cross-cultural psychology is to identify the various factors in the natural and man-made environments of humans which influence their behaviors in reliable ways. These factors comprise the context in which human behaviors occur. And that context includes some of the distal causes of those behaviors. The term culture (itself too gross, diffuse, and variously defined to be useful except heuristically) can be and is regularly dissected into various contextual factors, including basic institutions, social organizations, subsistence patterns, languages, rules governing interpersonal relations, educational systems, division of labor schemes, and the like. These sorts of variables comprise the man-made part of any human environment. In addition, there is the physical environment, and certain other man-made phenomena, like habitats (houses, tents, houseboats) and certain demographic features (e.g., population density) that are rather directly contingent on features of the physical environment. Together, all such characteristics comprise the ecocultural context, and all these characteristics constitute, potentially, the independent variables for cross-cultural psychology. Any one or any combination of them might, we assert at the outset, be relevant to our attempt to understand aggression. Nevertheless, we single out a few ecocultural contextual features as most pertinent for the study of aggression.

Probability of Conflicts Over Resources. Simply put, some environments are rich, some are poor. But within both rich and poor, allocation of resources may be more or less equitable, setting the stage for less or more conflict over their distribution. Thus, in the South Fore highlands of New Guinea, in the not-too-distant past, when the Fore people were hunters and gatherers, we are told by Sorenson (1978) that land was abundant, population sparse, resources sufficient for all, and, "aggression and conflict within communities . . . unusual and the subject of considerable comment when it occurred [p. 15]." By the same source, we are told, that later, with increasing population pressure and competition for agricultural land, adult fighting emerged [p. 16]. This example, which could be duplicated many times over, is the basis for our asserting that contexts vary, over both time and space, in the likelihood of realistic, intragroup conflict.

Probability of Frustration. Many features of a culture can determine the probability that numbers of individuals will experience frustration. Distribution of resources, mentioned above, is only one. Certain features of child-rearing practices comprise others. So do prevalent attitudes governing acquisition and consumption of valued goods. For example, in many large-scale technological societies, characterized by consumptionist values, reinforced by advertising and other marketing practices, unrealistically high levels of aspiration (for goods) may set the stage for high levels of personal frustration among large portions of a population. Conversely, communal ownership in a setting that lacks all but the most essential of commodities may produce lower levels of frustration.

Together, the probability of conflict over resources and the probability of individual frustration, and whatever variables determine those probabilities, either make likely or prevent the occurrence of conflict and frustration. In this manner, the interpersonal situations in response to which aggression and violence may occur are culturally conditioned. Thus, the first set of linked concepts in our framework is as shown in figure 1.1.

Cultural Norms for Conflict-Resolution. Every society has traditions, institutions, and rules that pertain to the resolution of conflicts. These include systems for adjudicating disputes, when the prime actors in them are unable to reach a settlement. There are likely also to be widely shared expectations about the behaviors of persons engaged in such disputes. These expectations may be clearer in some societies than in others, and their actual content may differ. Various subgroups within societies may have different rules, as would be the case with various religious groups that might stress nonviolence or various regional groupings that might encourage vigilante-like efforts to resolve conflicts. Closely allied to these features are sanctions for or against aggression, which clearly vary across societies. For example, from data on maternal behavior collected in the six cultures study (Minturn & Lambert, 1964), marked differences could be found across six comparable communities in punishment for peer-directed aggression among children; mothers in an American New England town were very unlikely to do so. Numerous other examples could be adduced from the cross-cultural literature that sustains the proposition that societies vary in the nature of sanctions pertaining to

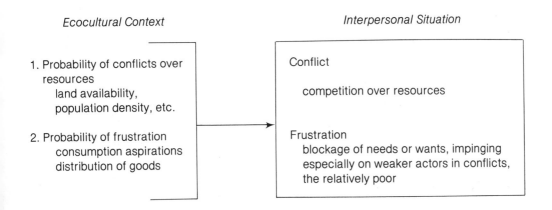

Ecocultural Context   *Interpersonal Situation*

1. Probability of conflicts over
   resources
       land availability,
       population density, etc.

   Conflict

       competition over resources

2. Probability of frustration
       consumption aspirations
       distribution of goods

   Frustration
       blockage of needs or wants, impinging
       especially on weaker actors in conflicts,
       the relatively poor

Fig. 1.1. Conceptual framework, Part One: Cultural roots of conflict and frustration

aggressive behavior and in other norms that relate to strategies for conflict resolution. These would also include, as we saw earlier in this chapter, variations in aggression-inculcation. This proposition is illustrated in figure 1.2.

Child-Rearing Emphases. The literature on differences in content, timing, targets, and agents of socialization across cultures is vast. Very little about socialization is universal beyond the bald fact that children everywhere are socialized. There is also evidence of considerable consistency across cultures in differentiation between the two sexes in child rearing emphases; e.g., *if* a society places more emphases on nurturance training for one sex than for the other, it is nearly always, if not always, females who receive more nurturance training than males (Barry, Bacon, & Child, 1957). But, even in this regard it must be noted that some societies differentiate between the sexes much more than do other societies (Barry, Child, & Bacon, 1959). So, it is clearly safe to state that one of the most striking differences across cultures is in child-rearing practices. In a variety of rather obvious ways, such differences have implications for aggression, by affecting the experiences individuals are likely to have growing up. A culture and personality framework, whether of a Freudian variety or of a more contemporary learning theory sort, provides linkages that run from socialization emphases to individual experiences to prevailing behavioral dispositions. We shall illustrate such linkages in our own framework, but not before introducing one more cultural context variable.

Availability of Models. In any society, children learn not only from deliberate teaching, as occurs in socialization, but in other ways as well. Among those other ways surely is emulation of models, including adults, older siblings, and some peers under certain circumstances. That

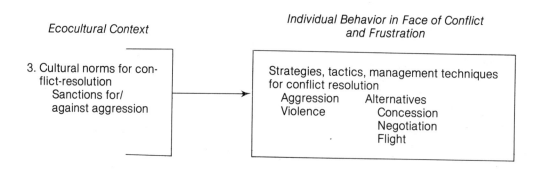

Fig. 1.2. Conceptual framework, Part Two: Cultural norms and conflict-resolution strategies

such learning "by imitation" occurs is a central tenet of social learning theory (e.g., Bandura, 1971) to which the editors of this volume, along with many other students of aggression, subscribe. As will be noted in our chapter on the United States, social learning therapy has proved very useful to American students of aggression. We believe that it is universally useful. Some of the variations in aggression described in this volume are best understood in terms of differential availability of aggressive models. Clearly, societies vary in the availability of models for aggressive behavior, as well as for alternatives to aggression as means for conflict resolution. This variation, like variations in child-rearing emphases, sets the stage for different individual experiences, particularly during childhood. Variations in individual experiences which concern us most as students of aggression are shown in figure 1.3, as deriving from cultural context variables.

Individual Experiences During Childhood

As was just suggested in figure 1.3, the experiences of individuals occur in cultural contexts and are shaped by them. Some of these culturally-shaped individual experiences are singled out for special attention because they bear directly on aggression.

   Reinforcements for Aggressive and Protoaggressive Responses. Every individual, in every society, has a unique reinforcement history, of course. But, as discussed above, the parameters of those reinforcement histories derive from the cultural context in which they occur. Of particular interest here are the histories that pertain to aggressive responses and to what we

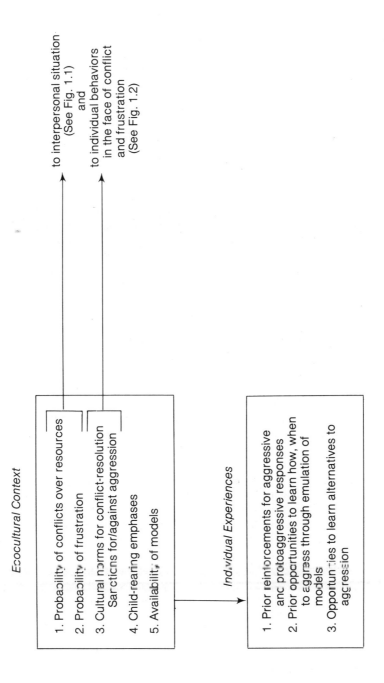

Ecocultural Context

1. Probability of conflicts over resources
2. Probability of frustration
3. Cultural norms for conflict-resolution Sanctions for/against aggression
4. Child-rearing emphases
5. Availability of models

to interpersonal situation
(See Fig. 1.1)
and
to individual behaviors
in the face of conflict
and frustration
(See Fig. 1.2)

Individual Experiences

1. Prior reinforcements for aggressive and protoaggressive responses
2. Prior opportunities to learn how, when to aggress through emulation of models
3. Opportunities to learn alternatives to aggression

Fig. 1.3. Conceptual framework, Part Three: Ecocultural context and individual experience

have called protoaggressive responses. Since protoaggression is, by definition, chronological-ly the earliest manifestation of aggression in all individuals, and since the concept is a key part of our conceptual framework, but not a standard part of the vocabulary employed by students of aggression, we shall deal with protoaggression first and in considerable detail.

Infantile Experience with Protoaggression. In a recent discussion of the role of social forces in the etiology of human aggression, Segall (1976) after having rejected the concept of an aggressive instinct, suggested that a social learning theorist must offer an alternative answer to the question of how aggressive responses come to occur and get rewarded in the first place. It was suggested that, during early childhood in every society, responses with *some* of the components of aggression are very likely to occur and very likely to be rewarded, with the result being a gradual transformation from protoaggression. The essence of the argument is presented in the following excerpts.

> The human infant starts life with an incredibly wide behavioral potential, but it can actually produce a very narrow repertoire of responses. . . . Those responses that it can and does make are the only ones subject to reinforcement. . . . Among the limited repertoire of responses at birth are actions that possess, in a primitive way, some of the basic attributes of what later in life are recognizable as aggressive responses. The infant can cry, pull, push, thrash about wildly, and struggle. It does so whenever it needs something. Later in life, . . . the child may come to emit similar responses when-ever it *wants* something, . . . but for the moment we are concerned . . . [only] with *need*, . . . the in-fant responds in one of the very few ways it can respond; these ways just happen to possess [some] features of aggressiveness—especially, *intensity* and an emotional state similar to what in everyday language is labeled *anger*. These responses further possess, albeit unknown to the infant who emits them, very strong demand characteristics. . . . The infant's responses serve as compelling stimuli for certain classes of responses by his caretakers. A very likely outcome of the infant's be-havior is that someone will respond sooner or later by satisfying the need. It is of little or no impor-tance that the infant is unaware in the beginning that this will be the outcome. It matters not that the struggling lacks intentionality. [p. 200]

Thus, it is argued, the infant responds to needs in the only ways it can and these ways involve rather consistently reinforced behaviors which we label protoaggressive because they are pre-cursers of genuinely aggressive behavior. What happens to these protoaggressive behaviors?

> Whenever a caretaker responds to these need-signalling behaviors of an infant, not only are the needs attended to (which has an immediate impact), the behaviors are reinforced (which has a long-range impact). During all those months before the baby matures sufficiently to acquire linguis-tic competence, it thus receives considerable reinforcement for its primitive, protoaggressive be-haviors. . . . [Assuming that] early experience is crucial in shaping the psychological development of the organism, . . . there is good reason to predict that all humans will acquire a strong and contin-uing disposition to respond "aggressively" whenever in some state of need. . . . the protoaggres-sion of the infant is subject to precisely the kind of reinforcement schedule that produces exceed-ingly strong response dispositions or habits. Because few caretakers are able to reward *every* need-signalling response of a discomforted infant, such responses are subject to a partial reinforcement schedule, just the kind that has long been known to make a response highly resistant to extinction. . . . Not only that, in the intervals of delay between the first distress call and the response of the care-taker, the infant's responses are likely to increase in intensity, so that it is often a very strong re-sponse that receives the reward. [pp. 201-202]

This argument proceeds to deal with the slow, erratic transformation of protoaggression to ag-gression:

As socialization proceeds, caretakers become increasingly demanding; [they] elicit and reward more sophisticated responses and endeavor not to reward the more primitive ones. Still, there is a long and difficult period of learning the more socially acceptable ways of signalling need, during which the child often regresses to earlier response patterns, which the caretaker sometimes in desperation reinforces. So . . . the child is inadvertently being taught that if all else fails, he can get what he needs by making a fuss.

As he acquires linguistic skills, which enable him to label his needs, the concept of "want" is gradually acquired. Whatever distinction there is between want and need, it becomes blurred, and all the behaviors associated with need-reduction generalize to want-satisfaction. And these behaviors must surely include the protoaggressive responses originally linked to need-signaling.

For one reason or another, asking often fails to produce the wanted object. When this is the case, the likely alternative to asking will be an earlier reinforced response . . . when frustrated, the child will regress to earlier behavior . . . [so] it turns out that a highly probable response to frustration is protoaggression.

[w]hat was once a diffuse protoaggressive response will subsequently become a directed, bona fide aggressive response, focused on another human being. Whereas earlier, the frustrated child responded by flailing aimlessly about, complaining, as it were, to no one in particular, the discovery that the ability to satisfy his wants resides in persons serves to sharpen his complaints so that they are directed to persons.

In the first instance, the persons most likely to be the targets of such responses are the child's caretakers. . . . As the child comes into contact with more and more people, . . . he is likely to encounter other persons who from time to time stand between him and his satisfaction. Other children especially are likely to have something he wants, or want to take from him something he has. The interaction that is likely to ensue . . . will almost inevitably involve interpersonal struggling because one or both of the actors will previously have struggled under similar, frustrating circumstances. Regardless of the outcome of the struggle, . . . the child will learn from it that aggression has a payoff. . . . learning this particular lesson is further facilitated by the simple fact that the child will often find himself in the company of other children who learned it before he did. . . . Thus, his learning . . . will be buttressed by what he learns by imitation. [pp. 202–203]

According to this account, what the child will have learned thus far in his or her development is simply to respond in an aggressive manner in order to get what he wants. This kind of aggressive responding is similar to the behavior that Aronson (1972) pointed to and termed instrumental aggression (see discussion above). Next we consider how a child can learn to perform responses that have as their obvious consequence (and perhaps intent) the infliction of harm.

Any instrumental response can become "an end in itself." Simply because a particular response has more than occasionally led to reinforcement, that response can come, via conditioning (via secondary reinforcement) to be intrinsically rewarding. As applied to instrumental aggressive responses, children who learn to make them successfully can learn also to make them for no reason other than to make them, because, as it were, it "feels good" to make them. [Segall, 1976, p. 204]

Thus, without postulating an aggressive drive, aggressive energy, or an aggressive instinct, we have followed the human infant from a helpless being who can only struggle aimlessly in an effort to satisfy his needs, through an intermediate stage where he learns to seek want-satisfaction by attacking others, through to a subsequent stage where he learns to inflict harm apparently for the sole sake of doing so.

We believe that this account describes a process which must occur in every society. We believe that what we have termed protoaggression, since it is so fundamentally a characteristic of the human animal during infancy, occurs everywhere, and that the process by which it is transformed into aggression must be the same, in at least outline form, everywhere. However, to the degree that early socialization practices and techniques vary from society to society, the manner and degree to which the universal protoaggression becomes aggression may vary considerably. It is for this reason that we highlight the reinforcement of protoaggressive responses in the *individual experiences* portion of our conceptual framework; and link it to the *ecocultural context* portion of that framework. Thus, we find the notion of protoaggression useful, potentially, for efforts to explain both the cross-cultural pervasiveness of human aggression and the intercultural differences in its frequency and intensity.

By the same token, we believe that differences across cultures in aggression are better explained by the reinforcement contingencies related to bona fide aggressive responses, and it is to these that we now turn.

Socialization of Aggression. In every society, sooner or later, caretakers probably decide that they will no longer tolerate certain behaviors from children—behaviors which, rooted in infantile protoaggressive behavior, more and more resemble acts with the potential for inflicting harm. Almost certainly, when such acts are directed against caretakers themselves, they come to be viewed as undesirable, if not intolerable. Lambert (1971), commenting on some of the findings from the six cultures study, noted that generally speaking, one of the most intolerable behaviors is aggression against a parent, as compared with aggression against child peers. On the other hand, even in the case of aggression against mothers, there were found, among the six societies studied, differences in the degree to which mothers punish or aggress toward their children when the children express anger toward the mothers. The clearest contrast in this regard, it will be recalled, involves the Gussii of Kenya, who put great pressure on children to obey and respect adults and who punish maternal defiance very severely, and the Khalapur of India, who are very nonpunitive (Minturn & Lambert, 1964, p. 287).

As regards other forms of aggression among children, responses by caretakers vary even more. Peer aggression is sometimes punished, and sometimes not. In some societies, punishment for aggression is fairly consistently applied, but in many it is not. In any case, the socialization of aggression is largely an exercise in discrimination learning, whereby the child is expected to learn when, where, and against whom he may or may not aggress. Once again from Lambert (1971), we know, for example, that in the United States, where mothers are not particularly permissive with regard to aggression toward mothers, they tend to be highly permissive, more so than any of the other five groups studied, with regard to peer aggression.

It is instructive to examine this last finding more closely. Minturn and Lambert (1964, p. 288) found that variation in socialization of peer aggression related to the degree to which families must live in close and constant contact with their relatives. Earlier, J. W. M. Whiting (1959) found that nuclear family cultures are least punitive of peer aggression, while extended family cultures are quite punitive. The key mechanism may well be fear that peer aggression might generalize to intrafamily targets. Whatever the mechanism, the finding serves to illustrate the basic point we wish to make in this section, that is, that reinforcement contingencies applied to aggression during childhood socialization not only vary across cultures but that the variance is rooted in ecocultural context variables, such as family structure and residence patterns.

If protoaggression occurs everywhere, the socialization of aggression will be a problem everywhere. Its solution, however, seems quite varied, when we view it in cross-cultural perspective. Thus, across cultures, children are apt to have very different experiences with reinforcement schedules when they behave aggressively. And there is more to the story of individual experience differences, as we point out in the next section.

Opportunities to Emulate Aggressive Models. As we stress elsewhere in this volume (see especially the chapter on the United States), we believe that much of the learning-to-aggress which occurs among human beings involves learning by observation. Hence, the availability of aggressive models, which may vary dramatically from place to place and from time to time, constitutes differential opportunity to have the kinds of experiences that promote or deter such learning. In societies in which adults or older children seldom aggress, younger children, obviously, will have few opportunities to emulate aggressive models. Consider, for example, the case of the Semai of West Malaysia and the following comments from a description of childhood in this nonviolent context (Dentan, 1978).

> Probably one of the most influential inhibitors of aggression is the fact that children see so few examples of it. In the absence of hierarchy, adults cannot even boss each other around. Parents make threatening gestures at children, but only rarely actually hit them. Therefore, even if a child wanted to become violent, it would have no very clear idea of how to proceed. [p. 132]

In contrast, consider the notoriously warlike Yanomamo of Venezuela, who, according to Chagnon (1968), express ferocity regularly and in diverse ways. And they actively teach aggression to young boys, both by example and direct tutelage as noted in the following description.

> Yanomamo boys, like all boys, fear pain and personal danger. They must be forced to tolerate it and learn to accept ferocity as a way of life. During one feast the adult men of two allied villages agreed to satisfy their grievances in a chest-pounding duel. They also took this opportunity to educate their small sons in the art of fighting and forced all the young boys from eight to fifteen years old to duck-waddle around the village periphery and fight each other. The boys were reluctant and tried to run away, afraid they would be hurt. Their parents dragged them back by force and insisted that they hit each other. [p. 130]

As these examples suggest, opportunities to learn to aggress through observation of aggressive adults are highly correlated with opportunities to receive reinforcement for aggressive responding, so that these two classes of experience that affect individuals probably function in the same direction and sustain each other. Nevertheless, given the importance that must be attached to the effects of learning by observation, we find it necessary and useful to single out that class of experience, as we have done here.

Opportunities to Learn Alternatives to Aggression. Just as aggression is learnable via reinforcement, both direct and vicarious, so, we presume, is nonaggressive conflict resolution. If examples of the latter kind of behavior abound, it will be emulated. If tutelage in concession, negotiation, or other nonaggressive conflict resolution skills is provided, those skills will be learned. In one sense, what we are talking about here is the obverse of what we discussed in the last two subsections, so that we should tend to expect opportunities to learn nonaggression to be negatively correlated with opportunities to learn aggression. But we treat opportunities to learn nonaggression separately, since the correlation just referred to is surely far from perfect. In many societies, there is a mix of the two. Surely in complex industrial societies, both kinds of opportunities coexist, and individuals learn both classes of behavior, however logically contradictory they may seem. Indeed, we suspect that in societies in which many opportunities to learn to aggress are provided, these are accompanied by many needs to learn to control, suppress, displace, or inhibit aggression. Some of these latter behavioral tendencies are probably reinforced directly or taught through example. In some of the most aggressive of societies, whole institutions are devoted to moral education, a central component of which is often proscriptions against violence of certain kinds, at least. These may be expected to contribute to the management of conflict by pointing persons toward nonaggressive alternatives, if only by contributing to some level of aggression inhibition. So, we single out opportunities to learn nonaggressive alternatives as one of the classes of experiences available to individuals that shape their behavioral tendencies.

Summary. In this section on individual experiences relating to social forces in human aggression, we have asserted that our tendencies to aggress are an end product of a complex socialization process in which our protoaggressive reactions to frustration are reinfroced in ways that make bona fide aggressive actions likely to occur under some conditions and less likely to occur under others. We noted that humans do not need to be taught to be aggressive, but that many almost unavoidably learn to be aggressive because they are first rewarded for prototypical aggressive responding during the helpless days of infancy. But just as many learn to aggress, some learn not to. If the key to aggression lies in socialization, so does the key to nonaggression. As we showed in figure 1.3, the key experiences are rooted in culture. What we suggest, now, as shown below in figure 1.4, is how these experiences are linked to prevailing behavioral dispositions.

Psychological Constructs

All psychological constructs of concern to us in our study of human aggression are presumed-to-exist states of the organism, never directly observable, but always inferred from individual behaviors in the face of conflict and frustration. These we place into two major categories: antecedent prevailing dispositions, and situationally provoked states. A third construct, genetic predispositions, will also be discussed.

Antecedent Prevailing Dispositions. In the first category, we place the more-or-less enduring dispositions of individuals—their acquired behavioral dispositions in the face of conflict and frustration, including their habits. Individuals who have "enjoyed" reinforcements for protoaggressive and aggressive behavior, applied via a schedule of reinforcement that strengthens such behavior, would be expected to be predisposed, more than others, to behave aggressively, and could be said to possess relatively strong aggressive habits. Taking a more cognitive orientation, we would add the concept of beliefs to this part of the story. Individuals whose experience has convinced them that it is in some sense good, at least under certain circumstances, to behave aggressively, would hold a belief that predisposes them to such behavior, under those circumstances. In addition, each individual may be thought of as characterized by some level of aggression-anxiety and aggression-inhibition. Again, these are presumed to exist enduring states of the individual brought about over time as a consequence of the cumulative experiences enjoyed by that individual. Finally, to round out the picture of prevailing dispositions, we suggest other personality traits, such as self-image, also products of past experience, and also conceivably related to the probability of overt aggression under certain circumstances.

To cite just one example of how antecedent prevailing dispositions need to be taken into account to understand aggressive behavior, the behavior of a terrorist (see descriptions in the chapters on Ireland and Italy) would be related to beliefs about the means justification provided by the alleged ends of the terrorist's "war."

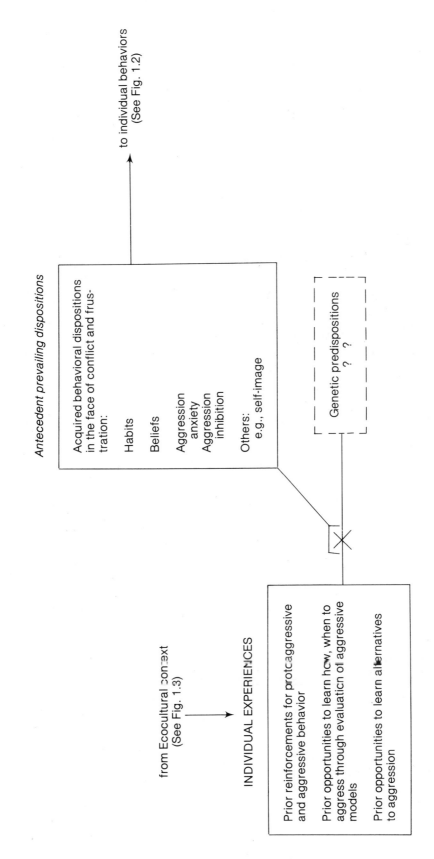

Psychological Constructs
Inferred states of the organism

Antecedent prevailing dispositions

Acquired behavioral dispositions
in the face of conflict and frustration:

Habits

Beliefs

Aggression
anxiety
Aggression
inhibition

Others:
e.g., self-image

to individual behaviors
(See Fig. 1.2)

Genetic predispositions
? ?

from Ecocultural context
(See Fig. 1.3)

INDIVIDUAL EXPERIENCES

Prior reinforcements for protoaggressive
and aggressive behavior

Prior opportunities to learn how, when to
aggress through evaluation of aggressive
models

Prior opportunities to learn alternatives
to aggression

Fig. 1.4. Conceptual Framework, Part Four: Individual experience and prevailing disposition

Situationally Provoked States. Whatever an individual's enduring predispositions, he may experience momentary states which lead to aggressive behavior. The first of these, it almost goes without saying, is awareness of conflict. Equally obvious is the desire to resolve it in some way. Without conflict awareness and desire to resolve conflict, neither aggression nor a nonaggressive effort to resolve conflict would be expected from the organism. Just how the conflict resolution attempt takes shape may depend on three other situationally provoked states—anger, hostility, and anxiety—any one of which is likely to increase the short-term potential for aggressive behavior. But, any one of them may also lead to other behaviors, such as flight and even attempts at negotiation and concession. In any event, these situationally provoked momentary states and the antecedent enduring states described above are all inferred from behavior and seen as products of experience imbedded in ecocultural contexts. Except as useful summaries of the residues of experience, these inferred psychological constructs add little to our conceptual framework. We have included them primarily because they are popular notions and because it seems useful to treat them as proximal antecedents of behavior. But it would be an error to infer from our treatment of these constructs that we attribute causal status to them. We do not.

Genetic Predispositions. Our picture is incomplete without some treatment of genetic predispositions. We include them here, as if they were inferred psychological constructs, but we treat them differently from the two categories of constructs just described. We have no idea which genetic predispositions are conceivably relevant to aggression. We doubt that there are any aggressive genes. We can't imagine genetic dispositions leading directly to behavior. But we allow for the very real possibility that certain inherited factors predispose individuals to react differently to the particular run of experiences they have during their lifetimes, including the kinds of experiences that influence aggression. So, in our conceptual framework, we show genetic predispositions *interacting with* individual experiences to produce prevailing dispositions, which in turn combine with situationally provoked states of the organism to set the stage for individual behaviors in the face of conflict and frustration. By so doing, we round out, and complete, our conceptual framework. An overall summary of it appears in figure 1.5.

As should be immediately apparent from this figure, and from our preceding discussion, the cornerstone of the entire framework lies in the ecocultural context, wherein reside the probability of conflicts over resources, the probability of frustration, cultural norms for conflict resolution, sanctions for and against aggression, child-rearing emphases, availability of aggressive or non-aggressive models, and the individual experiences which lead ultimately to individual behaviors in the face of conflict and frustration. And, since these contexts vary from society to society, the key to understanding intersocietal differences in the kind and amount of aggressive behavior lies there. We trust that the reader will find this framework useful as he or she encounters the array of behavioral descriptions contained in the following 18 chapters.

INTRODUCTION TO A CROSS CULTURAL SURVEY OF AGGRESSION

We turn now to an introduction to the 18 diverse accounts of aggressive behavior in particular contexts, most of them large, complex contemporary societies, in nearly every case a modern nation-state. Six of these are Western European nations, from Finland in the north, to Italy in the south, with Ireland, France, Germany, and Holland also in this category. Three are Eastern European or Middle Eastern, i.e., Hungary, Turkey, and Israel. Five are located in Asia—China, Japan, India, Hawaii, and New Zealand; two in Latin America—Brazil and

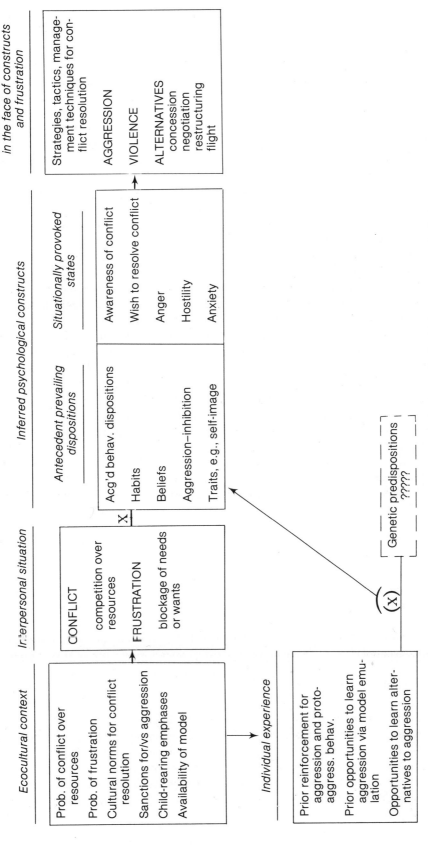

Ecocultural context

Interpersonal situation

Inferred psychological constructs

Individual behaviors in the face of constructs and frustration

Antecedent prevailing dispositions

Situationally provoked states

Prob. of conflict over resources

Prob. of frustration

Cultural norms for conflict resolution

Sanctions for/vs aggression

Child-rearing emphases

Availability of model

CONFLICT

    competition over resources

FRUSTRATION

    blockage of needs or wants

X

Acg'd behav. dispositions

Habits

Beliefs

Aggression–inhibition

Traits, e.g., self-image

Awareness of conflict

Wish to resolve conflict

Anger

Hostility

Anxiety

Strategies, tactics, management techniques for conflict resolution

AGGRESSION

VIOLENCE

ALTERNATIVES
concession
negotiation
restructuring
flight

Individual experience

Prior reinforcement for aggression and proto-aggress. behav.

Prior opportunities to learn aggression via model emulation

Opportunities to learn alternatives to aggression

Genetic predispositions
?????

(X)

Fig. 1.5. An Overall View of a Conceptual Framework for the Study of Aggression in Global Perspective

35

Peru; one in Africa—Nigeria; and one in North America—the United States. This geographic categorization could, of course, be different: Hawaii is actually one of the United States of America. But a large portion of the population of Hawaii is ethnically Asian. Israel, though located in the Middle East, has a majority Jewish population that is largely of recent European origin. But its Middle Eastern location is obviously a fact that has critical implications for matters pertaining to aggression in Israel. New Zealand, treated here as Asian, might also be thought of as European, since it has an overwhelmingly Anglo-Saxon population. So, the foregoing categorization is arbitrary. We use it primarily to indicate the geographic range of coverage provided by the contributors to this volume.

The contributions range not only geographically, but substantively as well. Nearly all—but not all—present facts regarding aggressive behavior, both individual and collective, in the nations or regions covered. Many—but again, not all—describe research on aggression that has been done by compatriate scholars. Several provide very rich historico-socio-contextual accounts. Some emphasize analyses at a micro level, others stress more macro analyses.

There are certain topics that show up in most of the contributions, such as crime statistics and socialization emphases; other topics show up in several, wherever relevant, such as terrorism and political violence; while some topics are treated either uniquely or only in a few contributions, e.g., vigilante activities.

Theoretical emphases also vary across the eighteen contributions, reflecting intellectual trends that are themselves imbedded in the cultural contexts which are of primary concern in this volume. For example, the ideas of Henri Laborit (cf. Laborit, 1978), the French biologically-oriented student of human aggression, are discussed critically in the analysis of recent experiences with armed acts of self-defense by individual citizens in France, but his ideas are not mentioned in any other contribution. Psychoanalytic approaches are referred to in several. Instinct approaches are frequently mentioned, but usually dismissed as unhelpful. Most often, but not always, the contributors employ one or another version of social learning theory, and many also find reason to refer to the frustration-aggression hypothesis.

So, the picture presented in the following 18 chapters is somewhat kaleidoscopic, rather than global in the sense of "comprising a gestalt." Therefore, before embarking on the journey through these diverse accounts, the reader might find useful the following preview of their contents.

Western Europe

In the chapter on *Finland,* Pulkkinen describes a very stable nation, with a remarkably non-aggressive foreign policy and an enlightened criminal justice system that makes no use of the death penalty. Noted also, however, is a very high rate of alcohol consumption, a high suicide rate, and considerable individual aggression including assaults and homicides, many of them apparently alcohol related. Pulkkinen pays special attention to the problem of youthful offenders in Finland, presenting a developmental analysis with suggestions as to how to deal with these youthful offenders. She suggests that the key might lie in more enlightened parenting.

Wiegman, Baarda, and Seydel consider parenting important also in *Holland.* A country which also eschews the death penalty, Holland has a relatively low crime rate, but there appears to be a recent increase in vandalism, some of it connected to football games, a phenomenon present elsewhere in Europe as well. Basing their chapter largely on research done in Holland, the authors consider influences on aggressive behavior that derive from schools, peers, sociocultural background factors, and the media. A discussion of terrorism is also present in the chapter on Holland.

Terrorism is discussed also in the chapter on *Germany*, the author of which, Groebel, emphasizes various forms of social stress as setting the stage for political violence and other forms of aggression. In this respect, his work relates to that of Landau and Beit-Hallahmi in Israel (see below). This Germany/Israel link is particularly interesting in the light of Groebel's references to the holocaust, both the event itself and the recent television drama concerning it that was shown in Germany. The author also offers some definitions and theories of aggression and describes some selected German studies, including one on effects of media violence. Notable also is an effective gun control law in Germany, a fact mirrored in several other countries included in this volume.

Perhaps the most dramatic instance of political violence is contained in the chapter on *Northern Ireland*, by McWhirter. She provides us with a very detailed historical account of the Irish "troubles," a lucid discussion of the underlying ethnocentrism and efforts at conflict resolution, and some intriguing studies of the impact of all of this on children growing up in this setting. In this respect, readers will perhaps wish to ponder why it is that Ireland has such a very low rate of homicide.

In the several discussions of political violence present in the chapters from Western Europe, reference is made to the student uprisings in France in May of 1968, with the suggestion that those events were a watershed, even a trigger for political violence elsewhere. In the chapter on *Italy*, by Ferracuti and Bruno, the failure of those well publicized events in France to generate major reforms in Italy is cited as a contribution to the emergence of terrorist groups in Italy, which the authors also analyze as a kind of fantasy war carried on by disaffected youth against their society. An interesting conceptual framework for the analysis of aggression in Italy (and perhaps elsewhere) is presented, one which takes into account some macro-level phenomena that have been characteristic of postwar Italy, including considerable internal migration, mostly from south to north and from rural to urban settings, with a marked decline in the numbers of agricultural workers, many of whom have helped to swell the unemployment rates. The authors also consider regional differences in aggressive behavior and highlight, in several regions, the well-known phenomena of vigilante activities and related criminal activities by such groups as the Mafia. Pertinent to our efforts to consider the possible impact of rigid sexual differentiation during socialization on individual aggressiveness (recall the discussion earlier in this chapter on "compensatory machismo") is the reference by Ferracuti and Bruno to the "unconsciously homosexual character" of some Mafiosi behavior.

If the events in France in 1968 were important for understanding political violence in Europe and elsewhere, the author of our chapter on *France*, DuLong, chose not to emphasize it. Instead, he provides an intriguing sociopolitical analysis of a relatively small but extremely interesting wave of individual vigilante-like behavior, the phenomenon in France known as *auto-defence*. He relates it to a form of hostility that he considers characteristic of adult-child relationships and person state relationships that he argues are very pervasive in France.

Eastern Europe and the Middle East

Ranschburg's chapter on *Hungary* consists primarily of a description of studies on human aggression done recently by Hungarian social scientists. These include research done on very young children (research which relates to our notion of protoaggression, as discussed earlier in the present chapter). Ranschburg also discusses sex differences in aggression, some research on catharsis, and he presents some interesting ideas about modeling effects due to observations of aggressive fathers.

Opportunities to learn aggression through male role modeling seem present to a high degree in *Turkey* also. While Fisek describes Turkey as a country undergoing rapid social change, her discussion points also to the tenacity of certain traditional structures and life styles, a salient feature of which is male supremacy and low status for women. She suggests that Turks may be threatened by fragile male self-esteem, which may be related to the quick, unrestrained expression of anger which is characteristic and which might further relate to crimes of honor, blood feuding, and political violence which are part of the picture in Turkey.

Landau and Beit-Hallahmi, in their chapter on *Israel,* focus on a framework that involves social stress, social support, and aggressive behavior. Sources of stress, such as war and high inflation rates (both common in recent Israeli experience), they believe set the stage for individual aggressiveness, especially when social support systems fail or malfunction. They note and offer tentative explanations for a steady increase in crime rates in Israel and a high level of verbal aggression. They call attention to increases in levels of internal aggressions following each of the recent wars in which Israel has been engaged, and related these increases to certain forms of social stress.

Asia

Another example of a nation which, like Turkey, has experienced profound social change but within which, nevertheless, tradition persists, is *China,* as described in this volume by Bond and Wang. The continued pervasiveness of Confucian ideology, with its emphasis on social order, is cited by them as reason for the nonencouragement of overt aggressiveness. In a manner reminiscent of the Israeli case, the authors of the chapter on China also call our attention to a form of verbal aggression which they see as characteristic of the Chinese—public abuse.

Japan, another Asian nation with a history of violence at the macro level, is described by Goldstein and Ibaraki as a very nonaggressive society at the micro level. It has an extraordinarily low crime rate, and individuals very rarely aggress within the society. So, the authors examine the issue of aggression controls within Japanese society and call our attention to the virtual absence of punishment in its socialization practices. They argue that internal aggression is obviously nonadaptive in Japan given its very high population density and the homogeneity of its population. It is also interesting to note the strict gun control laws in Japan.

Another homogeneous population is found in *New Zealand.* Although, as Ritchie and Ritchie remind us, some 250,000 Maori continue to live in what was their native land, the bulk of the population is Anglo-Saxon, which makes New Zealand very much like Western industrialized nations in many respects. And unlike Japan, with its homogeneous population, New Zealand suffers from increasing violence, which, while still lower in intensity than in many Western nations, resembles more the Western nations than its Asian neighbors. As in Finland, alcohol consumption is high in New Zealand. As in several European settings, certain socially sanctioned violence is described as rife in New Zealand, some related to football games and hunting, with drinking and other forms of machismo involved. The authors also describe a process whereby aggression is controlled in New Zealand. Thus, the country enjoys a gun control law and employs strict discipline in its criminal justice system and its schools. This strict discipline is reflected also in child-rearing patterns, but, according to Ritchie and Ritchie, the widespread belief in "punishment as the pillar of parenthood" merely contributes to a displacement of aggression into socially sanctioned arenas.

Socially sanctioned aggression is a feature of *India,* too, as described by Bharati, an anthropologist, whose chapter is very rich in details regarding the well-known Hindu norms of nonviolence and the less well-known, but perhaps more significant, Ksattriya norms which justify violence. Bharati provides numerous examples of a violent reality in India, and he resolves some apparent contradictions between that reality and the notions of nonviolence associated with Ghandi.

If Japanese are very nonaggressive individuals in Japan, this characteristic of theirs is not limited to those who live there. In *Hawaii,* we learn from Blanchard and Blanchard, Hawaiians of Japanese ethnic origin have particularly low crime rates. In this multicultural and multi-ethnic locale, the authors report marked ethnic differences in crime rates, probably related causally to unemployment rates and other indices of economic and social well-being that vary with ethnicity in Hawaii. In a chapter that provides considerable information about violence in schools and some clues as to its origins derived from self-reports regarding socialization emphases, the authors treat Hawaiian society as possessing a very high risk of violence which is effectively inhibited via various forms of social control. Also noteworthy is that Hawaii, despite certain forms of social stress, such as a severe housing problem, high cost of living, and a marked decline recently in the quality of life of most of its inhabitants regardless of ethnic background, still enjoys relatively low crime rates in comparison with the mainland United States.

Latin America

In *Brazil,* where Biaggio tells us students of aggression tend in the main to interpret aggression in the light of psychoanalytic theory and ethology, balanced somewhat by empirical research in a social-learning framework, urban violence is a growing concern. The author asserts that urban violence is escalating, a phenomenon which is perhaps rooted in socioeconomic problems. Traditional machismo in Brazilian culture is related by Biaggio to outbreaks of violence against women and to some seemingly very dangerous driving styles.

Difficult economic conditions in *Peru* are cited by Anicama as related there, too, to prevalent forms of aggressive behavior, as revealed by crime statistics, with special attention paid by the author to assaults, juvenile delinquency, strikes, and acts of political terrorism, all on the increase.

Africa

Perhaps the most dramatic examples of countries undergoing rapid social and political change exist today in Africa. *Nigeria,* however unique, is representative. Bloom and Amatu provide us with a very interesting analysis of aggression in Nigeria, this very heterogeneous, multi-ethnic society, which has known considerable violence rooted in politics. The picture they present is one in which overt aggression is volatile, occurring every now and again in a seemingly spontaneous fashion, then as suddenly gone and, as it were, forgotten. Their chapter also contains a report of a very interesting survey of beliefs about aggression held by Nigerians, both formally educated and not. Despite intergenerational, traditional vs. nontraditional differences in outlook, the survey reveals some interesting shared beliefs about the causes and appropriate responses to aggressive behavior.

North America

Finally, for the *United States,* Goldstein reviews some well-known kinds and instances of violent behavior, both individual and collective, which have peppered the 200-plus-year history of this major, industrial society. His review of the U.S.'s notoriously high crime statistics is accompanied by some observations that permit those disturbing data to be viewed in a context that offers some explanation and even some basis for optimism. Particular attention is devoted in this chapter to information pertaining to the control of aggressive behavior, a growing research interest among American scholars. The various theories of aggression and its control that have figured most prominently in American research on aggression are also reviewed in this chapter, with a particularly thorough presentation of social learning theory, which, in one form or another, has come to predominate.

A FINAL INTRODUCTORY COMMENT

As the foregoing preview has surely suggested, the chapters in this book comprise a sample of convenience from among a large population of contemporary societies, and the treatment of the topic in each chapter reflects decisions by the contributors themselves as much as it reflects their compliance with an outline we provided them when we solicited their contributions. So this volume ought to be considered an initial step in an effort to study aggression globally. It is, in our judgment, a long overdue initial step. The comparative literature dealing with aggressive behavior in complex nation-states is a slim one. Studies like that of Feierabend and Feierabend (1966), who studied internal conflict in a number of nations, including nearly all of those covered in the present volume, and those which have focused on intergroup conflicts within three East African Nations (Brewer & Campbell, 1976, and Levine & Campbell, 1972) are among the few that have tread similar ground. So we embark on this journey rather like explorers. The terrain is largely uncharted. But the rough outline maps that follow are eminently worth consulting.

REFERENCES

Ardrey, R. *The territorial imperative.* New York: Atheneum, 1966.

Aronson, E. *The social animal.* San Francisco: Freeman, 1972.

Bacon, M. K., Child, I., & Barry, H., III. A cross-cultural study of correlates of crime. *Journal of Abnormal and Social Psychology,* 1963, *66,* 291-300.

Bandura, A. *Social learning theory.* New York: General Learning Press, 1971.

Barry, H., III. Description and uses of the Human Relations Area Files. In Harry C. Triandis and John W. Berry (Eds.), *Handbook of cross-cultural psychology,* Vol. 2, *Methodology.* Boston: Allyn and Bacon, 1980.

Barry, H., III. Studies using the Standard Cross-Cultural Sample. In H. Barry, III and A. Schlegel (Eds.), *Cross-cultural samples and codes.* Pittsburgh: University of Pittsburgh Press, 1980.

Barry, H., III, Bacon, M. K., & Child, I. L. A cross-cultural survey of some sex differences in socialization. *Journal of Abnormal and Social Psychology,* 1957, *55,* 327-332.

Barry, H., III., Bacon, M. K., & Child, I. L. Definitions, ratings and bibliographic sources of child-training practices of 110 cultures. In C. S. Ford (Ed.), *Cross-cultural approaches.* New Haven: HRAF Press, 1967.

Barry, H., III, Child, I. L., & Bacon, M. K. Relation of child training to subsistence economy. *American Anthropologist,* 1959, *61,* 51-63.

Barry, H., III, Josephson, L., Lauer, E., & Marshall, C. Traits inculcated in childhood: Cross-cultural codes V. *Ethnology,* 1976, *15,* 83-114. Reprinted in H. Barry, III and A. Schlegel (Eds.), *Cross-cultural samples and codes.* Pittsburgh: University of Pittsburgh Press, 1980.

Barry, H., III, & Paxson, L. M. Infancy and early childhood: Cross-cultural codes I. *Ethnology,* 1971, *10,* 466-508. Reprinted in H. Barry, III and A. Schlegel (Eds.), *Cross-cultural samples and codes.* Pittsburgh: University of Pittsburgh Press, 1980.

Barry, H., III, & Schlegel, A. (Eds.) *Cross-cultural samples and codes.* Pittsburgh: University of Pittsburgh Press, 1980.

Berkowitz, L. Simple views of aggression: An essay review. *American Scientist,* 1969, *57,* 372-383.

Berry, J. W. An ecological approach to cross-cultural psychology. *Nederlands Tijdschrift voor de Psychologie,* 1975, *30,* 51-84.

Brewer, M. B., & Campbell, D. T. *Ethnocentrism and intergroup attitudes: East African evidence.* New York: John Wiley, 1976.

Campbell, D. T. Descriptive epistemology: psychological, sociological, and evolutionary. Unpublished lectures. Harvard University, 1977.

Chagnon, N. A. Yanomamo social organization and warfare. In Morton Fried, Marvin Harris, and Robert Murphy (Eds.), *War: The anthropology of armed conflict and aggression.* Garden City, N.Y.: The Natural History Press, 1968.

Chaney, R. P., & Revilla, R. R. Sampling methods and interpretation of correlation: A comparative analysis of seven cross-cultural samples. *American Anthropologist,* 1969, *71,* 597-633.

Coser, L. A. *The functions of social conflict.* New York: The Free Press, 1956.

Dahrendorf, R. *Class and class conflict in industrial society.* London: Routledge and Kegan Paul, 1959.

Dentan, R. K. Notes on childhood in a nonviolent context: The Semai case. In A. Montagu (Ed.), *Learning non-aggression: The experience of non-literate societies.* New York: Oxford University Press, 1978.

Divale, W. T., & Harris, M. Population, warfare, and the male supremacist complex. *American Anthropologist,* 1976, *78,* 521-538.

Eckhardt, W. Anthropological correlates of primitive militarism. *Peace Research,* 1973, *5,* 5-10.

Ember, M. Warfare, sex ratio, and polygamy. *Ethnology,* 1974, *13,* 197-206.

Ember, M. Statistical evidence for an ecological explanation of warfare. Paper presented at the 10th annual meeting of the Society for Cross-Cultural Research, Syracuse, N.Y., February 1981.

Feierabend, I. K., & Feierabend, R. L. Aggressive behaviors within politics, 1948-1962: A cross-national study. *Journal of Conflict Resolution,* 1966, *10,* 249-271.

Glueck, S., & Glueck, E. *Unraveling juvenile delinquency.* New York: The Commonwealth Fund, 1950.

Jahoda, G. Theoretical and systematic approaches in cross-cultural psychology. In Harry C. Triandis (Ed.), *Handbook of cross-cultural psychology.* Boston: Allyn and Bacon, 1980. Vol. I. *Perspectives,* pp. 69-141.

Kim, S. S. The Lorenzian theory of aggression and peace research: A critique. *Journal of Peace Research,* 1976, *13,* 253-276.

Laborit, H. The biological and sociological mechanisms of aggression. *International Social Science Journal,* 1978, *30,* 727-749.

Lambert, W. W. Personality development and socialization of aggression. In W. W. Lambert & R. Weisbrod (Eds.), *Comparative perspectives on social psychology.* Boston: Little, Brown, 1971.

Lambert, W. W., & Tan, A. L. Expressive styles and strategies in the aggressive actions of children in six cultures. *Ethos,* 1979, *7,* 19-36.

LeVine, R. A. Cross-cultural study in child psychology. In P. Mussen (Ed.), *Carmichael's manual of child psychology.* Vol. 2 (3rd ed.) New York: Wiley, 1970.

LeVine, R. A. & Campbell, D. T. *Ethnocentrism: Theories of conflict, ethnic attitudes and group behavior.* New York: John Wiley, 1972.

Levinson, D. *A guide to holocultural theory.* New Haven: Human Relations Area Files, 1977. 6 vols.

Levy, R. I. Tahitian gentleness and redundant controls. In Ashley Montagu (Ed.), *Learning non-aggression: The experience of non-literate societies.* New York: Oxford University Press, 1978.

Lorenz, K. *On aggression.* New York: Harcourt Brace Jovanovich, 1963.

Lumsden, C. J., & Wilson, E. O. *The coevolutionary process.* Cambridge, Mass.: Harvard University Press, 1981.

Maccoby, E. E., & Jacklin, C. N. *The psychology of sex differences.* Stanford, Calif.: Stanford University Press, 1966.

Maccoby, E. E., & Jacklin, C. N. Sex differences in aggression: A rejoinder and reprise. *Child Development,* 1980, *51,* 964-980.

Miller, W. D. Lower class culture as a generating milieu of gang delinquency. In M. E. Wolfgang, L. Savitz, and N. Johnston (Eds.), *The sociology of crime and delinquency.* New York: Wiley, 1958.

Minturn, L., & Lambert, W. W. *Mothers of six cultures: Antecedents of child rearing.* New York: Wiley, 1964.

Montagu, Ashley (Ed.) *Learning non-aggression: The experience of non-literate societies.* New York: Oxford University Press, 1978.

Moore, F. W. (Ed.) *Readings in cross-cultural methodology.* New Haven: HRAF Press, 1966.

Moore, O. K., & Lewis, D. J. Learning theory and culture. *Psychological Review,* 1952, *59,* 380-388.

Moris, D. *The naked ape.* New York: McGraw-Hill, 1967.

Munroe, R. L., and Munroe, R. H. Perspectives suggested by anthropological data. In Harry C. Triandis (Ed.) *Handbook of cross-cultural psychology.* Boston: Allyn and Bacon, 1980. Vol. I. *Perspectives,* pp. 253-318.

Murdock, G. P. World ethnographic sample. *American Anthropologist,* 1957, *59,* 664-687.

Murdock, G. P. *Ethnographic atlas.* Pittsburgh: University of Pittsburgh Press, 1967.

Murdock, G. P., & White, D. R. Standard cross-cultural sample. *Ethnology,* 1969, *8,* 329-369. Reprinted in H. Barry, III and A. Schlegel (Eds.), *Cross-cultural samples and codes.* Pittsburgh: University of Pittsburgh Press, 1980.

Naroll, R. *Data quality control—A new research technique: Prolegomena to a cross-cultural study of culture stress.* New York: Free Press, 1962.

Naroll, R. On ethnic unit classification. *Current Anthropology,* 1964, *5,* 283-312.

Naroll, R. Holocultural theory tests. In R. Naroll and F. Naroll (Eds.), *Main currents in cultural anthropology.* New York: Appleton-Century-Crofts, 1973.

Naroll, R. *The Moral Order.* Vol. I. Unpublished manuscript. n.d.

Naroll, R., & Cohen, R. (Eds.) *A handbook of method in cultural anthropology.* Garden City, N.Y.: Natural History Press, 1970.

Naroll, R., Michik, G. L., & Naroll, F. Holocultural research methods. In Harry C. Triandis and John W. Berry (Eds.), *Handbook of cross-cultural psychology,* Vol. 2. *Methodology.* Boston: Allyn and Bacon, 1980.

O'Leary, T. J. A preliminary bibliography of cross-cultural studies. *Behavior Science Notes,* 1969, *4,* 95-115.

O'Leary, T. J. Bibliography of cross-cultural studies: Supplement I. *Behavior Science Notes,* 1971, *6,* 191-203.

O'Leary, T. J. Bibliography of cross-cultural studies: Supplement II. *Behavior Science Notes,* 1973, *8,* 123-134.

Otterbein, K. F. Internal war: A cross-cultural study. *American Anthropologist,* 1968, *70,* 277-289.

Otterbein, K. F., & Otterbein, C. S. An eye for an eye, a tooth for a tooth: A cross-cultural study of feuding. *American Anthropologist,* 1965, *67,* 1470-1482.

Prescott, J. W. Body pleasure and the origins of violence. *Bulletin of the Atomic Scientists,* 1975, *31,* 10-20.

Rohner, R. P. *They love me, they love me not: A worldwide study of the effects of parental acceptance and rejection.* New Haven: HRAF Press, 1975.

Rohner, R. P. Sex differences in aggression: Phylogenetic and enculturation perspectives. *Ethos,* 1976, *4,* 57-72.

Rohner, R. P. Worldwide tests of parental acceptance-rejection theory. An overview. *Behavior Science Research,* 1980, *15,* 1-21.

Rohner, R. P., & Nielsen, C. C. *Parental acceptance and rejection: A review and annotated bibliography of research and theory.* New Haven: HRAFLEX Book No. W6-006, 1978. 2 Vols.

Rohner, R. P., & Rohner, E. C. Coping with perceived parental rejection: Correlates of social cognition. In L. H. Eckensburger, Y. H. Poortinga, and W. J. Lonner (Eds.), *Cross-cultural contributions to psychology.* Amsterdam: Swets and Zietlanger, 1979.

Ross, M. H. Cross-cultural sources of internal conflict and external warfare. Paper presented at annual meeting of the American Political Science Association, Washington, D.C., August 1980.

Russell, E. W. Factors of human aggression: A cross-cultural factor analysis of characteristics related to warfare and crime. *Behavior Science Notes,* 1972, *7,* 275-312.

Schaefer, J. M. The growth of hologeistic studies: 1889-1975. *Behavior Science Research,* 1977, *12,* 71-108.

Schlegel, A., & Barry, H., III. Adolescent initiation ceremonies: A cross-cultural code. *Ethnology*, 1979, *18*, 199-210. Reprinted in H. Barry, III and A. Schlegel (Eds.), *Cross-cultural samples and codes*. Pittsburgh: University of Pittsburgh Press, 1980.

Segall, M. H. *Human behavior and public policy*. Elmsford, N.Y. Pergamon Press, 1976.

Segall, M. H. *Cross-cultural psychology: Human behavior in global perspective*. Monterey, Calif.: Brooks/Cole, 1979.

Segall, M. H. On the search for independent variables in cross-cultural research. Paper presented at the Human Factors Panel, NATO Conference, Kingston, Ontario, August 1981.

Sillitoe, P. Land shortage and war in New Guinea. *Ethnology*, 1977, *16*, 71-81.

Skinner, B. F. Selection by consequences. *Science*, 1981, *23*, 501-504.

Sorenson, E. R. Cooperation and freedom among the fore of New Guinea. In Ashley Montagu (Ed.), *Learning non-aggression: The experience of non-literate societies*. New York: Oxford University Press, 1978.

Storr, A. *Human aggression*. New York: Atheneum, 1968.

Strauss, M. A. Measuring intrafamily conflict and violence: The conflict tactics (CT) scales. *Journal of Marriage and the Family*, 1979, *41*, 75-88.

Sumner, W. G. *Folkways*. Boston: Ginn, 1906.

Textor, R. B. *A cross-cultural summary*. New Haven: HRAF Press, 1967.

Tieger, T. On the biological basis of sex differences in aggression. *Child Development*, 1980, *51*, 943-963.

Triandis, H. C. (Ed.) *Handbook of cross-cultural psychology*. Boston: Allyn & Bacon, 1980. 6 Vols.

Van Leeuwen, M. S. A cross-cultural examination of psychological differentiation in males and females. *International Journal of Psychology*, 1978, *13*, 87-112.

Van Velzen, H. V. E. T., & Van Wetering, W. Residence, power groups and intra-societal aggression. *International Archives of Ethnography*, 1960, *49*, 169-200.

Whiting, B. B. (Ed.) *Six cultures: Studies of child rearing*. New York: Wiley, 1963.

Whiting, B. B. Sex identity conflict and physical violence: A comparative study. *American Anthropologist*, 1965, *67*, 123-140.

Whiting, B. B. & Edwards, C. P. A cross-cultural analysis of sex differences in the behavior of children aged three through eleven. *Journal of Social Psychology*, 1973, *91*, 171-188.

Whiting, B. B. & Whiting, J. W. M. *Children of six cultures: A psycho-cultural analysis*. Cambridge, Mass.: Harvard University Press, 1975.

Whiting, J. W. M. Cultural and sociological influences on development. In *Growth and development of the child in his setting*. Maryland: Maryland Child Growth and Development Institute, 1959.

Whiting, J. W. M. Effects of climate on certain cultural practices. In W. H. Goodenough (Ed.), *Explorations in cultural anthropology*. New York: McGraw-Hill, 1964.

Whiting, J. W. M. Method and problems in cross-cultural research. In G. Lindzey and E. Aronson (Eds.), *Handbook of social psychology*. (2nd ed.) Reading, Mass.: Addison-Wesley, 1968.

Whiting, J. W. M., Kluckhohn, R., & Anthony, A. The function of male initiation ceremonies at puberty. In E. F. Maccoby, T. M. Newcomb, and E. L. Hartley (Eds.), *Readings in social psychology*. (3rd ed.) New York: Holt, 1958.

Wilson, E. O. *Sociobiology*. Cambridge, Mass.: Harvard University Press, 1975.

2

Brazil: Competing Theories of Aggression and Initial Research Findings

Angela M. B. Biaggio

A sociology college professor I had in the early 1960s used to tell us jokingly that Brazil was perhaps one of the few countries that did not have to fight a war of independence. The United States fought England and several Latin American countries fought Spanish rule, but the independence of Brazil was proclaimed by the Portuguese emperor's son himself, who had been advised by his father, "Pedro, take hold of the crown yourself lest some adventurer gets it." Then, at the margins of the Ipiranga river, Pedro took his sword and cried to his soldiers: "Independence or death!" "Now," said my old college professor, "Since nobody wanted to die, Pedro put his sword back and we became independent. Although told out of context, this story is essentially true. Obviously, before the situation got to that point, there had been several uprisings. But the implication of my professor's story was that the Brazilian national character is basically not an aggressive one.

Brazilians have long liked to consider themselves as peaceful, ethnically tolerant, good-natured, and relaxed. Should a street fight break out, soon the "let that go" gang comes along. However, in the last decade, violence has been escalating, especially urban violence. In 1979, the Minister of Justice called upon a panel of jurists and social scientists to study the problem and prepare a report to the federal government. The publication of this report in the "Diário Oficial da União" (official daily of the federal government) was authorized on February 22, 1980. I will draw on this report for some factual information as well as for interpretations, explanations, and suggestions offered by the jurists and social scientists.

In the second part of this chapter, as a psychologist, I will focus on the views Brazilian psychologists have on aggression. I shall describe in detail a few research studies which illustrate the popular lines of theory and research on aggression in Brazil. I will also suggest how these scientific views affect lay conceptions of aggression and how to deal with it.

FACTUAL DATA AND SOCIOLOGICAL VIEWS

The social scientists' report to the Minister of Justice treats cautiously the available statistical data. Parga Nina (1980), in this report, cites several studies, mostly by U.S. experts such as Eleanor Sheldon, Albert Reiss, and several others, that have contributed to the improvement of information gathering regarding criminality and social change in the United States, and points out the need for comparable efforts in Brazil. In general, most authors cited by Parga Nina question the accuracy of statistical information on violence in different countries. With respect to the Brazilian situation, Parga Nina reports having visited the Division of Statistics, in the Office for Documentation and Information of the Ministry of Justice, where he talked to specialists; he asserts that the consensus is that Brazilian statistics on criminality are rather bad [p. 318]. He offers several suggestions for improvement of the system, but I will not review them here. My purpose in citing Parga Nina is to underscore the need for caution in making inferences from statistical data reported in this section. The following table is reproduced from the social scientists' report. It seems to be the best data available on different types of crime in each state of Brazil, although no information is given about which years it covers or about the population size of the states reported upon.

The overall tone of the analysis made by the social scientists emphasizes socioeconomic problems as the main causal factor, with which I agree. Low salaries, unemployment, concentration of people with low schooling living under subhuman conditions in the *favelas* (slums), and rural exodus to the cities are some of the conditions pointed to as responsible for increasing urban violence.

To put things simply: Brazil is a large country, with an area which is larger than that of the continental United States, a population of 110 million inhabitants, and an economy in bad shape. The inflation rate closed at around 110 percent in December 1980. Most of the population is concentrated in large cities, to which come rural migrant workers, unable to live off the land, hoping to find a job in the industrial centers; not only are they unskilled, but there are not enough jobs. This kind of population ends up in the *favelas,* that are expanding rapidly in comparison with the upper and middle-class areas in the large cities, due in part to differential birth rates, too. Migrant women usually resort to prostitution or work as maids. Men are lucky if they find employment as unskilled construction workers or similar jobs; many of them, unemployed, resort to alcoholism and crime. Juvenile deliquency is rampant and the number of abandoned or underprivileged children far outstrips the ability of the government to alleviate the problem.

A few church organizations are trying to help the poor. Thus, we have the Catholic ecclesiastical base communities, which are cells of lay people who try to build up community spirit and make the poor politically aware. Protestant groups seem to be more conservative and, by their rigid adherence to their interpretation of biblical principles, try to develop community friendships and to restrain aggressive behavior, alcoholism, and so on.

A governmental policy which would encourage rural workers to remain in rural areas is advocated by many as part of the solution to the country's economic and criminality problems. This is illustrated by the theme of the 1980s Catholic Bishops' National Conference Annual Fraternity Drive, the "Migrant Worker," with the slogan "Where are you going?"

Urban Violence

The newspaper *Correio do Povo* of Porto Alegre reported on January 11, 1981, about the city of Rio de Janerio:

> Rio and the Great Rio area are undergoing a real fear neurosis in these first few days of 1981, as if the whole population were living the emotions of a Hitchcock movie. Robbery and murders multiply themselves in a terrifying manner from day to day. . . . Today, Rio de Janeiro has become a difficult city to live in, in spite of its natural beauty. The atmosphere of revolt, fear, and apprehension are constant among people who had always been happy, irreverent, and relaxed—the "cariocas." Only during the past week, recrudescing violence did not respect a Navy officer, murdered at

Table 2.1. Number of Infractions in the Last Few Years*

Type of Infractions

STATES	INTENTIONAL HOMICIDES	AGGRESSION	SEXUAL INFRACTIONS	KIDNAPPING	ROBBERY	THEFT (WITHOUT VIOLENCE)	TRAFFIC OF DRUGS
Acre		502	4	210	10	1,690	21
Rondônia							
Roraima							
Amapá							
Amazonas	250	280				1,304	23
Pará							
Maranhão							
Piauí							
Ceará	81			1	17	235	18
Rio Grande do Norte							
Paraíba	2,009	4,027	240				
Pernambuco				13	115	674	
Alagoas	90	95	24				
Sergipe					1	1	1
Bahia	401		737	9	62	486	460
Minas Gerais	1,284	2,465	720	14	472	1,241	323
Rio de Janeiro	833	10,194	811	78	10,012	12,051	985
Espírito Santo							
São Paulo	2,195	51,029	2,343	2,869	20,203	86,040	1,096
Paraná	4,331	741	3,341		15,057		420
Santa Catarina	709	2,614	241		1,083		163
Rio Grande do Sul	8,902	6,123	2,984		3,802	14,247	1,336
Mato Grosso	227				103		14
Mato Grosso do Sul	49		2				
Goiás					17	38	58
Distrito Federal	173	2,763	59		834	9,181	

* No dates are provided.

Source: Reproduced from J. A. Rios, "Mosaico Brasileiro do Crime," in *Criminalidade e Violência*, Vol. 1. Brasília: Ministry of Justice, 1980, p. 197.

Pepino Beach at 11 a.m. An Army General had his house in Gavea broken into, was gagged and handcuffed along with three members of his family. An Air Force official was kidnapped with a shot in his head in Tijuca, another middle-class neighborhood in Rio.

Jornal do Brasil, one of the major newspapers in the country (from Rio de Janeiro) reported on January 13, 1981, on its first page: "Yesterday's Robberies," a list of nine major events, plus an editorial.

As a foreign visitor recently commented, in most cities of the world you know where the dangerous areas are, and what are the dangerous hours, but in Rio de Janeiro, you can be shot anytime, anywhere. There have been murders inside a city bus at 6 p.m., and they can happen during the afternoon or night, in nice residential areas such as Ipanema or Copacabana.

Violence Against Women

Many forms of aggression in Brazil are still not much talked about, although they certainly occur, in degrees that are impossible to know. For example, there are isolated reports of child abuse, especially among the poorest and least educated strata of the population, but this has not yet been a major preoccupation of authorities or the mass media and there are no reliable statistics about it.

Violence against women is becoming more talked about because of a burgeoning feminist movement. Violence against women is by no means restricted to the lower class. One case that received great publicity recently was that of an upper-class husband from Minas gerais, a very conservative stronghold of "machismo" in Brazil, who killed his wife. He got by with a very mild sentence. According to *Veja* magazine (December 31, 1980), six other "mineiro" husbands from the upper-class followed his recipe: some good bullets, running away, reappearance among tears and expensive lawyers, a thorough investigation of the victim-wife's past of infidelity, and unconditional swearing of love to the assassinated woman. This has been called by defense lawyers as "legitimate defense of honor" and many have been acquitted on these grounds.

According to *Veja* magazine, none of the gunfighter husbands had to celebrate New Year's Eve in jail. These episodes provoked strong reaction from educated women all over the country, with organizations such as the Association for the Defense of Women springing up. Wall paintings with slogans such as "If you love, you don't kill" began to appear in many streets in Rio de Janeiro. Marital violence had its feminine counterpart with one famous actress shooting her husband to death recently. All in all, these cases have illustrated violence against women in the upper-middle class and gave the feminist movement a boost, but there is not much information about the overall level of occurrence of wife-battering, which is probably especially high among lower-class members.

Homicide, Suicide, and Traffic Violence

In the earlier cited issue of *Correio do Povo,* another headline catches our attention: "São Paulo is a City of Death." This piece of writing refers to a doctoral thesis by Maria Helena Prado de Melo, Professor of Epidemiology on the Faculty of Public Health at the University of São Paulo, who investigated major causes of death which occurred during a period of fifteen years. Some of the data she cites show that traffic accidents, especially involving pedestrians, comprise the major category of violent deaths in São Paulo.

In 1975, traffic violence caused the death of 2,375 people in the city of São Paulo, an increase of 455 percent in relation to 1960. Eighty percent of the victims were pedestrians and 32.9 percent were below age 14. Data from 1980 show that these figures remain about the same in the city of São Paulo. So, the traffic there kills 8 times as many as in New York, and 17 times as many as in Tokyo. According to the National Department of Traffic (DETRAN), 18,130 people died in 1978 because of traffic accidents (mainly running over of pedestrians) in the whole country and this number increased to approximately 20,000 in 1979.

Traffic violence was followed by homicides, suicides, and other accidents as major causes of violent death. Melo found that 5,422 people died from what she categorized as violent death. From the 1960s to the 1970s, the increase in violent deaths was over 70 percent. Homicides have increased, and suicides are the only form of violent death that is decreasing.

In 1960, homicides represented 11 percent of violent deaths. In 1975, they reached 14 percent, and ongoing research covering the first half of 1980 indicate an increase to 27 percent. Fire arms were utilized in 60 percent of the homicides; knives and other cutting instruments came second. From 1960 to 1975, the increase in homicides with fire arms was 268 percent while, in the United States, analysts considered an increase of 152 percent from 1960 to 1973 as alarming. Melo concludes that, in view of the time accidents occur (evening, weekends) and the age bracket most hurt (20 to 30 years of age), educational programs of a preventive nature would be useful in reducing traffic violence.

Although traffic accidents may not be generally thought of as a form of aggression, they were included here because it was felt that the way many Brazilians drive really constitutes aggressive behavior. Or perhaps the poorly organized traffic, terrible jams, low rate of punishment for infractions, and disregard for traffic rules on the part of fellow drivers along with the automobile industry boom a few years ago may have led to aggressive driving.

The Juvenile Problem

Regarding juvenile delinquency, we found that the jurists had more to say in the 1980 report than did the social scientists. Aside from a few hypotheses that interpret crime in psychoanalytic terms, the psychologists offered little. The sociologists linked crime to poverty and slum living conditions, as they usually tend to do.

The jurists, on the other hand, emphasized that juveniles constitute a major problem in Brazil, and their report notes that a distinction must be made between the *abandoned minor* and the *delinquent minor*. Statistics estimate approximately 25 million abandoned or deprived minors, which means about one fourth of the total population of the country.

There is a consensus that the major causes of juvenile delinquency are: disorganization or non-existence of a family group; inadequate personality conditions of the parents, leading to the absence of affect and authority; insufficient family income; unemployment and underemployment; lack of instruction and professional qualification of family members; inadequate housing conditions; and precarious hygienic conditions.

These considerations appear also in an excellent study by the Justice of Minors of the capital of São Paulo, Dr. Nilton Silveira, who also added these observations, regarding the high level of delinquent minors: moral and material abandonment; precarious conditions of physical health and harm to emotional structure; null or incomplete schooling; excessive perambulating in streets, in bad and damaging environments; lack of available professional services; and practice of marginal and antisocial activities. After emphasizing the family, personal, and social nature of the problem, Silveira went on to state:

> Before it is a criminal problem, the problem of the juvenile is eminently a social one, and as such, its survey, its study, its solutions are inherent to the Public Power. The Public Power cannot alienate

itself from the problem, not even with the so-often heard excuses of lack of resources. Let us find the resources where they are. Because there are always resources. Let them be applied to the problem of the juveniles, and let us see what good use public men will have done with public monies. [p. 33, translation by the author]

Though a great deal remains to be done, awareness of these aggression-relevant issues in Brazil appears to be growing. As awareness continues to expand, it is hoped that needed knowledge, services, and facilities for the amelioration of these problems will be forthcoming.

THE VIEWPOINT OF PSYCHOLOGY

As discussed by Biaggio and Benko (1975) and Biaggio (1980), Brazilians are eager to apply psychology to solve relevant social problems and, as a rule, do not dedicate themselves to basic research and original theorizing. As a result, the kind of basic psychology one sees in Brazil comes from the United States or from Europe, especially from France. The Tavistock variety of British psychology also constitutes one of our major European imports. From the United States, influences are more eclectic, ranging from Skinner's radical behaviorism, through drive theory, through Bandura and Mischel's cognitive behaviorism, all the way to Carl Rogers' humanistic viewpoint.

How do all these influences affect Brazilian psychologists' view of aggression? I will discuss this topic briefly and cite in more detail a few examples of research on aggression which is carried out in Brazil.

Of all theoretical currents mentioned, psychoanalysis is by far the most influential in Brazilian psychology. Possible exceptions to this generalization are the University of São Paulo and the University of Brasilia, where a behavioristic approach has caught on, mainly through the influence of psychologists Robert Berryman and Fred Keller, more recently, and earlier through the influence of Otto Klineberg and David McClelland.

Most of the research reported here consists of graduate theses since Brazilian research tradition is recent, and graduate programs, as they are conceived of in the United States, only began here in 1966. I have tried to sample research done in the six major graduate centers in the country: Rio de Janeiro, São Paulo, Brasilia, Porto Alegre, Paraiba, and Recife, although it was not possible to obtain in-depth materials from all of them.

Some of this "research," especially the psychoanalytic work from Rio de Janeiro, takes a broad definition of the term research in the sense that it is speculative rather than empirical.

Psychoanalytic Theory

An example of psychoanalytically oriented research is Sattler's (1979) thesis on children's accidents and aggression. The author argues that safer environments do not solve accident proneness problems, because there are psychological factors leading to accident proneness. As evidence for this, she cites studies on childhood and adolescent suicide which link them to self-destructive behaviors in early infancy. Heinmann (1969), Menninger (1971), Knobel (1972) and others provide the theoretical and previous research background of the study.

The explicit hypothesis was that the incidence of aggressive manifestations in the Test of Familial Attitudes (Jackson, 1973) is higher among children who have had accidents than among those who have not had them. The sample was made up of 60 subjects, ages 6 to 11, of both sexes. Group I was made up of children who had accidents and were helped at the Municipal Emergency Hospital for wounds not caused by others or by the environment.

Group II was made of up children from three public schools and one private school, who had not received medical help for nor, presumably, had they had such kinds of wounds. The scoring system developed by Cibils (1978) was used, and blind scoring was done by another researcher. The results showed that "accident" children reveal more feelings of rejection and persecutory anxiety.

Sattler concludes that self-directed aggression contributes to accident proneness, and discusses her results in the context of theoretical notions by Melanie Klein and other psychoanalytic authors. This study was chosen to be reviewed here because it represents one of the few Brazilian psychoanalytic studies that involve empirical data.

Vasconcelos (cited in Fleck, 1981), in her M.S. thesis, studied aggression in institutionalized minors of Porto Alegre. Her main point is that, contrary to what one might expect, 16 to 18 year-old youngsters who steal show the same amount of aggressiveness as those who kill, and both show significantly more aggression than a control group. Based on psychoanalytic theory, she suggests that internal factors such as anxiety, guilt, and depression lead to delinquency. Although she admits the role of environment—especially poverty conditions, learning of more aggression in reformatories, and so on—her emphasis is clearly on internal factors. In line with psychoanalytic theory, she treats delinquency as an effect of insecurity which leads to anxiety. When anxiety becomes unbearable, it needs to be expressed, and the person becomes aggressive. Internal aggression predisposes to stealing or killing. Once the crime is acted out, more anxiety generates guilt and depression, and the person is caught in a vicious circle.

As these pieces of empirical research show, the psychoanalytic theory of aggression seems to be very popular among Brazilian psychologists. Jablonsky (1978) devoted a master thesis to a critical examination of the notion of catharsis of aggression. Jablonsky defends the notion that, although Freudian theoretical framework should allow for a notion of catharsis of aggression, Freud himself never explicitly asserted that, not even in his famous letter-response to Einstein, "Why War." Jablonsky thinks that Freud assumes that the possibility the human being has of aggression decreases as energy is channeled to other objectives in a process which is similar to the sublimation of the libido. It is a hydraulic model, but it is interesting to note that Freud never spoke of sublimation of aggression, as he spoke of sublimation of libido. This may have led to confusion and to the popular notion that catharsis of aggression is a Freudian notion. To sum it up, Jablonsky says that catharsis of aggression is theoretically possible as implicit in Freud's theoretical framework, but not asserted by Freud.

The Ethological Approach

Another popular theoretical notion about aggression among Brazilian psychologists is that of Lorenz (1973, 1974), who believes that there is an aggressive drive in animals and humans. His instinctivist position distinguishes itself from that of Freud, especially in regard to the aim of the aggressive drive. To Freud, aggression was a death drive; to Lorenz, aggression is an instinct whose goal, as that of all other instincts, is the preservation of life and the species. Lorenz's model is also an hydraulic one, and his solutions to control aggression are similar to the Greeks' notion of catharsis and the psychoanalytic notion of sublimation. Thus, sports competitions, such as Olympic games, Soccer World Cups, and so on, are suggested as preventive measures. However, in 1974, Lorenz revised his position, as evidenced in an interview with R. Evans (Jablonsky, 1978), at least as far as vicarious catharsis was concerned ("Nowadays, I have strong doubts whether watching aggressive behavior, even in the guise of sport has any cathartic effect at all, p. 16)." In spite of the well-done analysis by Jablonsky, the idea of catharsis dominates scientific and lay thinking about aggression among Brazilians.

Obviously, psychoanalytic work is rather elite-oriented, dealing with problems of the intellectually sophisticated upper-middle class and offers little help to alleviate the problems of urban violence and social unrest described earlier. Also, psychoanalytic work, even when empirically oriented, shows much less methodological rigor than neobehavioristic studies as the ones to be described later in this chapter.

Social Learning Approach

As an example of social-learning oriented research on aggression, I shall discuss a study by a former advisee of mine. Socci (1977) investigated the effects of the observation of film-mediated aggressive models in a natural setting. Subjects were institutionalized adolescents from a government institution (Funabem) which cares for abandoned and poor youngsters. Within this particular institution, there were no youngsters with records of antisocial behavior problems. The school was located in Rio de Janeiro. The study was based on Bandura's (1973) well-known work on aggression, which considers aggression as learned rather than innate, and emphasizes the role of modeling and to a lesser extent of reinforcement of aggressive behavior. Socci's study was innovative because it was conducted in a natural setting, the subjects being unaware that an experiment of such kind was being carried out. The sample consisted of 48 adolescents (both boys and girls) from ages 11 to 18 years and in grades 5, 6, and 8, presenting no schooling problems. All subjects came from the lower socioeconomic group.

The hypotheses of the study were: 1) There is a higher number of imitative aggressive behaviors in the younger age groups than in the older; 2) Boys exhibit a higher number of aggressive behaviors than girls. Both hypotheses are based on Bandura's work and on other specific research studies, such as Fein's (1973) who found that younger children imitate more than older children in situations of problem-solving and competition. Thus, Socci wanted to investigate whether these findings are generalizable to other types of samples.

The procedure was described as follows: After daily activities and supper, the students are free to use the recreation rooms where they can play, watch TV, go to the auditorium to watch a movie, play sports, stay out in the patio, or even, in the case of the oldest, go to a movie or a party outside of the institution. In the male pavillion, twelve inspectors in each of the three classes supervise the discipline during this free period. In the girls' pavillion, there is also a recreation period before bedtime. This was the time scheduled for the experimental work.

Categories of aggressive behavior were operationally defined in the following way: Direct physical aggression (fighting, slapping, socking, kicking, scratching, pinching, biting, hitting with the elbow, throwing an object, hitting with an object); indirect aggression (refusing to do a favor, refusing to obey, derogating, slamming doors or windows, throwing objects on the floor, destroying someone else's property, offending gestures); and direct verbal aggression (verbal provoking with or without swear words, defying, criticizing, humiliating, making fun of, ridiculing, swearing, saying bad things about a classmate to another, disturbing).

The inspectors who worked regularly with the children were trained to be the observers. During the observation training period, the six most efficient inspectors were selected to participate in the research project. The experimenter emphasized the importance of not discussing the topic of the research with the subjects. During the training period, the reliability among the observers was found to be 92 percent (mean value).

The subjects were taken to the projection room and watched certain movies (described below) together with the six inspectors who had been trained as observers for the research purpose. The observation began right after the end of the projection, as the subjects left the room, filled out a questionnaire, and walked to their quarters.

The experiment was presented to the subjects as a survey of adolescents' preferences regarding commercial movies. The questionnaire distributed at the end of the session justified this explanation, although its real purpose was to check on whether the aggressive movies were really perceived as aggressive, degree of interest aroused, etc. The experimenter, who watched the movie from the operator's booth, left the institution after gathering the questionnaires. The experimental procedure did not interfere at all with the students' routine, since it was customary for them to see a movie once a week. Two neutral films were shown before the experimental procedure itself began.

The movies were regular commercial movies obtained from a TV network, chosen by the experimenter according to their aggressive content. The first movie was a neutral one, for the purpose of establishing a baseline of aggressive behaviors. In the second week, an "aggressive" movie was shown. The "aggressive" movies were chosen not only in terms of aggressive content, but also with an attempt to rule out culturally irrelevant contents, such as war movies, westerns, gangsters, and Indians. Two weeks later, another aggressive movie was shown, in order to allow the verification of a cumulative effect of aggressive models. A fourth movie, one week later, was neutral, and served the purpose of follow-up. A content analysis of the answers to the questionnaires confirmed that the "aggressive" movies chosen by the experimenter were perceived as more violent, brutal, aggressive, and cruel; the neutral movies were considered equally entertaining.

The design was a $2 \times 3 \times 4$ factorial design, with two levels of sex, three levels of age, and four levels of the manipulated independent variable (films: neutral, aggressive, aggressive, neutral). An analysis of variance revealed significant main effects for sex and type of film, and an interaction between sex and type of film. Thus, hypothesis 2 was confirmed, with boys showing more imitative aggression than girls.

Hypothesis 1, however, was not confirmed. There was no significance for the age factor. The use of the Neuman-Keuls a posteriori test to check differences between pairs of means revaled a significant difference between the 14-15 year olds and the 17-18 year olds for the first aggressive movie. Testing for follow-up effects showed that, after one week, there were no residues of exposure to the aggressive model by age group. Cumulative effects of the aggressive movies did occur for boys but not for girls. Socci (1977) speculated that the age difference may not have shown up because the younger age group was obviously smaller, and may not have expressed imitative aggressive behavior because of fear of retaliation from the older groups.

We consider this study an illustration of carefully done research on aggression done in Brazil according to the social-learning framework, having as its major contribution the fact that it was conducted in a natural setting, but preserving much of the experimental rigor.

Another well-done study along these lines was that of Aragão (1975) who tried a behavior modification procedure employing cooperative models presented in eight sequences of slides, each series comprising a meaningful cooperative episode, accompanied by sound recording. An example of such sequence shows a boy and a slightly younger girl who is trying to open a yogurt container, obviously having trouble with it. The boy helps, they succeed, and both enjoy the yogurt out of two straws from the same container.

Kindergarten children suggested by school authorities as aggressive were first observed for baseline sessions, on operationally defined aggressive behaviors. Then, one group, randomly selected, was exposed to the slide sequences (cooperative model condition), a second group saw the same sequences plus two additional slides in each sequence, which introduced an adult reinforcing figure (model plus reinforcement). A third group, also randomly selected from the original group suggested by the school, whose level of aggressive behavior had also been comparable during the baseline sessions, acted as a control group, watching sequences of slides which showed neutral (no elements of cooperation or aggression) stories.

Reduction of aggressive behaviors carefully observed was significantly higher in the two ex-perimental groups than in the control group, which remained at the baseline level. There was no difference between the two experimental conditions, highlighting the powerful effect of sheer modeling, even in the absence of reinforcement.

This type of work by Socci and by Aragão, although common in the United States, is rarely done in Brazil. Because of the earlier French humanistic tradition and because of political un-rest, behaviorism, experimentation, and behavior modification are not well-accepted, except in a few circles. In my opinion, it is unfortunate that this is so, since behavior modification could be much more useful in clinics, schools, and especially large institutions for the aban-doned minors than the techniques currently used. The studies by Socci and Aragão were con-ducted in Rio de Janeiro, but they had their initial training in São Paulo and Brasilia, respec-tively, thus confirming the regional theoretical tendencies of Brazilian psychology discussed earlier in this chapter.

Eclecticism

An example of drive-theory combined with attribution theory is described below (Rodri-gues & Jouval, 1969). With a rationale based on Heider's attribution theory (1958) and on Berkowitz's additions to the frustration-aggression hypothesis (1962), the following hypothe-ses were tested: 1) In any frustrating interpersonal relation, the affective bond between the frustrating and the frustrated persons will determine the latter's attributions. There will be more attribution of personal causality when the interpersonal relation is negative than when it is positive; 2) Any frustrating interpersonal event always leads to anger in the frustrated per-son; 3) Aggressive reactions will only occur when the frustrated person attributes personal causality to the frustrating agent.

The experimental procedure consisted of showing a slide depicting a slightly modified ver-sion of the Rosenzweig's Picture Frustration Test to 84 freshmen from Catholic University of Rio de Janeiro. Two experimental conditions and one control condition were run, each hav-ing 14 males and 14 females, randomly assigned. The subjects were instructed to put them-selves in the position of the frustrated person shown in the slide, and write their spontaneous reaction to the frustrating agent. Next, they were asked to indicate on a 90 millimeter scale: a) the probability of a motive indicating personal causation having been the reason for the frus-trating event; b) the probability of a motive indicating impersonal causation having been the reason for the frustrating agent; c) the intensity of the anger aroused by the frustrating event; and d) the intensity of the aggression instigated by the frustrating event.

In one of the two experimental conditions, the subjects were informed that the two persons involved in the interpersonal interaction were friends, and, in the other, that they were ene-mies. Nothing was said about the affective bond between the two people in the control condi-tion. The results confirmed the first hypothesis and gave relative support to hypotheses 2 and 3.

A second reflection of an eclectic orientation to aggression is the work at Paraíba, a gradu-ate center in the northeast of Brazil, which has produced interesting research such as that of L. Camino, who also does work that could be classified as a mixture of drive theory and attribu-tion theory. Camino, Leyens, and Cavell (1979) add a social and political flavor to this combi-nation that seems to be a current preoccupation among Brazilian social scientists, and of a great number of the general population for that matter.

In an experimental study on the aggressive reactions of minority groups, Camino et al. (1979) tested three hypotheses: 1) Resorting to violence is more likely to occur as a sense of competence is raised among minority groups; 2) Violence is stronger when minorities attrib-ute responsibility for their situation to the majority rather than to an impersonal cause; 3) Control of aggression appears among minorities who expect an improvement in their situation, this improvement depending on the majority group.

The subjects were volunteer students from the Federal University of Paraíba who were told they were participating in a game of economics. These groups lost in a continuous fashion, and the two independent variables were attribution of responsibility and probability of improvement in the future.

The procedure was ingenious and merits detailed description. In the first experiment, 30 groups of four subjects participated, five groups in each experimental condition. Eight subjects were called at a time. They were received in a waiting room by the experimenter, who presented the study as dealing with group decision in economics. The game consisted basically of a competition between two groups, the goal being to get the most money as possible at the stock market. Each group started with the same amount of money and shares of fictional industries. The game was supposed to consist of seven trials of 15 minutes each, during which the groups should buy and sell shares from each other. The groups could not communicate directly but had to go through the intermediary of the change agency, who, after each trial, would inform the groups of the new values of their shares. The reasons invoked by the experimenter in order to explain the change of value of the shares constituted the manipulation of "attribution of responsibility." In the "personal responsibility" condition, the experimenter explained that the changes of value depended on a random program established by a computer located at the change agency.

The game proceeded, and after four trials, all groups were in the situation the authors called "minority." They lost consistently, and it seemed they had no control over the situation. At this point, the second independent variable was introduced. Because of the repeated losses of the group, the agency sent an expert in economics who called the attention of the players to their catastrophic situation and explained their eventual future. To a set of groups, the expert declared that, according to a well-known law of economics, they had a 100 percent chance of improvement because the group had bought shares in such a way ("personal responsibility") or because the computer program had devalued in such a way ("impersonal responsibility"). To another set of groups, the expert invoked the same reasons to declare that they had a 50 percent chance of improvement. To the third set of groups, the expert explained that it would be impossible to reverse the situation of continuous losers (0 percent condition). In all three conditions, the expert's talk was supported by graphs illustrating the respective tendencies.

At this point, the expert said that they could express their feelings and make pressure on the other group by means of electric shocks. After that, two questionnaires were filled out by each individual. The first questionnaire involved evaluating the other group on the basis of a list of 12 bipolar adjectives presented in seven-point scales. The second questionnaire was meant to evaluate one's own group.

The hypothesis regarding strategic control was the only one to be supported when data were viewed by means of an analysis of variance. The groups who were uncertain about their future and who believed that their future depended on the "majority" groups showed the least aggression. The discussion is centered around the frustration-aggression hypothesis and on methodological points.

In another study, Camino and Troccoli (1981) investigated the perception of violence as a function of level of belief in a just world and of the kind of motivation underlying violent acts. Three samples (psychology instructors, introductory psychology students, and intermediate level students) answered questionnaires about belief in a just world and types of violence. Violent acts were categorized into four kinds as to motivation (self-preservation, social change, self-interest, and vandalism). Subjects were classified as low, medium, or high, in "belief in a just world." Results regarding non-legal violence indicated that psychology instructors and introductory psychology students of low belief in a just world perceived violent acts motivated by social change as less violent than those of high or medium belief. There were no significant differences regarding the other types of motivation. Concerning violence exercised by legal social agents, psychology instructors of low belief in the just world classified violence motivated by social change as much more violent than did those of medium and high belief. In addition to this, a negative relationship was found between belief in the just world and participation in political activities.

The studies reported here by no means comprise a complete review of research on aggression in Brazil. It was my goal to illustrate research tendencies which cover a variety of theoretical positions, as well as regional representativeness. I have reported research done in the major graduate centers of psychology in Brazil, from the northeast (Federal University of Paraíba), through Rio de Janeiro, São Paulo, and Brasilia, to the south (Porto Alegre).

CONCLUSION

Although psychoanalytic studies may seem to have been deemphasized in favor of empirical research and more rigorous methodology, it is my feeling that psychoanalytic thought is certainly the most influential among Brazilian psychologists.

These ideas are filtered down to the lay public through several channels such as TV interviews, popular books, and magazines dealing with child rearing. The notions of catharsis, trauma, frustration, repression, and so on are thus distributed in more or less distorted form to the lay public of the middle and upper-class—among whom a high percentage undergo psychoanalysis themselves, by the way. This information and misinformation sometimes leads to some permissiveness regarding childhood aggression, and even adolescent and adult verbal aggression. On the other hand, subhuman conditions of health, housing, and education among the numerous poor people who are not affected by psychologists' views directly lead to social unrest, crime, and violence. So, on the whole, my pessimistic view is that aggression is on the increase in Brazil. How does the culture deal with this? No consensus has been reached among authorities.

The report by jurists and social scientists to the federal government in 1980 makes several recommendations including reforming the penal system, more humane conditions in the penitentiaries, preventive measures, social reforms, and so on. On a more immediate level, some politicians and authorities recommend more crime fighting through an extensive police apparatus. The situation has become so critical in Rio de Janeiro that many have asked for the resignation of the state's Secretary of Security and even wanted the federal government to intervene.

In the middle of all this, many still advocate that soccer games and the Carnival* are the best outlets for channeling aggression into sports and recreation—again, the old hydraulic model and the idea of catharsis, under the influence of Lorenz, perhaps. Although Brazilians, especially the *cariocas* from Rio de Janeiro love the Carnival and soccer games, I have yet to see that the net result of these activities includes diminishing aggressive behavior. Solutions are hard to find but, to me, they would lie along the lines of social justice, education, and the application of social-learning theory.

---

*The Carnival is a four-day event, preceding Lent, consisting of samba, all-night costume balls, street parades, drinking, etc.

REFERENCES

Aragão, W. M. Efeitos dos processos de modelção e reforço na diminuição do comportamento aggressivo e aumento do comportamento cooperativo. Unpublished masters thesis, Pontificia Universidade Catolica do Rio de Janeiro, 1975.

Bandura, A. *Aggression: A social learning analysis.* Englewood-Cliffs, N.J.: Prentice-Hall, 1973.

Berkowitz, L. *Aggression: A social psychological analysis.* New York: McGraw Hill, 1962.

Biaggio, A. *Psicologia do desenvolvimento.* Petropolis, Rio de Janeiro: Ed. Vozes, 1975.

Biaggio, A. Psychology in Brazil. Paper read at symposium on Psychology in Latin America at the annual meeting of the American Psychological Association, Montreal, Canada, 1980.

Biaggio, A. and Benko, A. American and European influences on Brazilian psychology. Paper read at annual meeting of the American Psychological Association, Chicago, 1975.

Camino, L., Leyens, J. P., and Cavell, B. Les réactions aggressives de groupes minoritaires. I. Études préliminaires: L'attribuition de responsabilité at le sentiment de competence et le controle stratégique. *Recherches de Psycholoqie Sociale,* 1979, *1,* 83-97.

Cibils, Z. Enurese infantil e agressividade. Unpublished masters thesis, Pontificia Universidade Catolica de Porto Alegre Rio Grande do Sul, 1978.

Criminalidade e Violência, Vol. I. Brasilia: Ministério da Justiça, 1980. (Jurists and social scientists' report).

Fein, O. O. The effect of chronological age and model reward on imitation. *Developmental Psychology,* 1979, *9,* 283-289.

Fleck, R. A. Sociedade gera círculo vicioso que leva ao crime. *Correio do Povo,* Feb. 24, 1981.

Freud, S. *A general introduction to psychoanalysis.* New York: Boni and Leveright, 1920.

Freud, S. *Group psychology and the analysis of the ego.* New York: Boni and Leveright, 1922.

Freud, S. *Standard edition of the complete works of Freud.* J. Strachey (Ed.). London: Hogarth, 1955, 20 vol.

Fromm, E. *Anatomia da destruição humana.* Rio de Janeiro: Zahar, 1975.

Gillespie, W. H. Aggression and the instinct theory. *International Journal of Psychoanalysis,* 1971, *52,* 155-160.

Heider, F. *The psychology of interpersonal relations.* New York: Wiley, 1958.

Heinman, P. Sobre a teoria dos instintos de vida e de morte. In *Os progressos em psicanáolise.* Rio de Janeiro, Zahar, 1969, p. 344-360.

Jablonski, B. Catarse de agressão: um emame crítico. Unpublished masters thesis, Pontificia Universidade Catolica do Rio de Janeiro, 1978.

Jackson, L. Instruçöes para o Teste de Atitudes Familiares. Mimeographed report, 1973.

Jones, E. *Vida e ubra de Sigmund Freud.* (2nd ed.) Rio de Janeiro: Zahar, 1975.

Knobel, M. *Infancia, adolescencia 7 familia,* Buenos Aires: Granica, 1972.

Lorenz, K. *A agressão.* Lisbon: Martin Fontes, 1973.

Lorenz, K. *Civilização e pecado.* Rio de Janeiro: Artenova, 1974.

Maridos Mineiros. *Veja* magazine, December 31, 1980.

Menninger, K. *Eros e tanatos, O homem contra si mesmo.* São Paulo: Ibrasa, 1971.

Us assaltos de ontem. *Jornal do Brasil,* Jan. 13, 1981.

Parga Nina, L. A. Estatísticas en informaçöes na área da criminalidade. In: *Criminalidade e violencia.* Vol. I. Brasilia: Ministerio da Justica, 1980.

Rios, J. A. Mosaico Brasileiro do crime. In: *Criminalidade e Violência,* vol. 1. Brasilia: Ministério da Justiça, 1980.

Rodrigues, A., and Jouval, M. V. Phenomenal causality and response to frustrating interpersonal events. *Interamerican Journal of Psychology,* 1969, *3,* 193-194.

Sattler, M. Acidente infantil e agressao. Unpublished masters thesis, Pontificia Universidade Catolica do Rio Grande do Sul, 1979.

Sao Paulo: uma cidade de morte. (Report on doctoral thesis by Maria Helena do Prado Melo), *Correio do Povo,* University of São Paulo, January 11, 1980.

Silveria, N. Jurist's and social scientist's report. In *Criminalidade e violencia,* Vol. 1, Brasilia: Ministerio da Justica, 1980.

Socci, Vera Vecchiatti. Efeitos da observação de modelos aggressivos em adolescentes de nível socio-cultural inferior. Unpublished masters thesis, Pontificia Universidade Catolica do Rio de Janeiro, 1977.

3

China: Aggressive Behavior and the Problem of Maintaining Order and Harmony

Michael H. Bond
and
Wang Sung-Hsing

家 和 萬 事 興 —When a family is united, everything prospers;
家 衰 口 不 停　When a family argues, everything fails.

(Traditional Chinese proverb)

INTRODUCTION

To undertake an overview and explanation of aggressive behavior in Chinese culture may appear to be the height of intellectual temerity. After all, there are more than 1 billion Chinese people scattered throughout the various countries of the world, each influenced to varying degrees by the climate, the economic resources, the political concerns, and the agencies of socialization found in these various countries. So, social scientists, when discussing the data base for their observations on a Chinese culture, dutifully provide a disclaimer for the generalizability for their conclusions to Chinese people as a whole.

This cautionary note is entirely appropriate. There is no question, for example, that industrialization has led to an increasing erosion of the extended family system and to a rising economic status of women (Wong, 1975). These changes will have important consequences for the husband-wife relationship and, thereby, for the socialization of Chinese children within the family. It is also clear that the recent ideological reorientation of mainland China will lead to changes in educational and commercial priorities (Ho, 1979) and, thereby, for the socialization of children outside the family. These changes must be studied and their impact assessed.

Despite these, and similar caveats, we discern a unity in the results from the various explorations of aggressive behavior in Chinese culture. Ho's (1980) conclusion bears repeating in this context:

Whatever regional or ethnic differences there may be, important though they are, they appear less significant when gauged against commonalities in the general pattern. Even among acculturated Chinese Americans, features of the traditional pattern are still apparent. Despite undeniable changes that have taken place, traditional conceptions and values, however modified and disguised, continue to exert their influence on the socialization process and leave their indelible marks on the child to the present day. [p. 48]

We believe that this commonality derives from traditional Confucian ideology, itself consistent with an ecology of limited resources and high population density (Foster, 1965; La Barre, 1945). Ideal character types are those who can fit smoothly into a collectivist social orientation (Hofstede, 1980, Ch. 5) where the paramount concern is for the integrity and advancement of the group, not the individual. The basic group is the family, however defined, and the various *modi operandi* found functional in this context are then generalized elsewhere, resulting in a consistency to Chinese behavior.

During the Cultural Revolution this Confucian ideology was vigorously attacked in Mainland China (Louie, 1980). These attacks were not surprisingly directed at the class system inherent in the Confucian social structuring. What impact the attacks may have had on socialization practices so far, especially within the family, is a moot point, however. In a recent analysis of village and family life, Parish and Whyte (1978) draw the following conclusion: "Changes have occurred, but much about the nature of child rearing, and particularly the role of the family in child rearing, appears relatively unchanged [p. 233]." We thus believe that a Confucian analysis has continuing validity toward an understanding of Chinese interpersonal behavior.

Obviously, our decision to perceive consistency and continuity within various Chinese subcultures is a deliberate one. It certainly is not blind to the wealth of evidence supporting the situational control of behavior (Bandura, 1969; Mischel, 1968). Nevertheless, we are impressed by the coherence in the various sources of evidence we have reviewed. As the social philosophy of Confucius provides the organization for this unity, we will begin with a discussion of its relevant features.

THE SOCIAL PHILOSOPHY OF CONFUCIUS

At the heart of Chinese culture lies the Confucian concept of filial piety. As a child, the son is nurtured by his parents to whom his debt of gratitude can never be repaid. In partial recompense, the son is expected to show unquestioning obedience to the parents, to strive for their interests, and to care for them when they are less able to do so. These requirements were continually underscored in folk wisdom, the classroom, and classical writings such as the *Twenty-Four Models of Filial Piety*. In an agricultural economy marked by scarcity of resources and little social mobility, they carried considerable force. An unfilial son had nowhere else to go and little opportunity for self-support.

In contrast to the Western family dynamic, the imperative was not to train the child for eventual independence from his or her family of origin. Instead, the family unit, with the exception of daughters, ideally remained intact throughout the life cycle of its members. In consequence, the development of different, non-independence-oriented, character traits was emphasized in the socialization of the child. Essentially, these were the personal attributes that promoted group harmony—deference to authority, responsibility in leadership, self-abnegation, emotional restraint, and cooperativeness. It is in this sense that we may regard Chinese people as socially oriented—they are trained to promote the harmony and integrity of the group, with the parent-son grouping as the basic model. The socialization of children is aimed at promoting interdependence, not independence.

Implications for Socialization

In distinction to many Western socialization practices, the training of aggressiveness has no place in the Chinese system. Solomon (1971) puts it this way:

> In cultures which tolerate or encourage the development of a sense of autonomy in children, aggressive impulses play an important role in the child's efforts at self-assertion, his attempts to establish an identity for himself independent of the adults who bore and reared him. But, as we have stressed, self-assertion was the one thing which Chinese parents would not tolerate. Hence every indication of willful, assertive, or aggressive action on the part of the child would be severely discouraged. By inhibiting the expression of aggression in their children, Chinese parents (consciously or unconsciously) were seeking to insure the continued dependence of these guarantors of their future security. [p. 69]

So we can see the rationale behind the link between filiality and lack of aggressiveness—the owner of the hand that is to feed one in later life must be taught not to bite, for fear that he might also attack (and abandon) his parents.

Aggressive behavior toward the parents and older siblings is thus seen as part of a larger danger—disruptive self-assertion. This self-assertion is dangerous because it undermines the authoritarian structuring of family relations legitimized by Confucian social philosophy.

The Chinese view is consistent with a recent conceptualization of aggression within the framework of coercive control (Tedeschi, Gaes, & Rivera, 1977). From this perspective, aggressive behavior is one of a group of influence tactics that can be used by an actor to assume power over another. Clearly, all such influence attempts by children must be closely monitored to protect family order and harmony. The more dramatic and obvious forms of coercive influence, such as physical assault in particular, must be suppressed.

Although we have focussed on a desire to limit, if not eliminate, children's aggression within the family unit, this concern extended to relations with neighbours. Margery Wolf (1970) has shown how arguments between neighbour's children could escalate as the "face" of their respective families quickly became involved, thereby fanning the initial conflict. There was no question of whether the aggressive behavior was justified—merely to be involved in an altercation led to parental punishment (A. Wolf, 1964). So great was parental concern that one child could often retaliate against another simply by informing the other child's parents about their child's transgression (M. Wolf, 1970). The parents would then punish their child, reinforcing their discipline with aphorisms from the folk culture, such as 君 子 動 嘴 不 動 手 (A civilized person should use his mouth but not his hands).

The issue here is not one of maintaining hierarchical order but, rather, one of preserving harmonious relations between families in a situation of interdependence. As one Chinese proverb puts it, 對 口 對 面 (We see each other every day). Psychological studies have shown that the expectation of future interactions with a target person reduces the amount of pain a subject is willing to administer to that person (e.g., Bond & Dutton, 1975). Presumably, this reluctance to inflict pain operates because the receiver of pain can later attack the initial aggressor. It is, therefore, in everyone's interests to suppress any aggressive behavior since everyone is potentially vulnerable.

This dynamic would obviously apply to any society with high population density, low residential mobility, and considerable interdependence (Whiting & Whiting, 1975). Chinese society is hardly unique in these respects. Constraints against aggressive behavior outside the family add further support, however, to the constraints operating within the family.

Emphasis on Social Order

The structuring of traditional Chinese society would also seem to amplify the sanction against disruptive aggression. In the Confucian tradition, social integration was ensured by organizing social relationships into hierarchical dualities, for which the father-son relationship was the ideal case. In effect, everyone was locked into a consensually accepted dominance hierarchy. As Hinde (1974) has argued, the existence of such a hierarchy precludes the need for aggressive behavior to be used as an instrument to establish and maintain power relations. "It is as though aggression is shown in relation to the need for asserting rank. . . . the more uncertain the rank, the greater the need to confirm it [p. 343]." Although Hinde was discussing the behavior of nonhuman primates, his argument is suggestive when extended to cross-cultural human comparisons. It may be hypothesized that there will be less overall aggression in societies where hierarchical relationships are widely found and generally accepted.

When such relationships of power are not accepted by subordinates, we have the recipe for revolution. Aggressive acts become instrumental in overturning established authority. Violence is thus seen as the precursor of anarchy and ultimately a redistribution of power. As a Chinese proverb puts it, . . . 讒 口 交 鬥 ， 爲 亂 之 階 梯 . . . (It is a step toward confusion when a quarrel begins). By this logic, aggressive behavior in general must be controlled in order to maintain the status quo.

From many avenues, then, we can see the rationale for a general condemnation of aggressive behavior in Chinese society. If violence is suppressed, families will remain intact, neighbourhood relations will be peaceful, and the wider social order will be protected. In short, harmony will be maintained.

POSSIBLE GENETIC INFLUENCES

Throughout this chapter we will focus on social determinants of aggressive behavior. Possible genetic inputs should not be overlooked, however. In 1971, Freedman reported the results of a study comparing Chinese-American and European-American newborns across a wide spectrum of behaviors. The Chinese babies were less emotionally reactive, habituated more rapidly to aversive stimuli, and were more easily consoled when upset. There were no differences between the two groups, however, in sensory development, maturation of the central nervous system, motor development, and social responsiveness. Given the absence of covariates to explain the differences in emotional lability, Freedman argued for a genetic explanation.

Under the endogamous pressures of Chinese culture (Hsu, 1953), it is possible that a gene pool has developed favouring genotypes predisposing to less emotionally responsive behavior. Such behavior is certainly more adaptive in a culture which places such a premium on self-control and emotional restraint (Solomon, 1971, Ch. 4). Indeed, data show that Chinese versus American differences in activity level, irritability, and lability continue well into infancy (Freedman, 1974; Green, 1969; Kagan, Kearsley, & Zelazo, 1978). We expect that these differences would be found with adult samples also given the dynamics of the Chinese social system.

The question for our purposes involves the relationship between these possible genetic differences and aggressive behavior. As Hinde (1974) has concluded, "In man, also, some individual differences in aggressiveness may be basically genetic, though precisely how the genetic factors operate is far from understood [p. 282]." With the present state of knowledge, then, the issue must remain unresolved. Throughout the following discussion, however, readers should keep in mind that aggression as observed in the Chinese may have some hereditary foundation.

COMPARATIVE DATA ON CHINESE SOCIALIZATION OF AGGRESSIVE BEHAVIOR

The quality of the data on aggressive behavior varies considerably—from retrospective comparisons of interview data to self-reports of behavior. In general, the comparisons involve American subjects as the yardstick against which the various Chinese samples are compared. The implications of the Chinese social orientation are diametrically opposed to the American self-orientation (Yang, 1980) and so this limitation in cultural samples is not altogether unfortunate. It does, however, narrow our perspective.

As our analysis of Confucian traditions suggested, Chinese parents are consistently shown to limit aggressive behavior in their children. In a retrospective comparison, Sollenberger (1968) used the interview schedule developed by Sears, Maccoby, and Levin (1957) with Chinese-American mothers. Their data were then compared with the original Cambridge sample studied by the Harvard group. Obviously, such a comparison is fraught with methodological difficulties, but the differences are so dramatic as to preclude any explanation based solely on extraneous variables. For example, fully 74 percent of the Chinese mothers reported putting no demands on their children to behave aggressively or to fight back under any circumstances. The majority of the American mothers, however, reported demanding aggressive behaviors from their children in "appropriate" circumstances and to fight back. This contrast is supported by data from university students of five cultures who responded to a 28-item attitude inventory developed by Cox (1971) and reported in Ryback, Sanders, Lorentz, and Koestenblatt (1980). More American (61 percent), Israeli (46 percent), and Indian (38 percent) than Ethiopian (22 percent), Chinese from Taiwan (19 percent), or Thai (5 percent) students indicated that they were likely to allow aggressive behavior in their children. The Thai (5 percent) and the Chinese (6 percent) were also the lowest in encouraging aggressive behavior (Israelis– 10 percent, Indians–22 percent, United States–29 percent, Ethiopians–32 percent). When specific forms of aggressive behavior were questioned (e.g., fighting with other children, temper tantrums, saying bad words, property damage, disobedience to parents or to other authority), the Chinese sample consistently showed the lowest incidence of support for the practice. At the level of verbal reports, then, there seems to be a consistent disapproval of children's aggression among older Chinese.

Given such parental attitudes, it is hardly surprising to find, as Solomon (1971, p. 68) reported, that for his respondents the most frequently recalled reason for parental punishment was quarreling or fighting (44.5 percent). Niem and Collard's (1972) results support our previous assumption that Chinese parents are more prone than American parents to discipline their children's aggressive behaviors. They asked Chinese mothers from Taiwan and American mothers from Massachusetts to record their disciplining of children's aggression over a thirty-day period. Given roughly the same number of aggressive episodes from the seventeen children, Niem and Collard found that the Chinese children were more likely to receive some form of parental discipline in response. Clearly, Chinese adults regard aggressive behavior in children as undesirable and respond with socializing pressures.

Type of Discipline

The method that such control takes, however, is an important issue because the parents can inadvertently model the very aggression they are attempting to suppress (Bandura & Walters, 1959; Sears et al., 1957). Data on this point are conflicting. Seventy-nine percent of Solomon's (1971) sample reported receiving frequent physical punishments from parents. Arthur Wolf's (1964) analysis confirms that of Solomon. After observing a Hokkien village in Taiwan, he asserted, "Rather than rewarding their children for the absence of aggression, or shaming them with reference to cultural models, the Chinese parents choose to use harsh physical punishments [p. 7]." Sollenberger (1968), however, concluded that exclusion from the social life of the family or withdrawal of rewards were more frequently employed than physical punishment by Chinese-American parents. Also, Niem and Collard (1972) found that:

> The Chinese parents reported using physical punishment 15 times, while the American parents reported 33 instances. Only 2 of the Chinese children were spanked (a total of 6 times), while 11 of the American children were spanked (a total of 23 times over the same period). [p. 96]

Social-class, rural-urban, or subethnic variations may account for these inconsistencies in the literature (Olsen, 1975; Ward, 1965).

Regardless of the methods used, the single minded intent is clear. As Arthur Wolf (1964) puts it," [t]he primary goal of child training practices in Hsia Chi Chou is the inhibition of physical aggression [p. 6]." We believe this conclusion is applicable to all Chinese societies. Partial confirmation comes from Niem and Collard (1972). They found that the largest difference between their middle-class American and Taiwanese samples lay in the subcategory of physical attack on another. This lower level of observed aggression in these younger Chinese children (4-4.5 years) confirms similar findings about aggressiveness in general using older children and different methodologies. Hsu, Watrous, and Lord (1961) used Rorschach responses; Hwang (1968) used responses to Rosenzweig's picture-frustration test; and Scofield and Sun (1960) used retrospective reports and global comparisons by judges.*

RELATED SOCIALIZATION PRACTICES

We should not overlook socialization practices which probably affect the expression of aggressive behavior in less direct ways. For example, Ward (1970) has described the often provocative and frustration-inducing behaviors of adults and elder siblings toward younger children in the family. In the tantrum that follows, the enraged child is ignored and left "to cry himself out." A succession of these experiences is likely to result in a low likelihood that aggressive behaviors will become a probable response to frustration (Bandura, 1973). This interaction pattern is also a technique for inducing a state of "learned helplessness' (Seligman, 1975), at least vis-a-vis higher status agents of frustration. Regardless of how it is conceptualized, this

---

*A. Wolf's (1964) report was based on voluminous data collected as an extension of the six cultures study (Whiting and Whiting, 1975) into a Chinese cultural setting. Unfortunately, this gold mine of information remains unanalyzed beyond the 1964 presentation. In a recent meeting with the authors, Wolf recollected that Chinese levels for certain types of physical aggression were *higher* than comparable American levels. One only wishes that Wolf's data were available in the public domain, so that appropriate modifications could be made in our present analysis. Such changes will clearly be required.

pattern of socialization probably helps to increase the apparent frustration tolerance of the Chinese by making aggressive and other active responses to provocation much less likely.

FUTURE DIRECTIONS

Reflection on the studies to date yields a number of suggestions for research into the area of aggression. First, information is needed about school-aged children to supplement what is available on preschoolers. Ho (1977-78, 1980) and A. Wolf (1964), among others, have noted the dramatic increase in socialization pressures that are applied to the Chinese child upon entry to primary school. If parental discipline, especially physical discipline, increases at this age, then there may be a concomitant increase in the aggressiveness of these children outside their families. This, in fact, is exactly what Arthur Wolf has observed. Contrasting his data with those from the six cultures study, he asserts that, "The Chinese appear to be the rare case in which aggression and age are positively correlated [p. 15]." Further confirmation of this finding would be most illuminating and reflect on the discontinuity of socialization pressures.

Secondly, greater attention must be paid to various types of aggressive activity at various ages. Niem and Collard (1972) found that their Chinese sample showed more frequent *verbal* aggression than comparable American children. This finding is consistent with A. Wolf's (1964) observation that Chinese children rarely received punishment for verbal attacks. (See later section on public abuse.) Some care will be required in constructing scales to measure such aggressive behavior, however. As Solomon (1971) has pointed out, "To be sure, such aggression (among the Chinese) is usually masked behind the forms of propriety 禮 貌 : the subtle twisting of good manners into an insult; the verbal abuse before a subordinate. . . . (pp. 79-80)." Also implicit in Solomon's remarks is the need to record the target of the aggression. One might well expect greater use of covert aggression toward superiors with the Chinese, for example, as this pattern of aggressive behavior is more compatible with Confucian social dynamics.

These suggestions for finer analyses reflect our concern that the question of aggression requires much more sophisticated consideration in cross-cultural studies than it has previously received. Simply asking whether members of culture X are more aggressive in terms of a particular operational definition than members of culture Y is not productive. Actors aggress against classes of targets using various methods, all within a social context. This reality underscores the usefulness of the conceptual analysis of aggression in terms of coercive control (Tedeschi et al., 1977). Such a model focuses our attention on critical features of the social context such as the relationship of the interactants, the normative structure regulating the interaction, and the type of influence tactic used. By so doing, it directs our attention to more articulated dimensions on which cultures may be expected to vary in their impact on aggressive behavior.

PSYCHOLOGICAL EXPERIMENTATION

When we move to the area of psychological experimentation, we find a paucity of studies on aggressive behavior itself. There have been no within-study cross-cultural comparisons and only a few investigations involving Chinese subjects alone. Given this situation, we will supplement the available material by referring to studies whose subject matter has suggestive although indirect implications for the understanding of aggressive behavior in Chinese culture.

Competition

A series of studies has involved the perception of a future opponent (Bond, 1979; Bond & Hui, 1980, 1981). In this research paradigm, subjects are placed in a competitive situation against another subject and asked to evaluate their opponent prior to the contest. Zero-sum situations such as this have a clear relationship to aggression as one can win only by preventing one's opponent from obtaining the available pay-off. This connection is even more marked for the Chinese. As Solomon (1971) put the matter, "Competition among peers is seen to be troublesome for social unity for the expectation is that rivalry will bring out bad feelings and lead to unrestrained conflict [p. 131]."

Thus, we could anticipate that an unavoidable competition against another would present Chinese subjects with an awkward situation. One solution was to rate higher the likability of a stimulus person described as a future opponent compared to those of the same stimulus person described as a nonopponent (Bond, 1979). It appears as if subjects were compensating their future opponents for a possible defeat by enhancing their opponent's personal qualities. This strategy allows Chinese subjects to observe the requirement of "Friendship first, competition second" (友 誼 第 一 ， 比 賽 第 二).

This ambivalence about competition is underscored by the results from an experiment by Li, Cheung, and Kau (1979). They instructed Chinese children in Hong Kong and Taiwan how to use Madsen's Co-operative Board (Madsen, 1971). They found that their subjects, in contrast to American subjects, continued to co-operate even when the reward structure was changed from a co-operative one to a competitive one. Evidently, it is relatively difficult to elicit competitive behavior from those reared in the Chinese tradition.

One's private wishes, of course, may be quite different from one's public behavior. The enhancement of a future opponent mentioned before (Bond, 1979) occurred across all subjects only when the ratings were made publicly to the experimenter. The higher ratings of a future opponent disappeared when subjects were allowed to make their ratings anonymously to the experimenter (Bond & Hui, 1980). Aggrandizing an opponent's personal qualities thus appears to be a strategy of proper self-presentation to a higher status person such as the experimenter. In fact, Chinese subjects who describe themselves as "competitive" denigrated their future opponent's competitive skills when allowed to make their ratings anonymously (Bond & Hui, 1981). This finding alerts us to the distinction between public face and private self among the Chinese, a phenomenon entirely consistent with their "social orientation" (Yang, 1980). One may harbor negative impressions about another, but these divisive perceptions should not be given a public voice. For, as a common adage puts it, "A team of four horses cannot drag back a word once uttered" (一 言 既 出 ， 駟 馬 難 追).

Conformity

Behavior that reduces the distance between one's opinion or behavior and that of some reference group can be viewed as satisfying various motivations. One is to regard the perception of one's deviance as a cue eliciting anxiety in persons trained to be dependent on groups or authority figures for guidance (e.g., Meade, 1970). Early cross-cultural comparisons found Chinese to be more conforming than Americans, and explained the results by using the dependency construct (Chu, 1966; Huang & Harris, 1973; Meade & Barnard, 1975).

It is equally plausible to view conformity behavior as a characteristic strategy designed to forestall open conflict. Solomon (1971) has argued that the socializing of Chinese children to accept the dictates of paternal authority without question ill-prepared them as adults to resolve differences without escalation into conflict. "In a society that teaches its children that avoidance of a dispute is preferable to moderated resolution of interpersonal differences, there is little between the poles of harmony and confusion . . . [p. 132]." To avoid confrontation and possible aggression, then, Chinese would be inclined to moderate their public position when they are seen to hold a deviant position vis-a-vis some important reference group.

Support for this alternative explanation comes from a study by Meade and Barnard (1973). In a carefully controlled setting high in experimental realism, they arranged for Chinese and American students to appear as deviates from group opinion on six different issues. Contrary to previous results, the American sample conformed more than the Chinese *on the average*. This difference occurred despite the fact that the Chinese subjects conformed *more frequently*. What happened was that the Chinese subjects generally moderated their stance in the face of group pressure, but only slightly. Americans, on the other hand, conformed less frequently but to a much greater extent when they did so. Americans appear to have responded to the issue, changing their opinion dramatically either in agreement or in opposition to the group. The Chinese, on the other hand, appear to have responded to the process element of group difference, attempting to circumvent conflict by compromising slightly on almost every point of contention. One wonders what forms of attitude change might have been found had private, rather than public, measures been taken.

Distribution of Resources

Use of the equity principle (Adams, 1965) for allocating resources is obviously disruptive in an economy marked by scarcity. The equality principle functions to maintain group integrity by preventing differences in members' ability from leading to unequal rewards. Conflict, and possible aggression, can thereby be displaced from the individual level to the group level where it is less immediate and less disruptive. Consequently, it is not surprising to find a proverb from the *Confucian Analects* stating, " 不 患 寡 而 患 不 均 " (Don't worry about scarcity but about distributing what there is equally).

Such reasoning was confirmed in a series of studies using students from the United States and Hong Kong (Bond & Leung, 1981; Leung & Bond, 1981). They allocated rewards, such as grades and future friendship choices, to group members whose inputs were varied; both groups used an equity solution. Chinese responses, however, were more moderate for the same input—less punitive when inputs were very low, less rewarding when inputs were very high.

Even within collective societies, it is probable that strict equality solutions will only be found in extremely cohesive groups interacting across an extended time perspective. The family is the prime example. This egalitarian press, however, is generalized in a modified way to other groupings. The result is an equity solution which is less extreme than that found in more individualistic societies. Its function is to promote the integrity of the group, rather than the welfare of the individual. Its outcome is to minimize conflict, especially when resources are perceived as limited (see also Chu & Yang, 1976).

OTHER OBSERVATIONS OF ADULT BEHAVIOR

Public Abuse

As mentioned previously, socialization pressures against verbal forms of aggression seem less intense than those against physical attack. One consequence may be the frequently observed activity of reviling another in public. Arthur Smith gave a lively description of the Chinese practice of Machie (罵 街) or "reviling the street." Although Smith observed the practice at the end of last century, it is still widespread. According to Smith (1900/1972):

> [T]he moment that a quarrel begins abusive words of this sort are poured forth in a filthy stream to which nothing in the English language offers any parallel, and with a virulence and pertinacity suggestive of the fish-women of Billingsgate. . . . it is in constant and almost universal use by all classes and both sexes, always and everywhere. . . . Women use even viler language than men, and continue it longer. . . . The practice of "reviling the street" is often indulged in by women, who mount the flat roof of the house and shriek away for hours at a time, or until their voices fail. . . . If the day is a hot one the reviler bawls as long as he (or she) has breath, then proceeds to refresh himself by a session of fanning, and afterwards returns to the attack with renewed fury. [pp. 219-221]

Chinese vocabulary seems well suited for this type of performance. Although very few publications have dealt with this topic, Eberhard's study (1968) indicates that Chinese has a rich treasure of abusive terms. The most well-developed terms, according to Noboru Niida (1968), a Japanese scholar on Chinese legal history, are the derogatory terms concerning *Geschlecht-sehre* (sexual honor) which hurt Chinese people more than any other type of abuse.

As soon as such a quarrel starts, it attracts the attention of busybodies who play the role of mediator and pass judgment on the dispute. A Chinese proverb says that three mediators are equal to an official, or three blockheads are equal to an above-board man and three above-board men are equal to a magistrate (三 個 中 人 當 一 官 ， 三 個 愚 人 當 個 明 人 ， 三 個 明 人 當 個 知 縣). Thus, the disputants concerned pay attention to the opinion of the on-lookers, as it is through this agency of social judgment that the issue can be settled.

Surprisingly to some observers, such quarrels rarely turn physical. For example, Kanayama (1978) noted:

> In China you can frequently meet wrangling and quarrelling in the street. If they were Japanese they would have already come to blows. The Chinese are just threatening to hit, but rarely do. Instead, the noise is horrible. [p. 111]

Should the quarrel lead to physical assault, the second function of the observers immediately becomes apparent. The following is a description of a family dispute which M. Wolf (1968) regarded as typical:

> Gioq-ki (the wife), of course, answered him (her husband) word for word, their verbal exchange disintegrated into a physical one, and the listening neighbors were obliged to enter the house and separate them. Chang (husband) left and Gioq-ki stood on the doorstep yelling curses after him.
> It was the stereotype of a Chinese family quarrel, from the listening neighbors to the wife yelling curses at her husband's departing back. Gioq-ki took her neighbor's teasing calmly enough until the neighbor slyly commented on her swollen eyes and hoarse voice, "just like someone who has lost her lover."
> This made Gioq-ki angry. "I should have such good luck! Don't worry about me! When he went out, I told him to hurry off and get himself killed." [p. 68]

Thus, the observers become participants, separating those quarreling before any physical damage can be inflicted and then trying to mollify the combatants. One wonders if such disputes are conducted publicly precisely in order to prevent them from degenerating into physical assault. If so, then this approach to containing physical assault combined with the socialization practices discussed earlier seems remarkably successful.

We do not know if these types of public quarrels occur more frequently in Chinese societies than in others and whether the incidence of private disputes is concomitantly lower. Given the Chinese concern about physical aggression coupled with the difficulty of resolving conflict in the absence of a recognized authority, we expect so.

Collective Violence

Confucian social philosophy functions to maintain the harmony of the in-group. Guidelines for behavior toward members of out-groups are conspicuously lacking. Of the five relationships discussed by Confucius, only that between friends could conceivably extend beyond an established grouping. If we couple this lack of guidelines with the ethnocentrism typically seen in authoritarian social systems (Thomas, 1975), it is not surprising to note numerous examples of seemingly excessive and unrestrained violence against out-group members.

As a probably behavioral reflection of these practices, the homicide rate in Hong Kong for 1975 was 2.3 per 100,000; the comparable United States rate was 12.3. In 1979, the respective Hong Kong and United States rates were 1.0 and 10.5 homicides per 100,000. (Census and Statistics Department, 1979).

An additional feature of Chinese social structuring is the relative lack of clear boundaries for defining an in-group (Ward, 1968). Even the sense of Chia (家), or family, sometimes includes only the members of a nuclear family, but can be extended to include all members of a lineage or a clan. This ambiguity gives disputants considerable leeway in generating a power base from which to struggle with one another. By appealing to those defined ad hoc as members of the same surname, locality, dialect, occupation, or whatever, one can muster considerable support before the battle is fully engaged. Thus, considerable attention is always paid by the participants in a dispute to defining and claiming their respective group memberships, often leading to "classificatory feuding" (Ino, 1901).

In premodern China, when the full power of the central government had not penetrated down to the village level, the disputes of people in the countryside often escalated into open feuding. The most common type of feuding in traditional China was the blood feud between two lineages. A typical example is given in Arthur Smith's *Village life in China* (1890/1970):

> A few villagers were returning late on a moonlight night from a funeral in another village. Nearing their own hamlet, they came on two young fellows chopping down small trees of the kind called date (a jujube or rhamnus). They were getting ready clubs for the combined hare-hunt next day. On being hailed, the youths, who were trespassing on the territory of their neighbouring village, fled to their home pursued by the others. The latter returned to their own village and maliciously spread the report that the young men had been cutting pine-trees from the clan graveyard. Although it was late at night a posse was soon raised to go to the other village (about a mile off) and demand satisfaction. The village was asleep, but some headmen were at last aroused who begged their visitors to postpone the matter till daylight, when the case would be looked into and the culprits punished, and any required satisfaction given.
>
> To the reasonable request, only reviling was retorted, and the band returned to their own village filled with fury. A gong was beaten, every man in the village aroused and every male of fit age forced to accompany the mob armed with clubs, poles, etc., to attack the other village. The latter happened to have a mud wall and gates kept closed at night. So large a band made a great noise, and soon aroused their antagonists by their abusive language. The village elders struggled to keep the gates closed, but they were overborne by the hot blood of the youth, who were resolved, since they must have it, to give their assailants all the satisfaction they wanted. The gates once opened, a furious battle ensued, and the women who clambered to the flat-house tops and struggled to see what was going on heard only the dull whacks of heavy blows. Several men were knocked senseless, and on the cry that they had been killed, the battle was renewed until the attacked were driven

inside their village, each side having several men wounded, some of them severely. One old man had his skull beaten in with a carrying-pole and was borne home unconscious, in which condition he remained for a week or two.

The next morning the attacking village went out and chopped down three little pine-trees growing in their own cemetery (as "proof" of the injury done by the other party), and preceeded to the District city to enter a complaint. The other village of course did the same. The first village took with them the old man, unconscious, and apparently in a moribund condition. Each party had to arrange its yamen expenses before a step could be taken, and as the case was a serious one, these were heavy. The Magistrate dared not decide either way until it was seen whether the wounded recovered. An epileptic, half-witted boy captured by one side, who avowed his responsibility for the trouble (perhaps scared nearly to death) was cruelly beaten till he was half dead for so doing. The matter dragged on for a long time, and at length was decided on no principle either of law or of equity—as is the case with so many suits—each side settling its own debts, and neither side winning. The village attacked had squandered at the yamen 300 strings of cash, and the attacking party 500! The old man at last recovered, and peace reigned in Warsaw and its suburbs. [pp. 131-132]

What seems noteworthy in this example is the absence of peaceful modes of conflict resolution between out-groups and the excess of the consequences in proportion to the provocation (Ward, 1970). One can appreciate the often-voiced wish for a strong authority among the Chinese if the consequences of its absence are so extreme.

Since the communist regime took over China in 1949, local villages have been nested within an administrative system that can step in to put down such rural conflicts. Nevertheless, some of the old physical conflicts between local groups still remain (Parish & Whyte, 1978, pp. 308-311), underscoring the power of these traditional in-group out-group distinctions.

Collective physical attack was also used to punish criminals in the past. Once found guilty, an adulterer or a thief would be attacked by a large band of his villagers, often ruthlessly (Smith, 1900/1972, pp. 194-216). This collective form of physical attack on "the people's enemy" was adopted by the communists and is a copy of the punishment used against criminals in traditional times. The most striking cases were seen at public meetings for the struggle against traitors and landlords. The communist cadres came into a village where there was no class antagonism before to mobilize the masses. The first step was to define the target as a traitor to, or an exploiter of, the community, an out-group member and consequently a non-person against whom violence could thereby be legitimized (Zimbardo, 1970) and where alternative norms of conduct were undeveloped. As soon as the target person was so classified, cadres mobilized some peasants who would speak out and lead the meeting. Many scenes of this kind of meeting were reported by William Hinton in his book *Fanshen* (1966). The following is one of the cases:

Wang Ch'ung-lai was an adopted son of the landlord Wang Lai-hsun's mother. Lai-hsun's mother bought a child wife for Ch'ung-lai. The couple were driven out by the family and forced into beggary. They had lived in another village for 20 years. When they heard that the landlords would be brought to account and debts repaid, they hurried home to the village in 1945, and looked forward to the day when the struggle against Lai-hsun would come.

Lai-hsun was brought to the tribune. Ch'ung-lai's wife was standing in the front row. She was the first to speak.

"How was it that you stayed at home while we were driven out?" she asked, stepping in front of the astounded landlord on her small bound feet.

"Because Ch'ung-lai had a grandfather. He had another place to live," said Lai-hsun looking at the ground. He did not have the courage to look her in the face.

"But you too had in-laws. You too had a place to go. Why did you drive us out and make beggars of us? During the famine year we came to beg from you, our own brother, but you gave us nothing. You drove us away with a stick and beat me and the children with an iron poker."

"I remember that day," said Lai-hsun.

"Why?" shouted Ch'ung-lai's wife, tears rolling down her dirt-stained face. "Why?"

"I was afraid if you returned you would ask to divide the property with me."

This answer aroused the whole meeting.

"Beat him, beat him," shouted the crowd.

Ch'ung-lai's wife then took a leather strap from around her wasting body and she and her son beat Lai-hsun with the strap and with their fists. They beat him for more time than it takes to eat a meal and as they beat him Ch'ung-lai's wife cried out, "I beat you in revenge for six years of beatings. In the past you never cared for us. Your eyes did not know us. Now my eyes do not know you either. Now it is my turn."

Lai-hsun cringed before them and whimpered as the blows fell on his back and neck, then he fainted fell to the ground, and was carried to his home. [pp. 139-140]

Other landlords were beaten to death at large public meetings by aroused groups of their accusers (Hinton, p. 142). The level of public rage mobilized at such meetings can be gauged from the following report of Akiyama (1977):

After a public struggle meeting, the landlord (a former village-head) was executed by shooting. The mass rushed to the corpse. Some threw stones at it, some kicked it, and others spit on it. The mass trampled upon the corpse for four hours until the head and the feet were indistinguishable. . . . [p. 53]

In contrast to the individual form of public abuse discussed earlier, these types of collective action typically result in physical attack, often of a brutal sort. Given the strong socialization against such physical abuse discussed earlier, it is significant that the physical violence occurs in a group setting. In mass action, individual responsibility can be diffused to the other participants, thus lowering restraints against assault (Zimbardo, 1970). In this regard, it is interesting to note Sugg's (1975) surprising finding about twenty representative juvenile delinquents in Hong Kong: all twenty committed the act of violence for which they were jailed when accompanied by one or more members of the group, never alone.

Furthermore, the group often provides a legitimizing function for the participants who see themselves acting to protect and maintain the group, be that group the family, the clan, or the proletariat. It is probable that the actors do not construe their actions as "aggressive," but instead see themselves as engaged in a just defense of community interests, a formulation which helps mobilize the instruments of coercive social control (Tedeschi et al., 1977).

The relative lack of guidelines concerning behavior toward out-group members completes the picture by permitting the violence to occur without opposition from social norms. It is for all these reasons that such a vast proportion of Chinese violence is undertaken by groups and appears unusually excessive and extreme (Smith 1890/1972). One can easily appreciate the terror with which Chinese people regard such violent outbreaks (Ward, 1970).

The Use of Mediators

We have discussed the Chinese concern about maintaining harmonious community relations. We have also presented examples to underscore the extreme and spiraling violence that often occurs when potential conflicts are not quickly checked. Given this backdrop, it is understandable that mediators are extensively used by the Chinese as a strategy for short-circuiting aggression between contending parties.

The advantages of using a mediator are clear. As Brown (1977) has pointed out, "By separating opposing sides during periods of intense conflict, the likelihood that insult or other affronts will occur may be reduced [p. 295]." In addition, the calling-in of a mediator allows respective parties to disengage without any loss of "face," a well-documented concern of the Chinese (Bond & Lee, 1981). If the mediator has sufficient face, then his prestige may be used by the leaders of the parties concerned to force a reluctant peace upon their followers. The followers, thereby, do not lose face in ceasing hostilities because they can construe their peacemaking as protecting the mediator's face (Cohen, 1967). Other advantages are listed by Raven and Rubin (1976).

The need for mediators was heightened by the relative absence of civil law and by the Chinese distrust of the "legal" process for resolving disputes. As we have previously seen, the results of any judgment were often costly to both parties (Gallin, 1967) and the process was usually protracted. Furthermore, Chinese officials were notoriously corrupt (Lau & Lee, 1980), so that the result of any legal action was frequently decided on the basis of which contending party could muster the greater amount of bribery. Thus, one can appreciate the wisdom in the folk proverb, " 餓 死 不 作 賊 ， 屈 死 不 告 狀 " (Better to die of starvation than to become a thief, better to be vexed to death than to bring a lawsuit). The consequence of this situation was to encourage disputants to seek a quicker and more economical resolution through the offices of a mediator.

CONCLUSION

We have sampled from a wide selection of sources in this survey of aggression in Chinese people—philosophical writings, folk wisdom, anthropological observations, sociological surveys, and psychological experimentation. We have argued that the fundamental concern of the Chinese has been to maintain the harmony of the in-group, however defined. The source of authority in these groups is not the rule of law but an individual acting as a leader. Consensual validity about the characteristics of these leaders is achieved through traditional Confucian teachings with the consequence that, " 長 幼 有 序 " (Each person has a ranking). The use of aggressive behavior to challenge these sources of authority is suppressed from an early age. High-density living and low residential mobility contribute their additional inhibiting effects on aggression. The net result is a low incidence of aggressive behaviors that present any challenge to this social ordering, e.g., physical violence toward peers or superiors.

The obverse of this picture is the existence of two dramatic and extreme forms of aggression: public reviling and collective violence toward an out-group. The former, although colorful, has a ritualized quality and rarely leads to physical assault. This is not the case with collective violence where the aggression takes on what Zimbardo (1970) has called a "de-individuated" character—unrestrained, spiraling, and excessive. Paradoxically, both forms of aggression validate the importance of group membership in controlling the behavior of the actors. Public reviling is public to the group which can then pass judgment on the disputants; collective violence is undertaken by persons acting in a group which functions to legitimize its members' violence toward those in the out-group.

Such group violence is extremely destructive, as Chinese history testifies. Given the Confucian hierarchical paradigm, however, social harmony can only be realized if one group emerges superior over the other or if both are brought under the authority of a third party. Neither solution is likely to please everybody; but, as one Chinese proverb puts the issue, " 寧 爲 太 平 犬 ， 莫 作 亂 世 人 " (It is better to be a dog enjoying peace than a man in troubled times).

REFERENCES

Adams, J. S. Inequity in social exchange. In L. Berkowitz (Ed.), *Advances in experimental social psychology*. Vol. 2. New York: Academic Press, 1965.

Akiyama, Y. *Experiences during land reform in China*. Tokyo: Chuokoronsha, 1977. (In Japanese)

Bandura, A. *Principles of behavior modification*. New York: Holt, Rinehart and Winston, 1969.

Bandura, A. *Aggression: A social-learning analysis*. Englewood Cliffs, N.J.: Prentice-Hall, 1973.

Bandura, A., and Walters, R. H. *Social learning and personality development*. New York: Holt, Rinehart and Winston, 1959.

Bond, M. H. Winning either way: The effect of anticipating a competitive interaction on person perception. *Personality and Social Psychology Bulletin*, 1979, 5, 316-319.

Bond, M. and Dutton, D. G. The effect of interaction anticipation and experience as a victim on aggressive behavior. *Journal of Personality*, 1975, 43, 515-527.

Bond, M. H., and Hui, H. C. C. Rater competitiveness and the experimenter's influence on ratings of a future opponent. Unpublished manuscript, The Chinese University of Hong Kong, 1980.

Bond, M. H., and Hui, H. C. C. Anticipating competition: Competitive self-schemas and ratings of a future opponent. Unpublished manuscript, The Chinese University of Hong Kong, 1981.

Bond, M. H., and Lee, P. W. H. Face saving in Chinese culture: A discussion and experimental study of Hong Kong students. In A. King and R. Lee (Eds.), *Social life and development in Hong Kong*. Hong Kong: Chinese University Press, 1981.

Bond, M. H., and Leung, K. Varying both task and maintenance inputs: How does collectivism influence reward allocation? Unpublished manuscript, The Chinese University of Hong Kong, 1981.

Brown, B. R. Face-saving and face-restoration in negotiation. In D. Druckman (Ed.), *Negotiations: Social-psychological perspectives*. Beverly Hills: Sage Publications, 1977.

Census and Statistics Department. *Crime and its victims in Hong Kong*. Hong Kong: Hong Kong Government Printing Office, 1979.

Chu, G. C. Culture, personality, and persuasibility. *Sociometry*, 1966, 29, 169-174.

Chu, J. L., and Yang, K. S. The effects of relative performance and individual modernity on distributive behavior among Chinese college students. *Bulletin of the Institute of Ethnology, Academia Sinica*, 1976, 41, 79-95.

Cohen, J. A. Chinese mediation on the eve of modernization. In D. C. Buxbaum (Ed.), *Traditional and modern legal institutions in Asia and Africa*. Leiden: E. J. Brill, 1967.

Cox, D. R. Child rearing and child care in Ethiopia. *Journal of Social Psychology*, 1971, 85, 3-5.

Eberhard, W. Some Chinese terms of abuse. *Asian Folklore Studies*, 1968, 27, 25-40.

Foster, G. M. Peasant society and the image of limited good. *American Anthropologist*, 1965, 67, 293-315.

Freedman, D. G. An evolutionary approach to research on the life cycle. *Human Development*, 1971, 14, 87-99.

Freedman, D. G. *Human infancy: An evolutionary perspective*. Hillsdale, N.J.: L. Erlbaum, 1974.

Gallin, B. Mediation in changing Chinese society in rural Taiwan. In D. C. Buxbaum (Ed.), *Traditional and modern legal institutions in Asia and Africa*. Leiden: E. J. Brill, 1967.

Green, N. An exploratory study of aggressive behavior in two preschool nurseries. Unpublished master's thesis, University of Chicago, 1969.

Hinde, R. A. *Biological bases of human social behavior*. New York: McGraw-Hill, 1974.

Hinton, W. *Fanshen: A documentary of revolution in a Chinese village*. New York: Random House, 1966.

Ho, D. Y. F. Traditional patterns of socialization in the Chinese culture. *Psyche*, 1977-78, 2, 27-39.

Ho, D. Y. F. Psycho-social implications of collectivism: With special reference to the Chinese case and Maoist dialectics. In L. H. Eckensberger, W. J. Lonner, and Y. H. Poortinga (Eds.), *Cross-cultural contributions to psychology*. Lisse, Holland: Swets & Zeitlinger B. V., 1979.

Ho, D. Y. F. Chinese patterns of socialization: a critical review. Unpublished manuscript, University of Hong Kong, 1980.

Hofstede, G. *Culture's consequence: International differences in work-related values*. Beverly Hills: Sage Publications, 1980.

Hsu, F. L. K. *Americans and Chinese: Two ways of life.* New York: Abelard-Schuman, 1953.

Hsu, F. L. K., Watrous, B. G., and Lord, E. M. Culture pattern and adolescent behavior. *International Journal of Social Psychiatry,* 1961, *7,* 33-53.

Huang, L. C., and Harris, M. B. Conformity in Chinese and Americans: A field experiment. *Journal of Cross-Cultural Psychology,* 1973, *4,* 427-434.

Hwang, C. H. Reactions of Chinese university students to Rosenzweig's picture-frustration study. *Psychology and Education,* 1968, *2,* 37-47.

Ino, K. Bunrui Kaito (Classificatory feuding). *Taiwan Kanshukiji,* 1901, *1,* 25-25. (In Japanese)

Kagan, J., Kearsley, R. B., and Zelazo, P. R. *Infancy: Its place in human development.* Cambridge, Mass.: Harvard University Press, 1978.

Kanayama, N. *Japanese and Chinese.* Tokyo: Sanshodo, 1978. (In Japanese)

La Barre, W. Some observations on character structure in the Orient. *Psychiatry,* 1945, *8,* 319-342.

Lau, C. C., and Lee, R. P. L. Bureaucratic corruption and political instability in nineteenth-century China. Unpublished manuscript, Social Research Centre, The Chinese University of Hong Kong, 1980.

Leung, K., and Bond, M. H. How Chinese and Americans reward task-related contributions: A preliminary study. Unpublished manuscript, The Chinese University of Hong Kong, 1981.

Li, Mei-chi, Cheung, See-fat, and Kau, Shwu-ming. Competitive and co-operative behavior of Chinese children in Taiwan and Hong Kong. *Acta Psychologica Taiwanica,* 1979, *22,* 27-33.

Louie, K. *Critiques of Confucius in contemporary China.* Hong Kong: Chinese University Press, 1980.

Madsen, M. C. Developmental and cross-cultural differences in the co-operative and competitive behavior of young children. *Journal of Cross-cultural Psychology,* 1971, *2,* 365-371.

Meade, R. D. Leadership studies of Chinese and Chinese-Americans. *Journal of Cross-Cultural Psychology,* 1970, *1,* 325-332.

Meade, R. D., and Barnard, W. F. Conformity and anti-conformity among Americans and Chinese. *Journal of Social Psychology,* 1973, *89,* 15-24.

Meade, R. D., and Barnard, W. A. Group pressure effects on American and Chinese females. *Journal of Social Psychology,* 1975, *96,* 137-138.

Mischel, W. *Personality and assessment.* New York: Wiley, 1968.

Niem, C. T. I., and Collard, R. R. Parental discipline of aggressive behaviors in four-year-old Chinese and American children. *Proceedings of the Annual Convention of the American Psychological Association,* 1972, *7,* 95-96.

Niida, N. *Law and morality in Chinese society.* Tokyo: Kobundo, 1968. (In Japanese)

Olsen, N. J. Social class and rural urban patterning of socialization in Taiwan. *Journal of Asian Studies,* 1975, *34,* 659-674.

Parish, W. L., and Whyte, M. K. *Village and family in contemporary China.* Chicago: University of Chicago Press, 1978.

Raven, B. H., and Rubin, J. Z. *Social psychology: People in groups.* New York: Wiley, 1976.

Ryback, D., Sanders, A. L., Lorentz, J., and Koestenblatt, M. Child-rearing practices reported by students in six cultures. *Journal of Social Psychology,* 1980, *110,* 153-162.

Scofield, R. W., and Sun, C. W. A comparative study of the differential effect upon personality of Chinese and American child training practices. *Journal of Social Psychology,* 1960, *52,* 221-224.

Sears, R. R., Maccoby, E. E., and Levin, H. *Patterns of child rearing.* New York: Harper, 1957.

Seligman, M. E. P. *Helplessness.* San Francisco: W. H. Freeman, 1975.

Smith, A. H. *Village life in China.* Boston: Little, Brown, 1970. (Originally published, 1890).

Smith, A. H. *Chinese characteristics.* London: Oliphant, Anderson and Ferrier, 1972. (Originally published, 1900).

Sollenberger, R. T. Chinese-American child-rearing practices and juvenile delinquency. *Journal of Social Psychology,* 1968, *74,* 13-23.

Solomon, R. H. *Mao's revolution and the Chinese political culture.* Berkeley, California: University of California Press, 1971.

Sugg, M. L. Adolescent aggression in Hong Kong. Unpublished manuscript, Social Research Centre, The Chinese University of Hong Kong, 1975.

Tedeschi, J. T., Gaes, G. G., and Rivera, A. N. Aggression and the use of coercive power. *Journal of*

Social Issues, 1977, *33,* 101-125.

Thomas, D. R. Authoritarianism, child-rearing practices and ethnocentrism in seven Pacific Islands groups. *International Journal of Psychology,* 1975, *10,* 235-246.

Ward, B. E. Varieties of the conscious model: The fisherman of South China. In M. Bauton (Ed.), *The relevance of models of social anthropology.* London: Tavistock, 1965.

Ward, B. E. Sociological self-awareness: Some uses of the conscious models. *Man,* 1968, *1,* 201-215.

Ward, B. E. Temper tantrums in Kau Sai. In P. Mayer (Ed.), *Socialization: The approach from social anthropology.* London: Tavistock, 1970.

Whiting, B. B., and Whiting, J. W. M. *Children of six cultures: A psychocultural analysis.* Cambridge, Mass.: Harvard University Press, 1975.

Wolf, A. P. Aggression in a Hokkien village: A preliminary description. Paper presented at a seminar on "Personality and Motivation in Chinese Society," Bermuda, 1964.

Wolf, M. *The house of Lim: A study of a Chinese family.* New York: Appleton-Century-Crafts, 1968.

Wolf, M. Child training and the Chinese family. In M. Freedman (Ed.), *Family and kinship in Chinese society.* Stanford, California: Stanford University Press, 1970.

Wong, F. M. Industrialization and family structure in Hong Kong. *Journal of Marriage and the Family,* 1975, *37,* 985-1000.

Yang, K. S. Social orientation and individual modernity among Chinese students in Taiwan: Further empirical evidence. *Journal of Social Psychology,* 1981, *113,* 159-170.

Zimbardo, P. The human choice: Individuation, reason and order versus deindividuation, impulse and chaos. In N. J. Arnold and D. Levine (Eds.), *Nebraska symposium on motivation.* Vol. 18. Lincoln: University of Nebraska Press, 1970.

4

Federal Republic of Germany: Aggression and Aggression Research

Jo Groebel

INTRODUCTION

One major stereotype of the German is that of an aggressive human being. It is still the *Landsers* to a high extent that represent Germany on TV screens around the world. Different periods in German history contributed to this picture, especially the Third Reich and the holocaust. Currently, the danger of aggression in one of its extremest forms, war, is more or less continuously present in the media and in public discussion due to Germany's geographical position in the middle between rival political hemispheres.

In this chapter, aggression will be considered in two ways, one that describes the different forms of actual aggressive or aggression-related acts, and one that primarily deals with the variety of scientific approaches to the problem. Each of these aspects can be subdivided into categories that represent the content of this chapter. A later section will present a theoretical and empirical strategy of how to construct such a taxonomy.

SOME FACTS ON AGGRESSION IN WEST GERMANY

In general, it is difficult to obtain "hard facts" on the actual aggressive state of a society. One exception seems to be official crime statistics. But even here, criteria are often very unstable and vary with changing definitions of crimes and with different "observer" (police) categorizations. However, in this cross-cultural context, it will be interesting to analyze the percentages of certain crimes in West Germany.

Even more difficult from an empirical point of view seems to be the analysis of "trends" in the public's discussion of aggression-related topics. There are, however, some general highlights, events, or periods that can be judged as significant with respect to aggression.

Aggression Related Topics in the Public Discussion After World War II

After one of the most aggressive periods of German history, at least with respect to collective aggression—the Third Reich (1933-1945) with the holocaust and World War II—Germany faced a completely unstructured situation. Large parts of the country were destroyed, most

Germans were demoralized by famine, death of relatives and friends, and all factors that resulted from the war and the Nazi regime. The period shortly after the war saw a desperate economic situation, an unstable social structure, a rampant black market, and political lynch laws in some parts of Germany—in general, a picture not unlike the atmosphere described in Carol Reed's movie about Vienna, "The Third Man." At the same time, however, a growing economic and political reorganization took place with the help of the Allies.

Finally, in 1949, two new German states were founded, the Federal Republic of Germany in the West with West Berlin politically connected to it and the German Democratic Republic in the East. This separation into two independent entities at the same time effected one of the major political conflicts of the following decade. Especially during the 1950s, the cold war influenced the political climate on both sides. Each accused the other of being offensive and aggressive and, at the same time, used at least verbal aggressive means itself. A step-wise decrease of the cold war took place beginning in the second half of the 1960s and finally led to a more "normalized" relation between the two states.

A "latent" conflicting factor for many Germans was and is Germany's political past. An often deep suspicion about the role of their parents and the older generation in general during the Third Reich period contributed to the conflicts of many young Germans with the state, its institutions, and its representatives. Also, in meeting people from other countries, Germans and even young Germans often experience a sense that the Nazi period is not forgotten and that they are still suspected to be violent and power oriented. While some of these stereotypes may originate in simplistic media content, such as Landser-comics and Nazi-comedies, the real consequences of the holocaust and war are still salient for many people inside and outside Germany. A later section will deal with specific aspects of how Germans cope with this period of their country's history.

Since the late 1950s and early 1960s, growing segments of the younger generation were engaged in the peace movement that followed a strong pacifistic tendency. Many elements of this movement also could be found in the leftist student organizations of West Germany that finally, during 1967 and 1968, hit the front pages with demonstrations against the Vietnam war. Confrontations with the police led to severe riots, especially in the major cities of Berlin, Hamburg, and Frankfurt. The following years saw a decline in street riots. While most of the students expressed themselves by means of political discussions, a small group turned to terrorism, a major topic in the German media during the 1970s and at the beginning of the 1980s.

Other trends in the public debate about aggression in West Germany since 1945 include youth violence, violence in the media, and violent crime. Shortly after the war, youth gangs with pro-Nazi orientations called "Werewolves" got some attention. However, it is not clear if there were really many of these groups or if their existence was largely a myth. The "Halbstarken" (Teds, Rockers) of the 1950s comprised another reportedly aggressive youth movement. They used aggressive poses and also were engaged in violent group conflicts, but again it is difficult to judge whether their aggressiveness was a real threatening factor or rather was a media attribution to this group. This was probably the case for the "punks" who, in the 1970s, at the beginning of their movement, seldom were engaged in real violence but, rather, could be found in antiracism campaigns. In 1981, however, a growing number of them participated in conflicts with the police.

The economic situation, loss of values, and low identification with the political system are among the factors that seem to have been responsible for youth violence and also, perhaps, for the reportedly increasing amount of aggression in the family. While it is difficult to test these hypotheses due to the absence of valid statistical data on noncriminal aggression, more can be said about the actual occurrence of criminal violence.

German Crime Statistics (1953-1980)*

It was mentioned earlier that official crime statistics may suffer from (systematic) over- or underestimations of the crime rates. This may occur because not every single crime is recorded by the police, e.g., the actual number of rapes is said to be much larger than the number appearing in official statistics because of victims being ashamed or being afraid of the examinations. In general, one can assume that the more severe the crimes are—with the probable exception of rape—the more official statistics will represent their actual number.

Looking at crime statistics, the question arises to what extent the data reflect the aggressive structure of a society in general. Different theories deal with the relation between societal influences and violence. Among some theories, a social stress hypothesis play a major role. Numerous international studies deal with this kind of theory. Three of them shall be mentioned here.

Merton (1957) relates pressure resulting from social structure to violence as one form of deviant behavior. In this theory, turning to criminal acts is one possibility for certain individuals or groups (e.g., minorities) to achieve goals that are highly valued by society (e.g., monetary success) but cannot be attained by them through legitimate means. Landau and Beit-Hallahmi (1982) extend the frustration-aggression theory (Dollard, Doob, Miller, Mowrer, & Sears, 1939) to social stress and aggressive behavior in populations. In their analysis, they found a correlation between stressors such as inflation rates and criminal activities. Scherer, Abeles, and Fischer (1975) discuss violence using different aspects of social structure. The social stratification system and subcultural systems contribute to the probability of interpersonal violence. All these approaches have in common that social stresses (e.g., anomie) are major factors influencing (criminal) aggressive behavior. While this relation seems to be plausible, and has some empirical support (e.g., Krebs, 1971), the question arises how the additional influencing variables interact and how they are structured in the individual's perception. One solution could be the use of multidimensional scaling procedures as described by Groebel (1981) for different facets of perceived threat, individual stress, and their structure. Factors, such as social stress, subcultural pressures, individual behavior preferences, etc., are possible dimensions that interact in affecting the occurrence of a criminal act. Each of these dimensions may be constituted by subelements, e.g., perceived gap between general and individual availability of monetary success or perceived social status. Feger (1979) uses a similar paradigm in his theory of attitude components.

At this point, however, some general data on the development of criminal activities in Germany between 1953 and 1979 will be presented without postulating causal relationships between single factors and the change of crime rates.

As shown in figures 4.1 to 4.5, there is a general increase in violent crimes during the period reported here. The combined measure of murder and attempted murder shows a strong increase between 1953 and 1975 and a slight decrease since that year, as shown in figure 4.1, which also shows that the number of attempted murders is much higher than the number of actual murders. Whether this difference denotes some psychological inhibition or pure luck cannot be answered by the data.

From the rape rates reported in figure 4.2, it is evident that, after a peak in 1961 and a decrease until 1965, the "official" annual rate has varied between 10 and 11 per 100,000 population.

---

*The data, tables, and figures reported in this chapter are based on the "Polizeiliche Kriminalstatistik fur die Bundesrepublik Deutschland," Wiesbaden, 1980. The author would like to thank Mrs. Junkers and Mr. Selhausen of the *Bundesministerium des Innern* for supplying him with the material.

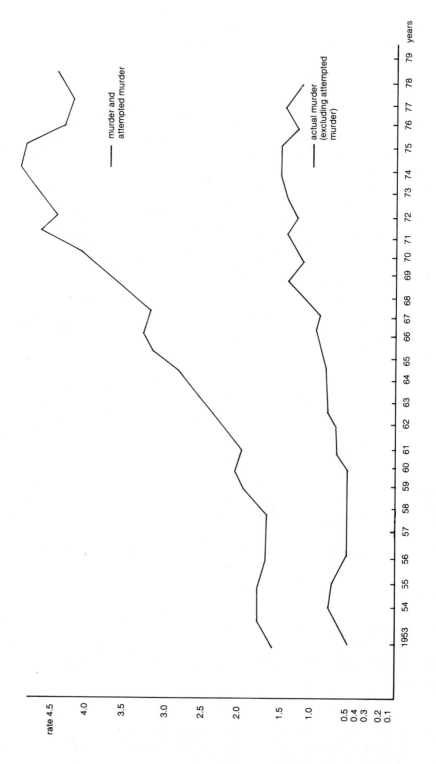

Fig. 4.1. Annual Rates of Murder and Attempted Murder in West Germany (per 100,000 population)

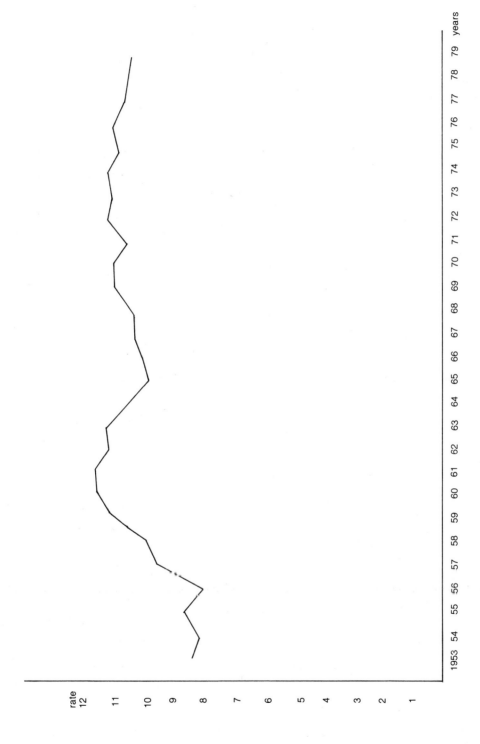

Fig. 4.2. Annual Rates of Rape and Attempted Rape in West Germany (per 100,000 population)

Table 4.1. Demographic Characteristics of Offenders (%), 1979

	SEX		AGE			
	MALE	FEMALE	−14	14–18	18–21	21+
murder	89.9	10.1	0.1	5.0	13.0	82.0
rape	99.4	0.6	0.5	7.6	16.3	75.5
robberies	93.2	6.8	7.7	22.2	22.1	48.1
strong physical assaults	90.8	9.2	1.9	12.5	17.5	68.2

However, while most crimes of all kinds are committed by males (see table 4.1), rape is almost exclusively a male crime. So, the rates for rape have to be corrected for this. Also it is probably underreported.

The most likely crime subject to a relationship with "social stress," (such as unavailability of monetary success by legitimate means) is robbery. Here, a steady increase (with two minor exceptions in the 1970s) can be observed (Fig. 4.3). There is a correspondence between these data and the increase in unemployment rates and an above average percentage of adolescents engaged in this kind of criminality (table 4.1), who also are particularly effected by enemployment. But this does not per se justify assuming a simple causal relation. There may be other factors and their interaction that can be effective, such as "loss of values."

Figure 4.4 represents the annual rates of strong physical assaults against the person; figure 4.5 illustrates the development of *all* criminal activity, including nonviolent crimes, between 1953 and 1979. Both figures show a general increase (with some annual exceptions) in crime within this period with a particular rise since 1970.

A more specific geographical analysis for 1979 shows an above average percentage of big cities and urban areas as places of crime (tables 4.2 and 4.3). Different theories deal with the possible impact of urban environments on violent behavior. Crowding theory assumes that the high density of people on small space creates aggression similar to the behavior of too many rats in the cage. Milgram (1970) suggests that higher social isolation and anonymity increase the occurrence of aggressive behavior. Whether it is these factors or the specific urban subcultures as Scherer et al. (1975) hypothesize is hard to decide. Actually, one can assume that every crime has its specific history and that each of the above mentioned factors are affective under certain circumstances at least for certain violent acts. It is interesting to note, however, that West Germany follows that same pattern as the United States—though not to the same extent—with respect to the disproportionate occurrence of violence in urban settings.

The significant increase of criminality rates during the 1970s was accompanied by the appearance of strong political terrorism for the first time since World War II. It had an immense impact on the media and is perceived as one of the major threats against the political system. Although the effects of terrorist activity are high—at least with respect to headlines and public discussion—the actual number of offenses is quite small compared to the percentage of nonpolitical crime (see figures 4.6 and 4.7). However, the proclaimed threat to the whole political system, the spectacularity and cleverness of the terrorist acts, the prominence of some of the terrorists (like Ulrike Meinhof who committed suicide) and their victims (Schleyer, Ponto, Buback) contributed to the intense coverage of terrorism by the media.

Later, I shall consider the factors which might prompt someone to terrorism. So far, it can be concluded that violent crime has become an increasing concern in West Germany, but annual rates are still far from reaching American standards.

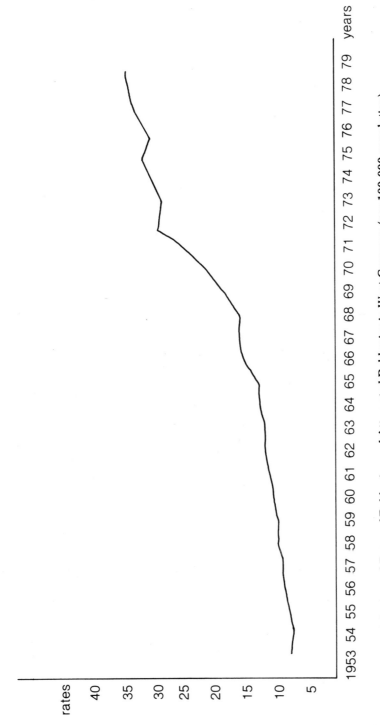

Fig. 4.3. Annual Rates of Robberies and Attempted Robberies in West Germany (per 100,000 population)

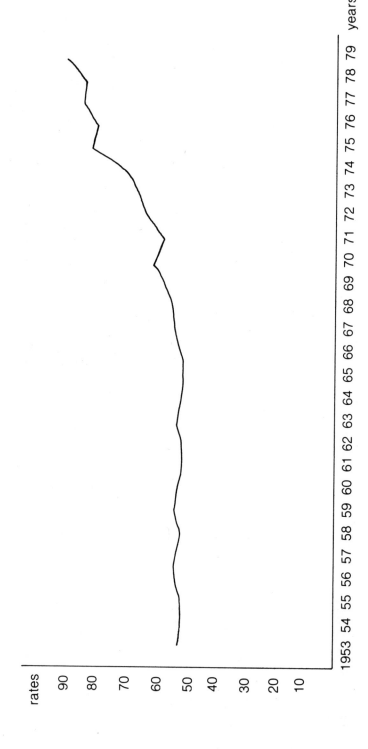

Fig. 4.4. Annual Rates of Strong Physical Assaults Against the Person in West Germany (murders excluded, per 100,000 population)

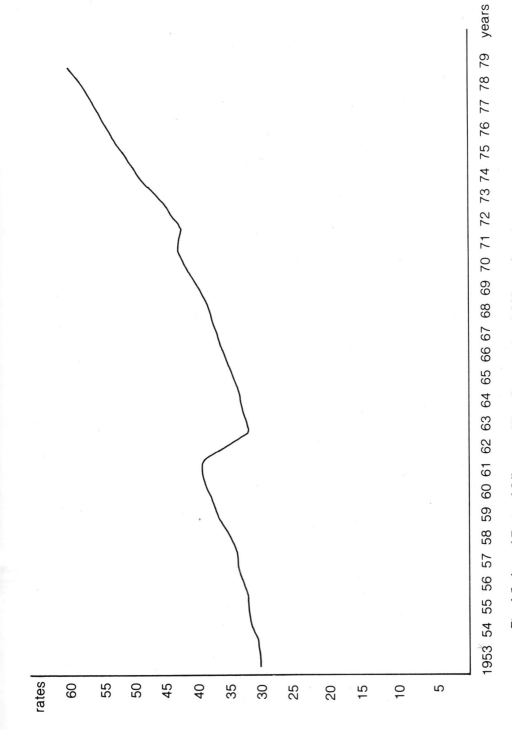

Fig. 4.5. Annual Rates of Offenses in West Germany (per 1,000 population)

Table 4.2. Geographical Crime Structure in West Germany (1979)

	PERCENTAGE OF TOTAL WEST GERMAN POPUL.	PERCENTAGE OF TOTAL OFFENSES	PERCENTAGE OF MURDER	PERCENTAGE OF RAPE	PERCENTAGE OF ROBBERIES	PERCENTAGE OF STRONG PHYSICAL ASSAULT
Cities with 500,000 population and more	17.2	27.9	22.9	28.2	41.7	32.7
Cities with 100,000–500,000 population	17.0	21.6	19.2	21.2	25.5	23.7
Cities with 20,000–100,000 population	25.8	27.1	25.1	25.6	21.8	22.3
Regions with 20,000 population and under	40.0	22.6	32.6	24.7	10.9	21.2
Place of crime unknown		0.8	0.2	0.3	0.1	0.1
	100.0	100.0	100.0	100.0	100.0	100.0

Table 4.3. The Five German Cities (population 100,000 and more) with the Highest and the Five Cities (100,000 and more) with the Lowest Crime Rates (per 1,000 population), 1979 (percent)

HIGHEST			LOWEST		
CITY	CRIME RATE	RANK	CITY	CRIME RATE	RANK
Frankfurt	127	1	Wuppertal	50	65
Berlin	116	2	Witten	47	66
Hamburg	111	3	Berg. Gladbach	46	67
Heidelberg	110	4	Remscheid	42	68
Offenbach/M.	110	5	Siegen	37	69

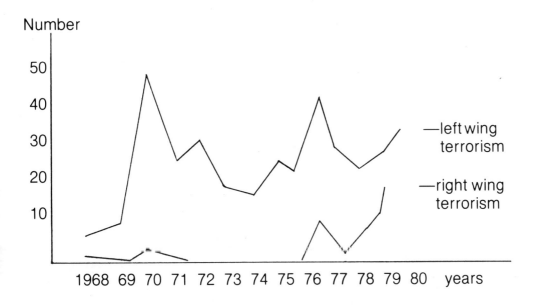

Fig. 4.6. Total Annual Number of Terrorist Offenses in West Germany

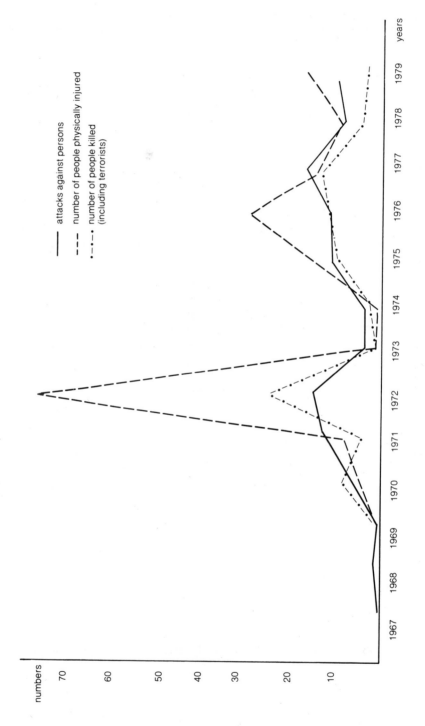

Fig. 4.7. Total Annual Number of German Terrorists' Physical Attacks

attacks against persons

number of people physically injured

number of people killed (including terrorists)

One important difference between West Germany and the United States should be noted. No guns or any other dangerous arms can be bought without an official permit which is very hard to obtain. Another factor may be the more homogeneous social structure of the population, which does not produce social conflicts to the same extent as in the United States, with its underprivileged ethnic minorities.

A growing number of conflicts, however, can be observed in some years which involve "house-kraking" people, primarily of the younger age groups, who squat in empty houses to demonstrate against real-estate and property speculations. Some severe riots took place over this, peaking in 1980 and 1981. While environmental and societal factors may be identified as important causes of aggression in this case, in general, the problem of its origins is mostly unsolved. Also problematic is the official and institutional treatment of aggression and "alternative" extra-institutional approaches. Further, it is difficult to make any diagnoses or predictions of future aggressive trends, or to develop strategies for prosocial alternatives to aggression. Nor have scientific theory and research yet faced the difficulty of insufficient generalizable results. However, there are some approaches in different disciplines that could offer further leads for dealing with the aggression problem.

AGGRESSION THEORIES

In general, empirical psychological aggression research in West Germany since 1945 has been done mostly within a frame of reference that was determined by American theories. The frustration-aggression hypothesis (Dollard, Doob, Miller, Mowrer & Sears, 1939) and the social learning theory (Bandura & Walters, 1964; Berkowitz, 1962b) were major influences. However, there is a growing number of theoretical approaches in Germany that work with different paradigms. Some of them will be presented in the following sections.

While purely psychoanalytical theories have had relatively little influence on empirical psychological research during the last decade, they still influence popular understanding of aggression as in the popular-scientific book market and in many clinical institutions. Following Freudian and Adlerian terminology, an aggressive drive is postulated by Mitscherlich (1969) and Fromm (1974) among others. These views have received much attention in West Germany.

Another prominent German figure who has written about aggression is Konrad Lorenz. In his ethological theory, he assumes the existence of a general aggression instinct (Lorenz, 1966). The conception of an innate aggressive drive (see also Eibl-Eibesfeldt, 1970) is widely criticized, however, in psychological and also ethological circles.

An important contribution to aggression research is made by brain researchers, biochemists, and physiologists. The amygdala and the hypothalamus could be identified as "aggression centers" by using electrostimulation (see, e.g., Holst, 1957). But again, the assumption of neurological processes as the *prime* source of aggression without taking into account environmental influences seems to be too limited.

Although monocausal interpretations of aggression may be attractive, one can rather assume that aggression is a multifaceted variable affected by many factors. The problem seems to be that very different phenomena are categorized as aggression, because their effects or the behavior associated with them appear to be similar, while their origins may not be connected at all. This may be explained by the fact that here science has to deal with a term originating from a "naive" description of rather complex acts where not only behavioral consequences but all conditions of this behavior should be considered. This demands, in my opinion, an interdisciplinary approach or at least an openness to the different facets of the causal relationships within the field of aggression.

The Definition of Aggression

Arguments about the definition of aggression reflect this problem. German authors like Werbik (1971) or Mummendey (1981a) criticize definitions that concentrate on only one aspect of an aggressive act, e.g., the *consequences* of an aggression, as Buss (1961) does in his "classical" definition, "Aggression is defined as a response that delivers noxious stimuli to another organism [p. 1]."

Selg (1968, 1974) offers a similar definition that focuses on the aspect of injury and defines aggression as a "distribution of injuring stimuli that are directed at an organism or an organism-surrogate [Selg, 1974, p. 15]." While some authors miss the inclusion of "intention" in his definition he stresses that by using the term "directed" a purely accidental injury is excluded from the definition. At the same time, he refuses to accept the necessity of the intentional aspect. A definition centered around "intention" would not consider ethological approaches (Selg, 1981).

However, for the definition of *human* aggression, "intention" is generally assumed as a necessary element (see Irle, 1975). Werbik (1981) and Werbik and Munzert (1978) use the terms "intention" and "intentional" with reference to *action theory*. Following a cognitive point of view, they speak of an action as a form of behavior that can be induced or can be changed through *argumentation;* an action is called aggression only if its consequence or its effect contradicts another person's will (Werbik, 1981). A similar definition is given by Kempf (1981). Werbik (1981) mentions different kinds of aggressive acts:

- "intentional destructive acts" describe a behavior where the acting individual expects destruction of another individual (death)
- "intentional partly destructive acts" means that the attacked individual is expected to be physically injured
- "intentional aversive acts" denotes a behavior where the aggressed other is expected to suffer from a (permanent) state he would like to avoid.

Mummendey (1981a) focuses on what he terms "interaction suggestion," when, in addition to an actual injury or intended injury, there is a dissent between the acting individual and the individual affected by the action with respect to the situational-normative adequacy of the action.

While these definitions may concentrate on different aspects such as injury, intention, or interaction, in many of them the role of the observer in labeling an act as aggressive is emphasized (see Hilke & Kempf, 1981b; Jütteman, 1981; Werbik, 1981). This interpersonal interpretation of an action is also stressed by Kornadt, Eckensberger, and Emminghaus (1980): "Aggressive behavior requires that the other persons involved attribute it to an aggressive motive, otherwise, it will have another meaning [p. 256]." The problem of defining aggression is extensively discussed in a German publication edited by Hilke and Kempf (1981a), *Menschliche Aggression* ("Human Aggression"). Instead of going into more details of these definitions or adding another one, an integrating scheme for different aspects of an aggressive act—injury, intention, observer—is presented below.

If a motive and/or act is to be called aggressive it can be represented in a three-dimensional space with the three axes: "actor" (intention), "victim" (injury), and "observer" (judgment, measurement), each running from zero to one. Zero (0) denotes no aggressive intention, no injury, or no observation of aggression, respectively. "1" means that the respective factor is true to a maximal extent. Also, the different definitions of aggression can be placed in this schema according to the particular terms that are used. The three-dimensional space depicted in figure 4.8 stands for two kinds of aspects—one that is related to the factual actions, consequences, and norms; and one that is related to their representation in an empirical and/or a numerical system (for the principles of measurement see Suppes & Zines, 1963).

At least for empirical research, the study of aggression cannot be separated from its measurement. To call an act aggressive, it is necessary to have adequate methods for measuring it. Measures can be analyses of the actor's and/or the victim's statements, such as in interviews or questionnaires (probably using statistical norms), systematic behavior observations, or other methods. A "1" on the observer/method dimension would represent a totally valid judgment; however, one can rather expect that most observations, at best, will fall short of this

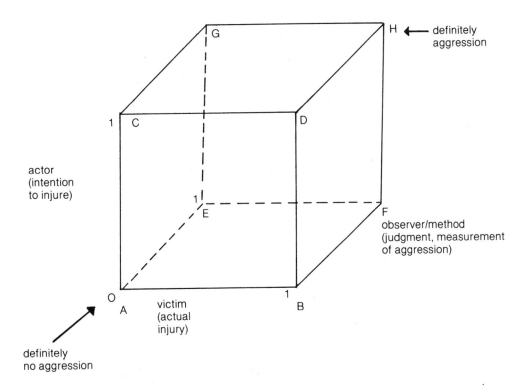

Fig. 4.8. Three-Dimensional Space to Represent Aggressive Acts/Intentions

point. Corresponding to this, the actor and the victim dimensions represent statements on the respective levels of aggressive intention (actor) and perceived injury (victim).

Given valid measures, it is possible to place an aggressive act/motive at the correct representing point of the geometrical space with the three dimensions: actual intention, actual injury, and actual judgment by an observer (normative aspect). A, B, C, . . . , H are the extremes with the following characterizations of different acts:

A. not intended—no injury—not judged as aggressive: definitely no aggression
B. not intended—injury—not judged as aggressive: wrong attribution by victim; non-aggressive injury, e.g., operation
C. intended—no injury—not judged as aggressive: aggressive "state" of a person, not subject to external observation
D. intended—injury—not judged as aggressive: misjudgment
E. not intended—no injury—judged as aggressive: misjudgment
F. not intended—injury—judged as aggressive: pathological aggression, animal aggression (if intention defined as purely related to human cognitive processes)
G. intended—no injury—judged as aggressive: aggressive intention only, e.g., threatening someone without injuring him directly; aggressive "state" of a person, aggressive gestures
H. intended—injury—judged as aggressive: definitely aggression

As a consequence, one can conclude that the more similarly an act is rated by an actor, a victim, and an observer, the more clear-cut its representation on the "definitely aggression-definitely not aggression axis" (connecting A with H). (An analysis of aggression ratings by actors, victims and observers using conjunctive or disjunctive scaling techniques, see Coombs, 1964, could contribute to a more exact classification of different aggression terms.) While this may sound like a tautology, it actually denotes the problem of the correspondance among different perspectives. Any deviation from the A-H axis indicated an ambiguity in calling an act aggressive. These problems hold not only for the definition of aggression but have consequences for aggression theory.

The "Classical" Theories

Numerous books and publications deal with the classical aggression theories (among others, Bandura, 1973; DeWit & Hartup, 1974; Kornadt, 1981b; Mummendey, 1981b). These mostly include reviews of studies by well-known German-language authors, such as Adler, Freud, and Lorenz. Although some of them actually were of Austrian origin, they either worked in Germany or at least had a major impact on thinking about aggression in Germany—often creating strong controversies about the respective conceptions. Here, we will provide a brief consideration of their works, and present a few additional "classical" studies.

Freud had different consecutive ideas about aggression. In the early stage of his psychoanalytic theory, he assumed aggression to be one component of sexuality. After 1915, aggression was regarded as a reaction to frustration in trying to satisfy the ego-drives—a preformulation of the frustration-aggression hypothesis (Dollard et al., 1939). Finally, he offered a revised definition and treated aggression as one of two dual drives—the other being the "eros" (see Freud, 1950).

Adler (1908) postulated many primary drives that, if not satisfied, would release the aggression drive. A major critique of the drive conception of aggression, related to the frequently voiced objection to orthodox psychoanalytic theories, is that they are not open to an empirical falsification and thus cannot be subject of a real scientific analysis (see Popper, 1934, 1959;

and many others). Accordingly, these drive conceptions have received little attention in modern German experimental psychology.

Konrad Lorenz (1963, 1966) also assumes the existence of an innate aggression drive. Beside the often criticized fact that Lorenz and another prominent German exponent of the ethological aggressive-drive theory, Eibl-Eibesfeldt (1970, 1977), have drawn their conclusions mainly on the basis of results from animal studies, they also face the argument that they had not considered alternative interpretations to their observations. For example, the occurrence of aggression in isolated animals, judged as "proof" for the "spontaneity" of aggressive behavior by Eibl-Eibesfeldt (1977) can also be interpreted as reaction to a stressful situation (isolation). Hassenstein (1981) considers this aspect and presents an ethological aggression theory that differentiates between at least eight biological causes for aggressive animal behavior, such as sexual motivation, group-defense aggression, aggressiveness as reaction to fear, pecking order aggression, and frustration aggression. In addition, he also views the simple transfer from "animal" results to human behavior as rather problematic and demands that it include an abstraction from the animal functional principles to the human level, and a test if these principles also could be observed in humans (for a further discussion of Lorenz' and Eibl-Eibesfeldt's theories see Dann, 1967; Scherer et al., 1975; Schmidbauer, 1972).

One of the most influential psychological aggression theories in West Germany dealt with aggression as a reaction, and was introduced as frustration aggression theory by Dollard and his colleagues in 1939. It is interesting to note, however, that earlier, Tamara Dembo (1931) had used "frustrating" conditions in her experiments on anger at Kurt Lewin's psychological department of the Berlin University. Subjects were asked to solve a reportedly manageable problem which actually could not be solved (grabbing certain flowers that were out of reach for the subjects). Dembo observed different kinds of reactions to the "frustration." Some solved another problem they had *not* been asked to solve (grabbing *other* flowers), some started completely different activities, and some verbally attacked the experimenter. Dembo's studies can be regarded as some of the first *systematic* attempts to observe frustration-induced human aggression in the laboratory.

As a whole, most of the early German studies on aggression either assumed an internal aggressive drive (Freud, Adler, recently Lorenz) or stressed the importance of cognitive processes (Dembo, Buhler). After World War II, the classical American learning theories influenced the aggression debate in Germany to a relatively high extent. However, in recent German research, motivation and cognition play a major role again.

Recent Trends in German Aggression Theory

After an era of an often polemically led debate between rival theories, the international aggression discussion of the late 1970s and the early 1980s is widely characterized by a growing demand for an integration of the different theoretical approaches. Brain physiologists (Ervin, 1981; Mark, 1981), psychologists (Berkowitz, 1978) and representatives of other disciplines either postulate or actually formulate theories that include varied combinations of, inter alia, hormonal, environmental, cognitive factors, and/or factors related to learning processes. A similar trend can also be observed in recent German approaches (see Kornadt, 1981a; Michaelis, 1976; Mummendey, 1981b). In this context, a special role is played by action-theory (see Werbik, 1978) and motivation-theory (see Heckhausen, 1980).

Action theory postulates that an individual does not react directly to an actual environment, but that he or she perceives coded information out of this environment and acts after information processing thus "creating" a new environment through his action. The emphasis, therefore, lies in the interaction between person and environment and the mutual influencing process between the two. An action results from the perceived discrepancy between an actual state and a desired state. Accordingly, an aggressive act will occur when a person perceives a discrepancy between actual and desired states and assesses the situation so that aggression is expected to be the adequate means to achieve the desired state. In this context, Werbik (1974) introduces a formalized cognitive theory whereby each goal of an individual's action can also be seen as means (goal on a lower level, "subgoal") for a more general goal (goal on a higher level). These goals form a hierarchical system with different levels. Using the system, the cognitions associated with aggressive acts as well as the roles of frustrations and learning processes can be explained (Werbik, 1974). Belschner (1981) reports an empirical attempt to test the theory: Subjects' evaluations of a potentially aggression-inducing situation and their willingness to act aggressively were investigated in interviews. The results supported the theoretical assumptions. However, the possibility of a totally adequate representation of the very complex and detailed theory in an empirical system has yet to be demonstrated. We will return to this point in the section on "measurement of aggression."

Another complex integrative theory is presented by Kornadt (1980). In his "motivation theory of aggression," he assumes the existence of a permanent motivational system consisting of an approach and an avoidance component. According to the specific stimulus characteristics of a certain situation and the expected outcome of an action in this situation, the aggression motive will be affective similar to the principles postulated for the achievement motive (see Atkinson & Feather, 1966; Heckhausen, 1967):

The motivation for a certain situation-related aggressive act is a function

- of the stable aggression motive (M_A),
- of the expectation that the respective aggressive act can be successfully performed in the situation (E_A),
- of the anticipated positive value associated with reaching the actual goal of the aggressive act (A_A), and on the other hand
- of the stable motive to avoid aggression (M_{AV}),
- of the expectation of negative consequences (punishment) after having performed the aggressive act (E_S),
- of the negative value associated with the anticipated negative consequences after having reached the goal (A_S): . . . A motivation for an aggressive act $= f(M_A. E_A. A_A) - (M_{AV}.E_S.A_S)'$. [Kornadt, 1980, p. 13]

Kornadt indicates, however, that the connection between the approach and avoidance components may not necessarily be additive. Still, the underlying principle would hold and would describe aggression-motivated, intended hostile human acts. Thus, "instrumental" aggressive acts performed for goals other than to satisfy aggression motives have to be separated from the "real" aggression motivation in this theory (see also Feshbach, 1964). In the first stage, anger is activated by the perception of situational cues that are usually associated with anger, e.g., aggressor-induced frustration. Learning processes as well as genetic factors may determine the association between these cues and anger. The activation is subject to a cognitive control; emotion and situation are evaluated. Another element of this evaluation is the perceived intention of the aggressor (intention-attribution). If the result of the evaluation denotes that the situation is relevant with respect to aggression, the aggressive motive is activated. Dependent on the cognitive evaluation of the situational adequacy, an aggressive (counter-) act is performed. If the outcome of the action is equal to the intended goal, a deactivation of the motivational system takes place. During the whole evaluation and action process, the aggression-avoidance motive is also activated (see above) and can inhibit the aggressive act.

The strength of Kornadt's theory lies in the fact that he has offered a system where seemingly contradictory theoretical approaches and results can be integrated and where the interaction of person and situation, cognition and emotion is considered and defined. In addition, he formulates hypotheses that can be tested in iterative procedures (see also Kornadt et al., 1980). Different studies provide evidence for his theoretical system and illustrate a possible integration of his theory into a more general motivation theory (Heckhausen, 1980; Kornadt, 1974).

ON THE MEASUREMENT OF AGGRESSION

A general goal of aggression research is to relate theoretical assumptions directly to an adequate methodology. Such a systematic approach could also include iterative assumptions on strategies aimed at changing aggressive behavior. In addition, *structural* aspects (of the situations, of the different dimensions of aggression, and of inter- and intraindividual differences) definitely have to be included. A structural taxonomy then could be added to the theoretical systems. One possibility for constructing such a taxonomy is given by a combination of facet theory and multidimensional scaling techniques. Before we describe a design for such a taxonomy, some measurement procedures should be briefly discussed.

Beside many adaptations of Anglo-Saxon tests, there exist different newly constructed German aggression measures, either for experimental purposes in psychological research or for diagnoses in the applied field. However, some of the diagnostic techniques fail to take into account intercultural characteristics, structural or processual aspects of aggression, or even test-theoretical criteria (though this may not be a specifically German problem). H. D. Mummendey (1980) reports an experimental study which proves the relatively low relation between results based on "aggression-machines" (see Buss, 1961) and aggression questionnaires. He postulates the use of combined measures—including "bogus-pipeline" situations to reduce social desirability effects—in which each could record a specific aspect of aggression. In table 4.4, we provide a survey of different method-related categories with respective examples of procedures applied in Germany plus the hypothesized aspects of aggression in-

Table 4.4. A Survey of Some German Aggression Measures

PROCEDURE	NAME (ABBREVIATION ONLY)	AUTHOR(S)	ASPECT MEASURED
aggression machine	—	Mummendey (1981b)	overt behavior
questionnaire	AMAF	Krebs & Groebel (1976)	attitudes, intentions
	EAS	Petermann & Petermann (1980)	evaluation of situation
physiological measures	—	see Lischke (1975)	emotional arousal
projective tests	TAT	Kornadt (1974), see also Zumkley (1978)	motivation
behavior observation	—	see Mees (1977)	overt behavior, social interaction
interview (situation related)	various	see Hilke and Kempf (1981a)	action processes

vestigated. A combination of these or similar procedures, assuming they are valid, could contribute to more adequate measurement of aggression. However, some of the listed methods have yet to prove their usefulness.

Directly related to the measurement problem is the structural aspect. As the theoretical discussion in previous sections has demonstrated, there are many different facets of aggression. *Aggression is not one-dimensional.* Accordingly, it is not possible to measure *the* aggression. Rather, one can assume different dimensions on the motivational, behavioral, and situational levels, respectively. Theoretical classifications were introduced by Buss (1961) for aggressive behavior and by Werbik (1971) for aggressive intentions. A preferred procedure to test such structures has been factor-analysis. Krebs and Groebel (1976) found three clearly separated factors in their aggressive-attitude scale: *destructive aggression, legitimated aggression,* and *reactive aggression.* In this context, "destructive" denotes a spontaneous aggression (just for fun), "legitimated" refers to an aggression against social "deviants," and "reactive" is an aggression after frustration. Yet, apart from the fact that the factor-analytical model is often criticized for the shortcomings of its algorithms (see Schönemann & Steiger, 1978), it is not able to represent an interlocked structure adequately.

A possible solution is given by the use of facet theory (see Jordan, 1978). At the same time, a direct link between theory and measurement is offered. In this context, Guttman (cited in Levy, 1980) defines theory as an "hypothesis of a correspondence between a definitional system for a universe of observations and an aspect of the empirical structure of these observations together with a rationale for such an hypothesis." Thus, the "universe of observations" is part of the structural theory defined for specific elements. The elements are written as a "mapping sentence," whose structure can be tested by multidimensional scaling (MDS) procedures (for details see Green & Rao, 1972). It is important to note that this method also allows one to measure structural changes over time and could be related to a more general theory as is demonstrated for threat stimuli by Groebel (1981). To illustrate the principle of the construction of a structural aggression taxonomy by means of facet theory, we suggest the "mapping sentence" shown in figure 4.9.

The extended and/or modified version of this mapping would be presented as items/observation categories, the results (e.g., ratings) could then be analyzed using MDS. Representing the obtained structure in an n-dimensional geometrical space would allow one to test the assumed taxonomy. The more precisely the structure (i.e., the relation of single elements) can be analyzed the more exact will be the measurement of intra-/interindividual differences and the testability of complex theories.

SELECTED STUDIES ON VIOLENCE AND AGGRESSION

The problem of measurement also affects research in the applied field. The "paper-and-pencil paradigm" is of limited use when it does not consider the already mentioned situational, structural, and processual aspects. In the German studies described below, different strategies were chosen to deal with this problem.

Aggression in the School

Violence and aggression in the schools have reportedly increased over the last decade in West Germany (Heinelt, 1978). Psychologists and teachers have to examine ways to reduce student aggression. In this context, the teacher's and the student's classification of a certain

A
A
(person)   of   B
(group)   (male)
                       (female)   sex with

a
C
(very high)
(. . .)   aggressive disposition
(very low)

and
D
(normal)
(abnormal)   brainfunctions

who is confronted with a
E
(very frustrating)
(. . .)
(not frustrating)

stimulus in a situation
F
(being with others)
(. . .)
(being alone)

G
(attributes)
(does not attribute)   the frustration to

another
H
(person)   I
(group)   I
(intends)
(does not intend)

to attack the
J
(frustrating)
(not frustrating)   other

and shows a
K
(physically aggressive)
(verbally aggressive) reaction
(non-aggressive)

which   (injures)
         (does not injure)   the other.

Fig. 4.9. Example of a "Mapping Sentence."

behavior as aggressive is an important issue, as are the antecedents of these definitions—as the studies which follow illustrate.

Linneweber (1980) focuses on the interactional definition of aggression (see above) and presents results on the effects of situational factors on the judgment of possibly aggressive student interactions. In the first stage of the study, using student and teacher ratings, Linneweber and his colleagues got a classification of different situational characteristics that (a) are given in the school environment (b) are likely to evoke aggressive behavior. The respective variables are density, spatial mobility, presence of by-standers/observers, presence of controlling persons, stress of performance, and time during the lessons. Every possible combination of these dichotomized variables (with a total of 64 different combinations) was formulated as a situational description of possible aggression instigators. In addition, each of these situations included the description of physically or verbally "aggressive" acts, respectively. A total sample of 1,200 10 to 16 year old students rated these aggressive acts as to their situational adequacy, their intentional content, and their degree of injury. Using hierarchical cluster analysis, the results prove that the situational context has a strong effect on the judgment of the aggressive acts. For example, verbal attacks in situations with high observer attention are rated as more aggressive than verbal attacks in situations with little attention. The practical relevance of this finding lies in the fact that teachers' reactions to aggressive acts will often be directed by their interpretation of the situational characteristics only, thus probably creating misjudgments and reactions that cannot effectively reduce aggression.

Directly related to this problem is a study by Dann, Humpert, Krause, Olbrich, and Tennstädt (1981). The authors investigate the influence of teachers' "naive" aggression theories on aggressive student behavior and teacher-student interaction. In addition, they discuss ways to correct these theories so that the probability of an occurrence of aggressive acts can be reduced. In this context, the term "naive" denotes implicit theories such as Heider's (1958), i.e., an individual's implicit cognitive conceptions of the origins and conditions of others' behavior. The analysis of teacher statements showed that five elements contribute to the impression that an act has to be called aggressive: provocation of the potential aggressor, intensity of the judged act, the potential aggressor's intention to injure, his emotional arousal, and the actual injury to the potential victim. In a manner similar to Linneweber's study, these elements were combined with situational descriptions and presented to teachers. Each specific profile of these elements denoted aspects of the teacher's personal implicit aggression theory. At least one conclusion can be drawn at this point. If a teacher has a relatively stable transsituational "aggression theory," he often may face an "aggressive" student behavior that appears to be similar to the one in previous situations and he may react according to this implicit theory while another reaction would have been more adequate to solve the situation. Thus, a *systematic* critical analysis of these individual theories of aggression *and* the respective coping strategies could increase the validity of the teacher judgments and could contribute to the development of more effective ways to manage student aggression. If we assume that the situational judgments, the aggression ratings, *and* the supposed adequate reactions to the aggressive acts can be represented in a common geometrical space for numerical analysis, then the empirical data can be obtained by similarity judgments of the respective variables. The geometrical representation would represent the structure of the teacher's aggression assessment and coping system.

The Effects of Media Violence

Many international publications deal with the effects of violent television programs on aggression. Although American studies (Bandura et al., 1963; Berkowitz, 1962a; Feshbach, 1961) had a strong influence in this area of research, an unrestricted generalization of all their findings to Germany is dubious. While American networks offer a choice of many different programs with nearly 24-hours service and a high percentage of commercials, the structure of German television is quite different. Two major networks present prime-time broadcasting from 7 pm to 10 pm including a high percentage of documentary and news programs. A third network primarily offers programs for an intellectual public. Commercial broadcasting averages twenty minutes *per day* for each of the two major networks. After 8 pm there are no commercial programs at all. The percentage of violent content on television is relatively low compared to American standards. However, the news programs are often said to draw too much attention to the violent aspects of certain events instead of focusing on the background information. As a whole, the percentage of aggressive content presented on German screens exaggerates the probability of becoming involved in an actual aggressive situation. In addition, German children and adolescents show a high preference for violent programs. Therefore, television used to be one of the major factors that were accused of creating adolescent violence. Laboratory experiments partially proved this assumption (see Bergler & Six, 1979). However, personal and situational factors and their interaction also have to be considered when investigating media effects. In addition, aggressive behavior is only *one* possible effect of watching violent programs. The high percentage of aggressive information can also be related to anxiety (see Gerbner, Gross & Jackson-Beeck, 1978; Groebel, 1978; Sturm & Grewe-Partsch, 1978).

To test the causal relationship between the different factors, Krebs (1980) and Groebel (1981) conducted a longitudinal field study with a random sample of approximately 2,500 11 to 15 year old German students. The students were investigated three times over a period of two years by presenting them with a questionnaire which included personality, situation, and television variables, and aggression (aggressive attitudes) and anxiety (anxious cognitions) measures. The empirical data were analyzed using longitudinal path analyses. As could be expected, the results showed that television is *not* the main factor influencing aggression and anxiety; nevertheless, it has an effect on both variables. Personality factors, such as high neuroticism and low self-esteem, and factors of the social environment, such as previous experience with actual aggressive situations, play the major role for the development of aggressive attitudes.

The degree of influence of television is dependent on the respective dimension investigated. "Destructive aggression" and "legitimated aggression" (i.e., police aggression) were not affected by television, but the amount of television watching—especially violent programs—had a reinforcing effect on "reactive aggression" (Krebs, 1980). This seems to be plausible, for aggressive reactions to an attack are likely to be presented as adequate means on the screen in contrast to purely destructive aggressive acts. Here, one can assume a modeling effect controlled by personal and situational factors. For the relation between violent television content and anxiety, the "modeling" concept does not seem to offer a sufficient interpretation: Over time, the level of physical and social anxiety affects the amount of television watching. High-anxious children seem to use the programs to "escape" from problems with their actual environment, the (threatening) television content then reinforces their anxiety (Groebel, 1982). Again, personality factors and previous experience with actual threat situations have a stronger effect on anxiety than the television variables. It is interesting to note, however, that this medium has become a major factor for children to cope with problems in their actual surroundings. As aggressive and threatening elements are highly represented in the medium, the effect may be something like a closed control loop—the results of this study show that anxiety is increasingly reinforced by media information. The respective cognitive processes can be described by the assumption of an "internal model of the environment" whose structure is dependent on the perceived characteristics of the individual's surrounding situations. The perception of these characteristics is a function of direct and indirect informa-tion. "Direct" denotes actual experience with the situations, "indirect" denotes "vicarious ex-perience," e.g., formed through watching television. If an individual spends much time wat-ching television, it may become a prime source for structuring his perception of the environ-ment. The respective processes can be illustrated by different sets—representing dispositional factors, the actual situation, the media information, and the perception structure—whose elements are more or less similar to each other. Not only the actual surroundings of the perceiving individual but also the situational embedding of the perceived information deter-mine the individual's reaction. Groebel and Krebs (1982) found a highly anxious, emotional response to a reportedly realistic television program which described violent crimes actually happening in Germany's present (Aktenzeichen XY . . . ungelöst). Another program that also offered realistic violent content but was related to Germany's past was the American-produced "Holocaust." It did not create anxious reactions; rather, Germans having watched this program reported deep shock and thought-provoking effects. Before we turn to some selected results regarding "Holocaust," it can be concluded at this point that violence informa-tion creates very different responses depending on the situational context and interpretation of both the individual and the information.

How did a German audience react to a television program which describes a violent stage of Germany's history, the Third Reich? In the context of the broadcasting of "Holocaust," an American documentary teleplay on the genocide of the Jews, different studies tried to in-vestigate this question. Among others, Magnus (1980) reports the following results of a poll regarding the program. Although "Holocaust" was presented on the "minority" channel (see above), it was viewed by more than 35 percent of the total adult audience. A representative sample of adults was investigated in consecutive stages: two weeks before the program was on the screen, the week after it was broadcast, and four months later. Seventy-five percent of the interviewed viewers gave a positive judgment and appreciated the informative content of "Holocaust." Negative reactions were related to the violence of the program. About 50 per-cent reported that they had received facts about the Third Reich and especially the KZ's and the violence toward the Jews that they had not known before. Two-thirds of the audience were "deeply shocked," 40 percent were "very ashamed of what Germans have done or tolerated." As a whole, the effects of this program in the public discussion were higher than those of any other single program broadcast during previous years. This may be partly ex-plained by the fact that, for the first time since World War II, a broad German audience was confronted with Germany's violent past in a "popularized" way. In contrast to the usual docu-mentaries or television discussions with little mass attention, "Holocaust" presented personal fates that a younger audience could emotionally identify with.

Especially the aspect of "popularization" may be criticized considering this specific topic. However, an additional effect of the program was the wide attention drawn to "serious" publications dealing with genocide and holocaust.

Terrorism

As noted earlier, Germany was confronted with political terrorism in the 1970s and the 1980s. To analyze the origins and conditions of German terrorism, an interdisciplinary group of scientists investigated biographical characteristics of the terrorists, their respective group structures, societal factors possibly creating terrorism, and terrorist ideologies and strategies. Most of the results of this effort are based on official documents, descriptive analyses of ter-rorist acts, and governmental reactions to these acts, as well as on analyses of the terrorists' publications and publications related to terrorism. The findings indicate that terrorism is a multifaceted phenomenon and cannot be explained by a single factor. Only some selected studies are reported here.

For the supposed ideological background of left-wing terrorism, Fetscher, Münkler, and Ludwig (1981) could show that, while terrorists often use Marxist theories in their argumentation, their actions cannot be *logically* deduced from these theories. Hence, even from the theoretical point of view many of them are relying on, German terrorist acts have to be called irrational. Sack (1982) views left-wing terrorism, apart from other factors, as one outcome of escalation processes between the actions of an extraparliamentary opposition and often inadequate police and governmental reactions.

Of 250 persons prosecuted for terrorist activities in West Germany, 43 percent had a higher education (academic secondary school, college, or university) while only 20 percent of the normal comparable age group (20 to 40 years old) have the same education. In separating left-wing from right-wing terrorism, however, a remarkable difference occurs: only 9 percent of the right-wing terrorists belonged to the well-educated group, while 47 percent of the left-wing terrorists had a higher education (Schmidtchen, 1982). Another distinction between the two groups has to be made with respect to the sex of the terrorists: one-third of the left-wing members were women, the prosecuted right-wing terrorists were nearly all male. In addition to these demographic differences, the group structures of the two show different patterns. The Neo-Nazis group has a low degree of organizational stability (till 1980), while the groups on the opposite political extreme can be described as relatively well organized. However, the left-wing terrorists do not have a completely homogeneous structure: each of the violent left-wing groups has a different theoretical and strategic conception that is embodied in the respective organization pattern. The *Rote Armee Fraktion* (RAF, Baader-Meinhof group) can be characterized as the most influential and the ideologically most explicit group. Sociometric status and clique analyses by Feger and Groebel (1982) prove that it had a hierarchical structure in the beginning. The leaders, most of whom were well-educated, determined the actions; "normal" members found a relatively stable organization but did not have much freedom to develop their own theories and strategies. Another important group, *Bewegung 2. Juni,* was less hierarchically organized. It started as a movement whose primary goals were spontaneous actions without an ideological legitimation. Accordingly, the group only had a loose structure and every member had equal chances to participate in the planning and performing of terrorist activities. In the beginning of the 1980s, RAF and *2. Juni* had lost much of their influence. Since then, a third left-wing grouping, *Revolutionare Zellen*, which concentrated on regional, often violent activities, and new right-wing terrorist groups got more attention in the public and in the media.

The structural differences between the groups correspond to the varied factors that created terrorism. In addition to misinterpreted, ideological influences and the escalation processes, the individual preterrorist experience that society cannot be changed into the wanted direction by nonviolent means has played a major role in the development of left-wing terrorism, e.g., many of the "RAF" members had been engaged in prosocial activities before turning to violent actions (Neidhardt, 1982). Realizing the relative inefficiency of these activities on a more global level may have meant a strong frustration leading to aggression, and also a suppposed personal liberation.

Apart from the probably low frustration-tolerances, *clear-cut* biographical factors relating to terrorism cannot be identified. However, the need for identification with a group (Neidhardt, 1982), external and internal group pressures, and the tendency to "forced compliance" of a theoretically postulated violent change of society (Groebel & Feger, 1980) appear to have contributed to German terrorism.

Table 4.5. A Classification of Anti-aggression Strategies

	RELATED TO VERBAL ARGUMENTATION	RELATED TO ACTUAL BEHAVIOR
International level	Political conferences	Modeling of *successful* non-aggression-led politics
Intersocietal level	Avoidance of polarization through systematic analysis of consensus chances	Control of individual aggressive power by nonaggressive means; systematic reduction of permissiveness toward aggression
Group level	Avoidance of a dissociating labeling of other groups or single group members	Modeling of prosocial behavior
Individual level	Education, systematic communication centered therapy	Nonaggressive socialization, behavior modification

Aggression Control and Prosocial Behavior

It probably reflects the actual state of the problem, that this section on "aggression control and prosocial behavior" is our shortest one. Really effective means to reduce aggression on a large scale have not yet been discovered. There are attempts to find a solution for the individual and societal openness to aggressive actions; but, instead of reporting single approaches, whose efficiency has often yet to be demonstrated, we will outline the different levels where anti-aggression strategies should start. Table 4.5 gives an ad-hoc classification of these different levels and of the usually attempted means to reduce aggression. The boundaries between the categories are fluid. However, the "individual-international" scale appears to be a scale of increasing "naivete" in expecting successful solutions. For development of aggression control strategies on the different levels, the systematic analysis of the situational contexts, the *exact* classification of the aggressive acts, person and group related diagnoses, and systematic tests of different argumentation and prosocial-behavior chains are necessary. In this respect, the iterative solution of the problems outlined in the sections on "definition," "theories," and "measurement" is a basic requirement for further steps toward an improvement of aggression control. This seems to be a relatively easier task on the individual level but a most difficult and complex one on the international level.

REFERENCES

Adler, A. Der Agressionstrieb im Leben und in der Neurose. *Fortschritte der Medizin*, 1908, *26*, 577–584.

Atkinson, J. W., & Feather, N. T. *A theory of achievement motivation.* New York: Wiley, 1966.

Bandura, A., Ross, D., & Ross, S. A. Imitation of film-mediated aggressive models. *Journal of Abnormal and Social Psychology*, 1963, *66*, 3–11.

Bandura, A., & Walters, R. *Social learning and personality development.* New York: Holt, Rinehart & Winston, 1964.

Bandura, A. *Aggression: A social learning analysis.* Englewood Cliffs, N.J.: Prentice-Hall, 1973.

Belschner, W. Aggression als problemlösende Handlung für eine Situation. In R. Hilke and W. Kempf (Eds.), *Menschliche Aggression.* Bern, Stuttgart, Wien: Huber, 1981.

Bergler, R., & Six, U. *Psychologie des Fernsehens.* Bern, Stuttgart, Wien: Huber, 1979.

Berkowitz, L. Violence in the mass media. In *Paris-Stanford studies in communication*. Stanford: Stanford University, 1962.a

Berkowitz, L. *Aggression: A social psychological analysis*. New York: McGraw-Hill, 1962.b

Berkowitz, L. Introductory speech at the ISRA-meeting. National Academy of Sciences, Washington, D.C., 1978.

Bühler, Ch. *Das Seeleneben der Jugendlichen*. Jena: Fischer, 1922.

Buss, A. H. *The psychology of aggression*. New York: Wiley & Sons, 1961.

Coombs, C. H. *A theory of data*. New York: Wiley, 1964.

Dann, H. D. Genetische Aspekte aggressiven Verhaltens. *Zeitschrift für Erziehungswissenchaftliche Forschung*, 1967, *3*, 3-37.

Dann, H. D., Humpert, W., Krause, F., Olbrich, C., & Tennstädt, K. Ch. Alltagstheorien und Alltagshandeln. Ein neuer Forschungsansatz zur Aggressionsproblematik in der Schule. In R. Hilke and W. Kempf (Eds.), *Menschliche Aggression*. Bern, Stuttgart, Wien: Huber, 1981.

Dembo, T. Der Ärger als dynamisches Problem. *Psychologische Forschung*, 1931, 15.

DeWit, J., & Hartup, W. W. (Eds.) *Determinants and origins of aggressive behavior*. The Hague, Paris: Mouton, 1974.

Dollard, J., Doob, L., Miller, N. E., Mowrer, O.H., & Sears, R. R. *Frustration and aggression*. New Haven: Yale University Press, 1939.

Eibl-Eibesfeldt, I. *Ethology: The biology of behavior*. New York: Holt, Rinehart & Winston, 1970.

Eibl-Eibesfeldt, I. Evolution of destructive aggression. *Aggressive Behavior*, 1977, *3*, 127-144.

Ervin, F. R. Theoretical models of aggression: A comprehensive review. Paper presented at the meeting of the International Society for Research on Aggression, Boston, 1981.

Feger, H. Attitude structure and attitude change: Results, problems, and a theory of attitude components. Unpublished manuscript. Aachen, 1979.

Feger, H., & Groebel, J. Analyse von Strukturen terroristischer Gruppierungen. In *Analysen zum Terrorismus 3. Gruppenprozesse*. Opladen: Westdeutscher Verlag, 1982.

Feshbach, S. The stimulating versus cathartic effects of a vicarious aggressive activity. *Journal of Abnormal and Social Psychology*, 1961, *63*, 381-385.

Feshbach, S. The function of aggression and the regulation of aggressive drive. *Psychological Review*, 1964, *71*, 257-272.

Fetscher, I., Münkler, H., & Ludwig, H. Ideologien der Terroristen in der Bundesrepublik Deutschland. *Analysen zum Terrorismus 1. Ideologien und Strategien*. Opladen: Westdeutscher Verlag, 1981.

Freud, S. *Gesammelte Werke*. London: Imago, 1950.

Fromm, E. *Anatomie der menschlichen Destruktivität*. Stuttgart: Deutsche Verlagsanstalt, 1974.

Gerbner, G., Gross, L., Jackson-Beeck, M. Cultural indicators. Violence profile 9. *Journal of Communication*, 1978, *28*, 176-207.

Green, P. E., & Rao, V. R. *Applied multidimensional scaling*. New York: Holt, Rinehart and Winston, 1972.

Groebel, J. Perceived situations, anxiety, and their effect on aggression. Paper presented at the National Academy of Sciences, Washington, D.C., 1978.

Groebel, J. Cognitive dimensions of environmental threat. Paper presented at the 39th Annual Convention of the International Council of Psychologists, UCLA, Los Angeles, 1981.

Groebel, J. Vielseher und Angst: Theoretische Überlegungen und einige Längsschnittergebnisse. In H. Sturm (Ed.), *Aspekte des Vielsehens*. München, New York, London, Paris: Saur, 1982.

Groebel, J., & Feger, H. *Analyse sozialer Beziehungen in terroristischen Gruppen*. Bonn: BMI, 1980.

Groebel, J., & Krebs, D. A study on the effects of television on anxiety. In C. D. Spielberger and R. Diaz-Guerrero (Eds.), *Cross-cultural anxiety*. Vol. 2. New York: Wiley, 1982.

Hassenstein, B. Menschliche Aggressivität—insbesondes des Kindes und Jugendlichen—in der Sicht der Verhaltensbiologie. In R. Hilke and W. Kempf (Eds.), *Menschliche Aggression*. Bern, Stuttgart, Wien: Huber, 1981.

Heckhausen, H. *The anatomy of the achievement motivation*. New York: Academic Press, 1967.

Heckhausen, H. *Motivation und Handeln*. Berlin: Springer, 1980.

Heider, F. *The psychology of interpersonal relations*. New York: Wiley, 1958.

Heinelt, G. *Umgang mit aggressiven Schülern*. Freiburg: Herder, 1978.

Hilke, R., & Kempf, W. (Eds.) *Menschliche Aggression*. Bern, Stuttgart, Wien: Huber, 1981.a

Hilke, R., & Kempf, W. Naturwissenschaftliche und kulturwissenschaftliche Perspektiven der Aggressions—forschung—Versuch einer Integration. In R. Hilke and W. Kempf (Eds.), *Menschliche Aggression*. Bern, Stuttgart, Wien: Huber, 1981.b.

Holst, E. von. Die Auslösung von Stimmungen bei Wirbeltieren durch "punktförmige" elektrische Erregung des Stammhirns. *Die Naturwissenschaften*, 1957, *44*, 549–551.

Irle, M. *Lehrbuch der Sozialpsychologie*. Göttingen: Hogrefe, 1975.

Jordan, J. E. Facet theory and the study of behavior. In S. Shye (Ed.), *Theory construction and data analysis in the behavioral sciences*. San Francisco: Jossey-Bass, 1978.

Jütteman, G. "Aggression" als wissenschaftssprachlicher Begriff: Versuch einer Explikation. In R. Hilke and W. Kempf (Eds.), *Menschliche Aggression*. Bern, Stuttgart, Wien: Huber, 1981.

Kempf, W. Formen der Aggression und das Problem des inneren Friedens. In R. Hilke and W. Kempf (Eds.), *Menschliche Aggression*. Bern, Stuttgart, Wien: Huber, 1981.

Kornadt, H. J. Toward a motivational theory of aggression and aggression inhibition: Some considerations about an aggression motive and their application to TAT and catharsis. In J. De Wit and W. W. Hartup (Eds.), *Determinants and origins of aggressive behavior*. Den Haag: Mouton, 1974.

Kornadt, H. J. Grundzüge einer Motivationstheorie der Aggression. Unpublished manuscript, Saarbrücken, 1980.

Kornadt, H. J. *Aggression und Aggressionshemmung*. Vol. 1. Bern, Stuttgart, Wien: Huber, 1981.a

Kornadt, H. J. (Ed.) *Aggression und Frustration als psychologisches Problem* I. Darmstadt: Wissenschaftliche Buchgesellschaft, 1981b.

Kornadt, H. J., Eckensberger, L. H., & Emminghaus, W. B. Cross-cultural research on motivation and its contribution to a general theory of motivation. In H. C. Triandis and W. Lonner (Eds.), *Handbook of cross-cultural psychology*. Vol. 3. *Basic processes*. Boston: Allyn and Bacon, 1980.

Krebs, D. Anwendung der Stress-Theorie in einer Felduntersuchung an Obdachlosen. Unpublished manuscript, Mannheim, 1971.

Krebs, D. Die Wirkungen von Gewaltdarstellungen im Fernsehen auf die Einstellung zur Gewalt. Aachen: Forschungsbericht des Instituts für Psychologie, 1980.

Krebs, D., & Groebel, J. Erstellung und ansatzweise Konstruktvalidierung eines Fragebogens zur Erfassung der Einstellung zur Gewalt. Aachen: Institut für Psychologie, 1976.

Landau, S. F., & Beit-Hallahmi, B. Aggression in Israel. A psycho-historical perspective. In A. Goldstein and M. Segall (Eds.), *Aggression in global perspective*. New York: Pergamon Press, 1982.

Levy, S. Lawful roles of facets in social theories. Unpublished manuscript, Jerusalem, 1980.

Linneweber, V., Klassifikation feld- und verhaltensspezifischer Intraktionssituationen: Umgebungsbedingungen aggressiver Interaktion in Schulen. Bielefeld: Beilefelder Arbeiten zur Sozialpsychologie, 1980.

Lischke, G. Psychophysiologie der Aggression. In H. Selg (Ed.), *Zur Aggression verdammt?* Stuttgart: Kohlhammer, 1975.

Lorenz, K. *Das sogenannte Böse*. Wien: Borotha-Schoeler, 1963.

Lorenz, K. *On aggression*. New York: Bantam Books, 1966.

Magnus, U. Ergebnisse der Begleitforschung zur Fernsehspielserie "Holocaust." Köln: WDR, 1980.

Mark, V. H. A multidisciplinary perspectus on aggression. Paper presented at the meeting of the International Society for Research on Aggression, Boston, 1981.

Mees, U. Zur Validität von Verhaltensbeobachtungen. In U. Mees and H. Selg (Eds.), *Verhaltensbeobachtung und Verhaltensmodifikation*. Stuttgart: Klett, 1977.

Merton, R. K. *Social theory and social structure*. New York: Free Press, 1957.

Michaelis, W. *Verhalten ohne Aggression? Versuch zur Integration der Theorien*. Köln: Kiepenheuer & Witsch, 1976.

Milgram, S. The experience of living in cities. *Science*, 1970, *167*, 1461–1468.

Mitscherlich, A. *Die Idee des Friedens und die menschliche Aggressivität*. Frankfurt A.M.: Suhrkamp, 1969.

Mummendey, H. D. Einige Probleme der Erfassung aggressiven Verhaltens im psychologischen Labor.

Bielefelder Arbeiten zur Sozialpsychologie, 1980.

Mummendey, A. Der Stand der psychologischen Diskussion um das Konzept aggressiven Verhaltens. In W. Michaelis (Ed.), *Bericht über den 32.* Kongress der Deutschen Gesellschaft für Psychologie. Göttingen: Hogrefe, 1981.a

Mummendey, A. Aggressives Verhalten. In H. Thomae (Ed.) *Handbuch der Psychologie.* Vol. 2: *Allgemeine Psychologie II-Motivation.* Göttingen: Hogrefe, 1981.b

Neidhardt, F. Linker und rechter Terrorismus. Empirische Ansätze zu einem Gruppenvergleich. In *Analysen zum Terrorismus 3. Gruppenprozesse.* Opladen: Westdeutscher Verlag, 1982.

Petermann, U., & Petermann, F. *Erfassungsbogen für aggressives Verhalten in konkreten Situationen.* Braunschweig: Westermann, 1980.

Popper, K. *Logik der Forschung.* Wien: Julius Springer, 1934.

Popper, K. *The logic of scientific discovery.* London: Hutchinson, 1959.

Sack, F. Der Beitrag staatlicher Reaktionen zur Erzeugung politischer Radikalität und Gewaltsamkeit in der Bundesrepublik. In *Analysen zum Terrorismus 4. Gesellschaftliche Prozesse und Reaktionen.* Opladen: Westdeutscher Verlag, 1982.

Scherer, K. R., Äbeles, R. P., & Fischer, C. S. *Human aggression and conflict.* Englewood Cliffs, N.J.: Prentice-Hall, 1975.

Schmidbauer. W. *Die sogenannte Aggression.* Hamburg: Hoffmann und Campe, 1972.

Schmidtchen, G. Die Terroristenkarriere. In *Analysen zum Terrorismus 2. Lebenslaufanalysen.* Opladen: Westdeutscher Verlag, 1982.

Schmidt-Mummendey, A. *Bedingungen aggressiven Verhaltens.* Bern: Huber, 1972.

Schönemann, P. H., & Steiger, J. H. On the validity of indeterminate factor scores. *Bulletin of the Psychonomic Society,* 1978, *12,* 287-290.

Selg, H. *Diagnostik der Aggressivität.* Göttingen: Hogrefe, 1968.

Selg, H. *Menschliche Aggressivität.* Göttingen: Hogrefe, 1974.

Selg, H. Aggressionsdefinitionen und kein Ende? In R. Hilke and W. Kempf (Eds.), *Menschliche Aggression.* Bern, Stuttgart, Wien: Huber, 1981.

Stern, W. Psychologie der frühen Kindheit bis zum sechsten Lebensjahr. Leipzig: 1914.

Sturm, H., & Grewe-Partsch, M. Das Fernsehen: Vermittler von Gewalt und Angst? Theorien, Thesen, empirische Befunde. *Fernsehen und Bildung,* 1978, *12,* 28-41.

Suppes, P., & Zines, J. L. Basic measurement theory. In R. D. Luce, R. R. Bush, and R. Galanter (Eds.), *Handbook of mathematical psychology.* Vol. I. New York: Wiley, 1963.

Werbik, H. Das Problem der Definition 'aggressiver' Verhaltensweisen. *Zeitschrift für Sozialpsychologie,* 1971, *2,* 233-247.

Werbik, H. *Theorie der Gewalt.* München: Fink-UTB, 1974.

Werbik, H. *Handlungstheorien.* Stuttgart: Kohlhammer, 1978.

Werbik, H. Zur terminologischen Bestimmung von Aggression und Gewalt. In R. Hilke and W. Kempf (Eds.), *Menschliche Aggression.* Bern, Stuttgart, Wien: Huber, 1981.

Werbik, H., & Munzert, R. Kann Aggression handlungstheoretisch erklärt werden? *Psychologische Rundschau,* 1978, *9,* 195-208.

Zumkley, H. *Aggression und Katharsis.* Göttingen: Hogrefe, 1978.

5

Finland: The Search for Alternatives to Aggression

Lea Pulkkinen

FINLAND AS A NATION

Finland, an independent republic in Scandinavia, is, after Iceland, the most northerly country in the world. Average temperatures in Finland are, however, considerably higher at all seasons than in other countries of the same latitude. The country is snow-covered for about five months of the year in the south and up to seven months in Lapland (Facts about Finland, 1979). Finland's population was 4,757,500 in 1979. The country is rather sparsely populated with 15.5 inhabitants per sq. km. (40.3 per sq. mile). Up to the middle of the nineteenth century, farming was the main source of livelihood, supplemented by fishing and hunting. At present, agriculture comprises approximately 6 percent of the GNP (gross national product). The primary importance of the forest for the national economy of Finland is readily understandable, as the forests cover 65 percent of the land area. However, a diversification of industrial production and increasing exports have been characteristic features of development since World War II, during a period when a rapid economic growth appeared in Finland. In 1975, the per capita GNP was $5,100, the seventeenth highest in the world. As late as 1974, unemployment was only 2 percent of the entire labour force. In 1978, it soared to a record figure of 8 percent.

Racially, the Finns are mixed. The main stocks apparently derive from the East Baltic and Nordic races. The Finnish language belongs to the Finno-Ugrian group. Finland has a Swedish-speaking minority (6 percent in 1978). In 1970, 2,240 persons spoke Lappish and 1,680 persons Russian as their mother tongue.

Between the ninth and thirteenth centuries, Swedes entered the country and consolidated the position of Christianity. Until 1809, Finland was a province of Sweden. In 1809, Finland became an autonomous Grand Duchy of Russia and, in 1918, an independent republic. In 1979, 8 parties were represented in a parliament of 200 members; 113 representatives for non-socialist and 87 representatives for socialist parties.

In spite of the authority of other nations until 1918, Finland maintained its own culture. Old Finnish culture is reflected in the national epic, Kalevala. "Heroic but human, its men and women march boldly through the fifty cantos, raiding, drinking, abducting, outwitting, weeping, but always active. . . . [Kalevala, 1977, preface]." Imagination is perhaps the outstanding talent of the characters, who prefer skill or guile or magic to the use of force. Music is

104

an important part of life, and the laws of hospitality are well understood. The influence of Kalevala on Finns has been strong. At present, Finnish culture is characterized by Western culture with a relatively high standard of living and the Lutheran religion.

NONAGGRESSIVE FOREIGN POLICY AND AGGRESSIVE DRUNK BEHAVIOUR OF FINNS CHARACTERIZED BY "*SISU*"

Finland has long sought security by remaining outside international conflicts and entanglements. Neutrality and friendly relations with its neighbours built on mutual confidence are the basis of Finnish foreign policy. Nevertheless, security does not mean isolation; promoting the peaceful settlement of conflicts and developing international co-operation are integral parts of Finnish policy.

The lack of collective violence and internal coercion in Finland was also shown by a comparison of 86 countries by Gurr & Bishop (1974). Finland, with the other Scandinavian countries, was among the least violent countries in structural violence (particularly in economic and political discrimination and military intervention or its support), and also below the average in physical violence (protests, civil wars).

Individual Finnish behaviour is not, however, as nonaggressive. Severe individual aggression including homicides and suicides is more common in Finland (particularly in males) than in other Scandinavian countries. However, the assault rate, including petty assaults, is nowadays a little higher in Sweden than in Finland. In 1978, the number of assault offences per 100,000 inhabitants was 276 in Sweden (243 in 1974), 247 in Finland (291 in 1974), 97 in Norway (89 in 1974), and 78 in Denmark (56 in 1974) (*Criminality in Finland 1979*, p. 94).

The suicide rate in Finland is one of the highest in the world. In 1961-1963, 29.0 suicides per 100,000 inhabitants aged 15 and over (47.7 in males and 12.3 in females) occurred in Finland, 33.9 in Hungary, and 24.7 in Japan (Apo, Lönnqvist, & Achte, 1973). In 1977, 1,222 suicides were committed: 962 by males and 260 by females. This is almost twice as high as deaths in traffic accidents (709 in 1977) in a country where the number of cars per 1,000 inhabitants was 258 in 1977 (276 in Japan).

Finland also has a high homicide rate. It is not a recent phenomenon. Since the sixteenth century there have been extremely violent periods in Finland (Ylikangas, 1973). The number of homicide victims reached its peak, for example, in the period 1861-1877 in certain western parts of Finland. At that time, the use of a knife (*puukko*) became common as a weapon. In addition, during the time the prohibition law was in force (1920-1932), the frequency of crimes against life reached another peak. During the latter period, their number was about 16 times higher than the number committed in Sweden, in which there was no such law (Verkko, 1951). During the last years of prohibition, smuggling was widespread and strong spirits were consumed excessively. The conflicts between the authorities and the smugglers and drinkers of smuggled alcohol were often violent.

The increase of violence has been explained by economic changes which threaten status expectations and drive individuals to search for intensive experiences and compensatory values (Ylikangas, 1973). The congenital inability of Finns to use alcohol moderately was regarded by a Finnish criminologist, Verkko (1951), as the main reason for the high homicide rate. He connected it with the negative aspect of Finnish "*sisu*" (perseverance). It has been stated (Verkko, 1951, p. 92) that *sisu* is the energy of emotion and will, mental fervour, and power. *Sisu* is the faith and will to win, "negative *sisu*" is its counterpart. Although no national characteristic or constitutional ability to use alcohol moderately can explain changes in violence nor differences between areas, the alcohol factor is certainly crucial in explaining violent crime in Finland (Törnudd, 1978). Table 5.1 presents some features in Finnish society from 1950 to 1975. These figures show a correlation between alcohol consumption and assault offences, although there were also other factors which affected the increase of crimes, such as internal migration and the increase of unemployment.

The proportion of offences carried out under the influence of alcohol or other drugs was 68 percent of homicides, 65 percent of aggravated assaults, and 59 percent of robbery in 1979 (*Criminality in Finland 1979*). The study of victimization by Sirén (1980) also showed a very clear relationship between the frequency of hangover days and victimization. The heavy use of alcohol is an indicator of a life style that is characterized by a high risk of victimization. The way in which time is spent is one of the factors explaining differences in victimization rates among different population groups.

About 40 percent of the incidents of violent offences in Sirén's study could be called "street violence" (the incident took place outdoors, and the offender was a complete stranger), and 25 percent "other type of random violence" (e.g., in a restaurant, where the offender was a stranger or casual acquaintance). One third of the victims were close acquaintances of the offender. About 9 percent of all victimizations involved "violence in the family." These cases were more serious on average, especially among female victims. Sirén generalized that, although violence in close social relationships or in primary groups is not as common as street or other random violence, when it does occur it is more serious on average. Most homicides in Finland are committed against victims who knew the perpetrator, such as a family member, friend, or acquaintance.

Based on the data given by the respondents, of all the incidents of victimization to violence 14 percent were reported or otherwise brought to the attention of the police (Sirén, 1980). In his representative sample, 24 percent of the male respondents and 14 percent of the female respondents had been victims of some type of violence in a scale from threats to injury during the previous twelve months. In the young age group (15-21 years), victimization to street violence was more general than in the older age groups. However, the proportion of those who had been victimized in private apartments was almost constant among the different age groups.

The proportion of offences committed by 15 to 20-year-olds of all offences committed in Finland varies, depending on the type of offence. In 1979, for assaults it was 20 percent, for thefts 29 percent, for car thefts 50 percent, for robbery 36 percent, and for drunken driving 14 percent. In children under 15 years old, thefts and car thefts were relatively the most common offences (about 12 percent of all such offences in Finland in 1979). For robbery, their proportion was 5.6 percent and for assaults 1.8 percent (*Criminality in Finland 1979*).

At the beginning of the 1960s, the rate of violent offences was about the same for both young people and adults. During the 1960s, however, the number of violent offences committed by young people, and specially 18 to 20-year-olds, increased very rapidly; since that time, the rate of violent offences per 100,000 inhabitants has been much higher for young offenders than for adults (Joutsen, 1976). The general increase in juvenile crime can be attributed to the fact that the young are particularly susceptible to recent societal changes (table 5.1) which increase the opportunities for crime and give earlier modes of social control less opportunity to operate (Törnudd, 1978, p. 34). In addition, drinking has increased among young people.

CRIME CONTROL IN FINLAND

Finland ceased to use capital punishment in times of peace 150 years ago (in 1826). At that time, Finland was an autonomous Grand Duchy of Russia. The Czar of Russia declared that sentences of capital punishment were from that time to be commuted to banishment to Si-

Table 5.1. Crime Trends in the Changing Society of Finland, 1950-1975

	1950	1955	1960	1965	1970	1975
Total population in millions	4.0	4.3	4.4	4.6	4.6	4.7
Urban communities: population %	32	35	38	44	51	59
Agriculture and other primary production %	40	40	31	27	21	15
Gross domestic product per capita in 100 Fmks (1974 value)	60	75	89	108	137	161
Alcohol consumption: 100% litres of alcohol per capita	1.7	2.0	1.8	2.4	4.5*	6.2
Assault offences per 100,000 inhabitants	147	132	125	127	243**	278
—Males sentenced for 100,000 males	154	149	112	122	167	302
—Females sentenced per 100,000 females	6	4	3	2	4	10
Assault which caused the death of the victim: absolute number	63	33	46	31	–	83
Intentional homicide (including attempt)	56	50	45	43	52	83
Larceny offences per 100,000 inhabitants	504	432	675	934	1251	2145

*In 1969 the alcohol legislation was liberalized. The new law eased the restrictions on sale and consumption, and introduced the so-called "middle beer," which, unlike other alcoholic beverages, could be obtained through outlets other than the State Alcohol Monopoly and licensed restaurants.

**From 1970 on the figures include offences which caused the death of the victim; fewer than 100 cases a year.

Source: P. Törnudd, "Crime Trends in Finland 1950-1977," *Reports from the Research Institute of Legal Policy, 1978.*

beria. After some decades this procedure was, however, replaced by life imprisonment (Anttila, 1978).

At present, life imprisonment is Finland's most severe punishment in both peace and war. In practice, life prisoners are pardoned after 10 to 15 years of imprisonment. Life sentence is used rarely. During the 1920s, 30 to 40 life imprisonment sentences were passed annually; at present, only one or two. Life imprisonment is given only as a murder sentence. Even many of those found guilty of murder are not sentenced to life imprisonment. Out of a recent prison population of 5,700 in Finland, only 16 were serving a life sentence (Anttila, 1978, p. 28).

Long-term imprisonment is also rarely used in Finland. The average length of all prison sentences was 4.7 months in 1978. The corresponding average sentence in Sweden is less than 2 months. The average length of imprisonment sentences has been decreasing constantly in Finland. For example, in 1950, the average length of imprisonment was 7.6 months (Anttila, 1978; *Criminality in Finland 1979*).

The number of imprisonments given each year is almost 12,000 in Sweden and Denmark, of which 60 have been over four years in length. In Finland the corresponding numbers are 15,000 and 60. In addition, the offender is generally released from prison after two thirds or even half of the original sentence. More and more imprisonment sentences are also being set conditionally. In 1978, this was true of more than half (53 percent) of the imprisonment sentences. In spite of the decrease in the use of imprisonment, its rate is still considerably higher in Finland than in the other Scandinavian countries (Anttila, 1978; *Criminality in Finland 1979*).

Of all imprisonments, the proportion for assault offences was 3 percent in 1978 (45 percent of them unconditional). Most imprisonments (35.5 percent, 28 percent unconditional) were given because of drunken driving, the next category was thefts (19.7 percent, 64 percent unconditional). The proportion of solved crimes has continuously been high in assault offences, about 83 percent. In thefts, for example, this proportion has been about 36 percent (*Criminality in Finland 1979*).

In addition to imprisonment, day-fines are used as sentences. The average fine in 1978 was 9.5 day-fines. Each day-fine depends on the income of the offender. While the minimum amount for one day-fine is about $2 US (8 marks), there is no maximum size; day-fines of over 50 marks ($15 US) are, however, rare (*Criminality in Finland 1979*).

In Scandinavia, young offenders have in some respects been dealt with as a special group. In the "Scandinavian system," age is the mark of responsibility, and those above a certain age limit (15 in Finland, 14 in Norway) are dealt with by the same courts that deal with adults, while those below this age limit come under the jurisdiction of child welfare authorities (Joutsen, 1976). It does not, however, mean that young offenders are treated as adults before the courts. There are many special provisions concerning young offenders, some of which even apply to young adults.

Special legislation on young offenders was passed in 1940 in Finland. Under this legislation, the "young offenders" concept came to mean an individual who had committed an offence between and including the ages of 15 and 20. Before 1940, the ordinary courts ordered some reformative measures also for children aged 7 to 14. In Sweden, the age limit for criminal responsibility had already been raised to 14 years in 1864, and later to 15 years, and in Norway to 14 years in 1896. In addition, special acts were passed to create a new instititution, the juvenile prison.

As Anttila (1978, pp. 62–63) remarks, two decades ago it was regarded as self-evident that young offenders should be sentenced to lighter punishments than adults, penal sentences should be replaced by measures taken by social welfare authorities, all punishments should include treatment, the sentence should be individualized to "fit" each offender, the punishments should be based on a careful personal history investigation, priority should be given institutional to noninstitutional sanctions with long-term supervision, an institutional sentence should be an indeterminate sentence in a juvenile prison, and solely punitive fines were not recommended. The special system for young offenders was believed to constitute an historic reform. The system of probation for young offenders was seen as especially promising, since no probation system for adults was applied in Finland. It was thought that a totally new kind of punishment, "treatment in freedom," had been developed. The opinion of the time reflected strong "treatment optimism," which emphasized the responsibility of the social welfare authorities.

In the 1960s, the climate of the crime control policy changed (Anttila, 1978, p. 64). In part, this was due to joint Scandinavian studies of hidden criminality and to research on the detrimental effects of prison. The results on hidden criminality with army recruits showed that, at a certain age, it was statistically normal to commit offences. It was not considered a symptom of a deviant personality. The results seemed to cast doubts on the doctrines on the need of treatment. Instead, it seemed that those who were caught, and particularly those who were sentenced to institutions, became recividists. It was asked whether or not society should react to offences as leniently as possible instead of as harshly as possible, as the process of being labeled as an offender seemed to lead to recidivism.

The critical evaluation of the criminal justice system continued into the 1970s. The emphasis was placed on the offence instead of the offender, and on the criminal intent instead of the personality of the offender. Juvenile imprisonment as a special punishment was abolished in Norway and Denmark in 1973, and in Sweden in 1977. In Finland, the abolition was proposed by committee reports in 1977. A thorough reform of the system of probation and parole has also been proposed in Finland.

One of the principal purposes of the recent proposals has been to do away with the special legal status of young offenders. The sentence would not be based on a supposed need for treatment but on the offence and the guilt shown in the offence. Another trend of the 1970s emphasized the necessity of separating coercion and social services. In addition, the scope of the open institutions has been broadened. The prisoner's contacts with the outside world, as well as the prison facilities for education and leisure-time activities, have been increased for all age groups. Young offenders no longer need special provisions (Anttila, 1978).

DEVELOPMENTAL BACKGROUND OF YOUNG OFFENDERS: A FINNISH LONGITUDINAL STUDY

Young Offenders

It was possible to investigate the developmental background of young offenders in a Finnish longitudinal study in which features of social behaviour were followed from the age of 8 to 20. In the beginning of the study by the present writer (Pitkänen, 1969), the emphasis was on children's aggressive behaviour and nonaggressive alternatives to it. On the basis of the data, it was possible to study how aggressive and nonaggressive behaviour at the ages of 8 and 14 predicted the number and type of offences committed by the age of 20. The results also gave information about the life conditions of young offenders.

The original sample of subjects consisted of 196 boys and 173 girls, with an average age of 8 years 3 months. They were drawn from the second-grade pupils of 12 school classes of the town of Jyväskylä, which has about 60,000 inhabitants.

With the consent of the Ministry of Justice, criminal records of the 369 subjects who belonged to the original random sample were searched at the age of 20. Nineteen boys and 4 girls
were in the government register including information about offences the sentence for which
has been imprisonment. One girl and one boy had committed homicide; others forgery, violence against an official, and sexual offence.

The local criminal register held by the police also includes information about petty offences for which the person was not necessarily prosecuted, although the police have sought
punishment. Altogether, 71 boys and 17 girls (23.8 percent of the original sample) were found
in these two registers.

To make the criminal behaviour quantitatively comparable, the offences were categorized
into three classes: alcohol, theft, and violence. Thereafter, a scale for each category was constructed and a weight for each type of offence was given. This allows the calculation of a criminality score for each individual. Table 5.2 presents the scales, weights, and frequencies of the
offences obtained in the sample. The total number of offences was much higher (311) than the
number of individuals (88) who had committed them.

Figure 5.1 shows the distribution of offences in the sample. It can be seen that two thirds of
the boys and three fourths of the girls who were in the criminal registers had committed only

Table 5.2. Scales for Offences and the Frequency of Offence Categories in the Sample of 369 Subjects Ages 20 Years

CATEGORIES AND SCALES FOR OFFENCES	WEIGHT	FRE-QUENCY
Alcohol offences		
Arrested because of drunkenness; not prosecuted	1	127
Illegal disposal and sale of alcohol; 3–10 day-fines	2	13
Drunken driving (& unauthorized driving);* 40–50 day-fines	3	7
Aggravated drunken driving (with car theft); imprisonment for 3–4 months	4	1
For 57 males and 11 females, total		148
Theft offences		
Pilfering, not prosecuted or 1–8 day-fines	1	7
Theft, 8–14 day-fines	2	21
Theft, 15–25 day-fines	3	31
Theft, document forgery (2); imprisonment for 1–2 months	4	45
Robbery, car theft & unauthorized driving; imprisonment for 6–10 months	5	11
For 26 males and 9 females, total		115
Violent offences		
Disturbing general order; nor prosecuted	1	8
Disturbing entertainments, damage to property; 8–15 day-fines	2	27
Assault, domestic peace offence; 15–20 day-fines	3	5
Violence against an official, sexual offence; imprisonment for 2–3 months	4	2
Homicide; imprisonment for 3.5–4.1 years	5	2
For 17 males and 2 females, total		48

*A driving licence can be given at the age of 18 in Finland.

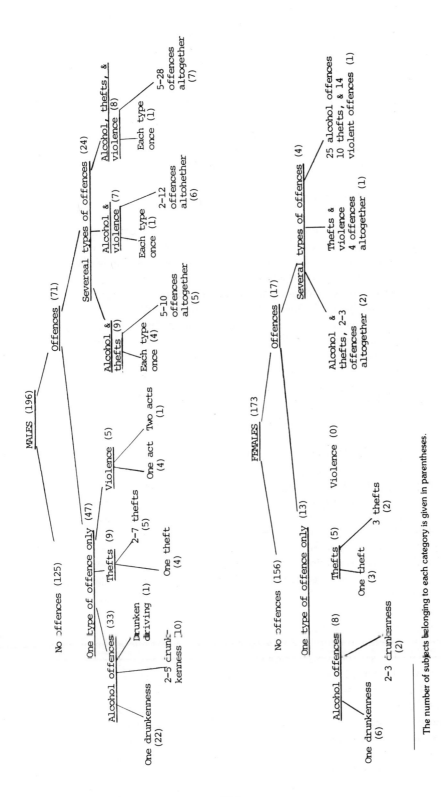

The number of subjects belonging to each category is given in parentheses.

Fig. 5.1. Distribution of Offences in the Sample.

111

one type of offence. Almost one half of the subjects had committed a single offence only, usually an alcohol offence.

Questions posed in the present study were as follows:

1. How predictable was criminal behaviour on the basis of behavioural indicators collected at the ages of 8 and 14?
2. What was the way of life of young offenders at the age of 20?
3. How predictable was the criminal behaviour on the basis of the data concerning child rearing and environmental conditions collected at the age of 14 by interviews?

Theoretical Frame of Reference

The present longitudinal study was started as a cross-sectional study of differences of 8-year-old children in reactions to frustrating situations (Pitkänen, 1969). In searching for alternatives to aggression, Pitkänen came to the hypothesis that there are two kinds of aggression inhibitory tendencies when external events instigate aggression in an individual. The psychological processes of these inhibitory tendencies and their assumed behavioural indicators have been described in detail elsewhere (Pitkänen, 1969; Pulkkinen, 1982).

In figure 5.2, the psychological processes of the aggression inhibitory tendencies are described within a two-dimensional model. When excitation is produced by a stimulus, an individual may either express his feelings without any inhibition or choose (often unconsciously) one of the inhibitory tendencies. *Suppression of aggression* was assumed to be dependent on the experienced power of external controllers, while *neutralization of aggression* was assumed to be dependent on an individual's cognitive mastery of the situation. An individual's behaviour may vary according to the situation. Alternative behaviour is described in this figure in terms of the theoretical constructs.

In spite of the fact that an individual's behaviour may vary from one situation to another, there was thought to be some consistency in his behaviour due to constitutional and socializing factors. In addition, although the two-dimensional model presented in figure 5.2 was based on the psychological processes concerning coping with aggression impulses, it was regarded as possible that the interpretational applicability of the theoretical constructs was not limited to the derivatives of the aggression inhibitory tendencies. Instead, an individual's way of controlling his impulses might be more general, concerning sexual drives, etc., and it might be generalized in time to characterize his relationships with other people and his life attitudes.

The personality parameters presented by Block & Block (1979) closely parallel the theoretical constructs presented in figure 5.2. They call for attention to integrational structures which children must construct for dealing with their interpersonal world, and distinguish two constructs; ego-control and ego-resiliency.

In the framework depicted in figure 5.2, it was hypothesized that adolescent ways of life were predictable on the basis of the subject's previous aggressive and nonaggressive behaviour and the life conditions which were found in various studies to promote either aggressive or prosocial behaviour. Thus, strong self-control was expected to manifest itself in adolescence as dependency on the parents and responsible behaviour, and weak self-control in problem behaviour and learned helplessness. Differences in life conditions between the individuals with strong and weak self-control were particularly expected. The child rearing methods for adolescents with strong self-control were supposed to be those which had appealed to the child's cognitive processes more than the methods used with adolescents characterized by weak self-control. Correspondingly, the life conditions of adolescents with strong self-control were ex-

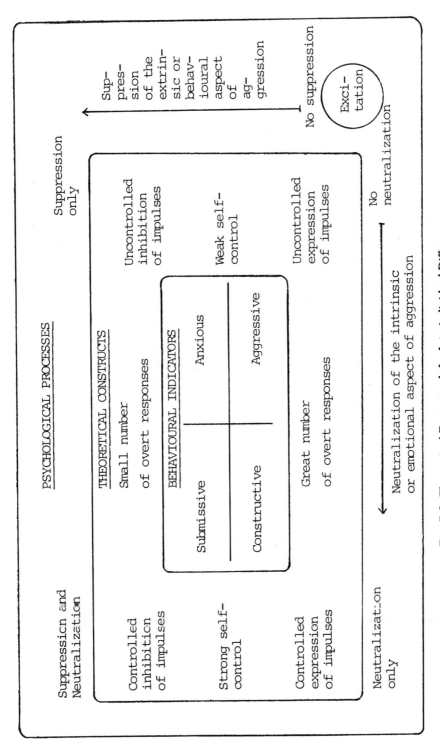

Fig. 5.2. Theoretical Framework for Interindividual Differences

pected to be steadier and more favourable in terms of cultural enrichment and social security. Criminal behaviour was expected to be related to the manifestations of weak self-control, as well as to the life conditions and child rearing methods which contributed to the development of weak self-control in children.

Stages of the Follow-Up Study

Behavioural indicators of the subjects were studied at the ages of 8, 14, and 20. The methods at the age of 8 were peer nomination, teacher rating, and two personality inventories with 16 scales. At the age of 14 a follow-up study of social behaviour was made with 189 boys and 161 girls, 96 percent and 93 percent of the original sample, respectively. Peer nomination and teacher rating were used again. In addition, 154 subjects and their parents (mainly the mother) were interviewed. Instead of using randomization, this sample was chosen deliberately on the basis of the results of peer nomination, as explained elsewhere (Pulkkinen, 1982). The aim was to draw a sample which represented the variation of behaviour found at the ages of 8 and 14. At the age of 20, 135 subjects were studied again by interviewing them and by collecting self-assessed reports on social behaviour. As mentioned above, criminal records of the whole original random sample (N = 369) were also searched.

The interview made at the ages of 14 and 20 was carried out as a conversation along chosen themes, which covered both the subject's life conditions and behavioural indicators, for example, school attendance, spare time activities, friends, intoxication, and the relationships with parents. The self-assessed reports on social behavior collected at the age of 20 included self-rating on variables closely parallel to those used in peer nomination and teacher rating at the age of 14. In addition, a Self-control Inventory and Self-control Check List were constructed. A clinical rating on the subjects' adjustment at the age of 20 was also made by the interviewers, who were allowed to use all the material they had gathered from the subject. The rating was made on a 5-point scale from good adjustment and co-operation to problems of adjustment such as antisocialness and unwillingness to co-operate.

Life Conditions. Interview data were collected at the age of 14 concerning child rearing and environmental conditions. Environmental conditions covered the family's socioeconomic status, the parents' working conditions, the day-care arrangements in childhood, the parents' leisure activities, the emotional climate of the family, and the stability and change in family life. In discussing child-rearing conditions, emphasis was laid on the interactions between the family members, the parents' interest in and control of the child's school attendance and leisure activities, and the type and consistency of guidance, reward, and general child-rearing atmosphere.

Analysis of Data. Since the number of variables for behavioural indicators at each age level was high (87-91), the data without criminal records were analyzed by the method of a principal factor analysis and varimax rotation. The connection of criminal records with behavioural indicators was studied on the level of individual variables and factor scores.

Correspondingly, two separate factor analyses were calculated for life conditions: one for child rearing, another for environmental conditions. Thereafter, the correlations between the background factors and behavioural factors were calculated by using factor scores for them. Life conditions correlated significantly with behavioural indicators at each age level. Their relationships with criminal records were also studied on the level of both individual variables and factor scores.

PERSONALITY PROFILES OF YOUNG MALE AND FEMALE OFFENDERS AND NONOFFENDERS

Aggressive and Nonaggressive Behaviour at the Age of 8

The word "offender" refers here to a subject who was found in either the government or local criminal register at the age of 20. The study of differences between offenders and nonoffenders in peer nominations and teacher ratings made at the ages of 8 and 14 revealed several significant differences. In most variables, the characteristic in question was in a linear relationship with the number for the types of offences committed by the individuals (tables 5.6–5.9). Those eight individuals (see Fig. 5.1) who by the age of 20 had committed all three types of offences differed from the others most clearly already at the age of 8.

Aggression. Aggressive behaviour was studied at the age of 8 by using peer nomination and teacher rating. Twelve variables were chosen to represent different types of observable aggression in the framework of the model presented in figure 5.3 (Pitkänen, 1969). The model had been previously used in a study of 5 to 6-year-old boys' (N = 216) aggressive behaviour which was observed and rated by their kindergarten teachers (Pitkänen, 1969).

Three dimensions were included in the model: the intensity (defined as the quantity of noxious stimuli delivered by an act), the direction (direct/indirect), and the aim (initiative/defensive) of aggression. In addition, more specific discriminations were made on the basis of the modes of aggression (e.g., physical). Each mode of aggression may occur toward a target more or less directly, with different intensities, and with either an initiative or a defensive aim. For example, beating somebody for taking a favourite toy is a defensive, direct response using a physical mode.

The variables for aggression used at the age of 8 are presented in table 5.3, which also shows the means of male and female nonoffenders and offenders in peer nomination. In addition, the significance of the variance due to the grouping and the test of linearity are given for teacher ratings.

In general, peer nominations discriminated more clearly than teacher ratings the future nonoffenders and the individuals who were to commit different numbers or types of offences. Both male and female multitype offenders, in particular, differed from the others in aggressiveness at the age of 8. The largest difference in males and females was in indirect aggression (teasing smaller and weaker peers, teasing behind somebody's back). In males, physical and initiative aggression discriminated the groups also clearly. In teacher ratings, the female offenders were verbally more aggressive; for example, they exaggerated and told lies about other children and said naughty things to others.

In most variables, the individuals who were to commit one type of offence only did not differ from the nonoffenders in aggressiveness, possibly because of a high amount of hidden criminality (Magnusson, Dunér, & Zetterblom, 1975). It is accidental, for instance, to be caught in drunkenness or pilfering.

Nonaggression. Nonaggressive alternatives to aggression (table 5.4) were studied at the age of 8 by formulating four items for anxious, submissive, and constructive behaviour corresponding to the theoretical framework (fig. 5.2). Their intercorrelations showed, however, that only for submissiveness did all variables correlate significantly; for example, apologizing (20) correlated more highly with constructiveness than with anxiety. In the other categories, the sum scores were calculated only for those items which had significant positive intercorrelations.

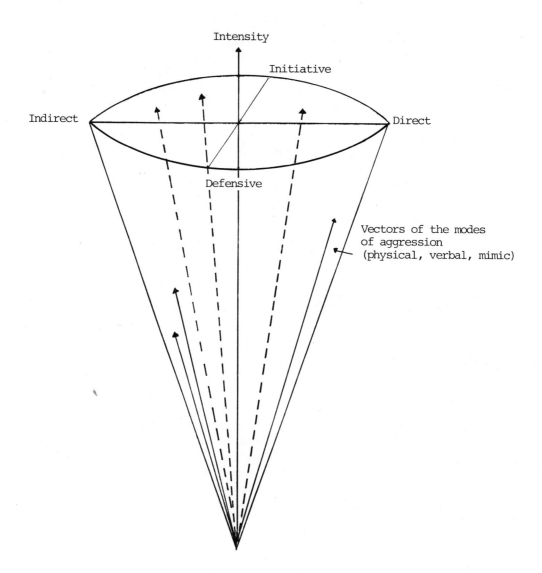

Fig. 5.3. A Descriptive Model of the Characteristics of Observable Aggressive Acts.

The means of peer nominations showed that male offenders had been less submissive at the age of 8 than nonoffenders. This was not so for females. Female offenders who had committed only one type of offence were more feminine and altruistic than the multi-type offenders (table 5.5). The latter showed the same pattern of behaviour in nonaggression as well as in aggression as did the male offenders, except for peer nominations in activeness and fearfulness.

Both the male and female offenders disobeyed the teacher (table 5.5). Peers interpreted that the future multi-type male offenders tried to attract attention by making fun. They were not regarded as good leaders for an excursion. Future offenders had difficulties in concentration and their school success was poor, particularly in girls.

Behavioural Indicators at the Age of 14

As mentioned above, 95 percent of the boys and girls of the original sample were found for a follow-up study at the age of 14. Except for one criminal boy, all those subjects who were later found in the criminal registers were included in the follow-up sample. Peer nominations and teacher ratings were available for all of them. The number of variables in peer nomination and teacher rating was reduced.

Table 5.6 presents the means of the male and female nonoffenders and offenders in these variables for peer nomination. The significance and linearity of differences are also given for teacher ratings. This table shows that still at the age of 14 the male offenders were more active and aggressive, and less controlled, submissive, constructive, and anxious than the other boys. Their school reports were poor, and they were disinterested in school attendance. They were often illicitly absent and also often punished at school. They smoked and took alcohol more than the other boys. Their social behaviour had worsened and good hobbies were lacking; they spent their spare time in streets more often than other boys. The multitype offenders had also been in contacts with police as far as the teachers knew.

In contrast, the female offenders differed less significantly from the other girls at the age of 14. Their behaviour was less controlled and they expressed more initiative aggression and maladjustment to school than the other girls, but in other variables they did not differ from them. In anxiety and passiveness, the same curvilinear trend could be found as at the age of 8; the one-type female offenders tended to be more passive and fearful than the multitype female offenders.

The interview of the subjects themselves and their parents confirmed the findings presented above. The sample of 77 girls and 77 boys interviewed at the age of 14, happened to include 26 boys and 10 girls who were later found in the criminal registers. The interview data showed that the future male offenders differed from the other boys in aggressiveness both according to the parents' conception of it and their own self-concepts. The parents of the male offenders considered that they behaved more aggressively in failure, were less able to laugh at themselves, and had generally been more difficult than the other boys. The male offenders themselves told the interviewer that their moods changed easily, they became easily angry, and often teased and fought with others. There were no significant differences between the female offenders and nonoffenders in these variables but the former felt themselves more passive than the other girls.

The interviews concerning leisure activities confirmed the findings that the future male offenders smoked more than the other boys (table 5.7). They also mentioned that they had been drunk more often and that their peers used more alcohol and smoked more than the other boys. No differences were found in girls.

The choice of friends of the future male offenders caused worries to their parents according to both the subject and parent interview. The parents considered the influence of peers

Table 5.3. Means in Peer Nominations for Aggression at the Age of 8 of Male and Female Nonoffenders and Offenders Committed Different Number of Types of Offences; One-Way Analysis of Variance.

VARIABLES AGE 8			PEER NOMINATION (PERCENTAGES)						TEACHER RATING	
			NON-OFFEND.	TYPES OF OFFENCES			BETW. GROUPS $p <$	LIN-EARITY $p <$	BETW. GROUPS $p <$	LIN-EARITY $p <$
				1	2	3				
MALES N			125	47	16	8				
FEMALES N			156	13	4					
1. Direct, defensive, physical: Hurts another child when angry	M		17.4	19.0	26.7	42.7	.007	.002	.06	.01
	F		17.5	18.0	35.6		n.s.	.1	.03	.08
2. –verbal: Quarrels with other children for a slight reason	M		17.6	16.7	24.0	36.5	.007	.007	.02	.00
	F		20.4	16.2	32.3		n.s.	n.s.	.04	n.s.
3. –facial: Starts sulking easily	M		17.2	18.6	17.4	26.0	n.s.	n.s.	n.s.	n.s.
	F		20.2	20.7	28.8		n.s.	n.s.	n.s.	n.s.
4. Indirect, defensive, physical: Teases smaller and weaker peers when angry	M		16.0	20.1	28.4	48.9	.000	.000	.02	.01
	F		15.7	20.0	42.3		.004	.003	.01	.007
5. –verbal: sneaks	M		18.4	19.9	16.6	28.2	n.s.	n.s.	n.s.	n.s.
	F		22.7	21.3	31.0		n.s.	n.s.	.09	n.s.
6. –object-oriented: Kicks pieces of furniture or other objects when angry	M		14.6	14.8	21.1	36.7	.002	.002	n.s.	.09
	F		16.1	23.1	21.5		n.s.	n.s.	.04	.03
7. Direct, initiative, physical: Attacks somebody without any reason	M		18.1	18.9	28.9	51.5	.000	.000	n.s.	n.s.
	F		16.7	16.2	36.0		.04	.07	n.s.	n.s.

Variable	Sex								
8. —verbal: Says naughty things to others even if these had done nothing wrong to him	M	17.2	20.0	23.4	39.5	.01	.004	n.s.	n.s.
	F	19.2	17.5	35.5		n.s.	n.s.	.006	.006
9. —facial: Keeps sneering and making faces at other children	M	17.7	14.5	27.6	29.8	.1	.04	n.s.	.09
	F	17.8	13.8	30.5		n.s.	n.s.	n.s.	.07
10. Indirect, initiative, physical: Teases others behind their back	M	17.9	19.6	25.0	50.3	.000	.000	.09	.02
	F	18.0	13.9	42.5		.005	.08	.02	.06
11. —verbal: Exaggerates or tells lies about other children	M	19.4	19.6	17.7	41.4	.02	.09	.1	.06
	F	20.7	19.3	46.0		.02	.05	.004	.03
12. —object-oriented: Takes other children's possession	M	13.4	14.3	21.2	44.1	.000	.000	.003	.000
	F	15.2	19.2	27.3		n.s.	.08	n.s.	n.s.
Sum for aggression (Z score) (1-12)	M	-1.07	-0.34	2.96	16.25	.000	.000	.02	.004
	F	-0.22	-0.86	10.22		.05	n.s.	.02	.02
Direct defensive aggression (1-3)	M	52.3	54.3	68.1	105.2	.02	.007	.09	.02
	F	58.1	54.9	96.5		n.s.	n.s.	.07	.08
Direct initiative aggression (7-9)	M	53.0	56.3	80.2	120.8	.001	.001	.02	.002
	F	53.7	47.5	102.0		.08	n.s.	n.s.	.08
Indirect aggression (4-6, 10-12)	M	99.9	108.4	129.8	269.9	.000	.000	.02	.006
	F	108.4	106.8	210.5		.03	.06	.008	.01
Physical aggression (1, 4, 6-7, 10, 12)	M	97.3	106.7	151.2	274.2	.000	.000	.008	.001
	F	99.1	100.4	205.0		.02	.04	.02	.02
Verbal aggression (2, 5, 8, 11)	M	72.8	76.2	81.9	157.4	.1	.009	.06	.03
	F	83.0	74.3	144.8		n.s.	n.s.	.002	.02
Facial aggression (3, 9)	M	34.9	36.1	45.1	55.8	n.s.	.06	.08	.04
	F	40.0	34.5	59.3		n.s.	n.s.	n.s.	.08

Table 5.4. Means in Peer Nominations for Nonaggression at the Age of 8 of Male and Female Nonoffenders and Offenders Committed Different Number of Types of Offences; One-Way Analysis of Variance

VARIABLES AGE 8	MALES N / FEMALES N	PEER NOMINATION (PERCENTAGES)						TEACHER RATING	
		NON-OFFEND.	TYPES OF OFFENCES 1	2	3	BETW. GROUPS p <	LIN-EARITY p <	BETW. GROUPS p <	LIN-EARITY p <
	N / N	125 / 156	47 / 13	16 / 4	8				
13. *Activeness:* Is always busy and plays eagerly with other children	M	23.1	21.5	28.6	39.0	.008	.01	n.s.	n.s.
	F	25.7	22.8	3.5		.03	.02	n.s.	n.s.
14. *Weak self-control:* Is sometimes very touchy and sometimes nice	M	21.6	16.7	18.3	34.8	.04	n.s.	n.s.	.02
	F	21.7	18.4	33.8		.1	.02	n.s.	n.s.
15. *Passiveness:* Is always silent and does not care to be busy	M	21.1	16.2	12.3	14.5	n.s.	n.s.	n.s.	n.s.
	F	21.8	25.0	17.3		n.s.	n.s.	n.s.	.04
16. *Strong self-control:* Tries always to be friendly to others	M	22.6	17.4	16.5	13.8	n.s.	.02	n.s.	.09
	F	26.9	25.5	7.8		n.s.	n.s.	.1	.1
17. *Anxiety:* Thinks that he/she will certainly get revenge but never does	M	19.3	20.6	22.9	30.0	n.s.	.09	n.s.	n.s.
	F	21.7	17.7	39.3		.04	.05	n.s.	n.s.
18. Starts easily crying if others treat nastily	M	18.2	12.4	16.1	9.4	n.s.	.1	n.s.	n.s.
	F	17.9	28.5	15.0		n.s.	n.s.	n.s.	n.s.
19. Is afraid of other children	M	17.5	13.7	11.6	20.4	n.s.	n.s.	n.s.	n.s.
	F	16.3	21.5	17.3		n.s.	n.s.	n.s.	n.s.
20. Apologizes readily even if he had done nothing very wrong	M	20.5	15.3	12.3	11.6	.01	.001	n.s.	n.s.
	F	24.2	21.2	14.3		n.s.	n.s.	n.s.	n.s.
Sum score for anxiety (18–19)	M	35.7	26.1	27.7	29.8	n.s.	n.s.	n.s.	n.s.
	F	34.3	50.0	32.3		n.s.	n.s.	.06	n.s.
21. *Submissiveness:* Never quarrels with others	M	20.5	15.3	12.3	11.6	.01	.001	n.s.	n.s.
	F	25.7	20.4	9.0		n.s.	.09	n.s.	n.s.

No.	Item	Sex								
22.	Dislikes squabbling company and leaves it for something else	M	22.8	16.6	15.4	14.2	.06	.01	.006	.001
		F	27.6	23.9	14.0		n.s.	n.s.	n.s.	n.s.
23.	Is peaceable and patient	M	22.4	18.2	15.6	7.5	.09	.01	.07	.008
		F	26.1	22.8	6.8		n.s.	.1	n.s.	n.s.
24.	Is considered a reliable classmate	M	21.6	16.4	16.9	6.4	.06	.01	n.s.	.08
		F	25.0	19.7	9.0		n.s.	.1	n.s.	.08
	Sum score for submissiveness (21–24)	M	89.3	66.5	57.8	34.9	.009	.001	.03	.003
		F	104.4	86.8	38.8		n.s.	.07	n.s.	.07
25.	Constructiveness: Tries to act reasonably even in annoying situations	M	22.8	16.9	16.3	9.4	.04	.006	n.s.	n.s.
		F	25.3	20.9	5.3		.1	.05	.07	.03
26.	Thinks that if one negotiates everything will be better	M	21.3	17.8	14.3	21.0	n.s.	n.s.	n.s.	n.s.
		F	23.8	19.7	20.5		n.s.	n.s.	.003	.001
27.	Thinks that it is just a joke if somebody attacks him/her	M	18.8	18.7	20.2	19.8	n.s.	n.s.	n.s.	n.s.
		F	20.6	19.2	22.0		n.s.	n.s.	n.s.	n.s.
28.	Sides with smaller and weaker peers	M	20.2	18.6	22.2	9.2	n.s.	n.s.	n.s.	n.s.
		F	25.2	22.2	5.0		n.s.	.08	.06	.02
	Sum score for constructiveness (25–26, 28)	M	64.1	53.3	52.8	38.2	n.s.	.04	n.s.	n.s.
		F	74.3	62.8	30.8		n.s.	.06	.009	.002
29.	Thinks that he/she would be a good leader of an excursion	M	22.3	19.0	20.7	14.4	n.s.	n.s.	n.s.	n.s.
		F	23.7	21.8	5.0		n.s.	n.s.	n.s.	n.s.
30.	I would never choose as a leader of an excursion	M	23.5	22.3	23.7	44.4	.08	n.s.	n.s.	n.s.
		F	23.5	25.2	43.0		n.s.	n.s.	.08	.08
31.	Tries to attract attention by making fun	M	19.0	20.6	20.5	39.9	.03	.03	n.s.	n.s.
		F	19.9	23.8	20.5		n.s.	n.s.	.1	.09
32.	Disobeys the teacher	M	16.4	18.6	24.8	36.9	.08	.02	n.s.	n.s.
		F	20.7	19.3	46.0		.02	.05	.000	.01
33.	Cries easily, say, at the dentist's	M	17.7	16.5	13.4	12.7	n.s.	n.s.	n.s.	n.s.
		F	18.0	23.8	24.3		n.s.	n.s.	n.s.	n.s.

Table 5.5. Means of Male and Female Nonoffenders and Offenders in Some Teacher Ratings and Inventory Scales at the age of 8.

VARIABLES AND INVENTORY SCALES AT AGE 8		N	NONOF-FEND.	TYPES OF OFFENCES			BETW. GROUPS p <	LIN-EARITY p <
				1	2	3		
	MALES	N	125	47	16	8		
	FEMALES	N	156	13	4			
34. Teacher feels concerned about because of ensuing antisocial behaviour	M		0.30	0.45	0.63	0.88	.08	.009
	F		0.15	0.08	0.50		n.s.	n.s.
35. Is too withdrawn and timid	M		0.41	0.34	0.13	0.05	n.s.	n.s.
	F		0.56	0.85	0.25		n.s.	n.s.
36. Is unsteady and lacks concentration in his work and attentiveness	M		0.85	0.98	1.31	1.50	.1	.01
	F		0.47	0.54	1.50		.01	.02
37. Teacher thinks that this child will certainly be successful in later life	M		1.80	1.81	1.69	1.25	n.s.	n.s.
	F		1.93	1.54	1.50		n.s.	n.s.
38. Success at school (1 = poor, 5 = good)	M		3.10	2.96	2.81	2.63	n.s.	.1
	F		3.08	2.46	2.00		.04	.01
39. *Inventory:* Femininity	M		2.40	2.28	2.38	2.00	n.s.	n.s.
	F		6.63	7.75	6.00		.04	n.s.
—Fearfulness	M		2.64	3.00	2.94	1.13	.01	n.s.
	F		2.68	3.33	5.00		.01	.005
—Reluctant attitudes toward school	M		4.87	4.43	4.31	3.88	n.s.	.06
	F		2.63	2.83	3.00		n.s.	n.s.
—Self-confidence	M		4.39	5.13	5.06	4.38	.1	n.s.
	F		4.63	4.00	4.50		n.s.	n.s.
—Altruism	M		5.45	5.39	5.06	5.88	n.s.	n.s.
	F		6.53	7.33	5.00		.06	n.s.

important. The male offenders themselves told the interviewer that they spent their leisure in streets and discos more often and were at home more rarely than the other boys, and that they spent pocket money on cigarettes, alcohol, sweets, and entertainment. They had started heterosexual interaction at an early age without ever having any close friend. They were illicitly absent from school and did not take care of their homework. Consequently, success at school was poor.

The female offenders and nonoffenders did not differ in these variables except for the female offenders' conception of their parents' little knowledge about the place where they spent their leisure. They also had fewer hobbies.

Both the future female and male offenders watched TV for excitement more than the others. They also read more comic books and thrillers. Obviously, their imagination was filled by excitement more than that of young people on average.

Ways of Life at the Age of 20

At the age of 20, 135 subjects (67 males and 68 females) were interviewed again. They included 20 males and 5 females, who were found in the criminal registers: 13 males had committed only one type of offence (alcohol offences 7, thefts 3, violence 1) and 7 males several types of offences. This corresponded to the distribution found in all male offenders (cf. Fig. 5.1). Three females had committed one type of offence and two females two types of offences.

A comparison of the behavioural patterns of the offenders and nonoffenders revealed the same differences as at the ages of 8 and 14. The male offenders were socially more active than females, while the latter were more alienated from the society (table 5.8). The female offenders did not feel obliged to society, but passed their time by watching TV, and had few plans for the future.

Compared with the age of 14, it was found that smoking and the use of alcohol had increased among the female offenders. Both the male and female offenders had finished their schooling with basic school and were employed without vocational training. Consequently, they had been unemployed more than the other young people. They were lacking occupational plans, self-confidence was low, and expectations about the future were pessimistic.

CRIMINAL BEHAVIOUR IN THE THEORETICAL FRAME OF REFERENCE

Continuity in Social Behaviour

To study the structure and continuity of social behaviour, factor analyses were carried out at each age level and the correlations of the first two factors between the three age levels were calculated by using individual factor scores. The structure of interindividual differences confirmed the hypotheses presented in figure 5.2. Also interindividual stability proved to be statistically very significant.

At the age of 8, the variables included in the factor analysis consisted of peer nominations and teacher ratings in 33 items, teacher ratings in 5 additional items, and 16 inventory scales; 87 altogether. The number of subjects was 369. The first factor was mainly formed by the items for *aggression* vs. *submission* from peer nomination and teacher rating. Table 5.9 presents the variables for which the highest loadings were obtained in this factor. The second factor represented socially skillful, *constructive* vs. socially helpless, *anxious* behaviour (table 5.10). Both factors supported the hypotheses on interindividual differences in aggressive and nonaggressive behaviour (Fig. 5.2).

At the age of 14, 91 variables were included in the factor analysis. The first factor corresponded to the pattern of aggressive vs. submissive behaviour hypothesized in the two-dimensional model (Fig. 5.2). It was, however, completed by several characteristics of social behaviour. As table 5.9 shows, the first factor described differences in the *orientation towards peers* vs. *dependency on home* with adjustable and withdrawn behaviour. Orientation toward peers included roaming the streets, gathering together, aggressiveness, and seeking pleasure in smoking, alcohol, and heterosexual interaction at an early age.

The second factor, on the other hand, corresponded to the pattern of constructive vs. anxious behaviour. The ratings of self-control were particularly connected with success at school, responsibility for school work and other behaviour, and relationships with the father, as can be seen in the highest loadings of the factor (Table 5.10). The opposite end of the factor represented negative of indifferent attitudes toward school, failure, aggression, anxiety, and a lack of friends and hobbies. The factor was interpreted as *Orientation toward responsibility* vs. *Negativism*.

At the age of 20, the factor analysis was made with 89 variables. The first factor supported the hypothesis about the "impulse control" dimension, at the one end, the uncontrolled expression of impulses including various kinds of problem behaviour and orientation toward

Table 5.6. Means in Peer Nominations and Teacher Ratings at the Age of 14 of Male and Female Nonoffenders and Offenders Committed Different Number of Types of Offences; One-Way Analysis of Variance

VARIABLES AGE 14	MALES N / FEMALES N	PEER NOMINATION (PERCENTAGES)							TEACHER RATING	
		NON-OFFEND.	\begin{tabular}{c}TYPES OF OFFENCES\end{tabular}			BETW. GROUPS p <	LIN-EARITY p <		BETW. GROUPS p <	LIN-EARITY p <
			1	2	3					
	119 / 144	119 / 144	46 / 13	16 / 4	8					
Activeness: Is energetic, always on the go, often in contact with others	M / F	14.8 / 22.4	23.9 / 23.4	18.2 / 40.4	28.9	.03 / n.s.	.02 / n.s.		n.s. / n.s.	n.s. / n.s.
Initiative aggression: Attacks without reason, teases others, says naughty things	M / F	12.7 / 15.0	26.0 / 23.4	34.0 / 37.7	40.8	.000 / .1	.000 / .03		.03 / .03	.05 / .06
Weak self-control: Impulsive, lack concentration, changes moods	M / F	14.3 / 18.6	21.8 / 25.9	25.4 / 47.4	33.1	.02 / .04	.002 / .02		.004 / n.s.	.001 / n.s.
Anxiety: Fearful, helpless in others' company, target of teasing, unable to defend	M / F	20.5 / 13.0	10.7 / 17.3	5.2 / 7.9	1.7	.01 / n.s.	.001 / n.s.		n.s. / n.s.	n.s. / n.s.
Passiveness: Does not move much, stands alone, is silent	M / F	18.2 / 16.8	10.0 / 22.3	9.7 / 0.00	0.64	.03 / n.s.	.004 / n.s.		n.s. / n.s.	n.s. / n.s.
Submissiveness: Fearful, patient, adjustable	M / F	19.2 / 19.3	14.5 / 13.9	9.9 / 12.6	6.1	n.s. / n.s.	.02 / n.s.		n.s. / .001	n.s. / .003
Strong self-control: Reliable, keeps promises, does not get excited	M / F	20.3 / 22.7	15.9 / 11.6	6.7 / 6.9	8.2	.02 / .08	.003 / .03		.000 / n.s.	.000 / .04

124

Variable	Sex								
Constructiveness: Tries to solve annoying situations reasonably, negotiates, conciliates, strives for justice	M	18.6	14.1	12.5	5.8	n.s.	.04	.009	.002
	F	19.2	9.3	11.5		n.s.	n.s.	n.s.	n.s.
Defensive aggression: Defends oneself if teased, but does not attack without reason	M	18.9	19.6	13.0	14.2	n.s.	n.s.	.008	.01
	F	21.9	20.4	9.5		n.s.	n.s.	n.s.	n.s.
School reports: Average of marks (4 = poor, 10 = excellent)	M	7.06	6.74	6.39	6.08	.000	.000		
	F	7.64	7.23	6.83		.04	.01		
Attentiveness & carefulness (10 = very good)	M	8.05	7.60	6.86	6.83	.000	.000		
	F	8.77	8.42	8.00		.1	.03		
Teacher rating: Interest in school attendance (1 = no, 4 = very interested)	M	2.60	2.09	1.75	2.29	.000	.000		
	F	2.99	2.75	2.33		n.s.	.08		
Truancy (1 = plays truant often, 4 = no)	M	3.83	3.60	2.56	2.13	.000	.000		
	F	3.71	3.50	3.25		n.s.	n.s.		
Punishments at school (1 = often punished, 5 = no)	M	4.00	3.69	2.81	2.75	.002	.000		
	F	4.67	4.58	3.00		.002	.006		
Smoking (1 = smokes, 3 = no)	M	2.68	2.37	2.00	1.71	.000	.000		
	F	2.64	2.44	2.50		n.s.	n.s.		
Use of alcohol (1 = takes alcohol, 3 = no)	M	2.93	2.91	2.44	2.60	.005	.005		
	F	2.88	3.00	3.00		n.s.	n.s.		
Participates in activities (5), withdrawn (1)	M	2.83	3.28	2.75	2.50	.08	n.s.		
Social behaviour improved (7), worsened (1)	M	4.14	3.82	3.81	3.63	.006	.001		
Contacts with police (3 = no, 1 = yes)	M	3.00	3.00	2.38	2.14	.000	.000		
Good hobbies (5), spare time in streets (1)	M	2.60	2.35	1.88	1.33	.09	.01		

Table 5.7. Means of Male Nonoffenders (=51) and Offenders (N = 26), and Females Correspondingly (N = 67 and 10), in Some Interview Variables for Leisure Activities at the Age of 14.

INTERVIEW VARIABLES	MALES			FEMALES		
	NONOF-FENDERS	OF-FENDERS	p<	NON OF-OFFENDERS	OF-FENDERS	p<
Does not smoke (5), regularly (1)	4.30	3.35	.006	3.42	3.30	n.s.
Never been drunk (5), often (1)	4.06	3.60	.09	3.79	4.11	n.s.
Parents know the place of leisure (5), no (1)	4.61	3.81	.01	4.24	3.40	.07
Leisure in discos often (3), no (1)	1.40	2.00	.001	1.83	1.75	n.s.
Pocket money for amusements (3), saves (2)	2.40	2.79	.002	2.63	2.67	n.s.
No heterosexual interaction (3), started easily (1)	2.73	2.33	.05	2.29	2.22	n.s.
No illicit absence from school (3), yes (1)	2.86	2.29	.000	2.66	2.29	n.s.
Training hobbies (4), no (1)	2.78	2.44	n.s.	2.53	1.70	.007
Watches TV for spending free time (3), for excitement (2)	2.39	2.09	.01	2.69	2.29	.04
Prefers violent series (4), movies (2)	2.89	3.35	.03	2.43	2.67	n.s.
TV always open at home (4), rarely (1)	3.16	3.58	.02	3.37	3.56	n.s.
Reads fiction (3), comic books & thrillers (1)	1.90	1.52	.09	2.55	1.67	.004

Table 5.8. Means of Male Nonoffenders (N = 47) and Offenders (N = 20), and Females Correspondingly (N = 63 and 5), in the Behavioural Indicators Showing Significant Differences Between the Groups at the Age of 20.

INTERVIEW VARIABLES FOR BEHAVIORAL INDICATORS AND LIFE CONDITIONS AT AGE 20	MALES			FEMALES		
	NONOF-FENDERS	OF-FENDERS	P<	NONOF-FENDERS	OF-FENDERS	p<
Easy to make friends (1), difficult (3)	2.11	1.55	.001	1.94	2.25	n.s.
No conflicts with friends (1), often (3)	1.91	2.20	.07	1.72	2.00	n.s.
Leisure in discos, streets (3), no (1)	2.15	2.75	.000	2.06	2.00	n.s.
Many obligations toward society (1), no (4)	2.49	2.79	n.s.	2.44	3.40	.009
Close friends (1), no (4)	2.85	3.15	n.s.	2.79	3.80	.02
Watches TV 0–1 h/day (1), over 4 hrs. (3)	1.53	1.68	n.s.	1.41	2.40	.000
Clear plans for future (1), no (3)	1.87	2.05	n.s.	1.87	2.40	.07
Satisfied with oneself (1), dissatisfied (3)	1.54	1.76	n.s.	1.43	2.00	.09
Never smoking (1), regular smoking (5)	2.26	3.55	.004	2.52	4.60	.003
No use of alcohol (1), often drunk (4)	2.70	3.25	.007	2.40	3.20	.02
Studies (1), employed from basic school (3)	1.53	2.40	.000	1.71	3.00	.002
Never unemployed (1), more than 1 year (4)	1.45	2.00	.03	1.68	2.60	.07
Clear occupational plans (1), no (5)	1.85	2.50	.03	2.00	3.60	.001
Optimism toward future (1), pessimism (3)	1.49	2.10	.001	1.60	2.40	.02
Realistic attitudes (1), lack of self-confidence (3)	1.40	1.80	.04	1.51	2.40	.01

Table 5.9. The First Factor of Behavioural Indicators at the Ages of 8, 14, and 20; Items with the Highest Loadings

Age 8

Aggressive, short-spanned (+)	vs.	*Submissive, calm* (−)
Hurts another when angry		Never quarrels
Teases smaller peers		Peaceable
Says naughty things		Leaves squabbling company
Attacks without reason		Silent
Disobeys the teacher		Always friendly
Kicks furniture when angry		Dependent (Inventory)
Changes moods		Feminine (Inventory)
Anti-social symptoms		Submissive (Inventory)
Lacks concentration		Altruistic (Inventory)
Restlessness (Inventory)		Withdrawn
Impulsive extraversion (Inventory)		Apologizes

Age 14

Orientation toward peers (+)	vs.	*Dependency on home* (−)
Energetic, contacts with others		Stands alone, silent
Attacks without reason		Peaceful, patient, adjustable
Free time in streets and discos		Free time at home
Smoking started before age 8		Never smoking
Lacks concentration, moods change		Stable
Early and excessive use of alcohol		No use of alcohol
Boy/girl friend before age 13		No dating
Fit for leadership		Unfit for leadership
Many friends		Few friends
Punishments given at school		No punishment at school
Pocket money to spend on amusements		Pocket money saved
Many friends whom the parents dislike		No friends whom the parents dislike
Conflicts and distant relationship with the mother		No conflicts, close relationship with the mother

Age 20

Reveller (+)	vs.	*Loner* (−)
Sociability (Self-control Inventory)		Social tension
Use of alcohol many times a week		No use of alcohol
Often drunk		
Heterosexual interaction before age 14		No dating
Social activity (Check List)		Social passivity
Use of alcohol before age 12		
Regular excessive smoking		No smoking
Smoking before age 11		
Energetic, active (self-rating)		Shy, tense, quiet, withdrawing
Conflicts with parents		No conflicts with parents
Easily makes friends		Difficulty making friends
Many friends		Few friends
Premarital intercourse accepted		Not accepted
Not dependent on parents		Dependent on parents
Parents have no power over child		Parents have strong power
Weak tolerance and control (Inventory)		Never in discos, restaurants
Angry, quarrelling (self-rating)		Prefers marriage
Free time in discos, restaurants		
Prefers unwedded living together		

Table 5.10. The Second Factor of Behavioral Indicators at the Ages of 8, 14, and 20; Items with the Highest Loadings.

Age 8

Socially skilled, constructive (+) vs.	*Socially helpless, anxious* (−)
Fit for leadership	Unfit for leadership
Defends smaller and weaker peers	Cries at the dentist's
Acts reasonably	Afraid of others
Negotiates	Cries if treated nastily
Reliable	Withdrawn
Always friendly	Lacks concentration
School success	Poor school success
Busy and plays	

Age 14

Orientation towards responsibility (+) vs.	*Negativism* (−)
Good school reports	Poor school reports
Acts reasonably, negotiates	Lacks concentration, changes moods
Interest in school attendance	No interest in school
Reliable, keeps promises, never excited	Gives up or becomes aggressive
No illicit absence from school	Truancy weekly
Takes care of homework	Lazy with homework
Never attacks without reason	Attacks without reason
Fit for leadership	Unfit for leadership
Many friends	Few friends
Defends himself if teased but does not attack	Fearful, unable to defend himself
No friends whom the parents dislike	Many friends whom parents dislike
Talks about freetime activities	Does not talk about free time
No difficult periods	Continuously difficult
Reads fiction and newspapers	Reads comic books
Close relationship with father	Distant or conflicting relationship with the father
Takes part in organized activities	No hobbies

Age 20

Striver (+) vs.	*Loser* (−)
Well-adjusted (clinical rating)	Problems of adjustment
Optimistic about future	Afraid of future
Positive and realistic life attitudes	Lack of self-confidence, disappointed
Satisfied with choices	Dissatisfied with choices
School success	Poor school success
Clear plans for future	No plans for future, day by day
Studies continued	School interrupted
Realistic description of own character	Unable to describe oneself
Little TV-watching (0–1 hrs.)	TV-watching many hours/day
Chooses news and information on TV	Does not choose TV programmes
Never smoking	Regular excessive smoking
Feel obliged toward society	No obligations toward society
Opinions about politics	No opinions about politics
Strong self-control (check list)	
Constructive (Self-control Inventory)	
Dependable, balanced (self-rating)	Difficulties in concentration
Studying or regular work	Unemployed
Makes friends easily	Difficulty making friends
Sociability (Inventory)	Social tension

peers, and, at the opposite end, the controlled inhibition of impulses with dependency on parents and parental norms. Table 5.9 presents the variables for which the highest loadings were obtained in this factor, interpreted as the ways of life of peer-oriented *Revellers* vs. parent-oriented *Loners*.

The second factor described the subject's attitudes toward himself, the future, and society (table 5.10). Strong self-control and a controlled expression of impulses were related to optimistic expectations about the future, success in studies, and responsible attitudes toward himself and society. On the other hand, the other pole of the factor represented negative and alienated attitudes and a lack of plans for the future. The subjects had failed in their studies, self-confidence was low, and problems of adjustment were obvious. The ways of life which the factor described were also in accordance with the hypothesis and they were interpreted as life attitudes of *Strivers* vs. *Losers*.

The correlations of the first two factors between the three age levels (8, 14, and 20) showed that interindividual stability was statistically very significant (table 5.11). Aggressive behaviour in childhood predicted orientation toward peers (and to some extent negativism) in puberty and also in adolescence, as emerged in the behaviour of "Reveller." It means that the uncontrolled expression of impulses of the aggressive children was related to the early use of alcohol, smoking, and heterosexual interaction, i.e., seeking pleasure without moral constraints (see table 5.9).

The opposite to aggression, submission, predicted dependency on home, refraining from pleasure, few contacts with age-mates and responsibility for school work in puberty. The constraints of the expression of impulses remained strong over the time period studied.

The predictability of the positive life attitudes of the "Strivers" was correspondingly high on the basis of constructive social behaviour in childhood and assuming responsibility for school work and other behaviour in puberty (table 5.10). This line of development reflected a strong orientation toward reality.

In contrast, the alienation of the "Losers" was connected with socially helpless, anxious behaviour in childhood, and negative attitudes toward school work and other people in puberty. Poor success in school possibly lowered self-confidence and reduced expectations about the future. Interrupted schooling made it difficult to find a job. The future was seen as frightening.

Criminal Behaviour in the Two-Dimensional Framework

Offenders and Non-Offenders. The comparison of the factor scores of the nonoffenders and offenders for the factors of behavioural indicators at each level revealed that criminal behaviour was related to weak self-control as expected (table 5.12). The multitype male and female offenders had been more aggressive and short-spanned than the other children. Female offenders had also been socially less skilled and anxious; the second factor did not discriminate male offenders from the other boys.

In terms of the theoretical constructs (fig. 5.2), uncontrolled expression of impulses had been typical at the age of 8 to both the future female and male multitype offenders. In addition, uncontrolled inhibition of impulses had been typical to the future female offenders.

At the age of 14, the future male offenders were significantly more oriented toward peers than the other boys. The future female offenders did not differ from the other girls in this respect; the girls who were to commit one type of offence only tended even to be more dependent on home than the other girls. The future female offenders differed from the other girls especially in negativism; as was the case with the future male offenders. Uncontrolled expression of impulses was still at the age of 14 typical of the future male offenders. However, in both males and females a tendency could be found toward a concentration of criminal behaviour in

Table 5.11. Intercorrelations of the Factors for Behavioural Indicators Extracted at Ages 8, 14, and 20*

FIRST TWO FACTORS EXTRACTED AT EACH AGE	AGE 8		AGE 14		AGE 20	
	AGGR. I	CONSTR. II	PEERS I	RESPONS.	'REVELLER' I	'STRIVER' II
Age 8						
I Aggressive, short-spanned (vs. Submissive, calm)						
II Socially skilled, constructive (vs. Socially helpless, anxious)	−02					
Age 14						
I Orientation towards peers (vs. Dependent on home)	44xx	11				
II Orientation towards responsibility (vs. Negativism)	−24x	46xx	16			
Age 20						
I 'Reveller' (vs. 'Loner')	43xx	02	53xx	−15		
II 'Striver' (vs. 'Loser')	−08	40xx	−02	46xx	00	

xx=p< .001, x=p< 01
*The number of subjects in the correlations between the ages of 8 and 14 was 154; between 8 and 20, 135; and between 14 and 20, 116.

Table 5.12. Means of Male and Female Nonoffenders and Offenders in Factor Scores for the Factors of Behavioural Indicators Extracted at the Ages of 8, 14, and 20.

FACTOR SCORES		NONOFFENDERS	NUMBER OF TYPES OF OFFENCES			BETWEEN GROUPS $p<$	LINEARITY $p<$
			1	2	3		
Age 8							
	N	(125)	(47)	(16)	(8)		
		(156)	(13)	(4)			
Aggressive, short-spanned (−) vs.	I M	0.09	0.35	0.57	1.30	.007	.001
Submissive, calm (−)	F	−0.29	−0.38	0.85		.009	.05
Socially skilled, constructive (+) vs.	II M	0.02	−0.03	−0.03	−0.25	n.s.	n.s.
Socially helpless, anxious (−	F	0.06	−0.44	−0.63		.09	.03
Age 14							
	N	(151)	(16)	(6)	(4)		
		(67)	(6)	(4)			
Orientation toward peers (+) vs.	I M	−0.42	0.18	0.67	0.65	.008	.001
Dependency on home (−)	F	0.16	−0.48	0.05		n.s.	n.s.
Orientation toward responsibility (+)	II M	0.05	−0.17	−1.24	−0.59	.01	.005
vs. Negativism (−)	F	0.28	−0.70	−0.38		.04	.03
Age 20							
	N	(47)	(14)	(2)	(4)		
		(63)	(3)	(2)			
"Reveller" (+) vs. "Loner" (−)	I M	−0.17	−0.62	0.60	1.41	.001	.000
	F	−0.15	0.20	0.58		n.s.	n.s.
"Striver" (+) vs. "Loser" (−)	II M	0.17	−0.27	−1.24	−0.75	.02	.004
	F	0.15	−1.45	−1.10		.006	.004
*Specific factors**: use of alcohol, smoking,	M	−0.14	0.56	−0.91	−0.97	.008	.001
pessimism (+) vs. abstinence, optimism (−)	F	−0.20	0.83	−1.22		.02	.005
No interest in schooling, hobbies,	M	0.07	0.30	0.71	0.72	n.s.	.1
society (+) vs. strong interest (−)	F	−0.25	0.62	0.98		.04	.01
Parents have no power over the subject (+) vs.	M	−0.30	−0.31	0.23	1.14	.006	.003
dependent on parents (−)	F	0.15	1.32	−0.48		.06	n.s.

*From each group of data first two factors were extracted. In addition, all interpretable factors were extracted. If the groups differed in them, the means are given in this table.

132

weak self-control without a clear component of activeness or passiveness. For males at the age of 20, there was again a significant difference between the offenders and nonoffenders in the way of life.

Different Types of Offences in Males. Since the number of male offenders was large enough for correlational analysis, correlations between the variables for criminality and other data were calculated. Correlational analysis was not carried out with the female offenders because of their small number.

Thefts, alcohol offences, and violent offences were all positively correlated. The correlations between the ratings of aggression and the variables for criminality varied depending on the type of offence. Alcohol and violent offences correlated significantly with all 12 aggression variables at the age of 8, except for facial aggression and sneaking, while thefts correlated only with indirect or initiative physical aggression (table 5.13).

Most ratings of aggressiveness correlated with the amount of criminality also in the homogeneous groups of male offenders. For example, of those males who were found in the criminal registers at the age of 20, more alcohol and violent offences had been committed by those to whom teasing others in childhood was more typical.

At the age of 14, alcohol and violent offences still correlated significantly with initiative aggression but only in peer nomination. Instead, weak self-control correlated with alcohol and violent offences in both peer nomination and teacher rating. Teacher ratings of poor success at school, lack of interest in school, misbehaviour at school, smoking, and the use of alcohol were also related to alcohol and violent offences but not to thefts which correlated only with truancy and poor attentiveness and carefulness at school.

From the variables for nonaggression, only those for submissiveness correlated negatively with alcohol and violent offences at the age of 8. At the age of 14, both the frequency of offences and the number of the types of offences correlated negatively (on average .23, $p < .01$) with the teacher ratings of constructiveness and submissiveness, and with the peer nomination of anxiety.

The background of various types of offences in males is summarized by the correlations between the offence categories and the factor scores for the factors extracted from the data at the ages of 8, 14, and 20 (table 5.14). Of the behavioural indicators at the age of 8, aggressive, short-spanned (vs. calm, submissive) behaviour correlated particularly with alcohol and violent offences, but also with theft offences. Correlations of this factor with the criminality score and the number of types of offences committed by the individual were also significant.

At the age of 14, alcohol offences, the criminality score, and the number for the types of offences were related to peer orientation in particular but also to negativism. In contrast, violent and theft offences did not correlate with these behavioural indicators at the age of 14.

At the age of 20, all types of offences were related to the way of life called "Reveller." It also correlated highly with the criminality score and the number for the types of offences.

Aggression in Different Patterns of Behaviour. The results presented above, as hypothesized, suggest some developmental lines. For example, children who displayed strong self-control were later oriented toward the maintenance and advancement of society with its norms and values. As a contrast, aggressive and anxious behaviour in childhood that shared the characteristic of weak self-control was later oriented toward indifference to society and the individual's own future. However aggression was related not only to this developmental line. In puberty, it related also to negativism which stemmed from early anxious behaviour which reulted, in adolescence, in the way of life called "Loser." The latter line of development was especially pertinent to criminal behaviour in females.

Table 5.13 Predictability of Male Criminality on the Basis of Behavioural Ratings at the Ages of 8 and 14; All Subjects and Offenders Separately

VARIABLES WITH SIGNIFICANT CORRELATIONS FROM PEER NOMINATION (PN) AND TEACHER (TR) AGE 8	N =	ALCOHOL OFFENCES		THEFT OFFENCES		VIOLENT OFFENCES	
		ALL (196)	OFFEND. (57)	ALL (196)	OFFEND. (26)	ALL (196)	OFFEND. (20)
1. Direct, defensive, physical: Hurts another child when angry	PN	29^{xx}	48^{xx}	18	23	33^{xx}	54
	TR	23^{x}	37^{x}	13	23	26^{xx}	45
2. Direct, defensive, verbal: Quarrels with other children for a slight reason	PN	25^{xx}	41^{x}	12	08	24^{xx}	38
	TR	20^{x}	20	21^{x}	25	20^{x}	55
4. Indirect, defensive, physical: Teases smaller peers when angry at something	PN	33^{xx}	44^{xx}	29^{xx}	32	34^{xx}	60^{x}
	TR	23^{x}	28	29^{xx}	09	20^{x}	57^{x}
6. Indirect, object-oriented: kicks objects when angry	PN	31^{xx}	51^{xx}	23^{x}	37	28^{xx}	51
	TR	17	17	02	09	17	26
7. Direct, initiative, physical: Attacks somebody without any reason	PN	33^{xx}	42^{x}	30^{xx}	36	34^{xx}	56^{x}
	TR	20^{x}	29	13	21	26^{xx}	49
8. Direct, initiative, verbal: Says naughty things to others	PN	28^{xx}	42^{x}	11	06	27^{xx}	47
	TR	24^{xx}	33	17	25	23^{xx}	57^{x}
10. Indirect, initiative, physical: teases others behind their backs	PN	31^{xx}	47^{xx}	23^{x}	27	36^{xx}	62^{x}
	TR	25^{xx}	35^{x}	13	20	23^{x}	44
11. Indirect, initiative, verbal: Exaggerates or tells lies about other children	PN	23^{x}	49^{xx}	17	23	19^{x}	41
	TR	18	25	08	08	17	50

12. Indirect, initiative: Takes other children's possession	PN	30^{xx}	43^{xx}	17	12	28^{xx}	37
	TR	32^{xx}	38^{x}	12	11	23^{x}	23
Sum score for aggression (12 variables, see table 5.6)	PN	34^{xx}	57^{xx}	22^{x}	26	31^{xx}	50
	TR	25^{xx}	33	15	22	25^{xx}	53
Anti-social symptoms	TR	28^{xx}	44^{xx}	16	16	30^{xx}	65^{x}
Sum score for submissiveness (4 variables, see table 5.7)	PN	-18	-18	-12	-11	-20^{x}	-46
	TR	-24^{xx}	-31	-13	-28	-20^{x}	-41
Age 14	$N =$	(186)	(54)	(186)	(25)	(186)	(18)
Initiative aggression: Attacks	PN	31^{xx}	18	14	13	28^{xx}	61^{x}
Weak self-control: Impulsive, lacks concentration, changes moods	PN	31^{xx}	34	14	22	25^{xx}	65^{x}
	TR	23^{x}	14	08	09	19^{x}	28
Attentiveness & carefulness } school } report		-39^{xx}	-39^{x}	-22^{x}	-27	-27^{xx}	-46
Average of marks		-31^{xx}	-30	-17	-29	-22^{x}	-36
Uninterested in school	TR	24^{x}	10	12	10	16	46
Often punished at school	TR	23^{x}	14	14	22	23^{x}	29
Truancy	TR	34^{xx}	15	31^{xx}	32	32^{xx}	18
Smokes	TR	31^{xx}	24	19	06	19	06
Takes alcohol	TR	23^{x}	19	02	-05	39^{xx}	38

$^{x}p < .01$
$^{xx}p < .001$

Table 5.14. Correlations of the Offence Categories with the Factors Scores for the Factors Extracted from the Data at the Ages of 8 (N = 196 males), 14 (N = 186 males), and 20 (N = 67 males)

FACTORS		ALCOHOL OFF.	THEFT OFF.	VIOLENT OFF.	CRIM. SCORE	NUMBER OF OFFENCES
Age 8	Factors					
Aggressive, short-spanned (vs. calm)	I	28xx	17x	27xx	31xx	24xx
Socially skilled, constructive (vs. Anxious)	II	− 10	− 02	− 10	− 06	− 05
Age 14						
Orientation toward peers (vs. Dependency on home)	I	36xx	14	18	36xx	37xx
Orientation toward responsibility (vs. Negativism)	II	− 29x	− 12	− 26	− 32x	− 31x
Age 20						
"Reveller" (vs. "Loner")	I	34x	33x	31x	43xx	46xx
"Striver" (vs. "Loser")	II	− 28	− 16	− 24	− 29x	− 35x

xp < .01
xxp < .001

The type of aggression included in these patterns of behaviour was initiative aggression. Defensive aggression ("Defends himself if teased but does not tease others without reason") is typical of constructive (even submissive) children (Pitkänen-Pulkkinen, 1981). Of course, initiatively aggressive children also defend themselves aggressively, but defensive aggression alone does not predict criminal behaviour. Instead, initiative aggression, especially teasing smaller and weaker peers, is a very potent predictor of multitype criminal behaviour and different types of offences.

Life Conditions

Life Conditions in the Background of Social Development. To study the possible factors which might explain the stability of behaviour, the interview data collected at the age of 14 concerning child rearing and environmental conditions were factor analyzed and the correlations between the background factor scores and behavioural factor scores were examined.

Child Rearing. The factor analysis of child rearing conditions involved 49 variables: 22 from the parents' and 27 from the subject interview. The first two factors were interpreted as child-centered guidance vs. selfish treatment and concerned restrictiveness vs. unconcerned permissiveness (Pulkkinen, 1982). The former was related only to the characteristics of children's behaviour. "Selfish treatment" correlated significantly (.37–.53) with both types of weak self-control at each age level; and "child-centered guidance," correspondingly, with both types of strong self-control (Fig. 5.4).

"Child-centered guidance" included the parents' trust in the child, knowledge of the child's spare time company, place, and activities, interest in the child's school attendance, consideration of the child's opinions, consistency in child rearing, just restrictions and sanctions, giving advice, sympathy in the child's failure, and avoidance of physical punishment. Daily

conversations and democratic interaction appealed to the child's cognitive control of his behaviour and granted gradual independence. "Selfish treatment" included just the opposite:
the parents' little interest in the child's leisure activities and school attendance, distrustfulness
and conflict about the child's leisure, physical punishment, unjust and inconsistent treatment,
lack of consideration of the child's opinions, and rare conversation with the child. In this atmosphere, the child could not develop positive social skills.

Environmental Conditions. The factor analysis of environmental conditions was made
with 85 variables; 59 variables from the parents and 26 from the subject interview. The first
two factors were interpreted as "socioeconomic status" and "steadiness of life conditions."

In the factor of socioeconomic status, high status included the parents' highly-valued occupation, long schooling, high quality of housing, permanent job, harmonious climate at home,
and, in addition, the parents' participation in various activities. In low socioeconomic families, schooling was shorter and consequently the occupation was less-valued, the quality of
housing was poorer, the parents were culturally less active, and the emotional climate was less
harmonious than in high socioeconomic families.

The factor of socioeconomic status did not correlate significantly with the factors for uncontrolled expression of impulses vs. controlled inhibition of impulses (e.g., Aggression vs.

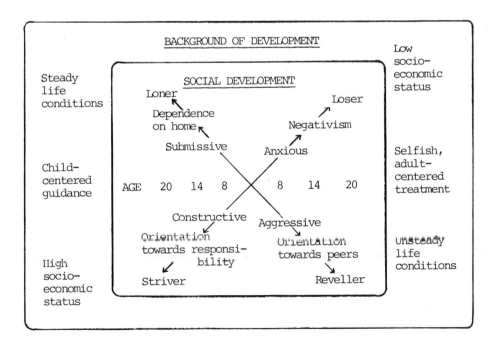

**Fig. 5.4. Schematic Presentation of Relationship of Social Development to Upbringing
and Environmental Conditions.**

Submission) at any age. Instead, high socioeconomic status was related to socially skilled, constructive behaviour (age 8, r = .33, p < .001), orientation toward responsibility (age 14, r = .22, p < .01), and the way of life of "Striver" (age 20, r = .25, p < .01). Correspondingly, low socioeconomic status correlated with socially helpless, anxious behaviour, negativism, and the way of life of "Loser."

The other factor, steadiness of life conditions, was constructed on two aspects: the mother's employment and the parents age. Mature parents had been better able to give the child steady conditions, a permanent dwelling, a stable family structure, etc., than young parents. On the other hand, the mother's employment easily caused unsteadiness and other problems in the child's life such as changing day-care arrangements, loneliness, and a lack of time for the child.

Unsteady life conditions correlated with socially helpless, anxious behaviour (age 8, r = .31, p < .001) and negativism (age 14, r = .92, p < .001), but not with the way of life of "Loser." Instead, unsteady conditions predicted at the age of 20 the way of life of "Reveller" (r = .32, p < .001). Correspondingly, steady conditions correlated with constructive and responsible behaviour in childhood and puberty but the way of life of "Loner" in adolescence.

Life Conditions of Young Offenders

The interview data concerning the future nonoffenders' and offenders' life conditions revealed many differences, particularly in child rearing (table 5.15). It could be found that the problems with leisure activities were related to the parents' little encouragement of their children's hobbies and control of their use of money. The parents did not even encourage their school attendance nor were they interested in the children's success at school — at least from the perspective of the children — and had no plans for their further schooling.

The offenders and nonoffenders did not differ in father's occupational status in any systematic way. Instead, the female offenders came from broken homes more often than the others. The parents of the female offenders were significantly younger at their birth than those of the female nonoffenders. The mothers of the female offenders had been employed more and their work with travel had taken more time; consequently, the mothers had less time for their daughters than the mothers of the other girls. If the father was at home he had inconvenient working hours more often than the fathers of the other girls. The female offenders had few shared activities with the father and they knew less about the father's work than the other girls.

If the physical or psychological absence of the father was characteristic of the female offenders, the male offenders, on the other hand, had more conflicts with the father than the other boys. The fathers of the future male offenders gave models for taking alcohol and smoking, and for violence through corporal punishment until the teens. The mothers of the male offenders had inconvenient working hours more than the mothers of the other boys. The absence of the mother in the evenings affected without a doubt the family atmosphere and the mother's possibilities of controlling the son's leisure activities.

The means in the factor scores for the factors extracted from the data at the age of 14 summarized the findings and also confirmed the applicability of the two-dimensional model to the prediction of criminal behaviour (table 5.15). Selfish treatment with conflicting, authoritarian atmosphere (corporal punishment, lack of guidance, conflicts between family members) were typical of male offenders as well as of the subjects with weak self-control in general; the multitype offenders did not differ in these respects as much as those offenders who had committed two types of offences. The latter came from lower socioeconomic status.

The life conditions which characterized female offenders consisted of unsteady conditions provided by young parents. These conditions were also more characteristic of the multitype male offenders than of the other male offenders. In general, unsteady life conditions were re-lated to weak self-control of the subjects.

DEALING WITH CHILD OFFENDERS

The results of the Finnish longitudinal study showed that criminal behaviour was predictable on the basis of both individuals' behaviour and life conditions, particularly child rearing. The findings were in accordance with other studies (Farrington, 1978; Feldhusen, Thurston, & Benning, 1973; Jessor & Jessor, 1977; and Magnusson, Dunér, & Zetterblom, 1975; among others) which have shown that aggressive behaviour tends to be associated with antisocial or problem behaviour, e.g., drinking, in males in particular. In girls, the symptoms of malad-justment were more related to anxious behaviour as in the recent Swedish study by Magnusson et al. (1975).

The results concerning child rearing confirmed findings by, for example, Olofsson (1973) who discovered in Sweden that young male offenders had suffered corporal punishment more than boys in the control group. In contrast, socioeconomic status was not related to the fre-quency of offences. No effect of socioeconomic background on criminal behaviour of 16-year-old boys were found by Magnusson et al. (1975) either. In general, criminality has been related to parent-centered, selfish treatment which is capricious: sometimes indifferent, some-times strict, depending on the parents' moods and energy available (Glueck & Glueck, 1950, 1962; McCord, McCord, & Howard, 1961).

The parents of antisocial youngsters control their children's activities less than in general. Conflicts between the parents are common (Olofsson, 1973) and, consequently, there are con-flicts about child rearing methods (Jonsson, 1970; Krüber, 1969). The relationships between antisocial boys and their parents, the fathers in particular, are conflicting (Bandura & Wal-ters, 1959), and the parents have few shared activities with their children (Krüber, 1969; Ol-ofsson, 1979; Vedel-Petersen, From, Løve, & Pedersen, 1968). The present results also showed that the parents of offenders were young and that these young parents (often divorced) were unable to provide the child with stable life conditions.

The pattern of aggressive behaviour in children and the risks of its further development are known. The question of what can be done remains.

Various kinds of training methods have been constructed for helping aggressive children and young people in positive development, e.g., Structured Learning Therapy (SLT) for ado-lescents (Goldstein, Sherman, Gershaw, Sprafkin, & Glick, 1978), a programme of Develop-ing Understanding Self and Others (DUSO) for preschool children (Dinkmeyer, 1970), and die Helferspiele (Tausch & Tausch, 1977). The present author has also made two experiments Pitkänen, 1974; Pitkänen Pulkkinen, 1977) for developing self-control in children. The main idea in the latter programme was to give parents and kindergarten teachers some material which would help them in guiding their children toward constructive behaviour: consideration of others, conciliating, role-taking, and empathy.

The empirical findings show that a systematic training of behaviour may be helpful at least in immediate effects (Mussen & Eisenberg-Berg, 1977; Staub, 1979). Long-term effects of the programmes are, however, less known. The child is emotionally so tight with his family that it is probably very difficult to change his behaviour permanently without improving the whole communication system at home.

Therefore, a better method would be to give future and young parents a thorough prepara-tion for parenthood. It can be seen as most important at present, when nuclear families live apart from grandparents who cannot transfer their life experiences on upbringing to the

Table 5.15. Means of Male Nonoffenders (N = 51) and Offenders (N = 26), and Females Correspondingly (N = 67 and 10), in Some Interview Variables for Life Conditions at the Age of 14 and the Factors Extracted from Them.

Interview variables P = parents, C = child, F = father, M = mother	MALES			FEMALES		
	NON-OFFENDERS	OFFENDERS	$p <$	NON-OFFENDERS	OFFENDERS	$p <$
M encourages C's hobbies (4), no (1) *	3.69	2.80	.01	3.45	2.22	.02
F encourages C's hobbies (4), no (1)	3.44	2.73	.07	3.08	1.56	.007
P control use of money (4), no (2)	2.96	2.57	.06	2.83	2.75	n.s.
P encourage school attendance (4), indifferent (1)	2.84	2.50	n.s.	2.86	2.22	.08
P proud of C's success (5), indifferent (1)	2.98	2.35	.006	3.27	2.70	.1
P have plans for schooling (4), no (1)	3.71	2.88	.08	3.73	2.20	.02
C's school success corresponds to expectations (4), no expectations (1)	3.27	2.61	.02	3.48	3.14	n.s.
F's occupational status low (9), high (1)	5.27	5.18	n.s.	5.48	6.50	n.s.
Normal family (2), broken family (1)	1.92	1.78	n.s.	1.78	1.29	.006
M's age at C's birth; in years	28.5	28.8	n.s.	28.4	21.1	.005
F's age at C's birth; in years	30.7	32.3	n.s.	30.7	23.0	.02
M at home (3), employed (2)	2.41	2.22	n.s.	2.49	2.14	.08
M at home after school hours (5), no (1)	4.04	4.19	n.s.	4.03	2.43	.006
M's time for C sufficient (4), insufficient (1)	3.39	3.30	n.s.	3.69	2.86	.08
F lives with the family (2), no (1)	1.90	1.92	n.s.	1.88	1.67	.09
Shared activities with F (4), no (1)	2.86	2.62	n.s.	2.24	1.60	.01
Knows the nature of F's work (5), no (3)	4.81	4.95	n.s.	4.63	3.80	.01
Number of dwellings in C's life time	2.71	3.09	n.s.	2.74	4.57	.02
Regular rhythm of life, meals together (4), no (1)	2.57	2.62	n.s.	2.51	1.90	.1
Close relationship with F (6), conflicting (2)	5.00	4.46	.01	4.36	4.00	n.s.

Factors		NONOFFENDERS	NUMBER OF TYPES OF OFFENCES			BETWEEN GROUPS	LINEARITY
			1	2	3	p<	p<
Number of people living at home at age 14		4.22	4.73	4.87	4.40	.07	n.s.
F takes alcohol abundantly (3), no (2)		2.09	2.26	2.24	2.33	.08	n.s.
F smokes (4), no (2)		2.87	3.29	3.20	3.33	.09	n.s.
M's shifts convenient (5), inconvenient (3)		4.49	4.11	4.29	3.86	.07	n.s.
Physical punishment never (4), until teenage (1)		3.07	2.30	2.90	2.60	.000	n.s.
P take C's opinion into consideration (4), no (2)		3.67	3.40	3.74	3.40	.08	.08
Praise for reward (2), no or material reward (1)		1.80	1.68	1.86	1.57	n.s.	.06
Upbringing							
I Child-centered guidance (+) vs. Selfish (parent-centered) treatment (−)	M	0.22	−0.17	−1.48	−0.52	.000	.000
	F	0.12	−0.51	−0.38	0.66	n.s.	n.s.
II Concerned restrictiveness (+) vs. Unconcerned permissiveness (−)	M	0.16	0.46	−0.16		n.s.	n.s.
	F	−0.17	−0.50	0.34	0.00	.000	.000
Specific factors*: Warm, supportive (−) vs. conflicting, authoritarian atmosphere (−)	M	0.02	−0.11	−1.56		n.s.	n.s.
	F	−0.13	−0.70	−0.08		n.s.	n.s.
Environmental conditions							
I Socio-economic status high (+) vs. low (−)	M	0.38	0.15	−0.74	0.86	.02	n.s.
	F	−0.26	−0.37	−0.24		n.s.	n.s.
II Stable life conditions (+) vs. Unsteady conditions (−)	M	−0.03	0.34	0.04	−0.96	n.s.	n.s.
	F	0.15	−1.51	−0.78		.004	.006
Specific factors: Mature parents (+) vs. Young parents (−)	M	0.01	0.17	0.61	−1.07	n.s.	n.s.
	F	0.04	−1.33	−1.62		.05	.02

*From each group of data first two factors were extracted. In addition, all interpretable factors were extracted. If the groups differed in them, the means are given in Table 5.15.

younger generation. Young parents generally admit that they know very little about child rearing and that they would like to have more information. Nevertheless, school education does not include such knowledge. Neither is it given in sufficient detail as a part of maternity care. Several proposals for increasing education for parenthood have been recently presented in Finland.

Social welfare is, from the international perspective, on a high level in Finland (*Finland — a Scandinavian modern country,* 1978). Child welfare, however, at present starts only when the neglect of a child is very obvious (there are about 2,000 such cases annually) or when the child's behaviour shows such problems of adjustment (truancy, use of alcohol and narcotics, committing an offence) that the environment cannot manage with him/her. Child welfare measures are the same for neglected and delinquent children, according to the 1936 Child Welfare Act. The measures mentioned in this 45 year old act are economic support, use of supervised leisure-time activities, a warning to either a child or his parents, protective supervision, and transfer of guardianship. In practice, several other measures have been adopted, for instance, counselling, open-care (long-term contact between the social worker and child's family), and special arrangements for schooling and placements.

As mentioned in the first part of this chapter, the minimum age for criminal responsibility in Finland is 15. Children below this age are dealt with solely by the local social welfare board. Offenders between 15 and 17 can be dealt with by both the courts and the boards. Norway was the first Scandinavian country which, in 1896, passed a special child welfare act establishing local child welfare boards as the authority in charge of dealing with neglected and delinquent children (Joutsen, 1980). Sweden followed in 1902, Denmark in 1905, and Finland in 1936. Joutsen explains that one of the main purposes of the reform was to halt the criminal development of children at as early an age as possible. The punishment of children was abandoned in theory and replaced by educational measures.

Originally, Norway included the local judge, priest, and physician on the board but, at present, the lay element is predominant. In Finland also, each commune sets up a social welfare board which consists of at least six members elected by the communal council, the commune's representative body. In practice, most members are laymen with no presumed knowledge of law, education, or child rearing (Joutsen, 1980).

The only criminal justice system branch that a child offender normally comes into contact with is the police. If the offence is not regarded as very petty and forgiveable, the police have an unconditional obligation to notify the child welfare authority of the investigation of the offence allegedly committed by the child or young person. A representative of the child welfare authority, as well as the guardian, is to be given the opportunity of being present when the child is being questioned. In practice, a social worker is present in only some of the police investigations. As Joutsen (1980) remarks, offences can be detected at any time of the day or night while social workers usually have established office hours.

From the perspective of child rearing, a great problem at present is the fact that in Helsinki, for example, the Child Welfare Office receives reports of about 500 child offenders (mainly 13-14 years old) each year, but in two-thirds of the cases no measures are taken by the Office: the child is not even contacted. In 14 percent of the cases, the child is counselled, and in some 8 percent of the cases, institutional measures are used (Joutsen, 1980).

According to Joutsen (1980), criticism has been leveled by those who call for a clearer distinction between social control and social services.

Child welfare in Finland clearly implies both social control and social welfare, and thus it can be expected that there will be increased pressure towards developing a clearer distinction. This can be seen in the proposals that the minimum age of criminal liability be lowered from the present level of fifteen years. Were this to be done, the criminal courts could take over the social control role, leaving social welfare to the child welfare authorities. [p. 121]

The results of the longitudinal study presented above strongly support conceptions of the need for reforms in the control of children's behaviour and factors influencing it. For example, children's (boys' and particularly girls') use of alcohol has rapidly increased in Finland: in 1960, 1,000 young people were arrested because of drunkenness, in 1975, 8,900. Criticism aimed at the policy of the State Alcohol Monopoly has been presented and changes in the legislation demanded. Consequently, a law was passed in 1981 according to which providing alcohol for people under 18 years old who are not allowed to buy it would be illegal. Indifference to the problem behaviour of children on the part of the society cannot produce better results in child development than indifference on the parent's part. The only alternative to it is not authoritarian control but preventive control and wise guidance. Children's nonaggressive, constructive behaviour, and more generally strong self-control is a result of mature child-centered guidance and stable life conditions. Their promotion promotes nonaggression in society.

REFERENCES

Anttila, I. Papers on crime control 1977-1978. Helsinki: *Reports from the Research Institute of Legal Policy*, 1978 (Whole No. 26).

Apo, M., Lönnqvist, J., & Achté, K. Yleistä itsemurhista. (On suicides.) In: *Itsemurhat ja niiden ehkäisy*. Helsinki: WSOY, 1973.

Bandura, A., & Walters, R. H. *Adolescent aggression*. New York: Ronald Press, 1959.

Block, J. H., & Block, J. The role of ego-control and ego-resiliency in the organization of behavior. In W. A. Collins (Ed.), *Minnesota Symposia on Child Psychology*. Vol. 13. New York: Lawrence Erlbaum, 1979.

Bronson, W. C. Central orientation: A study of behavior organization from childhood to adolescence. *Child Development*, 1966, *37*, 125-155.

Dinkmeyer, D. *Developing Understanding Self and Others*. Manual, DUSO D-1. Circle Pines, Minnesota: American Guidance Service, 1970.

Facts about Finland, (16th rev. ed.) Helsinki: Otava, 1979.

Farrington, D. P. The family backgrounds of aggressive youths. In L. Hersov, M. Berger, & D. Schaffer (Eds.), *Aggression and antisocial disorder in children*. Oxford, England: Pergamon Press, 1978.

Feldhusen, J. F., Thurston, J. R., & Benning, J. J. A longitudinal study of delinquency and other aspects of children's behaviour. *Journal of Criminology and Penology*, 1973, *1*, 341-351.

Finland — A Scandinavian modern country. Helsinki: Finnish-American Cultural Institute, 1978.

Glueck, S., & Glueck, E. *Unraveling juvenile delinquency*. Cambridge, Mass.: Harvard University Press, 1950.

Glueck, S., & Glueck, E. *Family environment and delinquency*. Boston: Houghton Mifflin, 1962.

Gurr, T. R., & Bishop, V. Violent nations, and others. Paper prepared for delivery at the International Society for Research on Aggression meetings, Toronto. 17-18 August 1974.

Goldstein, A. P., Sherman, M., Gershaw, N. J., Sprafkin, R. P., & Glick, B. Training aggressive adolescents in prosocial behavior. *Journal of Youth and Adolescence*, 1978, *7*, 73-92.

Jessor, R., & Jessor, S. L. *Problem behavior and psychosocial development. A longitudinal study of youth*. New York: Academic Press, 1977.

Jonson, G. *Det sociala arvet*. Stockholm: Tiden-Barnängen, 1970.

Joutsen, M. Young offenders in the criminal justice system of Finland. Helsinki: *Reports from the Research Institute of Legal Policy*, 1976 (Whole No. 14).

Joutsen, M. Dealing with child offenders in Finland. Helsinki: *Reports from the Research Institute of Legal Policy*, 1980 (Whole No. 39).

[*Kalevala. The land of the heroes.*] (Translated by W. F. Kirby.) London: Everyman's Library, 1977. (Originally published, 1849).

Kohn, M., & Rosman, B. L. Cross-situational and longitudinal stability of social-emotional functioning in young children. *Child Development*, 1973, *44*, 721-727.

Krüber, H. Über den einfluss familiärer bedingungen auf die entwicklung des sozialverhaltens von schülern. *Probleme und Ergebnisse der Psychologie*, 1969, *31*, 81-101.

Lazarus, R. S. *Psychological stress and the coping process*. New York: McGraw-Hill, 1966.

Magnusson, D., Dunér, A., & Zetterblom, G. *Adjustment: A longitudinal study*. Uppsala: Almqvist & Wiksell, 1975.

McCord, W., McCord, J., & Howard, A. Familial correlates of aggression in nondelinquent male children. *Journal of Abnormal and Social Psychology*, 1961, *62*, 79-93.

Mussen, P., & Eisenberg-Berg, N. *Roots of caring, sharing and helping. The development of prosocial behavior in children*. San Francisco: Freeman, 1977.

Olofsson, B. *Ungla lagöverträdare 3. Hem, uppfostran, skola och kramratmiljö i belysning av intervju-och uppföljningsdata*. Stockholm: SOV, 1973.

Pitkänen, L. A descriptive model of aggression and nonaggression with applications to children's behaviour. *Jyväskylä Studies in Education, Psychology and Social Research* (Whole No. 19). Jyväskylä, Finland: University of Jyväskylä, 1969.

Pitkänen, L. An aggression machine. III: The stability of the aggressive and non-aggressive patterns of behavior. *Scandinavian Journal of Psychology*, 1973, *14*, 75-77.

Pitkänen, L. The effect of stimulation exercises on the control of aggressive behaviour in children. *Scandinavian Journal of Psychology*, 1974, *15*, 169-177.

Pitkänen-Pulkkinen, L. Effects of stimulation programmes on the development of self-control. In C. F. M. van Lieshout and D. J. Ingram (Eds.), *Stimulation of social development in school*. Amsterdam: Swets & Zeitlinger, 1977.

Pitkänen-Pulkkinen, L. Long-term studies on the characteristics of aggressive and non-aggressive juveniles. In P. F. Brain and D. Benton (Eds.), *A multidisciplinary approach to aggression research*. Elsevier, North-Holland: Biomedical Press, 1981.

Pulkkinen, L. Self-control and continuity from childhood to adolescence. In P. B. Baltes and O. G. Brim, Jr. (Eds.), *Life-span development and behavior*. Vol. 4. New York: Academic Press, 1982.

Rikollisuustilanne 1979. (Criminality in Finland 1979.) Helsinki: Research Institute of Legal Policy, 1980.

Seligman, M. E. P. *Helplessness. On depression, development, and death*. San Francisco: Freeman, 1975.

Sirén, R. *Väkivaltagallup 1976*. (English summary: Victims of Violence: Results of the 1976 National Surveys.) Helsinki: *Reports from the Research Institute of Legal Policy*, 1980 (Whole No. 40).

Staub, E. *Positive social behavior and morality. Socialization and development*. Vol. 2. New York: Academic Press, 1979.

Tausch, A., & Tausch, R. On becoming partners in preschool and school teaching. In C. F. M. van Lieshout and D. J. Ingram (Eds.), *Stimulation of social development in school*. Amsterdam: Swets & Zeitlinger, 1977.

Törnudd, P. Crime trends in Finland 1950-1977. Helsinki: *Reports from the Research Institute of Legal Policy*, 1978 (Whole No. 29).

Vedel-Petersen, J., From, A., Løve, T., & Pedersen, J. Børns opvaekstvilkår. En undersøgelse of de 9-12åriges problemer og hjemmemiljø. Copenhagen: Socialforskningsinstituttets publikationer, 1968 (Whole No. 34).

Verkko, V. Homicides and suicides in Finland and their dependence on national character. *Scandinavian Studies in Sociology*, 1951 (Whole No. 3) Copenhagen: G. E. C. Gads Forlag.

Ylikangas, H. Väkivallanaallon synty: Puukkojunkkarikauden alku Etelä-Pohjanmaalla. (Emergence of violent periods.) *Reports from the Institute of History*, University of Helsinki, 1973 (Whole No. 3).

6

France: Auto-Defence *

Renaud DuLong

Between Tuesday night and Wednesday morning, the small town of Mons-sur-Seine was confronted with yet another drama of "self-defence." Awakened by a suspicious noise in the middle of the night, M. Grandin, Manager of "La Civette," a bar and tobacco shop, went out to the terrace in front of his establishment. Convinced that it was a burglar, he returned to his bedroom and took the 22 carbine rifle which he had bought after a recent attempted robbery. Returning to the terrace, he addressed the intruder who at first hid himself in the corner protected by the door; then, at the moment when the latter tried to make his escape, the manager fired two shots. The burglar fell a few metres away. He was Michel X, aged 17, resident of Mons-sur-Seine. Wounded in the spleen, he was taken to hospital where the doctors certified that his life was not in danger. The keeper of the cafe was charged by the Public Attorney with willful shooting and wounding and was consigned to the prison of Versailles. The incident gave rise to strong feelings in Mons-sur-Seine where a number of thefts had been committed recently, and the debate on the issue of self-defence, which had diminished in the past several months, emerged once again. A petition was circulated among the tradesmen of the town demanding the immediate release of M. Grandin.

France has experienced all forms of aggression characteristic of modern society. But I shall discuss only one—"auto-defence." My decision to conduct research on this phenomenon reflects several factors. First, it is salient in France today. It enters into most discussions of violence and aggression. Secondly, its appearance in recent years has influenced lawyers and politicians to attend to the reaction of the general public concerning the evolution of penal practice. In addition, in the local communities where various incidents of self-defence have occurred, they have given rise to considerable discussion and in some cases, where judicial action has been taken against the perpetrator, to movements in support of the latter. Finally, the most visible actors in these movements are tradesmen and artisans and the arguments which they advance to justify self-defence are very much in line with *Poujadist* ideology. All this suggests that self-defence is a phenomenon rooted in contemporary French society, and is, in some sense, a typically French form of aggression.

An analysis of this phenomenon is also prompted by more theoretical reasons. Self-defence is, above all, a reaction to aggression, an aggressive response to an attack. The perpe-

*I am grateful to Professor Bernard Seuault, psychopharmacologist, for reviewing and commenting on an earlier draft of this chapter.

145

trator of self-defence does not apparently take the initiative, he merely responds to an attack of which he is the object. Even the notion of victim in each case becomes ambiguous since, while the person who is wounded or killed is a victim, it is the man who shoots who was in the first place victim of a malicious action. It was only when prospective victims of burglary started taking actions for damages and compensation from their aggressor/victims that the press began to write at length on self-defence.

Given the situation of the protagonists, it has been common to regard self-defence solely as a response to attack, an expression of a stimulus-reaction pattern well known to psychophysiologists and behaviorists, whereby the perpetrator reacts according to an instinctive pattern of behavior, which, when carried to extreme, leads to his act being considered as a reversion toward prehominid forms of behavior. This popular argument virtually excludes sociological analysis.

For a sociologist to enter into the discussion on self-defence, it is necessary to question these popular theories. Their explanations of human behavior have so permeated popular ideology that a large number of people believe that this reaction to aggression is instinctive. My purpose is to show that it is the manner in which the facts are presented that casts self-defence into the mould of a stimulus-reaction pattern. I will present and criticize the psychophysiological theory of self-defence, then I will raise pertinent questions that must occur to a sociologist. I will then put forward the principal elements of sociological analysis, drawn from the results of a study which I conducted by examining a dozen or so incidents of self-defence.

WHAT IS AUTO-DEFENCE?

Unable to examine police documents, the sociologist studying self-defence must be content with information given by the press. Newspapers in France began to report cases of self-defence during 1959. Up to 1976, the annual number of cases increased steadily, rising from single incidents to fifteen or so. Since then, the number of incidents has dropped to an average of about 2.5 a year.

It is exceedingly difficult to give a more precise evaluation of the importance of this phenomenon because journalists label as self-defence all armed acts aimed at a malefactor, even when carried out by a policeman or an official guard, and sometimes even when it is a question of settling accounts between hoodlums. For reasons which will become evident in the course of this chapter, the definition of the phenomenon is restricted here to cases of private persons defending their property—house, shop, or workshop—and who themselves alert the police after committing the act.

Since the result of this definition is to reduce the estimated number of cases, we come to a first conclusion: self-defence, so defined, is an extremely small matter compared with the attention which has been devoted to it by the press on the one hand and by political debate on the other. Road accidents, and even various forms of crime, have given rise to less discussion although many more are killed and wounded by them. Therefore, it is not the sheer frequency of self-defence that makes it a significant social phenomenon.

We should recall, however, that the number of incidents increased suddenly after 1977. It was then that the press began to give prominence to self-defence, echoing the local stir that it caused, raising questions, and reporting the views of lawyers and politicians. This increase in journalistic attention to self-defence may not merely reflect the increase in the number of incidents; in devoting more space to self-defence, the press may have contributed to legitimizing this method of response to crime. It is appropriate to speak in the regard of a press campaign, even if all the papers, including those whose politics are not inclined to the Left, contain expressions of regret that citizens have come to the point of killing their aggressors.

The papers deplore it all the more since burglars are not the only ones to die from this use of firearms. In October 1978, at Courtnay, a small town in the centre of France, a man fired a shot in the night against what he thought was a burglar, and killed his small son who had gone down to the kitchen to get a drink. This drama marks a turning point in the history of self-defence. Reference to it came to be used as an argument against self-defence, naturally by those who declare themselves in opposition to the practice, but also by journalists who do not fail to recall the incident when other similar "errors" occur—a man kills his wife, a grandfather his grandson, a brother his brother, etc. Mistakes such as these clearly do not fit the definition that I have given to the act of self-defence, but the fact that they are present in people's minds makes it necessary to take them into account in the analysis. Frequently in the course of this study, people have said to me "Self-defence, it is stories of fathers who kill their children."

The Legal Debate

The public debate on the subject has revolved principally around articles 328 and 329 of the French penal code, which define the conditions in which a citizen may exercise his right of legitimate defence. This debate concerns, above all, a juridical discussion, therefore discussion among lawyers. On the one side are the Syndicate of Magistrates, an organization of young magistrates which was formed following the political protests of May–June 1968, and on the other the association, "Legitimate Defence," which came into being early in 1978, when cases of self-defence were at their height. This association originally brought together magistrates and lawyers who wished, by proposing a new working of the text, to improve the penal code in regard to self-defence of victims. However, popular support very quickly transformed this intellectual club into a pressure group which adds the weight of its tens of thousands of adherents to the debate to defeat the attempts at reform of the Syndicate of Magistrates. In their efforts to legitimize self-defence, the members of this association denounce all improvements in the penal provisions introduced on the advocacy of the young magistrates: choice of prevention in preference to punishment, educational measures for juvenile delinquency, conditions concerning leave for prisoners, etc. On the one side, therefore, are those who wish to redefine the penal system in the direction of rehabilitating a delinquent into society; and, on the other, those who desire to accentuate the repressive measures of the code in the direction of a more radical exclusion of delinquents including a wider application of the death penalty.

The Popular Debate

To find discussion bearing directly on the problems raised by the private exercise of justice, one must turn to the local communities in which the incidents have occurred. Self-defence appears to take place with greater frequency in villages or in perimeter urban zones around large cities. In these local communities, probably owing to the high level of sociability that exists in them, the incidents become veritable events, causing an atmosphere of excitement which can lead to large demonstrations and producing animated discussions. I will return to this point at length in the final parts of this chapter; it is important here to underline the gap that exists between the central/political level and local levels of the discussions. The partisans and opponents of self-defence in the two spheres argue on different grounds. On the political level, partisanship revolves around the efficacy of the judiciary system, the choice between prevention and punishment, the definition of the sentence; on the local level, it is more a question of people's safety and of the right they have to kill an aggressor. This gap is indicative of the separation that exists between the political sphere and social sphere of society, a phenomenon which, as I will demonstrate, in part explains self-defence.

However, above and beyond this separation, the explanations that are advanced to justify self-defence come together again: it is a question of response to aggression, of people's reaction to the increase in crime. This view is put forward equally to explain the global development of the phenomenon and to account for each particular case. In itself, this assertion is not false, since the victims of self-defence, exception being made for the mistakes already mentioned, are criminals. However, it is necessary to make an appraisal of it, that is to say, to show the type of argument it reflects, in order to place it in a sociological analysis. Self-defence is certainly a reaction to criminal intent, but it is more than that.

THE PSYCHO-PHYSIOLOGY OF SELF-DEFENCE

On innumerable occasions I have heard people use the term "instinct": "This sort of thing cannot be explained—it's instinctive." "People react from fear like animals." Or further: "You know, when one finds oneself in situations like that, one does not think, one defends oneself as one can." In the same way, those who fired the shots justify their action by reference to fear: "It was night . . . I saw something . . . I was frightened . . . I fired." And, as if to summarize all this, the president of the association "Legitimate Defence" writes: "In the night you see a shadow, you fire, it's normal."

This way of considering self-defence is so simple that it calls for some comment. In the first place, one may remark that self-defence is in fact somewhat premeditated. It is always a question of defending oneself with a gun, never with a bludgeon, a knife, or fists. To use a gun you have first to have bought it, procured the ammunition, loaded it, and have it within reach. All this reflects a behavior that is socially complex, quite the opposite of a reflex action. It is possible that the act of pulling the trigger, at the moment when he catches sight of the burglar, is an automatic one for the perpetrator, but all that preceded this action and made it possible for him to find himself in the middle of the night, armed, in front of his attacker, indicates a premeditated sequence of conduct.

The only cases which do not fit this description make instinct irrelevant to self-defence. These are cases which involve not guns but explosive traps. The best known case was that of a garage owner in Troyes, a town in the east of France, who had transformed his transistor radio into a bomb, so that the thief who took it was killed by the explosion of the device and his comrade seriously wounded. The intention to kill or hurt was not present at the moment when the bomb exploded, but in the actions which preceded this moment. Likewise, aggressiveness toward the intruder does not lie in the act of pulling the trigger, but in the decision to buy an arm and to keep it in readiness.

If it is easy to refute in this way the instinct argument, it becomes more difficult to counter more elaborate theses on human behavior, those drawn from the observation of the behavior of animals and extrapolated to human conduct. In such accounts, self-defence would no longer be an instinct, but it would bring into play behavioral mechanisms that man allegedly has in common with many animals. This phenomenon would be thought to provide a particularly good illustration of biological theories concerning the interpretation of social behavior.

A pertinent example is the work of the French psychophysiologist, Henri Laborit, who is an outstanding figure in this line of thought. Of course, the works of Konrad Lorenz (1966)—to cite only the best known of foreign researchers—have had a strong influence in France, but, with the appearance in 1980 of the film of Alain Resnais, "My Uncle from America" ("Mon Oncle d'Amerique"), which presented the arguments of Henri Laborit, the latter stands out today in France as the best known of this line of thinkers (see Laborit, 1970, 1971).

The film of Alain Resnais treats the topic of aggression in the context of Laborit's theories. It relates the development of three people from birth to adulthood, when their lives merge. Retracing these biographies, the film stresses the socialization of two men and a woman, but it does this in order to more clearly underline, at the moment when relations become aggressive, how their social conditioning is obliterated by the eruption of animal instincts, of behavior which man shares with inferior creatures. There are scenes where a man tries to prevent a woman from leaving an apartment, sequences when two young business executives compete for the same post of authority, and the final tableau when a woman tries to strike the man whom she loves and who has decided to leave her. The producer compares each of these scenes with animal behavior by showing us experiments producing aggressive behavior or flight among rats. To emphasize the similarity more clearly, one sequence even shows the actors, disguised as rats, fighting each other. Off screen, Henri Laborit comments on the action voicing his ideas: man shares with other creatures a large part of his nervous system which controls eating, reproduction, flight, and struggle. What differentiates man is the neocortex, the seat of the nervous mechanisms which receive the imprint of education and social environment, the place where other people intervene in our behavior. In his books, Henri Laborit speaks in this regard of socioculture, the social environment of man, which is recorded in the conscious and unconscious aspects of his behavior and unites with the behavioral processes inherited from former phases of phylogenesis. It is this which gives rise to contradictions that can exist between instinctive impulses and the dictates recorded in the neocortex, contradictions that are the causes of serious psychological and physiological disorders. One of the characters in the film has an ulcer of the stomach and tries to commit suicide, another suffers an attack of nephritic colitis.

Self-defence does not enter into the film, nor into the books of Henri Laborit, but the number of scenes which present aggressiveness in one form or another leads us to extend the postulates of psychophysiological interpretation to all phenomena of aggression. Among them, self-defence would be a particularly suitable subject for the application of these theories insofar as it is a question of reaction to aggressive action. The reaction to a stimulus of attack provoked by the menacing presence of another is a form of behavior that, in its structure, perfectly fits the stimulus-reaction pattern which behaviorists such as Laborit have taken from psychophysiology.

One peculiarity of self-defence underscores its closeness to the model of animal behavior which psychophysiologists have built into their experiments. Reading the numerous reports on acts of self-defence, one is struck by the similarity in the accounts. Everything happens as if there were only one scenario for self-defence which is the one used by journalists to describe each case. This scenario may be described as follows:

> A man possesses a small property (residence, shop, or workshop) that he has obtained at the cost of a life's work. He is the object of repeated burglaries. On each occasion he appeals to the police without avail. He decides to arm himself, buys a gun, and keeps it near the place where he sleeps. One night he is awakened by a burglar. He takes his gun and shoots.

Small variations occur, in particular when the act of self-defence takes place in a bar or during the daytime, but the repeated experiencing of aggression, during which the individual becomes aware also of the impotence of the police, is never omitted. It is this phase that corroborates how Laborit's thesis may be applied to self-defence. On the one hand, the person attacked has experienced aggression which allows him to anticipate a further unpleasant episode, in the same way as an animal learns to relate a warning buzzer and an electric shock. On the other hand, his experience with the inefficacy of the responsible authorities leads him to disregard this control and revert to his "animal" behavior instinct of self-preservation.

However, this application of psychophysiological theories to self-defence ends in two stalemates. The first, already discussed, concerns instinct, which might make sense if the victim of the initial aggression were to knife the burglar, strangle him, or split his head open. But it never occurs in this way. The victim plans his action in advance, he prepares to defend himself by the use of a sophisticated firearm. The purchase, maintenance, and study of the use of this arm constitute a line of conduct that is very far removed from animal instinct.

The second point is that self-defence is *always* carried out by the purchase and use of a gun. If aggressiveness were really a regression toward a prehominid form of behavior, owing to the removal of the influence of others—socioculture, for Henri Laborit, is the presence of others in ourselves—the result would be a greater isolation of the individual. On this basis, one would expect that the choice of means of response would be more random, that it would result in the use of the whole variety of methods that man has invented to kill his fellows. Since it is almost invariably a gun, it is evident that self-defence calls other processes into play, a fact which the psychophysiological arguments fail to take into account. It is these processes which a sociological analysis of self-defence must bring to light.

I have not attempted to make an epistemological study of the validity of psychophysiological theories; I limit myself to challenging their pertinence in the explanation of self-defence. However, it does seem to me appropriate to stress that this challenge can be generalized. On the one hand, these theories echo common sense, and this may be merely theorizations of common sense—theorizations of the noncritical explanation that man gives to his own behavior. On the other, the theories isolate the conduct of the individual in relation to his social environment, reducing this environment to a secondary determining factor, susceptible to disappear when confronted with more primitive mechanisms. Without denying the existence of such mechanisms, my argument has been to show that to reduce behavior to its reflex dimension does away with the specific characteristics of a phenomenon.

THE IMAGE OF INSECURITY

When I spoke of popular justifications of self-defence, I drew attention to the arguments involving an alleged protective instinct. This signifies that the theories deriving from biology—those of Laborit, Lorenz, and others—have a certain influence on ideology, at least in France. However, side by side with these doctrines deriving from science, one finds other patterns of thought, also far removed from those of sociology, based on nonscientific concepts, which relate to the image of insecurity.

This image of insecurity was first revealed to me in conversations I held in the local communities where the incidents took place. These conversations were not recorded and, since they frequently took place on doorsteps or at cafe counters, it was difficult to conduct an analysis of them. Investigation into the ideological content of the question of self-defence only became feasible when I had access to a number of letters from its partisans. These letters are addressed to individual perpetrators, or to mayors who organized a militia of self-defence, in support of their cause in the face of opposition from the law and public authorities. The tone of this correspondence is very impassioned. Nevertheless, an analysis of the texts, despite their diversity, makes it possible to underline the recurrence of certain themes and to indicate a logic in the argument. This logic is composed essentially of three elements.

The Logic of Punishment. In describing the wrongdoers, the letter writers speak of "hooligans" ("voyous"). This expression in French can, at the same time, mean a criminal who kills, an adolescent who misbehaves in the street, and a child who is naughty at home. All the terms that the French language has used in the past to designate wrongdoers—bandit, scoundrel, swindler, pirate, etc.—are today, at least in working classes, applied by parents to their children. The authors of the letters, when commenting on the measures to be taken against the hooligans, frequently think of punishments which relate to a spanking. The expression often recurs: "Someone ought to fire a round of shot in their backsides." Here the form of upbringing in the family serves as a model for the punishment for juvenile delinquency, even if it results—and this is explicit in the letters—in the death of the wrongdoer.

One is struck by the number of cases where the victim of the act is an adolescent belonging to the same local community as his killer. It very rarely happens in an incident of self-defence that the person struck by the bullets is an adult criminal, an armed "professional," or a nonlocal. One can, of course, connect this with the characteristics of delinquents. But it is also quite justifiable to deduce from it that, in the minds of Frenchmen, self-defence is associated with the correction that a father should administer to his offending child. One is all the more justified in so doing given that the best remembered incident of self-defence is the one in which a father killed his own son.

The Call to Arms. This second theme is less evident in the letters than in the interviews, but it is implicit in the letters. People talk of their past as combatants, they recall the time of military conflicts. The phrase which best sums up this sentiment in regard to young criminals is "What they need is a good war." The image of war invoked here is that of a "good" war in the sense that it constitutes a place of purification for the new generation. The war myth in France serves as a testing ground to bring young males to manhood. Until recently, a man's political career was decided in terms of his military past. Here, the myth treats war as a kind of initiation rite.

Self-defence is indeed a war which honest men carry out against hooligans—in the name of law and justice obviously, but also in the name of the "Nation" which is threatened from within by those who have no respect for anything, who undermine the principal values of civilization, starting with property. At any rate, this aspect of the image explains why self-defence is carried out with guns, carbines, and pistols; and why, when the garage owner of Troyes placed an explosive in his transistor set, it was referred to as a bomb.

Denunciation of the State. Here, I suggest that self-defence is not directed only against hooligans, but that it aims just as much at the State and its representatives—the magistrates accused of cowardice, the police of impotence, and the government suspected of being in league with the criminals. The expressions that one finds on this subject in the letters are extremely varied, but they all bear witness to a change in the relationship of citizens to the State. More precisely, they reveal an ambivalence in this relationship: the State is, at the same time, the authority from which protection is expected against misfortune—and not only that of burglary—and also a point of weakness which is shown by its incapacity to reduce delinquency. Therefore, the State is at one and the same time revered and despised.

In acts of self-defence, the perpetrators themselves inform the police the act has been committed and submit themselves to the law for judgment. One may conclude that they expect from this a recognition of their right, and of the legitimacy of their act. And the decisions taken by the courts confirm them in this expectation, since almost all the court cases end in an acquittal or a decision that there is no ground for prosecution. The main point here is to clearly understand the contradiction in the perpetrator's relation with the State: he asks the State to legitimize an act in which the State's authority as holder of the monopoly for the legitimate use of force has been rejected. The perpetrator sets himself up as policeman, judge, and executioner before submitting his murderous act to the law and its representatives for ratification.

These three elements do not exhaust the images of self-defence contained in the letters. There are other themes. But the three were selected for several reasons: first their central position in the content of the letters, measurable by the frequency of the use of certain words—hooligans, war, or public authority—secondly, the links that can be established between the insecurity image and the acts of self-defence; and, lastly, the measure which they give of the extension of this image. It does not seem necessary to dwell further on the first two elements. The third, on the contrary, merits a more detailed explanation because it will enable us to expose the central question of a sociology of self-defence.

EXTENSIONS OF THE INSECURITY IMAGE

In France, there is extensive use of punitive practices in education and, in particular, corporal punishment. The influence of models of liberal education has been limited to certain intellectual circles. Each time the question of insecurity came up, the subject of youth, and then the education of children, had been discussed. This association of ideas hinges on an intermediary argument which introduces parental punishment as an educational norm: the aberration of the young emanates from the laissez faire attitude of the parents and from the growing permissiveness of education; the underlying inference is that parents are to blame for delinquency. At the same time, it puts the family back as the sole place where society is formed, and sets up parental strictness as a rampart against the destruction of civilisation, and physical punishment of the child as a measure of this educational requirement.

I mentioned earlier that the war was frequently evoked in the letters. The ideology of insecurity is demonstrated in practical terms in the development of the arms trade and, in particular, that of war weapons. Several French papers have carried out investigations on the number of persons holding weapons in France; they all conclude that there has been a marked increase in the last few years in the number of arms available to private persons. Nevertheless, while most of these arms have been acquired by recent purchases, a number came from the stocks distributed between 1942 and 1944 during the Resistance. In recent years, alarm systems, reinforcement of doors, and police dogs have become more noticeable. Even if not so obvious, the private weapon is of equal importance, at least among the less educated public where it is referred to in terms similar to those used for mobilization for war.

The ambivalence of the individual's relationship with the State is a characteristic common enough in French behavior to have been noted by foreign researchers as well as French (Hofmann, 1963). This is demonstrated by an attitude of defiance toward those who govern in particular and toward political parties in general, and also by an excessive expectation with regard to the State, which is looked upon as an authority capable of remedying all the ills from which its citizens suffer. In France, this attitude derives from a particular structural phenomenon; namely, the increasing gap between political and civil society, between that part of society which monopolizes public discourse and that which does not (Du Long, 1978).

It is in this context that I put the ideology of self-defence in the same category as self-management, which has served as a model for a number of the protest movements that have challenged society—ecological, antinuclear, regionalist, etc. If self-management derives more from a set of ideas associated with the Left, while that of self-defence is characterized as belonging to the Right, in both there is a denunciation of the State's incapacity to govern, an affirmation of a greater autonomy of society in theory and in practice vis-a-vis the State.

To place the image of self-defence in this way back in its context makes it easier to understand its importance. It concerns a group of ideas widely spreading in French society as a whole, but more particularly in the social strata to which one refers when one speaks of "the people"—workers, peasants, small tradesmen.

But, if this image of self-defence is so extensively held in French society, why is it that there are so few cases? Given the pervasiveness of the image of self-defence and considering the quantity of arms available to private individuals, it is surprising that the shootings are so few. Its relative scarcity, given the dispersion of the image which supports it, is a problem my analysis must address.

OPPOSITION TO SELF-DEFENCE

Through public debate, press accounts, and local demonstrations of support for the perpetrators, self-defence was subjected to a process of legitimization, which resulted in an increase in the number of incidents. Then the subsequent decline and, in most recent years, the standstill in the figures suggest that there may be a process of counterlegitimization. What I said about public discussion and the tone of the articles in the press underlines sufficiently clearly their contradictory character for one to be tempted to see in them the elements of this counterlegitimization. However, I have stressed the gap which exists between the political debate and that which occurs at the level of these small communities that the investigation must be pursued, in order to identify what it is that opposes the factors favourable to self-defence.

This is all the more imperative in that the legitimization of self-defence sometimes takes the form of groups demonstrating in support of a perpetrator, and that these demonstrations of force tend to show the community as unanimously behind one of its members when he is imprisoned as a result of his action. Often, in fact, the magistrate finds the perpetrator guilty, considering that a case for legitimate defence has not been proved. The combination of this accusation with some measure of imprisonment can give rise to a process of local mobilisation in support of the accused, implicitly approving his action. It is not self-defence that serves as the pretext for this mobilisation, but the decision of the judge who puts an honest man in prison when criminals are let off so lightly. This mobilisation takes the form of petitions, of public expressions of support, applications, at times collective assemblies, in which, in all cases, the local tradesmen play the leading role. Seen from outside, that is, through the accounts published in the press, the community seems unanimous in its support for self-defence. And it is because of this unanimity that I asked myself why such a movement in favour of a perpetrator did not lead other members of the community to imitate an action legitimized in this way. With possibly one exception, cases of self-defence have never occurred twice in the same locality. This exception was a town on the outskirts of Marseilles. The second incident gave rise to a series of demonstrations, directed this time *against* self-defence. For this reason, this exception also confirms the argument which I develop here.

To understand the problem, one must remember that self-defence takes place in villages or peripheral urban communities. These small communities differ in a number of ways from the town: sociability in them is intense and tends to bring people closer to one another, communication is essentially by word of mouth and functions under the cover of an established code of tradition; each member of the community is subject to the control of the group in his smallest actions. These communities are similar to traditional societies. Thus, self-defence is still more contradictory since judgment is passed by the group before it is passed by the public authorities; the act of self-defence even receives explicit approval before it is carried out since, in the conditions referred to above, it is not possible for the individual to defy the law of the group by an act of bloodshed. The measure of approval of self-defence, therefore, must be sufficiently great for the perpetrator to anticipate the support of his fellows. What then is the phenomenon that comes into play to counter this pro-self-defence factor and which prevents it from recurring? In what form does local opposition to taking justice into one's own hands present itself? What arguments enter the debate at this level to form a barrier to the image of self-defence?

My investigation showed that the unanimity is but a facade, that the mobilisation in favour of self-defence does meet with opposition. Here, once again, one does not find any of the themes which appear in the public debate, not even when militants of a strongly centralised party, e.g., the Communist Party, were questioned. Everything happens as if the opponents of self-defence had been forced to invent their arguments in terms of the line of thought attributed to its partisans. Here, too, it is possible to form the hypothesis that it is not a matter of a creation ex nihilo, and in presenting the inventory of the views expressed, one interprets them in the light of what may be assumed to be the working code of these microsocieties.

The first series of arguments evokes the eventuality of accident, which is always a possibility when firearms are involved. The image that comes up most frequently is that of the stray bullet. Or, again, reference is made to the numerous "errors" of self-defence which the papers have reported: the father who kills his son, the man who wounds his neighbor, the motorist who is nearly killed because he appears in the middle of the night seeking help after a road accident. Views of this kind do not make a frontal attack on the act of the private execution of justice but, rather, underline the danger an armed man presents to society. They recall the fact that there are safety rules which should be observed by those in possession of firearms, rules that are well known to sportsmen and game shooters for whom this type of accident is a constant danger. Given that the first of these rules is that a gun should never be pointed at a human being, one can consider that there is here already an implicit condemnation of self-defence.

The second series of arguments brings out what one might term a stereotype of America thought of as Chicago, the Texan, the Western, the sheriff, etc. America is here used as a bad example, as of a type of society where the relations between people are marked by violence and are the opposite of the kind of relationship existing in local society. Underlying these explanations is the idea that the community is threatened with destruction from the moment some of its members take up arms. The right to the private use of force risks a public outcry in the community since the fragile equilibrium with which it covers its cleavages threatens to break as soon as a clan asserts its rights to take up arms.

The third series of argument applies more directly to self-defence by weighing the value of the objects stolen against the life of a man. It is generally voiced by political militants or persons who are influenced by the parties of the Left. For them, it is not a question of repeating the arguments of the political debate, but the declarations of a principle fundamental to all life in society, namely, the interdiction against killing. In a certain way, this principle is implicitly present in the preceding arguments, and it is all the more conspicuous in that the victim is a member of the community. This argument also suggests that the perpetrator's claim to honesty which authorises him to set himself up as a judge of theft has much less foundation than he would like to claim. Insinuations of this sort—for it is more a question of insinuation than of accusation   are propounded by the declared opponents of small commerce, often those who challenge and contest the world of commerce as a whole. Therefore, they are less frequent. It is, however, significant that, at the moment when some individuals cling violently to their possessions, others proceed to a reevaluation of man's relation to property. Those who affirm that trade is founded on theft are, in fact, in making this claim, challenging one of the basic principles of rural society.

This inventory deals with the accounts gathered during the investigation. It may be supposed that many other things are said in the conversations evoked by the incident, and that other elements of the social code of the community are consequently highlighted. It is easy to imagine discussion revolving around the right to kill, discussions which are all the more contradictory and impassioned when the victim is a member of the community. In these conditions, it is permissible to conclude that a forum of this sort will be the place where the process of legitimization in favour of self-defence may tend to disappear. It is not a question of one camp being victorious over the other, but of an exchange of arguments sufficiently intense to deter members of the community from repeating the murderous act, to reaffirm the principles of life in society, and to restore to the State the monopoly of the use of legitimate force.

SELF-DEFENCE VERSUS THE STATE

Partisans and opponents of self-defence agree on one point: the State has failed in the matter of security. What is denounced by one side as treason, complicity, and surrender is translated by the other in more technical terms—lack of police force, absence of a policy of deterrence, inability or refusal to tackle the causes of delinquency. Shared by the two is a series of assertions indicating the shortcomings of the State concerning impotence of the police and the criminal justice system.

People in France seem to feel that the State is withdrawing from its role of protecting property. As the State disengages itself from its role of protector of private property, substitute methods for protecting possessions are devised. A system for financial compensation measures may be set up as well as alarm systems, door reinforcement devices, societies for the provision of surveillance, and, lastly, less sophisticated procedures which imply more personal involvement like training guard dogs. Self-defence—or at least the purchase of a gun—is an extreme in a wide panoply of measures taken by private persons to compensate for the State's withdrawal. The choice of one means or another is not simply happenstance; it reflects the social categories. Essentially, it involves small tradesmen and artisans. These occupations, including some who are retired, are represented in more than 70 percent of the incidents. And, tradesmen constitute the spearhead of local mobilisation movements favoring self-defence.

Of the range of means available for compensation or protection, none is a complete substitute for State protection. The various means chosen redefine the relationship of people to property. This is particularly evident in the case of insurance; which is quite different from a legal guarantee to have the stolen object restored and the criminal punished.

Between State protection and the substitutes for it, there are important rifts which have a bearing on the attitude to property, to life, and the relation between people and possessions. For tradesmen and artisans, a burglary concerns their shop or workshop, their stock or tools. The damage applies not only to their goods but to their means of production, which is regarded as an extension of their persons.

This argument may be extended to many other social groups in commerce, e.g., small agricultural cultivators and individuals who, though they may have left this domain, preserve the attitudes and values inherited from it. To explain the frequency with which shopkeepers are found to be self-defence perpetrators, other factors must be added. In the course of our investigations, we have noted that tradesmen, and particularly the perpetrators of self defence, frequently do not make use of the various technical means of protection offered commercially; and that, when they do, it is on the insistence of insurance companies. Recourse to the gun as the assured means of protection may be explained by the fact that the place of work is not distinctly separated in their minds from the home, from the family and dependents.

We have emphasized the aspect of protest against the State which fundamentally underlies the practice and ideology of self-defence. In my opinion, the perpetrator aims, at the same time, to punish the State and to correct the young offender, the correction being intended in some way to serve as a warning to the public authorities. This duality of purpose suggests that small tradesmen feel themselves robbed equally by the State and by the burglars, that the complicity between the two is a result not only of the slackness of magistrates, but also of the far greater dangers which the shop incurs because of the State.

Anti-statism among small tradesmen is very evident in French society. It has given birth to a social movement more or less peculiar to France, *Poujadism,* so called from the name of its first leader who effectively mobilised tradesmen and artisans against the State (Hofmann, 1956). The primary target of Poujadist demonstrations remains the State, even if, more recently, the demonstrators have turned their attention to large commercial enterprises. Susan Berger has shown clearly in how great measure this revolt of small tradesmen was linked with the State, in the same way as she has underlined the eminently defensive character of the claims they put forward (Berger, 1977).

Self-defence has many things in common with Poujadism: First of all, explicit links, since the Comité Interprofessionel de Défense de l'Union Nationale des Travailleurs Indépendants (the organisation which came from the movement) on several occasions intervened in local incidents in support of the perpetrator who had been charged. In addition, Gerard Nicoud, the present leader of the movement, adopted the word "self-defence" to describe a new form of action, "the brigades of fiscal self-defence," whose aim was to protect tradesmen from tax agents. But it is, above all, by its image that self-defence enters into the changing creed of Poujadism. Besides the traits which we have noted above, the discussions of partisans of self-defence have their roots in traditional values which the Poujade movement has publicly taken up as its own: the apologia for work—and particularly manual work—as the only form of fulfillment for man, the promotion of honesty as the foundation of community life, defence of the family against all the threats deriving from moral laxity, and appeal to the authoritarianism of the State against politicians.

It may be understatement that self-defence is connected with Poujadism. They are both, as it were, limbs of the dying figure that is the small merchant class. While the one asserts, in an organised form, the politicoeconomic arguments of this social class, the other acclaims by desperate acts the state of crisis brought upon them by the feeling of exclusion from the social group. I have developed elsewhere the hypothesis that acts of self-defence are described in terms of Poujadism as the "suicide" of small tradesmen—they are radical forms of the assertion of a break with society (Du Long, 1981). It is a question of two manifestations of the same phenomenon, the crisis of the relationship with the State experienced by a social class whose existence is in particular danger.

This analysis enables us to explain the excessive anti-State feeling in self-defence. The perpetrators not only claim that the State should act as guarantor of property; they demand recovery of its former capacity to assure the survival of the small holding, that is, the State should be restored to its former position in society. But this analysis also takes into account the identity of the victims who fall under the bullets of the guns. I have stressed that it involves, in general, adolescents rather than adults, and amateurs rather than professionals, and, in most cases, locals rather than outsiders to the district. Interviews confirm that adolescents are incriminated simply because they are young, and not that this group contains juvenile delinquents. They are accused of things of which many adults habitually accuse the young, but most especially that, by their attitude, they do not hold in high enough esteem the value of property and work. It is frequently said of this attitude that it resembles racism. I think that it represents the desperate feeling of those witnessing the disintegration of a world of values on which they have built their lives. The young become concrete targets of the anger because they render this change particularly visible. As for the young delinquents themselves, they translate more precisely into real terms the upheaval of the idea of property, an idea which, up to now, has been a cornerstone of the economic existence of small property owners. The violence in acts of self-defence is, of course, directed primarily against the delinquents, but is aimed also more widely.

One may notice in this part of the analysis the specific tone of self-defence, which ascribes the phenomenon as peculiar to French society. In the same was as Poujadism constituted a social movement particular to this society, so self-defence in general, as seen in both discussion and practice, represents a phenomenon not easily comparable with any encountered elsewhere. Not that each of the single elements into which I have tried to break it down does not find its corresponding element in other societies, but the specific characteristic of self-defence as it operates in the French incidents is precisely to consolidate this ensemble of values and attitudes into a single system and to reconstitute them as the form of response to crisis of a particular social category—the small producer-tradesman.

COMMENT

I would like to conclude by trying to relate my analysis of this peculiarly French phenomenon to the wider sphere of research concerning aggression in technologically developed societies.

For this we must return to the principal determinant of self-defence, the modification of the relationship which links the State to society, and must apply it more generally. The withdrawal of the State is not seen merely from the viewpoint of the protection of property, it is a withdrawal which is general throughout the whole range of social relationships and, as a result, these relationships are seen in their violent reality. Without leaving the domain of self-defence, we see that the disappearance of the State brings adults and adolescents into a generation conflict which can no longer be resolved through a superior consensus of values. The code by which one was accustomed to assess the wrongdoing of adolescents and assume it as a normal phenomenon has become null and void because it was meticulously written into the old order that was based on the family and guaranteed by the State. We are left with but a gloomy prospect of aggression between groups which will be all the more inclined to resort to force in that it permits them to give expression to their feelings of exclusion in relation to society.

In extending this generalisation of self-defence to include the development of a form of aggressive relationship among social groups, a question arises. It pertains to the close association of the State with aggression which is seen at the time when a change occurs in the relations between State and society—and this is true not only of the French experience. I have just mentioned how the withdrawal of the State exposes the relations between social groups; and, in describing the relations of the local communities to self-defence, I stated that these societies had realised to what extent their existence depended on the capacity of the State to preserve the monopoly of the legitimate use of force. Around these two facts we find an important field of thought which can easily be related to the questions raised in the study of other forms of aggression. Should the State, being the authority responsible for punishment, be regarded as a system that contains the violence which is inherent in social relations? Or, on the contrary, should the increased aggressiveness among different groups be attributed to the changes which the State itself undergoes through its inability to control modern forms of aggression?

The form in which I have phrased the question presupposes that one is taking up again the question put by Engels (1957) in *Anti-Duhring* on the relationship between aggression and the State, but in order to develop it in all its aspects, and in particular by examining how, on all levels of society, aggressiveness is in part restrained by and in part directed against the apparatus which specialises in repression. For example, self-defence suggests in some way a confusion of the role of the family and the State in the exercise of force between parents and children. It would seem, therefore, a question of deciding what is the mechanism which brings about agreement to replace this aggressiveness by a superior social authority.

This way of looking at the problem presupposes that force is the primary expression of social relationship, which invites the sociologist to review his attitude when confronting this phenomenon. At one point in my survey, I proposed a reversal in the terms of the question of self-defence. I said that it was not the phenomenon itself that gave rise to the problem but, on the contrary, the fact that it did not happen more often. In similar fashion, I indicated that aggression was the normal form of relationship between adults and children in certain social strata of French society. This inversion of the question, which was imposed on me by the results of my investigation, could open the way to a more general manner of treating the problem of aggression. Instead of asking how it comes about, it could be regarded as the natural form of social relationship, at least in capitalist societies, and thus investigated in terms of the acceptable mechanisms seen controlling aggression and channelling it into legitimate forms of expression.

REFERENCES

Berger, S. D'une boutique à l'autre. *Comparative Politics,* 1977, 121-136.

DuLong, R. *Les régions, l'état et la société locale.* PUF, 1978.

DuLong, R. Sens et non-sens de l'autodefense. *Déviance et Société,* 1981, 5, 211-222.

Engels, H. Anti-Duhring. In *F. Engels Werbe.* Berlin: Dietz, 1957.

Hofmann, S. *La mouvement Poujade.* Paris: Cahier de la Foundation Nationale des Sciences Politique, 1956.

Hofmann, S. *A la rocherche de la France.* Paris: Ed du Seuil, 1963.

Laborit, H. *L'aggresive detournée.* Paris: Union Générale d'Edition, 1970.

Laborit, H. *L'homme et la ville.* Paris: Union Générale d'Edition, 1971.

Lorenz, K. *On aggression.* New York: Harcourt Brace Jovanovich, 1966.

7

Hawaii: Violence, A Preliminary Analysis

D. Caroline Blanchard
and
Robert J. Blanchard

An integrated view of violence in any culture must take into account a host of interacting variables. On the level of cultural analysis, the values placed on different manifestations of violence for individuals of differing ages, social strata, sex, and situation provide a framework
against which the acculturated individual presumably measures his own behaviors. However,
there is also an economic side to violence in which material gain may promote acts in defiance
of cultural norms; as well as a political aspect with violence as the agent of power; and, above
all, a psychological view in which violence occurs as the expression of strong emotional states.
If one adds to these the possibility of biological factors, such as hormonal or constitutional differences associated with sex, or ethnicity differences which may also influence the incidence of
violence, then it is clear that a definitive evaluation of violence in any multicultural setting is
almost impossible.

Hawaii is the exemplary multicultural and multiethnic locale. What follows will necessarily be a tentative and preliminary analysis of some of the factors influencing the manifestation
of violence here. Although this analysis makes no claim whatever to either closure or elegance,
it may be useful in at least outlining some of the questions to be asked in further—and, one
hopes, more penetrating—investigations of violence in this fascinating community.

HAWAII—A BRIEF CULTURAL HISTORY

In order to provide a brief framework for consideration of ethnic, economic, political, and social factors as they may influence violence in Hawaii, here is a thumbnail sketch of some aspects of Hawaiian history.

The Hawaiian Islands were settled, beginning about 1,500 years ago, by several waves of
migrants from islands in the South Pacific. There remains considerable disagreement concerning the dates and numbers of different cultures involved, but it seems clear that as population pressures increased within the islands, the social structure became solidified into a rigid
class system involving an elaborate *kapu* (taboo) system and very fixed relationships among individuals with reference to common obligations, duties, and responsibilities. One important
aspect of this set of societal relationships was the *Ohana*, a group usually based on kinship

159

whose members shared food and other necessities freely. The opposite aspect was that all members of the *Ohana* were under the obligation to work for the good of the group. Self-advancement on an individual basis was not only not encouraged, it was a positive danger to the well-being of the *Ohana*.

This notion of sharing, without individual ownership of resources, was to have an extremely strong impact on the development of Hawaii after its rediscovery by Western explorers. The kingdom of Hawaii was unified early in the nineteenth century, and rapidly became part of a trading circuit between the West and the Orient. As the influence of Western missionaries and traders grew, the King of Hawaii, Kamehameha III, was persuaded to take the unprecedented step of dividing the land of Hawaii. Up to that point, all land had belonged to the monarchy but was traditionally cultivated by *Ohana* groups whose right to the land was unquestioned so long as they could use it and fulfill their obligations to the king. Parcelling out of these lands in the "Great *Mahele*" (division), in 1854, provided large portions of land to the king personally, to the monarchy, to a few families of high ranking *alii* (nobility), but only the barest minimum, about one acre each, to the 80,000 or so commoners, who depended on it for survival.

Predictably, much of this land, now privately owned, was quickly sold to the foreign traders, who were especially interested in large acreages for cultivation. In 1891, the monarchy itself was overthrown in a bloodless but much resented revolution instigated by powerful sugar-cane plantation-owners who wished political affiliation with the United States in order to receive preferential treatment in sales of sugar. Thus, although some few *alii* families had come through the nineteenth century with land and prestige more or less intact, the vast majority of native Hawaiians had gone from a position of great attachment to particular portions of land, cultivated and cherished by an *Ohana* group, to brief ownership of much smaller parcels. Most of these were quickly sold because the new owners had only a poor conception of the ownership of land, and because the smaller parcels were economically nonviable as farming units. As a result, most native Hawaiians found themselves dispossessed, while the political, economic, and social life of the islands was dominated by Caucasians.

A further focus of discontent for Hawaiians of Polynesian ancestry was provided in the famous Massie case, in 1931, in which the young Caucasian wife of a navy officer claimed to have been raped by a group of Hawaiians. Due to weaknesses in her story, the men were eventually released, but one of them was later kidnapped and fatally shot in an attempt by Mrs. Massie's socially prominent American mother to force a confession. The important aspect of this case to many Hawaiians of Polynesian ancestry is that Mrs. Massie's mother was not prosecuted, despite the fact that the killing undoubtedly took place while she and a companion were in the midst of a felony act, abduction.

During recent years, pure Hawaiians have almost disappeared, due to heavy intermarriage with other ethnic groups. However, part-Hawaiians have steadily increased, at a much higher rate than Caucasians, Japanese, or Chinese; and now constitute the third-most populous ethnic group in the islands. It is a testimony to the power of Hawaiian culture that many people with only one-fourth or less Hawaiian blood identify themselves consistently as Hawaiian. In some cases, there are material advantages such as a claim on Hawaiian homestead lands to foster this self-identification, but such advantages by no means account fully for the persistence of self-identification as Hawaiian for many individuals with only small proportions of Hawaiian ancestry.

Depending on whether the large military population is included, Caucasians are either roughly equal to Americans of Japanese ancestry in terms of population in Hawaii, or, are the largest single group. Although many *haoles* now resident in the islands can claim descent from the Caucasian traders, whalers, and missionaries who so greatly influenced the history of Hawaii in the nineteenth century, most Caucasians here are relative newcomers, due to heavy migration from the mainland United States since statehood was attained in 1959. Much of Hawaii's economy continues to be controlled by businesses and firms identified with Caucasians, but both "old money" and "new money" are represented, with the latter largely concentrated in the tourist industry. Moreover, this position of fiscal dominance is by no means as clear as in the past. The last ten years have seen massive investment by Japanese nationals and firms in the Islands' economy. On an individual basis, the per capita income of Caucasians ranks below Koreans and Chinese, and very close to Japanese, though still ahead of Hawaiians and recent immigrant groups. Income figures for Caucasians include a large proportion of low-income military personnel so this statistic is not terribly useful, but it does indicate that Caucasians are not an economically privileged group in Hawaii.

The Chinese, and later the Japanese, were first brought to Hawaii in the latter half of the nineteenth century (50,000 Chinese immigrants between 1850 and 1898; 180,000 Japanese between 1885 and 1907) to work on the sugar and pineapple plantations. Traditionally, Chinese workers left the fields as soon as possible, becoming merchants and independent businessmen. The Japanese immigrants stayed longer and, perhaps for that reason, were more favored by the important planters. At any rate, more of this group were brought to the Islands than were Chinese. Americans of Japanese Ancestry (AJA) are much more common than local Chinese.

After leaving the cane and pineapple fields, many second and third generation Japanese became teachers, civil servants, and skilled workers. After a brief threat during World War II, in which Hawaii's political future was much influenced by the refusal of the chief of police (later governor) John Burns to intern Americans of Japanese Ancestry, many of the AJAs served with distinction in the army, and returned to Hawaii to forge a political force in the Islands, which has continued to dominate Hawaii's politics until the present.

A few Koreans, about 7,000, arrived between 1903 and 1905. Though not numerous, they represent a highly-visible professional group in the islands.

Filipinos, like the Chinese, Japanese, and Koreans before them, came to Hawaii to work in the fields, this time beginning about 1910 and continuing for several decades. They continue to arrive in a steady stream; but, due in part to occupational requirements for immigrants, newer Filipinos are more likely to be professional people than unskilled workers. This is not an unmixed blessing. Physicians, dentists, and other professionals may not practice in Hawaii without undergoing strict relicensing procedures (even mainland dentists have filed discrimination suits with reference to ethnic bias in Hawaii's licensing examinations), and the number of professional-level Filipino immigrants who are unable to utilize their training is a continuing source of frustration.

In the past two decades, Samoans have also become a prominent feature of Hawaii's ethnic landscape. Most are recent immigrants, with only the children and sometimes young adults having been born here. Since there are no legal restrictions for immigrants from American Samoa, this group is in a somewhat different position than the continuing (but other than Filipinos relatively minor) influx from the Orient, in that sponsorship by residents of Hawaii is not required, nor are there applicable occupational restrictions. Additionally, American Samoa is not a high-technology area and the average education level is rather low. Thus, it might be expected that this immigrant group would have greater economic problems than most other recently arrived groups, and this in fact is true. Average income is lowest among Samoans, of all the groups surveyed in 1975 (Hawaii Department of Planning and Economic Development, 1976).

Another important aspect of an ethnic or cultural description of Hawaii is that there are several Hawaiian islands, with the other islands differing considerably from Oahu, with its major city of Honolulu. Oahu is not even the largest island, and its character is almost completely dominated by the urban and suburban sprawl of 700,000 Honolulu residents. In its central districts, Honolulu is a bustling, high-rise urban area with parking problems, in which rundown portions such as "Hotel Street" lie closely adjacent to multimillion dollar office buildings. The older residential areas contain gracious but somewhat decayed old houses, many of which are giving way to high-rise apartments. The more distant suburbs, built on virgin ground, are newer, but usually less "Hawaiian" in atmosphere, often housing large numbers of newcomers from the mainland, and giving much of the appearance and ambiance of a community in California.

As in other cities, the sense of "neighborhood" in Honolulu is very strong, and it is often clearly associated with a sense of ethnic identity as well. Although there has never been major legal or social sanctioning of discrimination in housing, self-segregation in the form of cultural preferences, age and stability of districts, and economic factors do have marked effects on the ethnic makeup of different areas of Honolulu. Thus, although part-Hawaiians live in every part of the city, they tend to cluster in two areas on Oahu, both semi-rural and located 20 miles or more from the city center. These places, Waimanalo and Nanakuli, are sites of Hawaiian homestead lands, made available to persons of qualifying Hawaiian ancestry by federal legislation. It probably goes without saying, however, that most of the descendants of *alii* families which kept much of their money and lands do not live on Hawaiian homestead lands; they live wherever they want to.

Other segregating factors include military status, with more military families and individuals (usually Caucasian or Black) living adjacent to the several large military bases, notably Pearl Harbor and Schofield; church identification, with many Samoans living near Laie, site of the headquarters of the Church of Latter Day Saints; and length of residence, with the tourist destination area of Waikiki almost exclusively Caucasian and of relatively recent arrival. In view of the great discrepancies in mean per capita income for different ethnicities, it is not surprising that economic factors influence ethnic distribution among districts. Most recent immigrant groups—including Samoans, the even newer Vietnamese, and Filipinos—plus economically disadvantaged older arrivals tend to cluster in relatively low-rent areas, while the most expensive districts house largely Caucasian, Chinese, and Japanese families. Honolulu, while it has been described as a "melting pot" in the sense of considerable sharing of cultural features, nevertheless is a city of economic, ethnic, and life-style contrasts, with different groups differing widely in the extent to which they are assimilated into either the local lifestyles, or to mainstream American life.

The city and county of Honolulu is a statistical unit, and figures to be given here for crime rates, etc. in "Honolulu" reflect both the city proper and some outlying areas. It is, however, a predominantly urban area, with a higher proportion of newcomers than are to be found in the outer islands. These outer islands, consisting of Hawaii, Maui, and Kauai counties, are very rural. The outer-island population consists almost exclusively of long-term residents, though small but highly publicized groups described as "hippies" were to be found, especially on Maui and Kauai, during the decade of the seventies. The ethnic mix is also different, with fewer Caucasians and almost no Samoans, Vietnamese, or recent immigrants. Japanese and Hawaiians are the dominant groups in almost all areas of the outer islands except for those localities in which recent developments in tourism have attracted a large number of persons—usually mainland Caucasians—in the tourist industry. Certainly, the dominant political force on the outer islands is a conservative "local" blend, made up of coalitions involving descendents of the early plantation workers—notably Japanese, but also including Portuguese who were brought to the plantations to serve as *lunas* or overseers of the oriental work force, and quite a few Filipinos.

Another set of forces which undoubtedly influence the incidence of crime in general, and violence and aggression more specifically, are economic. Since Hawaii became a state in 1959, economic growth has been generally spectacular, due largely to increased tourism but also reflecting a continued substantial military presence. Sugar cane and pineapple continued to provide a major portion of Hawaii's economy, but these did not expand at the rate of tourism or military expenditures. Efforts to diversify this economic emphasis involved attraction of multinational firms to Hawaii, an effort which has met with varied success.

However, the overall growth of the Hawaiian economy—in the past ten years especially—has not extended to individual betterment for the average worker. For one thing, tourism is a labor-intensive industry, but the average wage of tourism workers is relatively low. This is true also, in general, of agricultural workers. Finally, although military expenditures here have continued to be high, they do not produce jobs for local workers in the same proportions as do the other major industries. All of these act to keep wages low in Hawaii, although employment (at least in Honolulu) has usually been relatively high. In the last year or so, however, recession on the mainland and sharp increases in the cost of transportation have combined to produce a sharp drop in tourism, resulting in widespread worry and some loss of jobs in this important segment of Hawaiian economy.

The other side of the coin is that prices in Hawaii have always been high (Hawaii Department of Planning and Economic Development, 1967-1979). Food prices are consistently about 20 percent higher than on the mainland; and, while clothing is perhaps less expensive, due to the climate, two big-ticket items have consistently boosted basic living costs far above those in most of the rest of the United States. First, and most important, housing costs are so much higher. The average single-family house on the market in Honolulu in mid-1980 was priced at about $230,000; condominiums averaged over $120,000 (Honolulu Board of Realtors, 1980), that most families cannot afford to buy their own home without at least two incomes. Even when both husband and wife work, only about 50 percent of families can afford to buy housing. This situation would be problematic enough if housing prices were relatively consistent, although very high. However, they have risen so much faster than incomes, or even than other cost-of-living items, in the last 10 years, that this one item alone contributes enormously to the gap between a more affluent, home-owning group, and the other half, which could never afford to buy housing. Perhaps the major impact of this problem has fallen on the native Hawaiians and part-Hawaiians, who see others becoming wealthy on properties which once belonged, however briefly, to their families. Although Hawaiian homestead lands are designed to remedy this historic unfairness, the HHL is by no means filling the need. Many qualified families have been on the waiting list for years.

The other group which suffers because of this disproportionate housing cost increase is the newcomers. Those professional-level people who move to Hawaii because of employment opportunities cannot be said to suffer greatly, although they must often scramble to purchase housing and/or buy less than they had expected. However, the less affluent discover that rental costs are more than can be comfortably paid, and the level of accommodation much less than expected. In many cases, the situation is little short of desperate, and low-income renters often are forced to move from place to place as each (marginal) housing unit is torn down to make way for more expensive housing, or converted to other use.

The other big-ticket item, causing substantial dislocations for those families involved, is private schooling for children. For a number of reasons, some of which will be discussed later, proportionately more parents in Hawaii than in any other state in the Union, send their children to private school. Private school fees are not unreasonable, ranging from less than $1,000 to about $3,000 per year, but they are a consistent drain on family finances. Many working mothers make a direct connection between housing or school costs on the one hand, and their own decisions to work: "I'm working to send my kids to private school." Or, "I'm working so that we can afford this house" (or, "to be able to buy a house").

Housing and school costs are not only a major reason for the fact that over 50 percent of married women in Hawaii do work (the highest rate of any state, except Alaska), but these also constitute a very visible difference among specific families, a readily available means of assessing status, and a readily available source of resentment among those who cannot afford the cost. There may be reasons to suspect that these two items, one's home and one's children, are among the most sensitive topics in every culture. It is not surprising that people who feel they are being denied important advantages in these areas while others have them may be very angry about it.

The general economic picture for families and individuals in Hawaii may perhaps be best seen in comparison of pay and cost of living trends over the past five years. Relative to incomes of workers on the mainland, Hawaii's per capita income has steadily fallen from a high of 114 percent in 1975, to 104 percent in 1979 (Hawaii Department of Planning and Economic Development, 1967–79). During the same time, the relative cost-of-living has risen slightly to the present 131 percent of mainland costs. This trend is not just a little statistical sleight-of-hand. People in the Islands have been very cognizant indeed that the economic quality of life has deteriorated during this time frame. And this, perhaps, is the important factor. People tend to accommodate to any sort of relatively tolerable steady-state situation. However, the situation has not been stable in recent years. It has steadily gotten worse. This does not mean that people in Hawaii are destitute or living in direst poverty. Most people continue to lead a relatively comfortable life. However, aspirations have been changing, people are being forced to accommodate themselves to reduced buying power and often to simply do without items or activities which they had previously enjoyed and expected. Such accommodation is painful, and may contribute directly to frustration-based angers, and also to acts of violence based on expectation of material gain.

A final item of interest in this brief sketch of recent events in Hawaii is the short-term change in tourism patterns. Until the late sixties, almost all tourists to Hawaii came primarily to Oahu, and specifically to Waikiki. Since Waikiki was a tourist destination pure and simple, with very little in the way of other business activities, it was a place where the average tourist came into contact only with other visitors to the islands, or with local people who were there specifically as part of the visitor industry. When tourists did get outside Waikiki, something that many of them never managed to do at all, they still tended to go to places where they were welcomed for their contribution to the economy, such as cultural centers or shopping plazas.

In the late 1970s, however, an upsurge of tourism to the outer islands, particularly to resorts on Maui and to state and national parks on all the outer islands, began to bring these vacationers into more direct contact with the local populations there. On Oahu also, a trend toward independent travel not associated with tours resulted in larger numbers of visitors getting off the beaten track and away from areas in which tourism is the major employment of those whom they were likely to encounter. It is notable that visitors from Japan, although constituting almost one-quarter of all visitors during recent years, very seldom travel independently.

No one has attempted a specific analysis of the effects of this relatively new, widespread interaction of tourists and locals. Hawaii is famous for the hospitality of its people toward visitors, and experienced travelers continue to give high marks for courtesy and friendliness of Hawaiian residents. However, potential for confrontation and insult is a very real part of these meetings. As one, very mild, example, a friend of the author, a psychologist of Japanese descent, in his thirties, was recently approached in Waikiki by an elderly woman, obviously from the American mainland, who carefully inquired as to whether he could speak English, then asked him for directions. After he directed her to her destination, she rewarded him with thanks and a small tip. He was amused, but not everyone in his position would have been. References to Hawaii as different from "the States" are common, and commonly resented. Pejorative ethnic epithets such as "Chink" or "Jap" are virtually never used by Hawaii residents and are bitterly resented when they are heard, even by those of different extraction. Newcomers to the Islands usually have the tact to avoid such terms, but offenders—most of whom do not recognize the depth of insult they are offering—are naturally more common among recent arrivals such as tourists and the military, than among established residents.

This brief description of some important aspects of the history, economics, and geography of Hawaii provides just a bit of the information needed for analysis of recent changes in violence among Island populations. The measures of violence which we will examine include, first, statistics on violent crime; second, the results of a recent study of violence and vandalism in Hawaii's public schools; and, finally, results of a questionnaire designed to provide data on familial and nonfamilial violence which may be compared to similar results from both the mainland United States and from Japan.

HAWAII CRIME STATISTICS

Figure 7.1 presents rates for murder, forcible rape, robbery, and aggravated assault in Hawaii between 1975 and 1979 (Hawaii Criminal Justice Statistical Analysis Center, 1981). These four crimes all involve either damage to or severe threat of damage to another person and are combined as "violent crimes" for comparison with a group of selected "nonviolent crimes" in statistics published by the State of Hawaii and other sources. However, it is obvious that the four are a rather heterogeneous lot: Robbery is distinguished by the economic gain factor, rape involves a clearly sexual element, while murder is a crime involving many different motives. Aggravated assault is perhaps the most "pure" of these crimes, in the sense that material gain and sexual motives are minimally involved. As a preliminary speculation, it seems sensible to assume that most murders are linked to either the factors which are also involved in aggravated assault (anger, jealousy, desire for revenge) or to some type of profit motive (organized crime, murder incidental to robbery, etc.).

In this admittedly speculative context, it is interesting to note that the rates of change in the four crime categories over this five-year period are very different. Robbery showed a dramatic increase of over 50 percent in the last two years, while forcible rape went up about 37 percent with this increase almost totally confined to the last year of the period. In contrast, neither murder nor aggravated assault showed any dramatic rate increase, although aggravated assault did rise about 18 percent over the five-year period.

Statistics for all of 1980 are not yet available, but figures for the first nine months of 1980 may be used to assess the most recent trends for violent crime. For the first nine months of 1980, in comparison with the same period in 1979, murder rates rose 33.96 percent; forcible rape, 26.11 percent; robbery, 10.61 percent; and aggravated assault, 5.63 percent. Thus, these figures suggest a continuing, but somewhat slower rise in the extremely high rates of robbery, continued acceleration of rape cases, and continued slow increases in the rates of aggravated assault. Murder is the only crime category to show a change from the pattern established earlier, with a sudden increase during the first months of 1980.

Perhaps the first comparison that should be made of these figures is with crime rates for the United States as a whole. Table 7.1 presents rates per 100,000 population for the four violent crimes and for a selected group of nonviolent crimes, for Hawaii and for the entire United States, in 1975 (Hawaii Criminal Justice Statistical Analysis Center, 1981).

This comparison is particularly interesting because the trend it illustrates is so clear. In all categories of violent crime, Hawaii is consistently lower than the U.S. average. The discrepancy is least for rape, but very marked for aggravated assault, which is only about one-quarter as

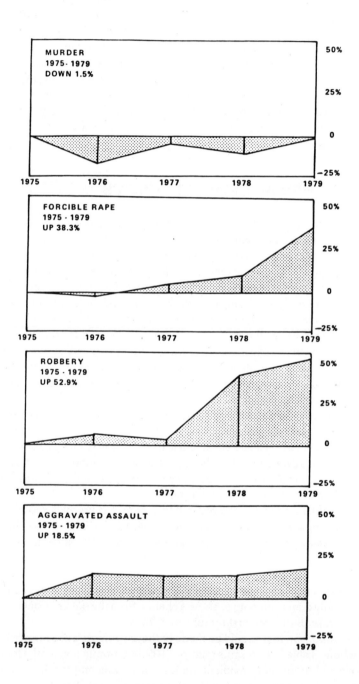

Fig. 7.1. Change in Rates of Four Crimes of Violence in Hawaii, 1975-1979.

Source: Hawaii Criminal Justice Statistical Analysis Center, 1981.

**Table 7.1. Rates of Violent and Nonviolent Crimes in Hawaii
and in the Total United States in 1975**

	RATES PER 100,000 POPULATION		
	HAWAII	U.S.	HAWAII/U.S.
Violent Crimes			
Murder	7.8	9.6	.81
Rape	24.7	26.3	.97
Aggravated assault	58.3	227.4	.26
Robbery	126.6	218.2	.58
Nonviolent Crimes			
Larceny-theft	3454	2805	1.23
Burglary	1827	1526	1.20
Motor vehicle theft	524	69	1.12

Source: Hawaii Criminal Justice Statistical Analysis Center, 1981.

high as for the U.S. average. When nonviolent crimes are compared, however, all categories show higher rates than the U.S. average, though none of them are startlingly higher. Nothing in the Hawaii trends visible in the five years after 1975 changes this picture, with the possible exception of rape. Rape increases in 1979 and 1980 may mean that rape rates in Hawaii are about the same, or possibly somewhat higher than on the mainland. Other than than, the general comparison continues to show lower rates of violent crime and slightly higher rates for nonviolent crime. Even the dramatic rise in robbery was not enough to bring it up to mainland levels.

One obvious potential factor in the different rates of violent and nonviolent crime for Hawaii as compared to the mainland is ethnicity. Table 7.2 presents the proportions of Hawaii residents in different ethnic categories, and proportions of persons arrested for different crime categories by ethnicity in 1979 (Hawaii Criminal Justice Statistical Analysis Center, 1981). As this table indicates, there are in general close relationships between the proportionate repre-

**Table 7.2. Ethnic Status of Hawaii Residents and of Persons Arrested
for Violent and Nonviolent Crimes in 1979**

		ADULT ARRESTS		
	% IN POPULATION	NONVIOLENT CRIMES*	ROBBERY	OTHER VIOLENT CRIMES
Caucasian	26.9	40.99	45.42	33.52
Black	1.1	4.24	6.73	8.71
Chinese	4.2	3.65	3.31	0.62
Japanese	25.2	7.26	8.89	5.69
Filipino	9.7	9.25	10.23	13.67
Samoan	.9	4.58	17.76	7.97
Korean	1.1	1.71	.42	2.36
Hawaiian/Part Hawaiian	18.7	19.66	28.65	14.85
Other	11.2	8.63	11.90	11.98

*Nonviolent crimes include burglary, larceny/theft, and motor vehicle theft.
Source: Hawaii Criminal Justice Statistical Analysis Center, 1981.

sentations of each ethnic group across the different crime categories. Thus, Caucasians tend to be somewhat overrepresented among those arrested. Blacks are severely overrepresented in each of these categories, and Samoans are even more strikingly overrepresented, while Chinese and especially Japanese are very much underrepresented. Filipinos, Hawaiians, and the "Other" category come in at rates close to their representation in the population, while Koreans alone show some inconsistency, with higher rates than warranted by their numbers, except for robbery which is lower.

Despite this very wide variation in crime rates for different ethnicities, it remains possible that there is also an effect of living in Hawaii—that is, that crime rates are lower for violent crime here not because the lower crime rates of specific ethnic groups tend to depress these overall statistics, but because there is something in the cultural make-up of Hawaii that tends to inhibit criminal activity. It is rather difficult to adequately evaluate a possibility with so many variables involved, but one way (admittedly not perfect) is to use violent and nonviolent crime figures for those groups which make up the overwhelming majority of the population on the U.S. mainland, and attempt to estimate what the Hawaiian crime rate would be if these groups, Caucasian and Black, were present in Hawaii in the same proportions.

This may be done by multiplying rates for each crime category by the overrepresentation of each of these groups (for each of them was overrepresented) among those arrested for crimes of that type, with this overrepresentation figure adjusted to fit the desired proportions of these two groups in the population. Thus, to take robbery as an example, Caucasians were overrepresented by 53 percent among those arrested for robbery, while Blacks were overrepresented by 512 percent. For a population consisting of 85 percent Caucasians and 15 percent Blacks, the robbery rate should be expanded by 135 percent, which would give a rate per 100,000 population of 297.5, which is 36 percent higher than the rate on the mainland. For other violent crimes, this procedure suggests that Hawaii's rate would be about 150 percent of the mainland rate (i.e., 50 percent higher), while the nonviolent crimes involving material gain (larceny/theft, burglary, and motor vehicle theft) would be nearly doubled in rate.

It should be admitted that this is not a perfect procedure. Since the ethnic status of all perpetrators in Hawaii is not known, these over- (or under-) representation rates can only be estimated from arrests. It is possible, for example, that Blacks, who are relatively uncommon in Hawaii, are identified by victims and arrested with greater ease than are individuals who "blend in" more easily. The same could be said of Caucasians; however, the opposite assumption might be made on the basis that "all Caucasians look alike" so that witness identification is more difficult to obtain for them, or for Blacks, than for locals: There is, in fact, no reason to suspect differential ethnic arrest rates as opposed to perpetration rates for the same crimes, but it should be noted that the first is here being used to estimate the second. A second problem with this procedure is that many of the Caucasians and, especially, Blacks, are young enlisted men in the military. Males between 18 and 30 have a much higher felony rate than women, or younger or older men, so their overrepresentation in crime arrests may reflect the peculiarities of Hawaii's age-sex pyramids for these two groups.

At any rate, these figures suggest that Caucasians and Blacks in Hawaii commit crimes at a rate at least equivalent to, and often considerably higher than, the rates they achieve on the mainland. This, in turn, suggests that the lower crime rates in Hawaii for violent crime basically reflect the relative nonparticipation in violent crime of some of the ethnic groups constituting a large proportion of Hawaii's population. Although Chinese contribute to this reduction, especially in the area of violent crimes other than robbery, examination of table 7.2 quickly suggests that the major reason is the extreme underrepresentation of the Japanese, whose numbers in all of these categories are only about one-quarter of what would be expected from their representation in the population.

Thus, it appears that ethnic differences have an enormous effect on crime rates of persons living in Hawaii. The next, and very intriguing, question is how? It is clear to those of us who live in Hawaii that the different ethnic groups here do maintain their cultural identities to a very striking degree. Before attempting to analyze these cultural differences, however, it might be well to start with some economic factors for these groups. The first graph in figure 7.2 represents proportional representation of the different ethnic groups in crimes of gain in 1979 plotted against the unemployment rates of these same ethnic groups in 1975 (Hawaii Department of Planning and Economic Development, 1980). Overall, the relationship is striking. There is a clear tendency for groups with higher rates of unemployment to be overrepresented among those arrested for crimes of gain. However, this relationship is equally apparent when the dependent variable is proportionate representation in crimes of violence, excluding robbery.

The second graph in figure 2 is especially interesting because the first graph, relating unemployment and crimes of gain, could so easily be interpreted as suggesting a very materialistic origin of the decision to commit economic crimes. "I am unemployed. I need money. Therefore I will rob/burglarize, steal, etc." Since the second graph specifically excludes robbery, leaving murder, rape, and aggravated assault as the violent crimes represented, it is clear that material gain was generally not an important direct consideration in the motivation of these crimes. Murder, perhaps, might have economic overtones in some cases, but murders represented only a small proportion of these crimes, and economically motivated murders must have been rarer still. Yet the relationship between unemployment and crimes without direct economic gain is at least as striking as the relationship between unemployment and crimes with direct economic gain.

There are two major interpretations of such a relationship, and each may contain some truth. The first hypothesis is that of a fairly direct relationship of unemployment to crime, in that the social satisfaction of an ethnic group—its feeling of competence, acceptance, and worth—may be tied to a host of economic indices, one of which is the rate of employment (and conversely, unemployment). The second hypothesis, probably not mutually exclusive of the first, is that the social acceptability of any group in a multiethnic culture is based in large part upon society's view of that group as law-abiding and trustworthy. When this view dips toward the negative pole and members of that group are regarded as law-breakers, untrustworthy, violent, and so on, then members of that group will have proportionately greater difficulties in finding jobs in that culture. This hypothesis suggests a relationship opposite to that of the first hypothesis, with crime rates acting back to determine employment rates for the different ethnicities.

Another potentially important determinant of rates of various types of crime in Hawaii is the urban/rural makeup of the state. Table 7.3 presents comparative population and crime rates for the city and county of Honolulu, and for the remaining three counties, each of which is a rural district on one or more outer islands (Hawaii Criminal Justice Statistical Analysis Center, 1980). These figures, for the first nine months of 1980, suggest that there is a considerable difference in the type of crime committed on the rural islands as opposed to Honolulu. For the island of Hawaii, both murder and aggravated assault are about twice the Honolulu rate, and aggravated assault is over twice the Honolulu rate in both Maui and Kauai counties. Only for murder, in Kauai, was the rate less than in Honolulu; and this particular figure, based on one murder during that period, is notably less than for equivalent periods in the past.

Rape was somewhat lower, proportionately, on the island of Hawaii than on Oahu. Rates on the other two islands were very close to what would be expected on a population basis. Since many of the rape cases reported involve female tourists, the lesser concentration of visitors to Hawaii may account for part of this difference. Maui, like Oahu, is a prime tourist destina-

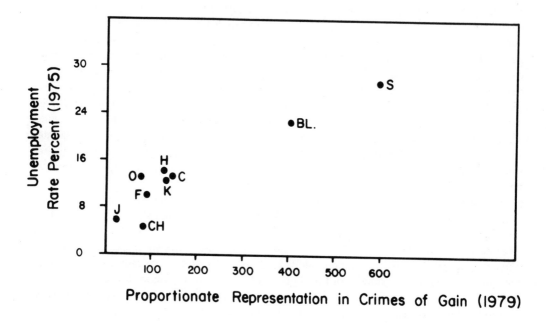

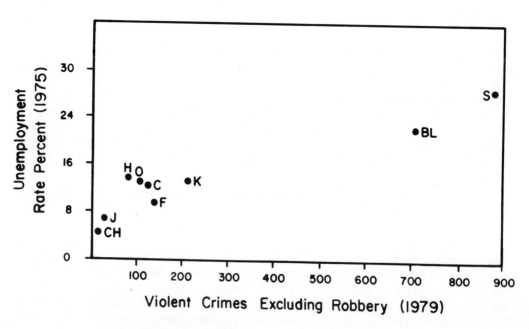

Fig. 7.2 Arrests in 1979 Plotted by Unemployment Rates.

Source: Hawaii Department of Planning and Economic Development, State of Hawaii Data Book, 1980.

Table 7.3. Comparative Population and Crime Rates for Honolulu and Outer Islands

	CITY & COUNTY OF HONOLULU	HAWAII COUNTY	MAUI COUNTY	KAUAI COUNTY
Resident Population	729,100	83,700	65,500	36,400
as % Honolulu	100%	11.48%	8.98%	4.99%
Violent Crimes as % Honolulu				
Murder	100% (54)	20.37%	9.26%	1.85%
Aggravated Assault	100% (315)	25.08%	20.95%	14.92%
Rape	100% (206)	7.77%	9.22%	7.28%
Robbery	100% (1,370)	3.21%	2.34%	.95%
Nonviolent Crimes				
Burglary	100% (10,245)	11.34%	12.36%	5.63%
Larceny-theft	100% (27,825)	8.95%	12.28%	4.82%
Motor Vehicle Theft	100% (4,166)	3.58%	5.88%	2.66%

tion, while Kauai, although it is not quite so marked as a destination area, has been noted for a tendency to attract young campers and hikers, and also "hippies." These people get off the beaten track, and are thus more vulnerable to potential assailants, which may account for the somewhat higher rape (and aggravated assault) rates there.

In notable contrast, robbery rates on all of the outer islands are strikingly lower than on Oahu. Since the outer islands tend to have unemployment rates at least as high as those on Oahu, this discrepancy is rather unexpected. However, burglary and larceny/theft rates are not lower, suggesting that economically motivated crime is as much a feature of life in the outer islands as on Oahu. The consistently lower robbery rates may perhaps reflect an element of rationality on the part of potential perpetrators. Robbery necessarily involves coming face to face with the victim; and, in a rural setting where people are individually more familiar with each other than in a large city, this tactic appears likely to lead to higher risk of identification of the criminal. This interpretation is supported by the figures on motor vehicle theft, which are also consistently lower on the outer islands. A stolen automobile is much more likely to be identified in an area in which people know each other's cars.

Comparison of figures from Oahu to the outer islands should be examined in terms of the notable demographic differences between these units: Oahu contains most of the newcomers to Hawaii, including recent arrivals from the mainland, military personnel, and immigrants from abroad. This is a very mixed group of individuals; but, on the whole, it might be expected that many of them would fit into the high-risk categories for crimes of violence. Thus, military are almost exclusively Caucasian or Black (both high risk ethnicities), and a disproportionate number are males between 18 and 30, which is again a high risk factor. Recent immigrants from abroad include Samoans (a very high risk group), plus others such as Filipinos, Vietnamese, and a continuing trickle from other countries, for which an average risk factor might be estimated. Recent nonmilitary arrivals from the mainland are predominantly professional-level individuals and probably fairly low-risk for crimes of violence. However, in terms of overall incomes, ethnicity, and possible "acculturation" problems, one might expect the newcomers as a group to push per capita violent crime statistics higher on Oahu.

The surprising thing is that this difference does not appear. With the exception of robbery and motor vehicle theft, which have already been briefly discussed, the outer islands' major crime rates are either equivalent to, or higher than, those on Oahu. Murder and aggravated assault are particularly high, especially on Hawaii and Maui. Two factors appear to be at least partly responsible for these rates; organized crime and other illegal activity, and relative economic depression.

Some portion of the murder rate difference between Oahu and the rural islands is due to organized crime. Before 1975, only 1 of the 42 murders attributable to organized crime occurred on the outer islands; from 1975 to 1977, 7 of the 18 organized crime killings were these outer islands (Hawaii Department of Planning and Economic Development, "Data Book," 1980). It is difficult to adequately analyze the factors leading to this partial change of locale for organized crime operations, but certainly the rise of *pakalolo* (marijuana) as an important cash crop on these islands may be a factor. *Pakalolo* is grown on all the islands. However, the island of Hawaii, because of its less stable economic base (nearly 19 percent of the population was located below the poverty line in 1974–75, in contrast to less than 12 percent for the other counties, (Hawaii Department of Planning and Economic Development, "Data Book," 1980) probably depends more on this crop. Certainly, the inevitable disputes and confrontations arising from a lucrative but illegal enterprise are most noticeable on Hawaii, though parts of Oahu share the same scenario.

Further insight into the dynamics of violence in Hawaii may be gained through analysis of the victims of violence here. Published descriptions of victims are not available for all violent crime. However, ethnic and age data have been published for murder victims in 1978 and 1979. Table 7.4 presents ethnic backgrounds for these victims.

Comparison of these figures with those in table 7.2, giving ethnic makeup of the population of Hawaii, suggests that Caucasians, Blacks, Samoans, and to some degree Chinese are overrepresented. For the first three of these categories, the overrepresentation among murder victims is very much in line with the overrepresentation of the same groups in arrests for crimes of violence. Chinese, however, tend to be somewhat underrepresented in arrests for crimes of violence. On the other hand, Japanese are somewhat underrepresented as murder victims, just as they had been underrepresented as arrestees. Hawaiians and part-Hawaiians and Koreans were represented in direct proportion to their relative numbers in the population. The only categories for which representation as victim was lower than representation as perpetrators of the violent crime were Filipinos and the "Other" category.

These statistics comparing arrest and victim rates for different ethnicities should be qualified slightly for Caucasians, in that at least some of the murder victims were visitors to the islands, and vacationers in Hawaii are largely from the U.S. mainland and mostly Caucasian. On any average day in Hawaii, about 11 percent of the persons actually present are visitors, so

Table 7.4. Ethnic Status of Murder Victims in Hawaii

	1978 (N = 60) %	1979 (N = 66) %	AVERAGE %
Ethnicity			
Caucasian	46.7	33.0	39.85
Hawaiian or Part Hawaiian	11.7	29.0	20.35
Japanese	11.7	12.0	11.85
Filipino	8.3	4.5	6.4
"Other"	8.3	4.5	6.4
Chinese	5.0	7.6	6.3
Samoan	5.0	3.1	4.0
Black	3.3	3.1	3.2
Korean	0	3.1	1.5

Source: Hawaii Criminal Justice Statistical Analysis Center, 1981.

the representation of murder victims should be adjusted to reflect the 8 percent or so more Caucasians present, given an overrepresentation of only about 14 percent, based on 29.9 percent resident Caucasians plus 8 percent visitors. Japanese visitors account for about 2 percent of the population at any particular time, and adding this figure in only increases the under-representation of Japanese ethnics among murder victims. A breakdown of murders and victims by tourist status is not actually available, so the decision to include tourists' ethnicity figures in analyses of proportionate representation of murder victims but not of perpetrators is based on the author's impression (arising from careful attention to reports of violence in the newspapers over a long period) that visitors are not infrequently the victims of violent crime, but they are seldom the perpetrators.

At any rate, comparison of perpetrator/victim proportions for different ethnic groups strongly suggests a close relationship of the two. Those groups which engage most actively in crimes of violence also provide a disproportionate number of victims, at least as far as murder is concerned. With the sole exception of the Chinese, those groups which are underrepresented as perpetrators are also underrepresented as victims. It is tempting to speculate that the slight overrepresentation of Chinese victims is related to their frequent status as proprietors of small businesses such as restaurants, which are very vulnerable to armed robbery.

In summary, statistics on crime in Hawaii pinpoint several ethnic groups, notably Samoans, Blacks, and Caucasians, as high-risk potential perpetrators. These same statistics suggest that both crimes of direct economic motive (robbery, burglary, larceny-theft, motor vehicle theft) and "crimes of passion" (murder, aggravated assault, rape) are closely related to a factor or factors associated with high unemployment rates. Certain patterns of different crime rates for Oahu versus the outer islands have also been explored.

VIOLENCE IN THE PUBLIC SCHOOLS

A second source of evaluation of these relationships, and additional information on violence in Hawaii, may be found in analysis of violence in the public schools. Like many systems on the mainland, Hawaii's public school system has been involved for many years in a controversy concerning the quality of education and the safety provided for students. This controversy has increased over the past ten years, and the proportion of students attending private schools has risen during the same period. "Violence and Vandalism in the Public Schools, a Report to the Hawaii State Legislature" recently (Hawaii Commission on Crime, 1980) summarized the results of a large-scale survey of public school administrators, teachers, and students.

This report suggests that the public's concern over violence in the schools is well-founded. Of 2,056 teachers responding to this survey, only 13 percent felt that violence and disruptive behavior of students had no effect on the quality of education at their school; 53 percent indicated a "moderately negative effect"; with 31.6 percent selecting a "serious" or a "very serious" effect on the quality of education. The proportion of teachers viewing the problem as either "serious" or "very serious" varied sharply from school to school, and in 8 of the schools surveyed (7 of them intermediate schools) 50 percent or more of teachers responding selected these categories.

It is clear that students share the teachers' concerns. A survey conducted for the Legislative Reference Bureau of Hawaii in 1976 questioned Oahu high school seniors. This study (reported in the "Violence and Vandalism" report) showed that "more than half the sample indicated that they personally worry about physical safety." In terms of ethnic factors in school violence, students were asked: "Do the students in your school who hassle you or "bully" other students tend to come from any particular ethnic group? If so, which ones?"

Of the 1139 respondents, 34.4 percent indicated that no group was more responsible, but of the 65.6 percent who did single out a group, the great majority selected either Samoans or Hawaiians as the bullies. The proportions selecting one or the other of these two groups differed from school to school. In an "urban high status" school and in a "suburban" school, 57.0 percent and 42.8 percent of the total respondents, respectively, indicated that Hawaiian students were the troublemakers. Samoans were selected by 23.6 percent and 24.9 percent of respondents in the two schools. In an "urban cosmopolitan" school, these proportions were reversed, with 52.8 percent singling out Samoans, and 20.4 percent accusing Hawaiians. In a rural school, about 25 percent of respondents selected each group. The only other ethnic group coming close to this percentage was "Filipino immigrant" with 17.3 percent in the "urban cosmopolitan" school.

With a sample of only four schools, these figures may not generalize. However, it is striking that both schools selecting Hawaiians as major perpetrators of violence appeared to serve higher income areas. Since Samoans tend to have quite low income levels, and to cluster in two or three major low-rent areas of Oahu, it is unlikely that either of these schools had many Samoan students. In the "urban cosmopolitan" school, where Samoans are probably more frequent, they were the group selected. Thus, school violence surveys agree with crime rate statistics in suggesting a high rate of participation of Samoans in violence.

Two other factors are notable, however. One is that Black students were *not* selected as "bullies." Interpretations of this finding may go in two rather different directions. First, although Blacks and Samoans are roughly equal in total numbers in the state (about 1 percent for each), they are very differently represented in the public school system, with only 835 Black students as opposed to 2,582 Samoans (1978-79). This difference reflects Black participation among enlisted military, with the few Black families frequently clustered near military bases. This demographic breakdown suggests that very, very few Black students go to public schools in nonmilitary areas. Thus, they are unlikely to be regarded as a major source of hassles for other students.

The second possibility is that there is a genuine difference between the participation in violent activities of Black children as opposed to Black adults. Demographic analysis also suggests that this may be true. As with any other group except Hawaiians, there is a potentially very important distinction to be made between "locals" and "newcomers." The newcomers—in fact, almost transients—among the Black population are usually military, especially young enlisted men. Age, sex, income levels, and the antagonism which fairly frequently erupts between local youths and the military contribute to the high risk status of this group. Although professional-level Blacks do contribute to both military and civilian immigration from the mainland, these new higher income individuals are probably a great deal less common than the low-income and frequently poorly educated Blacks in enlisted ranks.

In contrast, there is a small but stable Black population which has lived in the islands for years. These people tend to be well-educated professionals, well-integrated into the community, and enjoying a life style which appears to be very similar to that of other mainstream and middle or upper middle class groups. If income and education are major factors in violence, it is to be expected that the children of these families would not contribute disproportionately to rates of violence in schools. Thus, the lack of peer evaluation of Blacks as "bullies," in contrast to high risk for adult Blacks in crimes of violence, is very compatible with demographic data suggesting that Black school children in Hawaii, and Black adults, may be rather different cultural groups.

Young Hawaiians and adult Hawaiians obviously do not come from different populations. However, the school data and adult data on violence are again very different, with adult Hawaiians participating at levels very proportionate to their numbers, while school children are singled out by their peers as especially troublesome. To anyone who has lived in Hawaii for some time, these data are not a big surprise. The major difference between youthful and adult violence among Hawaiians is probably a cultural pattern which involves much freedom for youth to "sow their wild oats" early, then settle down to a much more stable and hard-working existence later on. Hawaiian girls, for example, tend to bear their first child at a considerably earlier age than Caucasians or Orientals (Hawaii Department of Health, 1980). Similarly, there appears to be greater acceptance of drinking, drug-use, and violence among children in their middle teens. It is not that any of these activities are necessarily condoned, but the Hawaiian teenager is aware that he or she will not be totally rejected for them. Caucasian families are less accepting, and traditional Oriental families are probably the least tolerant of these activities.

Second, there may be some difference between the subclass of Hawaiian children who attend public schools, and Hawaiian children in general. There has always been an Hawaiian aristocracy. The children of these families go to private schools, frequently Punahou, a school which has been associated with missionary, *kamaaina* (old landholding family), and *alii* (aristocratic Hawaiian) groups for nearly 150 years. There is another private institution, however, which selectively siphons students of Hawaiian or part-Hawaiian ancestry out of the public school system: Kamehameha School.

Kamehameha school is a large private institution supported by the enormous estate of one of the last members of the Hawaiian royal family. Its tuition fees are low enough to make private education available to most Hawaiian families, but until recently its admission standards have been high, and based on achievement and aptitude tests. Kamehameha has recently changed to a more "democratic" admissions policy, but there is still much self-selection by families of applicants.

The joint effect of the private schools in general and Kamehameha School in particular is to divert both higher income and high achieving Hawaiian children out of the public school system. Thus, the remainder, the public school Hawaiian youth, may be somewhat unrepresentative.

A final factor is individual size. One of the obvious differences between instances of violence in schools and crimes of violence among adults is that the latter involve weapons, while the former usually do not. A weapon—the usual instance being a gun—wipes out differences due to body build, size, or sex. When weapons are not used, these physical factors and the number of persons involved become much more important.

Here, we begin to come close to one of the important factors in the dynamics of personal violence. Hawaiians in general are very large people. So are Samoans. Both of these groups are about as tall as Caucasians, but they tend to be larger-framed. The differences in stature between Hawaiians and most Orientals of the same age and sex are striking. It thus appears likely that the average Hawaiian or Samoan youth has an obvious advantage in intimidation of his or her contemporaries. Since adult violence is much more often based on weapon use, this physical advantage is less important.

There is other data to indicate that physical size and development is a major factor in school violence. "Violence and Vandalism in the Public Schools of Hawaii" lists the specific schools in the state which are highest and lowest in terms of specific violence or vandalism criteria. The pattern is extremely consistent for violence directed toward students: of the 14 schools highest on threat to students, 13 are intermediate schools; of the 13 highest on beatings to students, 11 are intermediate schools; of the 20 highest in fear among students, 15 are intermediate schools. In contrast, of the 16 schools reported to involve most threats to teachers, 11 were high schools and 9 intermediate, while the 14 schools with most attacks on teachers involved 9 high schools and 8 intermediate schools (some were joint high and intermediate schools).

These data make it clear that the schools where students are worried about being attacked or threatened by other students are intermediate schools. Interviews with teachers, presented in the same report, make this phenomenon even more explicit: in intermediate schools, the 9th graders pick on the 7th graders. The mechanism here is obviously adolescence, and its associated great increase in size and strength for boys.

There are several corollaries to this phenomenon. First, the absolute levels of fighting in intermediate schools may not be higher than in elementary schools. The difference is that fights between 14 or 15-year-old boys are much more apt to result in serious injury than fights among younger children, with resultant differences in fear of onlookers as well as participants. A second aspect is that the participants are inclined to regard such fights as establishing a much more fixed relationship among winner and loser than equivalent fights among younger children.

One may well ask what happens to the anger or aggressivity of the children who fall low enough on such a dominance hierarchy that they cannot express themselves directly toward their peers (or other sources of annoyance). One possible outcome may be displaced aggression in the form of vandalism: of the 10 schools highest in ratings of vandalism, 8 were high schools; of the 13 schools with the lowest vandalism ratings, 3 were high schools, and 10 were either intermediate or elementary/intermediate schools. Thus, although vandalism is not an activity which relies on the greater strength, sophistication, or manipulative skills of senior high students, it is definitely more of a problem in Hawaiian high schools than in lower level schools.

In attempting to relate the violence levels in different schools to further school characteristics, comparison may be made of composite indices of violence for schools on Oahu versus the outer islands. Oahu schools were consistently more violent, with over 31 percent reporting that violence to students occured "often" while the outer islands reported from 18 to 26.27 percent ratings of violence "often." A rather similar picture was obtained for violence to teachers, with almost 20 percent of violence "often" in schools on Oahu, while Hawaii and Maui counties were both considerably less. However, 21.15 percent of respondents in Kauai schools reported violence to teachers "often."

This picture should, however, be analyzed in conjunction with another definite trend: smaller schools (251-500 enrollment) showed the lowest levels of ratings of violence toward other students (12 percent) or toward teachers (2 percent), while the largest (2,501-2,750 students) showed the highest levels (13 percent to students, 20 percent to teachers), with intermediate levels at schools of intermediate size. This suggests that at least some portion of the difference in violence ratings for the outer island schools versus Oahu schools may be attributable to the larger schools in Honolulu. Another factor may be the level of the school: combined intermediate/high schools tend to be large, while elementary schools are more numerous and smaller.

One variate which was—surprisingly—rather poorly related to violence in schools was the proportion of low-income (welfare) students in the school. For schools with less than 10 percent low-income students, nearly 20 percent gave ratings in the high violence group. For schools with 31 to 40 percent low income students, this had increased only about 10 percentage points. The increase in ratings of violence to teachers was proportionate, from 12 to 18 percent, but equally modest. Since most studies of school violence suggest a rather more substantial relationship between neighborhood incomes and violence levels, this finding is somewhat unexpected, but it probably reflects the Oahu/outer island difference: schools on the outer islands, which tend to be less violent have high levels of low-income students. One might expect that the relationship between income and violence for schools on Oahu only would be more striking.

Since ethnicity is generally viewed as a major factor in violence in the schools, one last feature of the "Violence and Vandalism Report" is of interest. How well do students of different ethnic backgrounds like school classes? The results are, again, rather unexpected. When asked to respond on a 5-point scale, from "Interesting" through "Useful," "OK," "Boring," to "Worthless," students of different ethnic backgrounds showed very little difference in selection of the "Interesting" and "Useful" choices, with the exception of Blacks, who chose these options considerable less often (35 percent). All other groups were tightly clustered together, with about 45 to 53 percent ratings in these favorable categories. On the "Boring/Worthless" end of the scale, Blacks again showed a difference, with an unusually high 26 percent selecting these categories. There is some evidence that groups selectively associated with school violence chose the unfavorable categories a bit more often than other groups (Samoans 16 percent; Hawaiians 13 percent; in contrast to 7 to 9 percent ratings for Chinese and Japanese students) but this evidence is hardly overwhelming.

These figures suggest that the extremely clear-cut stereotypes of Samoan and Hawaiian or part-Hawaiian students as responsible for much of the violence in schools are not matched by equally clear negative feelings for the school classes on the part of these specific groups. In fact, the one group showing systematically less regard for the school classes, Blacks, were not selected as major troublemakers by their fellow students.

Perhaps the most accurate way to characterize the relationship between these factors is to view them in the context of another theme persistently reiterated by the teachers, counselors, and principals interviewed in this school survey. These intimately involved onlookers frequently indicated that the overwhelming majority of instances of serious violence in their school were attributable to just a few individuals. The school officials further indicated that legislation making it difficult or impossible to get rid of these troublesome students was a major factor in the continuing high levels of violence at specific schools.

If this view is correct, and only a handful of students are responsible for much of the violence in schools, then the seemingly incompatible figures on ethnic groups responsible for these problems, and the attitude of the students of these ethnicities toward school classes, becomes understandable. A few very active and troublesome Samoan or Hawaiian students could be responsible for a widespread view that these ethnicities are responsible for the violence in schools, yet these few individuals would contribute little to the overall attitude of their own group toward school classes. This could be true even if the students involved were extremely negative in their own personal views of the value of school classes.

What these data suggest, then, is not that Hawaiians, or Samoans, necessarily share a general "subculture of violence" but that they tend to run to extremes, with a few individuals accounting for a wildly disproportionate amount of violent acts. However, this suggestion is based on the views of outsiders such as teachers and other school officials. The point will be reexamined in terms of self-report data in the next section.

In brief summary of the views of violence in Hawaii presented by these crime statistics and school reports, Hawaii is generally a less violent locale than the mainland United States, despite factors such as cultural differences within the state, a generally urban population, a large tourist industry, and a generally lower income to cost-of-living ratio, all of which might be expected to promote crime and violence. This lower rate for crimes of violence has been consistent for years, although current trends suggest that the gap between specific mainland and Hawaii violent crime rates may be narrowing.

The major factor in this generally lower rate of murder, aggravated assault, and robbery is the presence in Hawaii of large numbers of individuals whose cultures are associated with very low rates of violent crime. It is this, rather than an across-culture reduction in violence, that accounts for Hawaii's relatively favorable violence rates. Conversely, other ethnicities are represented at disproportionately high rates, up to 10 or more times their relative numbers, in arrests for violent crimes.

Data from school surveys was generally supportive of this view that cultural background is a major factor in violence in Hawaii, but some specifics of these data were quite different than those of adult crime. In the schools as in adult crime statistics, Samoans were singled out as an especially high-risk group. However, Hawaiian and part-Hawaiian students were also considered to be a major source of violence and fear in schools, although this group was not over-represented in adult arrests for violent crime. Conversely, Blacks, who are greatly over-represented in adult arrests, are not viewed as a threatening element in the schools, perhaps because there were so few in the specific schools sampled, or, alternatively, because Black school children in Hawaii represent a socially and educationally different group than does the largely military Black adult population.

In addition to information on ethnicity and violence, the school data provides the suggestion that there is a striking relationship of age to serious violence. Threats and fear of violence were consistently associated with intermediate schools (grades 7, 8, and 9) rather than elementary or senior high schools. Within intermediate schools, the specific problem was consistently identified as 9th graders picking on 7th graders. These findings suggest a strong relationship between the relative size and strength of opponents and the tendency to initiate threats or attack. This relationship is in good agreement with the identification of Samoans and Hawaiians (both physically large peoples) as the source of threats and harrassment in schools.

SELF-REPORTS OF VIOLENCE

How do these relationships compare with self-reports on aggression and violence by Hawaiian residents? As an initial step in obtaining self-reports of personal violence, we have given over 600 questionnaries to students at a local community college. This questionnaire was modified from the "Conflict Resolution Technique" scale used by Straus (1976).

In order to obtain comparisons of violent incidents within the family, as opposed to violence outside the family, the scale was given twice, once with each question involving activities aimed at a family member (scale presented in table 7.5) and again, with each question modified to involve actions directed at persons who were not members of the subject's family. These two scales were supplemented by questions on the subject's most violent familial and nonfamilial episodes, and by questions on ethnicity, age, sex, and parents' education and occupations.

Honolulu Community College is a two-year commuter college located near the center of Honolulu. Its enrollment of approximately 4,200 students is fairly evenly divided in educational emphasis between vocational-technical or paraprofessional training, and liberal arts studies. Students are quite varied in terms of ethnicity, age, and educational goals.

From the sample of 620 respondents, results were tabulated by ethnic identity. No group with less than 20 members of each sex in the sample was reported. Also, respondents over 24 years of age were eliminated, to reduce variability attributable to age. These procedures reduced the sample to 475, of which 277 were male and 198 female, representing five different ethnic groups.

Tables 7.6 and 7.7 present the average number of instances in each category of violent behavior reported by men or women of each ethnic group during the previous 12 months. Table 7.6 gives violence directed at family members, while table 7.7 is for violence outside the family. It is immediately apparent from examination of these two tables that considerable dif-

Table 7.5. Self-Report Violence Scale

For each of the following activities, try to remember how many times in the past 12 months *you* have done this to a *member of your family* (parents, brothers, sisters, spouse, children). If a given activity has not happened in the past 12 months, also indicate if this has *ever* happened, by checking the appropriate column.

ACTIVITY	INCIDENCES IN THE PAST 12 MONTHS							HAVE YOU EVER DONE THIS?	
	0	1	2	3-5	6-10	11-20	20+	YES	NO
12. You swore at or insulted a *family member*	—	—	—	—	—	—	—	—	—
13. You threatened to hit or throw something at a *family member*	—	—	—	—	—	—	—	—	—
14. You threw, smashed, hit, or kicked something (but not at the person) in a dispute with a *family member*	—	—	—	—	—	—	—	—	—
15. You threw something at a *family member*	—	—	—	—	—	—	—	—	—
16. You pushed, grabbed, or shoved a *family member*	—	—	—	—	—	—	—	—	—
17. You slapped a *family member*	—	—	—	—	—	—	—	—	—
18. You kicked, bit, or hit (with fists) a *family member*	—	—	—	—	—	—	—	—	—
19. You hit or tried to hit with a hard object a *family member*	—	—	—	—	—	—	—	—	—
20. You beat up a *family member*	—	—	—	—	—	—	—	—	—
21. You used or threatened to use a knife or gun against a *family member*	—	—	—	—	—	—	—	—	—

ferences exist between ethnic groups in some categories but not others, and that sex differences may be marked or insignificant, depending primarily on whether intra- or extrafamilial violence is tabulated. Beginning with ethnic and sex differences in violence within the family, Hawaiians and Caucasians, both men and women, tended to be highest in terms of lower-level conflict actions such as swearing at someone or threatening to hit someone. Oriental males and females (Chinese and Japanese) were somewhat lower on these scales, while Filipinos showed quite low rates for men, but the highest rates of all the groups for women.

Intermediate levels of within-family violence, including such activities as throwing objects, pushing, or hitting with the fist, were again most common among male Hawaiians (part-Hawaiians were included and probably constitute most of this category) and Filipino women. Except for Caucasian women, all other groups were relatively low on these intrafamily violence measures. Highest level violence, including hitting with an object, beating up, or using a

**Table 7.6. Mean Number of Reported Instances of Violence
Directed at Family Members for Males and Females
at Honolulu Community College**

	EUROPEAN	JAPANESE	CHINESE	FILIPINO	HAWAIIAN & PART-HAWAIIAN
Male					
Swore at	8.8	6.5	3.9	5.5	8.2
Threatened to hit	2.7	1.7	2.4	1.1	5.2
Smashed something	2.3	1.8	2.9	1.6	2.6
Threw at	0.7	0.5	1.4	0.1	1.8
Pushed, grabbed, or shoved	1.3	1.1	2.1	1.6	4.0
Slapped	0.5	0.2	1.4	0.2	2.0
Kicked, bit, or hit with fist	1.4	0.7	1.3	0.6	2.3
Hit with object	0.2	0.2	1.1	0.4	0.7
Beat up	0.3	0.0	1.2	0.0	1.2
Used a weapon	0.0	0.1	0.0	0.0	0.0
Female					
Swore at	7.2	7.4	4.8	8.3	8.8
Threatened to hit	2.7	1.3	1.9	2.5	1.9
Smashed something	3.0	1.4	1.3	3.9	2.6
Threw at	1.6	0.8	0.0	2.0	0.8
Pushed, grabbed, or shoved	2.4	1.7	0.5	2.0	1.2
Slapped	2.3	1.5	0.9	2.7	1.2
Kicked, bit, or hit with fist	2.1	0.8	0.7	1.6	1.2
Hit with object	0.7	0.7	0.0	0.1	0.3
Beat up	0.4	0.0	0.0	0.1	0.1
Used weapon	0.0	0.0	0.1	0.1	0.1

weapon on someone, was highest for Hawaiian males, and, rather surprisingly, for Chinese males. Such activities were quite uncommon among all females except Hawaiians who approached the averages for the male groups on this measure.

Because Filipino women's self-reports indicate high levels of activity in the low to intermediate violence categories, it should be pointed out that this particular trend did not continue when high-level violent acts were considered. Their intrafamilial pattern appears to involve many instances of relatively lower level violence. It is notable that male-female differences in low-level or even intermediate-level violence are not very marked for episodes within the family. For the highest levels, such as "beating up," there is greater self-reporting by males; but, overall, women in this sample reported rates which are quite similar to those of men when familial violence is considered. For extrafamilial violence, however, there is a clear difference between self-reports by men and women in almost every category and in each ethnicity. One exception, as in familial violence, is among Filipino women, who reported more incidents of low and intermediate-level violence than did Filipino men. The other exception was for Chinese women, who either tied or exceeded the rates for Chinese men in a number of report categories. It should be noted, however, that Chinese men had consistently low rates on all of these categories compared to men of other ethnicities.

Thus, for European (Caucasian), Japanese, and Hawaiian groups, men reported consistently and substantially higher rates of violence than did the women of the same groups. Even for Filipino men, high-level violence was more frequent than that for women, while Chinese men's low rates were generally equivalent to those of Chinese women.

Ethnic comparisons for extrafamilial violence suggest that the Hawaiian group was consistently higher. European and Filipino averages were rather close together, with somewhat greater contributions by European males and Filipino women. Japanese men, but not Japanese women, made scores quite close to those of this intermediate group of Caucasians and Filipinos. Chinese (men and women) were lowest as a group, but the Japanese women were the lowest subgroup.

In overall comparison of the intrafamilial and the extrafamilial violence data, men tended to be fairly stable in terms of violence within and outside the family, showing perhaps a bit more high-level violence outside their families. For women, the reverse relationship obtained—much lower levels of violence occurred outside the family than inside the family group. If these

**Table 7.7. Mean Number of Instances of Violence
Directed at Persons Who Were Not Family Members
for Males and Females at Honolulu Community College**

	EUROPEAN	JAPANESE	CHINESE	FILIPINO	HAWAIIAN & PART-HAWAIIAN
Male					
Swore at	8.1	6.3	3.8	5.5	8.4
Threatened to hit	2.4	2.7	1.7	1.3	2.7
Smashed something	2.0	2.4	0.6	1.1	1.2
Threw at	0.8	1.2	1.3	1.1	1.5
Pushed, grabbed, or shoved	2.0	1.6	0.8	2.2	3.6
Slapped	0.7	0.5	0.2	0.2	2.3
Kicked, bit, or hit with fist	1.0	1.6	0.2	1.0	4.5
Hit with object	0.3	0.9	0.1	0.5	0.3
Beat up	0.7	0.6	0.1	0.8	1.9
Used a weapon	0.0	0.1	0:1	0.1	0.1
Female					
Swore at	7.7	5.0	4.4	4.5	4.3
Threatened to hit	1.4	0.5	0.2	2.3	3.3
Smashed something	2.7	1.6	0.9	2.5	1.7
Threw at	0.3	0.1	0.2	2.2	0.5
Pushed, grabbed, or shoved	2.2	0.1	0.6	2.3	3.7
Slapped	0.7	0.5	2.0	1.2	3.3
Kicked, bit, or hit with fist	1.3	0.4	1.5	1.8	2.3
Hit with object	0.0	0.0	0.1	0.3	0.3
Beat up	0.0	0.0	0.1	0.1	0.3
Used weapon	0.0	0.0	0.1	0.1	0.1

had been older women, it seems likely that much of the slapping, hitting, etc. inside the family might be attributable to mothers' disciplining of children. Since all subjects over 24 years of age were eliminated from the analysis, however, few of these women had children, especially the older children for which a slap or blow might be considered a normal punishment.

Most of the group was unmarried, and for these individuals the most intense episode of familial violence was fairly evenly divided between siblings and parents. The data on targets of intrafamilial violence is still under analysis and cannot be reported definitively here, but one obtains a clear impression that physical violence involving parents is considerably lower among women of Oriental descent than among Caucasian or Filipino women. Women of Japanese or Chinese ancestry somewhat take in the slack, however, in encounters with sibs, particularly their sisters. One respondent, for example, contributed an extremely graphic description of how she had smashed a raw egg through her sister's carefully tended hair.

Such discrepancies between different ethnic groups in terms of the targets of violence may provide an interesting starting point for analysis of the effects of culture upon the expression of aggression. The intrafamilial violence data make it very clear that women of Oriental ancestry do become angry and are consequently aggressive, just as women of any ethnicity. However, these data suggest that some strong social inhibition is operating to reduce violence outside the family group. One indication of this inhibition was suggested to us in descriptions given by a student of Japanese ancestry, who sought help for the havoc created in her family as a result of her sister's attack on their father. The teenaged girl had broken a chair over her father's head, and the entire family was in a state bordering on panic. The girl was taken to a psychiatrist, who subsequently sent her for evaluation of neurological disorder, which was in fact confirmed. The remarkable feature of this situation was the swiftness with which the girl's behavior resulted in psychiatric evaluation. The behavior pattern was so clearly unacceptable in the context of a traditional American-Japanese family that it was immediately regarded as a symptom of mental illness. As a result of these clear cultural expectations, girls and women of Oriental ancestry tend to behave quite circumspectly toward their parents, and also with non-family members. This cautiousness has one additional benefit in terms of violence in Hawaii: women of Oriental ancestry are very, very seldom the victims of rape.

In order to compare overall results of this self-report survey to the Hawaii violent crime data, and to the results of the "Violence and Vandalism" report, a very rough summation might be made of the mean number of instances for each ethnic group in which an action occurred which might possibly lead to a violent crime charge, or, would likely inspire a reputation as a "bully." Such a comparison obviously involves a judgment as to the appropriate level of violent activity to be included, but we considered that slaps, pushes, grabs, or shoves were not violent enough acts to qualify, while the "kick, bit, or hit with fist" category was. The last four categories of violent activity in the self-report survey were therefore summed across sex and across intra-/extrafamilial incidents to obtain a mean number of instances per person Since numbers of men and women in the population are about equal, these sums were not weighted for the different numbers of males and females in the sample.

The result of this procedure is given in table 7.8. These results are in striking agreement with the "Violence and Vandalism" report, in that Hawaiians' self-reports for acts of fairly high-level violence are strikingly higher than those of the other four groups, which tend to be somewhat clustered together. The two groups of Oriental ancestry were the lowest, which certainly accords with the Hawaii crime statistics data, while Filipinos were somewhat higher and Caucasians higher still. Only the last group, however, exceeded 50 percent of the level of instances reported by Hawaiians.

Different portions of these data are, therefore, in agreement with violent crime statistics, or

Table 7.8. Mean Number of Incidents in Last Four Categories
of Behavior Rating Scale, By Ethnicity

Caucasian	Japanese	Chinese	Filipino	Hawaiian
4.2	3.05	3.2	3.75	7.8

with data on groups perceived as most threatening in the schools. Such agreement provides some evidence of validity of the self-report procedure. Particularly with reference to the participation of Hawaii residents of Oriental extraction (Chinese and Japanese) in acts of violence, the present data are in complete agreement with those of other sources, showing consistently fewer instances of violence than do other ethnicities represented, even in a setting for which the demographic makeup is probably biased against such a difference. This particular community college primarily attracts students because of vocational-technical training, which obviously involves blue-collar vocational aspirations, or (for students planning to transfer later) because of a combination of low tuition and open admission.

These factors suggest that such a school will attract different components of the various ethnic communities in Hawaii. For groups with low income and vocational levels, such as Samoans, Blacks, and recent immigrant groups, those students in any college probably represent the more success-oriented members of the group. For groups which strongly emphasize education, and high-status occupations, such as Japanese and Chinese, those young people who attend a community college rather than the traditional four-year institution probably represent either the lower-income members of those ethnicities or lower-achieving members of middle-class families. Since low income and blue-collar jobs are both associated with higher rates of violent activity (Straus, Gelles, & Steinmetz, 1980), these students are probably more violent than the average for their ethnic groups; conversely, the average Samoan student in college is probably less violent than his noncollege counterparts.

This view is supported by results of interviews with high-violent-profile students (to be described later) who were asked to describe how they personally compare, in terms of expressions of violence, with other members of their family. High-violent males of Oriental ancestry usually describe themselves as unusual, or even outcasts—no one else in the family is so violent as they, and the family may be in despair over the subject's behavior. The subject frequently reports considerable guilt at his own inability to "control himself." On the other hand, Caucasian men are likely to report that their violent behavior patterns are fairly typical of their families, as are part-Hawaiian males. The latter, however, seem most likely to report that other members of their families are more violent than themselves, and that these other family members are not represented in the community college sample. For example, one young man no longer lived at home because it was too violent there: "You have to watch your head at the table," he reported, "Every meal, you're likely to get hit with a beer bottle." This subject indicated that, in terms of his family norms, he himself was a very passive individual, an ironic characterization in terms of some of his recent activities.

These community college data indicate a continuing difference between students of Oriental ancestry (least violent), students of Filipino or Caucasian ancestry (intermediate levels of violence, around the norm), and students of Hawaiian or part-Hawaiian ancestry (highest level of the five groups surveyed) even for this predominantly blue-collar or low to middle income sample. The data also suggest that when occupational aspirations and family income for the different ethnicities are more or less equalized by the sample selected, there is some convergence toward the mean for students of Oriental ancestry. This, in turn, suggests that social and economic status factors are important here, as in other cultures sampled, such that between-culture comparisons of violence must pay explicit attention to the status characteristics of the groups examined.

A further sample, using the same self-report questionnaire, was given to students at the University of Hawaii (main campus at Manoa), Tokyo University of Education at Yokohama, and Klakamus Community College in Portland, Oregon. The Manoa campus is a large urban university with graduate programs, medical and law schools, etc., while the Japanese university sampled is one of the more prestigious in Japan. Students in the Manoa and Japan sample were demographically very similar, with the vast majority (90 percent or more) between 18 and 22 years of age, unmarried, with middle or upper income families. The 82 males and 71 females in the Japanese sample were ethnic Japanese, while 68.3 percent of the Manoa sample were Americans of Japanese Ancestry, the remainder being primarily Caucasian. The Klakamus sample were rather closer to the Honolulu Community College group, being more varied in age, and including a larger proportion of families of lower income than the two university samples.

Table 7.9 presents results for the Manoa sample, and relevant Honolulu Community College groups. Comparison of the incidents in each category for the Manoa sample, with the same data for the Honolulu Community College samples of students Japanese ancestry or Caucasians, provides a rough idea of the difference between a high aspiration, higher status sample, and a somewhat lower vocational aspiration group. For men, mid- to high-level intrafamilial violence was slightly higher for the Honolulu Community College sample, but a very large difference appeared in comparison of extrafamilial mid- to high-level violence for the two groups. Both Japanese and Caucasian males at Honolulu Commmunity College reported much higher levels of violence toward persons who were not members of their families than did male students at the University of Hawaii. For women, mid- to high-level violence within the family was more common for both Japanese and Caucasian groups at the Community College, but there was little difference in violence directed at individuals outside the family, this being very low in all cases. These results agree with the view that occupational and economic status are factors in the initiation or expression of violence. They also clearly indicate, however, that these factors differentially influence male as opposed to female behavior, and that sex may interact with target (family vs. nonfamily) in the determination of incidence of violence. These data, like those of the original HCC sample, suggest that intrafamily violence cannot be used as a good estimate of the tendency toward violent acts outside the family, and that ethnicity may have very different effects on the expression of violence in men as opposed to women.

Table 7.10 presents data from Klakamus Community College, in comparison with the Caucasian data from Honolulu Community College. This comparison, which should provide further evidence of similarity or difference between a largely Caucasian mainland population and a Hawaiian Caucasian group of somewhat similar demographic profile, suggests that, overall, the Hawaii group is a bit higher (considerably higher, however, in such activities as hitting with an object, and beating up) for male activities directed at nonfamily members. This finding, for rather similar groups at the community college level, is in agreement with the comparison of violent crime statistics for local Caucasians and Blacks as compared to mainland Caucasians and Blacks. Whatever the "climate for violence" of a particular community may involve, Hawaii appears to promote more, rather than less, violence than the mainland United States taken as a whole.

Comparison of self-reports for the Manoa students of Japanese ancestry to those of Japanese students at Tokyo University of Education is obviously relevant to such a "climate of

Table 7.9. Mean Number of Instances Directed at Family Members or Nonfamily Members for Students at Manoa and for Students of Japanese or European Ancestry at Honolulu Community College

	MANOA	MALES HCC		MANOA	FEMALES HCC	
		JAPAN.	EUROP.		JAPAN.	EUROP.
Toward Family Members:						
Swore at	4.0	6.5	8.8	6.6	7.4	7.2
Threatened to hit	1.1	1.7	2.7	1.8	1.3	2.7
Smashed something	2.4	1.8	2.3	1.9	1.4	3.0
Threw at	1.0	0.5	0.7	0.5	0.8	1.6
Pushed, grabbed, or shoved	1.0	1.1	1.3	1.5	1.7	2.4
Slapped	0.0	0.2	0.5	1.1	1.5	2.3
Kicked, bit, or hit with fist	0.2	0.7	1.4	0.4	0.8	2.1
Hit with object	0.0	0.2	0.2	0.1	0.7	0.7
Beat up	0.1	0.0	0.3	0.0	0.0	0.4
Used a weapon	0.0	0.1	0.0	0.0	0.0	0.0
Toward Nonfamily Members:						
Swore at	7.1	6.3	8.1	4.2	5.0	7.7
Threatened to hit	2.0	2.7	2.4	0.7	0.5	1.4
Smashed something	3.1	2.4	2.0	1.2	1.6	2.7
Threw at	0.6	1.2	0.8	0.2	0.1	0.3
Pushed, grabbed, or shoved	1.2	1.6	2.0	0.8	0.1	2.2
Slapped	0.3	0.5	0.7	0.9	0.5	0.7
Kicked, bit, or hit with fist	0.4	1.6	1.0	0.7	0.4	1.3
Hit with object	0.1	0.9	0.3	0.1	0.0	0.0
Beat up	0.1	0.6	0.7	0.0	0.0	0.0
Used a weapon	0.0	0.1	0.0	0.0	0.0	0.0

violence" notion. Table 7.11 presents these data, grouped into three categories of "threats" (items 1-3), "mild attack" (items 4-7), and "severe attack" (items 8-10). The basic pattern, of an interaction of male and female violence patterns with intra- versus extrafamilial targets, appears to hold here as well. Females, in contrast to males, showed higher levels of violence inside the family, but very low levels of extrafamilial violence. The pattern was not quite identical to that of the Japanese males at Honolulu Community College, however, in that men did not show greater violence outside their families. Since this pattern was also less marked in the Manoa sample, it appears to respond very selectively to vocational/economic status factors, with markedly more extra- than intrafamilial violence in lower or vocational aspiration groups.

Although the overall pattern of American-Japanese (Manoa) and Japanese (Tokyo) groups was very similar, the incidence data is different in virtually every category. The Tokyo groups, men and women, within and outside the family, reported fewer violent acts. This difference was smallest for threatening acts within the family, and of very high magnitude for all nonfamily violence. For this sample of 258 persons, every comparison was statistically significant, most of them at the .0001 level.

This comparison involves two samples of rather low-violence demographic profile individ-

Table 7.10. Mean Number of Instances Directed at Family Members or Nonfamily Members by Students at Klakamus Community College and Students of European Ancestry at Honolulu Community College

	MALES		FEMALES	
	KLAKAMUS	HCC	KLAKAMUS	HCC
Toward Family Members				
Swore at	6.2	8.8	8.6	7.2
Threatened to hit	1.4	2.7	3.7	2.7
Smashed something	1.7	2.3	1.2	3.0
Threw at	1.1	0.7	0.1	1.6
Pushed, grabbed, or shoved	1.4	1.3	2.9	2.4
Slapped	0.3	0.5	1.9	2.3
Kicked, bit, or hit with fist	0.3	1.4	1.0	2.1
Hit with object	0.2	0.2	0.5	0.7
Beat up	0.0	0.3	0.3	0.4
Used a weapon	0.0	0.0	0.0	0.0
Toward Nonfamily Members				
Swore at	6.9	8.1	3.9	7.7
Threatened to hit	1.2	2.4	0.6	1.4
Smashed something	0.7	2.0	0.6	2.7
Threw at	0.3	0.8	0.1	0.3
Pushed, grabbed, or shoved	1.1	2.0	0.3	2.2
Slapped	0.1	0.7	0.2	0.7
Kicked, bit, or hit with fist	0.4	1.0	0.5	1.3
Hit with object	0.1	0.3	0.0	0.0
Beat up	0.0	0.7	0.0	0.0
Used a weapon	0.0	0.0	0.1	0.0

uals. The fact that it still indicates differences, even at this level, suggests that one might expect even greater discrepancy if more representative groups were sampled. Certainly, the Honolulu Community College and the Manoa comparisons suggest that the Manoa group is unusually low in violence. The much greater violence levels in Hawaii than Japan again suggest that Hawaii is by no means a place where the initiation and expression of violence is inhibited. These data, of course, are very much in line with violent crime statistics for the two countries, but they go further in indicating that even a very personally nonviolent group such as individuals reared in traditional Japanese culture quickly respond to whatever violence-promoting factors are operative in Hawaii.

CAUSES OF VIOLENCE IN HAWAII

The obvious question, then, is "What are these factors?" Before going to a discussion of some of the potential promoters of violence in Hawaii, one variable often cited as contributing to generally higher rates of violence in the United States than in other countries, might be mentioned: Television. This is very pertinent to the difference between Japan and the United States, both in Hawaii and on the mainland. Television in Japan is, if anything, more violent than in the United States. It therefore cannot be a factor in the overall differences between the two cultures; and, if it has any major aggression-promoting effect, this effect must be more than counteracted by other variables differentiating the two cultures. Another finding not in agreement with the view that television is a major factor in cultural differences in violence is the consistently (though not markedly) higher level of violence of Caucasians in Hawaii as opposed to the mainland United States. The television programs in Hawaii and the mainland are virtually identical.

There are a host of phenomena influencing the complex cognitive processes involved in anger and aggression, and many aspects of life in contemporary Hawaii seem ideal for the fostering of jealousy, hostility, and indignation. Hawaii is a culture of material contrasts, in which very rich and comparatively very poor groups and individuals live almost side by side. Not many cities of less than one million population have sections of town in which the average price of a house is well over half a million dollars. Not many portions of the United States have thousands of new immigrants each year, many of whom cannot speak English or find employment. Comparatively few places in the world have a large population of "first settlers" who now feel themselves largely barred from economic, political, or social leadership of a land they once possessed. Certainly no other U.S. state can match Hawaii's multicultural mix, with all the tensions and misunderstandings that are a basic accompaniment to poorly-understood differences among peoples. Hawaii has all of these violence-promoting factors, plus the present trend of greater than average (for the United States) decline in standard of living during the past five years or more.

There is no way at present to link these factors in any direct, quantitative, and scientifically satisfactory fashion to differences between violence in Hawaii and elsewhere, or to differences between different ethnic groups in Hawaii. However, from an almost constant preoccupation with these relationships over a period of some years, facilitated by interviews with dozens of Hawaii residents, we think we can begin to see some outline of the dynamics—the psychology —linking cultural and economic phenomena to individual violence.

The factors cited above as potential promoters of violence may all act through their influence on a delicate and complex cognitive-emotional mechanism which controls anger. The central cognitive element in this mechanism is a sort of comparator which keeps a more-or-less accurate and very up to date check on how well the individual is faring with reference to his personally and culturally determined expectations of his own value, status, or rights. An "insult" is a symbolic violation of the individual's self-worth. Insults—as well as more immediate and nonsymbolic threats to self-esteem or to other prerogatives of the individual—result in anger. Insofar as these threats are perceived as stemming from the action (especially, the intentional action) of a specific person or group, such anger will become focused as the desire to harm that person or group: aggression.

Some quick examples: In our sample of college students, the more aggressive are almost always male; and, in many cases, these young adult males' most recent aggressive episodes stem from incidents involving cars. One almost infallible aggression-arousing event is for

Table 7.11. Mean Number of Instances of Threat, Mild Attack, or Severe Attack for Japanese-Ancestry Students at Manoa, and Students at Tokyo University of Education

	FAMILY VIOLENCE				NONFAMILY VIOLENCE			
	MALE		FEMALE		MALE		FEMALE	
	MANOA	TOKYO	MANOA	TOKYO	MANOA	TOKYO	MANOA	TOKYO
Threaten	6.4	6.1	9.4	7.5	12.8	4.1	4.8	1.8
Mild attack	1.8	0.8	4.3	1.7	3.3	0.7	2.9	0.2
Severe attack	0.0	0.1	0.1	0.1	0.2	0.0	0.2	0.0

someone to pass such a subject too closely, causing the subject to jam on his breaks or swerve. One high-violence profile subject felt himself completely justified in chasing such a car, forcing it off the road, and sending three of its four (male) inhabitants to a hospital with the aid of a pared-down baseball bat. The implication is that, when a person is driving, he perceives a certain road trajectory as "belonging" to himself. Passing too closely poses a (usually) minor threat to safety but is a major threat to this valued prerogative. For many individuals, the insult value of such an act is felt much more keenly when the insultor is of a different ethnicity, or when economic differences enter the picture. One informant described his anger in the following manner. Unemployed and feeling very left out of a materialistic society, he passed a Rolls-Royce parked outside an exclusive Honolulu Club. It was only a moment's work to rip off the "flying lady" hood ornament and use this to gouge out a groove along the side of the car.

These incidents and others like them, suggest that the basic relationship between such factors as unemployment or underemployment and violence is "psychological" rather than economic. Citizens of any culture—particularly males—base their self-worth in large part on the economic or achievement aspects of work. An unemployed or underemployed man (or, increasingly, the woman in similar circumstances) is a threatened individual. The vulnerability of self-esteem in such a person drastically lowers the threshold for perception of other events as "insulting" or "irritating."

For women, also, the incitement to anger may provide a penetrating glimpse into the specific areas of one's life which are felt to be especially important—and vulnerable. The incident referred to earlier, in which one sister smushed a raw egg into another's hair, resulted from a dispute over monopoly of the family telephone. The senior author's single most anger-arousing incident in recent memory was the complaint of a neighbor regarding her (then) 5-year-old son, accused of stomping around in some recently planted shrubs. This charge, accompanied by negative commentary on the child's character and habits, turned out to be untrue; a case of mistaken identity. The follow-up was a blistering telephone conversation followed by her refusal to speak to this person again until he left the neighborhood three years later. The author is certain that she would not have been so angry if she had not recognized the very real possibility that her son—no model child—could very well have been involved. The neighbor's complaint, while untrue in this case, was just a little "too close to the bone." Similarly, the "low man" on the ethnic totem pole—the Samoan, Hawaiian, or Black—constantly carrying a burden of resentment toward more favored ethnicities may be so ready to focus this resentment that he perceives insult even when one does not exist. This tendency is by no means restricted to these groups. Many Hawaiians of Oriental extraction are sometimes more than ready to resent the historically privileged Caucasians, while Caucasians are often paranoid about the Oriental's seeming monopoly of the state government bureaucracy. Privileged individuals worry about crime in the streets where they, too, are vulnerable, while the dispossessed and those who identify with them resent the social and economic power system.

As these examples suggest, most instances of aggression in people appear to reflect anger resulting from the perpetrator's view that he has been insulted, put down, or damaged with reference to some important right or prerogative. Violence by individuals threatened with severe bodily harm does occur, but it is much, much less common in our experience than anger-based aggression. With the important exception of professional or semi-professional criminals, most violence is not based on the expectation of direct economic gain.

It should not be overlooked, however, that a violent individual quite frequently "gets his own way" in other important matters through threats of violence, and this may be especially true for family violence in which a husband may totally dominate his entire family because of his brutality. A second source of real gratification for the violence-prone individual is simply that he is hurting someone (or some organization) which he perceives to be a threat to his values, prerogatives, or authority. We were recently much interested to hear a self-confessed spouse abuser, on a local television show, describe his personal reactions to the event. He said that he really "got off" on beating his "old lady," that it gave him a "buzz." There seems little reason to doubt that feelings of righteousness, power, virility, and self-esteem are involved in the overt expression of aggression, and that these are reinforced in some cultural settings by the admiring or fearful reactions of bystanders or victims. Every culture finds some place for the expression of aggression and, in this specific context, violence is an admired trait.

In a multicultural setting such as Hawaii, where persons of different cultures find somewhat different situations or stimuli insulting or anger-eliciting, it is hardly surprising that the occasions for aggression are multiplied. It appears to be an unfortunate fact of human nature that it is easier to expand a view of one's rights than to contract and abandon what were previously regarded as areas of personal control. As a rather analogous situation, it is very easy indeed for a man who has just made a great deal of money to begin to regard it as rightfully his own. The man who has just lost a great deal of money usually believes that it still "should" belong to him.

Multicultural societies thus run a higher risk of violence than those with a single, clear-cut view of the rights and privileges of the individual. Whether this risk will actually result in violence, however, largely depends on yet another factor: social control. A major cultural limiting factor for violence is the potential perpetrator's personal expectation that his actions will result in a high probability of significant punishment. Any culture contains factors which promote violence, though admittedly some contain more than others. Highly violent cultures, however, are those in which the perceived benefits of violence outweigh the perceived costs.

Societies provide many forms of punishment for undesirable behaviors, and these stem from a number of different sources. The family is certainly the first source of approval or disapproval for the aggressive acts of children, and it is clear that ethnicity is a major determinant of whether a given act of violence will be tolerated, punished, or even approved. In the traditional Japanese family, for example, girls fighting with their sisters are tolerated, fighting with brothers is less tolerated, while fighting with parents, especially the father, is least likely to be permitted. In Caucasian families, physical attack of a child or teenager against the parents is disproportionately more tolerated, and many more such attacks occur.

The pattern of tolerance for sibling fights but strong disapproval of attack toward elders in the family is also normative for Hawaiian families, although the overall attack level toward both types of individuals is much higher than in Oriental families. The specificity of this reaction is sometimes striking. One young part-Hawaiian man whom we interviewed described an incident in which he almost killed another man. Our informant had bashed this person's head against a car door until unconsciousness resulted. We asked why he stopped, rather expecting to hear that his anger had dissipated or some similar explanation. But, no: His aunt, it appears, had been driving by and stopped to intervene. "In my family," he explained, "if a grownup tells you to stop doing something, you stop." In fact, the clearest distinction between a "good boy" and a "bad boy" in the Hawaiian community may be that the latter is disrespectful to elders. Propensity of attack toward individuals of the same age level and sex, almost regardless of the force used, is compatible with being a "good boy."

This factor may provide something of an answer to one of the most perplexing questions raised by the present comparisons of Hawaii violence data. Why is it that ethnic Hawaiians, so often pointed out as "bullies" in the schools and self-reporting high-level violence at rates over twice as high as most other ethnicities, are not arrested disproportionately for crimes of violence? One possible answer—rather unpalatable to those of us who cherish this place—is that they may simply be arrested less often than they should: Much of the police force in Hawaii is Hawaiian, or part-Hawaiian, and there is certainly the potential for favoritism. Leaders of the

Samoan community have sometimes made the allied claim that Samoans are often blamed for violence committed by Hawaiians.

This possibility is obviously very difficult if not impossible to evaluate, and it is only fair to point out that it may not be true at all; Hawaiian's specific patterns of violence may be responsible. Briefly put, ethnic Hawaiians tend to live and move in areas and cultural institutions dominated by Hawaiian cultural mores. One such traditional dictum is that certain types of violence are quite acceptable and even expected. Moreover, even if an individual exceeds this acceptable limit, the family and friends of the victim are more likely to settle things themselves, rather than calling in the police. For example, a close friend belongs to a tennis club located in one such "Hawaiian" area. He described to us a tennis-loving but rather bad tempered individual who had acquired something of a reputation for serious fights with his tennis opponents. He had injured several young Hawaiian men over the years, but the police were never notified until he broke the jaw of one of his Caucasian opponents; this last victim totally failed to see such injury as a legitimate part of playing tennis, and notified the law.

For some violent acts, such as rape, this system is likely to produce more certain punishment than the police and judicial system can provide. The paucity of Oriental rape victims has already been mentioned, and this is almost certainly due to lack of opportunity for potential rapists. Girls of Oriental ancestry do not often put themselves into situations where rape is possible. Caucasion girls do, and the majority of women raped in Hawaii are Caucasian, often tourists who are so charmed by the ambience of the islands that they are less cautious than usual about finding themselves in isolated places with strange men. But Hawaiian and part-Hawaiian girls are also much less cautious than Oriental girls, and they too are seldom raped. When we have asked Hawaiian friends about this phenomenon, their answer has been consistent: Hawaiian girls don't get raped because, if they did, they would tell their father, and brothers, and uncles, and these men of the family would find the rapist, and exact very unpleasant penalties for the act. Many such crimes would not be reported to the police at all, but this lack of police involvement does not imply lack of punishment for the crime.

This factor was recently illustrated in a much publicized case involving gang-rape of a Finnish tourist by several young locals. In a newspaper interview, one of the defendants pointed out that the victim was "nobody's girlfriend." This statement was frequently interpreted by Caucasians and Orientals in the community to mean a lack of emotional tie between victim and assailant. To the persons involved, however, the implication may have been rather different: the victim had no local connections to seek revenge.

These considerations suggest that extra-legal sanctions for violence are complex, including threat of physical or material reprisal in addition to the disapproval and anguish of family, friends, and other persons important to the potential offender. These sanctions are very much influenced by ethnicity, and by the ethnicity and status of the victim. These two sanctions— family or social disapproval and fear of retaliation—constitute a major violence control factor, but one which is not applied equally to all acts of violence.

The second punishment control factor is external: the threat of legal sanction by society at large rather than the individual's family or friends, or the friends of the victim. In Hawaii, as elsewhere in the United States, the state-imposed costs of violence to the perpetrator are hard to assess accurately; delays and uncertainties in the process of arrest, prosecution, and clearing of legal appeals for offenders may mean that the final outcome of a particular violent crime may not be resolved for years. Moreover, when resolution does come, punishment is by no means certain. Conviction rates for rape and murder have been especially low in the recent past, due in large part to frequent use of insanity pleas, plea bargaining, and difficult standards of proof written into the relevant statutes. This combination of delay and uncertainty of punishment almost certainly dilutes the force of legal sanctions as effective punishment for violence. As one very recent example indicates, the existence of legal loopholes is clearly known to potential perpetrators. In this case, a man awaiting trial on rape charges threatened to kill one of the psychiatrists attempting to assess his sanity. When the psychiatrist responded that the prisoner would go to jail for such an act, the man calmly replied that everybody knew he was a psycho, so he would not spend more than a couple of months in a mental institution for the killing.

This dilution of effective legal punishment of violent crime means that family and culture-based sanctions for violence are more important than they would be if potential perpetrators were convinced of the certainty of significant external punishment. Thus, in the absence of a major external punishment threat, the family/friend/victim sanctions may provide the effective control for individual violence. This view agrees well with our interview data suggesting that Oriental families are least accepting of violence by their children, and Polynesian the most, with Caucasians in between. To investigate this factor further, we are presently collecting data on the relationship between parental reactions to intra- and extrafamilial violence by teenagers, and subsequent violence of their children as young adults.

It should be pointed out that a major discrepancy between the force of legal sanctions as opposed to familial sanctions for violence (or other undesirable behavior) is itself a mark of a multicultural society. In nonpluralistic cultures such as that of Japan, the attitude of the law usually reflects closely and accurately the attitude of individuals (or, perhaps, vice versa). A discrepancy between the two puts extra burdens on the family as a controlling agency; and, if an individual family fails, the potential for members of that family to go more or less "out of control" is high. In this summary treatment, there is no opportunity to go into the mechanisms by which such failure may occur, but it might be noted that single-family households, the decline of the extended family, and "culture shock" may all be factors.

SUMMARY

For psychologists accustomed to the possibility of laboratory experimentation in order to analyze behaviors, the most frustrating part of a composite demographic, sociological, and questionnaire data-set, such as this chapter has presented, is that there appears to be no easy way to get from suggestive data to the level of cause and effect relationships. Neither, of course, is there any adequate way of investigating the effects of cultural differences on aggression in a laboratory setting.

In summary, then, of these data on violence in Hawaii, perhaps it is adequate to state that they are very consistently in agreement with a model which we have begun to put together largely on the basis of animal analyses, with some speculative extensions to people (Blanchard & Blanchard, 1980, 1981). This model stresses the distinction between factors which initiate or elicit anger and aggressive urges and those which control it. The model indicates that anger elicitation, even for lower-level animals such as laboratory rats, is a complex event, linking experience and present circumstances with biological factors. The model also suggests that aggressive and violent behaviors may be both personally rewarding and advantageous in an evolutionary sense. All these aspects (except, perhaps, the last) may be demonstrated in human populations, given sufficient attention to the vastly greater complexity of human cognitive processes, and of the more varied control mechanisms inherent in any human society.

In summary of this preliminary view of violence in one highly diverse cultural setting, we are rather surprised at the specificity and inclusiveness of the connections that appear to exist between aggression in lower animals and in people. A meaningful evolutionary continuum does appear to exist, offering a real basis for meaningful comparison of animal experimental analyses with data on human violence. Only lack of persistence, or perhaps an outdated view that human aggression is "different," can keep us from understanding the causes, functions, and control, of this crucial behavior pattern.

REFERENCES

Blanchard, R. J., and Blanchard, D. C. Animal aggression and the dyscontrol syndrome. In Girkis, M. (Ed.), *Limbic epilepsy and the dyscontrol syndrome.* Elsevier, 1980.

Blanchard, R. J., and Blanchard, D. C. The organization of aggressive behaviors in rodents. In P. F. Brain and D. Benton (Eds.), *The Biology of aggression.* Nordoof, 1981.

Hawaii Commission on Crime. Violence and vandalism in the public schools of Hawaii/Hawaii Crime Commission. Honolulu, 1980.

Hawaii Criminal Justice Statistical Analysis Center. Crime trends in Hawaii. Honolulu, 1981.

Hawaii Department of Health. Statistical Supplement, 1979. Honolulu, 1980.

Hawaii Department of Planning and Economic Development. State of Hawaii data book; a statistical abstract. Honolulu, 1967-1980.

Honolulu Board of Realtors Multiple Listing Service. Weekly statistical report for week 27, 1980.

Straus, M. A. The CRT scales for measuring conflict in families. Paper presented at the meeting of the National Council on Family Relations, 1976.

Straus, M. A., Gelles, R. J., and Steinmetz, S. K. *Behind closed doors: Violence in the American family.* New York: Anchor/Doubleday, 1980.

8

Holland: Research on the Causes and Prevention of Aggression

Oene Wiegman
Ben Baarda
Erwin R. Seydel

In numerous publications dealing with human aggression, it has been demonstrated that external factors exercise a significant influence. In the Netherlands, too, investigations in this field have been carried out, mainly concerning the influence of the parents, the school, peers, sociocultural backgrounds, and the media.

INFLUENCES UPON AGGRESSION

Parents

That parents play an important role in relation to their children's aggressive behavior has been established in many investigations. In a study concerning the social rehabilitation of youths who had been in contact with the police, most of them having committed a rather serious criminal offence, the relationship with their parents was shown to be a major problem (Andriessen, 1978). This confirms an earlier study by Junger-Tas (1976), who found that of a group of young persons (n + 399) originating from a small Belgian suburb, juvenile delinquents came relatively more often from broken homes than nondelinquent youths.

As to the number, seriousness, and frequency of offenses, fatherless youths show significantly higher delinquency rates, whereas youths having a stepfather scored even higher. Of course, it is important to know which factors determine these differences. Both in an American (e.g., Lefkowitz, Eron, Walder, & Huesmann, 1977) and in a European study (Olweus, 1980), a number of variables are mentioned, the most prominent one being the degree to which parents accept their children, as well as the dominance of the parents, the degree to which they accept aggression, and their methods of punishment.

In the Netherlands, a limited amount of research on the influence of these variables was performed. A replication of the study by Eron, Walder and Lefkowitz (1971) was carried out by Stroo (1971). Data on 72 8-year-old children in Amsterdam were collected and the mothers of the children were also interviewed. The original American study was much larger; data were gathered on 451 8-year-old children. In the Dutch study, parental rejection also turned out to be the variable that correlated highest (.32) with the children's aggression scores (measured by means of peer-ratings). In the American study, this correlation was .25. A significant positive correlation ($r = .19$) with the punishing rate by the parents was also established. This correlation could not be demonstrated in the Netherlands. Perhaps the intensity range of punishments in the Netherlands might be smaller than in the United States. This might possibly be an explanation for the fact that, in the Netherlands, the correlation is markedly lower and consequently not significant.

A punishment termed "severe" in the Netherlands is probably rated "medium" in the United States. Dutch parents presented with the American questionnaire showed astonishment, and often embarrassment. A punishment such as flogging with a belt is hardly ever practiced in the Netherlands. Besides, parents who consider punishment to be a highly important discipline method, and those who credit it very low, generally have more aggressive children than parents taking a less extreme position in this respect (Stroo, 1971).

A variable playing an important mediating role in imitating aggressive behavior from the parents is the extent to which children identify themselves with their parents. Stroo found, for instance, in moderate punishment conditions, a clear trend toward less aggression becomes apparent if the child identifies him or herself more with the mother.

A remarkable difference between the American and the Dutch data concern the relation between the aggression scores and the activation level of the children. In the Netherlands, it was found that very active children are generally more aggressive ($r = .38$). True, this is quite understandable, since children who experience many interactions with peers have more opportunities to be aggressive. Yet, the correlation could not be demonstrated in the United States ($r + .07$). It is not clear which cultural differences might play a part in this.

Another important study on the effect of parental variables (Angenent, 1975) deals with delinquents convicted for assault. Angenent compared 100 delinquents with their nondelinquent brothers and their nondelinquent neighbors. In order to obtain good comparison data, the wife and one of the children of each of these men were also interviewed. Again, a correlation seems to exist between parental rejection and the manifestation of the child's aggression. This is also shown from the fact that the delinquent's family was described as relatively cold, both by himself and his brother. The neighbors, on the other hand, describe their parents in terms indicating that the atmosphere at home has been warmer. Angenent (1974) also studied a group of delinquents who had committed crimes against property. With the property-delinquents, however, none of these differences was found. The difference, then, only turns up with the physically aggressive delinquent.

This distinction between different forms of aggression seems to be of fundamental importance. Yet, in many studies, aggression is the general term used. The fact that Lefkowitz and his colleagues (1977) found the effect of the variable "rejection" strongly diminishes in time might stem from their not splitting aggression into these two subtypes. To them, aggression means both physical and verbal aggression. It is possible that, when only considering highly physical aggression, as is done by Angenent, the correlation between rejection and aggression remains present.

Angenent's study also included the factor of parental dominance. As regards the father's dominance, no difference exists between the three groups. The mother, on the other hand, is described to be the more dominant by the delinquent as compared to the other two groups. It is striking that, when the children of the three different families are interviewed about the dominance of their fathers, the delinquent's youngsters are slightly more inclined to typify their father as dominant. One would expect, then, that the dominance of a delinquent would also affect the aggressive behavior of his child. This appears not to be true: the children of the delinquent are not more aggressive than other children. They appear to be more neurotic, however. This aspect, in addition to his more aggressive behavior, also distinguishes the delinquent father from other fathers; just like his child, he appears to be more neurotic. His behavior of committing assaults is possibly influenced by a combination of aggressive and neurotic characteristics. The aggressive behavior is caused by a combination of factors. Those factors are not merely influences of the parental setting since, otherwise, brothers raised in the same domestic surrounding should be delinquent too.

School

In the Netherlands, research on the influence of the school and, consequently, of the teacher on the development of aggressive behavior has been limited. There is, on the other hand, a good deal of knowledge about truancy and negative experiences of pupils at school, by delinquent youths in particular. The fundamental question that cannot be answered, however, is whether the deviant behavior is caused by the negative school experiences, or are these negative experiences results of deviant behavior? From Angenent's study (1975) mentioned above, it appears that the delinquent convicted for assault has a lower educational level and, as a youth, had a higher truancy rating as compared to his present neighbor. In these respects, his brother holds a middle position between the delinquent and the neighbor.

Junger-Tas's (1976) study of a group of Belgian youths also showed a negative relationship between the number of offenses committed and the variable "liking to go to school and having a good relationship with the teacher." The general discord with respect to the school among delinquent youths also manifested itself in less time devoted to homework. Junger-Tas predicted that poor integration with society leads to delinquency. It is evident that the delinquent youths are poorly integrated in school life, but whether this brings on delinquency, or whether their deviating behavior results in poor school integration remains an open question.

Research bearing upon teacher influences in this domain is described by Wiegman and Seydel (1976). Two groups of children were shown either aggressive or prosocial films. These groups were selected on the basis of F-scale data about their teachers and mothers. One group comprised 44 young children with extremely authoritarian (high F) female teachers and mothers, whereas the teachers and mothers of the other 44 children had extremely low F scores. It was shown that the children of the authoritarian mothers and teachers were the least influenced by watching the aggressive film models. They reacted less aggressively after watching the aggressive film than the children of nonauthoritarian mothers and teachers. It remains obscure whether the effect is caused by the mothers, by the teachers, or by both. The conclusion that the children of the nonauthoritarian group were most susceptible to model behavior does not apply to the prosocial film, since a difference in prosocial behavior between the two groups could not be established.

Peers

Junger-Tas's study (1976) also contains data on the influence of friends on delinquent behavior. Committing an offense seems quite common among adolescents. Only one-third of the youth claimed to have a clean record. Junger-Tas defines an offense to be the commitment of punishable acts, including minor shop-lifting, stealing a bicycle, etc. Less than half of the acts are committed alone. It is clear that the influence of friends plays an important part. The genuinely physically aggressive offenses (threatening and fighting) are an exception, since these are mostly committed alone. This kind of behavior occurs relatively infrequently; youth delinquency concerns mostly crimes against property. It was found that delinquent youths generally have friends who are also delinquent. This is strongly connected with their leisure-time activities. These youths mainly spend their time outdoors, generally with a big group instead of going out with one close friend.

Social and Cultural Influences

Class. Here again, it is necessary to distinguish different forms of aggression in order to acquire a clear picture of the influence of social class. Many researchers have established that there is no difference between social classes with regard to, for example, the average number of offenses committed. The chance of conviction, though, is higher for people belonging to the lower social classes. Junger-Tas, for instance (1976), concludes: "No correlation could be ascertained between the social classes—taking the occupation of the father as a basis—on the one hand, and the number, frequency and seriousness of the offenses stated or the delinquency index on the other." (p. 37) When, however, the various forms of offenses are examined separately, she does find differences. The aggressive delinquents appear to come from the lowest classes more often. Angenent's study (1975), too, shows that assault delinquents originate in particular from the lower socioeconomic classes. Furthermore, when Angenent compares the delinquent with his neighbor, the former and his family appear to have a lower socioeconomic position than the latter. In the lower socioeconomic classes, aggression in terms of its sheer frequency is probably a more common behavioral pattern. This assumption is supported by Stroo's (1971) results, which indicated that the mothers of 8- to 10-year old children of the lower classes are more aggressive than the mothers in the higher class. Their children showed the same tendency.

Sex. An observation which is often explained from, in particular, sociocultural factors, is the difference in the manifestation of aggression between boys and girls. In the Netherlands, as in many other countries, physical aggression is regarded as a typically male behavior. It is not very surprising then, that Stroo (1971) found much higher aggressive peer ratings for boys than for girls. Junger-Tas (1976), too, detected differences, the boy/girl offense ratio being 3 : 2.

The ratio of the number of convictions is different, however. One girl to 2-3 boys is convicted. Again, there is considerable difference in the nature of the offenses. Boys commit aggressive and traffic offenses more frequently, but no difference exists as regards offenses against property such as shop-lifting. For boys, Stroo (1971) found a strong correlation between aggression at school and at home, while for girls this relationship was much less clear. Possibly at home, in a rather safe surrounding, girls are less hesitant to behave aggressively as compared to the school situation, where social control is probably stronger. Another remarkable fact established by Stroo is that boys seem to be more often rejected by their mothers than girls. As we have mentioned before, there is presumably a relationship between parental rejection and aggression. It may be possible that these differences in rejection may, to some extent, account for the differences in aggression between boys and girls.

Media Influence

Wiegman (1975) conducted a study on the effects of aggressive films on the viewer in the Netherlands. The subjects in this investigation were young children aged 4 to 6. The researcher used a film constructed for the investigation in three versions: an aggressive, a prosocial, and a neutral one. The films lasted about seven minutes and their contents were comparable:

two puppet-show figures meet each other and become involved in a number of odd situations. In the aggressive film version, these complications are solved in an aggressive way. In the prosocial film, they behave in a very cooperative, helpful way. In the neutral version, the puppets behave in a neutral, objective manner with respect to each other. In no instance are the puppets rewarded for their aggressive, prosocial, or neutral behavior in the films. Moreover, neither a victim nor a victor stands out in the aggressive film, while at the end of the prosocial film there is no question of someone having been favored. The degree of aggression displayed in the aggressive film by no means exceeded the TV violence usually observed by a child.

The test subjects were randomly assigned to the film-conditions. Afterwards, we sought to determine, through different methods, how far the aggressive or prosocial content of the film had contagiously affected the young viewers. One of these methods, the mask test, will be discussed here in detail. After the film was shown, the subjects were taken to a room containing a closed box in which the subject was told a child was playing. Actually, the box contained an adult, a researcher's assistant, behaving in such a way that the child got the impression that a child of its age was playing in the box. This mock child was invisible to the test subject. On arriving near the box, the experimenter showed two masks. One of these had the terrifying appearance of a witch, while the other represented an animal loved by children, i.e., a rabbit. Next, the experimenter showed the two masks to the mock child in the box. When looking at the witch mask, this "child" burst into tears, whereas it started to crow with delight when the rabbit mask came into view. After this, the subject was given the opportunity to decide which of the two masks he wanted to show to the mock child. If the test subject selected the witch mask, an aggressive act according to our definition had been committed, since the test subject knew that this act would have negative consequences for the victim. If, on the other hand, the subject chose the friendly mask, we may term this to be an act which is the opposite of aggression, and which we designate as prosocial. The results of this experiment are listed in table 8.1. In the aggressive film condition, the aggressive choice was made significantly more frequently than after viewing the prosocial film. The difference between the prosocial and the neutral condition was also considerable, but there was only a tendency toward a difference ($p < .10$, one tailed) after viewing the aggressive or the neutral film.

On the basis of these results, we might conclude that both the aggressive and the prosocial films contagiously affected the children. Other test procedures (drawing test and photo test) developed by us showed similar results. It was remarkable that, in general, the children were slightly *more* influenced by the prosocial than by the aggressive film. This implies that children are influenced in a prosocial direction just as well, if not easier, than in a negative (aggressive) sense. This result is opposite to Rosenhan & White's assumption (1967) that explicitly states

Table 8.1. Frequency of Choices on the Mask Test

CONDITION	CHOICE	
	AGGRESSIVE	PRO-SOCIAL
aggressive film	28	14
prosocial film	9	31
neutral film	21	19

aggressive-pro-social: $\chi^2 = 14.14$ df $= 1$, $p < .001$
aggressive-neutral: $\chi^2 = 1.71$ df $= 1$, $p < .10$
prosocial-neutral: $\chi^2 = 6.45$ df $= 1$, $p < .01$

that altruistic behavior can be modeled less easily—in their opinion this requires rehearsal—than aggressive behavior.

This series of experiments as well as the results obtained in other countries buttress the conclusion that aggressive TV programs may have harmful effects on children. If we subscribe to this conclusion, the next question will be how much aggression is displayed on Dutch television. To provide an answer, a number of programs presented during six weeks in 1977 was analyzed (Wiegman, Vries, & Gutteling, 1978). The selection criterion applied was that all the programs to be analyzed, 117 in all, were frequently (ratings higher than 10 percent) watched by children. Two independent judges scored the number of aggressive and prosocial moments (physical as well as verbal) occurring in each program. In this way, the predominant type of behavior (aggressive or prosocial) could be determined. It was found that, in the total of 117 programs, aggressive behavior was significantly more present than prosocial behavior (T-test: $T = 4.35$, $df = 116$, $p < .001$). Prosocial behavior had a relatively low score, but nevertheless constituted a very considerable part (43 percent) of the total number of actions.

We allude to those who make it appear that there is nothing but aggression on television. We hold that, in particular, the current manner of approach and research methods are the main cause of such a pessimistic judgment. For, if the television programs are analysed and scored only in respect to the number of aggressive events, as is common practice, it is not amazing to conclude that an overwhelming amount of murders, fights, and other severely aggressive scenes are displayed on the TV screen. The substance of the principle applied here is the "self-fulfilling prophecy," in the sense that the researcher will find and conclude exactly what he did induce by his own approach and research method, i.e., an abundance of aggression.

An objective impression is only obtained if several aspects of television programs are drawn into the scope of investigation. This means, essentially, that the researcher must judge all relevant aspects aspects of television events and formulate his conclusions accordingly. Some effort in this direction is embodied in our approach, which includes, in addition to aggression, the opposite behavioral component in the analyses.

However, the reader should not get the impression that we advance a plea for today's Dutch television programs. This is by no means the case. We already stated that the programs analyzed by us, and which have high ratings for children, contained an abundance of aggression. Even if we could have concluded that aggressive and prosocial moments occur at about the same frequency, the situation would still be open to criticism. We believe that, particularly when programs are frequently watched by children, television should perform a positive function. By this we have in mind that programs must be optimally directed at guiding the children's behavior into positive channels. This implies that the prosocial behavior must have more emphasis at the expense of aggression.

The results of our investigation also show that this consideration is hardly taken into account by the broadcasting companies, since we found that, in the early evening between half past six and half past seven, i.e., the prime time for children, aggression dominates more than in any other period (see fig. 8.1). We found that, during the afternoon, relatively few aggressive and prosocial actions were displayed, both having about the same frequency of occurrence. The evening hours, on the other hand, presented a different picture. There is a clear increase in aggressive and prosocial behavior as compared to the afternoon. Moreover, we see that the early evening hours contain a marked peak of aggression, which is not in any way compensated for by prosocial actions. Our results agree in a certain sense with those of Halloran and Croll (1971) in the United Kingdom. They discovered that 60 percent of the programs broadcast before nine o'clock in the evening contained acts of violence, whereas this figure was only 36 percent for programs broadcast after that hour. Halloran's investigation, though

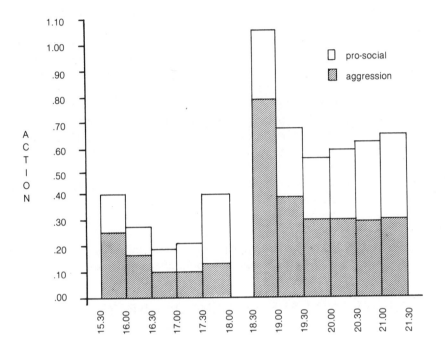

Fig. 8.1. Average Number of Aggressive and Prosocial Behavioral Elements per Minute, During the Afternoon and Early Evening

Source. O. Wiegman, S. Vries, and J. Gutteling, "Zes Weken Television. Aggressie en Affiliatie Nader Bekeken," *Pedagogische Studien* 55, 1979.

not quite comparable with ours because other time criteria are applied, also shows that, in the United Kingdom, too, a peak of violence is present early rather than in the late evening hours.

There is reason to be cautious when making statements as to Dutch television. By this we refer to the restrictions of our research method. It will be clear to the reader that a selection from a six-week television period cannot be held to be representative of the Dutch TV programs consumed by children throughout the year. A number of chance factors have undoubtedly affected the outcome of our investigation. It is, therefore, recommended that further analyses be conducted in the future.

Up to now, our attention has been focused on the overall aggression/prosocial content of TV programs. We will not enter in greater detail into the more specific part of our research. We established that the aggressive and prosocial content of the programs had a verbal character in over half of the cases. Most content analyses of TV programs, as for instance that done by Gerbner and Gross (1976), only score the nonverbal behavior. This approach might create the impression that verbal aggression is hardly displayed on television. Our results, though, point out that this impression is fully erroneous. Moreover, we studied whether the aggressive/prosocial contents of certain kinds of programs were different. We proceeded using the five program categories specified by the broadcasting companies; information, entertainment, sports, children's programs, and drama. The informative programs contained remarkably few aggressive/prosocial actions and, moreover, none of these predominated significantly. The latter statement also applied to the entertainment programs. In the sports programs, too, the aggressive part did not differ significantly from the prosocial part. As regards the last results, we must remark, however, that the number of sports programs analyzed was very small—there were no major sporting events during the research periods—while fighting sports such as boxing were not at all displayed, making any conclusion impossible.

The children's programs did show a preponderance of one of the two behaviors, in the sense that aggressive actions outnumbered prosocial ones. It is true that this difference was not statistically significant, but a tendency toward a difference did exist (T test; $t = 1.97$, $df = 30$, $p < .10$). In a way, though less pronounced, this result agrees with Schramm, Lyle, and Parker (1972), who remarked that violence is rampant in children's programs of commercial TV stations in the United States. In the drama programs category, aggression stood out significantly more than in the children's programs. A further detailed analysis of this category showed that serial programs contained significantly more aggression than drama which was presented once. The drama *produced* in the Netherlands did not differ markedly in this respect from the foreign drama; that is, ours contained an excessive amount of aggression as well.

THE EXTENT AND DEVELOPMENT OF CRIMINALITY IN THE NETHERLANDS

In order to assess the extent and development of the major forms of criminality in the Netherlands, one might consider using data available from the Netherlands Central Bureau of Statistics, i.e., the police statistics. These data involve those criminal acts that have been reported to the police. A large part of actual criminality, however, is never brought to the notice of the police. For a variety of reasons, people often just do not report to the police those things that have happened to them. We can only guess as to the extent of the "dark number" of criminal acts that remain in obscurity. Now the question is, how can the real extent of criminality, including the "dark number," be measured while not making use of police statistics. The answer is that we must ask a sample of the population of the Netherlands whether they have been a victim of an offense last year. However, it would be wrong to suggest that the results of such a victim survey would provide a complete picture of the crime rate. One problem is that it is unclear whether a victim survey would yield valid and reliable data reflecting real criminality. This problem involves questions concerning the degree to which, and the accuracy with which, the interviewed are able to recall the criminal events that have happened to them (Angenent, 1976; Fiselier, 1978). However, research work carried out in the United States (Turner, 1972), the Netherlands (Fiselier, 1974, 1978) and in Germany (Stephan, 1976) has demonstrated that it is, in fact, possible to obtain reliable results from victim surveys. The most important advantage of victim surveys is that—taking into account the reliability margins inherent to survey research—an estimate can be made of the total number of offences committed, including the "dark number."

The Police Statistics Versus Victim Survey: A Comparison

A nation-wide victim-survey has been carried out every year since 1973 (Van Dijk & Steinmetz, 1979), thus enabling us to compare police statistics with victim-survey estimates for crimes committed in the Netherlands. If we consider the development of crime-rates as reflected through police statistics (from 1970 on) and from victim-survey data (from 1973 on), then our conclusion is that there is a steady increase in the number of most kinds of offenses. Remarkable is the increase in vandalism (damage to property). Targets of vandalism are usually public objects, such as public transport, train stations, parking meters, etc. In these cases, the damage is usually considerable. The costs of damages to public telephones have shown an increase of 50 percent in three years time, while the number of public telephones has increased only 16 percent (Van Bergeyk, 1975). Acts of vandalism are often committed by youths. A substantial part of the literature on juvenile delinquency assumes that this form of delinquency is mainly a matter of group behavior. Theories on criminal subcultures which assume the existence of well-organized gangs are well known (Cloward & Ohlin, 1960; Cohen, 1955, 1971). In the Dutch language area, Junger-Tas (1972, 1978) demonstrated that the specific kind of offenses is highly related to the presence or absence of others; theft of money or stealing in school is usually an individual affair, while vandalism is in one-third of the cases committed by two or three persons and in one-third (36.5 percent) by larger groups. It is remarkable that most of those who commit vandalism cannot indicate any special reason for their destructive behavior. Only 23 percent of the cases of damage could be attributed to expressions of anger, frustration, or the result of a quarrel (Buikhuisen, Jongman, Schilt, & Schilt-Drost, 1972). Figure 8.2 also indicates that the data on the offenses "bicycle theft" and "pickpocket" show a clear increase. Theft of private cars, theft from private cars, and sexual assaults show a comparatively stable pattern.

Regarding the differences between police statistics and victim-survey methods, we notice that these differences are relatively small as regards offenses of burglary and car-theft. Since the financial damage is usually great in these cases, victims are quite likely to report them to the police (Angenent, 1976). In many cases, insurance regulations require official records (Van Dijk, 1979). The differences between the other data from police statistics and victim-survey data are considerable. A possible explanation is that one is less likely to report minor offenses which caused relatively little damage to the police. In addition, low report rates may indicate low confidence, on the part of the public, as to the capabilities of the police in finding the offender. For example, police statistics suggest a decrease in bicycle theft of 4 percent from 1976 to 1979, while the victim-survey, on the contrary, shows an increase of 39 percent. Apparently there is no steady relationship across different kinds of offenses between police statistics and victim-survey data.

Table 8.2 shows data on three categories of offenses on which no victim-survey data are reported: (1) offenses against public authority (obstruction of civil servants in the course of their duty, collectively committing overt aggression toward persons or goods), (2) insulting, and (3) crimes against life (murder, homicide). These data have been derived from police statistics. During the past ten years, offenses against public authority have increased 86 percent. The number of insults decreased substantially from 56 offenses per 100,000 inhabitants in the early 1950s to 17 insults in 1970 and 9 offenses in 1979 per 100,000 inhabitants. It is not very likely, however, that the Dutch have become more friendly toward each other. It seems more reasonable to assume that in Dutch society, maybe as a result of changing norms, certain ut-

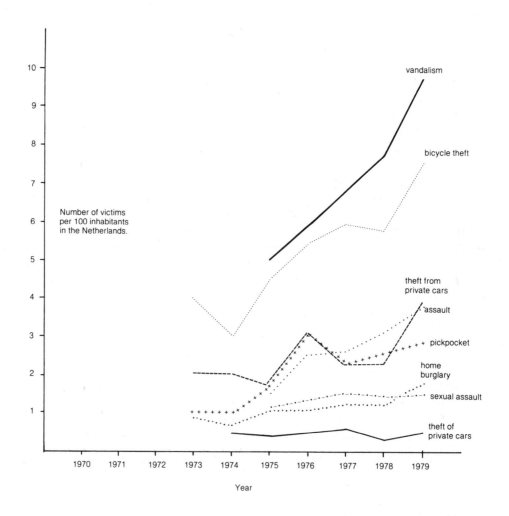

Fig. 8.2a. Extent and Development of Criminality in the Netherlands Based on Victim-Survey Data

Source: J. J. M. van Dijk, and C. D. H. Steinmetz, *De* WODC-slachtofferenquetes 1974-1979. (The Hague: Ministrie van Justitie WODC, 1979).

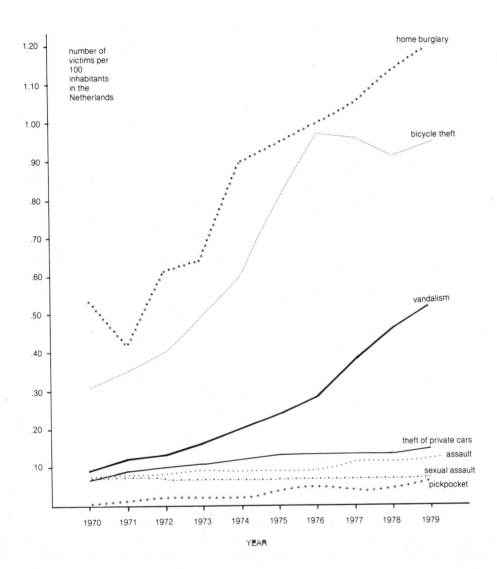

Fig. 8.2b. Extent and Development of Criminality in the Netherlands Based on Data from the Police-Statistics. (Note: The y-Axis Only Has a Range Here From 0% to 1.2%).

Source: "C.B.S., Maandstatistieken politie en Justitie," The Hague; 1970-1979.

Table 8.2 Crime Rates as Recorded by the Netherlands Bureau of Statistics
per 100,000 Inhabitants

OFFENSE	YEAR									
	1970	1971	1972	1973	1974	1975	1976	1977	1978	1979
crime against public authority	15	15	19	19	20	23	26	28	29	28
insult	17	13	12	10	10	10	9	10	11	9
crime against life (murder, homicide)	5	6	7	8	9	9	11	11	10	9

Source: C.B.S., "Maandstatistieken Politie en Justitie," The Hague, 1970-1979.

terances are no longer considered insulting. More serious are crimes against life, the number of which has increased from 5 per 100,000 inhabitants in 1970 to 9 per 100,000 in 1979. This is at least five times as much as in other European countries (Van Dijk, 1976). This high figure is a result of the fact that the police categorize any event in which a person has died under suspicious circumstances as murder or homicide. If we look at the actual conviction rates for murder and homicide, it is not very high in the Netherlands. In 1950, there were fewer than 3 convictions for every million citizens; in 1970, this number was 5 per million; and in 1979, it was 9 convictions per million Dutch inhabitants.

A Comparison with the United States

Because of the great difference in ways of defining crimes, in registration methods etc., it is infeasible and not justified to compare all international crime statistics. Lately, however, a start has been made with measuring crime rates in a number of countries by means of standardized victim-survey methods. Data are being analyzed now, so we cannot report anything as yet.

The original sources for the comparisons we now wish to offer are the Dutch National Crime Survey of 1977 and the United States National Crime Survey of Block (1980). Data from these two surveys are broadly comparable, but they differ in detail.

Table 8.3 shows that the rate of home burglary is five times higher in the United States than in the Netherlands. No difference is found between the two countries in burglary rates for homes where someone was there. However, burglaries of dwellings where nobody was at home are nine times more likely in the United States than the Netherlands. But once a burglary occurs, the Dutch householder is likely to suffer a greater loss than the American. The much higher rate for home burglary in the United States seems associated with the fact that far more American than Dutch women go out to work. In most American dwellings, there is usually nobody at home during daytime. The consequence is that at daytime it is relatively easy to break into homes. It was shown, indeed, that most burglaries in the United States take place at daytime (Lentzer, 1976), whereas in the Netherlands a peak is reached in the evening hours. In the Netherlands, rates of wallet theft and street assault are higher than in the United States. Rates of street robbery are about the same in both countries. Given the violent reputation of the United States, it is surprising that rates of street assaults are higher in the Netherlands. However, assaults in the Netherlands are less likely to gun attacks as compared to assaults in America (1.8 percent vs. 14.5 percent), and are half as likely to be attacks with other weapons than assaults in the United States (19 percent vs. 38 percent).

Sexual Offences

From victim-surveys (Van Dijk & Steinmetz, 1979), it appears that the number of sexual offenses must be much higher than the official police statistics suggest. There are reasons to
assume that even the victim-survey data are minimum estimates, since it is very well possible
that respondents do not consider a given offense as such (Van Dijk & Steinmetz, 1981) and/
or do not wish to mention it to the interviewer. Forty-two percent of the Dutch women say that
they do not risk going out on the streets at night, as compared to 19 percent of the men. More
than 50 percent of the women of less than 35 years old think they are most likely to be victim of
an indecent assault (Cozijn, 1976). Cozijn (1979) analyzed all reported cases of rape and
assault in a medium-sized Dutch town during five years. It appeared that assaults as well as
rapes were seldom committed by groups of attackers; most of these crimes were committed
by individuals. In the United States, on the contrary, rape seems to be committed much
more by groups. In Los Angeles, the percentage of rape committed by groups is 46 percent
(Chapel, 1977). Rape seems to be associated with such factors as time, day of the week, and
season. Rape rates are highest in summer, on the weekend, and at night. Such fluctuations
are less strong for assaults, which are relatively equally divided among seasons as well as days
of the week, and happen just as often during daytime as at night. The attacker is nearly always unknown to the victim, while in case of rape the victim is often acquainted with the attacker.

According to public opinion, the risk for a female of being assaulted or raped is highest outdoors, e.g., in the street, a park, or an open field. It is true that many females were raped during hitchhiking but not a single rape happened in a park. However, it was found that more
than half of the attacks happened *indoors*, during the evening and night. Especially young
women of 15 to 25 years old, actively taking part in social life, seem to have a high chance of
being a victim of these crimes, more than women of other age groups. Rape often seems to be
the result of a relationship that had developed, and gone out of control, during an evening
out.

Football Vandalism

One form of criminality that is not reflected through official statistics is what we call football
vandalism. During the last couple of years there has been a tendency of increasing aggression
among young football fans in the Netherlands. This can be observed on terraces, around the

Table 8.3. Rates of Four Types of Crime in the Netherlands
and the United States in 1976 and 1977

OFFENSES	UNITED STATES 1976	NETHERLANDS 1977
burglary per 100,000 households	6482	1253
wallet or purse theft per 100,000 inhabitants	927	2100
street assaults per 100,000 inhabitants	1309	2257
street robberies per 100,000 inhabitants	243	194

Source: Block, R. The impact of victimization, rates and patterns. A comparison of the
Netherlands and the United States. Unpublished paper, 1980.

stadium, at train stations, and in trains. During the 1975–1977 football seasons, respectively 4, 11, and 21 cases of vandalism committed by football fans in trains were reported, while the overall vandalism in trains seemed to decrease. Substantial theory and empirical research concerning football vandalism can hardly be found in the Netherlands at this moment. In the United Kingdom, however, more work has been carried out on this problem; the Harrington Report (1968) and the Lang Report (1969) present and overview on the subject. Taylor (1971) focused on theory, and field-research was described in the Milson Report (1976) and by Marsh, Rosser, & Harré (1978). In the Netherlands, some regard football vandalism as one aspect of youth vandalism, a social phenomenon, which should also be studied as such (Van Dijik, 1977). Others stress the influence of the massive character of the circumstances in which soccer takes place (CRM, 1977). Moll (1977) stated that this type of vandalism does not so much result from situational factors during the game, but that it should be explained as a result of an aggressive preoccupation of the football fans that existed beforehand. Others stress the relationship between these incidents and the specific course of the game: its excitement, unexpected events, the behavior of the referee and the players. These are all important factors in helping the fan behavior. Van der Brug (1981), using newspaper reports, analyzed all vandalism incidents that happened during eight soccer-seasons (from 1971 to 1979). It appeared that matches that had been exciting, i.e., those that resulted in either a draw or a one-point difference, were slightly more characterized by violent incidents on the side of the supporters, as compared to those matches that had been less exciting ($x^2 = 3.15$, df $= 1$, p $< .10$). Incidents were usually initiated by supporters of the losing team. Targets of these aggressive incidents were usually players of the opposing team or referees. The result seems to support the frustration-aggression hypothesis (Berkowitz, 1962).

Terrorism

During the past few years, several acts of terrorism have occurred in the Netherlands. Incidents have occurred involving small groups or individuals who kidnapped other people and threatened to kill them if certain demands were not satisfied. Often, these demands concerned political issues. In some cases, an action of this kind was carried out by a criminal or a prisoner without any political motive. In its purest sense, terrorism is an attempt to gain influence by means of violent and unlawful activities and by publicity. Hijackings and other forms of effective hostage taking are prototypes of terrorism, in that the terrorists are trying to put pressure upon a government by means of arbitrarily selected victims, and by influencing public opinion (Rosenthal, 1979). From 1970 on, nearly every year a hijacking or hostage case took place in the Netherlands. These were carried out by Palestinian, Japanese, South Moluccan, and other groups.

When we hear of hijackings or hostage cases, these often concern occupations of buildings, e.g., embassies, or airplane hijackings. However, the Netherlands have several times been confronted with the hijacking of a train. For example, in December 1975, heavily armed Moluccan youths hijacked a train. They got into the train with their weapons wrapped in St. Claus present paper. This hijacking lasted 12 days. Three people were killed and four wounded. In this and most other such actions, relatively few hijackers were involved (2 to 9). In one case, the intended kidnapping of Queen Juliana of the Netherlands, more South Moluccans were involved (45). The number of hostages in these cases ranged from 1 to 130. In some cases, one of the demands of the terrorists was the release from prison of persons from the same organization who had been captured during previous actions (Bastiaans, 1979; Cuperus, 1980).

PUBLIC OPINION

In the Netherlands, like in other countries, TV and newspapers pay considerable attention to the increasing rate of criminality. On October 18, 1980, the headline of one of the largest Dutch newspapers (*De Telegraaf*) stated: "Four crimes every minute. Minor criminality becoming major problem." Every time a murder is reported, this newspaper seizes the opportunity to stress the increasing level of danger in the Netherlands. This kind of information is reflected in everyday conversation. To the interview-question (Coenen & Van Dijk, 1978) whether one had discussed a crime during the previous day, 19 percent of the respondents agreed. Only for the items "sports" and "unemployment" were these percentages higher.

The Public

To the question as to what would be the greatest social problem in our society today, "crime" scored highest after "unemployment" (Cozijn & Van Dijk, 1976). Just as in Germany (Stephan, 1976) 15 percent of the Dutch respondents find criminality the greatest problem in the country. Seventy-five percent of the Dutch population think that crime rates have increased heavily. It appears that most respondents have violent criminality in mind when answering these questions. They are less pessimistic about the risk they run themselves in becoming a victim of crime. Only half of the subjects believe that this probability has increased, and this especially concerns crimes against property. They are even less concerned about the level of criminality in their own neighborhoods. On the basis of such seemingly inconsistent data, Fiselier (1978) stressed that the fear of becoming a victim of a crime has to be distinguished from feelings of anxiety as to crime being a social problem, probably because different kinds of offenses are concerned. The general assumption seems to be that crime as a social problem is connected to serious forms of violent criminality, while crimes that could be inflicted on oneself are likely to be minor offenses, i.e., offenses against property.

If people are asked whether they have every really felt threatened in the street, only 5 percent answer yes (Cozijn & Van Dijk, 1976). This suggests that there is a great discrepancy between the actual feelings of the population and what certain media suggest. It is true, however, that many take certain precautions. Approximately one-third of the population (30 percent) think that they would better stay indoors at night, and 46 percent find that they should be careful in the street (Cozijn & Van Dijk, 1976). There seems to exist a great difference between men and women; 42 percent of the women think that it is wise not to take an evening walk, while only 19 percent of the men hold this opinion.

Women's greater overall anxiety for violent crime is in particular based upon fear of rape. Fear of being raped is, for example, greater than the fear of becoming a victim of other aggressive offenses. If we compare this with the actual percentage of victims, we find, of course, that men are less often victims of sexual offences. The opposite is true for physical aggressive offenses such as threatening. Men are about three times as likely to become a victim of threat than women (see table 8.4). Fiselier (1978) also ascertained that men are twice as often victims of violent crimes than women. So the stronger anxiety that females have seems to be unrealistic; women have less chance of becoming a victim than men.

Place of residence also seems to play an important role in the fear of crime figures. In cities, this fear is twice as strong as in rural communities (see Talbe 8.5). The fact that people from cities are more afraid seems to be justified, since their risk is greater. The risk of becoming the victim of threat in our largest cities (Amsterdam, Rotterdam, The Hague) is nearly six times as large as it is for people from Dutch rural communities.

Table 8.4. Overview of Fear of Crime Index Data and Percentages of Victimization, Concerning Three Types of Crime for Males and Females

SEX	FEAR OF CRIME INDEX n = 1,219	% VICTIMS OF THREAT IN THE STREET n = 10,000	% VICTIMS OF INDECENT APPROACH n = 10,000	% VICTIMS OF ALL TYPES OF CRIME n = 10,000
male	1.15	3.5	0.8	19
female	2.24	1.2	1.5	14.3

Sources: Crime index data is derived from C. Cozijn and J. J. M. Van Dijt, *Onrustgevoelens in Nederland* (The Hague: Wetenschappelijk Onderzoeken Documentatiecentrum van het Ministrie van Justitie, 1976). Victimization percentages derived from J. J. M. Van Dijk and A. C. Vianen, *Omvang en ontwikkeling van criminaliteit, slachtofferenquetes 1974-1979* (The Hague: Wetenschappelijk Onderzoeken Documentatiecentrum van het Ministrie van Justitie, 1979).

There seems to be a relationship between age and fear of crime for women. Fear is highest for young women. It seems that this fear is based on fear of rape. The relationship between age and fear of crime does not exist for men while, in fact, young men are more likely to become victims. Fiselier (1978) computed that the percentage of aggressive incidents in which young people are involved (18 to 29 years old) is 8.3, while for persons of 60 years or more, this percentage is 0.6, which is fourteen times less.

Table 8.6 shows again that fear of crime is hardly contingent on the actual risk of becoming a victim. Young men from large cities, who run the highest risks, show very little fear, while elderly women from large cities, who run very little risk have a high level of anxiety. The rank order correlation between anxiety and real chance of becoming a victim (computed from Table 8.6) is even negative (− .27).

These Dutch findings agree with results obtained in other countries, e.g., Germany (Stephan, 1976), Canada (Courtis, 1979), the United States (Hindelang, 1979), and France (Peyeferitte, 1977). In all of these countries, it was found that the variable "fear of crime" is related

Table 8.5. Overview of Fear of Crime Index Data and Percentages of Victimization of Threat in the Street and of Criminality in General, for Different Residential Areas, for 1976 and Part of 1977

RESIDENTIAL AREA	FEAR OF CRIME INDEX n = 1,219	% VICTIMS OF THREAT IN THE STREET n = 10,000	% VICTIMS OF ANY TYPE OF CRIME n = 10,000
Amsterdam, Rotterdam, The Hague	NA	3.9	26.6
Towns of more than 50,000 inhabitants	2.1	3.1	21.8
Towns of less than 50,000 inhabitants	1.3	1.7	12.3
Towns of less than 5,000 inhabitants	NA	.7	7.5

Sources: Crime index data derived from C. Cozijn and J. J. M. Van Dijk, *Onrustgevoelens in Nederland* (The Hague: Wetenschappelijk Onderzoeken Documentatiecentrum van het Ministrie van Justitie, 1976); Victimization percentages derived from J. J. M. Van Dijk and A. C. Vianen, *Omvang en ontwikkeling van criminaliteit, slachtofferenquetes 1974-1979* (The Hague: Wetenschappelijk Onderzoeken Documentatiecentrum van het Ministrie van Justitie, 1979).

Table 8.6. Overview of Fear of Crime Index Data and the Rank Order of Risk of Becoming a Victim of Threat in the Street

SUBGROUP	FEAR OF CRIME INDEX	RANK ORDER FEAR OF CRIME	RANK ORDER OF RISK OF BECOMING VICTIM OF THREAT IN THE STREET
young women, city	2.73	1	3.5
young women, rural	2.43	2.5	5.5
elder women, city	2.43	2.5	7
elder women, rural	1.75	4	8
young men, city	1.55	5	1
elder men, city	1.48	6	3.5
young men, rural	.94	7	2
elder men, rural	.90	8	5.5

Source: Computed on the basis of data from J. J. M. Van Dijk and A. C. Vianen, *Omvang en antwikkeling van criminaliteit, slachtofferenquetes 1974-1979* (The Hague: Wetenschappelijk Onderzoeken Documentatiecentrum van het Ministrie van Justitie, 1977).

strongest to sex. One would expect that people who once have been a victim of a crime would be more anxious than people who have never been a victim. Yet Cozijn and Van Dijk (1976) only found a slight correlation (r = 0.14) between fear of crime and being a victim. This supports the idea that this fear is mainly based on ideas and not on experience. However, this research only concerned victims of minor crimes against property. Fiselier (1978) found that victims of violent crime do, in fact, have a strong anxiety about recurrence. The percentage of Dutch citizens who have been a victim of a serious physical aggressive offense is, of course, very small and hardly affects the average fear of crime index.

Fear of crime is also related to the faith that people have in the police (r = 0.15; Cozijn & Van Dijk, 1976). People who have faith in the police are less anxious. Junger-Tas (1978), however, remarks that the Dutch have strange ideas about the police. In general, the police are seen as criminal-hunters, while in reality this concerns only a limited part of their work.

It is, of course, not only interesting to find out how much anxiety there is among people, but also how aggressive behavior is judged. Walgrave and Kerckvoorde (1977) conducted a study in Belgium, in which they asked several groups of subjects (including policemen, group-leaders from reformatory schools, parents, youths, and youths from reformatory schools) to judge the seriousness of 25 different forms of juvenile delinquency. Physically aggressive offenses were unanimously judged most serious. Children's maltreatment was judged as the most serious offense, and mother beating scored second. Least serious were begging, sex in cars, and stealing of alcoholic drinks. Youths were very intolerant; they condemned the offenses most. Group-leaders, however, were the most tolerant. Of the adults, parents were the least tolerant and policemen occupied a middle position. One factor that played an important role in these judgments was the sex of the offender. In general, delinquent behavior was rejected more strongly for females than for males.

The Victims

In the Netherlands, three important studies have been conducted investigating consequences of offences for victims. Smale (1977, 1980) performed two studies on victims of serious aggressive crimes and serious crimes against poverty. These studies indicated that the consequences for victims are rather serious. Smale found that all victims suffered psychosocial damage.

Complaints concerned obsessive thoughts about the incident, insomnia, use of medicine, anxiety, and the like. These kinds of problems are encountered most frequently by victims of violent crimes, and they are contingent on the seriousness of the injuries they had suffered. If these injuries were more serious, the psychosocial damage is usually greater. Jaspers (1980) investigated the nature of consequences for victims of hijackings. Their complaints are almost the same as those of the kinds of victims we have described above, and were very persistent. Two-thirds of the ex-hostages continued to encounter negative consequences after a long time. They complain about anxiety, phobias, irritability, insomnia, and the like. The intensity of the negative consequences is greater if the period of being kept hostage had been longer. There seems to be a relationship between the number of complaints right after the hijacking and negative consequences in the long run. This indicates that early complaints have to be considered seriously, since they are indicative of possible long-lasting psychosocial problems. In case of a hijacking, not only the hostages themselves but their relatives as well are in a position of extreme stress. It is not surprising that the next of kin will encounter the same sort of problems that are encountered by the hostages themselves.

It is surprising that ex-hostages mention not only negative consequences; about one-third of them reported stronger ties with their relatives and acquaintances, the ability to see things more relatively, more enjoyment of life, and a reinforced self-consciousness. Jaspers (1980) also found that negative consequences are, in the long run, more serious for ex-hostages if they had a lower educational level and were younger. Smale (1980), however, could not ascertain such relationships for victims of serious crimes against property and violent crimes. Apart from that, consequences were greater for women than for men. One important factor that emerges from Smale's research is the degree to which the victim was acquainted with the offender. Violent acts induce more anxiety if the victim was unacquainted with the offender. In case of crimes against property, this relationship is reversed.

We have mentioned before that Cozijn and Van Dijk (1976) could find hardly any relationship between fear of crime and victimization. However, for victims of serious offenses, this relationship does exist. Victims of violent crimes frequently stated that they were afraid of the crime being repeated and that they would be the victim of revanche. Because of the seriousness of the consequences, among other things, one would expect these victims to have strong feelings of retribution. Yet, retributive feelings are less strong for victims of violent crime than for victims of crime against property (Smale & Spickenheuer, 1977). In general, feelings of retribution do not seem to be very strong. However, 70 percent of the victims from Smale and Spickenheuer's study say that they find the penalty to which the offender had been convicted too low, but the penalty that they would be suitable is rather low as well. A little more than half of the victims of serious crimes would suggest a sentence of no more than three months. We could expect that the degree to which a victim sees himself as being a cause of the incident influences the degree of retributive feelings. This is not the case; self-blame and feelings of retribution seem to be independent of each other. It is remarkable that retributive feelings are stronger as the injuries are more serious, but these feelings are not stronger if one has been a victim of a crime more often.

The Media

Concern about the increasing level of crime can hardly be based upon experiences. The chance for the average Dutch citizen to be confronted with a serious crime is very small. But we all are confronted with information concerning crime, through radio, newspapers, and TV. These are presumably the most important sources of information on which the Dutch base their opinions about criminality. This suggestion is supported by research data from Coenen and Van Dijk (1978). Being asked what source had immediately influenced their conversations about crime, two-thirds answered that this was a newspaper article. Especially newspapers seem to have a substantial influence in these kinds of conversations. Only 13 percent indicated that radio or TV broadcasts were the source. If a newspaper reports about crime, it concerns mostly violent crime. Twenty-six percent of the articles concern violence, while this form of criminality covers only 2.5 percent of the police-registered crime. It is also remarkable that Coenen and Van Dijk (1978) found that newspapers are paying more and more attention to crime. For example, while in 1966 the articles on criminality had an average length of 58 inches, in 1974 this was 81 inches. Pictures are more often included in the articles, and are more eye-catching. Although Dutch newspapers spend a smaller part of their editorial columns on subjects concerning crime as compared to foreign newspapers, Dutch papers, as well, present an image of criminality that is out of proportion. Of course, the most important question concerns the degree to which this influences anxiety among the Dutch population.

Table 8.7 shows that newspapers paying more attention to crime have readers who are slightly more concerned about the development of criminality. However, the question of causality has not been answered. Does reading a specific newspaper influence one's anxiety level, or does our level of concern make us choose a newspaper, or do these variables have a common cause? There are research data suggesting that newspapers affect feelings of concern. Coenen and Van Dijk (1978) found that, in a large group not reading a newspaper, more people said that they were less pessimistic about their personal victimization risk. This difference remained statistically significant when external factors were controlled. From a study on feelings of insecurity in the Netherlands (Coenen & Van Dijk, 1976), it appears that 40 percent of the people who sometimes consider the possibility of victimization indicate that newspaper articles are the immediate causes of their thoughts. In research carried out elsewhere, we can find support for the suggestion that newspapers reinforce feelings of insecurity (e.g., Davis, 1952; Peyeferitte, 1976). There appear to be three categories of people who have special interest in reading articles about crime: women, elderly people, and people with lower education (Van Dijk, 1978). These people also show higher fear of crime rates. The fact that they pay more attention to articles on crime may not arise from a greater interest in crime, but from the fact that these articles are usually easy to read and understand. Articles on such subjects as politics and the economy are much more difficult. For these people, "news" consists of accidents, murders, etc. This leads to a one-sided picture, which is possibly reflected in their higher fear of crime scores.

Table 8.7. Degree of Anxiousness of Readers of Newspapers, and Percentages of Articles on Crime in These Newspapers

NEWSPAPER	DEGREE OF ANXIOUSNESS	PERCENTAGE OF ARTICLES ON CRIME
De Telegraaf	+ 1,25	3,86%
De Provinciale Pers	+ 1,06	2,95%
Algemeen Dagblad	+ 1,05	3,46%
Trouw	− 0.03	2,30%
Volkskrant	− 0,36	2,63%
NRC-Handelsblad	− 0,60	1,40%

Source: A. W. M. Coenen and J. J. M. Van Dijk, "Politieverslaggeving, Koffiegraat en de angst voor misdrijven," *Tijdschrift voor Criminologie* 2 (1978).

PREVENTION OF CRIMINALITY AND GOVERNMENT POLICY

In Dutch studies on criminality, three periods can be distinguished. The first runs from the middle sixties to the early seventies. This phase is especially characterized by research on differential psychological properties of offenders. These studies stressed the humanization of care for delinquents, rather than legal punishment (Denkers, 1969).

In the second, during the first half of the 1970s, research on effectiveness of government policies and legal punishment took a central position. From a national survey in 1973 (Angenent, 1978), 71 percent of those interviewed felt that the government did not pay enough attention to crime prevention. Half of those interviewed had the opinion that penalties should be heavier. Some of them (6 percent) were in favor of labor camps, and 6 percent were in favor of introducing the death penalty. Twenty-five percent preferred social measures, i.e., better care for youths, reducing social and economic contrasts, improving mentality, etc. The question was whether criminality could be reduced through high penalties. A great number of studies from this period involve relative effectiveness of certain measures, e.g., short vs. long sentences, "open" vs. "closed" prisons, and imprisonment vs. fines.

Fiselier (1969) investigated whether a stay in an "open" prison would give rise to lower rates of recidivism as compared to the conventional, "closed" prison. In an "open" prison, prisoners are given more freedom. It appeared that open prisons did not lead to a lower recidivism-rate. Dijksterhuis (1973) investigated the extent to which traffic-delinquents, who had spent their confinement in such a special prison, relapsed less than those who had been in a traditional prison. No differences were found between the two groups. Steenhuis (1972) ascertained that fines were equally effective as imprisonment, as regards driving under the influence of alcohol. A general conclusion that can be drawn from these and other studies (Caminado, 1973; Van der Werff, 1974) is that the alternatives that have been investigated are at least as effective in preventing recidivism as the more traditional penalties. On the basis of this conclusion, a number of investigators suggest, especially in case of minor offenses, to replace traditional confinement with fines or a more humane sort of imprisonment, such as the "open" prison.

Although the studies that we mentioned were dealing with real offenses, the average citizen, when asked about inducement of heavier penalties, has more violent crimes in mind, such as murder, homicide, or rape, and not such offenses as driving under the influence. Apart from this, the research on the effect of alternative penalties is concerned with relatively small offenses. It is not clear whether the positive effects could also be found in the case of more severe criminality. It is interesting to note what the reactions of judges have been to these developments. In some groups in our society, a call for heavier penalities can be heard but, at the same time, these may partly be neutralized by research data. In order to gain some insight into the development and change in conviction measures for heavy violent crime, Van Dijk, (1976) compared sentences that were imposed for three types of crime (murder and homicide, rape, robbery) in 1969, 1972, and 1975.

Figure 8.3 shows that the total number of sentences for the three types of crime has slightly decreased from 1969 to 1975. Moreover, for rape and armed robbery it appears that the number of long sentences (≥ 1 year) has slightly decreased as well. This overview does not seem to support the idea that the Dutch judge is responding to the call for longer sentences for these kinds of offenses.

The question now is, whether the Dutch judge passes more or longer sentences than his foreign colleagues; in other words, what is the ratio between the total number of persons who are imprisoned in the Netherlands in a certain period and the number of people imprisoned in other countries? C.B.S. (1970) reports a comparison of 15 countries, including the Netherlands, to answer this question. Table 8.8 shows these figures in terms of proportions of the

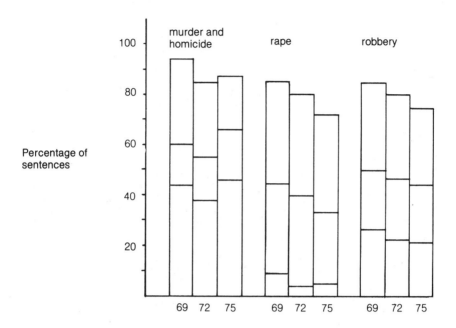

Fig. 8.3. A comparison of Sentences for Three Types of Crime.

Note: Each column is divided into three parts: the lower part represents sentences > 1 year, the middle part represents sentences ≤ 1 year and the upper part represents suspended sentences.

Source: "C.B.S., Maandstatistieken politie en Justitie," The Hague, 1979.

population in 1970, 1971, and 1972. It appears that the Netherlands have the lowest imprisonment rates of these 15 countries. So, compared with his foreign colleagues, the Dutch judge follows a relatively liberal course of action.

The third state, from 1975 to the present, is characterized by three main outlines: (1) the increase of criminality that has been suggested by the mass media, (2) the role of political parties, and (3) the growth of the security industry (e.g., guard services). The suggestion that the extent of criminality, including hidden crime, must be much greater than that officially registered has given rise to the so-called "dark number studies." The results of these studies (Fieselier, 1978; Jongman, 1978; Van Dijk, 1974; Van Dijk & Steinmetz, 1979) support the idea that one has to be careful in imposing legal sanctions because of their relatively arbitrary character. These results have raised some questions as to selectivity in legal decision-taking, because it appeared that only a rather small proportion of offenders was actually prosecuted. Apart from that, it appears that in Dutch society the stereotype image of the delinquent still exists. This image is characterized by a relatively low education, low social class, and male sex. An accused who fills this image is likely to get a longer sentence, even if he had committed the same crime as one who does not fit it well (Jongman, 1978).

Table 8.8. Selected Countires Ranked in Order of the Number of Persons in Prison per 100,000 Persons in the Population for the Most Recent Year Information Was Available

RANK	COUNTRY	YEAR	IMPRISONMENT RATE PER 100,000 POPULATION	(REMAND RATE PER 100,000 POP.)[6]
1	U.S.A.[3]	1970	406 531/203 200 000 = 200.0	
2	Poland[1]	1972	62 748/ 33 070 000 = 189.7	(88.8)
3	Australia[1]	1972	16 615/ 12 960 000 = 128.2	(9.2)
4	Finland[1]	1972	4 947/ 4 630 000 = 106.8	(11.0)
5	New Zealand[4]	1972	2 643/ 2 850 000 = 92.7	—
6	Canada[1]	1972	19 668/ 21 850 000 = 90.0	(11.0)
7	England and Wales[5]	1971	39 708/ 48 900 000 = 81.3	(6.1)
8	Denmark[2]	1971	3 350/ 4 800 000 = 69.8	(22.0)
9	Sweden[2]	1971	4 977/ 8 090 000 = 61.4	(6.9)
10	France[1]	1972	31 573/ 51 700 000 = 61.1	(21.8)
11	Italy[1]	1972	27 812/ 54 350 000 = 51.2	(27.8)
12	Japan[1]	1972	49 241/105 990 000 = 46.5	(7.9)
13	Spain[1]	1972	13 826/ 34 680 000 = 39.9	(16.6)
14	Norway[2]	1971	1 432/ 3 870 000 = 37.1	(13.7)
15	Netherlands[2]	1971	2 919/ 13 120 000 = 22.4	(10.4)

Data Sources:
[1]UN Census of Prison Population (1972). Population as of December 1, 1972.
[2]Great Britain Expenditure Committee Report (1971). Population as of January 1, 1971.
[3]Estimated from total of State and Federal Institutions, local jails, and juvenile institutions. Sources: *National Prisions Statistics Bulletin*, US Bureau of Prison No. 47 (1972); *National Jail Census* (1970) US Department of Justice; *Children in Custody* (1971) US Department of Justice. In 1965, the equivalent statistics were 404 049/194 240 000 = 208.0 (US Task Force Report 1967).
[4]Report of the Department of Justice, New Zealand (1973). Average daily population.
[5]Home Office. Report on the work of the Prison Department (1971). Average daily population.
[6]Remand rate is not restricted to those awaiting arraignment or their first trial. In some European jurisdictions such as Italy, this includes those awaiting a hearing in a court of second instance.
SOURCE: C.B.S. Maandstatistieken politie en justitie. The Hague, 1979.

The Effect of Publicity Campaigns

The Dutch Department of Justice originated an organization for the prevention of crime. The purpose of this organization is to contribute on a nationwide level to detection, removal, and prevention of situations and behavior which might stimulate criminality (Vader, 1979, 1980). For that reason, in 1977 and 1978, a nationwide publicity campaign was carried out by the Dutch Information Service. Some of the goals of the campaign were to increase the awareness of the Dutch population about the organization, and to enhance their willingness to cooperate and take security measures. In this campaign, mass media were used (e.g., television films). For instance, several times a week, half-minute announcements were broadcast on TV, just before the news, in which an item from the campaign was presented. Subsequently, advertisements in daily and weekly newspapers were published. One also could request extra information, for which a post-box number was displayed. Stickers of all sorts with a crime-prevention slogans and posters were available. Apart from that, free-publicity channels were used, e.g., newsreel programs on radio as well as TV, door-to-door papers, etc.

The evaluation research concerning the campaign was done by the Dutch Information Service of the Dutch Ministry of Justice (RVD/NSS, 1978, 1979; Van Dijk & Steinmetz, 1981).

Sixty eight percent of the population was able to recall one or more items from the campaign. The greater part (82 percent) of those who mentioned one or more items said that television was one of the sources of information for them. Newspapers (37 percent), posters (9 percent), radio and weekly papers (both 8 percent) were mentioned less frequently.

Among people who knew one or more items of the campaign and also stated that they would take preventive measures based upon it, a higher percentages were found for inhabitants of big cities (13 percent), among the highest social class (16 percent), and for the group under 55 years old (13 percent). Lower percentages were found among the inhabitants of small cities (10 percent among the lower classes (7 percent), and among older people (8 percent). Van Dijk and Steinmetz (1979, 1981) ascertained in an earlier study that the objective risk of victimization is higher when one is young and living in a big city, and when one belongs to a higher social class. So it seems that those population groups with the highest objective risks took the information most to heart. This research has provided some indication that the nationwide information campaign on crime prevention had a relatively positive effect on the reported intentionality to take preventive measures, e.g., paying more attention to locking doors, buying better locks, and marking down the frame number of one's bike. However, we suggest that information campaigns concerning crime prevention can be considered successful only if the practical application of the advice will objectively lead to a decreased risk for the groups involved; in other words, the campaign should result in a decrease in the number of victims. But, well-performed evaluation studies on this matter are still lacking. This can partly be attributed to the lack of a general theoretical framework which generates cues for the construction of prevention programs, as well as for the exact tuning in of these programs to the characteristics of high-risk groups. One question is, however, whether criminality just shifts place if crime prevention is effective in a certain area. Potential offenders will presumably search for other possibilities to commit their crimes. A well-known fact, for example, is that when steering column locks were introduced, joy-riders focused on older cars without such a lock. We are of the opinion, however, that the chance of shifting effects according to place, time, strategy, and offense is reduced by introducing public information measures on a national and international level.

Prevention with Respect to Youth

In the Netherlands, relatively little research has been carried out on prevention and treatment of aggressive behavior in children and youths. The research that was carried out has focused in particular on treatment of aggressive behavior of delinquent adolescents. Regarding the care of potential criminal youths in the Netherlands, just as in several other countries, an effort has been made to keep youths out of reach of the legal authorities. Behind this lies the idea that, when they have been in contact with authorities once, stigmatization will occur that might damage their future career and stimulate future criminal behavior. The solutions for these youths are usually sought in ambulant care. In the Netherlands, we believe that putting boys (these are more often involved than girls) into homes, together with other potential delinquents, stimulates their criminal behavior. Jongman and De Jong (1976) compared groups of youths from two parts of the Netherlands who had been in contact with the children's court magistrate. In one Dutch district, there was a tendency to place children in institutions, while this occurred less often in the other district. The two groups were matched as to age, social background, past experiences with institutions, etc. In this way, 41 of the mostly similar pairs were formed, of which one boy was placed in a home and the other one stayed with his family. Fifteen years later, the criminal records of the two groups were compared. The number of pairs of which the one who was placed in an institution had committed offenses, while the other had not, was 16. There were only five pairs of which the noninstitutionalized boy had committed crimes while the other had not.

These data seem to support the suggestion that putting delinquent youths into institutions only stimulates their delinquent behavior. Although these studies are, from a methodological point of view, not entirely sound, they support the idea that children should be kept out of the hands of the judge as long as possible. This idea is also reflected through official policies and statistics. The number of children placed in homes decreased from 19,000 to 12,000 between 1967 and 1976, while the number of persons under age hardly decreased in that period, and criminality slightly increased. At this moment, a solution is especially sought in ambulant social aid. Many of these programs come from England and the United States. In the Netherlands, too, we are acquainted with diversion projects, through which youths who have come into contact with the police receive early social aid. Especially through practical aid, e.g., dialogue with the school, search for a job and housing, etc., an effort is made to keep the youths away from legal authorities. It is striking that practical aid has become more and more prevalent, as opposed to talking with youths. In this form of aid, the police play an important role. A study among police in one of our big cities (Van der Zee-Nefkens, 1975) showed that 41 percent of the telephone calls concern requests for social assistance. If under-age persons are involved, the police usually contact the parents, or mention institutions of social assistance. The need for social assistance is greatest on the weekends. This has led to the appointment, in one of our big cities, of extra social workers during the weekends. Here, as well, it seems that social assistance is being stressed more than legal sanctioning. This, however, makes high demands upon the policemen.

In the Netherlands, we have several of these social aid projects, the effects of which have scarcely been evaluated systematically. There is only one exception to this: a project at the University of Amsterdam. A program has been developed there for boys between 14 and 20 years of age who have been in contact with legal authorities. The basic assumption behind this project is that many of the potentially delinquent youths have insufficient social skills. This results in incapabilities when it comes to applying for a job, developing social relationships, spending money, interacting with parents, etc. In a 10-session program, boys were trained in these kinds of skills. The training was focused on their specific situation. The results of this training were very promising. After a period of about 10 months, 29 boys from the control group had committed an offense again, while from the experimental group this number was only seven (Bartels, 1977). In Belgium, such a project was carried out as well. In this case, not only youths, but also their families were treated. Apart from psychological aid, practical assistance was offered. The family was taught how to spend money, allowances were arranged, etc. The result was that 80 percent of the boys who originally would have been placed into institutions could stay with their families (Verhellen, 1975). These training programs show that juvenile delinquency has much to do with such factors as maladaption in society, lack of skills, and related deficits.

Leisure time activities deserve our special attention. Buikhuizen, Jongman, Schilt & Schilt-Drost (1972) found that especially youths with lower educations indulge in vandalism during the weekend. Vandalism is one of the few ways of expressing and entertaining themselves. This has led to the decision by the public authorities to subsidize clubs for youths, with the purpose of keeping them off the streets. An effort is being made to infiltrate their subculture, with streetcorner workers, in order to locate groups of potentially criminal youths. By means of giving practical aid and information, they try to keep them straight. Apart from that, they try to induce understanding for these youths, especially in public authorities, employers, etc. They are functioning as a sort of bridge between the subcultural and, in the eyes of the youths, the hostile society.

Despite the noble objectives of these streetcorner workers, there is much criticism concerning their work, especially from the scientific side. The Dutch criminologist Jongman (1978) states: "This only deals with symptoms. The basic causes for their behavior remain unaffected." Streetcorner work can hardly be evaluated, since a clear theoretical framework is not available. Jongman states that the school has a special task in preventing juvenile delinquency. He suggests that the school should be rooted in the social environment from which the children are coming. Fortunately, these problems have the attention of the Department of Education. Money is available for so-called "stimulating schools." These schools can be found in other city areas with high unemployment figures. Apart from cognitive goals, there are also social objectives. An effort is made to minimize the psychological distance between schools and private environment, at the same time trying to raise the parent's interest in their children's development. Efforts are also being made to improve the sociocultural environment in cooperation with social workers. Hopefully, these preventive measures will result in positive effects in the long run.

This chapter has been devoted to a presentation and examination of aggression in The Netherlands. Its diverse expressions, current levels and social context have each been considered, as have the several constructive means currently employed in this nation for its reduction and remediation.

REFERENCES

Andriessen, M. RBS 38. *Hulpverlening aan jongeren met politiecontacten: Tweede verslag.* Groningen: Criminologisch Instituut, 1978.

Angenent, H. L. W. *Opvoeding, persoonlijkheid en gezinsverhoudingen in verband met criminaliteit.* Groningen, 1974.

Angenent, H. L. W. *Mishandeling in verband met opvoeding, persoonlijkheid en gezinsverhoudingen.* Groningen, 1975.

Angenent, H. L. W. Tehuisplaatsing en criminaliteit. *Nederlands Tijdschrift voor de Criminologie 1,* 1978.

Angenent, H. L. W., & Steensma, H. *Onveilig Nederland?* Callenbach, Nijkerk, 1976.

Bartels, A. A. J. Jongeren gewoon een handje helpen. *SJOW, 5,* 1977.

Bastiaans, J., Jaspers, J. P. C., & Van der Ploeg, H. M., (Eds.) *Psychologisch onderzoek naar de gevolgen van gijzelingen in Nederland (1974-1977).* The Hague: Staatsuitgeverij, 1979.

Berkowitz, L. *Roots of aggression.* New York, 1961.

Berkowitz, L. *Aggression, a social psychological analysis.* New York, 1962.

Berkowitz, L. Some determinants of impulsive aggression; Role of mediated associations with reinforcement for aggression. *Psychological Review, 81,* 1974.

Block, R. The impact of victimization, rates and patterns. A comparison of the Netherlands and the United States. Unpublished paper, 1980.

Buikhuisen, W., Jongman, R. W., Schilt, T. & Schilt-Drost, T. *Onderzoek aggressieve criminaliteit in Limburg.* Groningen: Criminologisch Instituut, 1972.

Bureau Landelijk Coördinator Voorkoming Misdrijven. *Voorkoming strafbare feiten, een oriënterings-nota.* The Hague, 1980.

Buss, A. H. *The psychology of aggression.* New York, 1961.

Buss, A. H. Physical aggression in relation to different frustrations. *Journal of Abnormal and Social Psychology, 67,* 1963.

Buss, A. H. Instrumentality of aggression, feedback and frustration as determinants of physical aggression. *Journal of Abnormal and Social Psychology, 17,* 1966.

Caminado, H. P. G. M. *Het PTK-Evaluatie-onderzoek.* Schippers, Nijmegen, 1973.

C. B. S. *Maandstatistieken politie en justitie.* The Hague, -1979.

Chapell, D., Geis, R., & Geis, G., (Eds.) *Forcible rape.* New York, 1977.

Cloward, R. A., & Ohlin, L. E. *Delinquency and opportunity, A theory of delinquent gangs.* New York: The Free Press, 1960.

Coenen, A. W. M., & Van Dijk, J. J. M. *Misdaadverslaggeving in Nederland.* The Hague: Wetenschappelijk Onderzoek- en Documentatiecentrum van het Ministerie van Justitie, 1976.

Coenen, A. W. M., & Van Dijk, J. J. M. Politieverslaggeving, koffiepraat en de angst voor misdrijven. *Tijdschrift voor Criminologie, 2,* 1978.

Cohen, A. K. *Delinquent boys: The culture of the gang.* New York: The Free Press, 1955.

Cohen, S. Directions for research on adolescent group violence and vandalism. *British Journal of Criminology, 4,* 1971.

Courtis, M. *Attitudes toward crime and the police in Toronto: A report on some findings.* Toronto: Centre of Criminology, 1970.

Cozijn, C. Verkrachting en aanranding. *Justitiële Verkenningen, 8,* 1979.

Cozijn, C., & Van Dijk, J. J. M. *Onrustgevoelens in Nederland.* The Hague: Wetenschappelijk Onderzoek- en Documentatiecentrum van het Ministerie van Justitie, 1976.

C.R.M. *Rapport van de projectgroep "Vandalisme door Voetbalsupporters."* (C.R.M.), May 1977.

Cuperus, J., & Klijnsma, R. *Onderhandelen of bestormen; het beleid van de Nederlandse overheid inzake terroristische acties.* Polemologisch Instituut, Rijksuniversiteit Groningen, 1980.

Davis, F. J. Crime news in Colorado newspapers. *American Journal of Sociology, 57,* 1952.

Denkers, F. A. C. M. *Ervaringen van gedetineerden in open gestichten.* Criminologisch Instituut, K. U. Nijmegen, 1969.

de Ridder, R. *Aggressie in sociale interactie: waarneming en reactie.* Leiden: Academisch Proefschrift, 1977.

Dijksterhuis, F. P. H. *De gevangenis Bankenbos II.* Assen: Van Gorcum, 1973.

Dollard, J., Doob, L. W., Miller, W. E., Mowrer, O. H., & Sears, R. R. *Frustration and aggression.* New Haven: Yale University Press, 1939.

Drost, T. R. de Jong, J., & Jongman, R. W. *Te lage aangifte voor de belasting; een onderzoek naar de opsporing en afhandeling van te lage aangifte voor de inkomstenbelasting.* Criminologisch Instituut, Rijksuniversiteit Groningen, 1980.

Ekkers, C. L. *Aktivatie en agressie.* Leiden: Academisch Proefschrift, 1977.

Eron, L. D., Walder, L. O., & Lefkowitz, M. M. *Learning of aggression in children.* Boston, 1971.

Fiselier, J. P. S. *Open gesticht en recidive.* Criminologisch Instituut, K. U. Nijmegen, 1974.

Fiselier, J. P. S. *Slachtoffers van delicten; een onderzoek naar verborgen criminaliteit.* Utrecht: Ars Aequi Libri, 1978.

Fris, T. *Gelegenheidsagressie.* Meppel: Boom, 1972.

Geen, R. G., & O'Neal, E. C. Activation of cue-elicited aggression by general arousal. *Journal of Personality and Social Psychology, 11,* 1969.

Gerbner, G., & Gross, L. The scary world of TV's heavy viewer. *Psychology Today,* April 1976.

Halloran, J. D., & Croll, P. Television in Great Britain. Content and control. In G. A. Comstock and E. A. Rubinstein, (Eds.), *Television and social behavior.* Vol. 1 Washington, 1971.

Harrington Report. Soccer Hooliganism. A preliminary report to Mr. Denis Howell, Minister of Sport, by a Birmingham Research Group, Bristol, 1968.

Hindelang, M. J. Public opinion regarding crime, criminal justice and related topics. *Journal of Research in Crime and Delinquency, 2,* 1979.

Jaspers, J. P. C. *Gijzelingen in Nederland.* Lisse, 1980.

Jongman, R. W. Geen straathoekwerk voor agressieve jongeren. *Jeugdwerk nu, 10,* 1978.

Jongman, R. W. *Klasse elementen in de rechtsgang.* Groningen: Criminologisch Instituut, Rijksuniversiteit Groningen, April 1978.

Jongman, R. W., & De Jong, N. Tehuisplaatsing als criminogene factor. *Nederlands Tijdschrift voor de Criminologie, 1,* 1976.

Junger-Tas, J. *Kenmerken en sociale integratie van jeugddelinquenten.* Brussels: S.C.J.M., 1972.

Junger-Tas, J. *Verborgen jeugddelinquentie en gerechtelijk selectie; een onderzoek in een stadsmilieu.* Brussels: Studiecentrum voor jeugd-misdadigheid, 1976.

Junger-Tas, J. Verborgen criminaliteit van jeugdigen. In *Geweld in onze samenleving.* The Hague: Staatsuitgeverij, 1978.

Junger-Tas, J. Preventie van jeugddelinquentie. *Delict en Delinquent, 9,* 1979.

Junger-Tas, J., & Van der Zee-Nefkens, A. A. *Publiek en politie; ervaringen, houdingen en wensen.* The Hague: Wetenschappelijk Onderzoek- en Documentatiecentrum van het Ministerie van Justitie, 1978.

Kelley, H. H. The process of causal attribution. *American Psychologist, 28,* 1973.

Lang Report. Report of the working party on crowd behavior at football matches. London, 1969.

Lefkowitz, M. M., Eron, L. D., Walder, L. O., & Huesmann, L. R. *Growing up to be violent.* New York, 1977.

Lentzer, H. R. *A national crime survey report: Criminal victimization surveys in Chicago, Detroit, Los Angeles, New York and Philadelpia.* U.S. Department of Justice, L.E.A.A., November 1976.

Marsh, P., Rosser, E., & Harré, R. *The rules of disorder.* London, 1978.

Milson Report. Football hooliganism and vandalism. An inquiry into experiences and attitudes of some young people in the West Midlands, reported by F. Milson, and R. Swannell, Westhill College of Education, Community and Youth Department, Birmingham, 1976.

Moll, H. De vreugde van het voetbalvandalisme. *Tijdschrift voor Criminologie, 5,* 1977.

Olweus, D. *Familial determinants of aggressive behavior in adolescent boys: A causal analysis.* Bergen, 1980.

Peyeferitte, A. *Responses à la violence.* Paris, 1976.

Rijksvoorlichtingsdienst. Nederlands stichting voor statistiek. *Onderzoek voorlichtingscampagne voorkoming misdrijven.* The Hague: Sociobus, 1978.

Rijksvoorlichtingsdienst. Nederlands stichting voor statistiek. *Onderzoek voorlichtingscampagne voorkoming misdrijven.* The Hague: Sociobus, 1979.

Rosenhan, D., & White, G. M. Observation and rehearsal as determinants of prosocial behavior. *Journal of Personality and Social Psychology, 5,* 1967.

Rosenthal, U. Terreurbestrijding in Nederland: Vijf thema's ter discussie gesteld. *Het Tijdschrift voor de Politie, 5,* 1979.

Schramm, W., Lyle, J., & Parker, E. *Television in the lives of our children.* Stanford, Calif.: Stanford University Press, 1972.

Siekman, R. Voetbalvandalisme. *Intermediair, 34,* 1978, pp. 1-9.

Smale, G. J. A. Psycho-sociale gevolgen en gedragsveranderingen bij slachtoffers van ernstige misdrijven. *Tijdschrift voor de Criminologie, 5,* 1980.

Smale, G. J. A., & Spickenheuer, H. Vergeldingsbehoefte en gevoelens van schuld bij slachtoffers van ernstige vermogens- en geweldsmisdrijven. *Nederlands Tijdschrift voor de Criminologie, 4,* 1977.

Steenhuis, D. W. *Rijden onder invloed.* Assen: Van Gorcum, 1972.

Stephan, E. *Die stuttgarter opferbefragung.* Wiesbaden, 1976.

Stroo, A. A. *Het verband tussen agressief gedrag bij kinderen van ongeveer 8 jaar en opvoedingsvariabelen van moeders.* Amsterdam: Vrije Universiteit, scriptie, 1971.

Taylor, I. Football mad: A speculative sociology of football hooliganism. In E. Dunning (Ed.), *The sociology of sport: A selection of readings.* London, 1971.

Turner, A. G. *Victimization surveying—Its history, uses, and limitations.* Statistics Division, NILECJ, 1972.

Vader, R. J. Voorkoming misdrijven: Enkele gedachten over deeltaak van de politie. *Het Tijdschrift voor de politie, 10,* 1979.

Vader, R. J. Politiële misdaadvoorkoming. *Justitiële Verkenningen, 2,* 1980.

van Bergeijk, G. A. Vandalisme. *Justitiële Verkenningen. 3,* 1975.

Van der Brug, H. Incidenten bij het publiek van voetbalwedstrijden in Nederland. Unpublished paper, University of Amsterdam, 1981.

van der Werff, C. *Huwelijksgratie en recidive,* deel I. Verkeersdelinquenten, intern rapport Ministerie van Justitie WODC, March 1974.

Van der Zee-Nefkens, A. A. *Onderzoek assistentieverlening gemeentepolitie Den Haag.* The Hague: Wetenschappelijk Onderzoek- en Documentatiecentrum van het Ministerie van Justitie, 1975.

Van Dijk, J. J. M. De geweldsgolf: Schijn of harde werkelijkheid. *Intermediair, 7,* 1974.

Van Dijk, J. J. M. Geweldsmisdrijven in Nederland. *Justitiële Verkenningen, 8,* 1976.

Van Dijk, J. J. M. *Dominantiegedrag en geweld: Een multidisciplinaire visie op de veroorzaking van geweldmisdrijven.* Nijmegen, 1977.

Van Dijk, J. J. M. *The extent of public information and the nature of public attitudes towards crime.* The Hague: Wetenschappelijk Onderzoek- en Documentatiecentrum van het Ministerie van Justitie, 1978.

Van Dijk, J. J. M., & Steinmetz, C. D. H. *De WODS-slachtofferenquêtes 1974-1979.* The Hague: Ministerie van Justitie WODC, 1979.

Van Dijk, J. J. M., & Steinmetz, C. D. H. *Crime prevention: An evaluation of the national publicity campaigns.* The Hague: Research and Documentation Centre, Ministry of Justice, 1981.

Van Dijk, J. J. M., & Vianen, A. C. *Omvang en ontwikkeling van criminaliteit, slachtofferenquêtes 1974-1979.* The Hague: Wetenschappelijk Onderzoeken Documentatiecentrum van het Ministerie van Justitie, 1979.

Verhellen, E., & Mylemans, M. *Een experiment van preventieve sociale actie en opvoedingsbijstand.* Brussels: Ministerie van Justitie, 1975.

Walgrave, L., & Van Kerckvoorde, J. Ernstevaluatie van jeugddeliquentie. *Nederlands Tijdschrift voor de Criminologie, 1,* 1977.

Walters, R. H., & Thomas, E. L. Enhancement of punitiveness by visual and audiovisual displays. *Canadian Journal of Psychology, 17,* 1963.

Wiegman, O. *Aanstekelijkheid van gedrag.* Utrecht, 1975.

Wiegman, O., & Seydel, E. R. *Agressie en helpen.* Antwerp/Amsterdam: De Nederlandsche Boekhandel, 1976.

Wiegman, O., Vries, S., & Gutteling, J. Zes weken televisie: Agressie en affiliatie nader bekeken. *Pedagogische Studiën, 55,* 1978.

Yablonski, L. *The violent gang.* London/New York: Pelican Books, 1967.

Zimbardo, P. G. The human choice: Individuation, reason and order versus deindividuation, impulse and chaos. In W. J. Arnold and D. Livine (Eds.), *Nebraska symposium on motivation 1969.* Lincoln: University of Nebraska Press, 1970.

9
Hungary: Aggression Research at the Institute for Psychology of the Hungarian Academy of Sciences

Jenö Ranschburg

Until the late 1970s, the psychological study of aggression was a neglected area in Hungary. Neither general-experimental nor developmental psychology was substantially concerned with aggression, though there did exist an effort to explore experimentally the role of personal space as described by Hall (1975) in the development of aggressive reactions (Münnich, 1977). Clinical psychology contained a few case studies of pathological aggression, as did criminal psychology, which included case studies that focused on the psychological aspects of violent crime. These were complemented by a few studies of aggression from sociological and legal points of view (Andorka, Ruda, Cseh-Szombathy, 1974; Huszár, 1964; Molnár, 1971; Vigh, 1964). There were only two Hungarian monographs that dealt with theoretical aspects of aggression (György, 1965; Popper, 1970), and both were concerned with the development of antisocial personality. There was only one experimental study concerning aggression in normal (i.e., nondeviant) people (Ranschburg, 1972), and in the early 1970s there appeared a monograph on the emotional background and behavioral manifestations of aggression from a developmental-psychological point of view (Ranschburg, 1973).

Then, in 1977, the Hungarian Academy of Sciences created the Department of Developmental Psychology of the Institute for Psychology. One of its two thematic groups, the Psychosocial Group is new in terms of both its personnel and its concept of research. The Psychosocial Group deals with the genesis of normative behavior and with the developmental-psychological questions of the internalization of social values and role-expectations; and within this general setting we have started three investigations which are concerned with developmental-psychological characteristics of aggressive behavior. However, since the department has been working for only three years, and since developmental-psychological research on aggression has such shallow roots in Hungarian psychology, the investigations described below are merely the first steps we wish to take in the study of aggression. The studies do not pertain to Hungary per se; they are studies of human aggressive behavior conducted in Hungary by Hungarian psychologists, but they have general, theoretical applicability. They relate to similar work done elsewhere, and to theoretical ideas known to psychologists everywhere.

THE DEVELOPMENT OF AGGRESSIVE BEHAVIOR IN CHILDREN RAISED IN OR OUTSIDE THE FAMILY

We have been studying the shaping and development of aggression in a population of several hundred babies from resident-nurseries and in two groups of 170 babies from day-nurseries. The day-nurseries groups were followed longitudinally for two years in order to record the shaping of aggressive behavior in similar populations. This project, under the direction of Dr. Boris Szegal, includes children under state care, brought up without parents practically from birth, and children whom the parents took home daily.

Our inquiries started at a particularly low age which is rarely treated in the literature. Is it appropriate to speak about aggression in such an early period of ontogenesis as the eighth to tenth month of life? Psychoanalysis, which assumes an aggressive instinct, asserts the existence of infantile aggression (oral aggression) quite axiomatically. The interpretation of dentition given by Erikson (1969) which states that biting diminishes the pain in the gums, and that this leads to masochistic or sadistic behavior depending on whether the baby bites himself or others, is an example. On the other hand, cognitive psychological theories (e.g., Kagan, 1969) assert that one cannot speak of aggression before the age of 1½ to 2 years. They suggest, and in my view with good reason, that the more or less explicit separation of "self" and "others" and the awareness of the possibility of inflicting pain are necessary for the commission of an "aggressive act" in the psychological sense. Thus, hitting, kicking, and biting in infancy cannot be called aggression. In any case, in our own inquiries we confined ourselves to human-ethological recording; any act of the child which appeared to cause pain to one of his partners (emotional aggression), or any acts from which he benefited at the expense of others (instrumental aggression) was called aggression. We take no stand on the degree of the child's understanding (and empathy) about the pain or harm caused.

At the very least, those acts which we qualify as aggressive acts are precursors, behavioral equivalents of the "real" aggression that unfolds at later stages in the development of the personality. It is known that socialization affects aggressive behavior from the early stage of development and that the amount of aggression produced by boys in the early years has prognostic value for later periods of socialization, while for girls, it does not (Kagan & Moss, 1962). The reason for this lies evidently in the different expectations and socializational pressures for the different sexes. We, however, wanted to know whether an effect of socialization on the quantity of aggressive acts of children can be detected as early as the first 20 to 25 months of age.

We found that, for children brought up in resident nurseries, the level of psychomotoric development correlated positively with the number of aggressive acts, while there was no such correlation for children brought up in families. For the latter group, the quantity of aggressive acts performed by the child correlates positively with the aggressivity of the father and the lack of anxiety in the mother. Langston (1961) argued that the aggressive behavior of the parent of the same sex motivates the child to imitate it, while the aggression of the parent of the opposite sex results in anxiety and the inhibition of aggression. Our results conform to Langston's for boys, but not for girls. Langston's conception may help explain these sex differences in aggression since, in most of our families, the father is the aggressive one, and he is the adequate model for the boy. But Langston's notion does not conform to the old-established fact of developmental psychology (Goodenough, 1931) that there is no difference in the aggression of boys and girls in the first two years of life, nor does it accord with the so-called "consistency hypothesis" (Kagan, 1964; Petersen, 1979), which is based on the child's comparing his own traits to the social stereotypes in the course of the evolution of gender-identity. Our assumption—which has to be verified by further investigation—is that, in the first two to three years of life, aggression is modeled after the father, regardless of the child's sex. In our opinion—which is in accordance with the consistency hypothesis—after the first three years, boys will be reinforced for modeling the aggressive father, while aggressive behavior will be responded to as inconsistent for girls, so they will gradually eliminate explicitly aggressive acts from their repertoire of behavior.

The fact that there is no difference in the aggression of boys and girls in the first two years is, as mentioned above, established knowledge in developmental psychology, and our inquiries have verified it again. At the same time, according to our dyadic analysis of aggressive acts, boys over two are more likely to be victims of aggressive acts than girls. We have not come upon similar results in the literature. Thus, from this age onwards—although the quantity of aggression is the same for boys and girls—most of the aggressive acts take place either in boy-boy dyads and in girl-boy dyads, where the girl is the aggressor and the boy is the victim. Our team has to confirm and refine this result with additional research. Besides other possibilities of interpretation, it is conceivable that this phenomenon marks a transitional stage in the development of gender-specific forms of aggression; the number of aggressive acts performed by little girls does not decrease before the development of gender-identity, while little boys, as a result of social learning, have already gleaned that aggression against girls is "unmanly" and "improper."

In conjunction with this work, we should comment on the results of Szegal's efforts concerning the relationship of emotional and instrumental aggression. Acts belonging to the category of emotional aggression (e.g., hitting, kicking, biting, pushing, pulling someone's hair) are clustered around "hitting"; while all types of emotional-aggressive acts correlate highly with hitting, there is no correlation between hitting and the instrumental form of aggression. Blurton Jones (1972) reached a similar conclusion. These data can be interpreted in two ways. The first interpretation amounts to saying that, to become conscious and aware of harming the other, one needs a much higher level of ego-development and empathy than is needed to acquire an "understanding" of causing pain. In this interpretation (which happens to coincide with the opinion of Hinde, 1974), seizing of objects cannot be regarded as aggression at the age of 20-24 months. The other interpretation is to say that emotional and instrumental aggression are different, and independently unfolding features of personality. Later on, we would like to contribute to the solution of the problem with the examination of groups of older children.

EXAMINATION OF GENDER-SPECIFIC FORMS OF BEHAVIOR

The aforementioned results relate to a fundamental question of aggression research: Is aggression a masculine feature, and if it is, do biological or social causes explain the differences between the sexes? In the last twenty-five years many theoreticians have attempted to subsume these masculine and feminine features under a unified concept. Parsons and Bales (1955) distinguished woman's expressive domestic activities (i.e., socially-oriented and home-centered) and the man's instrumental extra-domestic activities (i.e., object-oriented and centered outside the home).

Bakan (1966) described the "sense of agency" and the "sense of communion" as the two fundamental properties of living organisms. The former manifests itself primarily in self-assertion, self-protection, and self-aggrandizement, and is typically a "masculine principle," whereas the latter is a "feminine principle," marked primarily by selflessness, devotion, and desire for identification. (Naturally, these principles are not mutually exclusive; they indicate no more than that generally "sense of communion" is stronger in women than in men, while "sense of agency" is stronger in men than in women.)

McClelland (1975) expressed a similar idea about the feminine nature of interdependency and the masculine nature of assertiveness. McClelland also gave a much wider interpretation to the concept of interdependence than we do. He relied principally on a well-known finding of Witkin (1954) that, in many societies, women are more field-dependent than men. In McClelland's opinion interdependence means a particular contextual style, a constant openness to sensations from the external world, as opposed to the closed, analytic, masculine style. Thus, there appears to be a general consensus among various theoreticians that those characteristics that can be described in terms of goal-orientation and personal competence are masculine, while social-emotional sensitivity and interpersonal orientation are feminine traits. We emphasize that the theoreticians mentioned above do not claim that masculine (feminine) characteristics belong exclusively to men (women). For instance, in Bakan's (1966) opinion, if a strong "sense of agency" is not assisted by a "sense of communion," the result can be destructive for both the individual and the society. On the other hand, "sense of communion" can render the individual effective only when aided by agency. Johnson (1975) as well as Locksley and Colten (1979) criticised the above mentioned conception of Parsons and Bales (1955) primarily on the grounds that one needs a considerable level of instrumentality in order to fulfill the traditional feminine sphere of activity. In spite of the evident mingling of characteristics and roles (instrumental characteristics are needed for efficient functioning in the traditional feminine role, which is expressive), their opinion gives rise to several theoretical and methodological problems in research on masculinity–femininity.

Gender Specific Characteristics That May Relate to Aggression

A number of well-known cross-cultural studies are relevant to this domain. For example, Beatrice Whiting (1963) examined three-to-ten year old children from six cultures. In all of these, boys manifested more physical aggression and girls were more sociable, showed more readiness to help, and had a greater sense of responsibility. Sex-differences in socializing techniques may very well explain this phenomenon. Classifying ethnographical data from 110 cultures, Barry, Bacon, and Child (1957) reached the conclusion that the individual cultures show consistent differences in the socialization of boys and girls from the fourth year of life; e.g., in many cultures, girls are brought up to be obedient and to have a sense of responsibility, whereas boys, to have self-confidence and achievement-orientation. On the basis of such data from cross-cultural research one might ask: How can the fact that socialization for the (fe)male role (apart from a few exceptions) is essentially the same in different cultures be accounted for? The inquiries by Barry, Bacon, and Child modify the question as follows: How can we explain that consistent socializing procedures are in use in different cultures? Their answer is the "division of labor" hypothesis, stating in essence that the division of labor by gender which stems from the physical differences of the sexes will, in the course of the society's evolution, manifest itself in socialization emphases which prepare both males and females for their respective expected roles. Cross-cultural research involving Rorschach-records (D'Andrade, 1966) shows that, in the cultures examined, men are more anxious than women. This suggests that men must pay a considerable psychic price for their masculine privileges.

Thus, cross-cultural research describes aggression, achievement-orientation, self-confidence, and anxiety as masculine; while caring, sense of responsibility, and sociability are more feminine traits. Intracultural inquiries yield similar results, with but a few exceptions. Most of the researchers agree that boys are more aggressive than girls. For instance, for nursery-school children, this conclusion was shown in doll-playing situations by Gordon and Smith (1965), with projective tests by Jegard and Walters (1960), and with a complex methodology by Sears, Rau, and Alpert (1965). Sears (1961) demonstrated, with the aid of aggression-scaling techniques, that school-boys are more aggressive than school-girls; and Szegal (1981) reached a similar conclusion based on observational data of Hungarian children. For adults, Buss (1963), Buss and Brock (1964) verified in an experimental situation that men are more aggressive than women, and that women are more remorseful after an aggressive act.

Biological research—primarily experiments with monkeys (Resko, 1970; Rose, 1971, 1972; Rose, Bernstein, Gordon, & Catlin, 1974)—indicate a direct connection between the level of masculine sexual hormone (testosterone), aggression, and dominance. These results, together with the seemingly homogeneous nature of the above-mentioned psychological data might have influenced Maccoby and Jacklin (1974) in supposing that sex-differences in aggression are biologically determined. As early as 1961, Sears mentions that aggression-anxiety is stronger in girls and assumes that this is a result of conflict between aggressive drive and female behavioral stereotypes. His view is corroborated by his findings: girls manifest more socially accepted (prosocial) aggression than boys.

Experiments by Frodi, Macauley and Thome (1977) and Brodzinsky, Messer and Tew (1979) point to sex differences that can be explained on the basis of learning-theory. While boys show definitely more physical and verbal aggression, girls are just as aggressive if the aggression has an indirect form, i.e., aimed not directly at a person but, for instance, his belongings, instruments. It is to be noted that, if boys commit much more interpersonal open aggression and as much indirect aggression as girls, then the total of their aggressive acts is necessarily larger. The phenomenon can be explained on a learning theoretical basis (see, e.g., Feshbach, 1970): in an interpersonal situation (as a result of feminine role-expectations), aggression inhibition is more likely to occur in girls. At the same time, this finding is not contrary to biological interpretation.

Three-year-old boys are demonstrably more aggressive than girls, and Goodenough (1931), who found no difference before this age, explained it by the parents' being more submissive to boys' aggression. This claim is not supported by recent investigations; for example, Minton (Minton, Kagan, & Levine, 1971) evinced that two-year-old boys are more severely punished for aggression than girls of the same age in domestic environments, and Serbin (Serbin, O'Leary, Kent, & Tonick, 1973) found the same for three-year-old children in nurseries. However, we cannot leave our strong reservations about these studies unmentioned. First of all, the quantity of aggressive acts punished can be interpreted only in relation to the whole quantity of aggressive acts performed; that is to say, we must consider the adult more lenient toward the aggression of the boy if, from the far larger quantity of his aggressive acts, he is punished only as much as from the girl's. Our reservations are further motivated by the researchers' negligence of the metacommunicative features of the punishment's context. (When a father punishes his son for fighting, his behavior expresses probably much more satisfaction than when he has to punish his daughter for the same misbehavior.)

There are numerous investigations pointing to greater dependency in girls. It seems to us, we do not go beyond the domain of the much-debated notion of dependency (Ferguson, 1970; Maccoby & Masters, 1970) if we interpret the results proving that girls have a higher level of anxiety (Castaneda & McCandless, 1956; Knights, 1963; Olah, 1981; Rie, 1963), conformism (Allen & Crutchfield, 1963; Harper, Horving, Holm, Tasso, & Dubanovski, 1965), and social orientation (Adams, 1964) as the manifestation of stronger dependency in girls. The longitudinal investigation by Kagan and Moss (1962) offers clear-cut data indicating that the translation of dependency to someone outside the family (mostly from the same age

group) is a typically boyish trait. Girls until adult age tend to retain their close emotional relationships and strong dependency ties within the family. We have few but challenging data
about the origins of the girls' greater dependency. As Thomas (Thomas, Chess, Berch, Hertzig, & Korn, 1963) ascertained, the activity-passivity dimension of reactivity is a stable characteristic already shortly after birth, and one finds more boys on the activity side and more girls
on the passivity side of the dimension. The investigation seems to suggest that, as a result of
innate differences along the activity-passivity dimension, girls will be more likely to be reinforced in their contact and security-searching behavior than boys. Moss (1967) showed that
the greater activity in male infants manifests itself even in their crying more and being harder to
calm than girls. This property of male infants results in their mother's being more irritated and
letting them cry longer since their attempts to soothe them are successful less frequently. On
the other hand, little girls cry less often and stop sooner in the mother's embrace, which undoubtedly reinforces the mother's "nurturing behavior," i.e., increases the subjective importance of the mother-role.

In their important book, Maccoby and Jacklin (1974) do not concede that girls are more
socially oriented and conforming and less achievement-oriented than boys, and they do not
accept a few other sex differences claimed before but not mentioned here. At the same time,
they verify that boys are unquestionably more aggressive. Maccoby and Jacklin's results are
quite contradictory. They regard the characteristics used for comparing the sexes as independent, and this itself needs further consideration. For instance, dominance and competitive
spirit are related to aggression, although not indusputably (Mazur & Robertson, 1972; Plotnik, 1974; Plotnik, Mir, & Delgado, 1971); and it may safely be assumed that nurturing behavior and social orientation are interrelated. We note that they regard social orientation in
girls to be no stronger than in boys. This, however, can hardly be understood if we take into
account their result that self-rating of girls has social character while self-rating of boys has
object-character.

The Measurement of Masculinity-Femininity

The primary aim of our own gender-relevant research, conducted in Hungary, was to develop a standard masculine-feminine test (Horváth and Ranschburg, 1980). The traditional
ways of measuring the level of masculinity-femininity—the M-F test by Terman and Miles, the
Mf scale of the MMPI, the F scale of Gough and the M scale of Guilford (for a detailed examination of each see Constantinople, 1973)—all place the individual respondent at some point
on a masculinity-femininity scale. Thus, in giving M-F a single numerical value, they implicitly
assume that masculine and feminine characteristics are mutually exclusive (negatively correlated). This notion suggests that one can be *either* masculine or feminine to some degree (regardless of one's sex) but not both. The newer methods appearing in the second half of the
1970s (Bem, 1975, 1976, 1979; Spence, & Helmreich, 1979; Spence, Helmreich, & Stopp,
1975)—which treat masculinity and femininity as orthogonal dimensions, and thus make it
possible to place one in both—signify a new concept in the research of masculinity-femininity.
The MFSK, which is a masculinity-femininity scale constructed at our department both reflects
this more recent conceptualization of the measurement of M-F, and contains only socially desirable characteristics (like the PAQ test by Spence) but is composed of four main factors instead of two. These factors, together with the most weighted corresponding traits, are:

A. Violent factor: gentle, modest, peaceful, quiet
B. Career factor: ambitious, determined, striving for success, longing to get on
C. Einstein factor: versatile, talented, universal, havine fine prospects

D. Brood-hen factor: tender, understanding, warm-hearted, sympathetic

It can be seen that the attributes of the Violent and Brood-hen refer largely to passivity, and are traditionally considered feminine; while the more masculine-appearing factors are in apparent causal relation. The traits corresponding to the Career and Einstein factors seemingly function as the intellectual base for the extrovert, success-oriented, typically masculine behavior.

In this chapter, we would like to discuss briefly only the two masculine factors. In the course of our investigations with gender-role stereotypes (Ranschburg & Horváth, 1979a, b), we formed the hypothesis that career-orientation, which turned out to be a typically masculine trait, is closely connected to aggression, or, more precisely, with instrumental aggression which can be separated from emotional aggression in a very early age. The stereotype (or trait) we speak about here is essentially the one called self-aggrandizement by Bakan, assertiveness by McClelland, and instrumentality by Parsons. In our opinion, instrumental aggression is a very important element of the career-orientation. The Einstein factor emerging from the factor-analysis of our data indicates that career-orientation is closely related to intellectual self-ratings. The relationship of "stereotype" and "trait" complicates the problem. In one of our inquiries, we tested secondary-school children (aged 15–18) with a battery consisting of the MFSK and a sociometric test. We investigated five classes in three schools every year for four years with the following method: the children had to characterize their classmates, and themselves with the traits of the MFSK scale. The results showed that both sexes rated boys significantly higher in the Einstein factor, and children rated themselves the same way. Therefore, we might suppose that the lower self-rating of girls is as consistent with a feminine stereotype as the higher self-rating of boys with a masculine one. This indicates a problem in socialization, and can be interpreted with the aid of Kagan's consistency-hypothesis. In our belief, our results contribute new perspectives to the aforementioned research which analyze masculine-feminine differences in the general setting of "achievement-motivation" in the broader sense (Horner, 1974; Martin, 1973; Monahan, Kuhn, & Shaver, 1974). Finally, to conclude this section, we wish to indicate our awareness that our observation about instrumental aggression's hiding in the background of career-orientation is only a hypothesis which needs verification. In our coming inquiries—among which the investigation of the relationship between aggression and altruism has already begun—we would like to get closer to answering this question.

EXPERIMENTAL STUDY OF AGGRESSIVE CATHARSIS

The experiment to which we now turn is an attempt to study physiological effects that might underlie aggressive catharsis. We agree with Bandura and Walters (1963) that little has been added by the classical "frustration-aggression hypothesis" (Dollard, Doob, Miller, Mowrer & Sears, 1939) to the understanding of catharsis. According to Dollard and his colleagues, catharsis is nothing else but the reduction of the aggression instigation occurring in a frustrating situation effected exclusively by the aggressive act. Later, numerous experiments showed that aggression is not exclusively preceded by frustration; Bandura and his colleagues, in their "social learning theory" (Bandura, 1962; Bandura & Huston, 1961; Bandura & Walters, 1963) presuppose aggression not to be primarily a consequence of frustration, but learned through imitation by the child. The experimental research literature on catharsis includes many contradictions. The emotion-reducing effect of direct or vicarious aggression was disproved directly through the experiments carried out by Kenny (1952) and Feshbach (1956) on children, and indirectly through the works of Bandura, Ross, and Ross (1961-1962). Similar results were also obtained by Kahn (1960) with adults, while Feshbach's (1961) and Weatherley's (1962) investigations, also with adult subjects, seem to prove the original assumption relating to the cathartic value of aggression.

Berkowitz (1958), however, pointed out that reduction of the aggression could be caused by the inhibition of the behavior, too, occurring as a consequence of guilt. Possibility of a reduction of emotion through aggressive behavior is refuted by Arnold (1960), while Worchel (1957) favors the reduction-of-emotion view. This last interpretation is provided also by Hokanson and Shetler (1961), though with some qualifications. Central to the problems relating to catharsis is the concept of displacement of emotion. The Yale-group has adopted in its book this analytic conception of displacement. According to this, the degree of displacement depends on the intensity of the aggressive instigation: the greater the aggressive instigation, the greater the displacement. N. Miller later (1948) refined this view, and declared that the level of displacement also depends on two more factors: the checks against direct aggression, and the degree of similarity between the target and the surrogate. Feshbach and Singer (1957) suggested that displacement is also influenced by the individual or collective character of the danger which instigates the aggression. With this as background, we sought the answers to three questions:

1. Do aggressive acts reduce the emotion that is instigated by frustration?
2. Do aggressive acts reduce emotion, if it is directed not to the frustrator but to a different person?
3. Can emotion be reduced by verbal (non-aggressive) resolution of the frustrating situation?

Description of the Experiment

The participants in our experiment were 25 male students, all 17 to 18-year-old pupils in classes III and IV of the grammar school in Budapest. The instrument used during the experiment measured the galvanic resistance of the skin. The experiment was carried out in three phases.

Phase 1. Frustration. The student entering the room was told that he certainly knew that there are experiments taking place in order to introduce new testing methods for the entrance examinations. Now he will be a subject of one of these experiments. He has to solve a task that makes him think, and in all probability he will meet similar tasks at the entrance examination of the university, and the professional school, too. With his participation in the experiment, he supports our work in elaborating appropriate selection methods and, at the same time, it is useful for him to have an opportunity to judge what he can achieve at the real entrance examination. Following the presentation of this structuring statement, the electrodes were fastened to the student's palm and the back of his hand, and he was asked to relax himself for a time of apparatus calibration.

For the experimental tasks, one half of the participants were given a piece of paper with the assignment to connect nine points with four continuous lines; the other half got a paper with a square cut in five parts of different shapes, and they had to put the parts together shaping therewith the entire square as indicated in figure 9.1.

Two different, but similar and seemingly equivalent tasks were utilized as a means of counteracting negative effects on task performance resulting from unintended communication between students about the experiment's content and requirements. The tasks were chosen primarily on the basis of one criterion: they had to be soluble, but with such difficulties that during

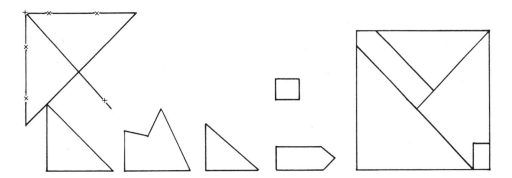

Fig. 9.1. Experimental Construction Task

the three to four minutes' space of time being at the students' disposal the solution would not be apparent.

Changes in the resistance of the subject's skin were continuously measured during the unsuccessful trials, during which they were further frustrated by disagreeable remarks: "Now you are not ready yet? Is it really nonsense, if a primary school child can solve a task like this in such a space of time!—Are you a grammar school student? In this way you certainly will have difficulties at the entrance examination. It is better if you leave it off!" Apart from some insignificant stylistic variations, these frustrative remarks were communicated to every study participant. Since success at the experimental tasks was shown to be a hopeless goal, every student was told to stop and was shown the right solution.

Phase 2. Aggression. Study participants were divided into five groups as follows:

a) Group "Aggression"₁ (5 Persons). The members of the group were asked to help us in another experiment. The participant was asked to think of a number between 0 and 10, and the experimenter had to find out what number it was. When the experimenter did not correctly guess the number thought by the participant, the participant administered an electric shock to the experimenter. The experimenter was sitting in a position so that the student could see his hand well. The experiment went on up to 10 trials. The average number of the experimenter's failures was from 8 to 10 trials, and the student pressing the button with each failure could see the twitch of the experimenter's hand. Hokanson and Shetler (1961) in their experiment applying a similar method, cut the circuit so the shock was not a real one. We were concerned that participants might discern such a ruse; therefore, we worked with a real, rather sharp electric shock.

b) Group "Aggression"₂ (4 Persons). The same procedure was applied as in the former group with the difference that the experimenter was replaced by a student of class IV, with whom the participants were well acquainted.

c) Group "Aggression"₃ (6 Persons). For participants in this experimental condition, a grammar school student who was cooperating with us sat as an indifferent participant during the phase of frustration and was a witness of the schoolmates' hopeless trials. The participants were not informed about the reason of their friend's presence.

d) Control-Group "Light" (4 Persons). Instead of the electric shock, a light signal was utilized in this condition. By pressing the key button, a small lamp on the wall was lighted. The participants were told when we did not find out the number they had thought of, the button was to be pressed, and that was the sign of unlucky trial.

e) Group "Verbal" (6 Persons). After the phase of frustrating, we begged the subjects' pardon for having used a shocking manner of speech with them. We admitted that the task was really not easy at all, and it was made much more difficult for them by our impatient remarks and by the short amount of time we put at their disposal. We referred to our weariness, to our having then been out of temper, and we asked the students to look at the events as if they had not occurred at all.

Phase 3. Recalling. The aggression phase was in all cases the recalling, wherein four standard questions were asked:

1. What sort of task did you get?
2. Did you succeed in solving it?
3. What was the leader's opinion of your production?
4. What is your own opinion about it?

Changes in the resistance of the skin were also measured in this phase of the experiment.

Results

The results of this experiment indicate that skin resistance declined from study phase 1 to study phase 3, on the average, for participants in the three "aggression" groups, while it increased, on the average, for control group participants. An analysis of variance confirmed that differences between the three aggression groups on the one hand, and the control groups on the other were statistically significant. There were no significant differences among the three aggression groups nor between the two control groups.

We then compared each aggression group with the "light" control group, and found that each aggression group, in fact, differed from this control. The largest difference involved aggression group #1. No significant difference existed between the verbal apology group (Group 5) and the control group (Group 4).

Discussion

Our hypothesis that the aggressive act reduces the emotions caused by frustration, thus having a cathartic value, is supported by our experimental results. The phenomenon can be defined also in this way: the temporal increase of the negative emotions was hindered by the aggressive act in the experimental situation that was brought about, it was even a decreasing tendency of the aggressive acts brought into force.

According to Hokanson and Shetler (1961), if the frustrator is a person "of high status," blood pressure remains at the prefrustrative level, i.e., it does not significantly differ from it. This was interpreted by Hokanson and Shetler (1961) with the statement that "Supposedly it had been appropriated by the subjects that there was very little possibility of being overtly aggressive against a person of high status, thus it happened that the minimal tendencies of reaction were only evoked by the frustration to an overt aggression." Comparing our groups "aggression₁" and "aggression₂" (in the former, the experimenter played the frustrator's role; in the second, the IVth class grammar school student who was co-operating with us), it can be seen that Hokanson's statement could not be confirmed by our results. The overt aggression was manifest as the most effective reductor of emotion in the group, the frustrator of which

Table 9.1. Intensity of the Negative Emotion in the Case of the Previously Treated Groups

AGGRESSION₁			AGGRESSION₂			AGGRESSION₃		
P	M	P-M	P	M	P-M	P	M	P-M
4.5	5.4	−0.9	23.5	17.6	+5.9	12.4	8.1	+4.3
86.2	22.0	+64.2	7.6	12.6	−5.0	10.5	15.0	−4.5
12.7	22.8	−10.1	17.8	0.7	+17.1	13.1	2.0	+11.0
6.3	24.5	−18.2	26.8	17.8	+9.0	8.4	9.0	−0.6
18.3	17.2	+1.1				20.1	6.2	+13.9
			75.7	48.7	+27.0			
128.0	91.9	+36.1				21.1	14.1	+7.0

	VERBAL				LIGHT		
	P	M	P-M		P	M	P-M
	4.3	34.3	−30.0		17.1	36.7	−19.6
	7.7	14.3	−6.6		12.0	38.6	−26.6
	16.2	33.4	−17.2		46.0	68.6	−22.6
	14.0	14.0	±0.0		7.5	49.0	−41.5
	42.2	96.0	−53.8		82.6	192.9	−110.3

P = Perception (Phase 1)
M = Memory (Phase 3)

Table 9.2. Partition of the Analysis of Variance I

SQUARE RAISED SUM		F	P
DE − ABC	3727.5	$\frac{3727.5}{293} = 12.72$	0.05
D − E	364.5	$\frac{364.5}{293} = 1.24$	0.10
A − B	0.0	—	0.10
A − C	8.4	$\frac{8.4}{293} = 0.03$	0.10

Key to the capital letters:
  A = aggression₁
  B = aggression₂
  C = aggression₃
  D = verbal
  E = light

Table 9.3. Partition of the Analysis of Variance II.

GROUP	F	P
aggression₁ − light	3.18	<0.05
aggression₂ − light	2.31	<0.10
aggression₃ − light	2.53	<0.10
verbal − light	1.19	>0.10

was the experimenter. According to our supposition, the different results can have a number of causes, but if we take into account that the dispersion in our "aggression$_1$" group was much greater than in the "aggression$_2$" group, certainly it seems possible that the cathartic value of an aggression manifested against a frustrator of high status depends on several, yet-to-be-specified, other characteristics of the reactor's personality and situation.

Through the fifth of the experimental groups, we inquired whether the emotion instigated by frustration could be diminished by verbal satisfaction, i.e., by the frustrator's appeal to the student for forgiving. Our results indicated that verbal satisfaction had nearly no emotional consequence; the group did not display any significant declination from the control-group.

We have examined research in Hungary concerned with the development of aggression in children, its gender-specific associations, and the function of cathartic opportunities following instigations to aggression. These completed investigations, as well as others in progress and planned, reflect the growing involvement of our department, as well as others in Hungary, to the systematic study of aggression—its development and its control.

REFERENCES

Adams, J. P. Adolescent personal problems as a function of age and sex. *Journal of Genetical Psychology*, 1964, *104*, 207-214.

Allen, V. L., & Crutchfield, R. S. Generalization of experimentally reinforced conformity. *Journal of Abnormal and Social Psychology*, 1963, *67*, 326-333.

Andorka, R., Ruda, B., & Cseh-Szombathy, L. (Eds.) A deviáns viselkedés szociológiája. *The Sociology of Deviant Behavior*. Budapest, Gondolat. 1974.

Arnold, M. B. *Emotion and personality*. New York: Columbia University Press, 1960.

Bakan, D. *The duality of human existence*. Chicago: Rand McNally, 1966.

Bandura, A. The influence of rewarding and punishing consequences to the model on the acquisition and performances of imitative responses. Unpublished manuscript, 1962.

Bandura, A., & Huston, A. C. Identification as a process of incidental learning. *Journal of Abnormal and Social Psychology*, 1961, *63*, 311-318.

Bandura, A., & Ross, D. Imitation of film-mediated aggressive models, *Journal of Abnormal and Social Psychology*, 1962, *66*, 3-11.

Bandura, A., Ross, D., & Ross, S. Transmission of aggression through imitation of aggressive models. *Journal of Abnormal and Social Psychology*, 1961, *63*, 575-582.

Bandura, A., & Walters, R. H. *Social learning and personality development*. New York: Holt, Rinehart and Winston, 1963.

Barker, R. G., Dembo, T., & Lewin, K. *Frustration and regression: An experiment with young children*. University Ia. Stud. Child. Welf., 18, 1941. (Quoted by: Baldwin, A.L., *Theories of child development*. New York: Wiley and Sons, 1968.

Barry, H., Bacon, M. K., & Child, E. L. A cross-cultural survey of some sex differences in socialization. *Journal of Abnormal and Social Psychology*, 1957, *55*, 327-332.

Bem, S. J. Sex role adaptability: One consequence of psychological androgyny. *Journal of Personality and Social Psychology*, 1975, *31*, 634-643.

Bem, S. J. Sex typing and the avoidance of cross-sex behavior. *Journal of Personality and Social Psychology*, 1976, *33*, 48-54.

Bem, S. J. Theory and measurement of androgyny: A reply to the Pedhazur-Tetenbaum and Locksley and Colten critiques. *Journal of Personality and Social Psychology*, 1979, *37*, 1047-1054.

Berkowitz, L. The expression and reduction of hostility. *Psychological Bulletin*, 1958, *55*, 257-283.

Berkowitz, L. Anti-semitism and the displacement of aggression. *Journal of Abnormal and Social Psychology*, 1959, *59*, 182-187.

Blurton Jones, N. G. *Ethological studies of child behavior*. Cambridge, 1972.

Brodzinsky, D. M., Messer, S. B., & Tew, J. D. Sex differences in children's expression and control of fantasy and overt aggression. *Child Development,* 1979, *50,* 372-380.

Buffery, A. W. H., & Gray, J. A. Sex Differences in the Development of Spatial and Linguistic Skills, 1972. Quoted by: Maccoby, E. E. and Jacklin, L. N., *The Psychology of Sex Differences,* 1975.

Buss, A. H. Physical aggression in relation to different frustrations. *Journal of Abnormal and Social Psychology,* 1963, *67,* 1-7.

Buss, A. H., & Brock, T. C. Regression and guilt in relation to aggression. *Journal of Abnormal and Social Psychology,* 1964, *66,* 345-350.

Castaneda, A., & McCandless, B. R. The children's form of the MAS. *Child Development,* 1956, *22,* 317-326.

Constantinople, A. Masculinity-femininity: An exception to the famous dictum? *Psychological Bulletin,* 1973, *80,* 389-407.

Corteen, R. S., & Blackman, A. R. Skin conductance change and sensory discrimination. *The British Journal of Psychology,* 1965, *56,* 431-437.

D'Andrade, R. G. Sex differences and cultural institutions. In E. E. Maccoby (Ed.), *The development of sex differences.* Stanford, Calif.: Stanford University Press, 1966.

Dollard, J., Doob, L. W., Miller, N. E., Mowrer, O. H., & Sears, R. R. *Frustration and aggression.* New Haven: Yale Univ. Press, 1939.

Erikson, E. H. *Childhood and society.* London: Penguin Books, 1969.

Eysenck, H. J., & Warwick, K. M. Situationally determined drive and the concept of "arousal." In H. J. Eysenck, (Ed.), *Experiments in Motiv.* 1964.

Ferguson, J. R. Dependency motivation in socialization. In R. A. Hoppe, G. A. Milton, and E. C. Simmel (Eds.), *Early experiences and the processes of socialization.* New York: Academic Press, 1970.

Feshbach, S. The catharsis hypothesis and some consequences of interaction with aggressive and neutral play objects. *J. Pers.,* 1956, *24,* 449-462. Quoted by: Bandura, A. & Walters, R. H. *Social Learning and Personality Development.* London: Holt Rinehart and Winston, 1963.

Feshbach, S. Aggression. In P. H. Mussen (Ed.), *Charmichael's manual of child psychology.* Vol. 2. New York: Wiley, 1970.

Feshbach, S., & Singer, R. The effects of personal and shared threats upon social prejudice. *Journal of Abnormal and Social Psychology,* 1957, *54,* 411-416.

Freud, S. Mourning and melancholia, 1925. In E. Jones (Ed.), *Collected Papers* Vol. IV. New York: Basic Books, 1959. Quoted by Dollard, J., Doob, L. W., Miller, N. E., Mowrer, O. H. & Sears, R. R. *Frustration and Aggression.* New Haven: Yale Univ. Press, 1939.

Freud, S. *Introduction to the psychoanalysis.* Internazionaler Psychoanalitischer Verlag, Wien and Somló Belá. Budapest: (No date).

Frodi, A., Macauley, J., and Thome, P. R. Are women always less aggressive than men? *Psychological Bulletin,* 1977, *84,* 634-660.

Goodenough, F. L. *Anger in young children.* Minneapolis: University of Minnesota Press, 1931.

Gordon, J. B., & Smith, E. Children's aggression, parental attitude and the effects of an affiliation-arousing story. *Journal of Personality and Social Psychology,* 1965, *1,* 654-659.

György, J. A nehezen nevelhetö gyermek *The problematic child.* Budapest: Medicina, 1965

Hajtman, B. Bevezetés a matematikai statisztikába. *Introduction to the mathematical statistics.* Budapest: Akadémiai Kiadó, 1968.

Hall, E. B. Rejtett dimenziok. *The hidden dimensions.* Budapest: Gondolat, 1975.

Harper, F. B. W., Horving, G., Holm, G., Tasso, J., & Dubanovski, D. Young children's yielding to false adult judgments. *Child Development,* 1965, *36,* 175-183.

Hinde, R. A. *Biological bases of human social behavior.* New York: McGraw-Hill, 1974.

Hokanson, J. E., & Shetler, S. The effect of overt aggression on physiological arousal level. *Journal of Abnormal and Social Psychology,* 1961, *63,* 446-448.

Horner, M. S. The measurement and behavioral implications of fear of success in women. In J. W. Atkinson and J. Raynor (Eds.), *Motivation and achievement.* New York: Halstead Press, 1974. Quoted by: McClelland, D. C.

Horváth, I., & Ranschburg, J. Maszkulin-Feminin értékelö dimenzió serdulöknél. *Masculine-feminine appreciating dimension in case of adolescents,* Magyar Pszichológiai Szemle, 1980, *21,* 323-333.

Huszár, T. Faiatalkoru bünözök. *Juvenile delinquents.* Budapest: Tankönyvkiadó, 1964.

Jegard, S., & Walters, R. H. A study of some determinants of aggression in young children. *Child Development,* 1960, *31,* 739-747.

Johnson, M. Fathers, mothers and sex-typing. *Sociological Inquiry,* 1975, *45,* 15-26. Quoted by Locksley, A. & Colten, M. E. Psychological Androgyny: A Case of Mistaken Identity?, 1979.

Kagan, J. Acquisition and significance of sex-typing and sex role identity. In M. L. Hoffman & J. W. Hoffman (Eds.), *Review of child development research.* New York: Russel Sage, 1964.

Kagan, J. Personality development. In J. L. Janis, (Ed.), *Personality dynamics, development and assessment.* New York: Harcourt, Brace and World, 1969.

Kagan, J., and Moss, H. A. *Birth to maturity.* New York: J. Wiley and Sons, 1962.

Kahn, M. A polygraph study of the catharsis of aggression. Unpublished manuscript, 1960. Quoted by: Bandura & Walters, *Social Learning and Personality Development.* London: Holt, Rinehart & Winston, 1960.

Kenny, D. T. An experimental test of the catharsis theory of aggression. Unpublished manuscript, 1952. Quoted by: Bandura & Walters, *Social Learning and Personality Development.* London: Holt, Rinehart & Winston, 1963.

Kimura, D. Speech lateralization in young children as determined by an auditory test. *Journal of Comparative and Physiological Psychology,* 1963, *56,* 899-902.

Knights, R. M. Test anxiety and defensiveness in institutionalized and noninstitutionalized normal and retarded children. *Child Development,* 1963, *34,* 1019-1026.

Langston, R. Children's overt and fantasy aggression toward peers as a function of perceived severity of parental punishment, 1961. Quoted by: Várkonyi, Zs. Tájékozottság és kompetencia. *Knowledge and competency.* Budapest, Akadémiai Kiadó, 1978.

Landsdell, H. 1968. Quoted by: Kagan, J. Sex Differences in Early Behavior: General Discussion. In: Schaffer, H. R. (Ed.), *The Origins of Human Social Relations.* New York: Academic Press.

Locksley, A., & Colten, M. R. Psychological androgyny: A case of mistaken identity? *Journal of Personality and Social Psychology,* 1979, *37,* 1017-1031.

Maccoby, E. E., & Jacklin, C. N. *The psychology of sex differences.* Stanford, Calif.: Stanford University Press, 1974.

Maccoby, E. E., & Masters, J. C. Attachment and dependency. In P. M. Mussen (Ed.), *Carmichael's Manual of Child Psychology, Vol. 2.* New York: J. Wiley and Sons, Pp. 73-159.

Malmo, R. B. Activation: A neurophysiological dimension. *Psychol. Rev.,* 1959, *66,* 367-386.

Martin, J. C. Competitive and noncompetitive behavior of children in beanbag toss game. Preliminary Draft. University of California, 1973. Quoted by: Maccoby and Jacklin, 1974.

Mazur, A., & Robertson, J. S. *Biology and social behavior.* New York: The Free Press, 1972.

McCandless, B. R. *Children and adolescents. Behavior and development.* New York: Holt, Rinehart and Winston, 1961.

McClelland, D. C. *Power. The inner experience.* New York: Irvington Publishers, 1975.

Miller, J. G. The experimental study of unconscious processes. In M. L. Reymert (Ed.), *Feelings and emotions.* 1950.

Miller, N. Theory and experiment relating psychoanalytic displacement to stimulus-response generalisation. *Journal of Abnormal and Social Psychology,* 1948, *43,* 155-178.

Miller, N., & Dollard, J. *Social learning and imitation.* New Haven: Yale University Press, 1941.

Minton, C., Kagan, J., & Levine, J. A. Maternal control and obedience in the two year-old. *Child Development,* 1971, *42,* 1873-1894.

Molnár, J. Galeribünözés. *Group crime.* Budapest: Közgazdasági és Jogi Könyvkiadó, 1971.

Monahan, J., Kuhn, D., & Shaver, P. Intrapsychic versus cultural explorations of the "Fear of Success" motive. *Journal of Personality and Social Psychology,* 1974, *29,* 60-64.

Moss, H. A. Sex, age and state as determinants of mother-infant interaction. *Merrill-Palmer Quarterly,* 1967, *13,* 19-36.

Mowrer, O. H. *Learning theory and the symbolic processes.* New York: Wiley, 1960.

Münnich, I. A gyermek- és fiatalkori bünözés. (Crime in the childhood and the youth.) In Münnich-

Szakács (Eds.), *Bünözö Fiatalok. (Juvenile Delinquency.)* 1977. a

Münnich, I. Vasszaesö bünözök személyes tere, perceptuális, orientációja, szorongásos szinvonala mint a nyilt, támádo viselkedés jelzései. (The Personality Range, the Perceptual Orientation and the Anxiety Level of Recidivists as Indicators of Undisguised Aggressive Behavior.) Budapest: *Magyar Pszichológia Szemle,* 1977, *18,* 245-256. b

Olah, A. Svéd és magyar fiatalok szorongás-profiljának összehasonlitó vizsgálata, -megjelenés alatt (Comparative Study of the Anxiety Profile of Sweden and Hungarian Young People) *Magyar Pszichológiai Szemle.* In press.

Parsons, J. E. (Ed.) *Psychobiology of sex differences and the sex roles.* Washington: Hemisphere, 1980.

Parsons, T., & Bales, R. F. *Family socialization and interaction process.* Glencoe, Ill.: Free Press, 1955.

Petersen, A. C. Biopsychosocial processes in the development of sex-related differences. In J. E. Parsons (Ed.), *Psychobiology of sex differences and the sex roles.* Washington: Hemisphere, 1979.

Plotnik, R., Mir, D., & Delgado, J. M. R. Aggression, noxiousness and brain stimulation in unrestrained rhesus monkeys. In B. E. Eleftheriou, and J. P. Scott, (Eds.), *The Physiology of Aggression and Defeat.* New York: Plenum Press, 1971.

Plotnik, R. Brain stimulation and aggression: Monkeys, apes and humans. In R. J. Holloway, (Ed.), *Primate aggression, territoriality and xenophobia.* New York: Academic Press, 1974.

Popper, R. *A kriminális személyiségzavar kialakulása. (The genesis of the criminal personality.)* Budapest: Akadémiai Kiadó, 1970.

Ranschburg, J. A frusztráció ébresztette interferáló emóciók intenzitásának változása frusztrátor illetve indifferens személy felé irányitott nyilt aggresszió hatására. (Changes in interfering emotions aroused by frustration as an effect of overt aggression directed at the frustrator or an indifferent person.) *Magyar Pszichológai Szemle,* 1972, *2,* 173-182.

Ranschburg, J. *Félelem, harag, agresszió. Fear, Anger, Aggression.* Budapest: Tankönyvkiadó, 1973.

Ranschburg, J. & Horváth, I. *Connection of sociometrical data with stereotypes of gender role.* IUPS XXII. Conference, Lipcse, DDR, 1979. a

Ranschburg, J. & Horváth, I. *Gender role stereotypes in adolescent boys and girls.* A Fifth Conference ISSBD, Lund, Sweden, 1979. b

Resko, J. A. Androgen secretion by the foetal and neonatal rhesus monkey. *Endocrinology,* 1970, *87,* 680-687.

Rie, H. E. An exploratory study of CMAS lie scale. *Child Development,* 1963, *34,* 1003-1017.

Rose, R. M. Plasma testosterone, dominance rand and aggressive behavior in male rhesus monkeys. *Nature,* 1971, *231,* 366-368.

Rose, R. M., Bernstein, J. S., Gordon, T. P., & Catlin, S. F. Androgens and aggression: A review and recent findings in primates. In R. J. Holloway, (Ed.), *Primate aggression, territoriality and xenophobia.* New York, London: Academic Press, 1974.

Rose, R. M., Gordon, R. T., & Bernstein, J. S. Plasma testosterone levels in the male rhesus: Influences of sexual and social stimuli. *Science,* 1972, *178,* 643-645.

Sears, R. R. Relation of early experiences to aggression in middle childhood. *Journal of Abnormal and Social Psychology,* 1961, *63,* 466-492.

Sears, R. R., Rau, J., & Alpert, R. *Identification and child rearing.* Stanford, Calif.: Stanford University Press, 1965.

Serbin, J. A., O'Leary, K. D., Kent, R. N., & Tonick, I. J. A comparison of teacher response to the pre academic and problem behavior of boys and girls. *Child Development,* 1973, *44,* 796-804.

Spence, J. T., & Helmreich, R. J. The many faces of androgyny: A reply to Locksley and Colten. *Journal of Personality and Social Psychology,* 1979, *37,* 1032-1046.

Spence, J. T., Helmreich, R., & Stopp, J. Ratings of self and peers on sex-role attributes and their relation to self-esteem and conceptions of masculinity and femininity. *Journal of Personality and Social Psychology,* 1975, *32,* 29-39.

Stephens, W. N. *The family in cross-cultural perspective.* New York: Holt, Rinehart & Winston, 1963.

Szegal, B. Az agressziv viselkedés fejlödése a korai gyermekkorban. (Development of the aggressive behavior in early childhood.) *Magyar Pszichológiai Szemle,* Budapest. I. 1978; II, 1981.

Szegedi, M., & Münnich, I. Szexuális motivációból elkovetett emberoles-sorozat pszichologiai elemzese.

(Psychological analysis of a murder-series committed for sexual motive) *Magyar Pszichológiai Szemle*, Budapest, 1970, *2*, 272-284.

Thomas, A., Chess, S., Birch, G. H., Hertzig, M. E., & Korn, S. *Behavioral individuality in early childhood*. New York, University Press, 1963.

Venables, P. H. Can arousal be treated as a psychological variable? *Bulletin of the British Psychological Society*, 1962, 47. Quoted by: Corteen & Blackman, Skin Conductance Change and Sensory Discrimination. *The British Journal of Psychology*, 1965, *56*, 431-437.

Vigh, J. A fiatalkoru bünözés és a társadalom. (*Juvenile delinquency and the society*. (Budapest, 1964.

Weatherley, D. Maternal permissiveness toward aggression and subsequent TAT aggression. *Journal of Abnormal and Social Psychology*, 1962, *65*, 1-5.

Whiting, B. B. (Ed.) *Six cultures: Studies of child rearing*. New York: J. Wiley and Sons, 1963.

Witkin, H. A., Lewis, H. B., Hertzman, M., Machover, K., Messner, P. B., & Wapner, S. *Personality through perception*. New York: Harper, 1954.

Worchel, P. Catharsis and the relief of hostility. *Journal of Abnormal and Social Psychology*, 1957, *55*, 238-243.

10

India: South Asian Perspectives on Aggression

Agehananda Bharati

One of the gravest problems of our day is the lack of commitment to common symbols. If it were merely a matter of our fragmentation into small groups, each committed to its proper symbolic forms, the case would be simple to understand. [Douglas, 1970, p. 1]

INTRODUCTION AND THEORY

South Asia means India, Pakistan, Sri Lanka, Nepal, and Bangladesh. I will be using "Indian" quite frequently and synonymously with "South Asian," since South Asian culture is the overarching matrix when it comes to so pervasive a theme as aggression and violence. I view aggression within the context of a cultural matrix; a single matrix for aggression exists in all South Asian countries regardless of their official boundaries and national identities. I hesitate to call the matrix a model, since a model should generate or account for each occurrence to which it applies. A matrix is more like a statistical model, in that it elegantly explains exceptions as it preserves the academic nobility of model use. Mary Douglas (1970), a few pages into her text, chides Smelser when "he puts the factor of strain into his explanation of mass movements, panics, crazes and religious movements [p. 6]." (What a relief! I thought Smelser's was the answer to many things relating to mass behavior, until I read Douglas' little volume.)

The South Asian aggression–violence matrix is not due to any strain, endemic or acute, but is a part of the symbolic maze which characterizes Indian culture. Theoretical analyses and the proposal of heuristic theories is an etic effort in anthropological terms; illustrations of theory are emic, and they have to be put between quotation marks. This is what I will be doing in this chapter.

The Indian matrix for aggression is uniquely Indian. Briefly outlined, it reads somewhat like this: autochthonous Indian (i.e., Hindu, Buddhist, Jaina) norms, both cognitive and conative, provide pervasively and powerfully for nonviolence (ahiṃsā in Sanskrit and modern Indian languages), but they do not provide norms for aggressive thought and behavior for Indian society as a whole. They do provide such norms, and very elaborate ones at that, for a defined segment of Indian society, i.e., the kṣattriyas or rājputs.[1] Killing, even murder, assault

---

[1]In the normative scheme of Hindu castes, the kṣattriyas are the kings, their military vassals, the landlords of actual or perceived royal descent. Rājput (literally "king's son" cognate with Latin regis puer) is a synonym of kṣattriya

and counterassault, and other sources of individual violence are part of the codified ethos of the kṣattriyas. For reasons again uniquely South-Asian, the kṣattriyas provide a model for all segments of Indian society which rank below them—and that comprises roughly 80 percent of the population. It is a model—and until recently[2] the only one which held out the chance for corporate advancement upward in the status hierarchy of the most highly stratified society in the world. Act like rājputs over a generation or two, make your neighboring castes higher and lower than you, forget that there was time when you didn't, and there is a chance that you will achieve the status and, hopefully, the power of rājputs as the decades go by. As you do so consistently, as you keep "upcasteing" yourselves the kṣattriyas-way, a very important part of your actions and feelings must be kṣattriyized—you must learn violence, must learn to feel aggression. The one-time segmentary model begins to apply for you. ("You" here of course is always plural, i.e., the group or caste in question—individuals can't do much about it.)

The modern templates of collective aggression suggested by the editors (terrorism, student and labor riots, perhaps even organized violent crime, juvenile gangs, vigilante groups) in South Asia today can be deduced from the kṣattriya norm as internalized by people who emulate the kṣattriya, and they are patently obvious where kṣattriyas or their surrogates (police, the armed forces, paramilitary organizations) embark on implementing the rājput norm. Once again, this is an etic proposal—police brutality as evinced in India at the time of this writing, the Naxalites hit and kill lists and their execution, the alarming growth of rape in the cities and in rural areas are not seen as extentions of a kṣattriyan matrix by Indians who articulate and oppose these events. Indian press and journalistic commentary never go beyond or beneath the simple explanatory packet of rumor, gossip, agitation; but their reports belong to the emic self-representation of modern South Asian countries. The angry rejection of such etic analyses as those provided by the anthropologist-sociologist or the psychologist, when they enter the ken of modern South Asian reportage, is part of the rejection of the alien, the erstwhile colonizers, the imperialists. But, of course, anthropologists—Indian or Western—are not fazed by such rejection. G. N. Obeyesekere, a Sri Lankan anthropologist at Princeton, has analyzed sorcery as aggression (Obeyesekere, 1975, pp. 1-24)—and even if Sri Lankan politicians or journalists read his study and protest, that would hardly make him change his approach. What I stress here is the gap between official South Asian and scholarly evaluations of aggression in the region. Few South Asians will agree with this analysis, and, for example, the Muslim column writer in Dacca or Karachi simply won't know what I am talking about, since he did not even have to reject the basic Hindu model any longer—the preceding generation has done this for him. Still, my claim is that the Hindu matrix is at work. All South Asian Muslims are culturally Indian Muslims, and all of their ancestors were Hindus.

There is one relatively small (about 10 million), highly visible community in India. They are visible for sartorial reasons—everyone recognizes the Sikh turban, whether in Delhi, Bombay, or Vancouver, B.C., and because of their aggressive, successful, and conspicuous mercantilism. Sikhism, an eclectic offshoot of North Indian Hinduism of the sixteenth century, has the least controversial and the least problematic set of rituals and doctrines of the Indian

---

and I will use these terms interchangeably. There is a highly complex relation between the normative kṣattriya concept first promulgated in the Vedas, the canonical texts of Hinduism, and the hundreds of castes (jāti) which claim kṣattriya status. The anthropological literature on this topic is enormous and still growing. Seminal texts on the situation are those by Andre Beteille (1971), G. M. Carstairs (1958), Louis Dumont (1970), Pauline Kolenda (1978), to mention but a few.

[2]Since roughly the end of World War I, and certainly since after independence and partition (1947), the merchant caste (vaiśya or banyā) model has begun to compete with the kṣattriya model for upcasteing purposes. See Gitel Steed (1955) and other authors in McKim Marriott's Village India anthology (1955) as well as my Asians in East Africa (1971).

religions. The ideal for the Sikh man is that of the *sant-sipāhī* "saint-soldier." At the *gurdvārā* ("gate of the teacher," the Sikh temple) he must act humbly and demurely, but outside he must be brave and heroic. He carries a sword (a miniature one stuck in his hair in modern-day urban Sikh society) at all times, and he should not unsheath it nor put it back into its sheath without having drawn blood of an evildoer. Here the *kṣattriya* norm is completely overt, undisguised, and brazenly displayed, regardless of the fact that very few Sikh castes today have actual *rājput* background. The *Jaṭs*, the largest and most dominant caste of Sikhs, are farmers; the *aroras* are merchants. The cultural identification, however, remains military-heroic-*rājput*. Sikhism's symbols are unambiguous and simple: the five Ks (the Pañjābi words for the comb, the sword, the long military underwear, the iron ring on the right ankle, and beard and turban all signify heroic virtues) identify a man as a Sikh; the ritualistic display of the gurus' swords in the main shrine of Sikhism does not need elaborate interpretation. Gandhi's *ahiṃsā* never found favor with the Sikhs; it was quite openly, and at times vociferously rejected during Gandhi's ministry and even after (Bharati, 1981a, pp. 89-91). During the postpartition riots, Sikhs killed many Muslims and never made any bones about it. During a sermon at Shishganj, the largest *gurdvārā* in Delhi, the preacher, addressing a crowd of close to five thousand, many of them highly modernized, professional people, on the occasion of Guru Gobind Singh's birthday, said: "*khūn kā badlā khūn*, the revenge for bloodshed is bloodshed, this is what the gurus said, this is what *vir* [heroic men] have to do. All that talk about *ahiṃsā* is children's prattle."[3]

H. Izmirlian's *The Politics of Passion* (1979) is an apt title for a book on contemporary Sikh villages. Violence is part of their ethos—it is not accepted with a shrug or legislated out of existence, but it is underwritten as part of the way things should be done. "The rivalry between these groups," Izmirlian writes reporting about two politically powerful groups in his village, "had resulted in violence in 1958. Two men of Ch. Singh's group were hacked to death; Ch. Singh was killed when a truckload of men pulled up and fired on him in his fields [p. 94]." Panjab's former Chief Minister, Pratap Singh Kairon, was assassinated by rivals, and just three months before this writing the leader of the dissident Nirankāri sect was shot dead in the middle of the busiest road in Delhi, in broad daylight. Both events had national coverage. Both events and reactions to them directly instantiate the *kṣattriya* model—they were witnessed with interest and understanding.

At the other end of the aggression scale with no indigenous symbol system to account for, we must observe movie production in India, the largest in the world, followed by Japan with the U.S. movie production only a third in annual size. *Sholay* is one of the most popular Hindi movies, about ten years old, with constant reruns. Some 30 million Indians have reportedly seen the movie, and some 5.5 million have seen it twice or more often. It is replete with incredible violence. There is no Indianness to it, at a first viewing. The heroes do not conform to any *rājput* model—their model, I assume, or the one the producers had in mind seemingly belongs to the Western genre or to gangland as conceived by Hollywood. I think its attraction, as well as that of more recent movies modeled on *Sholay*, is due to the fact of the utter alienness of such unrestricted, unideological aggression—just as bodily nudity or seminudity in American movies which go past the Indian censor attract large Indian audiences.

I suggested earlier that there is no pan-Indian model for violence; but it seems that the Hol-

---

[3]There is no such instruction in the *Guru Granth Saheb*, the holy book of the Sikhs. Some of the Sikh Gurus and their kin were martyred by the Moghul rulers, but this fact did not enter the holy writ. This is unimportant; in the Sikhs' perception, the historical event merges with scriptural injunction, very much as Klanners quote scripture in support of their mischief. This sermon, which I heard in person, was delivered only three years after partition, when the memory of the bloodshed was quite fresh in people's minds and when some legitimation was needed.

lywood-modeled Hindi movie does provide a pan-Indian model for aggression. The fact of its ideological provenance is unknown and unimportant—the actors are Indian, and they are the heroes of the Indian screen who receive virtually divine homage from the viewing public. The stories have an Indian setting. Whereas the culture-specific type of violence requires some side-taking, some ideological participation or tolerance, there is no need for that in the violent movie or the violent novel sold by the thousands in the vernacular languages all over the sub-continent. There does not seem to be any link between these two perceptions.

Millions of people were killed during partition, and this has become part of the accepted mythology of violence, similar to that of the great Hindu epics, the *Mahābhārata* and *Rāmāyaṇa*. Millions of Jews were killed by the Nazis, but those Indians who have heard about it view it with the same sort of mythical perception extended to the millions killed in the *Mahābhārata*. The holocaust seems to fit into the *rājput* model. Hitler is regarded as a *kṣattriya*-like hero by millions of orthodox Hindus who would literally not kill a fly (Bharati, 1965, pp. 74-78). These events do not exceed the boundaries of the *rājput* model—it remains part of a restricted code.

Sholay's sheer violence seems to fill a need for an elaborated code, where such need is felt in a complex society heavily exposed to internal and alien speech patterns which have discarded an earlier restricted code. That the elaboration of a code may lead to a new idiom, to a new restricted code after an interregnum of sheer cognitive confusion should not bother us, since we are not called upon to make any esthetic judgments. If we were to look for a new idiom of aggression, one that is alien to the known "restricted code" violence, I think we have to examine all the sources of alienation from the traditional code, from silly movies to political rhetoric. The only criterion here is *spread*.

Conceivably, there could be some such thing as random violence where the only etiology found was psychological and idiopathic. But this is simply not the case in India—the kind of street violence we fear in American cities is a new experience for the subcontinent. The template of violent thought and action is much more systemic in India than it is in the West. This is so both in its doctrinally negative evaluation in the *ahiṃsā complex* as well as in its statement. The epics and other ancient literature are replete with long and gory descriptions of bloody action between princes and their vassals, and there is more than the occasional elaboration on individual violence: Narasiṃha, half-man half-lion, the fourth incarnation of Viṣṇu, tears the entrails out of the body of the evil demon Hiraṇyakaṣipu, and this scene is represented in thousands of sculptures all over India, albeit in a highly stylized manner. The tutelary deity of Bengal is Durgā, the killer of the buffalo demon, astride a tiger, spearing the demon to death—again, this image is part of the eidetic storeroom of all Bengali Hindus, and the image is not only repeated in thousands of sculptures and paintings, but the goddess with her attendants, in her taurognatic posture, is moulded in clay and installed in the houses of the affluent every year in Bengal and wherever Bengalis live—worshipped by one and all, by women in their best finery, with sweets for the children, and a general display of joyous festivity, with male goats sacrificed to the goddess every day. The Durgā of Kalighat in Calcutta is the tutelary deity of Bengal, and she is a pretty awesome lady: a garland of skulls around her neck, entrails of slain demons as her girdle, a lolling tongue. Her violent epithets are numerous, but they are outweighed and outnumbered by benign, maternal appellations. The total mesh of the *Urmutter* with the total destructess of evil may account for the fact that Bengalis have never developed any brooding worry about the possible preponderance of the terrifying aspects of the Divine Mother. Kazi Nazrul Islam, a recently deceased Bengali Muslim poet, wrote some of the best modern poetry about the Goddess—a thing a good Muslim is not supposed to do; but, here, as in so many contexts, Indianness overrides Islamicity. He wrote a beautiful song *mahākāler kole e'se guari ho'lo mahākālī* "when the Great black goddess embraced the Great God (i.e., Śiva, her spouse, she became "Guarī" (i.e., "the white one").

Violence is seen as part of a cosmically necessary concatenation. The progression from the benign to the violent and back to the benign provides an ontic continuum which explains much of the Indian world view otherwise alien to Western observers. The mythological fact that demons must be killed but, since killing is bad, the killer must be punished is the reflection of a perennial theme, patent to the Indologist who can check it in hundreds of texts. Reporting on rituals in today's Bengali cities, Âkos-Östör writes vividly about the manner in which today's Bengalis view the violent involvement of the gods and of the supreme Mother Deity—Rāvaṇa abducts Sītā, the incarnate goddess; Rāma, the living supreme, kills Rāvaṇa, advised and guided by Durgā, he thereby becomes guilty of the gravest sin, the killing of a brahmin (Âkos-Östör, 1980). Rāma is the prototype of all *kṣattriyas* and his deeds are known to all adult Indians—Hindus and Muslims alike. Rāma, who stands for optimal justice as well as for divine power, is a *kṣattriya*, most of whose exploits are of a heroic, swashbuckling order. At least in the original Sanskrit Rāmāyana by Vālmīki, he merrily eats meat and drinks wine with his spouse and his vassals,[4] and he does kill one opponent from an ambush, unseen by the latter. In preparing this chapter, I tapped my closeby resources, the Indian community (not students at the universities, but settlers in Syracuse and Rochester, N.Y.) to get some input from them as to the rightness of Rāma's acts of violence. To 200 persons, I posed two questions only: (1) Was Rāma right in killing Rāvaṇa for abducting his wife? (2) Should everybody act in a similar fashion given a similar situation? I received 58 responses. Since a person's caste and religion can usually be told from his or her surname, I can present the statistics found in table 10.1:

(1) aye $49 \cong 85\%$
    nay $9 \cong 15\%$
(2) aye $34 \cong 59\%$
    nay $15 \cong 26\%$
    blank $9 \cong 15\%$

broken down into traceable caste and religion categories:

(1) aye: 4 brahmins, 9 *kṣattriyas*, 16 other Hindu castes, 2 Muslims, 1 Christian, 12 did not
           sign
    nay: 1 brahmin, 1 *kṣattriya*, 4 other Hindus, 3 did not sign
(2) aye: 2 brahmins, 9 *kṣattriyas*, 14 other Hindus, 3 Muslims, 6 did not sign
    nay: 7 brahmins, 1 *kṣattriya*, 3 other Hindus, 1 Christian, 2 did not sign
    blank: (which I read as undecided) no brahmin, no *kṣattriya*, 3 other Hindus, 1 Muslim, 5
           did not sign

Only 12 respondents wrote an additional note, five of them were *kṣattriyas*, no brahmin, 3 other Hindus, 1 Muslim, 3 did not sign. Of these elaborated responses, 9 or 75 percent said that *kṣattriyas* or "similar people" (which I read to mean strong, powerful, or power-seeking

---

[4]The original (Sanskrit) Rāmāyana scribed to the mythical seer Vālmīki does not many any bones about meat and liquor consumed among the *rājput personae dramatis*. This changed drastically in later times: in Tulsidas's Hundi Rāmāyana—the text which started the Hindi language as a literary idiom (fifteenth century)—the heroes are all strict vegetarians. Rāma's heroic exploits and his deeds of legitimized and morally approved violence are unchanged and intact following the Vālmīki Rāmāyana composed about nineteen centuries earlier.

Table 10.1.

	WAS RAMA RIGHT IN KILLING RAVANA FOR ABDUCTING HIS WIFE?		SHOULD EVERYBODY ACT IN A SIMILAR FASHION GIVEN A SIMILAR SITUATION?	
	YES	NO	YES	NO
Brahmins	4	1	2	7
Ksattriyas	9	1	9	1
Other Hindu Castes	16	4	14	3
Muslims	2		3	
Christians	1			1
Not signed	12	3	6	2
Total	44	9	34	14

N = 58
Of those who were undecided, Other Hindus = 3; Muslims = 1; Did not sign = 5

people, virile people) should act this way. Of the nay respondents to the second question, only one wrote a statement, and that one, strangely, and counter-intuitively, was a ksattriya, who wrote that taking revenge is bad under all circumstances.

Now, these people are successful professionals and their wives. They are all secure, and hardly any one of them plans to return to India during their active years. This goes a long way to show how very strong these cognitions are. In the process of acculturation to American ways, which includes the erosion of Hindu beliefs and practices in the generation born here or migrated at a very young age, the selective acceptance of violence endures as a clearly Hindu idiom. Their response seems to bear out my belief that the rājput model remains intact as a powerful, if not the only legitimation for violence. The one ksattriya who stated that taking revenge is bad under all circumstances wrote, of course, in a Gandhian or a general humanistic vein. The Gandhian model is part of modern India's official culture, and while ahimsā is an important, ancient part of the Hindu view of life, it is available to modern Indians who are not specialists, through the Gandhian model only. Since the rejection or at least the blurring of caste norms is part of Gandhian perceptions, there is a tendency to down-caste oneself if one's actual caste status is high and well established; this explains the ksattriya respondent's remarks.

THE *KSATTRIYA* MODEL

As I proceed to illustrate the ksattriya model of violence and its decreasing overtness, I will begin with "straight cases" of rājput aggressive behavior today, and will end with occurrences in patterns where the rājput segmentary model is either nonexistent or where it has been so thoroughly internalized that it is no longer perceived by the agents. I will also introduce the term "minimal symbolic trigger" to aid the explanation of acts of aggression where the rājput model is no longer evident to the agents, though certainly to this researcher.

G. M. Carstairs, a British psychiatric anthropologist, studied three well-defined castes in Rajasthan, a highly conservative region in Northern India. Rajasthan, formerly called Rajputana, is the center of classical ksattriya-dom and virtually all people on the subcontinent and right into Nepal who claim rājput status affirm or aver that their ancestors came from that area.

In Rajasthan, maharajas and landholders and brigands belonged to one and the same caste, and they were usually kin to each other. Violent behavior is part of their ethos, and a nonviolent *rājput* is regarded as something of a misfit not only by his fellow *rājputs* but also by the non-*rājput* castes in the area, and this despite of the fact that they have been suffering under *rājput* violence in an endemic fashion. "Local brigandage was not easily eradicated and still occurs" writes Carstairs (1958:13). "The history of violence and social disruption is still alive in the memory of the country folk. On several occasions villagers described dreams in which they had to take refuge in the hills while their homes were plundered by a passing warrior band." However, these warriors were *rājputs*, related to the ruling nobles, and highly admired for their violence. Women share in the exploits to this very day. One of them, a close affinal relative of the former ruler of Jaipur and a devotee of Durgā, is said to have killed hundreds of police, and taken tribute from hundreds of villages. When the woman brigand was finally mowed down by police bullets in 1979, the picture of her bullet ridled body made the cover page of the *Illustrated Weekly of India*.

Carstairs' *rājput* informant Vikram Singh said that a *rājput* must not only fight for the cause of religion, but also in self defense. He should be slow to anger, but formidable when roused. "They insist upon *rājput* heroism in battle, on their berserk fury when crossed . . . and upon the privileges associated with their caste—right to drink liquor and to eat meat. These substances, if taken in strict measure, add to the warrior's virility by helping him to acquire semen and with it the qualities of courage and strength which its possession conveys (Carstairs, 1958, p. 109)." A *rājput*, being defied by his younger brother (who is supposed to defer to him) "in a fit of anger (he) killed him, then killed his pregnant wife (p. 112)." Carstairs believes that this caused less revulsion among his caste fellows than the outsider might expect because it expresses the *rājput*'s firmest conviction, i.e., that of the unchallengeable authority of a ruler, or the father, or the elder brother.

Vinoba Bhave, an early associate of Gandhi, still alive at about 85, saw himself as the linear heir to Gandhi's philosophy in action. Famous for his *bhūdān* ("land-gift") movement where he prevailed upon landowners to give shares of their property to the disinherited poor, in the late 1960s he prevailed upon a large number of *dacoit rājputs* in the ravines of Rajasthan to give themselves up to the police and to surrender their weapons. He did not promise them any deal with the authorities, nor any leniency. He relied on his charisma as a holy man, a nonviolent master, a brahmin, and achieved what seemed to the public a phenomenal success. Some 200 long-wanted brigands did surrender their arms and themselves at an appointed place. Although there is probably a snag in the story,[5] it does support my basic theory of selective violence within the accepted framework of its radical opposite, i.e., *ahiṃsā*, and the deference of the traditionally violent to the traditionally nonviolent.

Until quite recently, I assumed that the violence of India was never sadistic. Recent events have made me suspend my judgment on this count. Some thirty persons, suspected or convicted of burglary, were blinded by the police; and, although this series of events evoked angry responses in Parliament and from Mrs. Gandhi, it raises questions of the sort germane to this study. The Calcutta based *Sunday Magazine* reported (November 16, 1980) that the police in

---

[5]The Deputy Inspector General of Police in Jaipur told me that he and his officers were rather unhappy with Bhave's scheme and its execution, since it disrupted their channels of communication and infiltration with the brigands. Many of the police officers were *rājputs* themselves, and related to both the robbers and the rulers. Also, it seems that on the very day, and at the very hour when those robber barons laid down their arms, attracting large crowds and large police contingents, other brigands belonging to the same corporate groups staged raids on several villages simultaneously, killing a few dozen people and making away with an unusually large number of spoils in the form of jewelry and women (personal communication, ca 1969).

Bhagalpur, State of Bihar, had found a unique way of punishing those they suspected as thieves and dacoits. "They blinded them with pins and acids," as they put it. Several persons, mostly young men, were blinded by police using bicycle spokes, syringe needles, and sulphuric acid. To make sure their operation was fool-proof, police bandaged the eyes of one of the victims with acid-slaked cotton. During the past three weeks, the Indian press has been replete with gory accounts of these events, and the government gave some aid to the victims' relatives to nurse them. *The Illustrated Weekly of India* (January 11, 1981) published an extensive opinion poll, presented with statistics covering seven pages, including such questions as "How important a national issue is the Bhagalpur blinding?" "Were the blindings justified?" The *Illustrated Weekly* is the largest publication of its kind in India. (Its importance roughly corresponds to the *Time Magazine* in the United States.) Both the report's content and its obvious fascination for a wide and diffuse readership support the kṣattriya-model suggested in this chapter.

In another part of India, in early 1981, cases of *sati* have been reported. *Sati* is the correct spelling for the official English spelling *suttee*. As a noun, it means "she who is good," and it is the name of the supreme mother goddess, spouse of Śiva. Since supreme loyalty to the husband is consummated in the widow's self immolation on her husband's funeral pyre, the act is also called Satī. It was outlawed by the British in the nineteenth century, but an average of ten cases a year are reported and the police do not always—or not always wholeheartedly—interfere. On the spot where a *sati* has taken place, the local people usually build a shrine to the woman, who is then venerated as Satī, an aspect of the great goddess. The Indian press has given full accounts of recent incidents of *sati*, including the publication of a photograph in the *Illustrated Weekly of India,* showing the immolation of a widow in the flames of her dead husband's pyre. The Hindu weekly *Dharmayug,* in its September 29, 1980 edition, reported that a young brahmin widow in Banda, Rajasthan, ascended her dead husband's funeral pyre and then ordered it to be lit. But at that time, the police, who had been informed about the widow's intention before her husband's demise due to an incurable illness, appeared on the scene, extinguished the fire, and removed the widow. However, 24 hours later she mounted the already extinct pyre again—her husband's body, of course, had been consumed by that time. And then the report says that, mysteriously, the pyre caught fire without being lit by human hands, and the widow succeeded—she became a Satī. Incidents seem to be on the increase, mainly in Rajasthan, the center of *rājput* culture and population.

What concerns us here is the degree of support the custom has rekindled. India, like other countries, has experienced a strong fundamentalist reaction during the past years, and such support, of course, instantiates the trend quite drastically. I think that the co-occurrence of unspeakable police brutality and *sati* has its roots in the overt or covert glorification, and introjection of kṣattriya ethos in India, not only by rājputs who, of course, didn't have to change their cognitions since they were kṣattriya, but also by lower caste groups who emulate rājput ways in the process of upcasteing.

These seemingly distant events, topically speaking, have a common base. India is still one of the most puritanical countries in the world, and the Hindu leadership, over the past three decades, has been complaining bitterly about the new lassitude of the young, the venality of the old, and the general permissiveness due to the movies and Western influence. Many years ago, I saw an interesting vignette in *Kalyāṇa Kalpataru,* a Hindu religious periodical with a large circulation. It showed two drawings side by side: on the left, several rājput women were ascending their dead husbands' pyres; on the right, modern Hindu girls in elegant saris were engaged in social ballroom dance. The commentary beneath read: "In a better age, women joined their husbands in glory and became *satis*; today, their descendants engage in dancing with men." The message was quite unambiguous; *sati* is desirable, social dance and contact with the opposite sex is undesirable.

The ideal for regeneration, however, has not been that of the brahmin, but that of the hero, the *kṣattriya*, the soldier. By extension, the police officer is a *kṣattriya*—he is more of a soldier than a layman.

The pan-Indian adulation of Subhas Chandra Bos over Gandhi and Nehru is a case in point. Bose "Netājī" (a literal translation into Sanskrit from "Herr Führer," made by Bose's associates in Berlin in 1942, and the one and only term of reference to that supreme charismatic of India's struggle for independence) belongs to this same bracket. So does the wide-ranging sympathy for the RRS (Rāṣthrīya Svayamsevā Sangh, "national self-help party") which, as an ideology more than as an organized party competing at the polls, has been a thorn in the sides of Indian governments since its inception soon after Independence. Its founder, Guru Golwelkar took paramilitary training in Nazi Germany and studied the Hitler Youth, consciously emulating it in the creation of the RSS youth groups. Until the RSS was outlawed under Nehru, the party symbol read R ϟϟ i.e., the two s'es being the Nazi symbols for the SS. Golwelkar was a brahmin, belonging to the same caste as Nathuram Vinayak Godse and Apte, the two men who planned and executed Gandhi's assassination in 1948. The Chitpavan brahmins of Maharashtra in western India have a dual legacy of high scholarly ritualism and violence. M. N. Roy, one of the finest political minds of mid-century India, was shaving when his wife called from the living room to tell him that news of Mahatma Gandhi's assassination had just come over the radio. Without looking away from the mirror, he said "it must have been a Chitpavan brahmin." And so it was. Bengalis will shout and write poems, maybe mount the gallows in violent protest, he remarked. Others will only shout or shoot without a schedule. Chitpavans will plan and act, and see it as religiously motivated. (personal communication from M. N. Roy, about 1952).

Brahmin monks were the advisors of the *kṣattriya* chief, Shivaji, the powerful military leader who defeated both the British and the Muslims, who is a national hero of mythological dimensions. The tie between brahmins and *kṣattriyas*, their functional complementarity, and their ritualized interaction belongs to quite a different category than Latin American and other generals hobnobbing with the church, which is purely exigent and weakly ideological. Quite consciously, the RSS aligns brahmanical counsel (purity, piety, vegetarianism, continence) with *kṣattriya* performance (violent action, military training, un-Indian punctuality). Unlike the Naxalites (about whom later) whose models of violent action are imported as are socialism and all forms of communism, the RSS and other Hindu communal groups articulate their policies from an indigenous value hierarchy. They legitimize violent action as derived from the Hindu model of kingship and of royal values. Even when brahmins take to arms, the model is powerfully available in the revered story of Paraśurāma, ("Rāma with the ax") the Lord of the brahmin Bhṛgu clan, who lopped off the heads not only of his immediate enemies but eradicated the entire *kṣattriya* population, outdoing their endogenous prowess with his own, more ferocious albeit brahmin. (Professor R. Goldman (1977) of Berkeley has argued convincingly that the entire plot underlying the great epic is a Bhārgava, i.e., a brahmin story, not a *kṣattriya* matrix as has otherwise been taken for granted.) Paraśurāma is the seventh incarnation of the all-God Viṣṇu; his eighth was the better known Rāma, the archetypal *rājput*, hero of the epic Rāmāyaṇa, and idol of all Hindus, including Mahatma Gandhi. (In Gandhi's ashrams, the daily litany includes "Raghupati Rāghava Rājārām," invoking Rāma, lord of the Raghu clan.) Brahmins and holy men are rājākaras ("King-makers"), and the replication of this functional diarchy is very close to the Indian ideological climate.

Hindu fascination and unconcealed admiration for Hitler is a somewhat pathological extension of this syndrome. I wrote about this matter in some detail fifteen years ago (Bharati, 1965, pp. 74–78), but things have not changed it seems, in spite of increasing cosmopolitanization of modern Hindus. At the 12th annual conference of the Subhas Bose Society at American University in Washington, D.C. in December 1980, I presented a paper on Bose's alliance with the Nazis (Bharati, 1981b, pp. 73-85). It turned out that my discussant was a member of the American Nazi party, and some three or four articulate, aggressive American Nazis were present in the audience. All of them, and the Indian organizers of this conference, claim that they belong to an international society of "revisionist" historians, whose charge it is to show that there was no holocaust and the Jews were not killed except in military action, and (on the Indian side) that Netāji's Indian National Army constituted under the Nazis and the Japanese was solely responsible for India's independence. Mr. Ranjan Bora, the chief convener in that conference, said during the discussion that Ramesh C. Mazumdar (one of the most outstanding Indian historians) once said that India should erect three gold statues: one to Netāji Bose, one to Mahatma Gandhi, and one to Adolf Hitler. Regardless of whether Professor Mazumdar ever made this sagacious recommendation or not, the fact that a large audience of Indians and Indian scholars assembled in Washington, D.C. nodded unexceptional approval speaks volumes, and is, of course, grist to my mill: the kṣattriya-brahmin-divine hero model, however transmogrified, persists through the avid adoption of jeans and phony American accents.

At this point, I will elaborate the term "minimal symbolic trigger." It seems to me that it works very well in the Indian context and it extends to such baffling phenomena as the overt or covert admiration of many Indians for Hitler and Nazi Germany. Why is it that perfectly gentle, perfectly vegetarian, philosophical, highly "spiritual" (a modern Indian-English term for "religiously engagé") would praise Hitler as a hero with divine overtones? They know nothing about anti-Semitism; most of them have never seen a Jew, and wouldn't know if they saw one. Quite often when confronted with facts, modern Hindus would deny Auschwitz and the holocaust as an American invention. A famous holy man once rebuked me, coram populo (the listening crowd numbered roughly five thousand people), when I pointed out the cataclysmic violence of the Nazi system and the sadism of its leadership: "You have no right, Sir, to say such lies about Sri Adolf Hitler. These are all lies concocted by the C.I.A. The pictures of corpses were collages of dead people pulled out of cemeteries and off the battlefield, in order to throw a bad light on Herr Hitler." This is a gross example, and it occurred a quarter of a century ago. Yet, the Bose meeting in Washington, D.C. in December 1980 points to an ominous persistence of these notions. To the non-Indianist, such disquisitions must seem ghastly and inane. Yet they fall well within the ken of Indian parlance. Few if any facts are known about Hitler; but what is perceived as true information about him are behavioral vignettes conducive to triggering cultural empathy: Hitler was (so Hindus believe) a vegetarian; he was chaste; he used the svastika, a sacred Vedic symbol—and a pervasive one in Hindu ritual and art, a symbol of fertility and undifferentiated, general benevolence. Hitler conquered, or was about to conquer, India's oppressor.

This is a "minimal trigger"; so are the repeated occurrences of sati, and so are notions of witchcraft and sorcery as reported by Obeyesekere (1975). Factual sequences are neither known nor asked, and selected elements of the perceived sequence of events are clustered into a gestalt which is the "minimal symbolic trigger." The Reuter report said that the alleged incursion of pigs into Muslim religious space caused the deadly outbreak in Moradabad in August 1980. The Mutiny of 1857 broke out, so Hindus aver, because the British allegedly greased ammunition with cow fat and, so Muslims said, the British greased it with lard. Neither was true because, as any ammunitions expert will tell you, either fat would ruin any ammunition.

I insist that the kṣattriya norm extends beyond Hindu society into all Indian societies, including the Muslim. Getting angry, and feeling righteous about it, is part of the kṣattriya norm, and triggers are interpreted in terms of the norm, ex post facto. There are pigs in all Muslim countries; in Lebanon, Egypt, and Jordan, Christian herders drive pigs right through Muslim sectors of town or village, and nobody minds. But in India, getting angry because of a confrontation involving infractions on ritualistic purity is part of the indigenous value orientation which extols *kṣattriya* virtues that contrast with brahmanical and other Hindu core values.

Actions of physical force done severally by individuals tend to be detached and reassembled into the mould of the *Kṣattriya* hero, into the *Bhagavadgītā* doctrine of the liberated man who does not kill even though he kills thousands, to whom no sin attaches since he knows his true identity with the cosmic Spirit, since he does not identify himself with his bodily actions. Thus, the use of the svastika on the German flag, the rumor that the dead husband's pyre lit up by itself as the widow mounted it, or that pigs belonging to Hindus had been made to trespass Muslim space, all operate as "minimal symbolic triggers" either for violent action or to condone violent actions. This is a modal Indian situation, and it contrasts with other kinds of violence—political, ideological—generated and sustained by the aggregation of long-term *alien* inputs (the Naxalites, factory and student riots, for instance). These do not fit the model. This is of no concern since unicausal explanations do not work for South Asian complexities. The "communal" violence of the region, from before and through the mind-boggling violence of partition in 1947, right through the Morabad riots between Muslims and Hindus in 1980 is a different matter and fits into my paradigm. Both Hindus and Muslims emphasize their mutual tolerance in normal, day-to-day interaction: they attend each other's festivals, etc. Few Hindu or Muslim persons would see communal violence as the result of doctrinal differences. Informed Hindus point out that they, as opposed to Christians and Muslims, have never persecuted people on account of their faith. There is no notion of heresy in the Hindu tradition, certainly not in the semantic domain which incorporates official persecution or discrimination due to religious views held. Yet, "minimal symbolic triggers" did precipitate every single incidence of violence reported.

The late saintly Indian leader Jai Prakash Narayan wrote a preface to a book on riots in the industrial complex of Rourkela (Chatterjee, Singh, & Rao, 1967), where he stated "This range and magnitude of the mob-violence that took place in Rourkela is to oversimplify and misunderstand the complex social situation. Economic tensions, the imbalance created by social change. . . . (p. iv)." The people who oversimplify and misunderstand are Hindus, but Narayan himself did not pay heed, in this statement, to the fact that all the reports about the riots showed that each incident which snowballed into carnage was triggered by minimal symbolic displays belonging to the Hindu-Muslim 'communal' repertoire. No doubt, the economic infrastructure is part of the etiology; but, since this is the case everywhere, it isn't saying very much. Very wisely, Narayan wrote elsewhere at about the same time, "If the Indian Hindus kill Indian Muslims for no other reason than that Pakistani Muslims have killed Pakistani Hindus, it is a complete vindication of the two nation theory. It simply means that we affirm in action what we loudly repudiate in words (*The Statesman*, March 27, 1964, p. 7)."

In books and smaller tracts on violence written by Indians, psychologists, journalists, and others, it is always "tensions" and "rumors" that cause outbreaks of mob violence. Triggers are mentioned only in straight primary news media reports, not as "triggers," but as news starters. They are ignored in *ex post facto* analyses, and the linkage is invariably seen in simple socioeconomic terms. I think the reason why cultural or psychological concatenations are never mentioned even by psychologists is that such reasoning might reflect the "backwardness" or "superstition" of the population. To the modern Indian writer and spokesman, few things are more embarrassing than suggestions that actual decision making, including violent action, may be linked to an indigenous metaphysic. It seems much less objectionable to ascribe such events to the more down to earth, the more modern, the more Western modes of causal explanation, i.e., the social or economic.

POLITICAL VIOLENCE

What do we do with political violence rampant in India at all times, but violence without "communal" underpinnings? There is barely sufficient literature on revolutionary violence in South Asia (Bharati, 1976; Dhangare, 1974; Kearney, 1980). There is some critical writing by Indian Marxists (e.g., Mohanty, 1977) who speak about violence as part of a political program; and there is the Naxalite literature pro and contra.[6] This writing, of course, is detached from the agonies of violence; yet any reasoned parlance which condones or recommends violence should belong to the genre of this volume. There are at least two ways of handling this "other," noncommunal, violence which, incidentally, may be more visible at times in certain areas (particularly in Bengal and potentially in Bangladesh) than the more indigenous communal violence. The first, easier way would be to assign an import etiology to this sort of violence. Imported ideologies find their takers; yet, for the South Asian peasant, or the landless sharecropper at the whim of the landlord or the middleman, there is hardly any need for, nor any knowledge of Marxist-Leninist-Maoist doctrine. However, any articulation of such doctrine, when made by a charismatic, seems to suffice to generate violent outbursts of dimensions hardly known in the West. When the disinherited Indian suddenly begins to loot, set fires, torture, or kill at the suggestion or the mere connivance of ideologized, politicized leaders, neither of them sees this as an adaptation to the *kṣattriya* model. Rather, he might be said to delegate feelings of guilt to the leader, taking recourse to the ancient Indian parlance of the leader being like an ocean that can absorb the slimiest rivers without being sullied itself; or he may take the apologetic stance, also part of the indigenous dialect, of having lost equilibrium under duress, not being himself, having gone "*mast.*"[7]

The second, subtler, but to me at any rate more attractive reading of this sort of highly visible violence in South Asia comes within the template of the "minimal symbolic trigger," albeit via a detour. Dhangare reports (1974, p. 120) that a village leader Doddi Kommarraya was killed by *goondas* (goons) during the Telangana peasant insurrection in the late forties. "Komarraya's martyrdom sparked off the conflagration and thus marked the beginning for the insurrection." Then follows a description of the expected police brutality in retaliation and control, and further retaliation of violence by violence. The village revolutionary councils (created ad hoc) "discouraged, and later even prohibited, primitive forms of torture and retribution."

Observe this sequence and compare it with the blinding of suspects by the Bhagalpur police at the time of this writing. In each case—and of course in scores of similar cases over a long period of time—violence erupted because both the aggressors and the victims shared a *kṣattri-*

---

[6]Naxalism and Naxalites: From "Naxalbari" village which was the site of a violent peasant revolt in 1967. The founder of the movement, Charu Mazumdar, a Bengali Maoist or Mao-inspired leader, proclaimed "the formation of a new revolutionary party through uncompromising struggle." Uncompromising it turned out to be; the Naxalites prepared hit lists and a large number of landholders, petty officials, and opposing politicians were murdered. The Indian police took brutal action to retaliate and suppress them and, although Naxalism is either dead or dormant, the term has become synonymous with political, leftist, planned violence by a sort of metonymical process: all over South Asia, "Naxalite" mentality, "Naxalite" plans, etc., has come to mean just this, and state governments in both India and Bangladesh remain on their guard. Naxalism is no doubt the most highly polarized noncommunal and, by implication, anticommunal form of actual or potential violence in the region.

[7]*Mast* is a Hindi word properly belonging to the mahout's (elephant driver's) language: when the bull elephant enters his once a year period of sexual excitement (*masti*), a thick resin-like liquid exudes from his trunk, the smell of which supposedly makes him fierce, unpredictable, self-absorbed, yet somehow tender—the word is *mast,* and of course it has no translation short of such paraphrase. The term is freely used to characterize men who act in a similar fashion—it is *never* used for women, and the analogy contains an apologia on behalf of the *mast* person who, like the bull elephant, cannot help being *mast.*

ya idiom, however dormant: evil must be punished, and acute evil must be punished right away. The Sanskrit word for (royal) justice is *daṇḍa*, "stick." Acute justice in response to acute transgression does not tolerate anything like "due process," it requires speedy administration and execution, it requires *daṇḍa*. In the first case, a farmer was killed through the manipulations of the unjust, cruel, cunning landholder, and this provided the minimal symbolic trigger to instantiate *daṇḍa*—it is not that people took the law into their own hands (such diction is alien to the Indian situation), rather, the people saw a higher law at work, a divine mandate to mete out justice through immediate retaliation. The policemen in Bhagalpur, the paper reported, "saw it fit to prevent dacoitry and other crimes, not by killing the culprits, but by blinding possible offenders." It appears there was a lineup of suspects at one of the police stations, and one officer said "*ab Rāmrājya dikhlāne kā waqt āgayā*" (now is the time to implement the reign of Rāma)[8] and he tied one suspect to a pole and pierced his eyes with a bicycle spoke— his fellow officers then set about to do the same. "Though persons all over the country expressed shock at the behavior of the police," a New Delhi news report states, "one rickshaw puller told *Sunday Magazine* 'only after the police have blinded some criminals, have the roads become safe' (*India Abroad*, Dec. 5, 1980, p. 6)."

An intermediate summary of my points is in order now; and I will inverse the order of my presentation for the sake of balance. At first glance, contemporary violence is either politicized, as in the case of Maoified (Naxalite) violence; or it is seemingly nonideological police brutality toward both apolitical and political suspects or "culprits." Antithetically to it, there is fully sacralized violence, along the *kṣattriya* model and/or the model of the liberated soul who must act as an ordinary man—an Indian syndrome to which Wendy D. O'Flaherty very aptly refers as the *shazzam* effect (O'Flaherty, 1980). Still, underlying both or, if you wish, as a synthesis, there is the *kṣattriya* model which delegates violence (the police inspector to the policemen, the elected official to the police inspectors), or it *hypostasizes* violence (condoning the dictator, espousing his deeds as cosmically beneficial, etc.). Literature supporting each of these stances is abundant. Yet there is virtually no literature on human problems involved— no indigenous literature that is. I do not include the work of Obeyesekere (1975, pp. 1-23) or that of other social scientists trained and writing in a Western critical tradition.

SĀTI VS. SUICIDE

Whether there is such a thing as aggression genetically coded or whether there is no such feat in nature, the anthropologist is interested in violence mediated by the endocultural symbolic structure. This transcends the emic-etic division of recent anthropology which would say that, emically speaking, an act or set of acts is not violent if the cultural agent does not see, report, or think of it as violent. But this does not work in such important studies of violence as Obeyesekere's, for surely, the Sinhalese who wants to harm another person through *hūniyan* or some other magical strategem does not report his intentions in the parlance of aggression; rather, he thinks about them in terms of justice, retribution, etc., maybe in Buddhist Karmic terms.

---

[8]*Rāmrājya* is a term very much in vogue in India. The reference is again the epic Rāmāyaṇa, which is to India what the Iliad would be to Greece had it preserved its ancient identity. The divine kind hero Rāma's deeds have been sung and narrated and contemplated for at least two thousand years, and his rule epitomizes all that a just ruler should do; it is the Hindu Camelot, as it were. Mahatma Gandhi used the term very often; and although he rejected movies and the film medium in general as wicked, he did see and recommend *Rāmrājya*, a movie about the deeds of Rāma, which was a great success on the Indian screen in the forties.

Yet, etically speaking, it is every bit as violent as hiring a hitman to kill the opponent. Via such detour, we return once more to *sati*, widow immolation on the husband's pyre, which seems to be on the rise at this time over and above sheer increased media coverage. Writing about a different part of the world, Dorothy Ayrs Counts (1980) opines about the Indian parallel to ritualistically condoned suicide in her area of research: "The ritual killing of a widow at her insistence contains neither the element of criminal responsibility nor the element of social disruption which the Lusi associate with self-killing. The widow's death expresses strong positive social ties and is socially cohesive [p. 347)." Counts take a Durkeimian position here, but applied to the Indian situation it is either trivial or—more likely—wrong. The widow's "insistence" can never be known, but what is known is that there is a lot of pushing and shoving of the widow by the crowd, regardless of her degree of preparedness, which only phenomenologists would speculate about. By now, subtler instantiations of a *ksattriya* model should be apparent: a *ksattriya* male (or any male whose caste aspires to *ksattriya* status) must do violence to others in the manner adumbrated. *Ksattriya* females cannot do so, or very rarely (the woman dacoits, the Rani of Jhansi and some other warrior ladies are mentioned, but their number does not exceed a dozen in the history of India, I believe). Yet *sati* must be read as the institutionalized counterpart to male *ksattriya* aggression. The fact that not all women who commit *sati* are *ksattriyas* (though close to 89 percent are) supports the anthropological axiom for India that the *ksattriya* model pervades almost all processes of upcasteing; it is therefore explanatory as commending and condoning the highly structured violence of *sati*. From Vasco da Gama through the missionaries reports into our own day, the West has seen *sati* as a form of suicide— even anthropologists, who ought to know better, like to call *sati* "ritualized suicide." But, in the Indian vision, *sati* was never seen as suicide—no Indian term for suicide would ever be used to denote *sati*.

Female suicide—not *sati*—is a problem in India, however; by most Western standards, it is of epidemic extensions in certain regions of South Asia. Since I disavow monocausal explanations, I gladly grant that the *ksattriya* model does not apply, or in such an elliptical fashion that only Levi-Straussian zest could tract it. Ullrich (1977) thinks that female suicide (among the Havik brahmins of the Karnataka region in the South) "may be her only course . . . because she has no formal power [pp. 94-110]." Now, the "lack of formal power," I think, should be interpreted as the lack of social approval for any sort of violent expression, unless it is ritualistically structured as in *sati*. There are no Niobes in the Hindu tradition. "Mother India," an enormously popular movie on the Hindu screen, features Nargis (the Indian Ingrid Bergman) killing her son because he did wrong and wouldn't reform. But the popularity of the movie was due to its being totally unrealistic, contrary to all cultural norms. This has been explained as "reversal fantasy" by one of my Indian colleagues—coquettish women, unmarried, nubile, wealthy, healthy, with their marriages not arranged by parents are every bit as unrealistic as "Mother India" killing her son because of his being unrepentent.

Reactions to reports of *sati* range from romantic, occidental soap inspired reverie to straight reiteration of the *ksattriya* ideal. One example of each will suffice—both were letters to the editor of the *Illustrated Weekly of India*, which carried a photographic report of a *sati* that occurred in 1980.

> Recently I came across a case of a young lady, a mother of two very young children, locking herself up in her bathroom and setting fire to herself, after hearing about the sudden death of her husband. We have also heard of young couples dying together, out of sheer love for each other, of females sacrificing themselves for the sake of their male partners and vice versa. Is *sati* something different from such sacrifice? [G. L. Kakshi, *Illustrated Weekly*, May 11-17, 1980]

While congratulating you on the excellent photographic coverage of the *Sati* incident in Rajasthan, there are general questions which arise. It appears that the widow has chosen a glorious death, instead of suffering acute poverty and helplessness and dying inch by inch (sic). Since society could do nothing to alleviate her sufferings, it does not have any moral right to point an accusing finger at the incident in Orissa [H. Acharya, ibid.].

IDEOLOGICAL VIOLENCE

An eminent political scientist who specializes in Indian factional politics (Brass, 1980), muses about political violence: "The Indian political system is a rough and tumble one full of violence, injustice, narrow pursuit of self interest . . . [p. 650]." Explaining violent mass action by the kṣattriya model and, negatively, by the lack of any other model for mass action, violent or other is a hermeneutic effort; it does not claim to come up with an etiology, but it can show some kind of continuity in a longitudinal tabulation of actions, say, from the deeds of Rāma as reported and perceived in the epics, to the self-righteous dastardliness of the Bihari police officers blinding their suspects; or from the mythology of the original Satī, known to all Hindu women, to occurrences of sati in today's Rajasthan.

S. K. Ghosh (1971), a retired inspector general of police, avers that mobs get out of control due to "rumours" and their rapid spread. This is reiterated ad nauseum, with very little modification, by editorial writers, by politicians in and out of power, and by college teachers. Violence due to rumors must then be controlled by police violence, and we find such gems as "the proper direction of a heavy pierce is diagonal to the frontage of the mob. If the mob faces north, the proper direction for the heavy pierce is from northeast to southwest . . . [Ghosh, 1971, p. 9]." The author quotes Swami Vivekananda in the motto of the book, and he quotes long passages from Vivekananda's writings and speeches; a Hindu hierophant, Vivekananda talked about ahiṃsā, nonviolence, and also a proper rājput strength and martial virtues. "It is more important for India's youth to play a game of football than to read the Bhagavadgītā"—this sagacious statement is ascribed to the Swami. The erstwhile inspector general of police comments on the Swami:

The Ramakrishna Mission movement preached the basic unity of all religions and so did Mahatma Gandhi. In spite of the teaching of [names of three saintly teachers including Gandhi] we have not been able to shake off our fanaticism. Apart from communalism between Hindus and Muslims, studies of Indian life record the deep distrust and abundance of quarrels between members of different castes and sects. . . . Communal riots between Hindus and Muslims in India usually arise out of the questions of "music before mosques" or "cow-killing." [Ghosh, 1971, p. 14]

He then continues, "When rioting breaks out between the Hindus and the Muslims, the offences committed are: (1) assault, stabbing, and murder (2) arson in shops and houses (3) looting (4) rioting between hostile groups (5) defilement of places of worship and (6) rape and abduction of women [p. 15]." It does not seem to bother him that all but (5) are common to all rioting everywhere. Ghosh writes as a policeman, no doubt, with bureaucratic interests and expertise; but he also writes as a Hindu policeman, and his juxtaposition of religious charismatics with danda as enforced by the police force, the surrogate king's men, illustrates the kṣattriya model as a central Hindu paradigm.

On the other end of the continuum, Mohanty, a radical, probably Maoist political scientist teaching in the Department of Chinese and Japanese Studies at the University of Delhi, trained at the University of California at Berkeley, writes as an apologist for Naxalism, rejects other leftist groups as revisionist, and uses all the official rhetoric of the extreme left. He bills his book as belonging "to the era of post-behavioral revolution in social sciences" (Mohanty, 1977, p. x), and revolutionary violence, of course, is a virtue for him. We may either read this as a completely alienated use of the term—alienated in the sense of disindigenized from the Indian symbol system—an explanation of the Naxalite movement, an informed, highly ideo-logized statement of transnational alignment, etc. Mohanty himself, no doubt, sees it this way. However, he writes about the Sri Lanka insurgency: "The April uprising in Sri Lanka in April 1971 . . . was not Maoist insofar as it did not believe in protracted war. However, this does not mean that they were not Marxist revolutionaries. They were wedded to Marxist, and in fact Maoist analysis of the Ceylonese environment [pp. 20-21]." They were nothing of that sort. This writer happened to be in Sri Lanka as the only Western anthropologist present on the island at that time; Kearney (1980) and I wrote about it (Bharati, 1973, pp. 35-45; 1976, pp. 102-113), and more is yet to come. Though the political leadership of the insurgents was clearly communist, the agents and executors were hardly ideologists—the cause for the insurgency was linked to massive unemployment of literate Ceylonese. Mohanty must interpose a symbolic scheme. He cannot talk about *rājput* heroism and *kṣattriya* bravura, but he can talk about a packeted ideology of total solutions as though it had functioned as a symbolic trigger. Maoism replaces *kṣattriya* ideology, both make violence respectable, and both disencountenance the likelihood of a violent upsurge without ideological base.

A "rural Indian" reports in his diary how and why violence is part of routine transactions (Morrison, 1978):

> Mehar, Gurdyal, and Dalip were going to cross the field of Bigu (the water carrier, an untouchable) . . . but Bigu's son did not allow them to cross the ground. A struggle arose. Bigu arrived with a stick. Mehar snatched the stick from him and strongly with both hands struck him on the head. He became senseless . . . blood came out from his mouth and nose. . . . A Harijan (untouchable), who had become fresh with a woman schoolteacher . . . a garland of broken shoes was hung around his neck, and he was made to blacken his face. . . . Then he was given a harsh beating publicly and again taken to the lockup. [p. 151]

Assuming that Morrison, an anthropologist, selected the writer of this diary as a typical villager, and comparing it with my own experience during my peregrination through India's villages back in 1950, I can vouch for its typicality. We have here violence along caste lines and about caste ranking and discrimination. Two thousand miles south of Morrison's village, and four languages and two language families away, a Kallan (paddy merchant and petty cultivator of low caste):

> ran up a bill and was one day asked to pay (by the brahmin landlord). When he refused, promising to pay later, the brahmin slapped his face. The Kallan at once cracked the brahmin's head open with a staff and walked coolly out of the village. Streaming with blood, the brahmin was rushed by bullock cart to the Tanjore hospital, and came home vowing to file a suit against his aggressor. [Gough, 1955, p. 46]

The idea of personal, heroic revenge did not enter, since such would be *kṣattriya* ethos and the brahmin would not see himself or be seen as capable of or morally entitled to take physical revenge. Slapping a man's face is not violence, especially not if the slappee is a low caste.

Not too far from there, a younger generation "had gone to school in the hope of obtaining lucrative government positions; the depression years offered them nothing but a return to the land. The young people, bursting with new-felt needs, expressed their dissatisfaction by taking aggressive action against neighboring villages [Beals, 1955, p. 96]." I witnessed an almost identical, though aggravated situation during the 1971 Sri Lanka insurgency. These cases do not seem to follow the kṣattriya model by any stretch of the imagination. They did follow a "higher expectation" pattern which, in the Indian context, can be perceived as a claim to higher status; and, in a somewhat elliptical fashion, this violence turns out to be righteous, i.e., kṣattriya-ethos-legitimized violence, after all. Check this against instances of unmediated kṣattriya ethos. Says a Vaghela rājput kinsman about the lineage chief, the Thakur Saheb: "We believe in him as in our God. He is our King. If he calls ten thousand rājputs, we will go and give our heads to him [Steed, 1955, p. 114]." "Power, allegiance, sacrifice, bravery are interchangeable and related ideals of a dominant rājput theme," Steed comments. Now, if a real rājput (i.e., a person belonging to the high kṣattriya groups of Rajasthan, northwestern India) refuses to act aggressively or to represent himself as potentially aggressive in culturally postulated martial terms, his only alternative is radically nonaggressive, i.e., religious behavior, as in the case of one rājput in that same village, who in Steed's word "opted for religious bachelorhood." In that young man's own words, he began "to experiment with the Goddess," i.e., he shut himself up for many hours every day in a room in his house converted into a shrine to the Goddess, the tutelary deity of most rājputs. "Religious bachelorhood," however, is a misnomer, since becoming or being a holy man confers highest charisma superseding all other sorts of culturally sanctioned behavior. The mythological archetype is Viśvamitra, the rājput warrior leader who undertook the most gruesome and prolonged penances in order to become a brahmin. All actual and potential rājput violence is cancelled in nonviolent saintly comportment since Indian society does not—or not yet—inculcate stageless leaps into the metaphysically highest position which would be that of the nonviolent renouncer. Progress must be in stages, and the kṣattriya model, with its built-in formula for violent conduct, remains as the most pervasively emulated one. But if a person like Steed's "religious bachelor" already happens to be a bona fide rājput, he can make that step smoothly and without further delay.

THREE CATEGORIES OF VIOLENCE

I distinguish between "causes" and "triggers" of violent behavior. This is a hermeneutic device rather than a taxonomic exercise. The distinction never belongs to emic accounts of violence, be they a rural narrator's or a Naxalite socialist's. In emic accounts, trigger explanations are far more frequent or else triggers and causes are confused with one another. To the question "why did you (or X) beat up Y?" the answer "because I saw red" (which must do to interpret Indian expressions of many nuances) is more likely to occur than "because I am (or X is) a rājput." On reflection once removed, however, a cause would be stated more often than not; and this will predictably mesh with the kṣattriya posture as interiorized in the case of actual rājputs or equivalent castes, or as emulated in the case of "upcasteing" lower castes. I use "cause" and "causal" in the sense Melford E. Spiro does in his seminal paper on problems of definition and explanation of religious behavior (1966, 117ff). Applied here, kṣattriya ideology provides a motivation to act violently, hence it is a causal explanation; anything else, as we have seen, might trigger such action, but triggers are not causes in this sense.

The linguistic base for violent action, the vocabulary, and the syntax of aggression should provide further checks along this line. In Bengali, there are three linguistic categories for violent action, i.e., jhagrā, all sorts of quarrel regardless of the degree of violence encountered, as well as quarrel as a sequel of any violent action; it is the weakest and most general expression. Mārāmāri (literally, "hitting about") is physical violence with no bloodshed; khūnakhūni (literally, "bloodletting all-over") is violence with murderous intent and/or consequence. A.

K. Aminul Islam reports about a village in Bangladesh—a Muslim village, of course—where land disputes top the list of triggers for violent action, marital or sexual jealousy rank second, and taking sides in unspecified factional disputes rank third. Rape and the communal rioting often linked to rape is given more media spread, but seems to rank only as a fourth frequency trigger. Each of these four may engender *jhagrā*, *māramāri*, or *khūnakhūni*, and the sequence of intensification is fistfighting, *lathi*-(club) charge, stabbing and knifing of various kinds, and finally firearms. There is a limited variety of types of rural violence, and virtually all village studies of the last four decades (and their number is literally legion) refer to it. *Gutbandi* (literally "tying knees together," i.e., factionalism over land or women, petty politics, petty revence) seems to follow similar patterns in all South Asian regions. Political violence is more recent. It began during pre-independence politicization and continues unabated, but not more extensively, official and journalistic assertions notwithstanding. While rape and sorcery are ancient, they were seldom reported as violence until quite recently. It appears that rape for revenge is rather more frequent in the area than just rape for any of the other known and researched causes. Since sex across caste lines is highly polluting and ritualistically dangerous, rape across caste lines would logically follow patterns of perceived intensification. Islam (1979) illustrates typical Bangladeshi village violence in several case stories (pp. 114-135). I think the perceived causes he lists are modal in the South Asian context: stereotyping a *gushthi* (clan) by members of another *gushthi*, as being dishonest, cheats, and mean, etc.; grazing rights on a specific plot of land; resettlement of flood victims, sexual scandal, and jealousy; conflicts within the *gushthi* and between *gushthis*; sectarian conflict—which could be seen as a subcategory of "communal conflict," since Muslim Hanafis and Muslim Muhamadis detest one another every bit as much as each of them detests Hindus; conflict resulting from gambling; and conflict from the powerful "too big for his shoes" syndrome.

In a society which bases its moral norms as much on kinship as does South Asian society, internecine and ingroup violence is either largely controlled or else largely suppressed. "In spite of the stringent rules regulating the intercourse of mother's brother and sister's son," writes Kathleen Gough about the matrilinear Nayars of Kerala (Gough, 1959, p. 248), "physical aggression between them may occur. In spite of the supernatural sanctions against violence within the lineage, I heard several stories of nephews who poisoned or stabbed their mother's brothers." Setting fire to the sari of the daughter-in-law by the mother-in-law or, more pathetically, of the husband burning his wife to death by orders of his mother is an oft reported event all over the subcontinent. Emically, however, this is not seen as ingroup violence at all, since the wife (in all but the Dravidian groups of the South) does not belong to her husband's family at all and is a functional stranger. About brahmins, Gough continues, "Aggression against the parents seems to be too deeply repressed for them to be thought of, alive or dead, as themselves aggressive. Instead, the Brahmin seems to effect a reaction formation against his aggression which appears in his unusual concern for the ancestor's safety, and in the anxious needs to perform numerous rites which will ward off from them the punishment of the god of death [p. 253]."

Where parents have a strong and lasting influence over their offspring and where the status of the elders is also highly ritualized and respected, aggression tends to be displaced by cathartic ritual. This is particularly evident among *rājputs* whose fathers epitomize the Freudian father much more ideally than his Viennese Jewish father might have done. The *rājput* son is a kind of ideal type Jewish son in Freudian terms. The *rājput* does not have an independent sex life so long as his father is alive and in control of the family affairs, even when the son has already produced children of his own. Now it seems that political aggression in India during the decades of the struggle for independence, including attempted and successful assassinations of British officials and of hundreds of bomb attacks which have become part of the folklore of that struggle, could well be paraphrased in Freudian terms. (This is only a suggestion to enthusiasts, since I myself am less than sanguine about the use of Freudian models for the study of Indian society and culture, see Bharati, 1978, pp. 71-76.) The British were the enemies but the British *sarkār* ("Mr. Government") was also a father, just like *rājput* and Muslim rulers preceding them had cast themselves in that paternal role. But since the British were also the clearly defined enemy, you did not have to curb aggression against them nor did you have to ritualize it in the manner other societies ritualize repressed hatred of their agnates (Bradbury, 1966, pp. 127-155); rather, it could be expressed directly through violent acts, which also had positive sanctions galore in the *kṣattriya* ethos of vanquishing the unjust.

SORCERY AS VIOLENCE

Some may consider my assessment of sorcery as active aggression as farfetched. But I think Obeyesekere (1975, pp. 1-25), who is a psychology-oriented anthropologist—a Sri Lanka born scholar now at Princeton—sets a standard when he suggests that violence as intention and violence as premeditated action is not exhausted in the jural paradigm. He defines sorcery as "a technique of killing or harming someone, deliberately and intentionally, generally with homeopathic or contagious magic, accompanied by spells, charms, and incantations [p. 1]." He also informs us that "traditionally, both sorcery and premeditated murder were viewed as crimes and carried the identical punishment (i.e., death), which provides further evidence that the indigenous culture viewed these two practices as similar [p. 3]."

Obeyesekere salutarily suggests that anthropologists should attend on sorcery as premeditated, rationally planned violence. Many anthropologists and sociologists do not think of sorcery and witchcraft as "real" violence. They arrived at the erroneous syllogism "since sorcery is not effective, and since intention alone does not constitute violence, sorcery is not violence." But nobody should know as well as the field anthropologist that sorcery and witchcraft do indeed work among people whose belief system encodes their practice. The linkage is clear, of course. What Obeyesekere reports for Sri Lanka applies in similar proportions to India, Bangladesh, Nepal, and Pakistan, i.e., to roughly one-fourth of mankind today. It simply cannot be ignored without peril to this endeavor. Violence as sorcery is autochthonous; it does not fit any political matrix generated by foreign ideological imports (nationalism, socialism of all forms, liberalism). Though it does not immediately instantiate the *kṣattriya* model, it follows it elliptically, as it were: both the *kṣattriya* model and violence through sorcery and witchcraft can be subsumed into a wider, more general and pan-Indian scheme, which I would call the "metaphysical-orectic." You act violently, you harm another person or persons physically, ignoring or bypassing the esoteric norm of *ahiṃsā* (non-violence) by making the *kṣattriya* norm supersede it; or else you contract a tantric or other sorcerer to undo your adversary. In both cases, the etiological referend is the magico-religious web of Indian thinking. South Asian area anthropologists will at once recognize a helpful taxonomy: they will see *kṣattriya*-type direct violence as "great tradition," as Sanskritic violence, and they will see violence via sorcery as "little tradition." The "great" and "little" traditions model was first enunciated by Robert Redfield and Milton Singer. Together with "Sanskritization," a term coined by the Indian anthropologist M. N. Srinivas, it had its day and belongs to the realm of Kuhnian paradigms lost. I tried to salvage it in a book by elaborating on its subtler applications (Bharati, 1980). Just as the French Canadian can switch his linguistic code from French to English quite effortlessly, so the Hindu or Buddhist in South Asia can switch his orectic code of legitimation from the great tradition, *kṣattriya*, to the little tradition, sorcery-witchcraft code. In this light, it does not seem overly astounding that thoroughly modern South Asians—lawyers, physicians, delegates at the United Nations—believe in the objective effectiveness of sorcery.

NONVIOLENCE

The literature and the popular reflection on *ahiṃsā* (nonviolence) is enormous in India. Its intensity helps diffuse its doctrines, in one form or the other, across five continents. Martin Luther King, Jr. took his cues from *ahiṃsā* teachings via Gandhi. Few in the West who talk about nonviolence fail to acknowledge its Indian roots. Gardner Murphy, charged with explaining the gruesome violence that killed close to five million people during partition in India in 1947, opined that Indians could not handle that dimension of violence because, unlike Western nations, they lacked norms or models for violent action (Murphy, 1953, pp. 59-91). He did not know anything about the *kṣattriya* model nor, of course, about the "metaphysical orectic" in the Indian value system.

Most contemporary Indian writing and talking about *ahiṃsā* is apologetic; as part of the post-Gandhian rhetoric, it is ubiquitous on the subcontinent (except in Pakistan where it is rejected) regardless of the fact that it has little influence over its audience in India. It is an axiomatic stance, it is the official Indian and Sri Lankan doctrine of proper intergroup action.

Professor Unnithan, a well known Indian sociologist, lectured at Syracuse University in 1980. His topic was "Gandhi and Modernization," and I had expected a critical assessment of the social impact of Gandhian thought on modernization. But all he did was to reiterate Gandhi's reading of *ahiṃsā*—as an ideal, as an achievable state of mind, and as the only alternative to capitalism and communism. This is the official line of all Indian conservatives in politics, but it is rather different from the scriptural meaning of *ahiṃsā*, which dovetails with what I said earlier on the Hindu concept of the perfect man; he who has realized his essential identity with the cosmic spirit cannot do *hiṃsā* (harm, violence, aggression), since it is only his body apparatus that contrives *hiṃsā*, and the "realized soul" no longer identifies with the body. Now this scriptural reading is used by the Hindu fascist politicians (and by the Hindu version of a moral majority which shares the insidiousness of all moral majorities) that violence done through some metaphysically grounded apologetic is no violence. It must be remembered, however, that *ahiṃsā* is to indigenous Indian thinking what the decalogue is to Judaeo-Christian world views. When King Yuddhiṣṭhira, the paragon of royal justice and one of the heroes of the gigantic *Mahābhārata* epic was asked by a vassal king what he regarded as the most important moral commandment, he first said, in an amazingly relativistic mood, that every land and every time has its own norms and commandments. On being pressed harder, insisting on a universally valid norm, Yuddiṣṭhira then proclaimed *ahiṃsā paramo dharmaḥ* ("*ahiṃsā* is that supreme law").

J. H. Broomfield (1968) made one of the best etic statements about Gandhi's version of *ahiṃsā* when he wrote:

> Coming from a Gujerati trading caste, he (Gandhi) had been strongly influenced by the quietest doctrines of Vaiṣṇavism and Jainism[9] and, determined to apply the principle of *ahiṃsā* to politics, he developed a technique of passive resistance. . . . What he proposed was the application to national politics of a method of protest that was familiar in Gujerati society in which he grew up; self abasement and self-denial to force an individual who had given personal offence to realize the injury that had been inflicted and to see the error of his ways. [p. 148]

---

[9]Vaiṣṇavism is one of several traditional Hindu doctrinal traditions, with the deity Viṣṇu as its mythological center. Jainism, an older contemporary of Buddhism, stands outside the Hindu theological ambit in that it is atheistic. But both Vaiṣṇavism and Jainism emphasize total nonviolence and strict vegetarianism as their main commandments. Both Vaiṣṇavism and Jainism are strongly represented in the region of Gandhi's birth and his formative years. His family belonged to the Vaiṣṇava tradition. Vaiṣṇavas and Jains intermarry freely in that region provided they belong to the same caste.

Yet this does not sit well with many Indians. An important segment of Bengali intellectuals feels that the charismatic emotionalism he inspired was no aid to national strength. Broomfield quotes Bipin Chandra Pal, an outstanding Bengali intellectual who wrote:

> I am not blind to the possibilities of good in the great hold that Mahatmaji (i.e., Gandhi) has had on the populace; but there is the other side, and in the earlier stages of democracy these personal influences, when they are due to the inspirations of medieval religious sentiments, are simply fatal to its future. This does not remove the inherited slave-mentality which is the root of all our degradations and miseries. [Broomfield, 1968, p. 148]

This sentiment reflects contemporary Indian notions which neither reject nor espouse violence either directly or by implication, and where the *kṣattriya* model no longer fits, where it is consciously rejected, and where an imported model supersedes the indigenous—something analogous to Kuhnian paradigm erosion and replacement in the ideological sphere. This novel thought was shared by some Indian leaders in the final stages of India's struggle for independence, but they remained somewhat marginal; at this time, they have also moved into the mainstream of Indian political life where they constitute a core for alternative thinking. It postulates the moving away from religious and nationalistic ideology and toward a dejingoized, decharismatized set of cognitions and conations. Though these did originate in the colleges and salons of the West, no more than socialism and nationalism are seen as Western imports by their Asian protagonists.

The blend of humanism, intellectualism, objectivism, and genuine secularism with the London School of Economics as its probable center of diffusion does not proselytize as do religious or political ideologies. Its advocates eschew violence, but their cognitive matrix for such eschewal is humanistic, Fabian—it contrasts fundamentally with the *ahiṃsā* type of nonviolence which is religious to the core. The alternative is nonproselytizing, selective, and somewhat elitist. Its Indian doyens, Bipin Chandra Pal, M. N. Roy, and his "Radical Humanist" disciples are as skeptical about *ahiṃsā* as they are about violence, but violence is not ruled out *en principle* when it comes to questions of social improvement. The late M. N. Roy, at one time the founder of the Trotskyite party in Mexico, and the only Indian ever on the Comintern, as well as one of Mao's political mentors in the thirties, rejected and renounced any party affiliation during his prison term imposed by the British, dissolved his own party, and created a loose assembly of unpartied political thinkers, the "Radical Humanists." Many of today's political leaders in India, in power and out of power, identify themselves as radical humanists. At this time, V. Tarkunde, eminent lawyer and advocate to the Supreme Court of India, edits the monthly English language journal *The Radical Humanist* in New Delhi which, together with *New Quest* published in Pune (western India), provides highly sophisticated political commentary. Its readership is limited. The total subscription at this time is about two thousand, and that seems to be the number of bona fide "radical humanists."

Subhas Chandra Bose "Netāji," India's most charmastic political figure through life and death (like Emperor Barbarossa, Bose is thought to be alive and hiding), stood very much in the mainstream of Indian perceptions. His fascination with violence as well as his opposition to *ahiṃsā* had religious, doctrinal moorings to the core; it was a powerful exemplification of the *kṣattriya* model. This no doubt accounts for the fact that Bose retains charisma of mythological dimensions in India—he virtually coalesces with the *kṣattriya* model; he is not known at all in the West except to political scientists specializing in modern India. Gandhi and Nehru are known in the West, because theirs were modes for thought and action which are not uniquely Indian. Just how much Mr. Gandhi felt threatened by Roy's secularism seems borne out by the former's directive to Congress party leaders when he told them *in camera* in 1931 "you have to ignore and isolate M. N. Roy. He aims at our roots" (personal communication Sri Krishna Sinha, former Chief Minister of the State of Bihar).

American-style urban violence—mugging, rapes, gang violence without any ideological underpinnings—is as yet underrepresented on the subcontinent, although incidents are on the increase in such large industrializing cities as Calcutta, Bombay, and Delhi. I am not sure if the last attraction of *Sholay* and similar Hindi movies mentioned earlier is due to the total novelty of "violence for violence's sake," as a well-known Indian writer paraphrased American urban violence, or whether it is not felt to be a novel variation of *kṣattriya*-type dacoitry. Other than that, violence seems always caused by some highly visible chain of events triggered by a minimal symbolic event, land disputes, faction rivalry, theft of women and adultery, and the other standbys of Indian village studies provide pervasive themes—the *kṣattriya*-model provides both cause and legitimation.

CONCLUSION

Raymond Aron (1975) wrote in his *magnum opus* on violence "Man is freedom—and it is in rebellion, in the pure act, that this freedom is unequivocally manifest [p. 116]." Man is freedom—Hindu and Buddhism wisdom proclaim the same, but they imply the radical opposite. "Man" to them is not the empirical, social being, but a metaphysical essence or an ontological construct—and there is no rebellion in that essence. Empirical man, the social being, is bound by rules other than freedom. His ethos is set by the mythology inherent in the caste (*varṇa*) scheme. According to McKim Marriott (1976), brahmins optimize, *kṣattriyas* maximize, *vaiśyas* (merchants) minimize, and *śūdras* (menial castes) pessimize (pp. 107-114). Maximization condones and entails permissiveness. Violence and sensuality are beyond the limit of the permissible for all but the institutionalized maximizers, the *kṣattriyas*. A *kṣattriya* must eat hot food, *rājasik* (passion-increasing) nutrition, meat, spices, and liquor so as to be heroic, read violent. The process of Sanskritization for Hindus of the lower strata is tantamount with *kṣattriya*-ization. The brahmin model is unachievable and not really desired; for the merchant model, one needs capital, a commodity sadly lacking in South Asia. But the *kṣattriya* model is eminently accessible and the most successfully upcasted groups have espoused it. It inculcates violence; it permits rebellion and bashing heads.

"The deed of Adam," Aron wrote, "results in the essence of Adam and thus, according to Sartre, Adam carries no responsibility for it [1975, p. 167]." In Hindu India, one's own norm (*svadharma*) is given by birth, through the effects of karma. Unexpectedly, Sartre and the Hindu *kṣattriya* model intersect.

To summarize, the official, traditional ideology of India is that of nonviolence (*ahiṃsā*). Over the past two millennia, it kept being revitalized by charismatics, the most recent one being Mahatma Gandhi, the father of India's independence. Of all the virtues encoded in the Indian value system, *ahiṃsā* ranks highest. But there is a systemic problem: as traditional and as official as *ahiṃsā*, the ethos of the hero, the warrior, the prince, is one of martial violence; the very texts that extol *ahiṃsā* praise the king's and his vassals' right and duty to violent action, not only to punish evildoers, but because it is "in the nature" (*svabhāva*) of the *kṣattriya* (prince, warrior, soldier) to be violent. It is not, as superficial observers have thought, that violence sneaks into a basically nonviolent body politic; both *ahiṃsā* and violence are on the books, quite literally. We might compare it to an hour-glass: one of the bulbs marked violence, the other *ahiṃsā*. The substance flowing between the two bulbs is the same; it is the position of the bulbs that makes it flow into either direction. The hour-glass is overturned by "minimal symbolic triggers"—any of which tilts the *ahiṃsā* bulb, and the violence bulb gets atop. Much less frequently, yet well known in the Indian lore, a "minimal symbolic trigger" might convert a robber into a saintly vegetarian—the sight of the *dhoti* (loincloth) of Mahatma Gandhi and Vinoba Bhave did that to some famous brigands. The hour-glass analogy is an improvement over the idea I have often heard expounded in India—that Indians are ideologically non-violent, but pragmatically violent. This is both simplistic and wrong. The Indian ideology itself is two-valued; bivalent, chemically speaking, *ahiṃsā* and violence being its two valences.

However, a purely pragmatic factor is at work in the violent comportment, although it is perceived in ideological terms by the actors: social improvement of a corporate group in South Asia is achieved through the process of "upcasteing," and the *kṣattriya* model is the one emulated by a large segment of India's population. The close to two thirds of the population whose rank is below actual *kṣattriyas* hope for, and do quite frequently achieve, *kṣattriya*-status by consistently acting like *kṣattriyas*—and this means acting violently and psyching themselves up toward a violent repertoire. The TV Guide ad says "be a model—or act like one"; the Hindu model, suggests "be a *kṣattriya*—or act like one." And just as the maiden in the ad looks like a model, though she presumably isn't one yet, so the member of an upcasteing group acts as a *kṣattriya* is supposed to act; this includes the Bhagalpur policeman, the audience of *Sholay,* and the *sati.*

This is not a unicausal explanation of Indian violence, because some violent action (political, incipient, urban mugging) may well be inspired by perceptions of Mao's revolution or Central Park. And while *sati* is a patent extension of the *kṣattriya* ethos, regular suicide does not illustrate this model, though it is often culture specific: a very large number of female suicides are due to pressures young women experience from their in-laws. These, together with intrafamily aggression, are not peculiar to India—rather, they are shared cross-culturally in strongly agnatic, extended, land-based family systems. It is the *kṣattriya*-model alone which is purely South Asian.

REFERENCES

Aron, R. *History and the dialectic of violence.* New York: Harper and Row, 1975.

Akos-Östör. *The play of the gods. Locality, ideology, structure, and time in the festivals of a Bengali town.* Chicago: University Press, 1980.

Beals, A. Interplay among factors of change in a Mysore village. In McKim Marriott (Ed.), *Village India.* Chicago: University Press, 1955.

Bernstein, B. A Socio-linguistic approach to social learning. In J. Gould (Ed.), *Penguin survey of the social sciences.* London: Penguin Books, 1965.

Beteille, Andre. *Caste, class, and power. Changing patterns of stratification in a Tanjore village.* Berkeley: University of California Press, 1971.

Bharati, A. Nazi Germany, Hinduism, and the Third Reich. *Quest,* Bombay, 1965, No. 44.

Bharati, A. *The Asians in East Africa: Jayhind and Uhuru.* Chicago: Nelson Hall Publishers, 1971.

Bharati, A. Serendipity suddenly armed: The 1971 Sri Lanka insurgency. *Quest,* Bombay, 1973, No. 88.

Bharati, A. Monastic and lay Buddhism in the 1971 Sri Lanka insurgency. In Bardwell L. Smith (Ed.), *Religion and social conflict in South Asia.* Leiden: E. J. Brill, 1976.

Bharati, A. The anthropology of Hindi movies. *Illustrated Weekly of India,* January 30 & February 6, 1977.

Bharati, A. Psychological approaches to Indian studies: More cons than pros. *Indian Review,* Chicago, 1978, No. I/1.

Bharati, A. *Great tradition and little traditions: Indological investigations in cultural anthropology.* Varanasi, India: Chowkhamba Sanskrit Series, 1980.

Bharati, A. *Hindu views and ways and the Hindu-Muslim interface: An anthropological assessment.* New-Delhi: Munshiram Manoharlal, 1981. a

Bharati, A. Bose and the German I.N.A.—An unexplored chapter. *New Quest,* Bombay, 1981, No. 26. b

Bradbury, R. Ritualized aggression against agnates. *Ethnology,* 1966, 5, 127-155.

Brass, P. Review of S. J. Elderveld & B. Almond. Citizens and politics. *Journal of Asian Studies,* 1980, 39, 648-650.

Broomfield, J. *Elite-conflict in a plural society: Twentieth century Bengal.* Berkeley and Los Angeles: University of California Press, 1968.

Carstairs, M. *The twice born.* Bloomington: Indiana University Press, 1958.

Chatterjee, B., Singh, P., & Rao, G. (Eds.) *Riots in Rourkela: A psychological study.* New Delhi: Popular Books, 1967.

Counts, D. Fighting back is not the way. Suicide among the women of Kaliai. In *American Ethnologist,* Vol. 7/2, 1980.

Dhangare, D. Social origins of the peasant insurrection in Telangana (1946-51). In *Contributions to Indian sociology* (New Series). New Delhi, No. 8, 1974.

Douglas, M. *Natural symbols. Explorations in cosmology.* New York: Pantheon Books, 1970.

Dumont, L. *Homo hierarchicus. The caste system and its implications.* Chicago: University Press, 1970.

Ghosh, S. *Riots: Prevention and control.* Calcutta: Eastern Law House, 1971.

Goldman, R. *Gods, priests, and warriors. The Bhrgus of the Mahabharata.* New York: Columbia University Press, 1977.

Gough, K. The social structure of a Tanjore village. In McKim Marriott (Ed.), *Village India.* Chicago: University Press, 1955.

Gough, K. Cults of the dean among the Nayars of Kerala. Milton B. Singer (Ed.), *Traditional India: Structure and Change.* Philadelphia: American Folklore Society, 1959.

Islam, A. *A Bangladesh village: Conflict and cohesion.* Cambridge, Mass.: Schenkman, 1979.

Izmirlian, H., Jr. *The politics of passion. Structure and strategy in Sikh society.* Columbia, Mo.: South Asia Books, 1979.

Kearney, R. The Ceylon insurrection of 1971 (with Janice Jiggins). *The Journal of Commonwealth and Comparative Politics,* London, Vol. XIII/1, 1975.

Kearney, R. Youth protest in the politics of Sri Lanka. *Sociological Focus,* Vol. XIII/8, 1980.

Kolenda, P. *Caste in contemporary India: Beyond organic solidarity.* Menlo Park, Ca.: Benjamin/Cummings Publishing Co., 1978.

Marriott, M. (Ed.) *Village India:* Chicago: University Press, 1955.

Marriott, M. "Hindu transactions: Diversity without dualism. In Bruce Kapferer (Ed.), *Transaction and meaning: Directions in the anthropology of exchange and symbolic behavior.* Philadelphia: Institute for the Study of Human Issues, 1976.

Mohanty, M. *Revolutionary violence. A study of the Maoist movement in India.* New Delhi: Sterling Publishers, 1977.

Morrison, C. Masterji's journal: Selections from the diary of a rural Indian. In Sylvia Vatuk (Ed.), *American studies in the anthropology of India.* New Delhi: Manohar Publishers, 1978.

Murphy, G. *In the minds of men. The study of human behavior and social tensions in India.* New York: Basic Books, 1953.

Obeyesekere, G. Sorcery, premeditated murder, and the canalization of aggression in Sri Lanka. *Ethnology,* XIV/1, 1975.

O'Flaherty, W. *Women, hermaphrodites, and other mythical beasts.* Chicago: University Press, 1980.

Singer, M. *Traditional India: Structure and change.* Philadelphia: American Folklore Society, 1959.

Smelser, N. *Theory of collective behavior.* London: Routledge and Kegan Paul, 1962.

Spiro, M. Religion: Problems of definition and explanation. In M. Banton (Ed.), *Anthropological approaches to the study of religion.* New York: Praeger, 1966, pp. 85-126.

Steed, G. Notes on an approach to the study of personality formation in a Hindu village in Gujarat. In McKim Marriott (Ed.), *Village India.* Chicago: University Press, 1955.

11

Israel: Aggression in Psychohistorical Perspective*

Simha F. Landau
and
Benjamin Beit-Hallahmi

INTRODUCTION: A CONCEPTUAL FRAMEWORK

This chapter begins with a general framework within which to interpret aggression in Israel. Our most general theoretical starting point is the frustration-aggression hypothesis (Dollard, Doob, Miller, Mowrer, & Sears, 1939), which states that organisms often react to frustration with aggressive behavior, and that populations are more likely to turn to aggression when frustrations mount. Henry and Short (1954) presented the classical model for the analysis of aggressive behavior in populations, also starting with the frustration-aggression hypothesis.

Following previous work, we conceive of a variety of psychological stressors which will increase the prevalence of aggressive behaviors in a social unit. We will speak of overall stress, rather than frustration, as leading to aggression. This extension of the frustration notion to include social "instigators" or stressors, such as economic conditions, was first suggested by Hovland and Sears (1940).

We are using the terminology of stress originally coined in medical research (Selye, 1956), because we have found it to be a useful analogy in describing both social and individual processes, but its metaphorical nature should be kept in mind. Another common term used in connection with the prevalence of aggression is "social pathology." This is another useful metaphor, connecting the individual and society. The language of social pathology represents a view of crime, deviance, and aggression as symptoms of "sickness' in a social system, possibly caused by social stress. The stress model is a useful analogy or metaphor, moving from the body physic to the body politic. When stressors affect the social system, they bring about both social and individual reactions.

Social support systems (or support systems within the individual) are the factors mediating

*The authors would like to thank Menachem Amir, Stanley Cohen, and Steven Hobfoll for their valuable remarks. Miriam Neta assisted in the data collection. Preparation of this chapter has been supported by the Research Funds of the Faculty of Law and the Institute of Criminology, Hebrew University, and by the Social Science Research Committee and the Research Authority, University of Haifa.

between the stressors and the individual and social reactions they will lead to. More effective social support systems will lead to more effective coping. Less effective systems will lead to social or individual pathology, including noninstrumental aggression. We will deal with social support systems at the macrolevel and at the microlevel. Pervasive feelings of national solidarity can be regarded as a social support system on the macrolevel. A stable network of friends can be regarded as a social support system at the microlevel. Both systems will act as buffers against stressors affecting individuals.

Our social stress perspective follows the reasoning, though not the exact methodology, proposed by Brenner (1977, 1979) who considers macrolevel historical changes in social stress factors in relation to individual behaviors in the aggregate level. Thus, unemployment rates (social stressors) are related to mortality rates from specific illnesses. Similarly, we choose to look at macrolevel changes in social stress, e.g., wars and inflation, in relation to rates of aggressive behavior.

We conceive of the overall pressure pushing a population toward aggressive behaviors as stress, and specific pressure factors as stressors. A stress model has to include an accounting of pressure and frustration factors that might lead to aggression, together with a delineation of social support systems and alternative means of reacting to frustration. We assume that aggression will be the reaction to frustration and stress when social support systems fail or malfunction. Thus, measures of the functioning of social support systems, such as the family, are relevant.

Aggression in Israel: Topic Selection

As the reader undoubtedly knows, the whole history of the State of Israel has been one of international conflict and hostility. Israel, and the Zionist movement that has created it, have been in conflict with the Palestinian Arabs inhabiting the territory of Palestine, and also with neighboring Arab states. Describing and analyzing all the aggressive acts involved in this historical conflict are impossible here. Historical accounts of the conflict are available elsewhere (e.g., Cohen, 1976); we will deal with only a limited segment of the variety of aggressive acts carried out within the borders of Israel over the past 32 years. We ignore all aggressive acts which are a direct part of the Israel/Palestinian conflict, or the conflicts with neighboring Arab countries (except as sources of stress, as shown below). Moreover, since part of Israel's population (about 15 percent) is made up of Palestinian Arabs, we decided to exclude them from the discussion, because this sizable minority lives under special circumstances that require a separate analysis. Palestinian Arabs in Israel are a homogeneous group with a unique cultural identity, distinct from that of the majority, and involved in an ongoing conflict with that majority.

The two populations, Arabs in Israel and Israeli Jews, differ significantly in their characteristic rates of aggressive acts, for cultural and social structural reasons. Thus, rates for the two populations should not be combined without careful consideration. Analyzing aggression among Palestinian Arabs in Israel would require looking at their history and culture, as well as their present situation, with its unique pattern of aggression. We believe that there are also unique patterns of aggression in the majority group, on which we will concentrate. The salient differences between Jews and Arabs in Israel regarding the most extreme forms of aggression have been investigated elsewhere (Landau 1974, 1975b).

Our topic in this chapter is, then, aggression in all its forms among 85 percent of the current population in Israel, a group identified by a common cultural and national identity. The social unit we are examining does not correspond exactly to all the inhabitants of the State of Israel, geographically defined. It includes only those inhabitants who are likely to identify themselves without hesitation as Israelis, and who are also legally recognized by the state as Jews.

While it is true that certain Jewish inhabitants of Israel do not identify themselves as Israelis (the extremely orthodox Jewish minority), this group still enjoys the privileges accorded to Jews in Israel by law. The separation by Jews and non-Jews in Israel is clearly marked and legally defined. We are thus limiting ourselves to Israeli Jews only.

Stress Affecting Israeli Jews

As we shall see, this group lives under the impact of severe external conflict, and so we are not ignoring it, but treating it as a source of stress. For Israeli Jews, there are two major stressors: the threat of hostile actions from the outside, and the difficulties involved in internal social and economic problems. There is little need to defend the use of the term stress in this case, or to define it carefully. To paraphrase Shakespeare, all human beings are hurt with the same weapons, bleed when pricked, are warmed and cooled by the same winter and summer, are subject to the same diseases, and are healed by the same means. They are all subject to the same stresses and strains, with similar detrimental consequences. There is little need to prove that war, inflation, or unemployment are all stressors.

A major historical event that preceded the founding of the State of Israel and has affected life in it in major ways was the holocaust of European Jewry between 1939 and 1945. This cataclysmic event in recent Jewish history is part of individual and collective consciousness in Israel. As such, it still acts as a stressor, at least on psychological and ideological levels. At least 20 percent of the Israeli population in 1980 were holocaust survivors; for them, at least, its effects remain (see Miller, 1967; Rakover & Yaniv, 1980).

The effect of a more-or-less permanent war situation must be detrimental to humans. We take this assertion to be self-evident and beyond debate. We do not need any scientifically designed, well-controlled experiments to show us that a continuing threat of war is psychologically disruptive and destructive. The permanence of the threats of war does have a considerable effect on Israel society. A state of belligerence has been the most stable aspect of the history of the Israelis—they have come to regard themselves as a society at war, if not a society of warriors.

The large-scale conflict in which the Israeli population has been involved against neighboring groups may have at least two consequences as far as the level of aggression in this population is concerned. It may serve as a legitimized outlet for aggression, turning it outside the group, or it may serve as a stimulus or a stressor, creating more internal aggression, or both. It may reduce internal aggression by providing an outlet outside the system (a displacement hypothesis). It may increase aggression by making it more habitual or legitimate, or by providing aggressive stimuli (an instigation hypothesis). It may increase aggression by affecting the whole social system negatively (a stress hypothesis). Let us turn now to some basic facts about aggression in Israel.

Aggression in Israel

The cultural meaning of aggression is an important factor in determining levels of actual aggression in any society. Cultural variables can be regarded as the mediators between structural social factors and the behavioral outcomes of aggressive acts (see Clifford, 1978; Curtis, 1978). The traditional cultural attitude toward physical violence in Israeli society has been definitely negative. Historically, Jews have always had low rates of physical violence. The creation of the State of Israel in 1948 involved Jews in a major international conflict, and they have became accustomed to aggression directed toward the Arab out-group. In-group violence, however, remained low and negatively sanctioned. One of the first acts of the new Israeli government was to abolish the death penalty, which was part of the legal system under the British mandate in Palestine. The only exception to this rule occurred in the case of Adolf Eichmann, hanged in March 1962 for Nazi war crimes. The abolition of the death penalty certainly symbolizes and reflects traditional cultural attitudes to physical violence directed toward members of the in-group. Such violence is abhorred and denounced on the basis of millenia-old Jewish traditions, calling for complete mutual loyalty among Jews, and stemming from the long Jewish history of persecution and oppression as an undesirable minority.

The use of deadly force by the police toward Jews in Israel is almost unknown, especially if compared to police behavior in other countries (this is not the case in regard to Arabs). Verbal aggression, on the other hand, is much more acceptable in Israeli society in comparison to similar Western groups. Many observers have commented on the high level of verbal aggression in political discourse in Israel. The outward level of civility in political exchanges in Western countries seems strange to Israelis, who are used to blunt, almost profane, debates as part of the normal political process. The skilled political debater in Israel does not always stick to the high road, but is ready to insult and draw (psychological) blood if necessary.

Another aspect of nonphysical (or sometimes almost physical) aggression often commented on by visitors to Israel is the general lack of manners, or even rudeness, of Israelis in public places. Compared to the norms in most Western countries, Israelis do indeed seem to be inconsiderate and blunt in everyday social exchanges. This norm of verbal aggression can also be regarded as traditional, and may even be viewed as a constructive outlet for overall tensions, if it remains the only such outlet. This high level of public verbal aggression may in itself reflect a high level of social stress.

An Historical Perspective

This chapter will have the theme of a historical survey, examining trends in aggressive behaviors in Israel between 1948 and 1979. Why a historical survey? Why not just characterize the current situation to the best of our ability? We believe that any meaningful analysis of human aggression has to include a cultural-historical context. Ignoring history, and seeing human aggression as ahistorical and without a context leads to "neutral" abstractions of individuals engaged in meaningless acts (see Beit-Hallahmi, 1977). The society under review here has undergone such significant changes over the past thirty years that it may be regarded as actually being three different societies in three different decades. Each decade had its own spirit, flavor, political nature, economic developments, and its own types of violence and war.

Although we believe that the permanent conflict with the Arab world within which Israel exists has been the main stressor affecting the Israeli population, other historical changes must have contributed to fluctuations in levels of aggressive behaviors. When the analysis is historical, and time is the overall "independent variable," other aspects of social change must be reckoned with. In addition to the stress and upheaval caused by the continuing external conflict, other major transitions occurred in Israel between 1948 and 1980. First and foremost, major changes in the economy that led to a significant rise in living standards, an increasing gap between the rich and the poor, and increasing industrialization can all be regarded as adding to social stress.

The past few years have seen frequent expressions of public concern about violence in Israeli society. Two public opinion surveys regarding estimates of level of violence and expressions of concern about it, conducted in July 1975 and October 1977, showed a significant rise on both measures. As tables 11.1 and 11.2 show, the level of violence was considered "high" or "very high" by 62 percent in 1975 and by 68 percent in 1977. In 1975, 54 percent showed "high" or "very high" concern about violence while, in 1977, the respective rate was 68 percent. A similar repeated nationwide survey focusing on public opinion regarding the contribu-

Table 11.1. Public Estimates of the Level of Violence
in Israel, 1975 and 1977 (percentages)

LEVEL OF VIOLENCE	1975 RESULTS	1977 RESULTS
Very high	23	37
High	39	31
Moderate	34	29
Low	3	3
Very Low	1	1
Total	100	100

Source: Public opinion polls commissioned by the Interior Ministry,
Government of Israel as shown in E. S. Shimron, J. Harmelin, E.
Lankin, E. Mann, and M. Sela, *Report of the Committee for the In-
vestigation of Crime in Israel.* Jerusalem: Ministry of Justice, 1978.

tion of the police to safety from violence (conducted at five intervals between 1972 and 1977) revealed that while, in 1973 before the Yom Kippur war, 35 percent of the public were of the opinion that the police contribute considerably to safety, in 1977, this proportion dropped to a mere 10 percent (Shimron et al., 1978). These expressions of public sentiments, however subjective they may be, are in themselves a significant social fact. We may start with these tentative, "subjective" impressions, because they reflect social reality. If individuals experience what they perceive as anomie and lawlessness around them, their own involvement in aggressive behaviors is likely to be affected. When regarding himself as a potential crime victim, the average citizen may decide to resort to "passive" preventive measures, such as acquiring better locks and burglar alarms; and it is quite clear that burglar-proof locks and burglar alarms have become quite common in Israel in recent years. (He may go beyond "passive measures" by legally purchasing a handgun, as we will see below.)

We will go beyond the tentative first impressions, and we will attempt to clarify the situation with the help of reliable data. We will not deal with specific subgroups in this population, or with specific phenomena, such as juvenile delinquency and domestic violence. We limit ourselves to a historical, macrolevel analysis.

Table 11.2. Public Concern About the Level
of Violence in Israel,
1975 and 1977 (percentages)

LEVEL OF CONCERN	1975	1977
Very high	24	39
High	30	29
Moderate	31	24
Low	9	3
No concern	6	5
Total	100	100

Source: Public opinion polls commissioned by
the Interior Ministry, Government of Israel as
shown in E. S. Shimron, J. Harmelin, E. Lank-
ing, E. Mann, and M. Sela, *Report of the Committee for the Investigation of Crime in Israel.*
Jerusalem: Ministry of Justice, 1978.

METHODS OF MEASUREMENTS

Aggressive acts involve individual decisions, but these can be summarized as aggregate measures of aggression in a population. Aggressive acts conceived and carried out by individuals in the aggregate become "social problems" or "social pathology."

Selecting the appropriate indicators for the general level of aggression in a society, and selecting other indicators of relevant social processes is a complicated task, influenced by theoretical and practical considerations. What we are presenting here are selected measures reflecting aggressive behaviors in relation to certain other social variables, within a theoretical framework that sees aggression as determined by levels of social stress and moderated by social support systems.

That rates of aggression based on official police reports are underestimates is well known. The rate of underreporting for the population we are covering here was established in a victimization survey, conducted by the Israeli government Central Bureau of Statistics in 1980. This survey shows that 38 percent of the victims of violent crimes did not complain to the police. This means that the true rates of violent crime (excepting homicide) might be about one third higher.

When selecting appropriate measures for the general level of aggression in a given society, we should look for behaviors that are reasonably frequent and show some flexibility in their rates over time. Murder in Israel is a relatively rare occurrence, showing little change in rates over time. Assaults and robberies, on the other hand, are more frequent and more sensitive measures of aggression, and thus are more indicative of the level of aggression in Israeli society. We report the best available data on all our measures; but, for some years and some populations, no data are available. Some of the criminal aggression data are simply nonexistent for the years 1971-1973 and 1976-1979, due to some problems in data analysis by the Israel Bureau of Statistics. In all cases, we tried to infer our conclusions from overall trends, and not just point by point fluctuations.

MEASURES OF STRESS, SOCIAL CHANGE, AND AGGRESSION

We have not tried to measure the intensity of the Arab-Israeli conflict over time. However, we will see that the major outbreaks of fighting in this conflict (1948, 1956, 1967, and 1973) are clearly noticeable in their effects. The following will be used as indicators of social stress:

1. Unemployment rates
2. Per capita income
3. Automobile ownership
4. Inflation rates
5. Gap between rich and poor
6. Rates of hospitalization for drug abuse
7. Marriage and divorce rates
8. Rates of births to unmarried mothers
9. "Mental health" treatment contacts
10. Strikes and work stoppages

The following will be used as measures of aggression:

1. Rates of murder, manslaughter, attempted murder
2. Combined index of violence

3. Robbery and attempted robbery
4. Rape and attempted rape
5. General criminal activities
6. Citizens' complaints against the police
7. Suicide rates
8. Permits to carry firearms

Indicators of Social Stress

1. Unemployment rates. Table 11.3 shows that unemployment in Israel was high in the 1950s and in the mid-1960s. In the years following the 1956 and the 1967 wars, a significant decrease in unemployment rates is observed.

Table 11.3. Selected Measures of Stress and Social Change

YEAR	UNEMPLOYMENT RATE PER 100,000	CONSUMER PRICE INDEX (SEPT. 1951-100)	PER CAPITA INCOME IN U.S. DOLLARS	PRIVATE AUTOMOBILE OWNERSHIP % OF FAMILIES
1949	1,611.04	91	—	—
1950	1,645.94	85	882	—
1951	1,693.69	97	955	—
1952	1,806.44	153	798	—
1953	2,526.66	196	685	—
1954	2,101.93	220	479	—
1955	1,792.91	233	576	—
1956	2,008.17	248	658	—
1957	2,007.44	264	714	—
1958	1,614.81	273	787	—
1959	1,389.48	277	877	—
1960	1,199.40	283	952	—
1961	1,305.12	302	1,087	—
1962	1,285.02	281	755	4.1
1963	1,201.06	353	852	—
1964	1,104.81	371	923	6.9
1965	1,076.82	399	1,085	7.7
1966	1,425.30	431	1,151	10.5
1967	2,009.44	438	1,131	13.3
1968	1,378.30	448	1,145	13.1
1969	927.60	459	1,284	13.9
1970	790.41	487	1,443	15.4
1971	623.29	545	1,643	18.2
1972	574.57	615	1,820	19.1
1973	506.35	738	2,225	22.1
1974	493.19	1,031	2,792	26.1
1975	491.98	1,436	2,712	—
1976	528.84	1,886	2,931	—
1977	514.48	2,539	3,135	27.4
1978	495.51	3,823	2,884	—
1979	528.91	6,817	3,776	—
1980	—	—	3,936	—

Source: Statistical Abstract of Israel, 1949-1980; and Economic Planning Authority, 1981.

2. Per Capita Income. One of the significant changes in Israeli society over the past 30 years has been economic growth, reflected in per capita income. As seen in table 11.3, from a low point of $479 in 1954, it went up to $1,145 in 1968, and then jumped to $3,936 in 1980. Thus, Israel has gone from the status of a developing country in the 1950s to an advanced industrialized country in the 1970s. (See, International Bank, 1978).

3. Automobile Ownership. The percentage of families owning an automobile in any given year does serve, in the case of Israel, as a general measure of the change in living standards. The change on this measure is rather consistent and remarkable. Table 11.3 reveals that, while only 4 percent of the families in Israel owned a car in 1962, fifteen years later the figure was approximately seven times as large, 27.4 percent.

4. Inflation Rates. Table 11.3 shows also the changes in the Israeli Consumer Price Index between 1949 and 1979. What is evident from the figures is the steady but moderate rise between 1948 and 1972, and then an acceleration that can only be described as astronomical. Between 1972 and 1979, the change in the CPI was more than 1,100 percent (taking the September 1951 CPI was 100).

5. Gap Between Rich and Poor. Another significant factor in the socioeconomic structure of Israel is the gap between the rich and the poor in relation to the overall economic growth and the rise in living standards. While per capita income has been climbing, the gap between the top 10 percent of the families and the bottom 10 percent in income has been essentially steady since 1966. Data for the families of salaried workers only for the year 1979 show that the lowest 10 percent earned 2.7 percent of the total income, while the top 10 percent earned 23.5 percent (Israel Statistical Abstract, 1972-1980). No data are available for nonsalaried earners, but we can easily imagine that these will add to the picture of a large gap between rich and poor.

6. Rates of Hospitalization for Drug Abuse. According to Brenner (1977, 1979), drug use is correlated with high levels of social stress. While general levels of drug use in Israel are hard to assess, there is general agreement that there has been an historical increase in the use of prescribed tranquilizers, hashish, heroin, and alcohol in Israel over the past fifteen years. One measure of drug abuse that we have obtained is the rate of admissions for inpatient care of substance abuse (table 11.4). This rate shows an almost five-fold increase between 1966 and 1976.

The estimated annual admissions rate per 100,000 Jews 15+ years of age for inpatient care of substance abuse (drug, alcohol) increased from 7.4 in 1966 to 43.3 in 1975. Estimates based on the admissions for the first six months of 1976 give an admissions rate of 33.3. Official statistics on hospitalization rates for drug abuse since 1976 are not available, but we have no reason to doubt that the trend has continued.

7. Marriage and Divorce Rates. Rates of marriage and divorce are the best general measures for the strength of the institution of the family. Figure 11.1 shows that the peak years for marriage were the early 1950s and the early 1970s. There was a marked increase in marriage rates after the 1967 war, and a smaller one following the 1973 war. Since 1974, a steady decrease in the marriage rate has been observed. Divorce rates were relatively high in the early 1950s, with a subsequent decline, and a gradual moderate rise since 1974.

Table 11.4. Estimated Annual Admissions Rate
for Inpatient Care of Substance Abuse (drug, alcohol)
Israel 1966-1976

YEAR	NO. OF ADMISSIONS	RATE/100,000 (15+ YEARS, JEWS)
1966	118	7.4
1973	600	30.4
1974	625	30.9
1975	900	43.3
1976	700	33.3

Source: Epidemiological & Statistical Unit; Mental Health
Services; Ministry of Health, 1976.

8. Rates of Births to Unmarried Mothers. The rate of childbirths by unmarried mothers was used as another measure of family strength and stability. Figure 11.2 shows quite clearly a steady rise in births by unmarried mothers between 1951 and 1979. In 1979, the proportion of these births was about six times that in 1951. The rise is especially pronounced since 1965.

9. "Mental Health" Treatment Contacts. Rahav and Popper (1980) report a significant rise in the number of outpatient psychiatric treatment contacts and also a rise in contacts with all "mental health" professionals between 1966 and 1979. They suggest that one possible explanation for these remarkable changes lies in the increased levels of general stress in Israeli society. Figures presented by Rahav and Popper (1980) show that, between 1966 and 1977, the average number of monthly visits to outpatient psychiatric clinics has grown by 288.9 percent, while the population served increased by 37.5 percent. The increasing use of professional psychotherapy may be regarded as indicating a weakening of naturally existing social support systems. It may be seen as another symptom of growing anomie, as more and more individuals turn to "mental health" support systems for meaning and solace, with the failure of earlier integrative mechanisms in society.

10. Strikes and Work Stoppages. The rate of number of work days lost per total workforce, presented in figure 11.3, shows that peaks in labor unrest occurred in 1958, 1965, 1970, and the all-time high was reached in 1978.

Measures of Aggression

1. Murder, Attempted Murder, and Manslaughter Rates. From the murder and manslaughter reported in figure 11.4, we can see that the years of major external conflicts (1956, 1967) show lower rates compared to preceding years, but then are followed by substantial rises (in 1957 and 1968).

2. A Combined Index of Violence. This combined index measures the rate of felons convicted of any act involving violence against another person, from murder to assault between 1950 and 1975. Figure 11.5 shows the highest rate in 1950, the next peak in 1958, and another one in 1965. There is a sharp drop in 1967, followed by a rise in 1970 to the 1963 level.

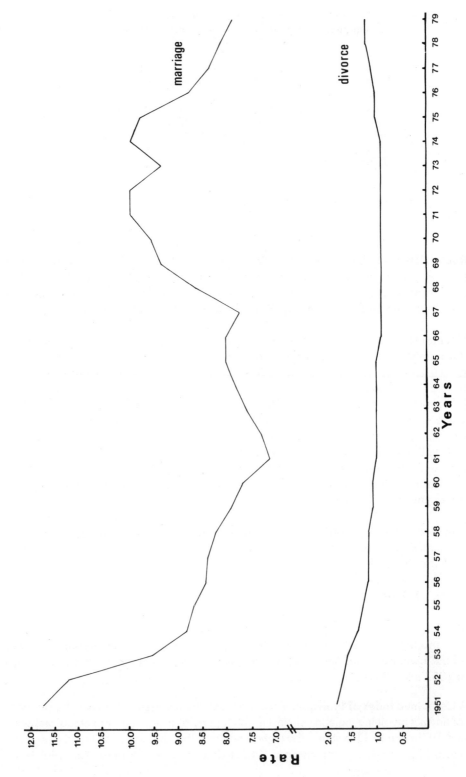

Fig. 11.1. Annual Marriage and Divorce Rates (per 1,000 population)

Source: *Israel Statistical Abstracts,* 1962–1980.

270

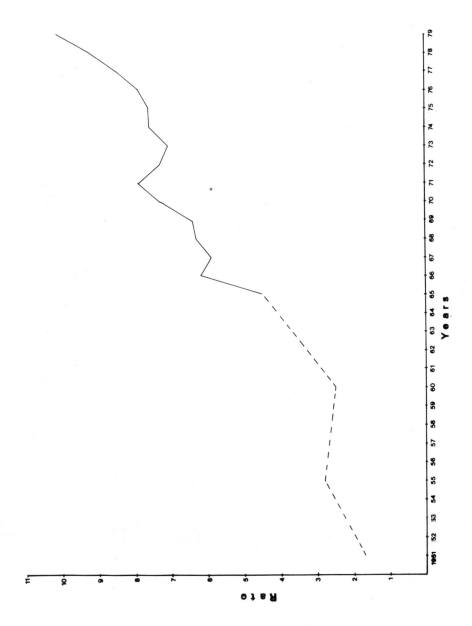

Fig. 11 2. Annual Rates of Births to Unmarried Jewish Mothers (per 1,000 Jewish childbirths)

Source: *Israel Statistical Abstracts*, 1951–1980.

271

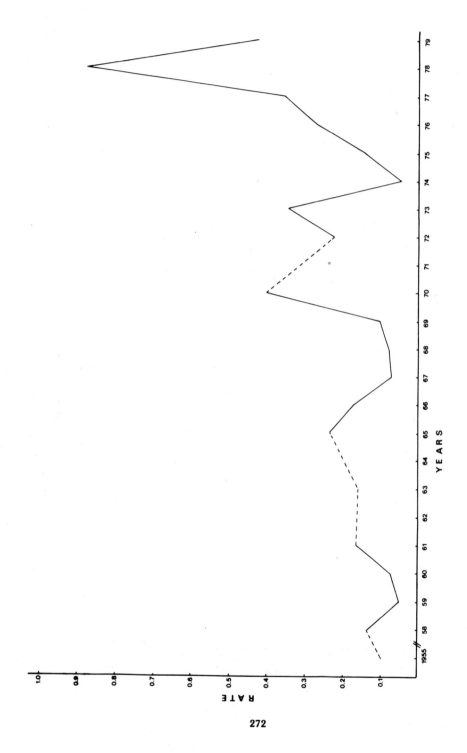

Fig. 11.3. Annual Rates of Workdays Lost in Strikes per Total Work Force

Source: *Israel Statistical Abstracts*, 1959–1980.

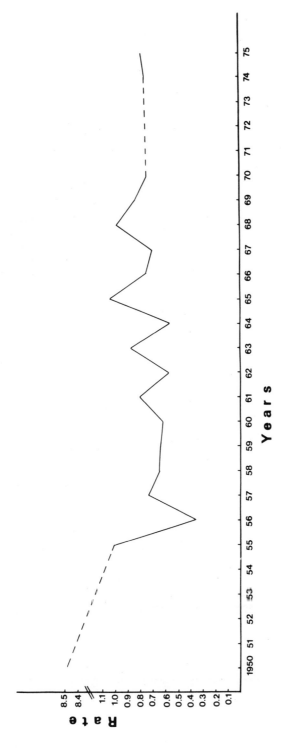

Fig. 11.4. Annual Rates of Murder and Attempted Murder by Jewish Offenders (per 100,000 Jewish population)

Source: *Israel Statistical Abstracts*, 1951–1976.

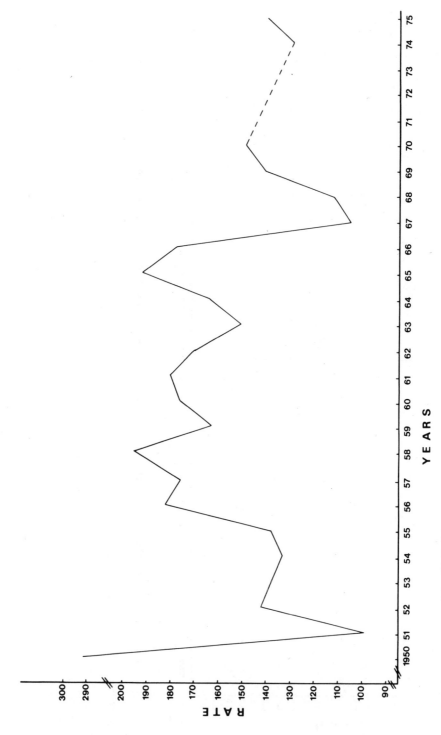

Fig. 11.5. Annual Rates of Jewish Offences Against the Person (per 100,000 population)

Source: *Israel Statistical Abstracts*, 1951–1976.

3. Robbery and Attempted Robbery. The offence category of robbery and attempted robbery is of considerable importance to our analysis as it includes a threat to human life and well being as well as to property. In addition, robbery and attempted robbery are of much greater prevalence than murder and manslaughter, thus they represent a much more concrete and visible threat. Unlike the previous figures, here reference is made to offences (and not offenders) regarding the total population (and not only the Jewish population) as separate rates for Jews were not available. Although the above differences should not be ignored, these figures can still be used in the present context. As stated earlier "pure" crimes of violence (and especially murder and manslaughter) committed by Arabs were omitted from the present analysis due to their strong relevance to cultural norms and values in the Arab society (and thus their much greater prevalence among this part of the population). This factor does not apply to the offences of robbery and attempted robbery.

As shown in figure 11.6, in the 1950s there was a sharp decrease in these offences in comparison to the peak in 1949. However, the 1960s and the 1970s witnessed a marked increase of these offences. From 1965 there is an almost unchanged steady increase of robberies and attempted robberies. The one marked exception is 1973 in which a considerable decrease can be observed. (Decreases of smaller magnitude are seen also in 1956 and 1967.) From 1973 to the late 1970s an unprecedented steady sharp increase is evident. These figures provide an objective and measurable support to the previously mentioned increase (between 1975 and 1977) in public estimates of violence in Israel, the increase in their concern about the level of violence in the country, and the parallel decrease (between 1973 and 1977) in the public's trust in police as an efficient social control agency.

4. Rape and Attempted Rape. Due to inconsistencies in the presentation of statistical data regarding sex offences (especially the combining of forcible with nonforcible sex offences), the figures presented here relate only to years 1972-1979. As in the previous figure, the data in figure 11.7 relate to offences in the total population. As can be seen in this figure, the 1970s have witnessed an increase in forcible rape and attempted rape, the peak years being 1975 and 1978. One has to keep in mind, however, that with regard to these offences the gap between the real number of crimes committed and those reported to the police is particularly large.

5. General Criminal Activity. Figure 11.8 presents the total annual rates of offences per 1,000 population between 1949 and 1979. This figure reflects all officially recorded criminal activity in the country during this period. As can be seen very clearly, there has been a steady increase in the crime rate during the last 30 years: in 1979 this rate was more than four times higher than in 1949. Another noteworthy phenomenon reflected in this figure is that the years of major wars (1949, 1956, 1967 and 1973) were followed by a sharp increase in the crime rate. This increase is particularly salient after the 1973 war.

6. Citizens' Complaints Against the Police. Table 11.5 contains data on complaints filed by the public against the police, for the years 1973-1980, for which information is available. What is quite clear from the table is that the proportion of complaints against police that allege brutality has been rising constantly and sharply in recent years. This proportion has risen from 21.8 percent in 1973 to 47.3 percent in 1980. This increase may represent a real change in the use of force by police, or a growing dissatisfaction on the part of the public. However, even if some of these complaints are untrue, they represent a real conflict between the police and the public.

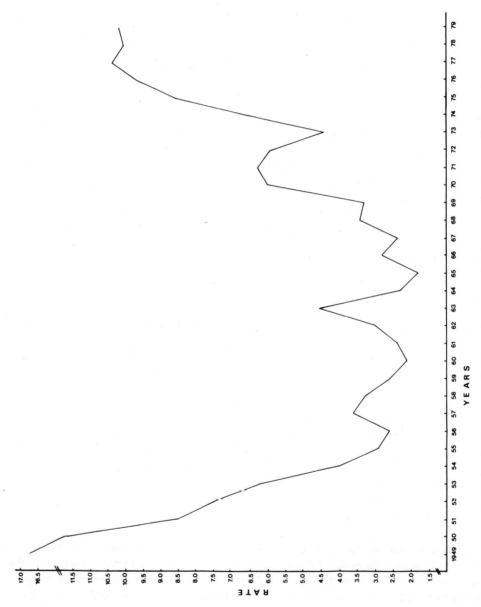

Fig. 11.6. Annual Rates of Robberies and Attempted Robberies (per 100,000 population)

Source: *Israel Statistical Abstracts*, 1960-1980.

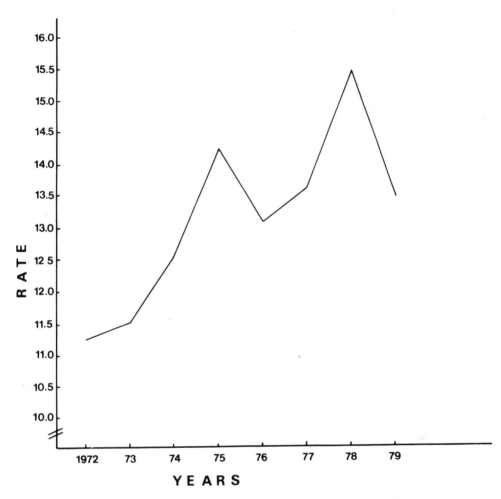

Fig. 11.7. Annual Rates of Forcible Rape and Attempted Rape (per 100,000 population)

Source: *Israel Statistical Abstracts,* 1973-1980.

7. Suicide Rates. Suicide rates per 100,000 of the Jewish population over 15 years of age are presented in figure 11.9. They show 1956 to be the peak year in the 1950s; 1969 as the peak for the 1960s; and 1975 as the peak for the 1970s. The lowest suicide rates are reported for 1967 and for 1973. The most likely explanation for the difference between the low suicide rates in these two years and the high rate in 1956 (in which there was also a peak in external fighting) is that, in comparison to the 1967 and the 1973 wars, the 1956 war was of a limited scale (total war dead were 175 compared to 750 in 1967 and 2,700 in 1973), and so the expected inverse relationship between a state of war and suicide was not found.

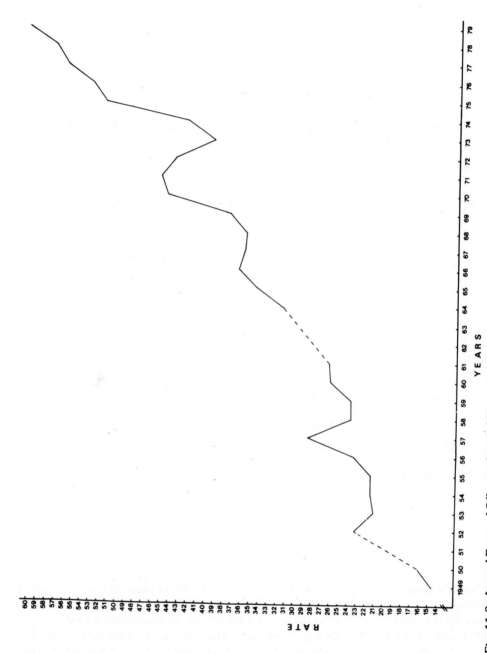

Fig. 11.8. Annual Rates of Offences (per 1,000 population)

Source: *Israel Statistical Abstracts*, 1950-1980.

Table 11.5. Complaints Against Police Brutality as a Proportion of Total Complaints Against the Police, 1973-1980

YEAR	TOTAL COMPLAINTS AGAINST POLICE	COMPLAINTS AGAINST POLICE BRUTALITY	% OF COMP. AG. BRUTALITY FROM TOTAL
1973	1,785	390	21.8
1974	2,410	531	22.0
1975	2,840	754	26.5
1976	2,955	872	29.5
1977	2,772	954	34.4
1978	2,858	1,104	38.6
1979	2,546	1,139	44.7
1980	2,220	1,050	47.3

Source: Israel Police Ombudsmann. Public Complaints against the Police. Jerusalem (mimeo), 1981.

8. Permits to Carry Firearms. The availability of firearms is widely and justifiably recognized as a factor in crimes of extreme violence (Danto, 1979). In Israel, firearms can be owned by permit only, and permits are issued by the ministry of the interior to individuals without criminal records. Figure 11.10 shows clearly that in recent years the legal ownership of firearms in Israel has grown significantly. It has more than doubled since 1973. Since these rates refer to legal ownership only, we can conclude that actual holding of firearms is more prevalent than indicated here. It is often remarked that actual holding of firearms in Israel is facilitated by the fact that almost all men between the ages of 18 and 55 are involved in some form of military duty where firearms are readily available. Most of the firearms used in cases of criminal violence in Israel are standard military rifles, submachine guns, and hand grenades.

Analysis and Interpretation

In order to facilitate understanding the many facts presented earlier, it is worth summarizing their most salient features.

Our most general finding is that the high points of the continuing conflict, namely outright war, are followed by high levels of aggression within Israeli society. The wars of 1948, 1956, 1967, and 1973 were all followed by periods of heightened internal aggression. It should be remembered, of course, that these wars were also followed by significant economic and political changes, or even upheavals.

As Fishman (in press) and others suggest that the outbreak of full scale, official war usually leads to a decrease in civilian kinds of aggression, as Thanatos is let loose upon the fields of war. When the war is over, "civilian" aggression returns to its normal levels. This is borne out by our data, as shown in all our figures regarding aggressive behaviors. Archer & Gartner (1967) also reported that homicide rates in many nations rise following involvement in a war. There are obvious reasons why rates of civilian aggression go down during a war in Israel. A large proportion of the population is mobilized, and for the nonmobilized population there is a strong sense of solidarity. Our own findings, as well as those reported by Archer and Gartner (1967) and Fishman (in press) show quite clearly that large-scale political aggression, and specifically full-scale war, do not really serve any "catharsis" function in their effects on individual aggression. The opposite may be true, and war may be an instigator of individual aggression toward ingroup targets. While external conflict does not serve a "catharsis" function

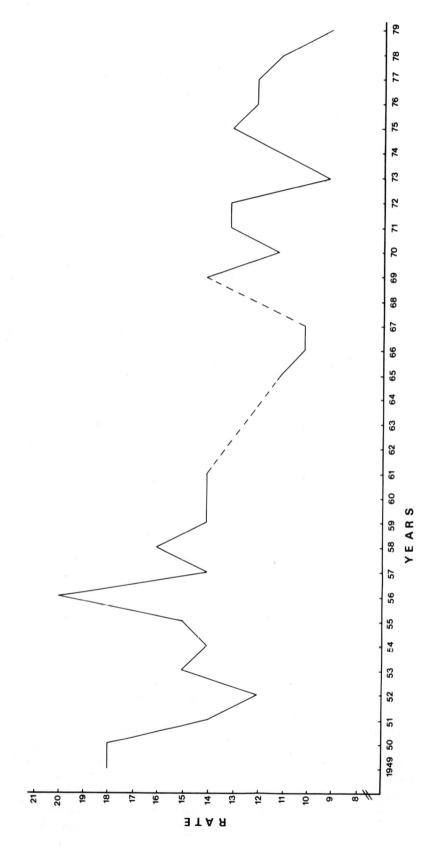

Fig. 11.9. Annual Suicide Rates per 100,000 Jewish Population Over 15 Years of Age

Source: *Israel Statistical Abstracts*, 1962–1980.

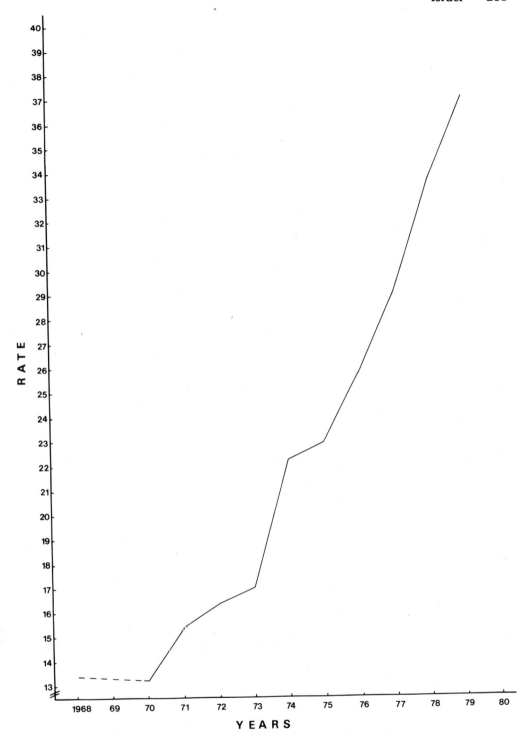

Fig. 11.10. Annual Rates of Firearm Permits (per 100,000 population)

Source: Israel Ministry of the Interior, "Firearm Permits," Jerusalem, 1980 (mimeo).

in regard to individuals, it may still serve this function in regard to subgroups within the same population.

If we regard the external conflict (i.e., Israelis versus Arabs) as displacing aggressive behaviors outwardly, we should hypothesize that, in times of relative peace, internal subgroup aggression will be on the rise.

The clearest internal divisions in the Israeli population include that between religious and secular Jews, and that between Eastern and European Jews (Peres, 1971; Smythe & Weintraub, 1971). The fact that these divisions, reflecting acute differences in culture, beliefs, and economic power, have not led to more open internal conflicts over the past thirty years calls for an explanation. One such explanation has been that the internal conflicts have been held in check by the external Arab-Israeli conflict (Beit-Hallahmi, 1972).

The effects of the external conflict in reducing internal divisions in Israeli society were explained by Peres (1971) in terms of three components: (1) interdependence of fate, as a national loss is perceived as a loss to all Israeli ethnic groups; (2) a common goal, since cooperation is perceived as necessary for survival; and (3) an outlet for aggression, as antagonistic impulses have a legitimate target. Heightened cohesiveness and the reduction of internal conflict as a result of external tensions was one of the results of the 1967 crisis according to Herman (1970). If this is the case, then we should expect more frequent expressions of these internal divisions during times of relative peace in the external conflict.

The most peaceful time in the history of Israel, the low point in terms of external hostilities, was the 1970-1972 period. This period was characterized by lowered levels of aggression, as compared to the preceding three-year period, 1967-1970. Beit-Hallahmi (1972) reported on the disturbances in the balance between external and internal conflicts. The cease-fire of August 1970 lowered the intensity of the external conflict, but was followed by a clear increase in the expressions of internal divisions. The 1971-72 period was indeed characterized by a rise in domestic unrest, in the form of strikes and dissident political movements, described by outside observers as "a homemade rebellion" (*Time*, 1971). The lowering of external stressors during that period was correlated with increased social tensions and a salience of differences among different segments of the population, such as the religious and the secular subcultures of Eastern and European Jews (Cohen, 1980; Cromer, 1976; Shama & Iris, 1977) and workers versus management. Demonstrations of Eastern Jews organized around claims for equality, wildcat strikes in considerable numbers and in public services, and tensions between secular and religious groups appeared with intensity during the first twelve months of the Suez cease fire.

Our assumptions about the relationship of domestic and external conflict lead us to assume that there would be a higher level of social unrest during periods of relative quiet and the borders. If we use our measure of labor unrest as an indicator, this is indeed the case, as was shown in our figure 11.3. Kimmerling (1974) reports identical findings. The two high points in working days lost to industrial strikes were in 1971 and in 1978, the two periods of almost complete peace in the Arab-Israeli conflict. The cease-fire was declared in 1971, following the 1968-1970 war of attrition with Egypt on the Suez Canal. The 1978 strikes followed the Sadat visit to Jerusalem, which signaled the possibility of a real resolution of at least one part of the conflict.

AGGRESSION CONTROLS AND ALTERNATIVES TO AGGRESSION

Following our above presentation of findings, and the discussion of their meaning, which we ourselves found quite sobering, we cannot be the bearers of good news at this point. Any serious suggestions for alternatives of aggression or for aggression controls in Israeli society, which go beyond exhortations and homilies have to deal with crucial social, economic and political problems. Historical changes in Israel over the past three decades can be described as unique in some aspects, so that it cannot be classified together with concurrent changes in other countries.

As we have seen in all our measures, the early 1950s was a period with the highest levels of aggression. This was an especially stressful period in the history of Israel, when the 1948-49 war was followed by 24 months of mass immigration, which doubled the Jewish population of the state. A large proportion of the immigrants came from Arab countries, and they suffered economic deprivation and cultural crises following their arrival. For this segment of the Israeli population, however, the major changes can be classified as those of "modernization" and integration into a developing capitalist economy.

Eastern Jews, those who immigrated from Arab countries such as Morocco, Algeria, Iraq, and Yemen after 1948, have undergone a process of rapid and painful social change, which involved the dismantling of their traditional culture. Thus deprived of the traditional social and psychological support given by the family and the close knit community, and relegated to the bottom of the socioeconomic scale, this group has reacted with all the symptoms of a social crisis, including high levels of criminal violence (see Odekunle, 1978). These immigrants and their descendants remained at the bottom of the social scale during the next thirty years, and their economic and cultural problems remain largely unsolved. Not too surprisingly, they contribute more than their share to criminal violence, and less than their share to political activity.

Today, while Eastern Jews constitute more than 50 percent of the Israeli population, they are underrepresented in the political, economic, and cultural elite (while individuals of Eastern origin made up 85 percent of elementary school pupils in 1980, they constituted only 15 percent of the students in higher education) but overrepresented to the point of monopolization in the criminal statistics (Landau, 1979). This stress-ridden group, which bears the brunt of economic and cultural insecurity, contributes most heavily to aggressive behaviors. Individuals of this group are most likely to be involved in acts of criminal aggression, and they make up over 90 percent of the prison population (Landau, 1975a). It is significant that the high level of individual aggressive acts by members of this group has been accompanied by a relatively low level of political action. We can reasonably assume some connection between the two phenomena. We may hypothesize that the stress and frustration which lead to political energy are expressed at the individual level in acts of criminal aggression, which is sometimes instrumental (i.e., economic).

The frustration of this lower class is channeled to criminal violence, rather than to political violence or political action. There were two noticeable periods of political violence on the part of Eastern Jews, one in 1959 and the other in 1971 (Shama & Iris, 1977). In both cases, street riots and attempts at political organizing around cultural background issues were quelled after a short period. Any serious attempt to lower the increasing level of aggression within Israeli society will have to deal radically with the main sources of stress within the system, which are the severe permanent political and economic pressures. It seems that social support systems are crumbling before the increasing burdens put on them, and aggression becomes the more likely response to stress.

CONCLUSION

How can the level of aggression in Israeli society during the period under discussion be characterized? As compared to most contemporary societies, it should be considered as mildly aggressive, when rates per population are used. The overall levels of aggression in Israel are still quite low in comparison with most Western countries (Sutherland & Cressey, 1974).

On further examination of the data, what is interesting to the observer are the fluctuations and historical changes in levels of aggression, and the correlations between aggression and social conditions. It is evident from our findings, and from findings of others (Fishman & Argov, 1980) that there is a long-term trend in the level of aggression in Israel, together with a few major historical turning points. Most observers point to the major wars of 1967 and 1973 as the turning points, and we can find support for this observation in our findings. What should be stressed, however, is that the turning points represent not just major outbreaks of violence in the form of wars, but much more than that. The whole social system we are looking at exists in the shadow of, and in the midst of, a major historical conflict, which colors all aspects of its existence. The effects of the permanent conflict are felt throughout Israeli society, and every aspect of life in Israel is overshadowed by it (Seliktar, 1980).

Kimmerling (1974) stated that the continuing external conflict affected Israeli society in two separate ways. It reduced the intensity of internal social conflicts, as measured by strikes, but it increased individual disintegration, as measured by suicides. It seems that the cost of social integration in this case was borne by individuals, who directed aggression toward themselves. Our findings support the notion that the external conflict serves to reduce large-scale internal conflicts (e.g., strikes and political violence), but it does not reduce, and even instigates, individual aggression toward both the self and others.

Because of the centrality of Arab-Israeli conflict for Israeli society, the turning points of 1967 and 1973 represent not only military gains and losses, but historical watersheds. Both wars led to major changes in self-perception, to major economic changes, and to major reassessments of the conflict with the Arab world. The military gains of 1967 did not lead to an increase in security but to a more direct confrontation with the Palestinian Arabs. Whereas before 1967 the conflict was between states, it later became a conflict between occupiers and occupied. This did not reduce the level of aggression related to the conflict. The 1973 war was a major crisis of confidence, leading to lowered morale and to a significant rise in internal crime and violence. Fishman and Argov (1980) report that there was a significant increase in certain categories of crime following the 1967 war, and describe a general "social crisis" in Israel following the 1973 war.

From our findings, the Arab-Israeli conflict can be seen as a most important factor in determining levels of aggression in the Israeli population. The picture emerging from the figures presented here in regard to the past ten years in the history of Israel is rather significant in its direction, and possibly enables us to say something about future trends. In terms of stress measures, these years have witnessed an unprecedented and enormous increase in inflation rates, and a large increase in hospitalization for drug abuse. This period also saw a decline in the role of the family as a natural support system. There was a decline in marriage rates, a parallel increase in births by unwed mothers, and a great increase in mental health treatment contacts. Among the measures of aggression used in our survey, a dramatic increase in crimes combining violence with threat to property (robbery and attempted robbery) was evident. This trend was coupled with an increase in public concern over violent crimes. In 1977, a special commission of inquiry headed by a former attorney-general was set up by the government to investigate the "crime problem" in Israel (Shimron et al., 1978). The public trust in the police's way of handling violence decreased while complaints about police brutality were on the increase. Strikes and work-stoppages were at a historical peak, and so was the legal acquisition of firearms.

The sharp rise in the number of firearms permits may reflect growing concern about crime and violence, or violent activities on the part of the Palestinians, together with a lack of confidence in the ability of the government authorities to control violence. The individuals who have purchased firearms legally are declaring themselves to be ready to use violence in what they perceive as their own defense. This phenomenon is unprecedented in Israeli society, and was almost unheard of in the 1950s. From what we know of the reality in other countries, the availability of firearms, even when legally acquired, is likely to increase homicide rates and other forms of violence.

This chapter is only a preliminary survey, giving a psychohistorical outline which should be followed by further work, but we can say that the subjective popular impressions of an increase in the rates of aggression in Israeli society in the past ten years seem fully justified by our findings. One may conclude from the data we have presented that Israeli society has reached an advanced state of anomie, and that some of the phenomena we reported on are symptoms of a growing solidarity crisis or social disintegration. The future will tell whether such inferences are warranted.

REFERENCES

A homemade rebellion. *Time,* October 25, 1971, p. 30.

Archer, D., and Gartner, R. Violent acts and violent times: A comparative approach to postwar homicide rates. *American Sociological Review,* 1967, *41,* 937-963.

Beit-Hallahmi, B. Some psychological and cultural factors in the Arab-Israeli conflict. *Journal of Conflict Resolution,* 1972, *16,* 269-280.

Beit-Hallahmi, B. Overcoming the "objective" language of violence. *Aggressive Behavior,* 1977, *3,* 251-259.

Brenner, M. H. Health costs and benefits of economic policy. *International Journal of Health Services,* 1977, *7,* 581-623.

Brenner, M. H. Influence of the social environment of psychopathology: The historic perspective. In J. E. Barrett et al. (Eds.), *Stress and Mental Disorder.* New York: Raven Press, 1979.

Clifford, W. Culture and crime—in global perspective. *International Journal of Criminology and Penology,* 1978, *6,* 61-80.

Cohen, A. *Israel and the Arab world.* Boston: Beacon Press, 1976.

Cohen, E. The black panthers and Israeli society. In E. Krausz (Ed.), *Studies of Israeli society.* Vol. 1. New Brunswick, N.J.: Transaction, 1980, pp. 147-163.

Cromer, G. The Israeli black panthers: Fighting for credibility and a cause. *Victimology: An International Journal, 1976, 1,* 403-413.

Curtis, L. A. Violence, personality, deterrence and culture. *Journal of Research in Crime and Delinquency,* 1978, *15,* 166-171.

Danto, B. L. Firearms and violence. *International Journal of Offender Therapy,* 1979, *23,* 135-146.

Dollard, J., Doob, L. W., Miller, N. E., Mowrer, O. H., & Sears, R. R. *Frustration and aggression.* New Haven: Yale University Press, 1939.

Fishman, G. On war and crime. In S. Breznitz (Ed.), *Stress in Israel.* New York: Van Nostrand, in press.

Fishman, G., & Agrov, M. Crime trends in Israel 1951-1976. *Crime and Social Deviance,* 1980, *8,* 25-35 (Hebrew).

Henry, A. F., & Short, J. F. *Suicide and homicide.* New York: The Free Press, 1954.

Herman, S. N. *Israelis and Jews: The continuity of an identity.* New York: Random House, 1970.

Hovland, C. I., & Sears, R. R. Minor studies of aggression: Correlation of lynchings with economic indices. *Journal of Psychology,* 1940, *9,* 301-310.

International Bank for Reconstruction and Development/The World Bank. *World Development Report 1978.* Washington, D.C., 1978.

Israel Economic Planning Authority. National income per capita. Jerusalem: Ministry of Finance, 1981 (Mimeo).

Israel Statistical Abstract. Jerusalem: Government Bureau of Statistics, 1972-1980.

Kimmerling, B. Anomie and integration in Israeli society and the salience of the Arab-Israeli conflict. *Studies in Comparative International Development,* 1974, *9,* 64-89.

Landau, S. F., Drapkin, I., & Arad, S. Homicide victims and offenders: An Israeli study. *Journal of Criminal Law and Criminology,* 1974, *65,* 390-396.

Landau, S. F. Future time perspective of delinquents and non-delinquents: The effect of institutionalization. *Criminal Justice and Behavior,* 1975, *2,* 22-36.

Landau, S. F. Pathologies among homicide offenders: Some cultural profiles. *British Journal of Criminology,* 1975, *15,* 157-166.

Landau, S. F. Do police discriminate in the handling of juvenile offenders? Some Israeli findings. *Crime and Social Deviance,* 1979, *7,* 159-168 (Hebrew).

Miller, L. The social psychiatry and epidemiology of mental ill health in Israel. In N. Petrilowitsch (Ed.), *Contributions to comparative psychiatry.* Basel and New York: Karger, 1967.

Odekunle, F. Capitalist economy and the crime problem in Nigeria. *Contemporary Crises,* 1978, *2,* 83-96.

Peres, Y. Ethnic relations in Israel. In M. Curtis (Ed.), *People and politics in the Middle East.* New Brunswick, N.J.: Transaction Books, 1971.

Rahav, M., & Popper, M. Trends in the delivery of psychiatric services in Israel in the years 1965-1979. Paper presented at the 1980 Pinhas Sapir Conference on Development, Tel Aviv University, December 1980.

Rakover, S. S., & Yaniv, A. Individual trauma and national response to external threat: The case of Israel. *Bulletin of the Psychonomic Society,* 1980, *16,* 217-220.

Seliktar, O. The cost of vigilance in Israel: Linking the economic and social costs of defence. *Journal of Peace Research,* 1980.

Selye, H. *The stress of life.* New York: McGraw Hill, 1956.

Shama, A., & Iris, M. *Immigration without integration: Third World Jews in Israel.* Cambridge, Mass.: Schenkman, 1977.

Shimron, E. S., Harmelin, J., Lankin, E., Mann, E., & Sela, M. *Report of the Committee for the Investigation of Crime in Israel.* Jerusalem, 1978.

Smythe, H. H., & Weintraub, S. Intergroup relations in Israel. In M. Curtis (Ed.), *People and politics in the Middle East.* New Brunswick, N.J.: Transaction Books, 1971.

Sutherland, E. H., & Cressey, D. R. *Criminology.* Philadelphia: Lippincott, 1974.

12

Italy: A Systems Perspective

Franco Ferracuti and Francesco Bruno

INTRODUCTION

The Italian Dictionary defines "aggression" as: "A predictory assault, where the victim is taken by surprise and overcome through violence." The English term "aggression," unlike its Italian equivalent, goes beyond a single definition of an aggressive act; it is identified in the Webster's Dictionary as: "A form of psychobiologic energy, either innate or arising in response to or intensified by frustration, which may be manifested by overt destruction, fighting, infliction of pain, sexual attack or forcible seizure."

In both English and Italian, the concept of aggression is connected to the concept of violence acted out against a person by another person. Dictionary definitions reflect the negative connotations which aggression and aggressiveness have been assuming through centuries in most cultures, but these terms imply also a much wider and less defined, deep psychological meaning, whose roots reach into the etymological derivation of the words.

Aggression derives from the Latin verb *aggredior*. This is composed by the prefix *ad* (meaning "to," "toward") and the word *gradus* (meaning "step," the act of walking particularly referred to military marches). Perhaps, this is the root of the violent connotation of the term; the Latin expression "*gradum inferre in hostes*," literally translated as "to march against the enemy," idiomatically means "to attack the enemy." However, the verb *aggredior,* in its original meaning, had not only a negative implication; in the Latin language it meant primarily "to get near," "to move toward" something or somebody, regardless of intent of harm or not, and it also meant "to begin," "to start."

In the Italian society, and not only in the language, this original meaning of aggressiveness is still present today, and expresses itself in a deep psychological and cultural ambivalence toward aggressive acts and attitudes. The understanding of this ambivalence is a necessary prerequisite to the study of the phenomenology and consequences of aggressiveness in the social context—in the Italian culture—as elsewhere.

METHODOLOGICAL CONSIDERATIONS

Most authors agree on the need for three basic elements in the definition of an aggressive attitude; biological, psychological, and social, although different authors tend to give different relevance to one or the other of these three components.

However, the multicausality and complexity of the phenomenon are the reason for the inadequacy of any single-factor approach to the scientific study of its basic characteristics. This is the first methodological difficulty to be overcome in the study of aggressiveness, as an object of scientifically controlled observation. Also, when we move from the study of aggressiveness to the study of its manifestations within the context of a specific national culture, a second, more difficult to overcome, obstacle is met. This is because, within a culture, aggressiveness is part of a system, and is a function of several component variables.

To overcome these difficulties, and at the same time to study with some degree of scientific adequacy aggression within modern Italian society, a conceptual framework is needed.

Italian contemporary society, like any other national society, can be defined as a "system." A system, in this context, is an aggregate of elements which concur, with varying degrees of coordination, in the performance of a function. In more general terms, therefore, a system can be viewed as a dynamic aggregate.

In the specific case of a national system, a society can be considered as a group of structural and cultural elements, relative to a given people in a given geographical region, at a given time period, activated by internal dynamics and engaged in external movements, which result from the interaction of the internal dynamics within themselves and with unavoidable influencing factors. Within the system, the interacting elements, for the sake of simplicity, can be grouped into three functional macroelements: employment; number of social interactions; and a third dynamic complex factor which includes both aggressiveness and needs.

If we attempt to describe the system, as outlined above, in terms of a logical function, the following abstract equation results:

$$\frac{S}{t} = \frac{c \neq s}{n} (r \neq w \neq f)$$

where:

S = system
t = time
c = cultural variables
s = structural variables
n = size of the population in the system
r = number and intensity of social interactions
w = total amount of available employment
f = the third dynamic factor (aggressiveness $\neq$ needs)

In other words, a system (a national society) in a given time period is the sum of its structural and cultural elements, considering the size of its population, multiplied by the dynamic pressure of the sum of the social, labour, aggressiveness, and needs which operate within its boundaries.

If we develop the equation in order to obtain "f," as equivalent to the aggressiveness operating in the system, the following expression can be written:

$$f = \frac{ns}{(c \neq s)t} - (r \neq w)$$

This expression, derived from the previous decription of the functioning of a society as a system, contains the conceptual framework which will guide discussion in this paper. It can be rephrased as follows:

Aggressiveness (as expressed by "f") within a national society, other conditions being equal, is directly proportional to the size of the population and to the decrease of employment and of the number and intensity of social interactions, while it is inversely proportional to the sum of the cultural and structural variables, and to the length of the time period to be considered. This hypothesis implies that aggressiveness in a given society increases as population increases, available employment and social interaction decrease, cultural and structural variables deteriorate, and the tempo of social changes increases. Aggressiveness will, on the contrary, decrease as the population decreases, available employment and social interactions increase, cultural and structural variables improve, and the tempo of social changes slows down.

The Contemporary Italian Society

It may be useful to attempt a brief and general description of the Italian contemporary society as a system. The time span of our observation is limited to the last 35 years, from the end of World War II to the beginning of the 1980s.

Historically, this is a relatively brief period, but it is also rather homogeneous in relation to the object of our study. In this period, Italy has not been involved in international conflicts. No national war having taken place, the specific explosion of aggressiveness and its legitimate channelling toward an external enemy has not taken place. Also, within the same period, there has been no constitutional change and the country has been governed according to the formal principles of republican representative democracy and electoral representation, through the political parties system.

In spite of this lack of political change, the period under consideration has witnessed deep social and structural changes which have allowed the country, first, to heal the many wounds left by the war, and, subsequently, to build a rather progressive society, although not free from imbalances and contradictions.

In the following description we will quote from the most reliable statistical sources, made available each year by the Central Statistical Institute (ISTAT) of the Republic of Italy, rounded up to the last thousand. We have selected, among the many available figures, those parameters which appear to be more reliable and more meaningful for our study. Obviously, the first parameter is the size of the resident population of the country, which was 47,516,000 in 1951, and 56,999,000 in 1979, with an increase, in nearly 30 years, of almost 11 million persons. This increase, however, seems to have taken place with a slightly decreasing average increase, from 7.4 percent in 1951 to 6.3 percent in the last year. Therefore, if we exclude a slight increase of the population in the 25–35 years age range, due to the natural demographic increase immediately following the end of World War II, the mean age of the Italian population tends to increase.

A second important parameter is internal mobility of the population, as expressed by the number of persons who each year change their residence from region to region. In Italy, the differences between the North-Center areas and the South are very pronounced. In the time span under consideration, each year 1 million persons have changed their residence, mostly moving from the South to the North and from the country to the large urban areas, thus causing an increase of the population in the North-Center area of the peninsula, and the aggregation of large metropolitan areas. Today, about 12 percent of the population lives in four cities, which each has over 1 million residents. This change was greater between 1950 and 1970, and has progressively decreased in the last decade.

The mobility of the population has coincided with such major changes in the field of employment that the general pattern of labor-related cultural values has been deeply modified. For example, the number of people employed in agriculture, which in 1951 was 8,261,000 (representing almost 40 percent of the active Italian population), already in 1961 had shown a decrease of 2,500,000 persons, and has continued to decrease, although at a smaller rate, reaching in 1979 the global figure of 2,840,000 (equal to 13.98 percent of the active population). Consequently, in the last 30 years, almost 5,500,000 workers, and their families, have abandoned agricultural employment, moving to industrial or service occupations. Considering that this process took place with the greatest intensity in the first 15 years of the period under consideration, a first important deduction emerges. Evidently, for a large section of the active population, there is a deep cultural gap between the generation of the fathers, of rural origins, and the generation of their offspring, now 15 to 30 years of age, born and raised entirely within the fold of a developed industrial society.

Simultaneous with the decrease of agricultural employment, but of much smaller size, has been the increase of the industrial sector. Statistical data show that persons employed in this sector were, in 1951, 4,720,000, equal to 22.8 percent of the active population. This figure increased constantly, reaching, in 1971, a total of 8,162,000 (42 percent of the active population), but more recently has gradually decreased, in absolute figures and in percentage, reaching in 1979 the figure of 7,532,000 persons employed in the industrial sector. Presumably, the industrial sector has not absorbed all the workers who have abandoned the agricultural field, and is less and less capable of doing so. Important segments of this displaced labor force have moved to other employments or, in many instances, are now unemployed.

Available data on the number of unemployed workers are not very reliable. However, some trends are evident. The official number of unemployed workers (i.e., recorded in placement offices) appears to remain fairly stable over the years, and varies between 200,000 and 300,000. However, the number of persons seeking first employment (this figure is estimated through periodic samples) is steadily increasing, moving from 100,000 to 200,000 in 1951 to 866,000 in 1979. Therefore, the total number of unemployed is about 1 million, but to this figure about 600,000 persons must be added, representing the estimate of the so-called "underground" employment, a phenomenon which is difficult to assess, since it is extremely variable and since these workers tend to hide their status, both when employed and when unemployed. Taking into account all these factors, it can be estimated that current unemployment is at the level of 1,600,000 persons.

In spite of increasing unemployment, the Italian economy, in the 30 year period under consideration, has experienced an accelerated expansion, as shown by available macroeconomic data. Gross national product, in U.S. dollars, at market prices for each year, increased from $28 billion in 1951, to $336 billion in 1979, with an (uncorrected for inflation) increase of 343 percent in the last ten years. At the same time, family expenditures, also in dollars, and uncorrected for inflation, have moved from $16 billion in 1951, to $64 billion in 1971, to $211 billion in 1979, with an apparent increase of 297 percent in the last ten years. In real terms, the increase is much smaller, of approximately 4 to 5 percent per year. The discrepancy between apparent and real figures is due to inflation, which has now reached the 20 percent per year level.

The energy and economic crises which have striken Western countries since 1973-74, appear to have, in Italy, influenced marketing more than production or consumption. In other terms, throughout the 1970-1980 decade, the country has continued to benefit in part from the strong expansionist push of the previous decade and in part from the extreme vitality shown by atypical economic structures and mechanisms, which have carried out a powerful, vicarious, and reserve action. It is as if there had been, alongside with the official economic system, a second parallel economic system, partially hidden, "submerged," and partly overlapping the official system. Thus, paradoxically, the very element of economic dysfunctionality of the official system appears to have, in the time of crisis, insured the functionality of the whole economy.

Expansion and the resulting economic changes have been accompanied, over the last 30 years, by a major cultural change, which has expressed itself both in quantitative terms as an increase in the level and diffusion of education and increase in the possibilities for communication and interchange, and in qualitative terms as change and leveling of cultural values.

As an example, university education, which in 1951 was limited to 1 to 2 percent of the student population, in 1979 has expanded to include 9.5 percent of the whole student-age population, with an increase, in gross figure, of 800,000 persons in the last 20 years. At the same time, the number of television sets (the most efficient of the mass media) has increased from 3 million in 1961 to 13 million in 1979, spreading the audience in both the cities and the rural areas.

Last, the roads network, which was 450 kms. per 1,000 square kms., already in 1971 reached the level of 955 kms. per 1,000 square kms., and the number of registered cars has increased from 1 million in 1951 to almost 17 million in 1979.

If we shift the analysis to the political scene, the Italian system has peculiarities that make it different from the systems of the other Western European countries. In the Italian system six distinct groups can be identified:

- A Catholic group, the Christian Democratic Party (DC), which occupies a center-right parliamentary area and, from 1951 to 1980 has gained a percentage of electoral support ranging between 40 and 36 percent with a slow but consistent decreasing trend since 1974-1975.
- A communist group, the Italian Communist Party (PCI), and other minor leftist parties with parliamentary representation, whose electoral support has been progressively increasing from 21 percent in 1951 to 33 percent in 1980, this trend increasing since 1974-1975.
- The third group is composed of Marxist and social-democratic socialists (Italian Socialist Party-PSI, and Italian Social Democratic Party-PSDI), which add up to 21 percent in 1951, decreasing to 16-17 percent in 1980, with alternating trends, and an increase in the last few years.
- A fourth, heterogeneous group, with a liberal-progressive matrix, includes several parties, from the Radical Party (PR), to the Republican Party (PRI), to the Liberal Party (PLI). Electoral support for this group has ranged from 5-6 percent in 1951 to 10-11 percent in 1979, with a general trend toward increase.
- The fifth political group includes the authoritarian-fascist right wing area, the Italian Socialist Movement (MSI), which has varied from 6 to 8 percent of electoral support, with, currently, a decreasing trend.
- The last political group, although outside of the political arena and without parliamentary representation, has lately acquired some weight in the Italian system. It is of primary interest because it postulates the use of violence to modify reality. This is the so-called "Armed Party," which includes various aversive and terrorist groups, the most notorious being the Red Brigades. Direct or indirect consensus with their line of political violence, not identical to belonging to a unit, or group, can be estimated to range between 0.5 and 1.5 percent of the electorate (200,000 to 600,000 individuals). This group began to emerge in Italy in the early 1970s, immediately after the 1968 youth and cultural movement and the labor struggles of 1969, and has lately shown a considerable operational capacity.

To sum up, the following dynamic trends can be hypothetically considered to exist in the contemporary Italian society:

- The social system has undergone deep transformations, whose tempo, fast in the 1960s and in the 1970s, tends to decrease in the most recent decade. The change has affected both the cultural and the structural aspects of the system, the former being more affected, and several imbalances have emerged between the basic structures and existing needs and trends. This has favored the emergence of new needs, which can be fulfilled in a contest of economic expansion, but which cannot be met during a prolonged economic crisis.

- The internal management of the system is characterized by a strong stability, which has never allowed major changes in the political leadership of the country. However, this stability, since 1974–1975, becomes precarious with a resulting leadership crisis.
- Last, some destabilizing forces are acting in the system, aimed ar rapid change at any cost, and stabilizing forces, aimed at status quo preservation at any cost.

Under these circumstances, aggressiveness can manifest itself within both the destabilizing and the stabilizing forces, thus increasing throughout the society. Also, and this would be a much more sinister development, the value of aggressiveness can change, from tool to symbolioc goal, from small-scale violence to terrorism.

THE FORMS OF AGGRESSIVENESS IN ITALIAN CONTEMPORARY SOCIETY

The assessment of the quantitative dimensions and of the qualitative forms of aggressiveness in a country are not easy, since there is no index of the phenomenon which can cover all its aspects, and since this index cannot be simply derived by figures of criminality trends.

Not all crime is aggressive, and aggressiveness is more than violent crime statistics. The limitations of existing criminal statistics are well known, and, in any case, both criminal and noncriminal aggressiveness should be assessed in the context of the society taken as a whole. Nevertheless, it is necessary to attempt an objective measurement, at least of the better defined aspects, to attempt some analysis and correlation with other social phenomena. Keeping the preceding considerations in mind, and the existing methodological shortcomings, the following data are offered, with some attempts at explanations.

Before presenting the data, some information on their format is necessary. Data concern reported crimes for which judicial action has been initiated (no reliable police statistics by crime are available in Italy). Among all possible crimes, we have selected those whose aggressive character is more evident. They have been grouped in the following way:

- *Crimes against the person* (this category includes mass murder, murder, attempted murder, manslaughter, wounding, defamation, and libel).
- *Rape and other violent sexual offences.*
- *Robbery, extortion, and kidnapping for ransom,* because of their violent connotations, although they are also property crimes.
- *Crimes against the state, or against public order* (this category includes most terrorism-connected crimes).

Pragmatically we have selected for analysis behaviors which, by common sense, before any theoretical consideration is applied, express aggressiveness. These behaviors, since they are dangerous for the development and survival of humanity, also fall into the definition of "crimes." However, a deeper analysis of their "aggressiveness" component is needed.

The category of "crimes against the person" includes behaviors whose final outcome is the death of the victim as well as behaviors whose outcome is a damage to the physical, psychological, or moral welfare of the victim. We have, as far as possible, kept homicide separate from other crimes against the person, because of its juridical and moral seriousness and because, biologically, it is the clearest expression of aggressiveness. Almost all behaviors in this category include the potentiality of homicide, from a practical viewpoint, and could be considered as "incomplete" or "failed," or "truncated," or "limited," but in any case, "possible" homicides. Thus, wounding is not homicide only because the amount of violence is limited, and defamation and libel are symbolic, and not acted out, violence.

Robbery, extortion, and kidnapping often do not end in homicide only because of the victim's behavior, but death is actually threatened.

Crimes against the state, and against public order, do not necessarily imply murder, "complete" or "incomplete." However, these crimes are particularly prevalent in Italy now, and they are also a good example of the relativity of the social perception of aggressiveness, and of its use in terrorist behavior. Anthropomorphically, there are the "murder" of the state.

Concerning the issue of the instrumentality of aggressiveness, human behavior cannot be identified as "instrumental" without considering the actor's interest and the social frame of reference. Killing of men can be the purpose of war, but war can also be the purpose of killing men. Killing in self-defense can be defined as nonaggressive, or *any* killing can be seen as aggressive. Table 12.1 gives the rate, per 100,000 persons, of some crimes for which judicial action was initiated between 1951 and 1976. The homicide rate is constant, while robberies, extortions, and kidnappings, in the last seven years, increase sharply. This is also evident in figure 12.1.

Table 12.1. Reported Crimes for which Judicial Action has been Initiated
(rate per 100,000 persons)

YEAR	MURDER	ROBBERY, EXTORTION, KIDNAPPING
1951	5.0	7.9
1952	4.5	6.9
1953	3.7	5.4
1954	3.7	5.7
1955	4.0	6.2
1956	3.9	6.2
1957	3.5	5.6
1958	3.4	6.0
1959	3.4	5.7
1960	3.2	6.0
1961	3.2	6.5
1962	3.0	5.9
1963	2.7	5.5
1964	2.7	5.8
1965	2.6	5.4
1966	2.3	5.3
1967	2.5	5.5
1968	2.4	5.6
1969	2.2	5.6
1970	2.4	5.8
1971	2.8	8.6
1972	2.7	9.0
1973	3.2	14.0
1974	3.2	17.2
1975	3.1	20.4
1976	3.5	25.0

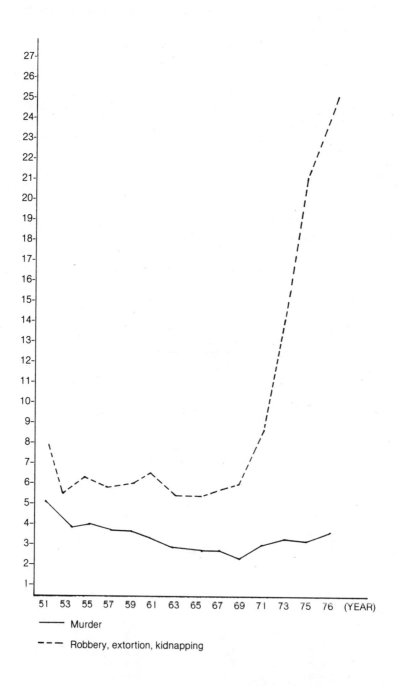

Figure 12.1. Trend of Reported Crimes for Which Judicial Action was Initiated
Between 1951 and 1976 (per 100,000 persons)

Robberies, extortions, and other forms of violence have increased rapidly since 1969. The change is so abrupt that an external cause appears likely. The social and cultural crises which the country is undergoing appear to coincide, chronologically, with an increase in instrumental violence.

Employing a different classification, table 12.2 presents rates per 1,000 persons of some crimes for the years 1972-1980. Crimes have been divided into four categories. Crimes against the person, including nondeadly ones, appear to have remained relatively constant for the time period under consideration. The increase or decrease variation is 23 to 24 percent. Sexual aggression also is relatively stable, the variation being 33 to 34 percent over several years. However, robberies, extortions, and kidnappings have steadily and progressively increased, with a 414 percent increase over the years. Crimes against the state and against public order show a 200 percent increase from 1972 to 1980. Finalized, or instrumental, violence appears to have increased much more than basic, homicidal violence.

Table 12.3 presents rates (per 1,000 persons) for the same categories of crimes (1972-1976) in six Italian regions. These regions have been selected because they differ from one another, as well as from the "average" Italian region. Lombardy has the highest rate of industrialization. Lazio, besides including the capital, Rome, has a high political and bureaucratic identity. Campania is the most industrialized of the Southern regions. Calabria and Sicily have the Mafia phenomenon. Sardinia has a specific and separate culture, and has a banditism phenomenon, originally linked to a cattle raising economy.

Crimes against the person in Campania, Calabria, and Sicily tended to decrease from 1972 to 1976. Sex crimes also decreased, except in Sardinia where in 1976 their rate was higher than anywhere else.

Robberies, extortions, and kidnappings, which were high in 1972 in Calabria, Sicily, and Sardinia, increased everywhere in 1976, and the increase was particularly pronounced in Lazio.

Figure 12.2 presents data on murder and on robberies, extortions, and kidnappings in 1972-1980 for the six regions under consideration, together with data on the size of the population. Calabria, with the lowest population, has the highest rate of crimes, followed by Sardinia and, partially, by Campania. Sicily, Lazio, and Lombardy show a closer relationship between the size of the population and the violent crime rates.

It is evident that the phenomenology of violent crime tends to become more homogeneous for the six regions in the period from 1972 to 1976. However, quantitatively and, as we shall see, also qualitatively, some Southern and insular regions show specific peculiarities.

ORGANIZED CRIME IN THE SOUTHERN AND INSULAR REGIONS OF ITALY

One of the most unique aspects of Italian criminality is, undoubtedly, the peculiar types of organized crime which operate in the Southern and insular regions of the country. The variety of aggressive behaviors within Italy as a whole, a fairly small geographical area, must be linked to deep ethnic, geographical, historical and social differences which, even in recent past, have created different realities in various regions of the peninsula.

However, as the data appear to show, an homogenization of the criminal phenomenology is taking place. This process seems to be caused both by the high mobility of the Italian population, with a South to North trend which has caused the diffusion of specifically Southern criminal behaviors in different Northern areas, and by the process of fast adaptation by the criminal groups to changes in the socioeconomic structure of the regions.

Table 12.2. Crimes Reported in Italy, for which Judicial Action was Initiated, 1972-1980 (rate per 1,000 persons)

CRIMES	1972	1973	1974	1975	YEAR 1976	1977	1978	1979	1980
Against the person	3.05	3.35	2.87	2.64	2.59	2.77	2.71	2.80	3.20
Rape and other violent sexual offenses	0.04	0.04	0.04	0.03	0.03	0.04	0.03	0.04	0.04
Robbery; extortion, and kidnapping	0.07	0.09	0.13	0.16	0.19	0.20	0.24	0.33	0.36
Crimes against the state or against public order	0.01	0.02	0.02	0.01	0.01	0.02	0.02	0.02	0.03

Table 12.3. Reported Crimes for Which Judicial Action was initiated in Six Italian Regions, per 1,000 persons (1972-1976)

CRIMES	REGIONS											
	LOMBARDY		LAZIO		COMPANIA		CALABRIA		SICILY		SARDINIA	
	1972	1976	1972	1976	1972	1976	1972	1976	1972	1976	1972	1976
Crimes against the person	2.9	2.8	2.03	2.1	3.88	2.3	3.8	2.4	2.2	1.6	3.03	1.4
Rape and other violent sexual offenses	0.04	0.02	0.05	0.02	0.06	0.03	0.04	0.02	0.06	0.02	0.01	0.04
Robberies, extortions, kidnappings	0.32	0.77	0.36	1.20	0.55	0.84	1.09	1.47	0.87	1.24	1.21	1.51
Crimes against the state and against public order	0.01	0.01	0.01	0.02	0.02	0.006	0.01	0.02	0.03	0.002	0.02	0.01

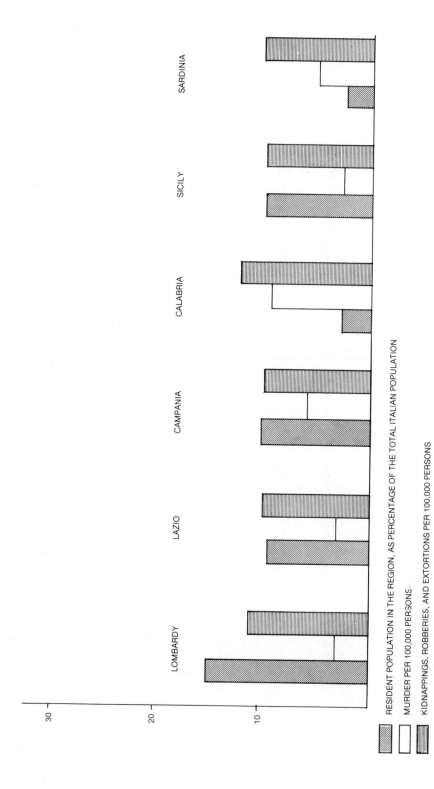

RESIDENT POPULATION IN THE REGION, AS PERCENTAGE OF THE TOTAL ITALIAN POPULATION

MURDER PER 100,000 PERSONS

KIDNAPPINGS, ROBBERIES, AND EXTORTIONS PER 100,000 PERSONS

Fig. 12.2. Reported Crimes for which Judicial Action was Initiated, in Six Italian Regions (1971 census)

The simplest way to discuss the phenomenon is to describe separately the major criminal organizations, trying to underline their similarities and their major differential characteristics.

Mafia

The Mafia is the best known Italian criminal organization because of its diffusion in foreign countries, particularly in the United States, following the great migrations from Southern Italy at the beginning of the century.

The Mafia was born in western Sicily between 1820 and 1848, originally for a defence of the interests of the great aristocratic landowners and of the interests of the middle class. In the following decades it evolved as a clandestine organization aimed not only at obtaining criminal goals, but also at imposing a certain degree of hegemony on all social and economic activities, both legal and illegal.

The etymology of the term "mafia" is controversial, but most authors concur in attributing its roots to the Arab word *Mahjus,* or "boasting," or "Excessive and exaggerated trust in one's own capacities and possibilities." In reality, the Mafia seems to imply not only a criminal organization but also a specific attitude, or set of attitudes, leading to the belief that the protection of the self and property is better achieved through personal actions and influences, independently from legal protection by the state.

The transformation of these attitudes into a value system, and their codification into an unwritten but widely adhered to code of behavior and the adoption of such a code by a group of individuals are the processes which translate into the spires of a modern criminal organization what is left of the medieval and feudal habits still surviving in a sector of the Southern Italian population. The state is absent, far away, and uninterested, and the Mafia steps into the vacuum.

The cornerstones of the Mafia organization are secrecy, *omertá* (silence), revenge, obedience, and terror. Secrecy, obedience, and *omertà* are the tools which enable the Mafia to exist, infiltrate, and act, in spite of legislative and police efforts. *Omertá* and revenge are the roots of the so-called "honor," which is a necessary prerequisite to be admitted into the organization. Specifically, revenge may be postponed in time, but must inevitably be carried out. The capacity to carry out the revenge is the essential feature of the "honorable man." Last, terror is the power tool of the leader and the group. This needs to be considered in any attempt to understand the brute violence which is the frequent trademark of the Mafia crime. This type of violence is highly symbolic, since it is meant as a message. This is the reason why many murders are ritualized and take place only in specific settings (in public, since the crowd must see and fear; *omerta* will protect the murderer from reporting witnesses), or with specific modalities (genitals cut off and placed in the mouth, or small coins over the body of the traitor who has spoken too much). Such violence is also void of any mercy (cruel executions are carried out on children, guilty only of belonging to a rival group), as if mercy would be a sentiment unworthy of man and proper only for women.

The unconsciously homosexual character of the Mafia organization, the identification of the organization with the protective powers of the maternal womb, appear to determine a deep anxiety whose compensatory mechanism, in dynamic terms, is the removal of any feeling perceived as too feminine and, therefore, anxiety-producing.

The Mafia structure is very specific. It is based on small groups (*cosche*) of 10 to 15 elements (*picciotti*), who are the armed executors of the will of the leader (*padrino*) to whom respect and almost absolute obedience are due. The leader tends to present a positive public image, based on the charisma of his authority and the appeal of his power.

Mafia activities, once centered on blackmail rackets and extortions toward farms and commercial or management establishments, an intimidation, exploitation of prostitution, and kidnapping, are now mostly directed toward drug trafficking and illegal political-economic activities.

The enormous wealth accumulated in recent years through criminal enterprises has been invested in international commercial and financial enterprises, which have greatly flourished, allowing the Mafia, in part, to integrate into, and infiltrate, some of the most delicate and sensitive political and economic structures of the country. In the last 30 years, the Mafia, after recurring struggles for leadership by one of the "families," has acquired a solid structure in Sicily where it appears to have established a base for drug trafficking toward the United States and, from Sicily, has extended its net of interests practically all over Italy.

The 'Ndrangheta

The slang term *'ndrangheta* indicates a criminal organization which exists in the Calabria region. This area, as shown in the preceding tables, has a high rate of aggressive crimes. The *'ndrangheta* is very similar to the Mafia both in its structural aspects and in its use of violence, and the two organizations are sometimes mixed-up in popular literature. However, there are some basic differences whose discussion will help to understand the roots of aggressive behavior in Southern Italy.

Calabria is a culturally and socially heterogeneous region and includes one southern area, similar to Sicily, and a northern area, more similar to the rest of Italy. The *'ndrangheta* is located in the southern area, while elsewhere crime resembles the patterns usually found in large metropolitan areas.

One distinctive aspect of *'ndrangheta,* when compared to the Mafia, is that it is smaller in size and more localized, with no extensions outside of Italy. The criminal activities are less diffuse and the "volume of business" is much smaller. Qualitatively, an important differential aspect is a lesser degree of solidarity among the members, and a prevalence of family and individual interests over the "social" interests of the organization. A consequence of this is the existence of *faide,* or chain revenges, which involve two rival families, and can cause a large number of murders over a long period, sometimes lasting for decades.

Also, the *'ndrangheta,* more than the Mafia, carries out a vicarious function for the serious gaps of production structures with resulting unemployment. In other words, many young Calabrians are attracted to the criminal organization by a malaise caused by the need to satisfy continuously increasing needs in a context of absence of work opportunities to achieve perceived goals.

The *Camorra*

Camorra is the name of a criminal organization mostly located in the Campania region, more specifically in the Naples area. This region has serious structural and social imbalances: a large city (Naples) with a disaggregated and inadequate urban structure, areas of recent industrialization, together with areas of backwardness and absence of services, etc. The recent earthquake (November 1980) has worsened an already unfavorable situation, causing unacceptable living situations for hundreds of thousands of inhabitants. In this frame of reference, *camorra* activities have sharply increased, so that, within Naples, over 200 persons have been killed in gang warfare in 1981.

The *camorra,* although structurally similar to the Mafia, has different qualitative aspects. Typical of the *camorra* member is a peculiar type of ostentation and braggadocio which is totally absent in the Mafia member, who, on the contrary, tends to hide the most conspicuous aspects of his power. Similar elements of ostentation are evident in urban juvenile gangs in Northern and Central Italy, where this pattern facilitates the identification process of the weaker boys with the leader, selected as a model for imitation because of his displayed strength.

Another differential characteristic between the *camorra* and the Mafia is that the former does not identify with the state and does not attempt to infiltrate governmental structures, as the Mafia does. The *camorra* has a tendency to present itself as an alternate power, contrasting that of the state. For this reason, alliances between *camorra* groups and marginal urban lower class groups, with aversive connotations, are not unusual. On the contrary, the Mafia tends to gravitate toward the most integrated and influencial classes, with a rather conservative posture. Within *camorra*, links are looser and activities are less coordinated than within the Mafia.

Sardinian Banditism

Violence in Sardinia is prevalently bandit activity, or gangstery, which is one of the simplest forms of criminal association. The aggregation of outlawed individuals in groups of varying size, led by whomever achieves leadership because of superior intelligence or greater criminal capabilities, is one of the most frequent criminal phenomena. However, for this to happen, life in a "sanctuary" is necessary, an impenetrable and secure area unknown and unreachable by the police. This presupposes a particular type of *omertá*, or at least some support by the local population, in order to escape police detection and capture over a long period of time.

Sardinia has both elements. On one side, there are large underpopulated mountain areas and, on the other, a population which is isolated, closed, bent to solve problems within itself and through deeply rooted and ancient folkways and deviant or criminal phenomenon. Originally, banditism was linked to cattle-theft and to extortions against rival farms but, more recently, it appears to be connected to increasingly frequent and diffuse kidnapping for ransom.

In Sardinia, this highly profitable crime has steadily increased, partly favoured by migration from Sardinia into the continent, and is now a most serious phenomenon. Occasionally, kidnapping has been used, particularly on the continent, not merely for profit but to fund and supply terrorist organizations. In the case of Sardinia banditism, the antistate quality, already noted in the *camorra*, is even more evident. In this case, it links with separatist feelings, deeply rooted in the Sardinian culture, and with initial terrorist activities.

More recently, Sardinia gangs appear to act in a more coordinated and better organized *modus operandi*, so that the phenomenology of violence appears more homogeneous than that prevailing on the continent. Thus, sex crimes have increased and violence is no longer limited, as it was the case in the past, to male members of the culture. In recent years, women and children have been kidnapped and rape (both hetero- and homosexual) of the kidnapped victims is more frequent.

TERRORISM IN MODERN ITALIAN SOCIETY

Most scholars place the beginning of modern terrorism in Italy on Dec. 12, 1969, when a bomb exploded in a Milan bank killing 16 persons and wounding many more. This date, however, not only marks the beginning of terrorism but also, conventionally, the end of the complex historical era termed "the '68." This period, in Italy as elsewhere, was characterized by the sudden rise of wide social problems, by the crisis of the established value system, and by the rapid change of many cultural models.

Some analysts believe that terrorism, deeply ingrained into Paleo-communist doctrine and ideology, and because of its temporal proximity to 1968, is nothing but a direct offspring of the revolutionary movements which, in the '68, emerged in most Western countries. For other analysts, the relationship between the two phenomena is not so close, and is more indirect; for yet others, no relationship exists.

In any case, the problem of the origins of terrorism in Italy has, so far, only controversial and partial solutions and up to now no uncontested factual explanation is available. However, in spite of the prevailing lack of consensus, some comments and reflections can be presented, at least as an heuristic attempt toward a scientifically adequate theoretical explanation.

First, however, the concept of "origin" and "cause" must be defined in this context. To know the former does not imply possessing adequate information on the latter. Certainly, Italian terrorism was born within the greater fold of the '68 movements. Many of the early terrorists had had a role in the students' and workers' revolt in the preceding years, but the true "father" of terrorism is yet to be identified. If we had adequate knowledge of the causes of terrorism, we would possess the basic knowledge necessary to defeat and eliminate it.

So far, few explanatory models are available for terrorism. On the other hand, a proper scientific approach in this field cannot differ from the approach adopted for the study of deviant phenomena, which D. T. Campbell and J. C. Stanley (1963) have so well defined as "quasi-experimental method," thus underlining the limitations of this type of investigation.

An added difficulty, in the case of terrorism, is the practical impossibility of assuming a sufficiently wide, objective, and nonpartisan viewpoint, free from the political and moral bias of the observer. The comprehension of the meaning of the observation, of a terrorist event, or of a terrorist motive, cannot avoid being influenced by the value system, the goals, and the motives of the observer.

Definitions of terrorism are many, and several underscore its relativity, as an *ex-post facto* only definable phenomenon, and more seems to cover all aspects of the terrorist activities in Italy.

Even one of the most comprehensive definitions (G. Pontano, 1979) appears to overlook some fundamental aspects of the phenomenon, which are particularly relevant in seeking to define or identify Italian terrorism.

> A terrorist act is only action carried out as part of a method of political struggle (that is, aimed at influencing, conquering or defending State power) implying the use of extreme violence (inflicting physical or psychological death or the infliction of physical or psychological damage) against innocent (non-fighting) persons.

Another element of its definition is its "theatrical" aspect, the show business quality of terrorism, which R. Kupperman (1979) has equated to a show, underlining the complex relationship between terrorism and the mass media.

One further element which appears to be characteristic of Italian terrorism deals with its organizational-structural aspects. In Italy, terrorism is not a sporadic and random phenomenon but, instead, appears to be the end product of the interplay of a complex system of interconnected political forces, linked by close organizational ties.

A third element, which appears to elude the definition by Pontano, concerns the psychological-motivational aspects or the subjective force which propels the individual toward the use of terror as a method of political struggle.

The last element appears to concern the ethical aspect, which involves all those considerations which go beyond the use and the political viability of the phenomenon, and expands into the moral value of the terrorist behavior.

The main interpretative theories of terrorism, as they have been summarized by B. Salert

(1976), are also not satisfactory. Briefly, according to Salert, the following theories can be postulated, to explain political violence:

a) An economic theory, which considers terrorism as a rational choice;
b) A psychological theory, based on the frustration-aggression hypothesis;
c) A theory of unbalance of the social system, based on the assumption that social systems are homeostatic and, consequently, if an unbalance takes place, and some specific conditions exist, such as, for example, insufficient capacity for self-corrective change by the system, a revolution may occur, to restore balance violently;
d) A Marxist theory, based on a dialectical-materialist conception of history.

An Italian political scientist, Luigi Bonanate (Bonanate, Marletti, & Migliorno, 1979), lists several interpretative hypotheses for terrorism and favors an approach based on the concept of "blockade" of the sociopolitical situation. In his view, terrorism is the symptom of a blockage of a system which has so firmly entrenched its basis and its organizational structure to negate any change. This interpretation does not appear to be totally acceptable in an Italian context since it is difficult to define the Italian sociopolitical system as "blocked," in view of the extensive changes which have taken place in the last 30 years.

Italian terrorism, as any complex social fact, should be interpreted on the basis of a multifactorial approach. Terrorist political violence, within a democratic system, is a human social behavior (perhaps more appropriately defined as antisocial), whose determining factors are many. The factors should allow for interpretation not only of terrorism but of the whole society where it takes place. This leads to the assumption that terrorism cannot be considered as external, alien to the society which harbors it, of which, instead, it is part and parcel. In this approach, a preliminary answer is possible to the first question which can be postulated on the origins of Italian terrorism: the roots of the phenomenon are not limited to the critical '68 time, but extend into the preceding historical period, when postwar Italian society was built. The origins of Italian terrorism are in the last 30 years of Italian history (rarely known are terrorists over 30-40 years of age).

However, although the terrorist phenomenon is part of the society where it originates, because of its adoption of violence as a method of struggle and its uprooting of traditional values, the interrelation between the society and the phenomenon resemble those which take place between a dominant culture and a violent subculture (Wolfgang and Ferracuti, 1967).

The subcultural interpretation of Italian terrorism allows the analysis of its relationship to the society, and some forecasting of its effects. The possible relationships are the following:

1. Terrorism has a destabilizing effect on the system, which interacts in all directions, uprooting the democratic structure and replacing it with a new authoritarian-revolutionary structure, thus reinforcing, through feedback, the strength and identity of the violent terrorist subculture.
2. Society can play a destructive role on terrorism, contrasting its destabilizing action and breaking the protective shell of the terrorist subculture.
3. Society can simultaneously carry out a destabilizing and reinforcing action, which, instead of destroying the violent subculture, helps it to spread its values and to gain acceptance among larger groups of individuals.

The second and third alternatives depend upon the processes which the society puts into action vis-a-vis the phenomenon. Thus, selective repression, political and individual social prevention, the strengthening of social values, group fragmentation and dispersal, and the co-option of individuals seem to favor the second alternative, disrupting the subculture. On the contrary, indiscriminate repression, the weakening of civil liberties and of democracy, and the worsening of political and social crises favor the third, destabilizing alternative.

Before analyzing the causal elements of Italian terrorism from the point of view of aggressiveness, it may be useful to indicate its extent and main trends.

Figure 12.3 indicates the general trend of the phenomenon, as expressed by the global number of events which occurred in Italy from 1969 to 1981. The 1981 figure is projected from data in the first six months. The declining trend should not induce any facile optimism. The fact that the total number of events tends to decrease does not mean that today terrorism is less serious than in 1977-78. The number of events is not a good index of the seriousness of the phenomenon. For example, by counting the events as units, the Bologna bombing, which caused over 80 deaths, is counted as a unit, and the same value is given to setting fire to a police car, with no casualties. An idex of seriousness of terrorist events is needed but has not, as yet, been developed.

However, figure 12.3 shows, over the years, the trend of diffuse political violence which, however, must not be confused with organized terrorism. The trend is biphasic, with two peaks, in 1970 and in 1978-79, and, consequently, two upward trends and two critical points. The trend is cyclical, increasingly high, but decreasing as soon as the peak is reached. This allows two alternative explanations: either the phenomenon decreases because spontaneously terrorists abandon diffuse violent behavior, or countermeasures by the state are carried out after a certain threshold level of violence is reached. In other words, it can be assumed that either the response of the state is inadequate, or that it becomes adequate only after a very high level of violence takes place. It should also be noted that the total number of terrorist events in 1980-81 has decreased by 58 percent. Another interesting aspect is evident: if one divides by semesters the total number of terrorist events since 1978, each year the second semester shows a reduction in number of events over the first semester.

Table 12.4 portrays the general trend of terrorism, by number of events per year, in the different major areas of the country. An analysis of variance by area and by years produces F values which show a nonrandom distribution of the figures ($P < 0.01$). Consequently, the dramatic decrease in the number of events in 1980 does not appear to be a chance event, but the result of the action of external factors. It could be the effect of countermeasures by the state, which have been at least partially effective. In a similar manner, the higher prevalence of the phenomenon in some geographical areas does not appear to reflect a chance process, and this would imply several considerations on the probable organizational structure of terrorism in several areas of the Italian peninsula.

The distribution of terrorist events over three years (1979 to 1981) in the various Italian regions is given in table 12.5, in raw figures and in rates per 100,000 residents. The table shows sharp differences in the distribution of the events over time and by regions, although some elements remain constant. Lazio remains fairly stable, with very high rates. Other "stable" regions are Trention A. A. and Veneto. In some regions, terrorism is increasing (Liguria, Calabria, Aosta Valley), and in others it is decreasing (Piedmont, Lombardy). In 1980, some level of homogenization appears to have taken place. Events decreased, but tended to spread out over previously less involved regions.

Of specific interest is the size of the phenomenon in Lazio and in Veneto. Interestingly enough, the only two regions where ethnic grievances exist are Trentino A. A. and Sardinia, providing some low level "separatist" causes for terrorist activities. However, Italian terrorism has always been political rather than ethnic or race oriented. And Veneto and Lazio have no ethnic minorities at all. Therefore, the high level of terrorism in these two regions does not appear to be chance determined and is probably linked to the presence, within their territory, of

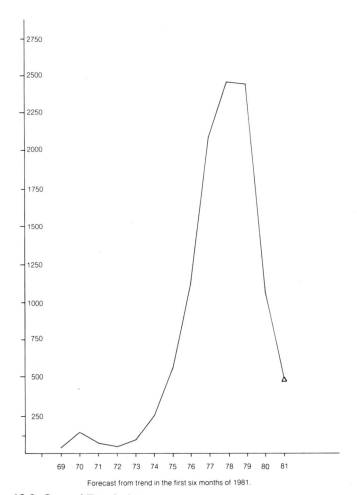

Forecast from trend in the first six months of 1981.

Fig. 12.3. General Trend of Terrorism — Global Number of Terrorist Events

major structures or of important targets, from the terrorist tactical and strategic perspective. This hypothesis is at least partially verified by well documented indictments of various terrorist units by the Italian courts.

In a recent book (M. Galleni, 1981), which contains the first available large data collection on terrorism, the Italian sociologist Ferrarotti identifies such peculiarities in three typically distinctive features of Italian society: (1) the existence of Mafia as a national power system; (2) kidnapping for ransom, as the residual of a disappearing rural culture, and (3) organized political violence by terrorist groups. Italian terrorism, according to Ferrarotti, can be distinguished from other forms of national terrorist activities, on the basis of the following features:

a. the vagueness of the targets;
b. the operational alliance between common and political criminality;
c. its urban character;
d. the high number of young members;
e. the existence of "repented" terrorists.

Ferrarotti stresses the need for an in-depth and structural multifactorial approach to understanding.

Table 12.4. General Trend of Terrorism — Global
Number of Events by Year and by Geographical Area

REGION	1978	YEAR 1979	1980
Northwestern Italy	641	697	281
Northeastern Italy	378	349	124
Center-North Italy	302	279	105
Center-South Italy	757	854	422
Southern Italy	105	170	57
Islands (Sicily and Sardinia)	184	175	70

Fc (variance among columns) = 9,227
V_1 (df-degrees of freedom of largest variance) = 2
V_2 (df$_2$-degrees of freedom of smallest variance) = 10
P < .01 (the probability of the variance being due to chance is less than 1/00)
Fr (variance among rows) = 12,486
V_1 (df) = 5
V_2 (df$_2$) = 10
P < .01

Table 12.5. General Trend of Terrorism — Number of Events per 100,000 persons

REGION	1978 NO.	%	YEAR 1979 NO.	%	1980 NO.	%
Aosta Valley	3	2.63	1	0.87	4	3.50
Piedmont	178	3.92	266	5.87	60	1.32
Lombardy	405	4.52	346	3.86	163	1.82
Trantino A. A.	48	5.47	45	5.13	39	4.45
Veneto	292	6.71	259	5.95	72	1.65
Friuli V. G.	38	3.05	45	3.61	13	1.04
Liguria	55	2.98	84	4.55	54	2.92
Emilia Romagna	145	3.65	93	2.34	44	1.10
Tuscany	126	3.50	122	3.38	49	1.36
Umbria	10	1.23	24	2.97	4	0.49
Marche	21	1.48	40	2.82	8	0.56
Lazio	647	12.78	659	13.02	355	7.01
Abbruzzo	17	1.37	18	1.45	5	0.40
Campania	89	1.63	174	3.18	62	1.13
Molise	4	1.19	3	0.89	0	—
Basilicata	5	0.80	6	0.97	2	0.32
Puglia	55	1.40	69	1.76	19	0.48
Calabria	45	2.16	95	4.57	36	1.73
Sicily	85	1.70	89	1.78	34	0.68
Sardinia	99	6.18	86	5.37	36	2.24
Mean value	4.15		4.41		1.87	

It is suggested that, within the terrorist scenario there is a specific point in time when the various factors coalesce and merge, creating the "conscience of war" in the individual and in the group, and transforming and adjusting the dynamic personality processes to the life style of the terrorist.

This is the most important point of the long journey which takes an individual outside of his social environment, to an external, aberrant status. To identify the conditions which lead to this crucial point is essential, not only to recover to civilization those who have chosen violence as a political expression but to plan any effective preventive measures.

In other words, aside from general (and normally unmodifiable) socioeconomic causes, the following questions beg for an answer:

1. What distinguishes terrorists from non-terrorists?
2. Are terrorists similar or different within the terrorist subculture?
3. How does a non-terrorist become a terrorist?
4. When, and given what circumstances, does this transformation occur?

These questions can be answered at present only intuitively. For too long a time, the basic and most elementary questions have been eluded: How can a well informed, and usually bright, modern young man (or woman), born and raised within a democratic society, choose the road to death and terror, sometimes reaching the extreme limit of conscious and intentional self-immolation? What generates and maintains this quasi-religious fanaticism? Can this enormous energy potential be redirected toward socially acceptable goals? The example of the I.R.A. inmates, who let themselves starve to death, expresses dramatically the paradoxical radicality of this choice.

To answer the first question, a preliminary distinction must be drawn between "normal" and so-called "pathological" terrorists, excluding the latter from further discussion. Mental pathology, however, is limited among terrorists, although its prevalence is higher in right wing groups (Ferracuti and Bruno, 1981).

The type of terrorist who can be defined as "pathological" is an individual affected by a nosographically identifiable mental disorder, to which his terrorist activities appear to be connected. This is a small but important minority for which murder and massacre are the outcome of deeply disturbed mental processes. These subjects are the lonely murderers of popular political figures, gifted with charisma and notoriety. Because of the uniqueness of the pathological mental processes, no generalizations are possible concerning this group, and their actions are unpredictable and unexplainable.

Our discussion must be limited to those terrorists in whom no obvious mental pathology exists. These are the subjects who must be matched with "normal," non-terrorist, individuals, and with common criminals, all other biological, social, and cultural conditions being equal.

Since Lombroso, comparative criminological research aimed at identifying the causes of criminal behaviors and the differences between criminals and noncriminals has produced a voluminous body of literature. However, practical, scientifically indisputable results are conspicuously absent. Crime and terrorism are not "natural" categories, but behavior classes which are arbitrary and normatively defined. For this reason, the current consensus of opinion is that no validly discriminating structural differences exist between deviant and criminal groups and "normals."

Consequently, if a single society, such as Italy, is examined, and if, within its context, subjects of similar age, sex, social class, culture, area of residence, and educational and political experiences are analyzed, it can be assumed that their biological and instinctual make-up will be similar, although they will include "normal," law-abiding citizens, terrorists, and criminals.

What varies is the behavior within the society, and a major difference in the attitude toward the use of aggressiveness and violence, and toward the acceptance of death. While the "normal" citizen restrains from violence and abhors death in any form, the terrorist and the criminal adopt violence and aggressiveness as a method and engage in a dialectical intercourse with death, both ideologically and in practice—the terrorist to destroy the society where he lives; and the criminal, in a more limited fashion, to improve his living standards. It is, however, a learned behavior, not an innate predisposition. It is a value, not an instinct.

The instrumental use of violence is not an anomaly, per se. It exists even in the most peaceful and orderly societies and can manifest itself in various contexts and at any time in human life, as is shown by aggressiveness in the educational process of children, or by the popularity of some violent sports, or of some violent media entertainments. However, most modern societies officially and conventionally prohibit physical aggressiveness, and replace it with competition and merit systems which adopt a variety of different cultural and value mechanisms. If a member of the society does not conform, and violates the ban on violence, he is labelled criminal or deviant and appropriate restraints are carried out.

The relationship with death follows a different dynamic pattern. The biological instinct to survive, for the individual and society, is the authority which vetoes the acceptance of death. Man escapes from death using every available mechanism, but particularly through a specific psychological attitude that has been defined as "the delusion of immortality" through which man lives day by day as if death did not exist or at least did not concern him.

The only condition where this attitude toward death is drastically changed, and the survival instinct appears not to operate, is war. In a war situation, man appears ready to kill and be killed, the most aberrant forms of aggression are carried out by highly civilized cultures and every soldier can engage in murder. War permits the rule of death over life, and thus legitimizes terror. The "normal" terrorist is like a soldier outside of time and space, living in reality a war which exists only in his fantasy. This is widely reflected in terrorists' writings and in their posture; when captured, they claim "prisoner of war" status.

At this point, to understand the differences between a terrorist, a "normal" citizen, and a criminal, it may be useful to analyze the elements which allow for living in fantasy, in a state of war within a reality of peace and democracy, confronting real war with the fantasmatic war of the terrorist.

Real war is a complex phenomenon involving the subversion of norms, values, and habits in life of two or more societies, trying to solve through strength a conflict based on opposite interests. A status of real war can take place only if certain conditions exist. The first is the need for two or more clearly distinguishable groups or societies with a clear and discrete social identity. War is a collective and organized phenomenon. One necessary and irreplaceable prerequisite for a collective event is the existence of a collectivity. But, in order for this collectivity to modify itself through a state of war, it must possess a certain degree of organization and sovereignty. The organization is needed to possess a minimum degree of viable social structure, and sovereignty ensures the independence of power from the structure.

A second condition, before a real war can take place, is the existence of a crisis due to a reciprocal conflict of interests involving two or more collectivities. In other words, for war to happen, the concerned groups or nations must experience the need for appropriation of something (physical object or instrumental asset) whose property is contested and which is considered indivisible.

The third condition is the transition from a state of peace to a state of war, with the acceptance of new values, new goals, and new behavioral patterns, which must be functional to the new, warlike, life style.

The last condition is the need for the use of strength, and all of the sophisticated technological aids that man has created to multiply his limited physical power to inflict harm.

The process which precedes entering a state of war involves the identification of the "enemy" as such, and therefore of its alienation into something different and hostile. Implied is a projection process of one's own dramatic anxieties over the loss or destruction of the contested object, and the decision to destroy the enemy to prevent his appropriation or destruction of the object.

Together and in parallel with the process of alienation of the enemy, the parties involved develop a maniac feeling of increasing power and invulnerability.

All these mechanisms produce what the Latin expression identifies as the *animus belli*, the will to wage war psychologically dominant in at least one of the contending groups. The opposite group, to survive, must assume a similar posture.

Franco Fornari (1966) has formulated a suggestive psychoanalytic interpretation of war, which he identifies as a paranoiac and manic elaboration of mourning. In his view, to hate the enemy is, paradoxically, the only possible form of love between conflicting groups, and this is explained as a mechanism of projection on the enemy of the guilt for the destruction of one's own love object, so that to hate the enemy is rightful and love-producing. To kill the enemy, in this perspective, is an act of atonement, since it is to destroy the "bad" parts of oneself which have been projected into the enemy. These processes may help to explain and understand terrorists' motivations.

Real war, in the end, manifests itself by carrying out projects of destruction through a chain reaction dominated by the need to kill in order not to be killed, until a new crisis point is reached through conquering or destroying the contested object, or through destruction or incapacitation of one of the contestants. The new crisis is solved with the return to a state of peace through political and sovereign negotiations.

Fantasy war, of course, is only partial war, and it is real for one of the contestants who adopts war values, norms, and behaviors against another, generally larger, group in an attempt to solve a conflict based on legitimate or illegitimate grievances. A fantasy war is neither accepted nor acknowledged by the other group who, in fact, tends to deny it. Fantasy war is, therefore, an ongoing phenomenon in continuous unstable balance between two possible stabilizing processes: either into real war, or as diffuse terror.

Fantasy war becomes real only if acknowledged by the "enemy"; and becomes terrorism when, being unable to compel the enemy to accept a state of war, it must limit itself to harass and destabilize the enemy through utilization and diffusion of fear. The operational conditions of fantasy war are similar to those of real war, but in part art artificially produced to mimic reality. For example, even fantasy war needs the existence of at least two groups, distinct and organized. Within the same society (Italy), since sovereignty can only be attributed to one group; that to which it is denied tries to achieve it, carrying out symbolical duties and privileges of the other, dominating group, and rejecting existing laws and prevailing values. So, it claims power of life and death over citizens, engages in criminal activities claiming their lawfulness, establishes courts of law, promulgates sentences, and applies new laws. A crisis is necessary (if none is taking place, it must be generated), solutions to the crisis are rejected ("reforms delay the revolution"), and the existence of a love object (perceived as in danger) is also necessary. This object is not contested by the other group, but it is threatened in its structure and functions. The process of singling out and alienating the enemy is identical to what takes place in real war, but it can assume much more serious pathological connotations because it is less subject to reality testing and criticism.

Last, fantasy war, as real war, is carried out by executing projects of destruction; but the chain reaction, not being completely maintained by counteractions by the other group, must be self-sustained through an escalation of terror that does not permit the participants to abstain from action or even to lower the level of conflict.

As already stated, two possible scenarios exist in fantasy war: either it changes into real war, and in this instance ends with the defeat of one contestant, or it stabilizes itself into terror, and in this case it can only move into a new crisis, which removes the threat to the object, or makes it accessible to both contestants, or the system changes, reducing or abolishing the prerequisites of war.

At this point, it can be hypothesized that the terrorist differs from the "normal" citizen and from the criminal because he perceives himself as different and alien vis-a-vis the ruling society; because he belongs to a group characterized by a strong ideological, cultural, and political identity; and because he feels that his love object is threatened by the rest of the society which he identifies as enemy and tries to destroy. To achieve this goal he chooses violence, which he uses to generate terror, this being, in his perception, the only option, open to him.

If the above hypothesis is accepted, the second question, of those listed above, can now be approached: Are terrorists different among themselves? Etiologically, several different types exist, but they can be grouped into two major categories.

The first category is the terrorist by despair, who chooses terror because of the frustration of all his expectations and of all his political actions. This type of terrorist is the portrayal of the failure of his political project, just as the nineteenth century individual anarchist could not accept that killing the king only meant that another king would step into power. For him, terrorism was simply a goal which exhausted itself in the act and in its symbolic value.

Terrorists of this type have not been infrequent in Italy, but they should not be confused with the second category—those who use terror not only as a goal but also as a tool to obtain and enlarge their power. This type of terrorist belongs to a cohesive and organized group with lucid political objectives; who use terror to declare a state of fantasy war, which they try to escalate into "real" war. The consistent attempt by Italian terrorists to force the government to assume a military control posture is well known, and is part of a broader political design.

The "Red Brigades" in Italy belong to this second type and, therefore, their danger is directly related to their planning and organizational capabilities, and to the capacity of the state to outmaneuver them.

The last two questions—How does one become a terrorist? and What are the conditions for the transition to terror to take place?—are the most important for the specific Italian situation, since they may help to explain how terrorism was born and how it remains active in the country. What follows is only a set of general considerations on the problem, from a strictly theoretical standpoint, without considering specific, local, events, and outside of any attempt at an historical analysis of Italian terrorism. Available data, in any case, would be inadequate to confirm or deny any hypothesis. Following the previously proposed model, and analyzing Italian terrorism as a fantasy war, a definition of the conditions of such war can be attempted.

First, taking into consideration what has been discussed earlier on the process of change which has been taking place in Italian society for the last 30 years, it is easy to note how deep the division has been between the two major political groups: the communist and the catholic-capitalist. The differences between the two groups, one always in an opposition role and the other always in government, have not been limited to ideological conceptualizations and to political action but have increasingly deepened, involving psychological and behavioral existential aspects and thus contributing to the development of different cultural identities.

Also, the rapid social change which the country has experienced and the tumultuous cultural innovative process, accompanied by the uneven diffusion of new and more affluent life styles, have produced new individual and social needs and have mobilized deep collective anxieties with persecutory contents, partly due to the crisis of the institutions and partly due to the awareness of the enormous increase of the destructive potential of man through technological progress. The economic and political crises which have exploded in the entire Western world in the second half of the 1960s, has triggered the rise of the youth movement, together with the pressing request for new structural social adjustments to the new demands. Here, however, contrary to what was simultaneously taking place, for example, in France and in Germany, the "'68 movement" not only did not generate major reforms but has been followed by an increasingly serious economic depression and, at the same time, by a flourishing right-wing terrorist activity.

The end result of these complex events has been a serious psychological cost paid by the new generation—the need for the Italian society to slow down or even temporarily halt its development.

The persecutory anxieties, already mobilized, have, for some young men, progressed to the elaboration of quasi-paranoic defense mechanisms, outside of any specific psychiatric nosography, and their ego-structure has retained sanity through adherence to a particularly supportive ideology, such as the Marxist-Leninist, which provides ready-made credoes and unshakable beliefs for the future. From this to the organization of terrorist groups is a small step. However, the phenomenon did not exhaust itself in the simple carrying out of sporadic terrorist activities. Should this have been the case, it would already have faded into oblivion. In Italy, it developed into a state of "fantasy war," as previously defined, and this has happened for the following reasons:

1. The substantial political consensus and backing which large sectors of the Italian population offer to the terrorists. In given points in time, this has reached the figure of 4.5 percent consensus and 1 percent direct or indirect backing. In recent analysis on values and behavior, of youth (G. Calvi, in press), 8.8 percent of the Italian population, aged 15 to 64 years, justified terrorism on ideological grounds, and 16.6 percent approved of diffuse political violence. A previous study of a representative sample from a junior college in Rome (Bruno, Grasso, & DeIorio, 1979) has found that 3.5 percent of the subjects approved of the *lotta armata* (armed struggle). This percentage increased to 12.4 in a smaller, less conformist subsample. In other words, it is evident that in Italy terrorism enjoys the open support of a few hundred thousand persons. A large-scale poll (1 million questionnaires) is being conducted by the Italian Communist Party. Preliminary results appear to confirm the data presented above. Obviously, these kinds of investigations must be duplicated and enlarged, with improved sampling and more sophisticated analysis.

2. The important ideological and cultural contribution of a new political conceptualization is spreading widely, not only among youth, and is being grafted to the old Paleo-Marxist-Leninist concepts of the terrorist groups, bringing them to the forefront of the debate on the new and changed situation of the developed and developing nations. This is the "theory of radical needs," which has introduced new social actors, such as the "worker in the society" and the "metropolitan proletariat," in their various stratifications. A discussion of these conceptualizations would exceed the scope of this chapter. It is, however, necessary to mention the enormous amount of theoretical publications that the "armed party" has produced and distributed through regular channels. The development of this relatively exhaustive ideological debate has allowed a rationalization of the terrorist movement which, at least in the beginning, has been ignored by the state and by the constitutional parties.

3. The organizational and programmatic level of the terrorist groups, on a national scale, cannot be overlooked. From military-style armed bands, a full-fledged "communist fighting party" has developed. This is a permanent structure, gifted with political imagination, and capable of self-preservation and expansion, independent from staging terrorist actions. This qualitative change, leading to a party formation, is extremely relevant since it gives to terrorism a much stronger and more effective political capability. Paradoxically, it decreases the need for terrorists to assert themselves through violence and murder. In other words, the

"armed party" is no longer compelled to kill and can now engage in negotiations and in dialectic differentiation of actions.

4. The unidirectionality of the countermeasures by the state and by its institutions has, so far, proved itself to be only partially effective at a military-control level, but has been deficient at the dialectical and political-social levels. The terrorists have shown a considerable ability to profit from mistakes and weaknesses of the system, deploying on short notice professional utilization of a range of techniques, from mass media to electronics, while the state has often overlooked and left unexploited weaknesses and mistakes by the terrorists.

CONCLUSIONS

A concluding remark is in order: Italian terrorism is a complex, lively, specific reality and its menace still weighs heavily on the future of the country. The "fantasy war" can be won by democracy, but only if the state chooses to give battle on the terrain where it is stronger—the terrain of democracy, freedom, popular participation, welfare, and reason. Reason normally overcomes unreason; but, if it grows careless, monsters are generated. Aggressiveness being learned, it can be unlearned, but not through overcontrol and counterviolence.

REFERENCES

Bonanate, L., Marletti, C., Migliorino, C., and others (Eds.) *Dimensioni del terrorismo politico*. Milan: Angeli, 1979.

Calvi, G. *Analisi dei valori e dei comportamenti giovanili*, Report to the Italian Sociology Meeting, Florence, 1980, *in press*.

Campbell, D. T., & Stanley, J. C. Experimental and quasi-experimental designs for research on teaching. In N. L. Gage (Ed.), *Handbook of research on teaching*. Chicago: Rand McNally, 1963.

Dollard, J., Doob, L. W., Miller, N. E., Mowrer, O. H., & Sears, R. R. *Frustrazione ed aggressività*. Florence: Giunti e Barbera, 1967.

Ferracuti, F., & Bruno, F. Psychiatric aspects of terrorism in Italy. In I. L. Barak-Glantz and C. R. Huff (Eds.), *The mad, the bad and the different*. Lexington, Mass.: Lexington Books, 1981.

Fornari, F. *Psicoanalisi della guerra*. Milan: Feltrinelli, 1966.

Fromm, E. *L'anatomia della distruttività umana*. Milan: Mondadori, 1975.

Galleni, M. (Ed.) *Rapporto sul terrorismo*. Milan: Rozzoli, 1981.

Heller, A. *Instinto e aggressività. Introduzione a un'antropologia sociale marxista*. Milan: Feltrinelli, 1978.

Kupperman, R., & Treat, R. *Terrorism*. Palo Alto, Calif.: The Hoover Institute, 1979.

Lorenz, K. *L'aggressività*. Milan: Il Saggiatore, 1969.

Pontana, G. Violenza e terrorismo, il problema della definizione e della giustificazione. In L. Bonanate (Ed.), *Dimensioni del terrorismo politico*. Milan: Franco Angeli, 1979.

Salert, B. *Revolution and revolutionaries*. New York: Elsevier, 1976.

Wolfgang, M. E., & Ferracuti, F. *The subculture of violence*. London: Tavistock, 1967.

13

Japan: Aggression and Aggression Control in Japanese Society*

Susan B. Goldstein
and
Toshio Ibaraki

INTRODUCTION

Almost all forms of verbal and physical aggression are strongly discouraged in Japan. Several forms of aggression control, especially familial and social pressure, as well as the system of law enforcement and criminal justice systems have been extremely successful in Japan, and the Japanese people today enjoy living in a country with one of the lowest crime rates in the world. Japan is one of the few industrialized nations where the crime rate is not only extraordinarily low, but for many crimes it is actually decreasing.

In 1980 in Tokyo, a city with a population of over 11 million, there was not one killing in the streets, parks, or subways, and only a single case of murder connected with a breaking and entering. Both men and women can travel alone at any time of day or night with relatively little fear of being attacked by a stranger. Crimes involving property are also comparatively few. The fact that one is 225 times less likely to be robbed in Japan than in the United States is evident in the thousands of commuters' bicycles left unlocked at city train stations, the many grocery bags in unattended privately-owned carts outside of supermarkets, and the virtual absence of burglar alarm systems in cars, stores, and private homes.

This atmosphere of personal safety is especially surprising in view of Japan's violent history, including warfare among Tokugawa feudal states, the extermination of Christians in the 1600s, the political assassinations of the 1930s, and the record of notoriously brutal behavior of many Japanese soldiers toward prisoners of war and civilian populations of occupied territories during World War II.

One might also speculate that the common practice of social drinking among Japanese men, as well as the uncensored violence depicted by the Japanese mass media (such as in the battles of the warrior television serials and movies, and the graphic depictions of sexually-ori-

*We wish to acknowledge, with appreciation, the assistance of Shotaro Kosugi, Hisao Osada, John Alex McKenzie, Michibo Kazuno, and Edward Norbeck.

ented violence toward women in so called "sports newspapers") would be related to a high number of aggressive incidents. It is unlikely that historical factors, drinking practices, and violence in the media are unrelated to aggression, but probable that the aggression controls inherent in Japanese society are so powerful that they greatly diminish the level of overt aggressive behavior. We shall now turn to a brief examination of those controls.

AGGRESSION CONTROL AND COOPERATION IN JAPANESE SOCIETY

Demographic factors, ecological and environmental factors, norms of socialization and of familial relations, and also practices of employment seem to have an important influence on the control of aggression in Japanese society. As we shall see, these factors have all helped to foster cooperative rather than individually assertive behavior and the repressing, rather than expressing, of aggressive tendencies.

Demographic Factors

Few countries today are as homogeneous as Japan. According to Edwin O. Reischauer (1977), "As early as the seventh century, [the Japanese] saw themselves as a single people, living in a united nation. This has always remained the ideal, despite long centuries of feudal divisions [p. 8]." The main exception to this homogeneity among native Japanese is the *burakumin* (or *Eta*), an outcaste group which comprises only about 2 percent of the population and which first became differentiated during early feudal times. According to Harumi Befu (1971),

> It is probable that among their original occupations more than a thousand years ago were such activities as dealing with the care of dead human and animal bodies, slaughtering animals, and guarding grave yards, and that this had something to do with placing them in a polluted status. [p. 107]

Of the approximately 117 million people in Japan, foreigners make up less than 1 percent of the population. The feeling of unity among the Japanese may be seen in the fact that foreigners, including long-term residents and people of foreign ancestry born in Japan, are categorized as *gaijin* or "outsiders." Of the various types of foreigners in Japan, the 600,000 Japanese of Korean ancestry are the main group that is the victim of discriminatory practices and occasional violence by Japanese citizens of Japanese decent.

Ecological and Environmental Factors

The importance in Japan of cooperation extending beyond groups of kin may well have much of its basis in the innovation of wet rice cultivation, about 200-300 B.C. The geography of Japan, with its small marshes, lakes, and streams, necessitated the use of complex irrigation systems by which many farms derive their water from common sources. In times of water shortage or surplus, as well as during the repair and cleaning of irrigation systems, cooperation is essential. Although technical innovations have weakened the solidarity of "irrigation cooperatives" (Befu, 1971), these associations still constitute an important part of the Japanese agricultural system.

Because Japan is a group of islands where fish is the main source of animal protein, it may also be important to consider the possible role fishing has played in the shaping of Japanese society. According to Befu (1971) "Just as there are ecological bases to unite farmers, there are ecological reasons for fisherman to cooperate [p. 73]." In addition to the fact that the seashore of a given village is communally owned, cooperation also comes into play in the fishing process itself. Deep-sea fishing requires a closely coordinated crew as does net fishing.

Another relevant feature of the Japanese environment is the relative frequency and the severity of natural disasters. Typhoons, which hit every year during late summer or early fall, are particularly destructive, but devastating earthquakes and even volcanic eruptions are also sprinkled throughout the historical records. Over the years, Japanese people have reacted to such catastrophes with what Reischauer (1977) calls the "typhoon mentality." Natural disasters and the repair of their destruction are accepted as a part of living. Survival from these catastrophes would be impossible if not for the ability of the Japanese people to mobilize the resources of the community during troubled times, a cooperative undertaking.

In addition to the agricultural and other natural disasters of Japan, a third environmental factor influencing cooperation may be its population density. Although the islands of Japan have an area of about 143,000 sq. miles, they are extremely mountainous with relatively little habitable land. The result is a population density of approximately 785 people per square mile (American Chamber of Commerce in Japan). Families live in small quarters, by American and European standards, and, except in the rural areas, there is little space between houses. Stores and public buildings are also comparatively more crowded as are the infamously congested trains and subways throughout Japan. Aggressive outbursts are seen to be maladaptive to living and working in close quarters and are kept at a minimum.

Another environmental factor is the lack of natural resources in Japan. Water is the only natural resource in abundance and, thus, reliance on international trade is unavoidable. This dependence on imports seems to have important implications relating to the reluctance of Japan in recent decades to become involved in aggressive acts or statements on an international level. Thus it seems reasonable to think that Japan's ecology and environment have strongly influenced the development of cooperative practices and the suppression of aggressive behavior among the Japanese people.

Socialization and Familial Factors

One of the most important factors in the control of aggression in Japanese society appears to be child rearing. According to Befu (1971),

> A consistent patterning of emotion develops, not simply because of a certain feeding practice or a specific weaning method, but through an accumulation of a large number of behavior patterns in which parents relate themselves to their children and which taken together tend to produce a clearly recognizable mode of handling emotion. [pp. 151-152]

Infancy is marked by physical restriction and contact with the mother. Reischauer (1977) has observed that "the Japanese child is nursed for a relatively long period, is fed more at will, is constantly fondled by its mother, in more traditional society is carried around on her back when she goes out, and sleeps with its parents until quite large [p. 140]." There are few physical or verbal reprimands from the mother, who is more apt to elicit proper behavior by cajoling the child with sweets or toys or by making the child feel ashamed of his or her behavior. She may even ask a teacher to reprimand her child rather than create any animosity between herself and her son or daughter. The father may be more apt to act in an authoritarian manner than the mother, but the image of the father as the tyrant of his home is more a vestige of prewar days than a realistic representation of present conditions. Most fathers are out of the home for six days of the week, working or socializing, during their children's waking hours. Sundays are most often used as a time for fathers to play with their children, rather than for any disciplinary actions. The results of a Japanese upbringing, then, would seem to be that the child grows to be eager to act in accordance with the parents' wishes and often feels insecure going against them or exercising individual will. According to Befu (1971):

> One sees in Japanese child-rearing practices the consistent avoidance of outright and severe punishment as a method of discipline . . . [punishment which if used would have] the effect of removing some of the positive affect from parents and of making them into potential sources of anxiety. As a result, Japanese children, much more than American children, tend to associate positive affects with their parents and seek and find emotional security in them. [pp. 158-159]

Furthermore, the child comes to feel a strong sense of responsibility, not only for his or her own behavior, but for how this behavior reflects on the family. This type of thinking is reinforced by Japanese society which tends to stress the achievements and failures of one's relatives when judging the individual. This sense of responsibility is deepened by a strong feeling of indebtedness (on) to one's parents. Feelings of responsibility and on would seem to have major implications for the degree and nature of expressions of aggression. An aggressive act may be far less likely to be committed if it brings shame and guilt to the individual for betraying one's responsibility to the family and one's indebtedness to one's parents.

Employment

Just as feelings of loyalty and indebtedness to one's family members inhibits behavior that would reflect on them badly, analogous feelings for one's firm of employment make it very difficult to act in ways possibly damaging to its reputation or causing disharmony among fellow workers. The Japanese employee, whether construction worker, doctor, or elementary school teacher, works within a system based on the combination of hierarchy and consensus. Individual disruption of this system through either legitimate or illegitimate means is seen as not only a lack of devotion to one's job but as evidence of selfish motives. A great many factors inherent in the Japanese employment system serve to discourage antisocial behavior or acts not in accordance with the policy of the employer. This is accomplished by making the employer central to the employee's life as well as by practices that facilitate solidarity among workers.

Let us look in greater detail at a Japanese company. One enters it after passing a battery of interviews and entrance exams and begins an intensive training period. This "training" may emphasize to a greater degree the building of emotional ties than it does the gaining of technical familiarity with one's job. Employees, married or single, are often housed in company dormitories during the training period. Japanologist Ezra Vogel (1979) describes this period in American terms as being ". . . perhaps like a combination of the behavior of the fraternity pledge, without the hazing, and the young doctor in residency training [p. 146]."

Many Japanese companies begin their day with a gathering of all employees to recite the company motto or sing the company song. Ceremonies and parties are an important part of company life. Employees may also go on trips or retreats together. Companies often have special housing available for employees and their families and many even offer home loans or mortgages. Companies often sponsor sports activities, clubs, or courses of instruction in various subjects for family members of employees. It is especially interesting to note that labor unions are organized within single companies, across vocations, rather than by vocation across companies. The intricate weaving of work life with home and social life makes it extremely difficult and unpleasant for an employee to think of behavior in a disruptive manner in any sphere of action.

Thus it would seem that demographic and environmental factors, socialization methods and familial factors as well as the employment system, have an important influence on the control of aggression in Japanese society. Both the homogeneity of the Japanese population and the necessity for cooperation imposed by environmental circumstances seem to have facilitated and formed a basis for cooperative and low-conflict interpersonal relations. This tendency toward group efforts is further enhanced by the sense of loyalty and indebtedness one develops toward one's family as a child and toward one's employer as an adult. We shall now turn to a more detailed examination of the frequency and expression of aggressive and criminal acts in Japan today.

FREQUENCY AND EXPRESSION
OF AGGRESSIVE BEHAVIOR

An overview of criminally aggressive behavior in Japan from 1966 to 1979 (fig. 13.1) shows that crime rates have decreased or remained relatively stable among adults, whereas the number of young offenders (under 20 years of age) has steadily increased. Juvenile crimes jumped from 23 percent of all crimes recorded in 1976 to 42 percent in 1980. This increase has mainly occurred in the categories of theft; assault and battery; extortion; rape; arson; and intrafamily, intraschool, and motorcycle gang violence. It is now useful to examine a breakdown of frequencies for specific criminal acts.

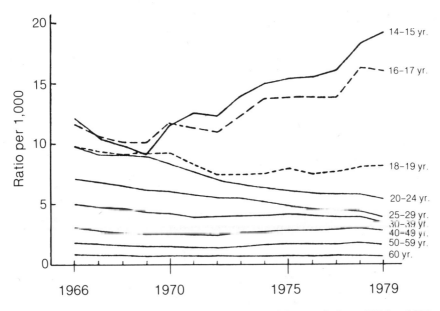

Fig. 13.1. The Change of the Number of Arrested Criminals from 1966 to 1979

Source: Statistics of the National Police Agency and "the Estimated Population of Japan" by the Bureau of Statistics of the Prime Minister's Office.

Assault

In official Japanese crime statistics, the term "assault" (*boko*) is equivalent to the English legal phrase, "assault and battery" and thus includes not only actual injury, but also verbal abuse such as threats and blackmail, and the assembling of weapons. The rate of assault increased from 1966 until 1973 (6.47 percent) but has slowly decreased since to a rate of 3.25 percent in 1980. This trend applies to juveniles as well as adults.

The rate of assault by females is relatively low but has increased gradually, most likely reflecting changed social restrictions on the behavior of women. Assaults by females seem to differ from assaults by males with regard to their motives. Assaults by females most often relate to interpersonal or familial relations, but assaults by males are usually reactions to perceived provocations while under the influence of alcohol.

Rape

Rape in Japan has decreased from 4,052 cases in 1975 to 2,876 in 1978 and 2,757 in 1979. Fifty-seven percent of the total number of reported rapes are group-instigated and, of these, 75 percent were committed by juveniles. These statistics, however, are grossly misleading since rapes are rarely reported in Japan. A recent informal survey* conducted by women found that 90 percent of all women interviewed said they would not report to the police if they had been raped. The most common reasons given were that reporting the rape would embarrass the victim and her family and that the apprehension of the rapist would be no consolation to the victim. Most youths arrested for rape are already known to the police for having committed theft, larceny, extortion, or crimes of violence other than rape.

Murder

As may be seen in table 13.1, the overall incidence of murder has decreased steadily between the years 1975 and 1979. The rate of murders committed by minors when taken separately, however, does not show this decreasing trend. It is noteworthy that only 11.7 percent of accused murderers were strangers to their victims. The majority of murders seem to occur within the family group. (See figure 13.2 which is based on a study in which "Family" was defined as all the members of a household, which, in Japan, often includes members of one's extended family.) According to Masataka Imaizumi (*N.Y. Times,* 1/17/81), Tokyo's chief of police, "Just

Table 13.1. The Occurrence of Murder in Japan

YEAR	NUMBER	INDEX
1975	2,098	100
1976	2,111	101
1977	2,031	97
1978	1,862	89
1979	1,853	88

Source: The Police White Paper, 1980.

*The authors wish to express their appreciation to Mr. Kunio Yamada for organizing and overseeing this survey.

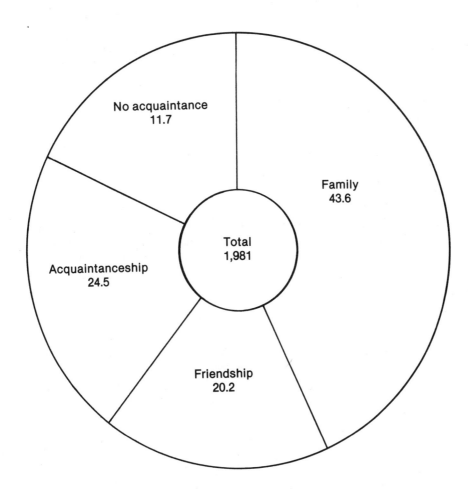

Fig. 13.2. The Offender-Victim Relationships of Murder

killing someone you have no connection with is extraordinarily rare. There were 180 murders here last year, but they involved relatives, quarrels in the family, that kind of thing." Imaizumi goes on to say that one reason for the rarity of murder in Japan is that murderers are usually apprehended. During 1980, 93 percent of murder cases were solved.

Intrafamily Violence

As Table 13.2 indicates, almost 50 percent of the victims of intrafamily violence (which includes both physical and verbal abuse) were mothers, and the perpetrators were males. This is not surprising in view of, (1) the relatively low status of the Japanese wives in relation to their husbands and the females with reference to males, and (2) the role of the mother with regard

Table 13.2. The Victims of Intrafamily Violence

VICTIMS	MALE NUMBER (%)		FEMALE NUMBER (%)		TOTAL NUMBER (%)	
Mother	725	(84.6)	168	(86.6)	893	(85.0)
Father	214	(25.0)	34	(17.5)	248	(23.6)
Grandmother	65	(7.6)	11	(5.6)	76	(7.2)
Smaller sister	62	(7.2)	9	(4.6)	71	(6.8)
Smaller brother	55	(6.4)	11	(5.6)	66	(6.3)
Elder sister	28	(3.2)	8	(4.1)	36	(3.4)
Other family members	21	(2.4)	6	(3.1)	27	(2.6)
Grandfather	21	(2.4)	5	(2.6)	26	(2.5)
Elder brother	13	(1.5)	0	(0)	13	(1.2)

Source: Statistics of the National Policy Agency, 1980.

to the education of her children. Many Japanese mothers feel responsible for the academic success or failure of their children and through constantly pushing their children to study, may become the target of expression of the children's frustration. Table 13.3 shows that most of the offenders in the category of intrafamily violence are 14 to 17 years of age, that is, junior high and high school students. According to Dr. Masahiko Otsuka, who served on the Tokyo Family Court for 30 years,

> From morning to night, the child is face to face with the mother and forced to study. The father works outside, comes home tired and doesn't involve himself much in family affairs. The mother thinks she must play both roles—putting twice as much pressure on the child in the belief that he will fail otherwise. . . . If he fails a test he thinks his mother is responsible for his failure. [*Honolulu Advertiser*, 4/11/81]

Table 13.3. Ages of Intrafamily Violence Offenders

AGE	MALE NUMBER (%)		FEMALE NUMBER (%)		TOTAL NUMBER (%)	
below 10	20	(2.3)	5	(2.6)	25	(2.4)
11	13	(1.5)	4	(2.1)	17	(1.6)
12	30	(3.5)	6	(3.1)	36	(3.4)
13	81	(9.4)	24	(12.4)	105	(10.0)
14	131	(15.2)	31	(15.9)	162	(15.4)
15	167	(19.5)	34	(17.5)	201	(19.1)
16	167	(19.5)	45	(23.2)	212	(20.2)
17	145	(17.2)	29	(14.9)	174	(16.6)
18	66	(7.7)	13	(6.7)	79	(7.5)
19	28	(3.2)	2	(1.0)	30	(2.8)
20	9	(1.0)	1	(0.5)	10	(1.0)
Total	857	(100.0)	194	(100.0)	1,051	(100.0)

Source: Statistics of the National Police Agency, 1980.

The offending youths usually lack a sense of guilt. Instead, they see themselves as the true victims in the family. They are often perfectionists, meticulous, worrisome, persistent, obsessive, egotistic, and dependent. Their mothers are overexpectant, overprotective, and doting toward their children. Their fathers, in contrast, often fail to show a sense of authority and are permissive.

With regard to the category of battered wives, concrete data are scarce and probably highly inaccurate. To report such an incident would bring shame upon the abused woman and her family. Shelters or services to help such women are almost nonexistent. The situation is similar for abused children. However, if the existence of an abusing parent is known, neighbors or family members would be somewhat more likely to intervene in order to protect the child than in the case of the battered wife. It is exceedingly rare that the police or other authorities would be called in either of these instances.

Intraschool Violence

Intraschool violence has recently gained much attention in the Japanese news media. Such violence consists of aggressive acts of students toward each other, toward teachers and administrators, and vandalism of school property. The fact that this kind of violence is increasing, as well as its reprehensible nature, have greatly alarmed the Japanese people. Although the incidence of intraschool violence remains considerably lower than in various other countries, assaults on teachers are up 70 percent and incidents of violence in schools as a whole have tripled since 1970 (Newsweek, 4/20/81, p. 40; and Honolulu Advertiser, 4/11/81). A recent survey conducted by the Kyodo News Service found an even higher rate of school violence in the records of the regional educational boards than was reported by the National Police Agency, which until recently had been regarded as authoritative. The Japanese educational boards reported a total of 3,645 incidents of violence at the junior and senior high school levels for the 1980 academic year, as compared with the 1,558 cases reported by the National Police Agency. According to social psychiatrist, Dr. Hiroshi Inamura (Honolulu Advertiser, 4/11/81), most of the disturbances involve groups. In one incident in Kanagawa prefecture, 18 students thrashed a teacher with bamboo swords (Japan Times, 5/1/81); in another, a group of 10th graders burned with a cigarette lighter the legs of a student suspected of informing to school authorities (Newsweek, 4/20/81). Often, violence is used as a means of revenge toward teachers at graduation time.

Statistics show no correlation between poverty and school violence; that is, the perpetrators are not poverty stricken. The Education Ministry attributes this new wave of intraschool violence to "parental indifference and the lack of unity among teachers." Others tie it to the pressures of the Japanese education system. Competition for good jobs is fierce in Japan, and gaining desirable employment is contingent upon the reputation of one's school. Admission to higher educational levels is almost entirely decided on the basis of entrance examination scores. Since the chances of getting into one of Japan's 34 most prestigious universities is only one in six, training for these entrance examinations begins early—sometimes as early as kindergarten. Many students spend all their free time and vacations preparing for the grueling high school and college entrance exams. Often, children will go to special cramming schools (juku) after regular school hours are over. Students who cannot keep up with the high pace of in-class and juku exam preparation drop out, if not physically, then psychologically. This phenomenon has been said to be the cause of suicide (approximately 800 Japanese students ages 5 to 19 committed suicide during the year 1978), the high incidence of stomach ulcers among Japanese school children, familial violence, and also may be the root of Japan's recent increase in intraschool violence.

Motorcycle Gang Violence

According to the National Police Agency, in 1979 there were 472 motorcycle gangs (*bosozo-ku*) in Japan. Of the total of 12,183 members, 77.6 percent were teenagers with full-time employment or high school students, both engaging in their frenetic change of pace on weekends only. Although most of their time is spent demonstrating their driving techniques and knowledge of the motorcycle, these gangs have committed crimes which range from damage to property to assault and murder.

Arson

Although arson accounts for less than 1 percent of all crime in Japan, it is seen as one of the most serious crimes and was punished by death during the Tokugawa era. Most Japanese homes, even today, are composed mainly of wood and paper, and a fire in one building could easily destroy an entire neighborhood. The incidence of arson in Japan has increased slowly since 1979.

Organized Crime

Organized crime in Japan is generally referred to by the term *yakuza*. According to Takie Lebra (1976),

> Most Japanese regard the *"yakuza"* as deviant and strongly disprove or fear any involvement with them. Nonetheless, some aspects of *"yakuza"* behavior are considered beautiful and morally valid and are still glorified in popular literature and films despite the strenuous police effort to exterminate *"yakuza"* organizations. [p. 170]

Although the term *yakuza* has been used in a general sense to describe the members of violent or criminal groups, Lebra goes on to state that "In the narrow sense of the word, however, *'yakuza'* refers to gamblers alone, and 'real' *'yakuza,'* in their pride and with regard for their honor, despise *'gurentai'* [violent gangs] and exclude them from the *'yakuza'* category [p. 170]."

Yakuza groups are secret organizations based on a system very much like that of the traditional Japanese household, with regard to hierarchical structure and obedience to superiors. In spite of large-scale imprisonments of *yakuza* group members, they are still the perpetrators of a significant portion of the crimes committed in Japan.

LAWS AND LAW ENFORCEMENT

One of the main reasons for Japan's low crime rate is the great efficiency with which the officers of the National Police Agency operate. As with murderers, the rate of apprehension of perpetrators of other crimes is much higher. Vogel (1979) points out that, because there are fewer crimes per person, more police can be assigned to a single case. To become a police officer, one must pass difficult entrance exams and meet strict requirements. The approximate length of training is one year in Japan, as compared to 8 weeks in the United States (Bayley, 1976). Codes of police behavior are strictly enforced, and few police are found violating them. Rather than operating solely from police stations, many Japanese officers work out of neighborhood police boxes (*koban*). People in the area always know where a police officer may be found should any trouble occur. Police travel by bicycle or on foot, making special efforts to become familiar with the residents and the goings on in their precincts in order to become aware of events which might lead to trouble. An officer from the *koban* tries to visit each resident in his/her area at least twice each year. In this way, relevant questions may be asked as a matter of routine without arousing feelings of resentment or suspicion. Most communities also have a Citizens' Crime Prevention Association which works closely with the local police. As a result of the existence of this police network in combination with the familiarity of citizens with their local police, most crimes are reported and dealt with quickly and efficiently. The National Police Agency also has a number of units of riot police (*kidotai*). These police have been used in controlling the violence which resulted from such events as the student takeover of Tokyo University in 1968 and the protests which have revolved around the construction of Narita Airport in recent years. The *kidotai* receive special training and are taught to avoid the use of force. According to Vogel (1979), "The essence of the strategy of riot police is to minimize the danger of injury, gain the support of the public, and reduce the threat posed by the resistors [p. 219]."

As Vogel explains, there are few loopholes in the Japanese legal system that would hinder the investigation or processing of criminal cases. There is no parallel in Japan to the American system whereby suspects may talk through their lawyers. Japanese people are more likely to settle disputes of any nature through means other than legal proceedings. Police are not restricted by the courts and would not hesitate to give informal warnings or to seek out information from friends or neighbors of suspects or victims.

Another factor which greatly aids the police in the control of crime in Japan is strict gun control and drug legislation. Pistols may be manufactured and sold to law enforcement officers only. In order to buy firearms for sport or marksmanship competition, one must go through complicated registration procedures. Japanese police estimate that there are now 50 pistols legally owned by private citizens. This may be compared to the more than 50 million privately owned handguns in America. The sentence for anyone found with an illegal handgun is 10 years or a stiff fine or both. In 1979, there were 10,715 homicides committed with handguns in the United States while there were only 48 in Japan.

The control of violent crimes in Japan is also facilitated by the virtual absence of drug abuse. Sentences for those found guilty of possession of illegal drugs are extremely severe, and most of the drug trafficking that does occur involves organized crime gangs.

In recent years, Japan, as a nation, has had a policy of nonviolence. An article in the new constitution "renounced war forever and the maintenance of any war potential." Japan has no armed forces except the Self Defense Force, which was founded in 1954 and now has approximately 277,000 members.

CONCLUSION

The low rate of criminal and aggressive acts in Japan would seem to be a function of a combination of different factors. First, the homogeneity of the Japanese people and, thus, the lack of cultural and linguistic differences facilitates conflict-free interpersonal relations. Second, persons who behave in nonaggressive ways receive the greatest material and social reinforcement. This phenomenon is most likely a product of the importance of groupism and consensus throughout Japanese society. In comparison with the Western proverb: "The squeaky wheel gets the oil," the Japanese have the saying: "The nail that sticks up gets hit."

When aggressive acts do occur in Japan, they appear to have certain patterns. One of these is aggression between groups due to Japanese values of loyalty and groupism. These values may be clearly seen in customs and ideals of appropriate behavior in the family, in the place of employment, and in the nation as a whole. Examples of intergroup aggression stemming from such loyalty and cohesion are violence between motorcycle gangs and violence between two schools or groups of students or between students and teachers. It may not be going too far to say the actions of Japan during World War II fit this same pattern of intergroup aggression with the aggressive group consisting of the entire Japanese people.

A second pattern of aggression seems to be intragroup violence stemming from a major conflict between one's sense of social obligation (*giri*) and one's personal feelings (*ninjo*). This type of aggression would be best represented by intrafamily violence in Japan, such as a son assaulting his mother who he feels is putting too much pressure on him to study, or a woman who kills an illegitimate child in order to be considered an eligible marriage partner.

This theme of inter- and intragroup violence may not encompass all types of aggression in Japan, but may serve as a useful model by which to examine a number of types of aggressive actions.

REFERENCES

Bayley, D. H. *Forces of order: Police behavior in Japan and the United States.* Berkeley, Calif.: University of California Press, 1976.

Befu, H. *Japan: An anthropological introduction.* Tokyo, Japan: Charles E. Tuttle, 1971.

Lebra, T. S. *Japanese patterns of behavior.* Honolulu, Hawaii: University Press of Hawaii, 1976.

Reischauer, E. O. *The Japanese.* Cambridge, Mass.: Belknap Press, 1977.

Vogel, E. F. *Japan as number one.* Tokyo, Japan: Charles E. Tuttle, 1979.

14

New Zealand: Developmental and Social Antecedents and Concomitants of Aggression

James Ritchie

and

Jane Ritchie

A woman with small children is half way across a busy intersection when the older child pulls back toward the curb they have just left. Without hesitation the mother pushes the younger child toward the curb ahead and delivers two heavy open-handed blows to the backside of the other who cries loudly while she drags him by the shoulder to the other side of the road.

A game of rugby football is in progress. To stop a driving rush in which eight players in a flying wedge take stabbing kicks at the ball, a frontline defensive player falls down on the ball to retain possession of it. He is overrun by the attackers who, gathering round in what is termed a "ruck," heads down, arms around each others' buttocks, attempt with their sprigged boots to take the ball from his grasp. He receives a concussion, two broken ribs, multiple bruising, and lacerations.

A three-year-old child, living alone with her grandfather, is brought to the hospital because of old scar tissue and recent burns over the entire surface of one hand. Grandfather held the hand of the screaming child over a gas flame to punish her for disobedience.

When she became pregnant with her fifth, her husband walked out, blaming and leaving her. The psychiatrist to whom she was referred when she wanted an abortion refused her plea. By then her pregnancy was too far gone to pursue that alternative further. Her husband returned and demanded sexual access, she refused; he beat her, raped her, and broke two of her ribs. Though she escaped to a women's refuge, two years later he was still harassing her.

Confronted with an embarrassing question, repeated and pushed home by a resourceful TV interviewer, a senior politician refuses to answer the question, verbally attacks the frontman for asking it, and tells the network that he will not be interviewed by that reporter again. The network relegates the interviewer to the children's programmes.

A Polynesian ethnic protest group, having repeatedly asked that a group of students desist from imitating Maori posture dances in crude and obscene lampoon style, during graduation festivities, finally attacks the offending students with fists, chains, and lengths of timber. Three students required hospital attention.

It is 9:45 p.m. and in the big room at the tavern, proudly publicised as covering half an acre, more than four hundred men and a few women are gathered in varying degrees of intoxication—but many fairly well on. Shortly, the bar will close and all will be disgorged into the crowded car park, many clutching six-packs or several quart bottles of beer. Everyone knows that this is the dangerous hour, certainly on the roads outside but also inside the vast drinking arena where uniformed bouncers and security men are becoming watchful and tense. In the crowd, a man carrying two jugs of beer brushes by the poised billiard cue of a man drunkenly trying to focus on the ball. A fist flies, beer splashes over a circle of people, a mini brawl erupts, and the bouncers and police move in.

THE SOCIAL BACKGROUND

While wife beating, child abuse, or any of these examples occur everywhere, it will be our task in this chapter to try to identify what is distinctive about aggression in this small, largely white, comparatively affluent, capitalist, export-dependent, postcolonial Western democracy— New Zealand.

Historical Background

Unlike such social melting pot countries as Canada, the United States, or Australia, the white people in New Zealand were either born here (in which case their ancestors predominantly came from the British Isles), or have emigrated directly from there. Tiny numbers have come from other European countries, notably Holland, Yugoslavia, Greene, and Central Europe. But the predominant culture is overwhelmingly Anglo-Saxon.

When white settlers arrived in the mid-nineteenth century, there were at least 250,000 native Polynesians, Maoris, living here, but through war, disease, and demoralisation, two out of three were wiped out by the turn of the century. At the present time, there are again about 250,000 New Zealanders who identify themselves as Maori and many more with some Maori blood. There are also close to 100,000 Pacific Island immigrants and their New Zealand-born descendants and a tiny proportion of Asians.

The pattern of ethnic relations is profoundly based on two features; Maori people were here first and they never lost their essential culture and the pride that flows from it. This is an important difference from the ethnic situation in either the United Kingdom or the United States.

As we discuss patterns of aggression in New Zealand, we will refer to cultural influences. Both authors are developmental and ethnopsychologists so that our approach will be not only descriptive but also concerned with the transmission of culture patterns. We will also discuss conflicts which generate aggression.

Statistical Background

In terms of the statistics of violence, New Zealanders display the same range of phenomena as any other Western industrial society (except extreme phenomena such as political terrorism, riots, and assassination). In the ways they bring up children, New Zealand parents try to control aggression in their children by means of aggressive acts because they rely on physical punishment as a general mechanism of child training. Behind these social, family, and personal phenomena lie two general cultural themes: an ideology of violence (which is a rationalisation for acting aggressively), and a general denial of the part that aggression plays in our personal and social lives. New Zealanders want other people to believe, and themselves want to believe, that they are peaceable, gentle, easy-going, pragmatic, phlegmatic, and not especially aggressive. This description does not fit the facts as we will present them in this chapter, and so a pattern of denial exists as well. We will now discuss the incidence of individual forms of the expression of aggression as seen in social statistics. These might form a functional kind of definition of the expression of aggression in New Zealand.

Violent Crime

What is the reported incidence of violent crime against the person? Table 14.1 lists all violent offenders appearing before the courts in New Zealand for the years 1967-1976. The first obvious and crucial finding is that common assault accounts for a very high proportion of the total, around 80 to 85 percent. Assault is defined in the Crimes Act (1961) as:

> The act of intentionally applying or attempting to apply force to the person of another, directly or indirectly, or threatening by any act or gesture to apply such force to the person of another, if the person making the threat has, or causes the other to believe on reasonable grounds that he has, present ability to effect his purpose; and "to assault" has a corresponding meaning.

Though from 1967 there is a progressive increase in violent offences as a ratio of total population, it is notoriously difficult to interpret such changes. We do not know, for example, how many detected cases of violence fail to result in either arrest or court proceedings. It is a well known feature of such statistics that they correlate most highly with the number of people in the police force (Nixon, 1974). In New Zealand there are 4,961 police, or approximately 600 per 100,000 population.

Table 14.1 show that heavy violence (murder, attempted murder, manslaughter, and infanticide) has generally increased. In the other categories, in spite of fluctuations, there is the same general trend, but hardly sufficiently dramatic to start one hunting for specific causes. With the exception of common assault, and actions which kill people, either more violent of-

Table 14.1. Violent Cases, All Courts

	1967	1968	1969	1970	1971	1972	1973	1974	1975	1976
Murder	3	4	2	7	5	2	9	5	8	13
Attempted Murder	4	2	3	1	3	3	0	3	2	1
Infanticide	1	2	2	0	0	0	1	2	2	2
Manslaughter	11	4	9	6	6	12	10	17	15	26
Causing Injury, etc.	1	4	1	4	7	9	3	12	12	10
Wounding with Intent	31	45	49	63	65	122	133	173	150	265
Aggravated Assault	39	58	47	62	77	65	121	107	177	144
Assault on Child	176	126	150	177	186	142	180	198	288	305
Common Assault	1,961	2,280	2,327	2,638	3,200	3,441	3,845	3,734	3,686	3,495
Robbery	28	63	65	61	110	140	98	103	91	91
Aggravated Robbery	16	16	15	19	17	49	41	36	64	74
Rape	12	18	11	20	20	22	31	42	38	40
Attempted Rape	21	11	15	6	13	12	18	23	13	21
Totals	2,304	2,633	2,696	3,064	3,709	4,019	4,490	4,455	4,546	4,457
Rate per 100,000 total population	83.9	95.0	96.1	107.4	137.0	135.7	148.33	144.0	144.2	141.3

fending is coming to the notice of the authorities (and thus the pattern is becoming more public and obvious) or there is actually more of it. Whichever may be the case, these data are sufficiently stable for us to have confidence that they arise from a general cultural pattern.

As in most other places, the statistics of offence are highest for the age groups under thirty. Serious violence, with the exception of murder, is almost exclusively committed by young males so that, with the entry of the post World War II birth increase into this age group, a surge of offending may have occurred. It will be interesting to see if rates decline for the years following the lower birthrate due to oral contraception, but this information is not yet available.

The Secretary for Justice (1978) reports that:

> Of all those persons arrested and subsequently convicted in the Magistrate's [lower] court for assault . . . nearly half of those arrested and classified as New Zealanders are Maori which is over six times the number one could expect in terms of their proportion in the total population aged fifteen years or over. [p. 10]

Similarly, 8 percent of the convictions were ethnic Pacific Islanders, four times the expected population rate (Table 14.2).

Rather than assume specific ethnic explanations for these figures one should note first the known association between recent urban migration, depressed urban living, and other lifestyle disturbances which particularly affect minority ethnic populations. The severity with which the courts treat young people from minorities is demonstrably greater (Acord, 1979), so these rates reflect both higher incidence and discriminatory visibility.

Domestic Violence. The extent of domestic violence is hard to judge since no specific statistics are kept by the Department of Justice and no research surveys have been undertaken here. The police department reports that home altercations occupy 10 percent of police time and, from the largest metropolitan city watchhouse in the country, statistics record that 60 percent of telephone calls to the police relate to domestic disputes. Unfortunately, we do not know who the participants in these disputes were since separate statistics for wife beating or other categories are not kept. However, the feminist and church organisations responsible for giving women refuge report a constant and growing demand for their services.

Child Abuse. The state of information concerning child abuse in New Zealand is summarised in the report of the symposium which undertook a national review of research and servicing (Geddis, 1980; J. E. Ritchie, 1980). The only extensive survey research, covering the year 1968, established a base rate of three cases per ten thousand children (Fergusson, Fleming, & O'Neill, 1972). This is about half the rate in Gil's national United States survey (1970). However, the research on which the New Zealand figure is based defined child abuse in a tight, medically-oriented way as that which comes to the attention of doctors, hospitals, or welfare agencies. At a conference of voluntary and state services concerned with the care of children, held in Auckland (the largest city, with some 1.4 million people in 1979), the likely figure for physical abuse was estimated to be four times that of the research study (Fergusson et al., 1972) or 12 per 10,000 children. Cohort studies already underway in New Zealand (Fergusson & Horwood, 1979; Geddis, 1978; Geddis, Monaghan, Muir, & Jones, 1979; Monaghan & Couper-Smartt, 1977; Silva, 1976) may ultimately yield information on both incidence and type of abuse and cover sexual abuse, neglect, and psychological cruelty as well. From the work of Geddis, it seems likely that one child in twenty faces a serious risk of being victimised in these ways, and in one family in ten there is reason for concern or remedial action.

Table 14.2. Birthplaces: Magistrates Courts Arrest Cases—Convictions for Assault Only

BIRTHPLACE	1970 NO.	1970 %	1971 NO.	1971 %	1972 NO.	1972 %	1973 NO.	1973 %	1974 NO.	1974 %	1975 NO.	1975 %	1976 NO.	1976 %
New Zealand														
Maori	1176	38.86	1373	40.50	1298	37.05	1712	39.97	1842	39.48	2090	39.32	2041	38.80
Non-Maori	1475	48.74	1552	45.78	1681	47.99	1959	45.74	2151	46.10	2455	46.18	2424	46.08
Australia	31	1.02	48	1.42	53	1.51	64	1.49	51	1.09	66	1.24	83	1.58
United Kingdom	123	4.06	150	4.42	139	3.97	148	3.46	165	3.54	157	2.95	151	2.87
Fiji	2	0.07	5	0.15	6	0.17	13	0.30	11	0.24	15	0.28	23	0.44
Western Samoa	85	2.81	105	3.10	138	3.94	187	4.37	196	4.20	225	4.23	258	4.90
Cook Islands	45	1.49	54	1.59	71	2.03	62	1.45	80	1.71	104	1.96	96	1.83
Niue Island	25	0.83	38	1.12	28	0.80	55	1.28	59	1.26	66	1.24	46	0.87
Tokelau Island	2	0.07	10	0.29	6	0.17	10	0.23	14	0.30	7	0.13	9	0.17
Tonga	1	0.03	7	0.21	10	0.29	24	0.56	33	0.71	62	1.17	53	1.01
Other	61	2.02	48	1.42	73	2.08	49	1.14	64	1.37	69	1.30	76	1.44
Totals:	3026	100.00	3390	100.00	3503	100.00	4283	100.00	4666	100.00	5316	100.00	5260	100.00

Note: In the 1971 Census, the total population of New Zealand 15 years of age and over was 1,953,008 of whom 1,794,289 (91.9%) were European and the remaining 158,719 (8.1%) were of non-European ethnic origin, a ratio of 11 : 1.

Table 14.3. Offence: Ethnic Group

OFFENCE	ETHNIC GROUP											
	MAORI		N.Z. POLYNESIAN		IMMIGRANT POLYNESIAN		PAKEHA N.Z. BORN		OTHER IMMIGRANT		TOTAL	
	M	F	M	F	M	F	M	F	M	F	M	F
PERSON												
Murder and Manslaughter	21	1	0	0	8	0	48	4	11	2	88	7
Serious Assault	104	11	2	0	14	0	112	10	13	0	245	21
Assault	354	19	8	1	29	1	428	26	28	2	847	49
Driving causing injury/death	10	0	0	0	2	0	24	0	5	0	41	0
Robbery	49	1	0	0	5	0	38	0	3	0	95	1
Homosexual	7	0	0	0	1	0	81	0	13	0	102	0
Other Sexual	126	3	0	0	16	0	240	1	31	0	413	4
Other Person	0	2	0	0	0	1	10	3	4	0	14	5
Total	671	37	10	1	75	2	981	44	108	4	1845	87
PROPERTY												
Robbery	42	10	1	0	1	0	42	1	3	0	89	11
Burglary	929	47	18	1	37	1	1224	43	125	4	2333	96
Theft as Servant	35	16	1	1	4	2	142	53	18	6	200	78
Theft	351	162	6	6	26	5	744	195	67	17	1194	385
Receiving	71	17	1	2	1	1	123	23	9	0	205	43
Fraud	94	38	2	0	7	2	298	62	47	7	448	109
Conversion	518	41	5	1	13	0	424	25	26	1	986	68
Willful Damage	45	7	2	0	0	1	118	7	3	0	168	15
Other Property	8	1	0	0	1	0	25	4	4	2	38	7
Total	2093	339	36	11	90	12	3140	413	302	37	5661	812

The detailed research on child abuse by Fergusson revealed nothing particularly idiosyncratic about the New Zealand pattern except in respect to ethnicity. Maori and Polynesian children are six times more likely to be physically abused than European children. Also, within this category there was a surprising frequency of assault on adolescent Maori girls by their fathers. We have elsewhere (Ritchie & Ritchie, 1979, 1981b) discussed the Polynesian background to child abuse and will return to some of these themes when we discuss physical punishment by parents later in this chapter.

Sexual Offences. One national retrospective study done by questionnaire in a popular women's magazine yields information on sexual abuse of young girls (Jackson, 1980). In this study, the Maori rate was no greater than one would have expected on a general population basis. This is at first sight surprising since the Maori incidence of sexual offences is high. Separate figures for rape are not available, but of the total of 409 convictions for sexual offences (other than homosexuality) committed by males in 1979, 126 or 31 percent were committed by Maori offenders (table 14.3). However, Maori women would be less likely to respond to a national magazine survey so that magazine figures do not mean much ethnically.

Jackson is also the author of the only empirical New Zealand study on rape, again conducted by means of a magazine survey (1977). Ninety-three percent of the rapists in the study were European, hence the incidence of Maori or Polynesian rapists in this survey is actually lower than one would expect on the basis of the total population. This finding may tell us more

Table 14.3. (*continued*)

OFFENCE	MAORI		N.Z. POLYNESIAN		IMMIGRANT POLYNESIAN		PAKEHA N.Z. BORN		OTHER IMMIGRANT		TOTAL	
	M	F	M	F	M	F	M	F	M	F	M	F
GOOD ORDER												
Drunkenness	1	0	0	0	1	0	7	0	2	0	11	0
Drinking and Driving	23	0	0	0	1	0	68	1	6	0	98	1
Indecent conduct and language	76	8	2	0	3	0	214	18	20	0	315	26
Idle and disorderly	89	74	2	3	4	2	104	51	12	7	211	137
Driving Offences	34	6	3	0	8	0	341	3	8	0	494	9
Other Good Order	10	0	0	0	1	0	13	0	2	0	26	0
Total	233	88	7	3	18	2	747	73	50	7	1155	173
ADMIN. JUSTICE												
Default of fine	28	0	1	0	2	0	36	0	3	0	70[1]	0
Search Probation/ Periodic Detention	53	12	2	0	2	0	55	6	5	0	117	18
Escaping, Breach Prison Regulations	11	0	0	0	0	0	25	2	0	0	36	2
Drugs	8	2	1	0	0	0	153	39	33	7	195	148
Child Welfare Act	0	1	0	0	0	0	0	0	0	0	0	1
Other Admin. Justice	13	3	0	0	2	0	16	1	1	0	32	4
Total	113	18	4	0	6	0	285	48	42	7	450	173
OTHERS												
Immigration Restriction Act	0	0	0	0	0	0	0	0	4	0	4	0
Shipping and Seamen Act	0	1	0	0	0	0	3	4	2	1	5	6
Others	14	2	0	0	2	0	41	4	5	0	62	6
Total	14	3	0	0	2	0	44	8	11	1	71	12
Total	3226	493	57	15	191	17	5200	590	514	56	9188[1]	1171

1. Excludes one male of unknown ethnic grouping
Source: Department of Justice, Annual Report, 1980.

about the people who respond to magazine surveys than about the ethnic backgrounds of rapists. In respect to the other characteristics of rape cases, New Zealand is no different from other Western countries since only 18 percent of the rapists were strangers to their victims, and most of the rapes took place in either the victim's or the rapist's home.

Clearly, it is difficult to sum up statistics and findings as scattered and tentative as these. More research is needed and more detailed police statistics are required. So far, then, New Zealand can be seen as a fairly characteristic industrialised and urbanised Western country, perhaps a little buffered by distance, by its small (3 million) population, and by a long history of good educational and welfare services. Let us now turn to noncriminal and often socially sanctioned institutional aspects of aggression.

The Sporting Scene

The sporting scene may seem an odd place to start, yet it is almost paradigmatic of the particular nature of aggressive expression in this as in other countries (Atyeo, 1979; Coakley, 1978; Sabo & Runfola, 1980; Snyder & Spreitzer, 1978).

Though netball, played exclusively by women, is undoubtedly the most frequent sport in which New Zealanders engage, it is by no means the national game. Pride of place goes to rugby football, a running-with-the-ball game, played by 15 men on a side whose size, strength, and speed (some would also add skill) are the critical factors in establishing supremacy over the other team.

The game involves four particular kinds of encounter where heavy body contact is allowed to occur. A player is permitted to fling himself at full tilt at another player carrying the ball in order to bring him to the ground. This is called tackling, and players willing to engage freely in it acquire a reputation for courage: they are called "spunky." Secondly, when the ball goes loose, a defensive player failing to pick it up may fall upon it. The forward players from both sides then gather round in a tight knot, heads down, arms around buttocks, and attempt to hook the ball out with their feet. During this manoeuvre, called a ruck, ground may be gained by the sheer weight of the heavier side pushing the rest, and the ball, forward. Rules proscribe picking the ball out of a ruck with the hands—it must be heeled or raked out with the foot. Rucks are not only a confused and poorly structured nexus of great physical power, but they give lots of opportunity for the individual player to let fly with fist or boot, especially when the referee can't see.

A scrum is a more formal setpiece of the same kind of activity. It consists of two identical sets of players locked in a power struggle for possession of the ball. Each set comprises a hooker whose head is locked beside the head and under the shoulder of his opposite counterpart and whose arms are lifted by two players on either side who push him up so that his feet are free to dangle over the ball and hook it backwards. He must keep possession of it with his feet, if he can, while the entire pack of eight forwards push behind to gain ground. At the right moment, the hooker then releases the ball back through his scrum who then heel it to the rear where the half-back is supposed to pick it up, kick it, run with it, or pass it to the backs. Those who support the hooker are called props and such is the stress upon them that cervical neck injuries resulting in paralysis are not uncommon. Death is also not unknown; there were five fatalities in 1978. The hooker and the two props are in the front row of the scrum with at least five men and sometimes more (amounting to about a thousand pounds of meat, muscle, and bone) pushing them up against the similarly implacable human wall of the other team, the other side of the scrum.

Tactically, various things can be done with this structure. A straightforward push is dangerous enough, particularly to those in the front line. The scrum may be screwed, that is, twisted around in a way that puts the opposing team offside. This sideways circular motion of the scrum is extremely physically dangerous to those involved. One can also collapse a scrum which halts its movement but creates a confusion of struggling bodies on the ground with the ball underneath, and a referee might permit rucking to go on in this situation until some infringement occurs.

Rugby is a fast, dramatic, athletic, male spectacle. The national representative team, termed "All Blacks" (because of the colour of the uniform, not their skins) are heroically idealised by the media and the public alike. In Spain, there are bullfights; in New Zealand, rugby football.

While the game of rugby itself is by nature competitively physically aggressive, the way the game is played provides additional opportunities, albeit outside the rules, for personal physical combat. This is deplored by rugby administrators, but nevertheless continues. One of the reasons for this continuance is the roar of response from spectators when someone lets fly with fist or boot. No All Black would wish to be known as a dirty player, but no one achieves All Black status who is unable to "dish it out." During a 1980 international series with Australia, two players exchanged blows and the New Zealander broke the jaw of the Australian. The commentator's remarks—"boys will be boys," "these things happen," "just a difference of opinion"—illustrate the acceptance of violence on the rugby field.

Protective clothing is not usually worn—not even mouthguards—such aids are "sissy." Volunteer paramedics regularly roam the sidelines to perform minor running repairs and resuscitations. Every winter's weekend brings a stream of injured players to out-patient clinics and doctors' waiting rooms.

Associated with the game of rugby is a considerable amount of club activity conducted in the locker room before or after the game, in taverns, and in private clubrooms. This is male mateship at its best and its worst, with a strong flavour of moral holiday as evidenced by the use of obscene language, bawdy songs, sexual and sexist bragging, plus much myth-making and reworking of the incidents of the match.

The same camaraderie exists in other privileged male enclaves, such as other sports clubs, service clubs, lodges, working men's clubs, even the regular groups that patronise the ordinary public drinking bars of hotels or taverns and the premises owned and operated by the R.S.A. (Returned Servicemen's Association).

Warfare

While New Zealand has never conducted a war outside its territory, of its own initiative, it has nevertheless participated willingly enough in every Western war since the Boer War in 1902. So identified have we been with our colonial origins that it never even occurred to us to ask whether fighting the Dutch in South Africa, the Germans in the two world wars, or Asians in Korea and later Vietnam was likely to gain us more than had we preserved a distant neutrality. Trade and treaty obligations in so small a country, heavily dependent on the sale of agricultural products to overseas countries, lie behind this history.

While New Zealand's involvement in these external wars does not shed much light on our pattern of aggressiveness, the maintenance of the romantic warrior myth by armed services clubs is beyond trade and treaty and is most indicative. Not only are such clubs very active, despite attrition in their membership, but they carry inordinate weight in the political sphere both as a lobby group and because they constitute the ruling generation, both politically and economically. The present prime minister was a corporal in the army; the leader of the opposition was an intelligence officer.

However, these macho male phenomena are not sufficiently belligerent to support a conclusion that we are a bellicose nation. War, even when we have engaged in it, hardly touched the national style or the majority of the population. More people died at home in the influenza epidemic following World War I than died overseas in action. Like the British, we tend to glorify the battles lost as much or more than those we won.

Police: Action and Style

In the British tradition, we have never permitted our police to carry weapons, neither handguns nor truncheons. Guns may only be used by specially deployed armed offender squads and truncheons may only be used on special duties. The New Zealand police do not use horses, hoses, or tear gas in crowd control as happens in other large metropolitan centres elsewhere. They primarily see their role as one of avoiding provocation, confrontation, or physical methods.

This said, there remain, however, notable occasions when the police have been required to act forcibly and physically, for example, to remove Maori protestors squatting on the grounds of Parliament over land rights or, similarly, to use force to shift a Maori protest group who occupied a golf course that was once ancestral land. The deployment of a force of 400 police, with army backup, to remove 120 Maori squatters protesting Maori land loss in Auckland City passed off without much public outcry, indeed, with tacit approval. Since all these confrontations are ethnic, related to the loss of land, occurred within a twelve-month period, and were clearly in two cases at the direct instruction of one man, the prime minister, they may constitute a special circumstance which we shall discuss shortly. They are not, however, evidence that the police have license to do anything more than keep the peace (though there is some doubt whether they can refuse political direction to the contrary). In all three of these confrontations, the police were unarmed—nor was there any suggestion that they should be armed. The Armed Forces cannot be used for peace keeping within New Zealand.

Gangs

More recently, concern over motorcycle gangs, largely an ethnic phenomenon, has led some within the police force to argue for riot control equipment of a kind now familiar in other Western countries. Equipment of this kind is deployed in Australia and Papua New Guinea but to date has not been used in New Zealand, though it has now been purchased, following police-gang confrontations. But neither plastic shields, tear gas, mace, nor cattle prods have yet been used here; there is nothing equivalent to the American National Guard. Riots, so far, simply do not arise.

Gang confrontations do contribute occasional threat to public order and occur somewhere or other in the country, perhaps about once every two weeks. The frequency is not great, but the attention given the phenomena gives them considerable notoriety, the more so because gangs and Maori protestors are the only identifiable social groups employing tactics of direct confrontation. Occasionally, student or other groups protest by carrying banners or doing a little chanting, but New Zealand has not experienced the shock of violent protest from either the extreme political right or left or from religious extremists.

Ethnic Status

Ethnic disadvantage and discrimination probably constitute the greatest area of institutional violence. European institutions continue to act in ways that are seen by many Maori, young and old, to deny Maori people their birthright, and aggressive social violence is, and will become more frequently, a prevalent response.

Behind this lies a history. By the time the British annexed the territory of New Zealand in 1840, the yoke of colonialism was already beginning to press upon the shoulders of authorities in England. Once in charge, however reluctantly, the British colonial office acted according to its responsibility, more from duty than with enthusiasm. The British crown had undertaken by treaty to protect the lands of the natives from exploitation. The settlers, however, wanted the lands. Rather than arm the settlers (with the lessons of the American colonies much in mind), the British deployed colonial troops in New Zealand, set up land purchasing machinery, and behind the advancing thin red line of the British army, uneasily, the land was populated.

Elements of this situation persist. It is against the crown and its treaty, not the white citizens, that the Maori protestors direct their grievance. To lose one's land and standing is to be the victim of violence, however civilly and legally it is done, and the targets are institutions not individuals. The expansion of New Zealand by white settlers was so rapid, so ruthless, and so successful by means of treaty, the courts, and the militia that there was never need to arm all the settlers or establish that right in law or constitution. It is, and has always been, illegal for people to carry arms, other than the armed forces, except for hunting. Every time the settlers pressed for the right to bear arms, the government became nervous of what wildcat vigilante groups might do or become and tightened arms control.

Arms and the Law

The law governing the sale and possession of arms in New Zealand is contained in a tight official statement issued by the Police Department which requires permits and licensing and prohibits possession of certain weapons altogether.

While there are 750,000 legally registered firearms in private hands, guns are not a major feature of homicides, robbery, or other crime, and are certainly not held for reasons of personal protection or to defend oneself from other citizens or sections of society. The police carry no guns and, should an incident with an armed offender arise, they must call in a special armed-offender squad.

Hunting

New Zealand law and practice concerning arms caters to one group and for one purpose only: the sportsman and hunter on whose behalf lobbying activity is constant but not strong. It is mainly concerned with the opening up to hunting access of government controlled areas of state park and forest, and with commercial and culling activities which might limit the populations of hunted species, mainly deer, ducks, and pigs. All three of these game species are not indigenous but have been introduced for hunting as a sport. The animals have caused serious ecological damage, and ducks maintain a disease pool of salmonella and destroy crops and pasture. The origins of hunting in New Zealand were twofold: food and sport. There has simply never grown up around hunting in New Zealand the kind of macho male mystique that appears to characterise it in the United States nor the aristocratic rituals that accompany hunting in Great Britain. It is a young men's recreation that they most outgrow!

A generation ago, practically every New Zealand male would have gone hunting at sometime in his life, with firearms for the birds and large and small game and a knife to slaughter wild pigs once hunting dogs had bailed them. Now all that is restricted to a much smaller population as urbanisation and population growth have limited such opportunities. Thus, hunting, if it ever was an aggressive outlet, figures now in only minor ways. There is no organised gun lobby as in the United States.

Similarly, whereas twenty-five years ago competitive team sport was almost a universal feature of growing up in New Zealand, there are now many young people engaged in more individual sports such as surfing and skiing where the aggressive and competitive element is much reduced if not entirely absent for most players.

Violence and Vehicles

However, there has undoubtedly been a vast increase in the number of young men for whom driving cars and motorcycles is an aggressive activity. The association of aggressive release with the power of the internal combustion engine is so intrinsically satisfying as to have many of the qualities of an addiction. Combined with alcohol, the mix can be deadly. The popular and the psychological theory of catharsis gains little in credence from the continuing activities of motorcycle gangs and drinking drivers.

Motorcycle gangs are primarily a peer group substitute for the extended family (Ritchie & Ritchie, 1979) and, through caring and sharing, satisfy much more than simply macho male aggression. The media and society generally see the leather jacketed menace on a high powered motorcycle as a threat to "law and order" when, most of the time, no such threat exists (Kelsey, 1980). However, when the gangs roar off to the local tavern and stake out their territory in the public bar, things can get a bit rough.

Violence and the Use of Alcohol

Research on drinking behaviour in public places (Graves & Graves, 1979) has shown that violent episodes are far less frequent than most people would believe on the basis of the publicity given when incidents do occur. Maoris and Polynesians tend to drink in larger groups; they drink more and spend a longer time in the pubs. Therefore, if fighting does occur, among or between ethnic minorities, it involves more people who are possibly drunker, and the incidents tend to occur close to closing time when police and bouncers are at their most vigilant. Polynesian and Maori pub brawls are more likely to involve the use of weapons and to result in injury than other fights.

The Graves discuss interesting cultural differences: in Polynesia, where there is a cultural emphasis on the power and the sacredness of language, physical resolution of conflict is regarded as less damaging than verbal insult or attack; from a blow or a wound you can recover, with no harm done, whereas verbal insult or damage to a reputation may hang around for generations. Proverbial sayings direct, in effect, that one seeks physical rather than verbal satisfaction for aggressive feelings. For example, there is a Maori saying that the shaft of a spear may be deflected but there is no defense against a damaging word. Compare this with the European saying, "Sticks and stones will break my bones but names will never hurt me."

The use of alcohol in New Zealand by all ethnic groups increases the likelihood of aggressive expression. Every culture has its own folk theory of the appropriate way to act when drunk (McAndrew & Edgerton, 1969). In New Zealand, there are three components in drunkenness: alcohol is thought to be relaxing, stimulating, and releasing. In ordinary terms, forget your worries, get high, respond to the excitement of the social situation, and let yourself go. "Letting go," naturally enough, is more likely to occur in psychological areas where individuals have trouble expressing themselves when sober such as anger and sexuality. The behaviour of New Zealanders when drunk, especially males, is diagnostic of serious flaws in both socialisation and in social control, especially in relation to authority, sexuality, and aggression.

Maoris and Cook Islanders, in their own situation, mostly use alcohol to have a happy time and, when they get drunk, go to sleep. One of us, some years ago, described the two predominant drinking patterns in a rural Maori community (J. E. Ritchie, 1963). In that locality and time, Maori drinking groups took off into hilarity in a party situation or drifted into a soporific and slightly depressive mood state which they called sessions. Urbanisation and more frequent drinking in the public social setting of taverns has changed all that but, when ethnic groups are able to drink in their own cultural setting, fighting is rare, hilarity common, and sleepiness often follows. In the within-group situations, cultural sanctions and controls operate through the authority structure, on the one hand, and the obligations of mateship, on the other. In the public situation, the first is absent or inoperative, and the second is likely to lead to trouble since one must defend one's mates against all comers.

Violence in Politics

Since the earliest days, political debate in New Zealand has contained two themes: the oratorical style of the British parliamentary tradition; and stand-up, knock-down, sock it to 'em, rabble-rousing mob oratory. Many of the major politicians in the country's history have prided themselves on their contact with common folk ("the ordinary bloke") and allowed an element of personal aggressiveness to enter into political discussion regardless of their political orientation. Argument *ad hominem*, the use of personal invective and character assassination, has been more evident in recent times. While this decline in the standard of political debate is quite clearly associated with the personal style of the present prime minister, there is no doubt that a good part of the population approves of his leadership qualities. One overseas commentator some years ago noted the common practice of newspapers to publish anonymous letters commenting on the personal characteristics of public figures (Ausubel, 1960).

In terms of overt violence, political punch-ups, assassinations, riots, and political furor, New Zealand is a good deal quieter than other Western countries. But we emphasise that verbal aggression is an ever-present aspect of the political scene and occasionally becomes quite nasty.

Sources of Violence

This survey of the social phenomena of aggression and violence in New Zealand may be summarised by saying that by both socialisation and social custom, the New Zealand style chops back the peaks of intense overt and explicit expression of aggression and channels such feelings into a socially approved range of expressive modes, notably, into a competitive sport, aggressive display when drunk, and hostile interpersonal relations, especially within the family. As a society, New Zealand has many distinctive features or attributes which lie behind this pattern: absence of territorial boundaries with another country, no great difficulties with diverse migrant populations, comparative affluence, and, until recently, full employment and a comprehensive welfare state which reduces poverty and other sources of social strain.

Until recently, great differentials in wealth scarcely existed and, even today, are not conspicuous; the social ideology would still maintain that Jack or Jill is as good as his (or her) master (or mistress) and, on this basis, relatively harmonious labour relations exist. New Zealand was placed quite low on the United Nations list (by country) of days lost through strike action. Political expression of industrial dissatisfaction is so low that, lumping all the various kinds of communist factions together, the total membership is less than 300, .001 percent of the population.

These favourable social circumstances might be considered sufficient explanation for the relative unaggressiveness of the ordinary New Zealander. But it is our contention that the circumstances themselves are only one set of factors and that socialisation practices in the New Zealand family shape the New Zealand character; in particular, punishment shapes anger. The New Zealand family has intensified the ideology of punishment we received from our Anglo Saxon tradition and background. As they grow up, New Zealanders are so frequently punished for showing anger that they stop showing it. But it does not go away.

The effects of this socialisation pattern, we will argue, do not make New Zealanders nonaggressive but create a situation where the expression of aggression must become indirect. Our problem is to explain why displays of direct, overt, physical aggression are low while there is substantial evidence of aggressiveness in sports, drinking behaviour, and violence in the streets and on the domestic scene. Our answer will be that, in growing up, New Zealanders are not taught to be nonaggressive; but they are taught to fear the reprisal of authority figures should they act out.

By this argument, we are proposing that what psychologists call "anger in" is more prevalent than "anger out." This hypothesis is difficult to test empirically and is one which should be associated with high levels of suicide and depressive illness. International rates in these areas are notoriously difficult to compare; it is not our impression that New Zealand rates are particularly high but we would, nevertheless, argue for the "anger in" hypothesis with prescribed social circumstances for aggressive acting out among some groups more than others, so that it is mainly in the case of women that the "anger in" depressive result shows up (Calvert, 1979). They, after all, do not participate in aggressive action sports, in loud aggressive behaviour in bars and taverns, punch-ups on the street, or the dominating behaviour of male bossiness in the marketplace. In domestic violence, their role is as stimulus and target more than as aggressor. In respect to aggression training, there is not a great deal of evidence that boys and girls are treated differently, so it is to the situational and role factors in adult life that one must look for gender differences in aggressive behaviour. There are differences in child training, however, particularly with regard to physical punishment, and these we will now review.

CHILD TRAINING AND AGGRESSION

For almost twenty-five years, we have been researching patterns of child training in New Zealand families, both Maori and Pakeha, urban and rural (J. E. Ritchie, 1963; Jane Ritchie, 1956, 1979, 1980; Ritchie & Ritchie, 1970, 1978, 1979). In our 1963 survey of child rearing practices, we included a number of questions on discipline and control (Ritchie & Ritchie, 1970). We were surprised by the major features which emerged from these data. New Zealand mothers relied on very few of the wide range of possible control techniques. Those they did use were, for the greater part, negative—scoldings, growlings, threats, reprimands, and punishment. Not only did they make infrequent use of positive or reward techniques but they had very negative attitudes toward these regarding them as bribes, evidence of "spoiling," and, not infrequently, expecting that good behaviour should be its own reward. Finally, physical punishment was a moral obligation in, and criterion of, good parenting in the 1960s. The first principle of parenting was "spare the rod and spoil the child" not "suffer little children to come unto me."

This is, of course, retrospective survey data in which respondents notoriously try to present themselves in the best possible light. It may be that these levels of physical punishment were inflated by the naive desire of our respondents to convince us that they took the burdens of parenthood seriously and conscientiously. They may not actually have punished as often as this, but they certainly wanted us to think that they did.

Fifteen years later we repeated the survey (Jane Ritchie, 1979). While many features of parent-child interaction and relationship appear to have improved over this period of time, physical punishment persists as the major pillar of parenthood. Indeed, though the percentage of mothers who never use physical punishment increased from 1 to 10 percent, 54 percent of the mothers in the 1977 restudy used physical punishment weekly or more compared to 35 percent fifteen years ago. Neither chance nor sampling differences can explain an increase on this magnitude. However, though mothers are now using physical punishment more frequently, they are less likely to regard it as effective. Only 14 percent of the 1977 group found it unequivocally effective compared to 41 percent of the earlier sample. Why on earth do they then continue to do it if most think it ineffective? A finding like this is a clear indicator that one is not dealing with a pragmatic world of rational matters but with a deeply entrenched belief system relatively impervious to change.

In 1963 mothers only were interviewed. Our 1977 restudy included fathers as well as mothers. Fathers appear on the surface to use the same amount of physical punishment as their wives; however, because they spend less time with their children, their overall rate of physical punishment per contact hour must be greater. And almost twice as many fathers (one in four) as mothers think physical punishment always works, and another 50 percent regard it as quite effective most of the time. Fathers feel much more morally justified than mothers in using physical punishment since 50 percent of the men consider they are doing the right thing compared to only 29 percent of the women. Women are much more likely than the men to feel guilty and bothered by the use of physical punishment.

Mothers smack their sons and daughters equally often, but fathers punish their sons more frequently than their daughters. But, when they punish their daughters, they are more likely to feel guilty about it; fathers of sons are much more convinced that they are doing the right thing when they physically chastise them. Daughters respond with hurt feelings when hit by their fathers; sons respond with anger. The fathers report fewer reservations about the effectiveness of physical punishment with their daughters; boys are punished more frequently and the punishment is less effective.

THE IDEOLOGY OF VIOLENCE

We have an ideology of domestic violence. People consider it right to hit children; it is considered good for their character. We may utter the mild "tut-tut" over violence on the rugby field but, make no mistake, we expect any real All Black to be capable of it. There are a host of justifications and rationalisations: "it never did me any harm," "the Bible says," "sarcasm is worse," "it clears the air," "it let's them know who's boss," "how else will they learn respect," "punishment is a sign of a loving parent," "they don't know any better," "children prefer it to other punishments," "if you give them an inch they will take a mile," "it's the only thing they understand," "don't let them get the upper hand," "if you don't start early you will never control them," "spare the rod and spoil the child" (Ritchie & Ritchie, 1981a).

The practice of physical punishment in New Zealand is a national neurosis. This is not an excessive statement but a precise one. A neurotic condition exists when a person persists in behaviour that has socially or personally undesirable consequences, regardless of evidence that the behaviour is dysfunctional. Since both parents and children tell us that physical punishment does little good, and since the psychological literature shows how clearly it is related both to immediate undesirable side effects such as lying, cheating, deceptions, anger, hostility, acting out (Winder & Rau, 1962; Yates, 1962) and to a broad range of social pathologies such as child abuse, criminality, violent offending (Bakan, 1971; Gil, 1970, 1971; Steinmetz, 1977; Steinmetz & Straus, 1975; Straus, Gelles, & Steinmetz, 1980), a rational and healthy society would by now have taken clear steps, if not to eliminate, at least to reduce the practices.

ETHNIC PATTERNS

When we turn to ethnic differences, we must go back to the data gathered in the mid-1960s (Ritchie & Ritchie, 1970) since no more recent ethnic data are available. The differences are startling. The Maori rate for regular punishment (at a level of once a week or more) was double that of the European. Two thirds of the Maori mothers smacked this often. Only a third of the Pakeha mothers did so. In the category of most frequent use of punishment (daily or more), we find only 10 percent of the European mothers but 37 percent of the Maori sample.

We have elsewhere (1979) described the cultural background of physical punishment in

Polynesian society. There is no doubt that whatever the historical cultural pattern in Polynesia may have been, the stresses of urban modern living, minority status, absence of traditional supports, the vigilance of the majority culture, and their perceptions of what they must do to meet European expectations lie behind the severity of punitiveness in Polynesian child training, the child abuse statistics, and the frequency of violent offending by Maoris.

There is no doubt that the level of personal and social violence tolerated in some Polynesian situations is very high, even in remote village situations (Wendt, 1979). From time to time, we have heard an argument advanced that the use of punishment in Polynesian child training is an essential component in the maintenance of cultural traditions and values, particularly respect for age and status. In our view, there are enough frustrations and circumstances that might generate aggression in the present situation of Polynesians in New Zealand without the added load that comes from punitive child rearing. In any case, we doubt that traditional Polynesian societies were as punitive as they have become because, in the traditional child rearing pattern, adults had relatively little to do with children once infancy had passed. Children grew up in their own world—a sort of children's culture.

CORPORAL PUNISHMENT IN SCHOOLS

Apart from the family, the other great socialising influence is the school. Here, as in most other institutions, New Zealand inherited Anglo Saxon traditions, heavily loaded with punitive ideology. We will discuss this as a general matter later, but let us now look at punishment in the setting of New Zealand schools.

Elsewhere (Ritchie & Ritchie, 1978, 1981a) we have summarised New Zealand data on the use of corporal punishment in schools. We should note that the only European countries still permitting this are the United Kingdom and Ireland. According to the Society of Teachers Opposed to Physical Punishment (STOPP), it is prohibited in all communist countries. New Zealand is among other former British colonies (Australia, Barbados, Canada, South Africa, Swaziland, Trinidad & Tobago, the United States, and probably others) which still allow the practice to continue.

In a recent study, we gathered information from 110 Form II intermediate school (seventh grade) children (Jane Ritchie, Payne, & Tourelle, 1980). Almost half of the boys had been physically punished at primary school compared to only 30 percent of the girls. What were the *crimes* for which they were punished? Boys were hit for damage caused to property or walking on the garden, for physical aggression, bad language, and failure to learn. Girls were also hit for being bad in class and for bad language but, in addition, for running away. Girls were most likely to say they were wrongly punished or were unable to remember the crime. Of the children who were hit at primary school, only 25 percent felt their behaviour improved; more than half (60 percent) felt it made absolutely no difference to their future behaviour at all, and 14 percent actually felt it made their behaviour worse. Fewer children had been physically punished at intermediate school level (grades 6 and 7). Education Board regulations actually forbid the use of physical punishment with girls over 10 years of age, and only 31 percent of the boys had been physically punished. Their transgressions include bad language, talking and laughing in class, fighting, being cheeky, being a pest, and failing to do homework.

Once again, from self-reports of the children, the effectiveness of physical punishment as a means of changing behaviour appears to be dubious. The majority (59 percent) of those hit in intermediate school felt it made no difference to their behaviour, 24 percent felt it made their behaviour worse, and only 18 percent said it made their behaviour better. These boys have not yet embarked on their secondary school careers so we do not know what physical punishments await them there.

We do have data on what happened to men of their father's generation. Of 45 males, ranging in age from 26 to 55 years, interviewed in 1979 as part of a survey of the families of one Hamilton primary school, 84 percent had been physically punished at secondary school, only slightly less than the 91 percent who had been hit at primary school.

This extraordinarily high percentage indicates that, at least in the past, corporal punishment was not reserved for use as a last resort and only inflicted upon a few persistent offenders; only 16 percent of these fathers escaped physical punishment during their high school years. There is considerable psychological evidence that those who are subjected to arbitrary force or authority, of which this is but one form, will develop and perpetuate such patterns (Adorno, Frenkel-Brunswik, Levinson & Sanford, 1950; Bandura & Walters, 1963; Button, 1973; Eron, Walder, Toigo, & Lefkowitz, 1963; Sears, Maccoby, & Levin, 1957; Welsh, 1976).

As the percentage of boys hit at primary school (46 percent) is less than that of the men (91 percent) and the percentage of girls hit (30 percent) is less than that of women of their mother's generation (56 percent), we have grounds for believing that the use of physical punishment is declining in our educational institutions. But though practices may be changing, community attitudes still endorse the use of physical punishment in schools. And in view of their personal experiences, it is not surprising that males are significantly less likely to advocate the abolition of corporal punishment in schools than females. Of our 1979 adult sample, one third of the women but only 15 percent of the men thought corporal punishment should be abolished in primary and intermediate schools. Only slightly more (40 percent of women and 16 percent of men) thought it had no place in secondary schools. It is interesting that 12 percent of the men believed corporal punishment should be used more at all levels of schooling, whereas no women thought it should be used more at primary or intermediate levels and only 3 percent of the women thought it should be used more in secondary schools.

The adult attitude pattern is repeated in the intermediate school pupils' views on the abolition of corporal punishment. Eighteen percent of the boys thought it should never be used in primary schools compared to 25 percent of the girls, but fewer children thought that it had no place in intermediate schools—only 9 percent of the boys and 13 percent of the girls. Once again, more boys (12 percent) thought it should be used more often at both levels of schooling than girls (3 percent).

Both adults and children were asked their views on the South Auckland Education Board's regulations on corporal punishment which forbid its use with girls over the age of ten. The majority of the males (49 percent of the adult men and a huge 76 percent of the boys) feel that girls should be treated the same as boys—i.e., hit. That's what equality of the sexes appears to mean! A large group of the adult women (39 percent) agree with that, too, as do a third of the intermediate school girls. Another third of the girls are happy with the status quo, and the remaining third felt that nobody should be hit. Twenty-eight percent of the adult women feel that nobody at all should be hit, and as many feel that only boys should be hit. A third of the men feel that way, and only 14 percent feel that nobody at all should be hit, a view shared by 19 percent of the school boys, only 6 percent of whom supported the present position where only boys are hit.

What do all these figures add up to? They indicate that the majority of both samples, male and female, adult and child, endorse the use of physical punishment in schools. Clearly, whatever generational change in practice may have taken place, we are still dealing with an entrenched ideology, carried particularly by men, that will not simply go away by virtue of liberal decrees or by hoping for change.

IDEOLOGY AND THE LAW

As we indicated earlier, New Zealand's social background, its history, and its institutions largely derive from the Anglo Saxon tradition. Its law, therefore, has its roots not only in Roman Law but in the way that system codified customary attitudes and practices of the common law of Britain. Whatever the other general values of that system may be, justice and its administration in this as in other English-speaking countries is associated with strongly punitive and retributive principles. For example, in New Zealand, 90 people in every 100,000 are in prison, whereas for the Netherlands there are 18, in Denmark 28, in Sweden 32. New Zealand's figure is the same as that for Canada and the United Kingdom's is slightly less at 84. Australia reveals an interesting variation with 140 in the Northern Territory, Queensland has 101, and the A.C.T. (Canberra) has only 23. Figures for South Africa are not available.

Punitive and retributive justice is not something imposed upon the New Zealand population by the oppressions of history, the bureaucracy, or politicians; it's as indigenous as our renowned oysters or famous trout—and considered by most as equally desirable and natural. Whatever the historical reasons for this may be, the contemporary supports lie primarily in the power and authority system of home and family and in the transmission of social attitudes from parents to children.

Section 59 of the Crimes Act still provides legal protection for parents, those acting in their place, and school masters when any of these hit children. This section states:

Powers of Discipline

59. Domestic discipline—(1) Every parent or person in the place of a parent, and every school master, is justified in using force by way of correction towards any child or pupil under his care, if the force used is reasonable in the circumstances.

(2) The reasonableness of the force used is a question of fact.

Section 59 clearly indicates that a parent cannot limit the authority of another adult. A teacher under this section is legally entitled to use reasonable force to correct a child with or without approval of the parents—the authority under Section 59 does not rest in any supposed delegation by the parent but arises simply out of the necessities of the case. The parent may, at law, have no say in this matter. The section infringes both parents' *and* children's rights.

This means that any adult can use physical punishment against any child if that adult can show that he or she is acting in place of a parent. And the parent or person in his or her place or school teacher is both judge and executioner until called to account by court proceedings. We should note that since 1891 a husband's right to chastise his wife has been held to have no existence in law, and that Section 59 has dropped former sections in the law of 1893 and 1908 under which masters could use force over servants or apprentices.

Thus, where adults relate to adults (as wives or workers), physical discipline is no longer allowed, but the human right to be protected by law from physical assault has not yet been extended to children in their relations with their parents and school teachers even though they are the least able to defend themselves and undoubtedly the most vulnerable.

THE SOCIAL EXPRESSION OF VIOLENCE

We have now demonstrated that many people in New Zealand, particularly males, experience a rather punitive upbringing that is supported by a retributive and punitive ideology expressed through major institutions such as schools and the legal system.

Given this background, one might expect quite widespread evidence of open aggressive expression, but this is apparent only in the area of organised sport, and among alienated urban youth and the ethnic disadvantaged. There is virtually no evidence of terrorist activities, student riots, violent labour unrest, mob violence, political assassination, or public disorder. There is, however, inescapable evidence of domestic violence to a surprising degree in so apparently peacable a country.

What, then, are the contexts which have patterned the situation here? The first is undoubtedly an extremely high level of awareness and concern about the social expression of aggression. A single outbreak of gang violence, for example, is enough to cause national widespread concern with repercussive discussions in the media and in parliament for weeks afterwards. Anything more (or even that) may well provoke a government committee of inquiry or a special departmental report. New Zealanders almost think of their country as though it were a very large family, which, if well run, will display no behaviour worthy of negative social comment. Government, therefore, acts rather like the typical New Zealand parent—it will punish for outward aggressive display. A government does not have to be dictatorial to be repressive; repression by consensus is more absolute. Acceptance of authority has been well learned in the context of the New Zealand home, indeed, overlearned.

Behind the ideology of punishment lies the belief that aggressiveness is wrong, that it represents something dangerous in the human condition and that it must be eliminated. To that end, New Zealand society has established remarkably efficient social machinery for suppressing social violence. This includes not only such apparent and explicit means as a large and highly controlling police force and wide range of criminal and family law but also a social welfare system which comes into operation well before the level of deprivation reaches flash point. In some cases, this system of welfare services and benefits becomes self-perpetuating by causing welfare dependency which the system then proceeds to satisfy. All these mechanisms fail, however, to prevent personal violence and, in particular, its expression within the domestic scene. There the state is reluctant to intervene because another ideology, that of privacy, has been carried to such lengths that it has, for example, been impossible to set up a national reporting system for child abuse cases or to require mandatory reporting. However, we react with horror and righteous indignation when a child is brutally treated. We personalise the situation and blame the abuser rather than attempt to understand the circumstances and then remove the cause.

At almost every national election "law and order" becomes a political issue. Every contender for political office promises the electorate to do something about it, and what they do is to set up committees. These, then, report, after a not inconsiderable time, and then nothing happens. For example, in 1977, gang violence was an issue of public attention because of the unusual appearance and other attributes of motorcycle groups and fuss in the media. A parliamentary select committee was set up to consider the incidence and causes of violent offending. This meant that the government could go to the polls in November 1978 and reassure the electorate that something was being done. That committee reported in December 1979 but, at the time of writing, the report has still not been debated by parliament. Meanwhile, a further governmental agency, the Social Development Council, produced another report on violence in families which, apart from media attention for a couple of days, followed its predecessor into oblivion (1980). Within a few months, a further group produced a report on child abuse (Geddis, 1980). To date, there has been no action on this either.

A visitor from Mars, confronted with this pile of paper, might well conclude that New Zealand was either in the grip of some unprecedented wave of violence which triggered off these reports and then subsided, or that the whole performance constitutes a sociopolitical ritual. Since the former was not the case, and the explanation as ritual more appropriate, one must ask what the ritual is all about. In a word, it is about authority.

The ritual is a device to seem to do something about a situation that could only be changed if one reached beyond tinkering or fine tuning of the mechanisms of police and punishment to actually confront changes in the cultural pattern and especially in family life. Since we are not prepared to make fundamental changes in those areas of society which produce aggression, we must live with the consequences. These are patterns of privacy and parenting within the family; sex role definitions which permit male aggressiveness in taverns, recreational activities, and the domestic scene; and an economic system which has punishing effects upon the young, the ethnic minorities, and the less able.

Confronted with unwillingness and inability to promote change in these areas fast enough to see some result, New Zealanders are left with no option but to deny that they are as they are. Thus, there are some ways of acting aggressively which are socially approved, indeed admired, such as the football player who can "give as good as he gets," the politician who savages a television interviewer, the magistrate who endorses the short sharp shock of corrective training for the young offender. Then there are aggressive outlets which are tacitly supported and their aggressive nature is denied such as corporal punishment in school and home, the "she must have asked for it" theory of rape or domestic violence, and the promilitary posturing of the veterans' lobbies. Because we do not confront the realities of violence, we have done very little to deal with some rather desperate human needs such as those of abused children, women who seek help, for family crisis centres, rape crisis centres, to mitigate the institutional violence that courts, police, and law effect against minorities and especially the young.

It is less threatening to engage in endless debate about the possible influence of violence in our television programmes, largely imported from Britain and the United States, than to look at the origins of violence closer to home.

AGGRESSION AND PERSONAL MYTH

New Zealand has only recently entered its postpioneer era. All those features that tourists now appreciate were once confronted in a rather different light. Twelve-thousand foot mountains were impassable barriers. Wild and scenic rivers were killers. The lush temperate rain-forest was dark, dank, alien, and no living was possible till it was whacked down and forced into retreat. Scrub-cutting, bush-burning, clearing and sowing, running fence-lines over rugged wild country; then building roads, bridges, houses, towns, cities, airports, industries—all this in 150 years built a collective myth of the New Zealand character and style.

The pioneer, isolated, outsider theme is by no means unique to New Zealand, but then by definition no myth can be unique. Yet, here, the hero takes on a special quality. It is clearest in John Mulgans' novel *Man Alone* (1949) in which the hero becomes victim of the man he works for as a back-country farm hand, of sexual jealousy, of authority that turns him into a hunted person. There is a passive anger throughout the novel.

Or, in the vernacular story-teller tales of Barry Crump, his Good Keen Men make their own rules, avoid those of others, engage in petty and rather adolescent anti-authority postures, and fall in and out of minor fights. The hero has been left behind, made redundant and anachronistic, left to make a quest for personal isolation and independence, that will leave him up the creek.

At the folk hero level, there is a significant glorifying of male outlaws. In the 1940s, Stanley Graham "went bush" after shooting a neighbour and, after a three-week manhunt during which he killed three times more, he was gunned down by police and a citizens' posse. Now, at last, there is to be a film about him; our own Jessie James or Ned Kelly. Then there is George Wilder, the man no prison could contain, who in his many escapes was helped, often, by otherwise law-abiding folk.

Not criminal but of similar character and quest is Sir Edmund Hillary, whose comment as conqueror of Everest was "We knocked the bastard off" and who later beat Sir Evelyn Fuchs to the South Pole driving a modified ordinary New Zealand farm tractor. He was an individualist, an isolate, an outsider, a good keen man, a man alone, living just where adventure begins. And in his steps, a generation of younger New Zealand men took off climbing other mountains, sailing solo here and there, running in international competition and, of course, as always, locked in rugby football competition with traditional foes—South Africa, the British Isles, and France.

What does this myth say of aggression? It says that an aggressive, criminal man is in pursuit of goals not too different in ethos or kind from climbing the "big one" or winning at the Olympics; that person and the authority of law rest in uneasy relationship; that anger and assertion lead to lonely isolation however great the achievement.

There are many elements in this national myth. For all the winning, it is a loser myth, dour, physical, hard, and male. Are New Zealanders like that? Well no, it is, after all, a myth. Mountain conquest, murder, and prison escape are not the stuff of daily life. Ordinary life requires other skills, makes lesser (or perhaps greater) demands. Yet, in the struggle to be significant, to break out, to go to the edge of the law, to reject authority is still the stuff which dreams are made of. Who made men insignificant to start with? What elements of frustration in ordinary life sustain and nurture the myth of man alone?

No longer is the great outdoors easy to reach. No longer can the pioneer struggle to be fulfilled. Now there is a peacable society, a little obsessed by law and order, intolerant of dissent, suspicious of difference, and basically puritan still.

CONCLUSION

Because of its isolation, comparative affluence, and progressive social policy, New Zealand exhibits fewer of the aggressive phenomena that characterise other urban industrial societies. Nevertheless, its cultural patterns, attitudes, and practices implicitly endorse the expression of anger in aggressive and sometimes violent ways. If, as a nation, we have any lesson to offer the world, it is that progressive and liberal welfare legislation and well-developed institutions of social concern, however desirable these may be, will not eliminate the harm that aggressive and violent individuals inflict on their kind. The roots of violence are close to home, so it is there that its expression gets its fullest flood. The beast lives at home and is ourselves.

REFERENCES

Acord (Auckland Committee on Racism and Discrimination) Children in state custody. Paper presented to the Human Rights Commission Conference, Christchurch, 1979.

Adams, F. B. *Criminal law and practice in New Zealand.* Wellington: Sweet and Maxwell, 1971.

Adorno, T. W., Frenkel-Brunswik, E., Levinson, D. J., & Sanford, R. N. *The authoritarian personality.* New York: Harper & Row, 1950.

Atyeo, D. *Blood and guts.* London: Paddington Press, 1979.

Auckland Committee on Racism and Discrimination. Children in State Custody.

Ausubel, D. P. *The fern and the tiki.* London: Angus & Robertson, 1960.

Bakan, D. *Slaughter of the innocents.* San Francisco: Jossey-Bass, 1971.

Bandura, A., & Walters, R. H. *Social learning and personality development.* New York: Holt, Rinehart & Winston, 1963.

Button, A. Some antecedents of felonious and delinquent behaviour. *Journal of Child Clinical Psychol-*

ogy, 1973, *2,* 35-37.

Calvert, S. Women and mental health in New Zealand. Unpublished doctoral dissertation, University of Waikato, 1979.

Coakley, J. J. *Sport in society.* St. Louis: C. V. Mosby, 1978.

Eron, L. D., Walder, L. O., Toigo, R., & Lefkowitz, M. M. Social class, parental punishment for aggression, and child aggression. *Child Development,* 1963, *34,* 849-867.

Fergusson, D. M., Fleming, J., & O'Neill, D. P. *Child abuse in New Zealand.* Wellington, N.Z.: Government Printer, 1972.

Fergusson, D. M., & Horwood, L. J. The measurement of socio-economic status for 1,109 New Zealand families. *New Zealand Journal of Educational Studies,* 1979, *14,* (1), 58-66.

Geddis, D. C. The role of the Plunket Society in preventing parenting difficulties. Paper prepared for the 2nd International Congress on Child Abuse and Neglect, London, 1978.

Geddis, D. C. (Ed.) *Child abuse.* Report of a national symposium. Dunedin, N.Z.: National Children's Health Research Foundation, 1980.

Geddis, D. C., Monaghan, S. M., Muir, R. C., & Jones, C. J. Early prediction in a maternity hospital— the Queen Mary Child Care Unit. *Child Abuse & Neglect,* 1979, *3,* (3/4), 757-766.

Gil, D. *Violence against children.* Cambridge, Massachusetts: Harvard University Press, 1970.

Gil, D. Violence against children. *Journal of Marriage and the Family,* 1971, *33,* 644-648.

Graves, T. D., & Graves, N. B. *Drinking and violence in a multicultural society.* Auckland: South Pacific Research Institute, 1979.

Jackson, M. Rape in New Zealand. *Broadsheet,* December 1977, p. 18.

Jackson, M. The sexual abuse of children project: Auckland. Unpublished paper, 1980.

Kelsey, J. The gang problem: A conflict of pride and prejudice. University of Waikato, N.Z.: Winter Lectures, 1980.

McAndrew, C., & Edgerton, R. B. *Drunken comportment.* Chicago: Aldine, 1969.

Monaghan, S. M., & Couper-Smartt, J. Experience of an anticipatory management programme for potential child abuse and neglect. *Child Abuse and Neglect,* 1977, *1,* (1), 63-69.

Mulgan, J. *Man Alone.* Hamilton, N.Z.: Pauls Book Arcade, 1949.

Nixon, A. J. *A child's guide to crime.* Sydney, Australia: A. H. & A. W. Reed, 1974.

Ritchie, J. E. *The making of a Maori.* Wellington, N.Z.: A. H. & A. W. Reed, 1963.

Ritchie, J. E. The social context of child abuse in New Zealand. In D. C. Geddis (Ed.), *Child abuse.* Dunedin, N.Z.: National Children's Health Research Foundation, 1980.

Ritchie, Jane. *Childhood in Rakau.* Wellington, N.Z.: Victoria University, 1956.

Ritchie, Jane. *Child rearing patterns: Further studies.* Hamilton: University of Waikato, 1979.

Ritchie, Jane. Speak roughly to your little boy and beat him when he sneezes. Unpublished paper, University of Waikato, 1980.

Ritchie, Jane, Paine, H., & Tourelle, L. Sex differences in physical punishment: The children's view. In Jane Ritchie, (Ed.), *Psychology of women: Research record III,* Hamilton, N.Z.: University of Waikato, 1980.

Ritchie, Jane, & Ritchie, James. *Child rearing patterns in New Zealand.* Wellington, N.Z.: A. H. & A. W. Reed, 1970.

Ritchie, Jane, & Ritchie, James. *Growing up in New Zealand.* Sydney: George Allen & Unwin, 1978.

Ritchie, Jane, & Ritchie, James. *Growing up in Polynesia.* Sydney: George Allen & Unwin, 1979.

Ritchie, Jane, & Ritchie, James. *Spare the rod.* Sydney: George Allen & Unwin, 1981.

Ritchie, Jane, & Ritchie, James. Child rearing and child abuse: The Polynesian context. In J. E. Korbin (Ed.), *Child abuse and neglect: Cross cultural perspectives.* Berkeley: University of California Press, 1981.

Sabo, D. F., & Runfola, R. *Jock.* Englewood Cliffs, New Jersey: Spectrum, 1980.

Sears, R. R., Maccoby, E. E., & Levin, H. *Patterns of child rearing.* Evanston, Ill.: Row, Peterson, 1957.

Secretary for Justice. Submissions to the Parliamentary Select Committee on Violent offending. Wellington, N.Z.: Department of Justice, 1978.

Silva, P. *One thousand Dunedin three year olds.* Dunedin, N.Z.: Medical Research Council, 1976.

Snyder, E. E., & Spreitzer, E. *Social aspects of sport.* Englewood Cliffs, N.J.: Prentice-Hall, 1978.

Social Development Council. *Families and violence.* Wellington, N.Z.: Government Printer, 1980.

Steinmetz, S. *The cycle of violence.* New York: Praeger, 1977.

Steinmetz, S., & Straus, M. *Violence in the family.* New York: Dodd, Mead, 1975.

Straus, M., Gelles, R., & Steinmetz, S. *Behind closed doors.* New York: Doubleday, 1980.

Welsh, R. S. Severe parental punishment and delinquency: A developmental theory. *Journal of Clinical Child Psychology,* 1976, *5,* (1), 17-21.

Wendt, A. *Leaves of the banyan tree.* Auckland: Longman Paul, 1979.

Winder, C. L., & Rau, L. Parental attitudes associated with social deviance in preadolescent boys. *Journal of Abnormal and Social Psychology,* 1962, *64,* 418-424.

Yates, A. J. *Frustration and conflict.* New York: Wiley, 1962.

15

Nigeria: Aggression, A Psychoethnography

Leonard Bloom
and
Henry I. Amatu

INTRODUCTION

A contemporary Fanon should have written this chapter, but a Fanon matured beyond his obsession with presenting aggression in Africa as though it were peculiarly purified, its function to create an African identity by the simple technique of countering white aggression with black revolutionary violence. Fanon (1966), in his *The Wretched of the Earth*, writes about violence as a "cleansing force. It frees the native from his inferiority complex and from his despair and inaction. . . . When the people have taken a violent part in the national liberation . . . yesterday they were completely irresponsible; today they mean to understand everything and make all decisions [pp. 73-74]." Aggression is seen as emotionally and politically cathartic, and there is no concern about how to control the energy of aggression so that it can be sublimated into sociopolitical activity where stability and tranquility prevail.

No matured Fanon has, however, appeared, so a caveat must be uttered that the analysis of aggression in Africa is still tainted by the persistence (even among academics) of Fanon's positive valuation of aggression. For example, Ali Mazrui (1980) in a widely published series of lectures on contemporary social and political conditions in Africa adopts two contradictory positions: he argues first that the solution to the African "crisis of habitability" lies in the "gradual acquisition of . . . the capacity for self-pacification . . . [involving] the continent in controlling its own political and social excesses, ranging from tyranny to corruption, from border wars between states to the exploitation of women [p. 22]." But he also argues that the Pax Africana depends upon developing "a small nuclear section in the military establishment of Nigeria for the time being, and in Zaire and in black-ruled South Africa later [p. 135]." Aggression is not, therefore, a social and political problem, soluble by rational and cooperative means; but can only be controlled by the most aggressive and destructive weapons that man has so far devised. We are most dubious whether there is any magic in Africa that can convert aggression into a purer, more peaceful political energy; on the contrary, aggression in Africa, far from having the noble-sounding or therapeutic qualities attributed to it by Fanon, Sartre

(1966), and others, has the same sociocultural and psychodynamic characteristics as aggression anywhere else in the world.

NIGERIA—SOCIAL STRUCTURE

The modern state known as Nigeria emerged as a sociopolitical entity in 1900, and was formed out of the fragment of several ancient states, some of which had existed from the eleventh to the nineteenth centuries, and all of which had had well organized economies, governments, and sophisticated technology. The Niger delta had not been officially regarded as an area worth much administrative effort. As recently as 1881, Lord Kimberly (then the British colonial secretary) refused to approve the proposals of the governor of the Gold Coast and Lagos to "pacify the warring tribes" behind Lagos (Robinson & Gallagher, 1965, p. 165) because the trading prospects were thought to be not worth the expenses of administration. Only a century ago, the tedious problems of imposing law and order, thus facilitating the consolidation of smaller groups into a larger modern state, was barely—and grudgingly—begun; but there was never more than a handful of administrators, traders, manufacturers, and missionaries sprinkled thinly about the enormous area of what is now Nigeria. The vertiginous speed with which later Nigerians have seized upon the social, political, and economic examples of Western industrialisation and modernisation is remarkable. And unsettling! For one major sociocultural determinant of aggression is the unsettling nature of rapid sociopolitical change unaccompanied by any comparable development of models for conflict resolution.

Nigeria became an independent state in 1960, and is now economically thriving and socially effervescent—even turbulent. It has an estimated population of between 65 and 80 million in an area about two and a half times that of France (0.9 m.sq. km.). It is already one of the world's fifteen most populous countries, and it is estimated that by the year 2050 its population will have reached at least 135 million (Todaro, 1979, p. 176). It's already baffling complexity—economic, geopolitical, cultural, linguistic, and religious—will be even more bewilderingly compounded.

As long ago as 1938, the Nigerian Youth Charter stated as a major political aim "the development of a united nation out of the conglomeration of peoples who inhabit Nigeria [Herskovits, 1962, p. 348]," but the "conglomeration" persists and is one of the causes of collective aggression. In 1979, after thirteen years of military rule, the first national presidential elections still revealed an entrenched (but weakened) allegiance to regional, tribal, national, or ethnic groupings; and no major political party could plausibly present itself as unambiguously resistant to localistic pressures. However, at national and local levels, and in all kinds of administrative structures, sensitivity is shown to the dangers of localistic allegiances by appointing officers from outside the area or who are not likely to be involved in local power struggles. But, of course, this policy often founders because of the shortage of such detached people.

Nigeria is now divided into 19 major local authorities known as "states," and more have been demanded. Overall is the authority of the federal-presidential government, but there is still frequent suspicion of the federal and state governments by political and even social organizations, much grumbling about the power exerted by governments, and continual allegations that other groups are more favoured by, for example, admissions to universities, the sharing of political offices, or the allocation of federal-controlled finances.

Superficially, this resembles the social and political squabbling that occurs in all societies, but the personalization and emotional intensity of the disagreements suggests that sibling rivalries underlying political and social relationships are unusually close to the level of consciousness.

Ethnicity

Although during the last twenty years there has been very rapid urban growth and socioeconomic class strata are beginning to be politically and economically significant, one of the most emotionally significant groupings is ethnic. The concept "ethnic" is no more than an operational category, referring to a group of people who share a common culture, usually including a common language, and who perceive themselves as belonging to an ethnic group because of their common culture. It is essentially a matter of identification, and this may be forced upon the group by other groups, or may arise naturally out of an untroubled and continuous history.

Nigeria is highly diversified, culturally and linguistically, and the ethnic groups have often been associated with some degree of political independence that still influences political conduct at both national and regional levels. The gravity and persistence of ethnic identification and ethnic rivalries in stimulating and focusing collective aggression in Africa generally has been described and analysed by Ismagilova (1978) and Uchendu (1977). Writing from a Marxist perspective, Ismagilova contends that:

1. Ethnic peculiarities, the erection of national barriers (often artificial), a morbid attitude towards national sovereignty, and the stirring up of old wrongs and of past mistakes in attempts to resolve ethnic problems all occur in Africa; [p. 7]

2. Tribalist attitudes can develop into outbreaks of fanaticism . . . [because] the traditional institutions often make it possible for reactionary circles to utilise ethnic antagonisms and the ideology of ethnic separatism in the struggle for power; [p. 11]

3. Ethnic conflicts will probably be compounded by class-contradictions as socio-economic development proceeds and intensifies separatism in the competition for wealth and status (on the one hand), and the struggle to reduce economic, political and social inequalities (on the other). The Nigeria civil war (1967-1970) is a salutary example of how both ethnic attitudes and economic-political considerations combined with the non-existence of nationally acceptable institutions for the resolution of political conflicts made war inevitable.

Ismagilova is, however, rather too ready to attribute ethnic conflicts to conspiracies of ex-colonial powers and traditional rulers seeking to maintain or to extend their influence, and minimizes the phenomenology of ethnicity in specific and sometimes unpredictable situations. Since the end of the civil war, traditional rulers and external influences are still strong and still, presumably, interested in extending their economic power and social-political prestige, but few signs are evident of any building up of tensions that would be likely to produce another civil war. Ismagilova warns the reader against misconceiving *all* intergroup hostility and conflict as though it were simply reducible to "tribalism" or to ethnic rivalry; but, like many sociologists, she ignores the many sources of unconscious tension rooted in ethnicity that can provoke hostility and aggression (e.g., Enemuoh, 1975; Fagge, 1982; Ntekim, 1980; Sanda, 1976; Van den Berghe, 1973).

For example, Thomas and Chess (1980) regard aggression as adaptive: it is a manifestation of the psychodynamic process of acquiring "social competence and task mastery." Individuals and groups may react to stressful demands in many ways, one which is slowly acquired is to learn methods to neutralise or deflect a threat without losing self-esteem. If the stress is neutralized effectively then self-esteem is preserved, a social skill is learned and feelings of potency are enhanced. From this point of view, much interethnic aggression, whether expressed in open conflict and fighting or indirectly in wrangling, rivalry, and systematised suspicion, is a function of inappropriate socialisation.

The learning of social competence and task mastery of dealing with members of the family has been mastered through the imposition of strongly stereotyped constraints upon the expression of aggression toward sibling rivalry and the challenging of the authority of seniors. Respect for authority, an almost ritualised deference to seniors and superiors, and their pressure to encourage sentiments of subservience, frustrates the individual's self-esteem, inhibits spontaneity in relationships to strangers, and fosters aggression toward strangers by excluding them from both the kinship patterns of deference and the strong inhibitory institutions and sentiments of the kin group. Moreover, the model of polarization between "elders-in-authority and youth-in-deference" within the family is taken as the model in society at large, and the repressed aggression against authority in the family is readily transferred to other social institutions. The squabbles about the allocation of national oil revenues, and the interminable (sometimes fatal) skirmishes and the rambling law suits about territorial claims over patches of land often have the bitter and angry intensity of sibling rivalries for a mother's limited love. Ethnic collectivities are the major focus for this extrapolation of intrafamilial, suppressed aggression and rivalry.

It can be argued, however, that *all* types of socioeconomic change create tensions, uncertainties, frustrated expectations of betterment, and collisions with emotional strangers, all of which exacerbate the traditional tensions and hostilities. But the emergence of socioeconomic classes is a stage toward the formation of a wider national identity, and unless they coincide with ethnic groups, they may modify the intensity of ethnic rivalries by providing an alternative focus for intergroup aggression and rivalry, including the projection of aggression on sociopolitical targets outside the society. South Africa is a mild contributor to the deflection of political aggressions from internal targets.

Politics and Aggression

A more sensitive social anthropological analysis, based indirectly upon Berkowitz (1962), is that of Uchendu (1977), who contends that the high degree of aggressive behaviour in modern African (including Nigerian) politics is the result of so fundamental a change in the rules of the political game that the traditional consensus in African politics has been replaced by coercion.

Uchendu bases his argument upon Berkowitz's modified frustration-aggression theory, and upon the theory of relative deprivation, as adapted by Gurr (1970) to his analysis of collective political violence in the United States. Modern Africa is exceptionally aggressive because it has failed to develop an effective system to manage social conflict, and many of the conditions that determine such conflict are insoluble in political terms. Africa experiences severe frustrations that encourage aggression; Africa is perceived by its peoples as relatively deprived compared with the richer industrial countries; and there are many political and social uncertainties that are inimical to the development of stable patterns of conflict resolution. For example, Uchendu refers to Africa's inheritance of erratic political boundaries and to the rapid growth of "strategic aggression." In the unsettled economic, political, and social condition of Africa, there are innumerable incompatible goals and no established means by which groups can reconcile these goals and achieve some of them other than by collective aggression. Thus, aggression becomes legitimated as a means to rectify the group's perception of its deprivation of its rights, many issues become politicized, and, consequently, discontent is articulated into politically aggressive forms. Among the specific features of modern African states that encourage aggressive and competitive politics is the fact that almost all the independent states are too young to have developed systems of conflict resolution; they are dominated by ethnically complex political systems and tend to have authoritarian leadership and government.

With some justice, Uchendu refers to the "appalling legacy of colonial rule" in Africa as the untidy patchwork of administrative systems and the extremism of political language. But it is arguable that Africa has had no worse a political start than other decolonised continents, and that the experience of political and socioeconomic instability is similar in its origins to that of the frontier days in the United States or the gold and diamond-rush days in South Africa, before urbanization and population began to stabilize. Africa does have many political and economic frustrations and disappointments, and it may be argued that "competitive politics will always tend to lead to aggression [Uchendu, 1977, p. 107]." But can one be so certain that Africa has suffered a more dramatically severe, swift, and unsettling period of rejected expectations, false political prophets, and the sheer chaos of change than other areas in the world?

What conditions, then, might account for the sources and direction of aggression? The most plausible answer probably lies in combining Uchendu's analysis of sociopolitical patterns and the conceptualization of self-esteem. Africa has had an exceptional, but not unique, history; but it has possibly experienced an unusually intense period of powerlessness that has persisted beyond the period of colonial rule to that of independence. Even if one discounts a certain tendency to self-pity that exaggerates problems and nourishes defeatist attitudes toward solving problems, a lack of self-confidence in a world surfeited with problems encourages outbursts of anxiously assertive collective aggression.

Secularisation and Uncertainty

Nigeria, like other countries experiencing rapid socioeconomic change, has experienced dramatic changes in its religious and belief systems. One consequence of this change has been the growth of many competing religious and *soi-disant* philosophical sects, with the explicit or implicit aim of protecting and furthering the terrestrial and celestial interests and welfare of their members.

As long ago as 1967, Barrett (1968) enumerated 500 distinct schismatic Christian bodies in Nigeria, and over 6,000 throughout sub-Saharan Africa. This is not surprising. As Berger (1969) demonstrated, when allegiance to religions is voluntary, then the religious group must "sell itself" to the potential consumer as must any other product. In such a society as Nigeria, which is intensely competitive and materialistic, the rewards of success are lavish and the penalties of failure severe; the traditional supports of the individual are decreasingly effective; the frustrations and uncertainties of dependence upon authority and upon strangers grow more pressing and more capricious; and now traditional and Western patterns of dependency often reinforce each other. Individuals and groups, therefore, seek protection against uncertainty and the prescription for success where they will, and schismatic sects have dual functions of offering protection against the ruthless aggression of competitiveness, and of providing God's backing for success.

Symington (1978), in an illuminating discussion of the effects upon personality of secularization in nineteenth century Europe, has suggested mechanisms that encourage aggression, and his analysis implies parallels with the current situation in Nigeria. He begins with the observation that "major segments of society became detached from the sphere of the sacred . . . the waters of the Jordan are used for irrigation rather than for baptism." This symbolizes a transition from *materist* to *spiritest* religion, each with its own distinct social psychological experience. The materist type is associated with church-oriented religions, is closely linked with social and geographical location, and has a constant and predictable cosmology and epistemology that is almost tangible for the members. The spiritest type arises when people become unsettled, detached from their social and geographical location; they turn to a spiritest God, toward a more personal religion, and away from the group devotions and group orientations that mark materist worship.

Symington associates the materist religion with "individuals whose mental life is found in different compartments . . . especially with the obsessional type who has no real satisfying relationships [pp. 5-6]." The intensely organised religion acts as a defensive structure against the uncertainties of entering into relationships, and the group activities and rituals protect the individual from having to cope with creating an identity of his own. This religion (in terms derived from Kleinian and object-relations theory) is an active "warding off of the danger of personal relationships. . . . The bad internal object is projected onto the external world . . . onto God who must then be propitiated and so controlled to avoid a renewed injury [p. 7]." In the spiritest religion, there is a relationship to a personal God and the Good God is closely identified with the individual's ego ideal.

Africans have been precipitated into a changing world replete with dangers and uncertainties and with fewer and fewer of the traditional, social, and religious ego-supports. The destruction of traditional religions and philosophies by Christianity and Islam, the erosion of the African identity and ways of life, and the successful temptingly-dangerous wealth of Western economic systems emphasize the powerlessness of Africa and make imperative the need to obtain the most effective supernatural protection to replace the decay of secular life. Materist religion is increasingly being found to be as little satisfying and as ineffectively ego-defensive as it was in late nineteenth century Europe; the active dissolution and formation of ever newer and ever unsatisfying sects indicates this.

Ekanem (1980), in a study of "consumer religion" in a small town in southeastern Nigeria, found that a major motivation for sects to split from the parent sect was that it was felt that the parent had failed to ensure for its members an adequate return of security, wealth, health, and the good things of life that are associated with a materialist-capitalistic society. Dissident members are angry: indirectly with God for disappointing his children, and directly with the head of the church for not controlling the bounty and protection of God on their behalf. The aggression is indicated by the frequency of reports in the press of law suits between sects about property rights; announcements about the infidelities of other groups; and occasionally (and not rarely) open conflict between sects, including burning or seizing of properties.

The Young and the Old

As in most of Africa, traditionally Nigerian elders were respected; and, as in most societies in which the family is weakened by economic and social change, the role of the elders is challenged and the elders, in their turn, strive to assert their waning authority. That "traditional African societies are well known for their socialization which places emphasis upon obedience, responsibility, and respect for societal norms [Okonji, 1981]," is documented in a review of the ethnographic literature by Okonji, who also cites the studies of Munroe and Munroe (1972) and Munroe, Munroe and Daniels (1973). Reference can also be made to Bloom (in press, a).

Titchener (1972) wrote a perceptive psychoanalytical study of "the revolutionary temper in the young" in the middle 1960s in the United States. Not quite twenty years later, many of his observations of the aggressive temper of those times have parallels in Nigeria. In Nigeria in the 1980s, as in the United States in the middle 1960s, young people are living in a world in which the traditional cultural signposts to the future no longer point clearly in directions that people want to travel, and the traditional guides and counsellors no longer have quite the authority that they had in societies in the past. Moreover, the internal mechanisms that preserve emotional stability are increasingly shaken by the changing external sociocultural supports of the ego and the super ego. Titchener refers to five factors that encourage aggression in an unstable and changing society. A brief discussion of each follows.

1. Internal Conflict. One of the most common topics of conversation among young people in Nigeria is of the frustrations that they experience in attempting to plan in a society with so many changing and conflicting goals and procedures, and with so little positive guidance to depend upon.

2. Conscious Resentment. It seems psychodynamically plausible to include in this category the "rational," aggressive political protest of the kind that Fanon was advocating. In Nigeria, it is manifest largely in the intensely persecutory concern with what other groups are earning: the other siblings are getting more rewards from God, and *this* is another unconscious score against God!

3. A Demanding Ego-Ideal. Youth (or other groups) may act aggressively against society and its symbols in order to establish a sense of autonomy or, at least, to resist becoming submerged by that society. This motivation is peculiarly important in Nigeria (and probably Africa generally) where, in heavily structured and communalised society, the boundaries between the individual and the social are often hazy, and only an aggressive self-assertion, or eccentricity, can maintain the individual's uncertain awareness of where he or she ends and society begins—or vice versa. Thus one finds an uneasy and erratic oscillation between conformity and anarchic self-assertion: youth in one aspect of life is conforming, obedient, subdued, and in other aspects is rebellious and seen by elders and authority as "difficult to control".

4. A Love-Hate Relationship with Authority. In Nigeria, the heavily authoritarian role of the elders is permeated by protective and often affectionate relationships, so that the intricate relationships of hating and loving are difficult for the individuals to separate. This ambivalence is suggested in situations in which within a power structure there are covert and overt opportunities for competition. Debate and argument are often vigorous, even violent and angry, but it is unusual that there is not an acquiescent sense of relief when authority has spoken, a decision has been made, father has shown what must be done. But a decision accepted is not the same as a decision willingly carried out, and part of the notorious "inefficiency" of African administration is an indication of the love-hate relationship with authority—authority is at once welcomed and resisted, accepted superficially but unconsciously resented.

Flugel (1948) has explored the development of love-hate in the nuclear family and has extended its applications to a wider social and political society. The most relevant of his conclusions are all in some way related to the struggle by the child for independence and by the parents to maintain the control of the child, and he shows how many of the manifestations of growing-up (however this be defined by a society) involve emotional conflict and compromise: both parents and children are compelled to relinquish their attachments to one another, at one time inhibiting the anger of the unconscious or conscious acts of rebellion, and at others inhibiting the fixation on an idealized parent or child. Both sentiments are doomed to disappointment and frustration: the hero or heroine substitute for the perfect authoritarian parent rarely is found, and never found without qualities that lessen his mystical loftiness. The child, the subordinate, nearly always wants to grow up and grow apart. And permeating this conflict is that of the inevitable competition for wealth, prestige and privilege.

In both group and individual relationships where authority is involved, this is manifested by an almost ritualized form of verbal teasing that often seems (to an outsider) to approach a dangerous provocation to violence, but where the aggression is defused by a joke or witty comment. A short while ago, for example, I, Leonard Bloom, was the only white person in an informal gathering of Nigerians, and not unexpectedly, the discussion turned to the results of colonialism. The discussion grew more and more heated, and I felt uneasy as the target of openly hostile attitudes toward colonialism generally, and Britain and the British more specifically. I responded with equal vigour, though less bravura, and I became aware of the mixture of emotions that was being expressed: anger for the colonial experience was manifest, a stereotyped anti-British (but probably not anti-white) sentiment was also overt, and there seemed some considerable emotional release in relatively junior colleagues feeling free to attack a senior colleague in circumstances that carried no danger to them. Underlying the anger was a hint of jocular and affectionate teasing, of gratitude for a people who had made possible the acquisition of education and the skill to resist the authority that provided it. Even at the level of university teaching, similar experiences can be encountered: the characteristic relationships of staff to students are distant and authoritarian. The relationship of students to staff is characteristically submissive. But, as an outsider, the relationships to me are more spontaneous and more ambivalent: gentle but overt resistance to authority (which is safe, because I am an outsider and have not the cultural, social, and emotional predisposition to react punitively or violently), mingled with a sometimes regressive affectionate submission.

Essentially, the emotional questions are: "How far can I go before authority, our surrogate father, loses patience and punishes or rejects me?" "How far can I, in my position as a father surrogate, go before I have to punish or reject the students, the protesters, the discontented workers . . . before I have to assert firmly my paternal authority?" Concessions are perceived as weakness, weakness as dangerous both to the socioeconomic and the emotional structure of the society. Further, "How much love and understanding can be shown before I, representing paternal authority, will appear to be weak, submissive (where should be assertive and dominant) and therefore unable to control my children, students, workers, subjects. . . ."

5. Guilt-Resolving. Tichener's (1972) final aggressive causing factor is guilt resolution. The characteristic pattern of authority dealing with its subjects is one in which aggression is provoked by a readiness to put obstacles in the path of the subjects' wishes, and thus a pattern has developed in which much of the interaction of authority and subjects begins with an aggressive posturing that may explode into open violence. On the other side, there is a collusion with authority, dealings with authority often begin with a ritualised presentation of a demand that is unlikely to be accepted and that is followed by a brusque refusal. It is known that such a refusal will be received, so the subjects provoke authority into a response that will be provocative—and so the cycle continues, until a compromise is reached, often by capitulation by one side. Guilt, therefore, at resisting the father is aroused, and is dissipated after the routine of provocation and ultimate agreement. Much of the emotional liability of meetings, discussions, arbitrations, and negotiations seem to indicate this mechanism.

This erratic and ambivalent relationship between authority (father surrogate) and other people (sibling-children surrogates) is made acutely emotional, and increasingly erratic and arbitrary by the democratisation of sociopolitical structures, particularly the extended family and education, and by the weakening of the grip of authoritarian religious and value systems. But the open employment of aggression to quell what is interpreted as unruly behaviour is still widely acceptable, and is reflected in the continuing debates on the educational system and its effects upon young people.

During the last years of the military regime, for example, the press and the radio reported again and again alarm at the outbursts of protest by school and university students, and the government posted soldiers in schools to keep order. One of my (Bloom's) students was flogged in his secondary school by a soldier because of failing to wear the school uniform, and the head of state himself publicly flogged a boy who was wearing an unbuttoned shirt at school. It is as though the cohesion of the generations depends upon authority fighting threats to the nation and through the nation to itself. If the mass media indicate the prevailing mood of the nation, then one would be persuaded that the major social problems of the nation were not, for example, such economic problems as the decline of agriculture or industrial efficiency, but that they were a war between elders and youth, authority and anarchy, sometimes smouldering and often overt. The media report and comment is generally of a nature that would earn a very high score on the F scale; and, because of its immoderate nature, it both reflects and exacerbates the tendency to indulge in somewhat apocalyptic interpretations of social differences of attitude and opinions.

A typical example is the wide reporting of a speech by the Archbishop of Lagos who, in May 1978, drew attention to the "present tension and upheavals in the country which are the results of indiscipline, greed and lust for money. . . . The nation is full of lawlessness, much of which is unrebuked and unchallenged. . . . Discipline was the genesis of an orderly society, and when parents prefer to run after money they lose their parental authority." The Archbishop was speaking when there was still a powerful military regime; and, shortly after, there had been clashes between police, armed forces, and students in which students were officially reported killed, and reports of deaths and violence circulated for some time after the events. A government enquiry, reported in *The Nigerian Chronicle* (May 2, 1978) observed that "all along, the student leadership and their collaborators have carefully planned a strategy of violent upheaval . . . to spread fear and panic. They believed that if students in Europe could bring about the collapse of government so could they." There are only about 25,000 university students in Nigeria, of widely varying socioeconomic backgrounds and political and religious beliefs. Further, the enquiry commented: "students forgot their situation in life and became totally lacking in humility in dealing with other people reasonably." The emotive language used by the enquiry matched the emotive language of the students, but the specific protests were about such uninflammatory matters as the payments of fees and the poor quality of facilities in education, and there was barely a word or deed reported that suggests plausibly that the students had even the mildest radical strategy and psychology in the sense of the 1960s protests in Europe and the United States.

But young people are expected to be humble and to remember and appreciate their lowly station in life, and authority expressed alarm verging on panic when youth had the temerity to demand a larger slice of the growing and not inconsiderable national cake, and to be accepted as equal partners.

An indirect result of this confrontation is that young people generally, and other groups who perceive themselves collectively as underprivileged or who have grievances to which they fear that authority will not listen sympathetically, are socialized into aggression. The Nigerian social system is still based upon the extended family and enjoys family-type relationships and organizations. The system is still permeated by patriarchal and authoritarian attitudes that foster an ethos unfavourable to growing up emotionally; and sibling relationships persist, both prosocial and antagonistic. If parents or parent surrogates refuse to respond to their children's requests, and if siblings are forced to struggle for a share of their parents' love and largesse, then the children who feel deprived may respond by expressing their feelings of deprivation and rejection by attempting aggressively to seize what they consider to be their rightful portion. If a society, therefore, tends to treat its adults as children, then it socialises them to employ childishly confrontatory and aggressive social and political strategies to achieve their aims, and it encourages the regressive emotional states (of both parents and children) that motivate such strategies. Authority, by acting the heavy father, arouses the children to rebel, and so brings about the aggressive behaviour that it intensely fears. Moreover, aggression reminds the father surrogate that his powers are waning while those of his younger rivals are growing. What Dahrendorf (1978) has described as a "stratification lag: that is, status structures may lag behind changes in norms and power relations, so that the upper class of a bygone epoch may retain its status position for a while under new conditions [p. 39]," acquires a deep emotional significance.

From a different psychological perspective, one can draw an emotional parallel with deuterolearning. In deuterolearning, the individual acquires habits or systems of learning, and builds systems of cognitive techniques and strategies. Aggression may be learned not dissimilarly; the responses to unfamiliarity, threat, insecurity, and frustration are not learned in specific stimulus-response units but according to generalised principles that are established by social-cultural norms and by the individual's early childhood experience. One learns in what general circumstances and with what targets to be aggressive or to be conciliatory.

Like all societies, Nigeria has targets for aggression that are socially, ideologically, and culturally sanctioned, and styles of aggression that are acceptable.

There have long been distinguishable social groups such as ethnic or national groups, youth groups, groups given to magic and witchcraft, religious groups (all other religions are heresies), petty thieves and delinquents, and there are increasingly distinguishable modern targets such as members of trade unions, students, and political opponents. Women are an exceptional target because of the complexity of their role in society, and because they are perceived in a number of irreconcilable ways: untouchable but adored mothers and goddesses, wicked and dangerous witches, tempting and evil prostitutes, unreachable but alluring. The cartoons of women in the mass media and their portrayal in TV and on the radio, the lampoons of girls at school and university, and the perjorative stereotypes uttered carelessly by men about women often reveal an intense ambivalence about their relationships with women, at once hostile, sometimes openly aggressive and violent, dependent, contemptuous, and yet idealized.

Development Aspects

Freud himself in 1915 professed to being baffled by the causes of group antipathies, although one would have supposed psychoanalysts to be immune to the shock of revelations of the nastier qualities of mankind; and, as late as 1933, he was still expressing surprise that so many psychoanalysts and the laity were reluctant to recognise aggression as a strikingly pervasive and easily aroused state of individuals and groups (Freud, 1915/1963 and 1933/1977). Fenichel (1946) adopted an orthodox psychoanalytical schema that aggression is essentially adjustive: internal demands and the external world are brought into relation by an organizing, integrating, and maturing ego. Aggression as a function of frustration or of self-assertion, or even if regarded as an instinct, is "brought about by the pressure of the social environment. . . . If society becomes unstable, full of contradictory tendencies, and the scene of struggles between its different parts, power alone determines how and towards what goals [p. 586]" aggression may be directed. The child learns to distinguish permissible goals for his aggression from an early age, and a major function of institutionalized education is to establish in the child a pattern of targets and nontargets, and the internal controls of aggression that the culture favours.

Aggression, therefore, partially crystallizes into personality, and the question arises whether there are characteristics of personality in Africans that might affect aggressive behaviour which are related to culture.

An early view was that of Henri Collomb (1965) who, on the basis of an extensive research and clinical experience in Senegal (West Africa), contrasted the Western and the African personalities. Collomb described the former as insulated, granular, ego-centered, and individualized, and the latter as diffuse and sociocentered. The Western personality is formed in societies that are urban, insecure, and based upon individual anguish and guilt; but the African is traditionally raised in communities in which there is not the same alienating separation between the self and others as there is in an urban society. Africans, according to Collomb, therefore, grow up to be acutely sensitive to their social world, and to the relationships between people in it. Indeed, he argued that the traditional African is essentially defined by his position in the society and only knows his identity by the "cultural codification" of his relationships with others. He is rooted in a world of other people. The community is then a reference point for the individual personality.

In Jungian terms, it seems that Collomb would suggest that Africans are more likely to be extrovert types than is the average Westerner, and are, therefore, more likely to express aggression spontaneously and overtly.

Corin (1980) disagrees; she takes a less sociocentered view of the African personality and shows how, even in traditional societies, communal life is less pressing than Collomb suggests and, within traditional social structures, there are disruptive factors that should encourage a rethinking of the notion of African personality to permit the "individual" or the "particular" to be considered. For example, she notes that: "le milieu dans lequel grandit l'enfant est dépendant marque d'emblée par une série d'oppositions dont la plus manifeste est celle entre la famille nucléaire et le clan. . . . Sur le fond de cette opposition se met en place une dualité des références: à l'oncle maternel et au père, ou a l'oncle maternel et au grand-père [p. 141]."

When, therefore, there are tensions in the social structure, one can expect to find psychological tensions focused upon the forced-choice situations of finding identity and satisfying a sense of loyalty. In much of Africa, including Nigeria, one would expect that where urbanisation and industrialisation are still actively in conflict with traditional-agrarian forms of society, then psychological tensions and the search for identity would be strong. In this, there are some indications of convergence between psychodynamically oriented psychiatrists and psychologists and those social anthropologists who have examined the problems of the motivation, direction, and control of aggression.

For example, Corin (1980) expresses the view commonly held among Francophone psychiatrists that in West Africa "conflict is not internalized and ought not to be interpreted along the lines of interpersonal dialectics as would be the case of symptoms of persecution in Western psychiatry [p. 147]," because of the strength of external conflicts that are often implicit in the genesis of the individual's tension. Corin cites four common categories of motives that may arouse tensions, of which the first is "the transgression of a social or cultural rule" and the second is "conflicts in interpersonal relationships." This broad view is supported by other Francophone writers, for example Corin and Bibeau (1975), Parin, Morgenthaler and Parin-Matthey (1963), Sow (1977), and Zomploni-Rabain (1974), who imply that in West Africa it may be highly dangerous openly to express aggression except where the collective has ritualised and legitimated the direction of aggression. Aggression is introjected, and may be manifested socially in collectively approved feuding and fighting and in the form of persecutory fantasies in the functioning personality. These observations are confirmed by my recent research in Nigeria, though it was addressed to other problems (Bloom, in press a, b).

The considerable volume of anthropological material can only be touched upon lightly; and, although Bohannan (1967) is almost alone in dealing directly with Nigeria, it is reasonable to assume that Nigeria is not radically different from other African countries in the *general* nature of the social context of aggression and violence.

The central theme is the functions of aggression, i.e., aggression as cohesive socially and explicable rationally. This theme, since Evans-Pritchard's studies of the Azande and the Nuer

(1940 a,b) fifty years ago, is that of showing that "many violent acts can be shown to be 'rational' in a Weberian sense, i.e., designed by the actor to achieve a social aim. Others are irrational because they are unlikely to succeed; nevertheless they too may be amenable to sociological explanation [Marx, 1972, p. 281]." Even in a society such as that of the Nuer, which Evans-Pritchard (1940 a, p. 6) described as being that of "ordered anarchy," there is the paradox of order and predictability within a disruptive activity in a context of a society striving (like all societies) for cohesion despite the aggressive forces that pull it apart. Describing and explaining the apparently (to Westerners) bizarre phenomena of magic and witchcraft among the Azende of the Sudan, Evans-Pritchard (1940 b) focused his discussion on the problem of rationality in a given sociocultural context; he asked, "Is Zande thought so different from ours that we can only describe their speech and actions without comprehending them, or is it essentially like our own thought expressed in an idiom to which we are unaccustomed? [p. 4]." The answer was that the apparently bizarre beliefs formed a part of a highly intricate complex of beliefs and practices which altogether form a system that makes sense of otherwise incomprehensible events, and prescribes appropriate behaviour to deal with those events. Much aggressive or violent behaviour in Africa may similarly be interpreted in rational terms, i.e., as expressing the societies' ways of making order out of disorderly and otherwise disruptive behaviour. Thus, even where there are spontaneous quarrels and disputes, in most African societies the corporate group to which the disputants belong may intervene, and as Bohannan (1967) reports of the Tiv of northeastern Nigeria, even a murder may be "ritually repaired." Lineage groups are particularly significant in maintaining their solidarity by defending their members; and, in all societies, there are well-established, neutral groups or individuals whose function it is to act as mediators—to reduce tensions and repair rents in the social fabric by adjudicating the appropriate compensation or penalty. The emphasis is usually upon reparation and compensation; and the notion of injury, of violation of rights or offence having been offered, is closely related to the social distance betweeen the parties to a dispute. Eventually, if peacemakers "prove successful and popular . . . they become indispensible and their pacificatory role acquires a political edge. This is essentially the genesis of the hagiarchal state realized by communities of saints in Muslim societies [I. M. Lewis, 1976, p. 352]."

ATTITUDES AND OPINIONS ABOUT AGGRESSION

This section reports some of the major findings of a survey of views on aggression carried out by Henry I. Amatu, in and around the city of Jos in northern Nigeria. There were two samples:

1. 200 students, equally divided between students at the university and at the local advanced teachers' training college; and
2. 100 local inhabitants with little or no formal education.

The survey was carried out by means of a questionnaire, divisible into three main areas:

1. the nature and causes of aggression,
2. the control of aggression, both ideally and as in Nigeria, and
3. the alternatives to aggression.

The first area included, for example, questions to elicit what the respondents understood by the term "aggression"—whether it was peculiar to Nigeria, how it was caused, and its forms in Nigeria. The second area included, for example, whether respondents thought aggression was adequately controlled in Nigeria, what methods were employed to deal with it, and what methods ought to be tried. The third area dealt with the broader issues of how Nigerian society encourages aggressive behaviour, or encourages alternatives to it.

Nature and Causes of Aggression

Amatu's findings confirm those of Bloom (in press a) that aggression in childhood is welcomed by parents because, in today's Nigeria, if the individual fails to be aggressive and assertive, he or she is unlikely to be able to cope. Thus, children are said to need to be opposed in minor ways so that they will learn how to test their strengths and weaknesses and how to overcome obstacles. Only by learning to deal with opposition in childhood can the child begin to define his identity and learn how to defend it. It was felt that an unaggressive child might grow up to be either abnormally underassertive or overassertive.

However, aggression is also said to be caused by rejecting or neglecting children, so that the neglected child grows up to be an adult unable to tolerate rejection, and who responds to it aggressively. Rejection in childhood was also seen as a major cause of the behaviour of adults who are so ready in Nigeria to fight over what might seem to be trivial deprivations, and to the frequency with which the weak and the helpless are coerced and bullied by those in authority. Other causes of aggression mentioned by respondents included heredity, the intervention of the gods, and learning—both in the family and in wider sociocultural contexts. Over 50 percent of the respondents believed aggression was inherited, so that it ran in families. It was said that "the blood of criminals runs in their veins" and examples were given of families in which aggressiveness was marked throughout several generations.

Among the Igbo people, it is believed that some gods, particularly the rascally *Agwu,* cause humans to behave aggressively or otherwise antisocially, and other gods (more malleable) if offered sacrifices or bribes may be persuaded to influence one's enemies so that they behave aggressively and are led to their own destruction. Those whom the gods destroy they first make mad—in Nigeria as in ancient Greece. The possibility of poisoning and witchcraft to direct aggression against one's adversaries was believed. Often, for example, when a Nigerian dies, a relative will consult a diviner to find out the cause of the death, because it is widely believed that in most cases death is the result of someone's wicked acts. The diviner informs the complainant of the culprit, and prepares a poison or magical object with which an attempt is made to destroy the wicked person. It is not unusual for Nigerian obituary or in memoriam notices in the press or on the radio to declare: "the wicked have done their worst." In an unpublished analysis of over 2,500 obituary notices, P. R. Shakespeare found that there was only one reference to a natural death, and in almost the entire sample there was implicitly or explicitly reference to death as violent or unnatural. Not surprisingly, there is a brisk trade in charms, amulets, and talismans prepared by traditional medicine men to cause evil to befall others or to protect oneself. Sacrifices are hidden on the roadside, at the foot of trees, in the eaves of houses, and elsewhere so that the persons against whom they are directed will experience a misfortune or disaster. Sometimes live birds or goats or sheep are offered to a wicked god, for example, the god Amadiacha, and allowed to roam the streets to spread misfortune to the intended targets.

Aggression is also understood to be learned; the young child or adolescent grows up in a world in which violence is common and comes to accept aggression as normal. An example is the area of the city of Enugu which is known as Katanga, after the war-torn region of Zaire. Similarly, the former practice of publicly executing criminals provided a model of socially sanctioned violence, and, even now, it is common for children and adolescents to share with adults the practice of lynching those suspected of robbery. Amatu has witnessed the stoning to death of a suspect in which, horrifyingly, children and adults took turns throwing missiles.

Associated with the commonplace acceptance of overt socially approved aggression is the acceptance of aggressive techniques to mitigate the failure of administrative, legal, and policing agencies to enforce the laws of the land. The public enforces "justice" roughly because they fear that no other agency will enforce it at all. Lynching is justified as a reminder to the police that the people have no confidence in the ability or willingness of the police to protect life and property (A. Lewis, 1981). This suspicion of the police is reinforced by the common belief that the police are often accomplices in robberies, supplying arms or giving cover to robbers by contriving not to be around areas where there is high crime; and there have been reports of men suspected of armed robbery who were caught wearing police uniforms.

Less tangible is the association of aggressive behaviour with rapid socioeconomic change. The respondents were well aware of a possible relationship between the chronic shortages of facilities, housing, goods, etc. so that one cannot fail to be struck by the frequency and intensity with which Nigerians struggle in a chaotic manner to get a share of what is usually chaotically offered—the bus stop, market, even the sharing of domestic goods and services is frequently verbally and physically highly aggressive. More specifically, aggression such as armed robbery and thieving is said to be caused by poverty, and the struggle to improve one's lot in life in conditions where it might be very difficult to do so honestly. Individuals see considerable wealth around them and, wanting to get rich as quickly as the rich, use violence to wrench from society that which society denies them. Ujah (1980), Igwe (1981), and Osundare (1981), writing in the popular press, illustrate the prevalence of these views. Associated with poverty as a cause of aggression is the awareness of rapid socioeconomic change. Most Nigerians have friends or relatives who have migrated from the country to the town; and, in the press and by the respondents, it was often lamented that the cities breed crime and violence because the family no longer exists in the city, and people who would be stopped from aggression in the village by the intervention of friends, neighbours, or relatives are seen by no one in the cities and are, therefore, kept in check by no one.

The wider sociocultural context includes ethnic and religious factors. Beliefs about the latter may have been influenced by the riots in early 1981 in the northern part of Nigeria, when fanatical religious groups rioted and caused deaths and were only subdued after a determined military intervention; even at a domestic level, there are reports from time to time of murders, apparently motivated by religious fanaticism. On a larger scale, it is still commonly believed that the anti-Igbo pogroms in the north before the civil war were partly motivated by religion. The respondents listed religion as a cause of aggression but, even more frequently, cited ethnic differences and prejudices. For example, there have been press reports of death threats made to university staff who were not natives of the state in which the universities were situated, and several recent outbreaks of student violence in universities have been attributed to political rivalries complicated by ethnic antipathies.

Both physical and verbal aggression were reported: provocation, teasing and annoying remarks or curses, as well as beating and fighting. It was widely believed that, although aggression is universal, Africans generally and Nigerians in particular are less aggressive and destructive than other races. The respondents distinguished between the propensity of the "white races" to "habitually destroy others everywhere," and the African tendency to confine aggression to each other. But ritual killing was said to be more common in Africa. Even as this paragraph was written, an apparently ritual murder of a university student led to demonstrations by the students, followed by more deaths, and this sequence of events was not reported as in any way unusual.

It was widely held that aggression is most commonly carried out by adults against each other, and children were rarely mentioned as victims or as aggressors. One has the impression, indeed, that early adolescents are infrequently involved in major forms of aggression, but this may be because there are more prosocial outlets than in other countries, or that controls are stricter. The respondents seemed to judge aggression by young people more tolerantly than it would be judged in the United States or Europe, however; but children who are aggressive at school or in the home are not infrequently beaten.

Controlling Aggression

Aggression is controlled in Nigeria in much the same ways as in other countries. It was reported that children who are aggressive may be ridiculed, beaten, sentenced to "time out" (i.e., made to go to bed early), and exhorted and otherwise persuaded to behave less aggressively. But only rarely did it seem that Nigerian parents feel that they should provide ways for the child to act or talk out aggression within the family by holding an active dialogue. This reflects the conventional distancing of parents from their children: schools are rarely visited, children are rarely consulted or helped with their schoolwork (Amatu, 1981). From adolescence, it is reported that in village communities there is a common practice for villagers to call on a family to warn or advise them of the aggressive behaviour of a member, and sanctions may be imposed, ranging in gravity from the mild restitution to the severer propitiation of the gods and the spirits of the ancestors. A traditional healer might be consulted. It was known that, in the towns, medical help could be obtained to help control a manifestly disturbed, aggressive person.

Most commonly, it was asserted that the most successful method of controlling aggression was to counter it with aggression, because "aggressive persons are not amenable to reason." So, although there are methods of law enforcement to control aggression, these are felt to be insufficient and ineffective and not to be trusted or relied upon. Lynching is often resorted to as being swift, instant, and final. This is not without the tacit encouragement of the police and the army. It was reported that the police (and formerly the army) tend to respond violently to situations that are perceived as violent, and the summary (and violent) punishment of alleged offenders is common. The political structure also tacitly encourages counteraggression; political protests, labour strikes, and student demonstrations tend to be met now with dialogue but with an often violent suppression. Aggression is thus institutionalised as a characteristic of the social and political processes of gaining individual and collective goals.

Armed robbery, as the ultimate act of aggression, was much discussed by the respondents and is frequently discussed in the press. Broadly, it was agreed that robbery was so frequent and so evil that even execution or lynching was a justifiable punishment, and that the failure of less drastic but more certain methods of apprehending robbers amply justifies such methods. Amatu (1980) has found that direct experience or knowledge of specific cases of detected and convicted robbers increases the estimation of the risk of detection in crime; it was not known how many respondents had really witnessed such apprehension or punishment of robbers, but they agreed that, as a method, execution or lynching is warranted because of its supposed deterrent effect—an opinion reinforced by the horrifying reports of lynchings and the heavily didactic public discussions of crime and punishment that provide arguments in favour of draconic punishments as deterrents. Consistently, the as-yet-untried methods of controlling aggression mentioned by respondents were mainly variants of degrading and torturing offenders, but a not insignificant number of respondents were aware of the need to improve socioeconomic conditions and to offer young people better employment opportunities.

Alternatives to Aggression

Nigeria is economically an intensely competitive society, and respondents agreed that economic competition was a healthy form of aggression. Competition is encouraged in other ways of which respondents approved: sports, athletics, and festivals arouse considerable collective excitement. There are, for example, a national football team and boxers of international standing engraved on a tomb where visiting politicians lay wreaths, as though on a shrine. Organised political competition was also approved, although the violence and disruption that accompany it were criticized. The performing arts, particularly drama, are very popular in Nigeria and are traditionally socially acceptable vehicles for aggression. Many dramatic performances, even many popular songs, are intensely moral in their intent; and there is a high degree of audience participation. Within a song or a dramatic performance, a principle, a group, or an individual may be attacked; and much drama, poetry, novel writing, and journalism is unrestrainedly aggressive by American and British standards. There is also a great deal of spontaneous creation of songs and rhymes, political and nonpolitical, that expresses anger in a manner that is socially acceptable. Every teacher, for example, soon gets accustomed to finding lampoons and teasing messages on his door or on the blackboard.

The survey failed conclusively to show if respondents believed that aggression, individual or collective, is preventable. Some respondents argued that aggression is genetically determined and is, therefore, unchangeable. Others noted that, if society were overhauled, aggression could be reduced. But over 80 percent of the respondents thought that aggression is a necessary condition of social life and could never, therefore, be totally eliminated from the behaviour of mankind. Almost all the respondents agreed that aggression was increasing in Nigeria, partly because of the richness of the rewards and partly because of the ineffectiveness of the police and of the brutalising effects of the civil war. But, again, it was implied that even this deterioration could be arrested if honest and competent government improved social conditions.

One happier note was sounded: it was widely appreciated that, at both the local and national levels, governments have made efforts to reduce collective aggression. For example, at the end of the civil war, the victorious federal government declared that there were neither victors nor vanquished, and there was no victory parade, while the head of state immediately toured the nation to encourage reconciliation between the Biafrans and other Nigerians. The local state governments have steadily opposed the sometimes violent border disputes between neighbouring states; and, despite the bellicosity of the press, the national government has consistently restrained any mass demand for retaliation against aggressive acts by neighbouring nations.

CONCLUSION

It is no more than a slight exaggeration to describe modern Nigeria as an "ordered anarchy"; and, in view of the degree of orderliness that has already begun to stabilize, such a description is not pejorative. The traditional techniques for resolving conflict and for channeling aggression persist and are unlikely to be rapidly and fully replaced by urban techniques. In a modernized form, many of the activities of policing, resolving disputes, moralising, and reducing tensions between individuals or groups still have the intimate and personalized intensity of family, clan, and village conferences. Even in 1981, there are traditional disputes about land and property, thefts and robberies are committed, people assault and murder each other, and families quarrel and fight and disturb the civic peace. So, even in 1981, even in cities the size of Lagos, there are family and neighbourhood groups which maintain, within the limits of an urban world in which those who are disposed to vanish can often do so, an orderly (if informal and erratic) system of controlling aggression. Until formal policing is greatly improved and until a national morality is more widely accepted, the occasional lynching of suspected thieves, the "informal" flogging of naughty children and youths by police, the communal aggressions against the tax collector or government inspector, the continual rows and wrangling within industrial and governmental organizations indicate the enduring power of traditional modes of pacification. "Riots," in the words of Martin Luther King, "are the language of the unheard"; in Nigeria, despite the innumerable collective rivalries, antipathies, and uncertainties might be expected to cause riots and other forms of collective aggression. However, apart from the civil war, such collective aggression is not (in my view) alarmingly prevalent.

Feierabend and Feierabend (1966), in a study of political aggression in 62 nations between 1948 and 1962, found that the rate of political instability is greater in societies that are moving from an agrarian to an industrial way of life. Nigeria is an example of such a society, yet, although the cultural and structural factors that stimulate aggression ebb and flow unpredictably, much of social and political life appears to an outsider (like the writer) to be a not unsatisfactory oscillation between aggressive destruction and love and concern. The civil war strikingly illustrates how psychological and sociocultural factors converge in transmuting aggression into a less violent equilibrium. In 1970, after three years of bitter fighting preceded by four years of erratic, localized violence and angry political conflict, the civil war suddenly ended. It is difficult to see how any of the social and political problems that brought about the war had been solved by it, yet, in an almost unprecedentedly short time (compare the post civil war period in the United States), Nigeria was functioning again as one nation. Almost immediately after the war, there appeared a widely circulated photographic history of the war. One photograph is still popular and still arouses strong emotions: a federal and a Biafran soldier are shown embracing their submachine guns hanging from their shoulders; the caption expresses relief that brothers no longer have to kill one another. The build-up of aggression during the war was in one moment dissipated; and, despite the continuing socioeconomic, cultural, and religious tensions of the last decade, there are few signs of the revival of the anger of the 1960s.

The anthropologist Gluckman, analysing the various forms of conflict in preindustrial, preurban Africa (see, e.g., Gluckman, 1973), suggested that beneath the surface of aggression and violence there are strong forces that encourage stability and that reduce aggression. Like Evans-Pritchard's analysis of the way that feuding and conflict are controlled by many groups in a society in a state of equilibrium, e.g., the competing lineage groups also provide a stable system of conflict, so does Gluckman find that conflict and aggression are ritualised means of co-existing in societies in which social and economic interests conflict sharply, but yet in which the survival of the society is too precarious to permit unrestrained violence. There can be "real" conflict because (and perhaps only because) there is an underlying unity and interdependence and a pervasive sense of shared identity based upon an intensely communal ethos and an intricately interlocking political, social, and economic system. Gluckman even refers to ritualised rebellion and license in Africa in which, as in mediaeval Europe, an element of controlled aggression against authority acts as an institutionalized catharsis. Moreover, even real rebellion and changes of political power share this collective abreaction because, once the dust and clamour of rebellion have subsided, it is frequently found that though feelings are discharged the power structures are effectively unaltered. Political tensions, even if they are temporarily relieved, will accumulate again. Thus, the aggressiveness and contentiousness of much of Nigerian political and social life is both aggressive and prosocial. The underlying, deep social and economic conflicts are damped down by the overt, superficial, and often highly dramatic, ritualized protest. So authoritarian and hierarchical a society can only survive emotionally the ferocious competitiveness, the suspicion of strangers, and intense fears about the future, if the social and political systems not only permit but tacitly provide outlets for a superficial and aggressive protest that is widely (even if unconsciously) accepted as not approaching dangerously close to the roots of structural socioeconomic conflicts.

REFERENCES

Amatu, H. I. Estimation of the risks of detection in crime. Paper delivered at National Conference of the Nigerian Association of Clinical Psychologists, University of Benin, Benin, April 1980.

Amatu, H. I. Family motivated truancy. *International Journal of Psychology,* 1981, in press.

Barrett, D. B. *Schism and renewal in Africa.* Nairobi: Oxford University Press, 1968.

Berger, P. *The social reality of religion.* London: Faber, 1969.

Berkowitz, L. *Aggression — A social psychological analysis.* New York: McGraw-Hill, 1962.

Bloom, L. Socialization and dependence in a developing country, Nigeria. *Journal of Social Psychology,* in press, a.

Bloom, L. Lying and culture. A West African case-study. *Journal of Psychological Anthropology,* in press, b.

Bohannan, P. (Ed.) *African homicide and suicide.* New York: Atheneum Press, 1967.

Collomb, H. Les bouffées délirantes en psychiatrie Africaine. *Psycho-pathologie Africaine,* 1965, *1,* 167–239.

Corin, E. Vers une réappropriation de la dimension individuelle en psychologie Africaine. *Revue Canadienne des études Africaines,* 1980, *14,* 135–136.

Corin, E., & Bibeau, G. De la forme culturelle au vécu des troubles psychiques en Afrique: Propositions méthodologiques par une étude interculturelle du champ des maladies mentales. *Africa,* 1975, *3,* 280–315.

Dahrendorf, R. On the origins of inequality among men. In A. Beteille (Ed.), *Social inequality.* Harmondsworth, England: Penguin Books, 1978.

Ekanem, E. U. *Consumer religion in Ididep.* Unpublished B.Sc. (Sociology) research paper, University of Calabar, Nigeria, 1980.

Enemuoh, P. E. C. The effect of education and occupation on ethnic prejudice in Nigeria. Unpublished research paper, University of Nigeria, Nsukka, 1975.

Evans-Pritchard, E. E. *The Nuer.* Oxford: Oxford University Press, 1940. a

Evans-Pritchard, E. E. *Witchcraft, oracles and magic among the Azande.* Oxford: Oxford University Press, 1940. b

Fagge, A. M. Ethnic factors in social distance: A theoretical perspective. Unpublished research paper, University of Calabar, Calabar, Nigeria, 1982.

Fanon, F. *The wretched of the earth.* New york: Evergreen Books, 1966.

Feierabend, I., & Feierabend, R. Aggressive behaviors within politics, 1948–1962: A cross-national study. *Journal of Conflict Resolution,* 1966, *10,* 249 271.

Fenichel, O. *Outline of the psychoanalytic theory of neurosis.* New York: Norton, 1946.

Flugel, J. C. *The psychoanalytic study of the family.* London: The Hogarth Press, 1948. (Originally published 1921.)

Freud, S. Reflections upon war and death. In P. Rieff (Ed.), *Character and culture.* New York: Collier, 1963. (Originally published 1915).

Freud, S. *New introductory lectures on psychoanalysis.* (J. Strachey, ed. and trans.) Harmondsworth, England: Penguin Books, 1977. (Originally published, 1933.)

Fromm, E. *The anatomy of human destructiveness.* Harmondsworth, England: Penguin Books, 1977.

Gluckman, M. *Custom and conflict in Africa.* Oxford: Blackwell, 1973.

Gurr, T. R. *Why men rebel.* Princeton: Princeton University Press, 1970.

Herskovits, M. J. *The human factor in changing Africa.* New York: Knopf, 1962.

Igwe, N. O. Armed robbery—Postwar phenomenon. *Nigerian Statesman,* Owerri, Nigeria, April 15, 1981, p. 3.

Ismagilova, R. N. *Ethnic problems of the tropical Africa. Can they be solved?* (A. N. Utheritt, trans.). Moscow: Progress Publishers, 1978.

Lewis, A. Has lynching come to stay? *The Daily Times,* Lagos, Nigeria, February 19, 1981, p. 7.

Lewis, I. M. *Social anthropology in perspective.* Harmondsworth, England: Penguin Books, 1976.

Marx, E. Some social contexts of personal violence. In M. Gluckman (Ed.), *The allocation of responsibility.* Manchester, England: Manchester University Press, 1972.

Mazrui, A. *The African condition: A political diagnosis.* London: Heinemann, 1980.

Munroe, R. L., Munroe, R. H. and Daniels, R. E. Relations of subsistence economy to conformity in three East African societies. *Journal of Cross Cultural Psychology,* 1973, *4,* 149-150.

Ntekim, E. E. Inter-ethnic contact hypothesis in a Nigerian university: An empirical study. Unpublished research paper, University of Calabar, Calabar, Nigeria, 1980.

Okonji, M. O. Psychological differentiation. In B. Lloyd and J. Gay (Eds.), *Universals of human thought: Some African evidence.* Cambridge: Cambridge University Press, 1981.

Ortigues, M. C. and Ortigues, E. Intégration des données culturelles africaines à la psychiatrie de l'enfant dans la pratique clinique au Sénégal. *Psychopathologie Africaine,* 1966, *2,* 441-451.

Ortigues, M. C., & Ortigues, E. (Eds.) *Oedipe Africain.* Paris: Editions Plon, 1973.

Osundare, N. Violence in the U.S.: Gun control not the answer. *The Sunday Times,* Lagos, Nigeria. April 26, 1981, p. 5.

Parin, P., Morgenthaler, F. and Parin-Matthey, G. *Der Weissen Denken Zuviel.* Zurich: Atlantis Verlag, 1963.

Robinson, R., & Gallagher, J. *Africa and the Victorians—The official mind of imperialism.* London: Macmillan, 1965.

Sanda, A. O. (Ed.) *Ethnic relations in Nigeria.* Ibadan, Nigeria: University of Ibadan Press, 1976.

Sartre, J. P. Introduction. In F. Fanon, *The wretched of the earth* (C. Farrington, trans.). New York: Evergreen Books, 1966.

Sow, I. *Psychiatrie dynamique Africaine.* Paris: Editions Payot, 1977.

Symington, N. Secularization and social change. Paper delivered at conference on Psychology of Religion, University of Lancaster, Lancaster, England, 1978.

Thomas, A., & Chess, S. *The dynamics of psychological development.* New York: Brunner-Mazel, 1980.

Titchener, J. L. The day of a psychoanalyst at Woodstock. In W. Muensterberger and A. H. Esman (Eds.), *The psychoanalytic study of society.* New York: International Universities Press, 1972.

Todaro, M. P. *Economics for a developing world.* London: Longman, 1979.

Uchendu, V. C. The cultural roots of aggressive behavior in modern African politics. *Journal of Asian & African Studies,* 1977, *XII,* 99-108.

Ujah, A. O. Armed robbery—A case to study. *The Nigerian Standard,* Jos, Nigeria. September 24, 1980, page 6.

van den Berghe, P. L. *Power and privilege at an African university.* London: Routledge and Kegan Paul, 1973.

Zempleni-Rabain, J. Expression de l'agressivité et processus de médiation dans la socialization de l'enfant wolof (Sénégal). *Africa,* 1974, *44,* 151-162.

ACKNOWLEDGEMENT

I am grateful to my collaborator, Henry I. Amatu and to Egwu U. Egwu, both of whom have discussed this and other topics in the broad area of psychology in Africa with me over many years; without their critical encouragement, I would years ago have given up trying to be a psychologist in Africa.

L.B.

16

Northern Ireland: Growing Up With the "Troubles"

Liz McWhirter

A PREVIEW

To practice social psychological research on . . . intergroup conflict and violence is to assume a critical social responsibility. . . . one concrete way of exercising such social responsibility is to speak out not only to other psychologists but also publicly. [Trew & McWhirter, 1982]

The children of "dirty Prods" and "filthy Fenians" carry messages, set fires, use guns and knives. But sometimes they speak with the startlingly premature wisdom of those who have seen people fight and die for what they believe. [R. Coles, 1980, p. 33]

No person growing up in Northern Ireland since 1969 has been untouched by the violence, whether they have participated on the streets or merely watched it on TV. For a few, it has meant a short sharp career in terrorism, ending in death or imprisonment, but for the vast majority, it is a background they have learned to live and cope with. [B. White, 1981]

Indeed, the annual toll of murders, shootings and bombings is distressing, but eloquent testimony of both the intractability of the Northern Ireland question and the failure of statesmanship throughout the British Isles. [P. Buckland, 1981, p. 173]

If blame is to be apportioned for today's situation in Northern Ireland, it should be laid not at the door of men of today but of history. [R. Kee, 1980, p. 248]

Although being "born and bred" in Northern Ireland is not a justification for contributing to an international volume, it at least answers one often repeated criticism of recent academic research on Northern Ireland—"unless you're from the place you can't start to understand it [Harbison & Harbison, 1980]." Due to my research interests, the principal focus of this chapter will be on the ongoing social conflict in Northern Ireland, more commonly known euphemistically as the "Troubles."

I am grateful to Karen Trew, John Whyte and Ken Heskin for their helpful comments on earlier drafts of this chapter.

Fig. 16.1. Ireland

The backcloth for any analysis of a complex, multifaceted social conflict should be a mosaic including the history, politics, economy, geography, and culture of the region. I will, therefore, present a brief digest of the features that I consider relevant as a context for more detailed analysis of some aspects of the conflict and its resultant violence.

The pictures and sketches of Northern Ireland portrayed by historians, politicans, economists, social geographers—and also by the media throughout the world since 1969—have yielded a collage of unrest, destruction, violence, and socioeconomic disadvantage. Such a collage is, of course, only a selection of events in Northern Ireland. In attempting to dissect the conflict, I shall move from control and power to people—from history and politics to social geography and psychology—but my account will also be discriminating. Since the focus will be on aggression-related issues, the sketch I shall depict of Northern Ireland, both past and present, will inevitably be biased and distorted. It is important to note that, as with all data selected for a particular purpose, this chapter fails to tell the whole Northern Ireland story. It also fails to tell the full story of aggression in Northern Ireland.

THE HISTORICO-POLITICAL CONTEXT: FROM UNION THROUGH DEVOLUTION TO DIRECT RULE AND DEADLOCK

Much of the history of Ireland since medieval times is the story of Irish rebellion against rule from Britain.

England's domination of Ireland began in the twelfth century, with an invasion by Henry II. It culminated in the middle of the seventeenth century with land confiscation by Cromwell. The English conquest and colonisation of Ireland was resented by the Irish from the beginning. An integral part of the Irish defiance was resistance against English society, with its different identity, language, culture, and social order. (Ireland's original unique culture had been derived from the influences and ideas of the conquerors and adventurers—Celts, Gauls, Vikings, and Normans, combined with a tradition of Catholicism.) Since the time of the Tudor and Stuart conquest during the Reformation and Counterreformation, a period of profound religious and political upheaval and passion, Anglo-Irish relations have been most complicated and disturbed. In a nutshell, Catholic Ireland was invaded by Protestant England (Downing, 1980).

The legislative union of Great Britain and Ireland in 1800 which had abolished the Irish parliament and provided for Protestant Irish members of parliament in London had been established in the middle of a desperate war. The principal British motive had been military reinforcement against Napoleon. Almost thirty years later, Catholics won the right to become members of the British Parliament. Following the potato blight and famine of the mid-1840s in which great numbers died of starvation and disease, the Irish were more bitter against the English than ever. A new movement, the Fenians (or Irish Republican Brotherhood) wanted Ireland to become a separate republic, while another party wanted a parliament in Ireland. When the British government finally agreed to introduce "home rule" in 1910, there was fierce opposition from the Unionist party in Ulster and Britain. World War I postponed the issue.

At Easter in 1916, a group led by the Fenians caused an uprising in Dublin. Much of the city was destroyed. A movement called Sinn Fein (meaning "Ourselves Alone") quickly gathered electoral support except in east Ulster. In January 1919, Sinn Fein met in Dublin and proclaimed Dial Eireann, the parliament of an independent Irish Republic. The Irish Republican Army (IRA)—a military organization composed of an active group of republican extremists who rejected constitutional methods in favour of martial methods—attacked British troops and police. The British armed forces, in return, burned large parts of several towns.

At last, however, the "Anglo-Irish" war was brought to an end politically. The Government of Ireland Act was introduced by the British parliament in February 1920, and the Anglo-Irish Treaty was signed in December 1921. The Act partitioned Ireland and set up two devolved governments—two subordinate administrations and parliaments: one in Dublin for southern Ireland, the other at Stormont in Belfast for northern Ireland (Buckland, 1981). Six of the counties of Ulster remained part of the United Kingdom along with England, Scotland, and Wales. The remaining twenty-six counties of Ireland gained independence from British rule to become the *Irish Free State,* with its own army and navy and total control of its own affairs at home and abroad, subject to membership of the British Commonwealth of Nations, with dominion status like Canada or Australia, and an oath of loyalty to the monarch. Sovereign powers over the whole of Ireland had been given technically to the Irish Free State, but these powers were temporarily suspended for one month in six of the nine counties in the northeast of the northern province of Ulster. (Historically, Ireland was divided into four provinces. The nine counties in the Northeast of the island were within the Province of Ulster. Northern Ireland is often referred to as "the North," while the rest becomes "the South.") At the end of that month, those counties which chose to opt out of the newly created Irish Free State could do so. As expected, they did, forming the political entity called *Northern Ireland* (Kee, 1980). The 1920 Act was imposed upon Ireland. Home rule was accepted reluctantly in Ulster.

The signing of the treaty did not put an immediate end to the fighting in Ireland. In the north, the Irish Republican Army (IRA) continued its military campaign against the new regime. England was its only enemy (Beckett, 1979). In the rest of the country, disagreement over the terms of the treaty led to the outbreak of a civil war within a few months. The anti-treatyites, beliving in a myth of the "indivisible island" (Arthur, 1980), viewed the treaty as betrayal and would not countenance an oath of loyalty to the monarch. The republicans* now used against the Free State all the methods that had been used in previous years against the British. However, as Beckett (1979) recounts, the outcome was very different. They could no longer rely upon the same public support; and their wholesale destruction of property and frequent bank robberies, together with the suspicion that they favoured a communist land policy, turned a population heartily sick of rule by the gun increasingly against them. In addition, the new government showed energy, determination, and courage, and, more important, a ruthlessness that the British had never dared to display. They executed scores of prisoners and left hunger-strikers to starve if they chose. These measures proved effective. May 1923 saw the end of resistance—but not, unsurprisingly, control of the forces which years of irregular warfare had unleashed. As a consequence, the threat of violence has remained part of the background of Irish political life.

The Anglo-Irish Treaty applied formally to the whole of Ireland, but the position of Northern Ireland was specifically safeguarded. If the Northern Ireland parliament should request to be excluded from the Irish Free State, then Northern Ireland should retain its constitutional status within the United Kingdom accorded to it by the Act of 1920 (Beckett, 1966). The Ireland Act gave a firm and specific guarantee of Northern Ireland's constitutional position, but partition was not meant to be permanent. No time limit was set, but the entire 1920 Act was framed on the assumption that Irish unity was both desirable and attainable, and various inducements were offered to the two Irish parliaments to ensure that partition would be only temporary (Buckland, 1981). Northern Ireland was by no means firmly wedded to the constitutional bedrock of the United Kingdom.

---

*"Protestants" in Northern Ireland are often equated with "Unionists" or "Loyalists," while "Catholics" are often referred to politically as "Nationalists" or "Republicans." While the two sets of terms are not synonymous, I shall use them interchangeably without spelling out the fine distinctions.

The Government of Ireland Act was concerned more with political pacification than with administrative efficiency. From the very start, the political and economic interests of Northern Ireland were subordinated to the interests of Britain and the need for a settlement in the South. It is, therefore, not surprising that, while the settlement inaugurated for Ireland a longer period of general tranquillity than it had known since the first half of the eighteenth century (Beckett, 1966), Northern Ireland was born amidst violence.

Between 1920 and 1922, nearly 300 people were killed in Northern Ireland, most of them in the main urban centre of Belfast. In 1922 alone, 232 people were killed (including two Unionist Members of Parliament), nearly 1,000 were injured, 400 were interned, and more than £3 million worth of property was destroyed. There was a curfew in Belfast until 1924 (Arthur, 1980).

Due to the problems occasioned by a virtual state of civil war in 1922, the Parliament of Northern Ireland enacted the Civil Authorities (Special Powers) Act. Allied to the existence of the Special Constabulary, this act gave the government powers similar to those current in time of martial law (apart from the establishment of military courts), since it transferred many peace-preservation powers from the judiciary to the executive. Power rested with the Minister of Home Affairs (or any Parliamentary Secretary or Officer of the Royal Ulster Constabulary (RUC) to whom he might delegate his powers) who could "take all such steps and issue all such orders as may be necessary for preserving peace and order [section 1]."

The Special Powers Act, introduced at the peak of sectarian violence in Belfast surrounding the formation of the Northern Ireland state, was intended to last for only a year, but the decline of violence did not bring an end of the act. It was renewed annually until 1928, then for a period of five years and, in 1933, it was made permanent. (The act was repeatedly invoked until 1972 and was replaced in 1973 by the Emergency Provisions Act.)

The boundary between Northern Ireland and the Irish Free State was settled in 1925, and in 1937 a new Irish Constitution was adopted which accorded a special status to the Roman Catholic church. It applied in theory to the whole of Ireland, but jurisdiction was limited to the twenty-six counties, now to be known as Eire, "pending the re-integration of the national territory." (The constitution was published in both Irish and English. In the English version, the name of the state is given as Ireland. However, in normal English usage, the Irish name Eire was used to indicate the twenty-six counties.) In 1948, a new government in the South severed the last constitutional link between Eire and the Commonwealth by repealing the External Relations Act, and the *Republic of Ireland* was formally inaugurated in 1949.

The removal of the crown from the constitution made no practical difference; but it is, perhaps, hardly surprising that the IRA and its supporters refused to accept the Republic of 1949 as a substitute for the Republic of 1916, to which they alone professed allegiance (Beckett, 1979). The new regime, like its predecessors, had to face the recurrent threat of internal violence.

The question of partition also had little practical effect on Anglo-Irish relations. The Republic constantly aired its sense of grievance at what it saw as the British imposition but, in practice, they accepted the existing situation as if it were a lasting one. In contrast, the extreme republican groups, of which the IRA was the most important, maintained a sporadic campaign of violence in the North. They were, however, condemned by the leaders of the northern nationalists from whom they might have expected support. In addition, the government in the South took strong measures to suppress their activities. It seemed as if old quarrels were dying.

In lieu of bitter political wranglings emerged a recognition by the South of the benefits of strengthening economic links with Britain. The friendlier attitudes were encouraged by the contemporary spirit of ecumenism, which affected Ireland as it affected the rest of Christendom.

A change in the Northern Ireland government in 1963, with a prime minister who was more forward-looking than backward-looking, seemed to herald a new era of peace and reconciliation. In pursuance of closer relations with the South he arranged an exchange of visits with the Prime Minister of the Republic. But any attempt to change established patterns of behaviour in the political arena is inevitably perilous. Almost suddenly, what had seemed like a hopeful situation had become one of violent conflict. On the one side, fear among the rank and file of the Unionist party interpreted the new policy as a threat to their own monopoly of power. On the other side, the Catholics became increasingly insistent that expressions of good-will should be translated into positive social and political reforms.

The growing alarm among some right-wing unionists found a militant spokesman in Ian Kyle Paisley, a Protestant preacher and powerful orator who had established a new sect calling itself the Free Presbyterian Church of Ulster. Extremism on the right almost inevitably stimulated extremism on the left. Those who demanded immediate reforms organized themselves, after the American example, into a Civil Rights Movement in order to demonstrate their impatience.

Fundamentally, Johnson (1980) suggests, the prime cause of the Ulster crisis was the relatively poor performance of the British economy, in relation to the rest of the developed world, which became increasingly apparent as the 1960s progressed. The general setting in Northern Ireland is that of a Western industrialised society. It has an infrastructure of industry, commerce, and transport which is recognisably European and a system of welfare closely modeled on Great Britain. By that measure, however, it has not been a success. Poverty and deprivation—through a combination of large families, poor standard of health, high prices, low earnings, high unemployment, and poor housing—has been found to be greater than in any other region in the United Kingdom (e.g., Berthoud, Brown, & Cooper, 1981; Evason, 1976, 1982). The latest figures for Northern Ireland (pre-Christmas 1981) show that overall 18.9 percent of the insured working population is unemployed: 23.2 percent of the male population, and 13.1 percent of the female population. As Evason (1982) has pointed out, the long-standing very adverse socioeconomic situation is hardly surprising. Northern Ireland has few —if any—advantages likely to promote economic prosperity. It is a small, peripheral region, lacking natural resources. The land mass is only 13,500 square kilometres (the area of England, including fresh water, is almost more than 130 thousand square kilometres). The population of Northern Ireland is only 1.5 million (less than 3 percent of the United Kingdom).

The Catholic minority felt that they were not getting their fair share of council houses and opportunities for employment. In addition, voting arrangements in local elections prevented them from being fully represented. The "civil rights" demands included fair voting, an end to discrimination in jobs and housing, and an end to the Special Powers Act; but the excitement aroused by the French effervescence, glamorised by intense publicity, gave the Civil Rights Movement a mass and predominantly youthful (and nonsectarian) following (Johnson, 1980).

The success of the demonstrations caused many who had not been politically active previously to view marching and demonstrating behind Civil Rights banners as a peaceful way of registering their frustrations and complaints against discrimination, but 1968 also detonated an explosion of discontent. Loyalists representing the campaign as a Catholic attempt to undermine the existence of the state, reacted to the civil rights marches with obstructions and counterdemonstrations.

A march was planned (McCann, 1974) for the City of Londonderry (or Derry, as the Catholics prefer to call it), pride of place in Protestant mythology and the epitome of Catholic grievance through the gerrymandering that produced a Unionist council despite a Catholic majority. Although the march was banned, it went ahead on October 5. It was broken up with gratuitous baton-charging of the demonstrators by the RUC. The history of Northern Ireland was thereafter changed irrevocably. That march proved to be a landmark, not only because it was the most violent confrontation between the state and the civil rights supporters, but also because it took place in full view of television cameras. The resultant publicity exposed the social inequities in Northern Ireland to a wider gaze.

Events began to gain momentum with an increasing number of confrontations between Protestants and Catholics. The most violent of the first sectarian confrontations occurred on January 4, 1969 at an isolated beauty spot, Burntollet Bridge.

A four day march from Belfast to Londonderry had been blocked by Paisleyites and re-routed at various points to prevent it moving through Loyalist villages and towns. At its climax it was ambushed by a becudgelled loyalist mob. The attack was planned and vicious. Many of the two hundred attackers were reported to have been off-duty B specials and some members of the RUC also joined in the foray. In retaliation to police attacks, the people of the Bogside area of Londonderry sealed themselves off with barricades, a "people's militia" was formed, and "Free Derry" was constituted.

For many demonstrators, Burntollet was the turning point. Within a week, the marchers who had suffered violence replied in kind. A march was planned for the largely Catholic town of Newry for January 11, 1969. When a section of the route was outlawed, the marchers' patience evaporated. Three police tenders, separating the parade from the RUC, were burned and there was some disorder.

Violence begat violence, and the Unionists claimed that Republicans had infiltrated the Civil Rights Movement and were using it as a front to destroy the state. Hardliners were convinced that too much had been conceded. In March and April, there was a series of bomb outrages that caused millions of pounds worth of damage to electricity supplylines and waterworks. It was assumed that the bombings were the work of the long-established Catholic paramilitary group, the IRA; but it later emerged that they were the work of an illegal extreme loyalist group, the Ulster Volunteer Force (UVF), who had attempted to remove the prime minister from office. Ironically, those explosions led to the first influx of British troops. The Ministry of Defence announced on April 20 that 550 troops would be dispatched to aid the civil authority but that they would not be used to quell demonstrations or maintain public order.

As violence spread, there was a significant change of tone (Beckett, 1979). At the beginning, the campaign for civil rights had received considerable support from Protestants, but it soon became a sectarian body, in fact, although not in principle. In addition, the early specific reforms became both more vague and more extensive. Many of its members and many of the groups and organizations associated with the movement were now not likely to be satisfied by any reforms carried out within the existing constitutional framework. They agreed that Unionism must be totally destroyed.

Faced with this situation, right-wing influence in the Unionist party grew stronger and culminated in a change of premiership, but not a change of policy. Several weeks of comparative tranquillity ensued, but the extremists on both sides were preparing to renew the struggle. In August, fresh fighting broke out on a scale that the police could not hope to control. The present "troubles" began in earnest in August 1969.

A ritual Protestant march held annually on August 12 in Londonderry resulted, predictably, in a riot. Stone-throwing began between groups of Protestants and Catholics, a Member of Parliament was hit in the face and knocked unconscious. The police responded by forcing Catholics down into the Bogside district. Barricades appeared and petrol bombs were thrown. A bitter feud ensued between residents and police. Both sides strove to hold their ground— the Bogsiders to keep the police out, and the Police to keep the Catholics from breaking out to attack the Protestant areas of the City. In the early evening, as the police drew up armoured cars and watercannons, the whole community rallied to the defence of their territory.

For the first time in the United Kingdom, the RUC used CS gas to try to control the rioters. Riot-control CS gas had been first produced fifty years earlier, but its use by Britain had previously occurred only in troublesome colonies. The Unionist government also mobilised the B specials. As the Bogsiders appealed to their fellow Catholics elsewhere in Northern Ireland to relieve the pressure on them in Derry, fighting erupted in other towns (Downing, 1980). On the evening of August 14, there was a riot in Dungiven, and in Armagh a man was shot dead by the B specials. Belfast was ripped apart by the worst sectarian clashes since 1922. Within the space of a few days, the destruction was the most extensive and the death toll the heaviest since the 1970s (Buckland, 1981).

Intimidation added to the problems of street rioting. Over the next few years, between 30,000 and 60,000 people were forced to leave their houses in the Greater Belfast area in what the Community Relations Commission considered to be the largest enforced population movements in Europe since 1945 (Arthur, 1980). One of the immediate consequences of the destruction and death was the agreement by Westminster that troops should be sent in as a temporary, emergency measure. At first, the troops were regarded with wary relief by the embattled Catholics; their arrival seemed to signal the defeat of the police and the removal of the injustices of Unionist rule.

The four days of intense rioting in August 1969 may not have shaken the world but, as Buckland (1981) has stated, they certainly shook Northern Ireland to its very foundations. They finally and emphatically underlined the inability of the Unionist regime to cope with the challenges which had emerged in the 1960s, born of historic divisions. The most obvious consequence of the events of August 1969 was that Northern Irish affairs ceased to be confined to Northern Ireland.

On the evening of August 13, the Prime Minister of the Irish Republic, addressing the nation on television, declared that the Republic could not "stand by" while Catholics were attacked over the border, recognising, however, that "the reunification of the national territory can provide the only permanent solution for the problem." On August 19, the British and Northern Ireland governments issued a joint statement that there would be no change in the constitutional status of Northern Ireland.

Overall responsibility for security was placed in the hands of the British Army in Northern Ireland. The RUC and the B specials were replaced by the Ulster Defence Regiment (UDR). A tribunal set up to enquire into the disturbances uncovered six occasions when the police, by act or omission, were seriously at fault.

Considerable resentment built up among Loyalists because the British army was protecting Catholics, even to the extent of respecting the existence of "no-go" areas in Belfast and Derry. Savage riots erupted in Protestant West Belfast in October 1969. Most of the 100,000 licensed guns were in Protestant hands; but, for the first time, the army and police turned against them. In return, the first policeman to be killed in the present period of civil strife was shot by Protestants.

Gradually, after gauging the complex sectarian geography of working-class Belfast, the army fixed the physical divisions between the streets and alleyways along sectarian lines, constructing barriers to separate them. In contrast to Derry, the topography of Belfast is complicated. Apart from a number of dense estates in West Belfast, many working class Catholics live in enclaves situated in different parts of the city, each surrounded by concentrations of Protestant working-class people. (The so-called "Peace Line" was a construction of barbed wire and high corrugated metal screens.) In the uneasy peace which followed the August battles, the armed forces kept the two sides apart.

The army's presence created novel problems. By its very nature, an army is little suited to the sensitive tasks of peace keeping and restoring respect for the law in a divided society. The "military security" (Boyle, Hadden, & Hillyard, 1975) approach used relied not on the normal system of justice but on methods often careless of ordinary legal rights. In consequence, Britain's direct involvement in the Northern Ireland problem was alienating both sections of the population.

It was at this time that the Irish Republican Army (IRA), dormant for many years, once again entered the political arena. Following upon its last military campaign which ended in 1962, the IRA had become an overtly socialist organisation. By the end of 1969, a clear split had emerged in the Republican movement between those who wanted to pursue a purely political campaign (later to be known as The Officials), and those who preferred to take up the armed struggle immediately to defend the Catholic minority. A new ultra-militant and pro-violence wing was formed to take advantage of the communal unrest. It called itself the "Provisional IRA" and was led by an Englishman, Sean Mac Stiofan, who lived in the South. It adopted all the traditional IRA attitudes—anti-border, anti-British, anti-Protestant, and pro-Catholic—dropped its social beliefs, turned to the conventional sources of finance in the American-Irish community, and began to arm itself in the winter of 1968-69 (Magee, 1974).

With the open appearance of the new Provisional IRA toward the end of 1969, the Catholic ghettoes became the natural habitat of the gunmen. As Conor Cruise O'Brien (1972) pointed out, the formidable thing about the Provisional IRA was its simple relevance to the situation. In addition, during the early part of 1970, attitudes of the Catholics to the British Army changed from an impartial presence to that of an occupying force which was there to support the Unionist establishment. The army's response to the sectarian mayhem was to get tough. Their strong tactics ensured the hostility of the Catholics. Recruitment to the Provisional IRA soared.

Army policy focused on curtailing the ability of the Provisional IRA to move arms and explosives around Belfast and Derry. The Provisional IRA extended its bombing campaign to the border with the Republic. The army replied initially by blowing up roads in the border area, making them impassable except on foot. This, not surprisingly, outraged the local rural and farming communities. As the bombing campaign of the Provisional IRA escalated, an increasing number of civilians were killed by mistimed explosions and inadequate warnings. By the end of 1970, the Northern Ireland Prime Minister was calling for an all-out onslaught. The Provisional IRA, which was by now well established in the Catholic areas of Belfast and Derry, felt able to take up the offensive against the British army.

In February 1971, the IRA defensive stance was exchanged for "an offensive campaign of resistance in all parts of the occupied area [Burton, 1978, p. 82]," which consisted of robbery, shooting, bombing, and assassination. The aim was to break the morale of the security forces and the will of the Northern Irish and British governments by disrupting social and economic life and by maiming and murdering civilians as well as members of the Crown forces, primarily in Northern Ireland but occasionally also in Britain (Buckland, 1981). Like the Fenians, the Provisional IRA had no doubt of their moral right to wage war against Great Britain, in order "to achieve independence and unification no matter what the cost [Moody, 1974, p. 71]." The Provisional IRA viewed itself as an army of liberation and acted as such.

The IRA was back in business with more plausibility than it had enjoyed for nearly half a century. The increased use of snipers led to the first shooting of a British soldier in February 1971; there was an immediate outcry. A group of Members of Parliament at Stormont called for block searches, curfews, and punitive expeditions. The new Northern Ireland Prime Minister (the third since the renewal of violence in 1968) announced on television that Northern Ireland was "at war" with the Provisional IRA (Farrell, 1976). Aware of the activities of the Provisional IRA, extensive arms searches in West Belfast by the army exacerbated the sharply deteriorating relationship between the Catholics and the troops. Searches provoked rioting which, in turn, led to an increase in the army presence. The army raids resulted in bigger arms hauls and more arrests of Provisional IRA activists.

As the spiral worsened, the new RUC chief wished the restyled police force—expanded but relieved of the B specials—to replace the army on the streets. He proposed unarmed RUC riot squads. The army was designed and trained to be aggressive, whereas a police force was more normal and more passive in its role. Unlike a military force, the Chief Constable thought the police force represented visible law and order. However, the General Officer in Command of the army feared that the RUC might run amok again and further endanger the relationship of the army with the Catholics (Downing, 1980).

The response of the Provisional IRA to the increasing number of army raids was to launch a bombing campaign against commercial targets, in order to stretch the security forces. Protestants bore the brunt of these attacks and, in West Belfast, retaliated with rioting. In the run-up to the forthcoming General Election in June, Westminster appeared to be losing interest in the situation in Northern Ireland.

The Labour government in Westminster prior to 1970 had been leaning toward direct rule of Northern Ireland from Westminster. The new Conservative government opted for "firm measures." They introduced the Criminal Justice (Temporary Provisions) Act which made mandatory the imposition of a six month jail sentence for rioting. This encouraged popular support for the Provisional IRA since the troops had to try to enforce the Act and make the arrests. At the same time, the Incitement to Religious Hatred Act was passed with the aim of countering Protestant sectarian bigotry.

The next response by the government was internment: on August 9, 1971, British Troops swooped on houses all over the province and detained some 342 men. A rattle of dustbin lids on the pavement in Republican areas of Belfast alerted sleeping households to the raids. Internment had been a well-tried security measure in the past but, in the 1970s, it was a political and security disaster. It failed miserably to control the full-scale Catholic insurrection it provoked and led to tremendous resentment.

The entire operation was seen by Catholics as yet another attack on their community. They responded with every form of civil disobedience—from boycotting parliament to not paying rent, rates, gas, or electricity bills. The Catholic reaction was not irrational (Buckland, 1981). The authorities continued to regard Catholic violence more seriously than Protestant violence. The police tended to charge Catholic rioters with riotous behaviour but preferred to charge Protestants with only disorderly behaviour, for which the penalty might be a fine or even a suspended sentence (p. 150).

To get rid of the embarrassment of internment while still trying to benefit from its effects (Coogan, 1980), the government introduced a Detention of Terrorists Order. The name of the internment camp was also altered from Long Kesh camp to the Maze prison—a cosmetic change not accepted by Republicans. Internment provided excellent fuel for propaganda. By excluding the courts and sentencing procedure, internment resembled capture in battle. Internees were, in a sense, prisoners of war who could confidently expect their freedom in exchange for some truce (Tugwell, 1981, p. 32). Tugwell also stated that Britain could be shown to be acting:

> unlawfully or at least immorally in her "oppression" of Catholic civil rights. The fact that this was a distasteful measure, imposed reluctantly and to be abolished as soon as the security situation allowed, made it difficult to defend and the theme was ideal for transferring guilt from the perpetrators of violence to those who were trying to oppose it. [p. 26]

Apart from newspaper accounts, there have been a number of major official reports dealing with the use of torture or "ill-treatment" against Provisional IRA suspects since internment, including reports by Amnesty International and the European Court of Human Rights. Coogan (1981) details five major reports which date between November 1971 and March 1979. Taylor's (1980) account of the "inside story" of interrogation by the police from 1976 to 1979 and the accompanying political cover-up makes disturbing reading.

Britain was taken to the European Court of Human Rights at Strasbourg by the Eire government and charged with torturing 14 men in army barracks in Northern Ireland between August and October 1971. In January 1978, the Court found Britain guilty of "degrading and inhuman treatment." The whole episode was extremely embarrassing for Britain.

A Commission of Inquiry was set up by the British government to look into the allegations of physical brutality. The committee sat in secret and its terms of reference excluded investigations of psychological ill-treatment. Their report said that, although "ill-treatment" had taken place, there had been no "brutality" because those inflicting the suffering took no pleasure from it. Furthermore, no punishments have been meted out, and no promotions—army or police—have been affected by those found guilty of using the so-called "deep interrogation" technique (Arthur, 1980).

The emphatic Catholic reaction to the 1971 internment also provoked an indignant response from the Loyalists. Paisley called for the formation of a people's militia and, toward the end of 1971, Loyalist groups came together under the umbrella of an organisation called the Ulster Defence Association (UDA), a paramilitary body with the ostensible aim of defending Protestant territory from Republican attacks. It was estimated that the UDA numbered 50,000 men within three months of its formation (Arthur, 1980). Extreme Protestants and Catholics were now arch enemies and, by the end of 1971, paramilitary activity, extensive on both sides, was taking a dreadful toll of property and lives (Downing, 1980).

The long-feared Protestant backlash did not get underway until February 1972. Henceforth, small Protestant groups assassinated, or tried to assassinate, Catholics suspected of IRA activities; shot Catholics associating "improperly" with Protestants; placed bombs in bars frequented by Catholics; and attacked Catholics more or less at random on the grounds that they had failed to rid themselves of the IRA. During the 1970s, various murder squads emerged. One of the most consistent was the old Ulster Volunteer Force (UVF), which resumed the activities it had left in 1966. Said to be well armed with a variety of weapons, its main centres of strength were the Shankill area of West Belfast, East Antrim, and County Armagh.

Whereas the IRA had its higher justification and ideal in the concept of *Irish* freedom, so the Protestant paramilitaries insisted that they were "patriots . . . fighting for Ulster's freedom." They said, "Like the Jewish people, each time an act of aggression is committed against our people, we shall retaliate in a way that only the animals in the IRA can understand [Dillon & Lehane, 1973, pp. 285-286]." "No surrender" remains their slogan. With the growth of the Provisional IRA and the Protestant paramilitaries, Northern Ireland was in danger of disintegrating into anarchy by the end of 1971.

In January 1972, an illegal anti-internment march in Derry culminated in the shooting of 14 male civilians by soldiers of the First Parachute Regiment. An official tribunal failed to prove that any of the victims had been carrying weapons and out-of-court payments were made to the relatives. Nationalist and Catholic Ireland exploded with anger at what was quickly dubbed "Bloody Sunday." The British Embassy in Dublin was burned down on February 5, while there were strikes and demonstrations in Northern Ireland and deadly bomb attacks in both Northern Ireland and Britain. Counterattacks by extremist groups of the Unionist side added to the rapidly escalating picture of violence. As violence increased, the role of the British army became more and more important and the rift between Belfast and Westminster grew bigger.

In March 1972, the British government (now once again in Conservative hands) decided that responsibility for security should be transferred to London. The Northern Ireland government resigned and the province was placed directly under the British government, with a secretary of state responsible for Northern Ireland affairs. At the end of March, an effective two-day protest strike shut off power supplies, stopped public transport, and closed most of the major industries. A massive rally also occurred at Stormont to coincide with the last sitting of the old parliament. These nonviolent reactions suggested that, although Unionists were to be denied Stormont, they had the resources to thwart any future plans for the government of the province which they considered a betrayal of traditional Unionism. Now that Stormont had been prorogued, the major restraint on Protestant violence was removed.

Both the establishment and dissolution of the union of Ireland with Britain, in 1800 and 1921 respectively, occurred in times of war. Both were expedient acts by the British government and both failed to settle Irish affairs. Direct rule of Northern Ireland in 1972 was also the result of political violence. It, too, was taken as the readiest means of getting around a difficulty. While the measure was envisaged as no more than a temporary expedient in London, it proved to be the end of an era—the final breakdown of the Irish settlement worked out in 1900-21 and confirmed by the governments of the United Kingdom, the Irish Free State, and Northern Ireland in 1925 (Beckett, 1979).

With the rapid increase in murders—80 Catholics and 38 Protestants were murdered in the nine months following Britain's takeover—the authorities had to act. Early in 1973, Loyalists began to be interned. The disaffected majority reacted by calling a one-day strike in February in which five people were killed. With the rate of violence increasing, a political solution became imperative. Toward the middle of 1972, Britain moved into what Arthur (1980) has called the "most creative period in Ulster since the regime was established [p. 16]."

Following a ceasefire by the IRA, an unsuccessful meeting of the Secretary of State in Northern Ireland and the Provisional IRA was held in July. The fragile truce ended only a few days later when a riot, accompanied by shooting, resulted from a sectarian housing dispute in Belfast. On July 21, or "Bloody Friday" as it became known, Provisional IRA bombs in the centre of Belfast killed nine civilians and injured more than a hundred. In the resultant atmosphere of horror, the Secretary of State moved against the "No-go" areas of Derry. Four thousand extra troops were assembled and on July 31, "Operation Motorman" was launched. The troops went in and the barricades came down.

A conference was held the following month involving the Secretary of State for Northern Ireland, moderate Catholics, and Unionists. The British and Irish Prime Ministers also had meetings. In October, a government paper stated that the constitutional position of Northern Ireland was guaranteed so long as the majority wished it. This led to a referendum, a Border Poll, on March 8, 1973. The Protestant electorate overwhelmingly endorsed the constitutional status quo while Catholics overwhelmingly abstained (Arthur, 1980). Still, during the latter months of 1972, tension between the two communities resulted in a welter of sectarian killings, averaging at the end of 1972, three Catholics for every Protestant.

The highest incidence of violence and death of the last thirteen years occurred in 1972. 1973 and 1974 saw the establishment and satisfactory operation of political power-sharing in an elected Northern Ireland Assembly, but this was brought to an end in May 1974 by a 'strike' orchestrated by the Ulster Workers Council (UWC). After two weeks Northern Ireland had been brought to a complete standstill. The Unionist members of the Executive resigned on May 28, thus bringing an end to the Assembly.

In July Britain decided to establish a constitutional convention to consider what provisions for the government of Northern Ireland would be likely to command the most widespread acceptance throughout the community. It met during the second half of 1975 but failed to reach agreement, and collapsed early in 1976.

In May 1977, Paisley and UDA paramilitaries led an unsuccessful "constitutional stoppage" to persuade the authorities to "begin a powerful and effective offensive against the IRA and to announce steps to bring back Stormont." It was an attempted rerun of the UWC strike, but this one collapsed within a week, defeated by Loyalist indifference and decisive leadership by the Secretary of State for Northern Ireland (Arthur, 1980). Paisley's political career seemed at an end but, within a fortnight, his Democratic Unionist Party made substantial gains in local council elections. In the 1979 general election, his party increased its representation at Westminster and in the direct elections, involving proportional representation, for the European Assembly held in Northern Ireland on June 7, 1979, Paisley himself was elected on the first count with 170,000 first reference votes—almost 30,000 more than the quota. The scale of his victory, Paisley believed, established him as the unchallengeable leader of the Protestant people of Northern Ireland.

On the Republican side, the Provisional IRA have maintained their strength, aided by an extremely effective propaganda campaign. In Ireland, this involves forcing British politicians into committing actions which would discredit them at home and bring down censure on them from abroad.

In 1972, Republican prisoners interned in Northern Ireland decided to challenge the British government over the issue of political status. A hunger strike brought huge popular support and, faced with widespread civil disturbances and the hope of a truce, the government once again conceded by granting "Special Category status" initially to Republican prisoners and later to Loyalist prisoners. Prisoners were allowed to receive unlimited mail, to wear their own clothes, and to do no prison work. They were segregated from prisoners convicted of criminal offences and were allowed free association with their colleagues. By January 1975, a government report declared that Special Category Status was a serious mistake. At the end of 1975, the Secretary of State for Northern Ireland announced the end of "political status." From March 1976, those found guilty of terrorist offences would be treated as "criminals."

In September 1976, a young man sentenced for hijacking a van was the first prisoner to be denied political status. In response he refused to wear prison uniform and wore only a blanket, having nothing else to cover himself with. Those who joined the protest were denied parcels, writing materials, newspapers, radio or television. Filth accumulated and so the "blanket demonstration" became the dirty protest. By the summer of 1978, more than 300 prisoners were on the dirty protest at the Maze. They were mostly Provisional IRA members but did include some members of Loyalist paramilitary groups (Downing, 1980). The 'dirty' protest spread to the women's jail in Armagh in February 1980.

The trial of strength between the British government and the Provisional IRA over the issue of political status culminated in a hunger strike in 1980, a tactic which has already claimed twelve Irish victims in this century. Seven men were originally chosen in correspondence with the number of signatories of the 1916 Easter Declaration (Arthur, in press). The first phase of the campaign ended on December 18, 1980, when the prisoners thought that they had won concessions from the authorities. When they decided that those concessions were insufficient, they embarked upon a second phase on March 1, 1981. The first striker died amidst a blaze of worldwide publicity on May 5, 1981. IRA supporters, angry at his death, reacted predictably with widespread rioting aimed against the forces of the British government. Before his death, he had been elected Member of the Westminster Parliament for Fermanagh/South Tyrone at a by-election. His seat has been retained by his political agent, a member of Provisional Sinn Fein. (Two further hunger-strikers became elected members of the government of the Irish Republic.) By the end of August, ten hunger-strikers had died. Each death was followed by rioting in Republican areas, but the campaign failed to achieve the reintroduction of political status. There were many unsuccessful interventions by various church and lay bodies both national and international, but eventually, when two more deaths seemed imminent, pressure by some of the strikers' families finally led to the end of the campaign on October 3, after 216 days. On October 10, Provisional IRA bombings were resumed in London and resulted in two deaths.

The hunger-strike campaign has probably been the most successful propaganda weapon to be used by the Provisional IRA. International interest was worldwide and media reports strongly suggested that world opinion was largely stacked against Britain; many demonstrations in support of the prisoners took place as far apart as the United States and Australia— two countries with a large Irish immigrant population. Reaction against Britain was so intense in the United States that one member of the British Royal Family was subjected to some abuse and the visit of another member was cancelled. The campaign also highlighted the close involvement of the Roman Catholic Church in politics in Northern Ireland. Reaction varied, but a number of Church leaders refused to condemn the prisoners' actions as suicide because the strikers did not really "intend" to die—the British government was their murderer.

Arthur (in press) suggests that it would be a mistake to see the hunger strike simply as an escalation of the "H Block crisis." In fact, it is a continuation of the Provisional campaign by other means in which talk of defeat is meaningless! As he said, there is no gesture more compelling than the hunger strike till death, with its use of symbolism and imagery and its powerful theme of sacrifice for the cause. There is, along with the IRA doctrine of force, a dual standard of endurance as well as infliction (Coogan, 1980, p. 14). Not only have they fought to the death but they have also inflicted upon themselves greatly increased hardships and deprivation in prison and have starved themselves to death.

While a political vacuum exists in Northern Ireland, the success of Ian Paisley and the Provisional IRA will continue to flourish. In the absence of a local elected representative assembly, Arthur (1980) proposes, extremism on both sides will grow. Recent events indicate increasing polarisation. In short, while political stalemate continues, the deadlock will operate in favour of the demagogue and the gunman. *Faute de mieux*, both can claim the role of spokesman and protector of their community.

PROFILES OF THE VIOLENCE: FROM DYNAMICS TO STATISTICS AND CONTEXTS

The tendency to regard the Northern Ireland conflict as static and immutable has, as Darby (1982) points out, been notable in many recent studies. The violence and the reactions it provoked, when they were considered at all, were viewed merely as a consequence of conflict rather than as a factor in its development. Darby stresses the need to consider the relationships between "the dynamics of violence and the peculiar forms and directions which it imposes upon the underlying conflict." He also proposes that "in a deeply divided community all campaigns of protest eventually come to reflect the basic division. When agitation starts and is resisted, *regardless of its original demands and forms,* it will inevitably revert to sectarian patterns and objectives."

The apparently remarkable shift in the Northern Ireland conflict during the 1970s—from liberal reform to republican revolution—Darby argues, exemplifies this process of reverting to familiar forms of conflict. As the selective chronicle of the last section showed, the conflict had all the characteristic features of a conventional reformist campaign in 1969 similar to the contemporary racial conflict—a minority seeking equality of rights through reforms; demands which were liberal rather than radical; passive rather than violent resistance; and aspirations toward consensus rather than separation. The early peaceful protest marches, novel in Northern Ireland, attracted liberal Protestant a well as general Catholic support. Gradually, though, the protests adopted more traditionally republican forms—barricades, violence against the police and army, and paramilitary groups. These types of protest, Darby postulates, both discouraged Protestant sympathy and helped move the demands of the protesters toward more traditional objectives. According to Stewart (1977), a slide into violence was almost inevitable as Northern Ireland's disturbed past and the selective history of the inhabitants caught up with the present. Stripped of the protection of the state, the "civil population turned instinctively to the only source of wisdom applicable to such circumstances—the inherited folk-memory of what had been done in the past, both good and bad (p. 155)."

The IRA campaign from 1970 against the security forces and the hunger strikes of 1981, with their emotive echoes of earlier struggles, did much to replace liberal reform with republican revolution. After twelve years, the very basis of the conflict has shifted from a liberal-conservative axis to a republican-loyalist one, and passive protest has given way to violent conflict.

The qualitative picture of the changing dynamics of the conflict is reflected, as would be expected, in quantitative analyses of the nature and extent of the violence, both temporal and spatial, over the 13-year period of the present troubles—already the longest period of civil strife in Ireland's very violent political history.

The fluctuations over time, as Murray's (1982a) analysis has shown, are the result of the fact that the relative contributions of the different elements in the destruction and death have varied as the conflict has progressed. Attempts by the police and army to control Protestant Loyalist violence were a characteristic feature toward the beginning of the troubles. The deep-rooted sectarian conflict between Protestants and Catholics predominated in the mid 1970s. The apparently straightforward struggle between the forces of the British government and republican paramilitary groups, particularly the Provisional IRA, has been the most evident of the three main themes in the late 1970s and the beginning of the 1980s. All three dimensions have been present since the outset of the present troubles, but the rise of various groups has led to struggles for control within each community—Protestant and Catholic—and added a further dimension to the violence.

Not only have there been considerable variations from year to year in the pattern of violence, but it has also been distributed unevenly (Darby & Williamson, 1978; Mitchell, 1979; Murray, 1982b, Schellenberg, 1977). The main regions of violence have been the urban areas of Belfast and Londonderry, and the rural area surrounding the border between Northern Ireland and the Republic of Ireland, comprising South Armagh, South Fermanagh, West Tyrone, and Mid-Ulster.

Murray's (1982b) analysis of the spatial patterns of violence from 1969 to 1977, based on the absolute levels of deaths and explosions for the three main regions of violence, highlights interesting differences in the relative intensities of the different forms and targets of the violence:

Belfast
The incidence of explosions directed at "classical" targets (the police and army, central and local government personnel and installations, communications, etc.) is less than expected in relation to the overall incidence, while that of "economic" targets (commercial and office buildings, industrial premises) and "sectarian" targets (private houses, schools, public halls, clubs and any other building or location identified with one ethnic group) is greater than expected. Similarly there have been fewer police and army deaths but more "sectarian" killings.

Londonderry
There has been a low level of "sectarian" incidents both deaths and explosions, but a high proportion of security force deaths.

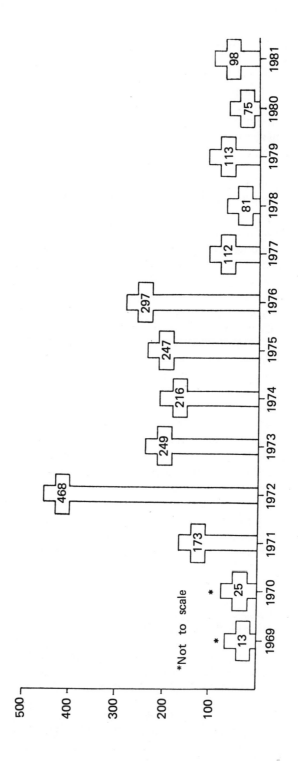

Fig. 16.2. Deaths in Northern Ireland connected with the security situation. (Adapted from *Belfast Telegraph*, January 7, 1982.)

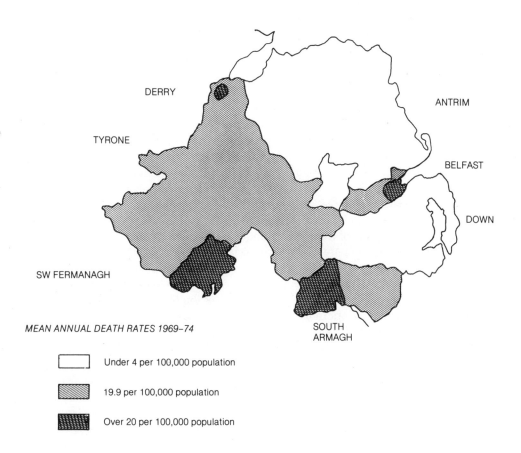

MEAN ANNUAL DEATH RATES 1969–74

☐ Under 4 per 100,000 population

▨ 19.9 per 100,000 population

▤ Over 20 per 100,000 population

Fig. 16.3. Violence Rates By Area: Northern Ireland, 1969-1974

Source: Adapted from J. A. Schellenberg, "Area Variations of Violence in Northern Ireland," *Sociological Focus 10*(1), (1977):69-78.

The Border Region
The incidence of "classical" explosions is particularly high whereas that for "sectarian" targets is lower than expected. Correspondingly, security force deaths are high, "sectarian" killings are low.

Consideration of the historical and political situation from which the statistics of violence in Northern Ireland emerge provides a coherent and an ecologically valid picture, but one cannot fully appreciate the severity of the troubles without viewing the resultant figures within the broader perspective of international violence, and comparing the data of the conflict with other violence and violent deaths which occur in Northern Ireland.

In world terms, the bald statistics of the last thirteen years—more than 2,000 deaths, thousands more injured, and over £200 million paid out for damage to property—are hardly momentous. Recent international reports suggest far more divided and violent communities than Northern Ireland: the old wars dividing Iran and Iraq, the Moroccans in the Sahara, the South Africans in Namibia and Angola, allied to the threats of war in Lebanon, South-East Asia, and Poland. Even where no threat of war or terrorism has recently prevailed, millions of people in the world continue to be ruled by the power of the gun and the secret police: South Korea, Uganda, large parts of Central and South America.

However, in order to compare different conflicts and incidences of violence, one needs to make relative—not absolute—comparisons. Americans, for example, have often pointed out that one is more likely to die violently in the streets of some American cities than in Northern Ireland. They will get a better idea of the magnitude of the Northern Ireland violence if it is translated into equivalent proportions for the United States. The population of the United States being 138 times that of Northern Ireland, the province's total causalty figures would mean, in U.S. terms, 276,000 deaths and over 1.5 million injured (Wilkinson, 1982). When viewed in this way, the figures suggest a very major internal war.

The grim statistics reflect a protracted period of violence. However, even within Northern Ireland, the number of people who have died violently in road accidents is even more horrifying, with fatalities more than 50 percent above the average in Great Britain. As figure 16.4 illustrates, in every year except 1972, more people have been killed on the roads in Northern Ireland than as a result of the political violence. While the road death toll for 1981 was the lowest since 1968 (221), it was still 2.25 times more than the number of deaths due to the violence (98) (*Sunday Times,* January 3, 1982).

Notwithstanding this sort of comparative exercise, the statistics do not detract from subjective reality or from the many concrete reminders of the ever-present threat of destruction, injury, and death. The most obvious signs of the threat of violence, particularly in urban areas, have been the ubiquitous security measures: posters warning about possible explosions or murders; soldiers; vehicle-check points; restricted vehicle parking zones; bag searching and body frisking at entrances to shops, bars etc. and in the Belfast city-centre shopping precinct; wire grills on windows; barriers outside buildings (to prevent vehicles from parking); ramps on roads; reduced slits in post-boxes; and barriers separating Protestant and Catholic areas.

Although there are large areas of Northern Ireland where the troubles scarcely impinge upon day-to-day life, these contrast sharply with other areas where the "normality" that has been achieved is at best an uneasy equilibrium between control and violence. The severity of the conflict is most evident in those relatively few districts which have witnessed the highest incidence of violence, where whole areas look as though they have been subjected to repeated aerial bombardment. Hayes (1981) suggests that one of the problems in Northern Ireland is the lack of perception in more peaceful, and by-and-large better-off areas, of the impact of an extended period of conflict in the poorer areas, both Catholic and Protestant, mainly in Belfast, which have borne the brunt both of intercommunal violence and of the measures used to

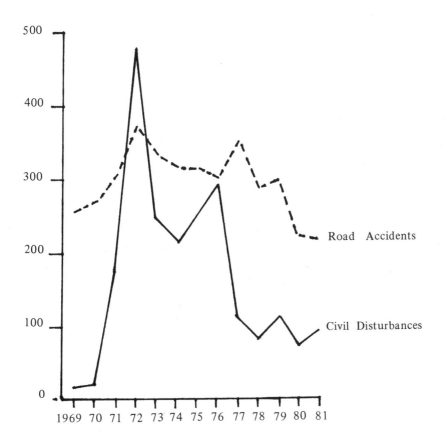

Fig. 16.4. Deaths in Northern Ireland Connected with Road Accidents and The Security Situation: 1969-1981.

Source: Modified from Fig. 1A, R.U.C. Chief Constable's Report, 1978.

control it, and which have shown themselves least capable of resolving conflict without resorting to violence. It is no coincidence that many of the areas that have seen the worst of the violence are urban regions suffering from severe socioeconomic deprivation.

However, no one in Northern Ireland has totally escaped the impact of the "Troubles"—it must be remembered that the country is a small land mass, with only a population of 1.5 million, which is composed of small, tightly-knit communities. As one of Murphy's (1978) interviewees put it, "Everyone in Northern Ireland—*everybody*—has been branded by our experiences since 1969. . . . you don't have to be damaged when you're branded. But we've all been painfully changed, us and our country. We'll never be the same again [p. 176]."

As the chronicles illustrate, the present troubles are merely the latest episode in a protracted and painful serial; but, while the theme remains essentially the same, the performers—the people—do change. It is, therefore, important to move beyond historic attitudes, political allegiances, religious categories, and the statistics of violence to look deeper, at a human level, at the conflict and violence. In the final section, I shall attempt to draw the threads of the web together and to look at the people—protagonists and victims of the violence—within the different dimensions of the conflict as given in the account. Within my research perspective, the emphasis will be on the young people growing up in Northern Ireland—they are the country's future.

THE IMPACT OF VIOLENCE: FROM CONTEXTS TO PEOPLE

As we have seen, the history of the island of Ireland illustrates the efficacy of violence in producing constitutional change. Violence led up to the establishment of the state of Northern Ireland and also caused its demise. Within the divided island, the political history of Northern Ireland depicts a divided society where religious affiliation, national identity, and political allegiance tend to coincide. The centuries-old roots of the ongoing conflict embrace relations between both Ireland and Britain and, within Northern Ireland, between Protestants and Roman Catholics. Most Catholics view themselves as Irish and aspire to a reunited Ireland, while most Protestants see themselves as British and have strived to maintain the state of Northern Ireland as a devolved part of the United Kingdom (Moxon-Browne, 1979).

The present period of civil unrest and violence has been described as "the worst protracted campaign of terrorism experienced in Western Europe in recent history [Wilkinson, 1981, p. 5]." As a consequence of the conflict since 1969, Wilkinson decided that, "A whole generation has grown up in the province under the shadow of the gunman and the bomber, constantly aware of the threat of a fresh eruption of violence [pp. 4-5]." Both statements require deeper analysis.

A necessary defining condition of terrorism is that it involves atrocious behaviour and a lack of normal regard for human life and property in the pursuit of some objective (Heskin, 1980a). Wilkinson (1974) characterized the concept of "political terrorism" as one of "amorality and antinomianism." Atrocious behaviour is not a sufficient condition of terrorism. As Heskin (1980a) states, "it is extraordinarily difficult to provide a definition of terrorism which makes a rational psychological distinction between what terrorists do and what governments engaged in conflict do [p. 75]." "Justified reaction," which insists that revolutionary violence is merely an unavoidable reaction to institutionalized violence by the state, has been common parlance in the propaganda of the Provisional IRA (Tugwell, 1981).

Indeed, although I have deliberately not used the terms "terrorism" or "terrorists" in my personal and historical accounts of the Northern Ireland conflict, I have used the term "violence" very freely. It is important to note that, in labeling acts of aggression as "violent," one is also making a subjective judgment. Legitimacy is a vital ingredient also in the definition of violence since violence legally refers to the unlawful exercise of force. It is the institution that legislates against violence. Thus, with both concepts, terrorism and violence, the judgment of illegality is in the eye of the beholder—violence may be what you use toward me but I merely use "force" toward you. The labels "terrorist" and "terrorism" have obvious pejorative tones and are, therefore, natural weapons in the armory of the state which tries to discredit its opponents. In contrast, terms such as "liberation fighters" or "guerillas" are used not by government officials but by illegal subversive organizations which oppose the state.

There are reported to be a large number of paramilitary organizations operating in Northern Ireland on both the Protestant and Catholic sides. Murphy (1978) reckoned that there were about 40 illegal paramilitary groups on the Protestant side alone, excluding the Ulster Defence Association (UDA) which has not been proscribed. Undoubtedly, however, the Provisional IRA has been the most active and the most important of these groups. I shall explore Wilkinson's (1981) assessment of terrorism in Northern Ireland a little further with particular reference to the Provisional IRA.

Although the Provisional IRA in Northern Ireland is often described as a terrorist group, the differences between it and other groups in Europe that are similarly named are noteworthy. The resilience and longevity of the Provisional IRA alone make it exceptional in European terms. The view held by the Provisional IRA of itself as "the legitimate Republic," and its belief that the existence of the Irish government and British presence in Northern Ireland are gross encroachments distinguish it sharply from other subservise groups in Europe such as ETA, the Brigate Rosse, the Baader-Meinhof gang, and the South Moluccans. Furthermore, none of these other groups can lay claim to the sort of ancestry which purports to make them the true repository of the nation's honour (Moxon-Browne, 1981). In addition, these other European groups wage campaigns that tend to be spasmodic, irrational, and apparently devoid of widespread support. Survey evidence (Davis & Sinott, 1979; Moxon-Browne, 1979) supports the contention that the goals and grievances of the Provisional IRA are shared by many (in both Northern Ireland and the Irish Republic) who would despise their tactics.

On the other hand, the IRA does manifest some of the characteristics of a guerilla movement, particularly what Wilkinson (1977) called "revolutionary" terrorism (as distinct from "repressive" or "subrevolutionary" terrorism). Their actions include classical guerilla tactics involving robbery and assassination, although they are unusual, as the statistics show, in engaging in both urban and rural guerilla warfare with equal success.

Thus, while the political aspirations of the Provisional IRA echo those of many Catholics in Northern Ireland, the methods they use have produced predictably a policy of "criminalization" of their campaign by the government. It has been argued, though, that the Provisional IRA is, generally speaking, not psychopathic (Burton, 1978; Heskin, 1980a). From what evidence is available on their personal characteristics, members of the Provisonal IRA appear to show neither "lovelessness" nor "guiltlessness." Indeed, Heskin (1980a) has argued that, "The behaviour of terrorists does not differ substantially from the behaviour of men in conflict-oriented groups generally, and that their behaviour is largely explicable, at a psychological level, in terms of the formalistic and authoritarian structure of conflict-oriented groups and the sole requirements of members of such groups (p. 93)." Also drawing on social psychological experiments, Heskin reminds us how similar behaviour can be elicited from ordinary people in the right, or wrong, circumstances.

The reasons and motives for joining paramilitary organizations include, it is believed, diffuse things such as boredom, desire for excitement, attraction by the glamour of membership, as well as more specific factors such as reaction to events (on the Protestant side this could be a political crisis, like Sunningdale or the current Anglo-Irish talks, but on the Catholic side it might be resentment of the activities and harassment of the security forces or the death of a hunger striker), intimidation, upbringing, indoctrination, a genuine belief in the aims of the group, or propaganda (e.g., Burton, 1978; Heskin, 1980a; Tugwell, 1981; White, 1981). In the words of Tugwell (1981):

> Both the Catholic and Protestant communities in Northern Ireland have for generations been organized into the types of isolated self-righteous and insecure groups that are ideal target audiences for the propagandist. An organized, closed group can easily strip the individual of his personal identity. . . . Conformity can be enforced by group dynamics and, if necessary, fear. [p. 20]

However, White (1981) suggests that:

There is nothing intrinsically evil, or even unusual about Ulster's paramilitary generation. It has grown up with violence as a means of achieving political ends and has seen the failure of conventional politicians to solve chronic unemployment, bad housing and poverty.

It knows what it is against—a British Ulster or a United Ireland—but what compromises it is prepared to make in the long term, no-one can say. It may look, and act, differently but its basic attitudes are those of its parents who bear the major responsibility for its problems. [p. 7]

What the eventual effect on the people and community of Northern Ireland will be when, or if, the violence ends can only be a matter of speculation. What is certain though, to paraphrase Heskin (1980b), is if the troubles were to end tomorrow Northern Ireland would still be a society under stress—socioeconomic stress. In some ways, though, the single most important question that must be raised about Northern Ireland is that of the effect of the troubles on the youth of the region and, in particular, on those most closely involved in or exposed to communal forms of antisocial behaviour. At its most fundamental, the question concerns whether the experiences of Northern Ireland children and adolescents have rendered them resistant to the control of law or even any control, and whether they will create havoc even in the event of a political solution—or whether their antisocial behaviour since 1969 is merely situationally determined. Some journalists and politicians have predicted that crime in Northern Ireland is on the brink of epidemic proportions as a result of the social unrest, and some researchers in psychiatry (e.g., Fraser, 1973; Lyons, 1973, 1978) and juvenile delinquency (e.g., Curran, Jardine & Harbison, 1980) have speculated on the emergence of antisocial behaviour as a major feature of life.

Several investigations in Northern Ireland on variables typically associated with delinquency, truancy and school absenteeism, reading retardation, antisocial and deviant attitudes, and teacher-rated antisocial behaviour (see Harbison and Harbison, 1980; and Heskin, 1980a)—together seem to make a *prima facie* case to substantiate the above fears of a consequent boom in youthful antisocial behaviour allied to the fact that vandalism and lack of discipline in Northern Ireland schools has greatly increased in recent years (ANIELB Report, 1976). However, as Heskin (1980a, b) rightly points out, there are difficulties in accepting the data at face value, in relation to larger, more general issues within the Northern Ireland situation, as well as in the specific terms of the particular studies.

These studies which have measured various characteristics of Northern Ireland young people in the post-1969 period have made two implicit assumptions: (1) high levels of indices which are known to be correlated with antisocial behaviour in other societies have arisen as a result of experience during the "troubles"; (2) these indices are predictive of future antisocial behaviour in the context of Northern Ireland.

The problem with the first assumption is that there is no pre-1969 data against which to test the hypothesis. Regarding the second supposition, perhaps the most relevant point is that correlates of delinquency and crime have never been good predictors in Northern Ireland. For instance, in spite of appalling social conditions, Northern Ireland has been a region of relatively low levels of crime and delinquency generally, and serious crime more particularly. At no time during the 1960s, prior to 1969, did the total number of murders reach double figures. Indeed, there was only one murder in the entire country in 1965.

Moreover, although criminal statistics are generally unreliable as valid indicators of real levels of crime and delinquency (e.g., Curran et al., 1980), and although differences in legislation render indictable/nonindictable distinctions problematic for comparative purposes, the figures in Northern Ireland compare favourably with those in England and Wales. As Jardine and his colleagues (1978) noted, the number of indictable offences known to the police in

Northern Ireland was still only two-thirds the rate in England and Wales in spite of a decade of social turmoil. Their data for *juveniles* found guilty, per thousand of the juvenile population, suggested that the rate in Northern Ireland for all offences was similarly two-thirds the rate in England and Wales and only one-third for all serious offences. Heskin's (1981) analysis of comparative levels of indictable crime from 1960 to 1978 in Northern Ireland, the Irish Republic, England, and Wales similarly reveals that there is no evidence to support the suggestion that Northern Ireland society is disintegrating.

On the other hand, though, from a temporal perspective, Northern Ireland has witnessed a level of very serious crime unprecedented in its troubled history, as a result of the conflict. As Curran's (1980) data illustrate, the increase in the official figures of crime for Northern Ireland has risen by 120 percent over the ten years from 1969 to 1978. In contrast, the comparable increase in England and Wales was 60 percent. While the total rate of serious crime has risen from 17,000 in 1968 to 40,000 in 1980, it is still about half the comparable figure for England and Wales (White, 1981). Research also suggests that a greater proportion of juvenile offenders in Northern Ireland engage in serious offending and that the increased level of juvenile deviance, measured in alternate ways, is closely associated with particular urban areas exposed to extremes of both socioeconomic deprivation and civil strife (Curran, 1982). These findings are not surprising in view of other studies outside Northern Ireland—particularly in the United States—which indicate behavioural correlates of urban deprivation and civil violence. Some reports in the press—e.g., *The Observer* and *The Sunday Times*—have also suggested that deprivation was one of the root causes of the serious race riots in some English cities during the summer of 1981. And yet, offences associated with political violence and terrorism constitute a relatively small proportion of all known offences. The extent of young people's involvement in political terrorism in Northern Ireland may appear considerable (Curran, 1982), but the vast majority of juvenile indictable offences are, in fact, crimes of dishonesty (Jardine et al., 1978).

It would seem, therefore, that fears of a serious growth in antisocial behaviour among the young people of Northern Ireland and the total disintegration of Northern Ireland society are largely unjustified. One likely factor that may account for the law-abiding nature of Northern Ireland society and the relative containment of crime is the strength of the churches' influence and the fundamentalist religious values espoused by both Protestants and Catholics in Northern Ireland (Rose, 1971). Another is the essentially traditional nature of Northern Irish society with respect to strong family ties and family support.

There is emerging now a rapidly growing body of research which continues the theme of resilience, coping, and "normality" with regard to children's and young people's awareness of the conflict and the violence. Focusing specifically on the troubles, rather than the socioeconomic stresses of Northern Ireland, Cairns (e.g., 1980, 1982a, b; Cairns, Hunter, & Herring, 1980), McWhirter and Trew (e.g., 1981, 1982a, b; McWhirter, 1982; McWhirter, Young, & Majury, 1982; Trew & McWhirter, 1982), and their co-workers have together illustrated the importance both of exploring social cognition and social behaviour in a protracted conflict situation, and of adopting an intergroup rather than an interindividual perspective. The belief is that evidence concerning people's social awareness, perceptions, knowledge, and understanding—of religious categories, of stereotyped cues used for group ascription, of intergroup relations, of the environment, of violence, and of death—provides an essential baseline from which to examine the socialization process involved and to approach an amelioration of some of the problems. The "problems" currently under investigation are being explored, not only in the self-selected, abnormal samples seen by researchers in psychiatry and criminology, but also in the representative samples of "normal" Northern Ireland young people. The emergent picture suggests that neither religious denomination nor conflict and violence are salient dimensions for Northern Ireland children. As McWhirter and Trew (1981) have interpreted, this "may be because after 12 years of 'troubles,' abnormality has become 'normality' [p. 309]"—everywhere.

Not only does the evidence suggest that people have become habituated—at least cognitively—to the conflict and violence but the spontaneous responses of the children and young people in open-ended 'disguised' tasks illustrate the extent to which their social perceived realities reflect the objective situation. For example, one study (McWhirter et al., 1982) asked Belfast children aged 3-16 years (n = 200) about the causes of death. The subjects attributed death more to sickness than to accidents or violence, just as frequently to heart disease and to old age as to explosions or shootings, and more to road accidents and cancer than specific local violence. Their perceptions, surprisingly, accurately reflected the official death statistics.

In another study (McWhirter, 1981a), 637 children, aged 9 and 12 years, from various areas in the province, were asked to write about "violence." Two-thirds of the subjects spontaneously censured it. Their conceptions of violence were global and embraced much more than the Northern Ireland troubles: 64.6 percent of the acts of violence described related to Northern Ireland situations, while 59.6 percent described general universal acts of aggression and violence which were either unspecific—bullying, kidnapping, killing—or occurred somewhere other than Ireland. Only 5.2 percent referred to Catholics and Protestants being violent to each other. In view of the nature of the conflict over the last few years, it was not unexpected that Catholic children from troubled west Belfast made more reference to Northern Ireland in type of violence—stoning, rioting, shooting, bombing, throwing petrol bombs, intimidation, etc.—than Protestant children also living in a neighbouring area of west Belfast and Catholic children living in a peaceful provincial town. In other words, the actual levels and types of violence which vary in different parts of Northern Ireland were quantitatively reflected in the writings of children living in more and less troubled areas. (This geographic variation is similar to the temporal variation which was found in an earlier study by Cairns et al., 1980.)

Two examples (with spellings etc. largely corrected) will help to illustrate this data. The first one was written by a 9-year-old Catholic from west Belfast.

> Violence is bad. It is about smashing windows. And rooking nest's (sic). Killing birds. Violence is breaking in to some one's house and wrecking the place. Some nights cars get stolen and crashed into walls or shooting people. Wrecking seats, cutting down trees and lying in flower beds. Starting forest fires, stealing things. Throwing at saracens. Throwing petrol bombs.

The second example was written by a 12-year-old from the peaceful area:

> All over the world there is one thing that has caused destruction and the breaking up of people—Violence. In many places like Iran and England and even in Ireland men and women cause hardship for others they kill and damage, they hurt and destroy. Many teenagers follow in these foot steps and I blame television. Things like TV-eye, Starsky and Hutch, Kojak and Vegas. They show bad examples even though they don't realise it. They kill and fight and it looks so real but they don't realise that children think they can do it and forget about getting caught. Violence begins at hate . . . then jealousy it tears peoples mind. Quiet places like Ireland, now have become a hell and a torment. Riping (sic) seats, bombing houses, suicide, murder, rape, kidnap, shooting and so on build up a world of terror for others. Violence has grown up since Julius Caesar till the Shah of Iran. I hate this world.

The apparent paradox which emerges from what might be called the "abnormal normality" interpretation is obviously resolved when one considers the relative nature of normality. When we think of the process of socialization into conflict, violence, and terrorism in Northern Ireland, we must differentiate not only between the majority and minority in Northern Ireland as a whole, or between the majority and minority religous group within specific locations in the country—variables crucial to an understanding of the *conflict*—but also between the majority and minority in terms of experience of the "troubles"—a variable vital to understanding the impact of the *violence*. For the vast majority, the violence is only a backcloth to everyday life.

To a large extent, most people in Northern Ireland have learned about the violence second hand—by word of mouth or via the media. But there is also the minority—reckoned by one television documentary to include, in 1974, about 30,000 children—who have been living at the heart of the troubles, where the wheels of violence grind relentlessly. They have obviously been unable to transcend the grim daily realities of continuing violence—sectarian and/or loyalist, and/or republican, and/or official police-army power and force. In such beleaguered communities where many people's lives are dominated by fear, it is not surprising that young people are sucked relentlessly into what is the "norm" for their area, and their "side."

Indeed, there is some evidence that those who became involved in the violence are quite "normal" in the psychological adjustment sense, or even above the psychological or personal norm.

In one analysis of people on trial for terrorist crimes in 1975, a group of researchers (Boyle, Chesney, & Hadden, 1976) found that overall, in terms of socioeconomic background, employment status, and previous criminal history, the defendants were broadly representative of the Protestant and Catholic communities from which they came. They concluded:

> Those coming before the courts on terrorist charges are not essentially different from those who might get into trouble in other ways in more peaceful times. But, because of the Troubles, *more* of these ordinary young people are becoming involved with the law on much more serious charges.

Nevertheless, it is difficult from an historical, legal, and psychological viewpoint to view those who commit terrorist-type offences in Northern Ireland as "ordinary" criminals. Although "political" or "special category" status may be anathema to the British government and although the government (e.g., Rees, 1981) claims that the system which has evolved in Northern Ireland should depart "as little as is possible from internationally agreed principles and from the traditions of British justice (p. 85)," scheduled (or terrorist) offenders are certainly not convicted or imprisoned in the normal manner in which "ordinary decent criminals" are in Great Britain or in Northern Ireland. Furthermore, not only does there seem to be no psychological evidence that those who have been involved in terrorist-type activities are diagnostically or otherwise clinically disturbed, but what little research data there is on the characteristics of juvenile scheduled offenders compared with "ordinary" delinquents suggests important personal differences. A small-scale study by Elliott and Lockhart (1980), for example, showed that, despite similar socioeconomic and family backgrounds and similar reconviction rates, a sample of juveniles charged with terrorist-type offences and sent to an assessment centre were older, more intelligent, with higher educational attainments. The same trend showed on various developmental indicators that the scheduled offenders were less prone to physical illness or accidents in childhood and were less likely to have been referred for psychiatric help or to have displayed a history of truancy.

Application of the Jesness Inventory of Deviant Attitudes by Curran (1980) to a sample of juvenile scheduled offenders sentenced to two institutions following conviction revealed them to be lower on the scale of manifest aggression (as well as lower on the "autistic" and "value orientation" scales) than a control group of "conventional" delinquents. On the other hand, the terrorist offenders were more "socially maladjusted" than a sample of secondary schoolboys. Curran (1982) interprets the finding of a lack of abnormal attitudes of aggression and alienation as contrary to many of the assumptions in the literature on political terrorism and suggestive of inadequate or disturbed socialization. However, those scheduled offenders who had a prior history of conventional offending scored more extreme on all five scales of the inventory than those scheduled offenders without such a previous criminal record.

To some extent, therefore, one might conclude that there is some evidence that a number of young people would not be involved in crime were it not for the "troubles." One can hardly say, though, that the young people who have become involved in such aggressive acts as arson, armed robbery, causing explosions, and intimidation do not know what they are doing or that they have simply drifted into a new kind of "aggro."

Northern Ireland children are exposed, of course, to more than events in Northern Ireland. Aggressive behaviour and violent deaths feature prominently in children's fiction (Opie & Opie, 1959) and in television fiction, as well as in world news. Aggression is also a salient characteristic of life throughout the entire history of childhood (de Mauser, 1976; Gruñnewald, 1981). The children of today still live in a violent world—violence toward children, as well as by children, is increasingly causing concern in humanitarian societies throughout the world (e.g., Rädda Barnen, 1980). There are far more violent and divided societies than Northern Ireland.

In considering the children of Northern Ireland growing up amidst conflict and violence, it is important not to lose sight of the general area of aggression and the development of aggression more specifically. As Shaffer, Meyer-Bahlburg, & Stokman (1980) conclude in their comprehensive overview, there is substantial evidence that there are certain individuals, more often boys than girls, who are characteristically aggressive throughout childhood and adolescence. The incidents that incite their aggressive behaviour are principally those that interfere in some way with the performance of an intended action or which cause them pain or humiliation. Such occurrences are more likely to lead to aggressive behaviour if experienced during a state of high arousal. This may include having watched violence on a film or television programme. These are also the main precipitants of aggressive behaviour in "good" children. There is, however, as yet no satisfactory explanation for why some children are more aggressive than others.

FROM THE PAST TO THE PRESENT AND THE FUTURE: DOES THE ALTERNATIVE TO VIOLENCE LIE IN PEOPLE, PROPAGANDA, OR POLITICS?

Within Northern Ireland there is no simple explanation for the conflict. Indeed, if analyses of Irish affairs were the keys to peace and prosperity, there would be no shortage of solutions. The Northern Ireland conflict, as this chapter has attempted to testify, is complex. It is so complex that observers inside and outside the country, who have exhaustively written about the religious, cultural, economic, political, and identity dimensions, disagree about the relative importance of the contributory factors. Nevertheless, it is certain that the political dimension is only the tip of the iceberg. This is the problem in its most basic form. The 1 million Northern Protestants have expressed their desire to remain British. The half million Northern Catholics have looked toward an all-Ireland context. What new political settlement will replace direct rule, only the future can reveal. Events since 1972 suggest that political endeavours to date are no nearer to solving the two basic problems which have prevented a permanent and peaceful solution to Irish politics:

1. The internal problem of relations between Roman Catholics and Protestants.
2. The external problem of relations between Ireland and Great Britain.

Both problems involve political and social psychological factors. They concern interpersonal and intergroup relations.

These problems appear in various forms, but they have a common root in the long-standing division within the population and the disagreement by the two sides on what each thinks the other side should reasonably accept. During the 1960s, such a recognition had seemed finally to be emerging, but events between 1969 and 1972 revived all the old antagonisms. Not only have recent events done nothing to weaken traditional hostilities, but there are few groups in any part of the island of Ireland which are willing to accept the fact that a workable solution must be a compromise and that compromise involves a partial surrender of one's position. It is important to note the complexity of the issues which divide the North and South. They include the suspicion deeply held on *both* sides of the border that the other side provides a haven for terrorists; the deep and abiding religious differences between the two majorities with all the accompanying historic matters; the growing economic crisis on both sides of the border; the legal differences which render agreements on anything from trade to security a bureaucratic nightmare (*Sunday Times*, November 1, 1981). As Whyte (1981) has recently argued, not only do the different sets of actors in the conflict pursue policies that tend to prolong it but both political and psychological pressures prevent them from changing course.

The British presence in Northern Ireland is the result, if not the cause, of division in Ireland. As Beckett (1979) concludes: "It is hard to see how the division can be removed from the map until it has been removed from the minds of men (p. 176)." To paraphrase two recent writers, a conception of politics as the conciliation of divergent interests has never taken root in Northern Ireland. It has been much simpler—and more deadly—to settle conflicting claims by traditional methods (Arthur, 1980, p. 106). As the resultant spiral of bitterness and death cuts deeper on all sides, attitudes appear to be locked into intransigence and the way toward a solution is blocked by an obduracy bordering on hopelessness (Coogan, 1980, p. 154).

Some months ago, Lord Dunsany was reported (*Belfast Telegraph*, August 8, 1981) to know only two insoluble problems: one was infinity; the other was Ulster. In moments of despair and frustration at the unending saga of attack and counterattack—verbal from the politicians and violent from the men of bomb and bullet—I have reluctantly agreed with this sentiment, especially when hoping for a peaceful solution. Resorting to violence may be a symptom of the failure of politics but, however unpalatable the fact, violence—and often only violence—appears to have been effective in achieving progress throughout the history of Northern Ireland (Downing, 1980). As Northern Ireland continues to search for a constitution in fruitless open convention or private negotiations, involving London and/or Dublin, it seems condemned to suffer a level of political violence totally unacceptable in part of the oldest parliamentary democracy in the world. The annual toll of murders, shootings, and bombings may be distressing but it is eloquent testimony to both the failure of statesmanship throughout the British Isles and the intractability of the Northern Ireland problem (Buckland, 1981). However, one historian concludes that, if nothing else has been achieved during the present period of civil strife, the British army has continued to prove, by its conduct over the past decade, that Britain has no other object in Northern Ireland but to secure a just settlement and a lasting peace. Perhaps this is a more important object gained than military victory because: "If there is one lesson the history of Ireland teaches, it is that military victory is not enough [Johnson, 1980, p. 193]." However, while the continued presence of troops maintains the state of war, most would agree that the withdrawal of the army, unless accompanied by a longer-term political programme that is acceptable to all sides, would result in a blood bath.

What should be recognized is the possibility that, given the position of the contending political factors in Northern Ireland at present, there is no *political* solution to the problem. No proposals, however sophisticated, can bring together or satisfy parties that fundamentally disagree. Therefore, as Downing (1980) suggests, if the political parameters defy solution, the only approach, in the context of a society that has agreed to disagree, is to begin to change those parameters themselves. Politics in Northern Ireland perhaps ought not to be about solutions but about how to change the situation sufficiently to make talk of solutions realistic. The *resolution* of conflict need not involve negative—or violent—behaviours and events.

> As regards conflict (social), *destructive resolution* treats the situation as an adversary contest—a fight between opponents one of whom must destroy, injure, or demean the other. In *constructive resolution* the situation is treated as a shared problem which can be solved with mutual benefits— benefits which exploit the advantages of cooperating in diversity. [Rosenzweig, 1977, p. 382]

Lantz's (1981) recent paper distinguishes between these issues. Attempts to handle conflict may focus on the conflict attitudes or the conflict behaviours involved. *Attitude* change can be attempted in a negative way by manipulation or propaganda, or the conflict may be smoothed over or even excused. A more positive and fruitful approach, Lantz suggests, involves information and education, or the parties may be brought together in an attempt at improving mutual understanding. Conflict *behaviour* may be changed by intervention from a third party in order to calm the conflicting parties or to keep them apart.

> This can be brought about by a third party which acts as a messenger, a mediator or a judge. Or it can be done by the conflicting parties themselves in some kind of bargaining. Or their aims can be changed by transforming the conflict to a meta-conflict, a substitute conflict. The fight between David and Goliath was a substitute for a war between the two people. Perhaps forms of peaceful competition could be such meta-conflicts. All forms of representative democracy can be looked upon as different kinds of conflicts transformed to meta-conflicts. And most forms of positive non-violence methods aim at forcing or persuading the opponent to change his aims. [pp. 12-13]

Nonviolence does not merely refer to the absence of violence. It can also refer to positive nonviolence—the use of nonviolent means for defence or intervention or for social change.

Lantz (1981) suggests that positive nonviolence (which presupposes a higher degree of community interest and values than violent fighting does) would be more effective against an antagonist whose ideals and valuations are diffuse and heterogeneous, than in a situation characterized by hard and clear-cut ideological antagonism on both sides, that is, when the conflict is greatly polarized and when it is a conflict of aims more than a conflict of interests. "And I think this is the case in the conflict in Northern Ireland [p. 10]."

The danger is not from thinking people who need to keep their nerve in the face of politically orchestrated violence, but from those whose emotions will over-rule their heads. The realities of the last thirteen years suggest that peace should be the prime goal. Reconciliation begins with stopping murder and incitement to murder. Once the killings have stopped, political discourse might have a chance to succeed (Editorial, *The Observer,* November 22, 1981). Perhaps, though, it is a chicken-and-egg situation: the politics-peace equation, as Ireland's history testifies, defies easy or simple solutions.

A concentration on the immediate situation induces pessimism and cynicism but, if the events of the past decade are viewed in their wider historical context, a sense of realism *may* be seen to be creeping into Anglo-Irish relations. After all, there has been more political movement in the last decade than there has been since the 1920s (Arthur, 1980).

It was not until 1979 that any prominent Dublin politician addressed loyalist Ulster for the first time on the advantages of Irish unity. A united Ireland thesis is unlikely to win many loyalist converts, but it illustrates that persuasion rather than coercion has become the keynote in North-South relations. In October 1981, the Irish Prime Minister, Garret Fitzgerald, launched a "Crusade" to end the turmoil of a divided Ireland. "With the initial impetus you start the debate, you make people think about things they haven't thought about before, you achieve something right away. . . . Then you've got a long slog thereafter as you develop the theme [*Sunday Times,* November 1, 1981]." Part of this theme is a proposed amendment of the Republic's constitution in order to appease the Northern Unionists. He has also challenged his people to shake off the sectarian Catholic attitudes which make the South unattractive to the majority of the North.

British attitudes toward Ireland, North and South, are also changing. For the first time since the 1880s, no major British political party unequivocally supports the union (Arthur, 1980). Also after six years of excluding the Republic from any consideration of British policy in Ulster, London and Dublin are once again holding talks. Among the radical proposals that are emerging is the concept of an Anglo-Irish Intergovernmental Council, an institutionalized recognition that the Irish Republic is inextricably bound into the problem of Northern Ireland.

Finally, in Northern Ireland itself, there has been both paramilitary and political movement. Not surprising is the reaction by Paisley and his party to the ongoing Anglo-Irish talks. To protest the alleged "sell-out" of Northern Ireland by London in the direction of Dublin, Paisley organized a "day-of-action" on November 23, 1981. The Loyalist protest was peaceful, but the day produced the first appearance by a new Loyalist paramilitary group organized by Paisley —"The Third Force."

However, there has been some surprising political movement among a few paramilitary groups in Northern Ireland (Arthur, 1980). Three paramilitary groupings are engaged in discussion rather than violence. Two Loyalist groups have recommended negotiated independence. In the past few years, Sinn Fein, The Workers' Party (formerly the Official Republican Movement) has been contesting, with little success, parliamentary and local elections. This offers some hope—even if it only leads to a breakaway by the Catholic militants.

Perhaps the deteriorating socioeconomic state and the harshness of the levels of unemployment in Northern Ireland—the worst since the depression of the 1930s—will succeed in uniting working class Protestants and Catholics. They did come together once before—in joint violence—for a common cause in the mightiest demonstration of unity that has ever been seen in Belfast, which occurred during the deep recession of the 1930s.

It may be sensible to concede that Ireland can be united—mentally rather than politically— in any constructive and lasting sense only by the will of *all* the people, and to conclude that the restoration of peace must therefore be the first priority. Terrorism and the themes of fear, hatred, and misunderstanding hamper progress. Indeed, every year of violence makes the task of finding a just and peaceful solution more difficult. The myths on *both* sides of the divide (McWhirter & Trew, 1982b) act as psychological barriers to the imaginative initiative which may be needed. Extremist propaganda and the politics of violence, both Protestant and Catholic, compose the greatest obstacle to psychological and political unity, and, as such, testify to the bankruptcy of such a philosophy.

Unfortunately, the alternative process—the politics of peace—is generally boring and tedious. Furthermore, its product does not sell well. Whereas a well-placed bomb can create world attention, individual peace efforts often do not attract the attention of politicians. The awesome logic of violence can create political attentiveness and a will to find a solution which the more boring process of peace may not achieve—as the history of Ireland demonstrates.

There have, of course, been some well-publicised peace efforts from time to time. The most spectacular, the Peace People, emerged in August 1976 after three small children were killed when a Provisional IRA car, fleeing from the army, went out of control and crashed. An overwhelming emotional protest attracting tens of thousands of people from all walks of life registered their disgust with violence and joined numerous demonstrations. The news media unanimously welcomed this manifestation. The Peace People leadership built up strong international contacts which culminated in an award of the Nobel Peace Prize for two of its founders. Fundamentally, however, it has not succeeded because of a failure to build at the community level, although Peace People are still active at a community level in performing welfare services, for example, for the families of prisoners who decide to renounce their paramilitary membership.

Like the vast majority of people in Northern Ireland, I abhor and despise violence. Also, I am not afraid, as a person, to say that extremists on both sides are wrong. Elsewhere (e.g., McWhirter, 1981b), I have emphasized the importance, for a professional academic researcher, of distinguishing between personal aspirations of peace and harmony in Northern Ireland and a genuine understanding of the causes, concomitants, and consequences of the ongoing social conflict.

Furthermore, to practice psychological research on such topics as religious and national identity, sectarian division and sectarianism, intergroup conflict and violence is to assume a critical social responsibility. One concrete way of exercising such social responsibility is to speak out. While maintaining due caution, I suggest that researchers working on real-life problems involving human aggression and social conflict must popularize their findings and make explicit the basis of whatever ideas are offered, so that statement of opinion, researched fact, judgment, and value can be differentiated.

While many others are engaged in very practical, pragmatic ways (see, for example, Bleakley, 1981; McCreary, 1981), both as individuals and in groups, of working for peace—"building bridges" is the fashionable phrase—I wish to assert that, although terrorist acts are readily condemned by those who follow the Western definition of terrorism, the specific conditions which lead to those acts need to be investigated. If violence emerges as a symptom of society, then, as Nelson (1975) states, the whole system has to be changed.

While politicians in Northern Ireland, Great Britain, and the Republic of Ireland continue to battle with the political conflict and the political systems, both intergroup relations within Northern Ireland and the prolongation of violence require further research by social scientists, especially social psychologists. As a political scientist concluded a few years ago (Whyte, 1978), at the end of a critical appraisal of interpretations of the Northern Ireland problem, in which social psychological models were significant by their absence:

> Anyone who studies the Ulster conflict must be struck by the intensity of feeling. It seems to go beyond what is required by a rational defence of the divergent interests which undoubtedly exist. There is an irrational element here, a welling-up of deep unconscious forces, which can only be explained by an appeal to social psychology. [p. 278]

In theory, peace may come from the top down—from the politicians and leaders. Hence, people are wont to look toward the politicians or the community leaders—the big people. But, in fact, peace may be a gradual thing that may well sweep right through society, slowly, at all levels. There is no harm in dreaming that this "something" might involve a genuine *reassessment,* if not change, of the aims, interests, and values of the people and politicians in Northern Ireland which have prolonged the Northern Ireland conflict for centuries, and the present "troubles" for the last thirteen years.

In order to cope with the harsh, uncompromising reality of violence, and continuing negative conflict one must not lose hope—even in an apparently hopeless situation. At times, Northern Ireland has seemed to be teetering on the brink of a real catastrophe but, in the event, a sense of realism and good sense has prevailed: like a strong elastic band, tension has recoiled rather than snapped. However, as McCreary (1981) concludes:

Those who hold out at the prospect of peace, who refuse to accept that war is the natural condition of the Irish or indeed mankind, can point to a better way which will require sacrifice on all sides. Whether their work can help to divert a catastrophe, or whether the words and ways of peace are those which will build up a new society after a catastrophe, is one of the major imponderables in the broad sweep of Irish history. [p. 96]

A more optimistic note to end on is the fact that December 1981 is the first month since June 1971 in which no deaths occurred due to the "troubles"—in spite of the recent upsurge in tension due to Protestant Loyalist protests.

REFERENCES

Arthur. P. *Government and politics of Northern Ireland*. Essex: Longman, 1980.

Arthur, P. Irish Myths and Political Realities. In L. McWhirter and K. Trew (Eds.), *The Northern Ireland conflict: Myth and reality. Social and political perspectives*. Ormskirk and California: G. W. & A. Hesketh, in press.

Association of Northern Ireland Education and Library Boards (ANIELB). *Vandalism and Indiscipline in Schools*. Report of a working party set up by the ANIELB, Belfast, 1976.

Barnen, R. *Children and violence*. Stockholm: Abedemilitteratur, 1980.

Beckett, J. C. *The making of modern Ireland, 1603-1923*. London: Faber and Faber, 1966.

Beckett, J. C. *A short history of Ireland*. (6th ed.). London: Hutchinson, 1979.

Beit-Hallahmi, B. Overcoming the "objective" language of violence. *Aggressive Behaviour*, 1977, *3*, 251-259.

Beloff, H. A place not so far apart. In J. Harbison and J. Harbison (Eds.), *A society under stress*. Somerset: Open Books, 1980.

Berthoud, R., Brown, J. C., with Cooper, S. *Poverty and the development of anti-poverty policy in the United Kingdom*. London: Heinemann, 1981.

Bishop, P. The muscle of Paisley power. *The Observer*, November 22, 1981.

Bleakley, D. *Saidie Patterson. Irish peacemaker*. Belfast: Blackstaff Press, 1981.

Boyle, K., Chesney, R., & Hadden, T. Who are the terrorists? *New Society*, May 6, 1976.

Boyle, K., Hadden, T., & Hillyard, P. *Law and state: The case of Northern Ireland*. Amherst, Mass.: University of Massachusetts Press, 1975.

Buckland, P. *A history of Northern Ireland*. Dublin: Gill and Macmillan, 1981.

Burton, F. *The politics of legitimacy: Struggles in a Belfast community*. London: Routledge and Kegan Paul, 1978.

Cairns, E. The development of ethnic discrimination in children in Northern Ireland. In J. Harbison and J. Harbison (Eds.), *A society under stress. Children and young people in Northern Ireland*. Somerset: Open Books, 1980.

Cairns, E. Intergroup conflict in Northern Ireland. In H. Tajfel (Ed.), *Social identity and intergroup relations*. Cambridge: Cambridge University Press, 1982. a

Cairns, E. The Northern Irish conflict: Social psychological perspectives. In L. McWhirter & K. Trew (Eds.), *The Northern Ireland conflict: Myth and reality. Social and political perspectives*. Ormskirk and California: G. W. & A. Hesketh, 1982.

Cairns, E., Hunter, D., & Herring, L. Young children's awareness of violence in Northern Ireland: The influence of Northern Irish television in Scotland and Northern Ireland. *British Journal of Social and Clinical Psychology*, 1980, *19*, 3-6.

Coles, R. Ulster's children waiting for the Prince of Peace. *Atlantic*, December 1980, 33-44.

Coogan, T. P. *On the blanket. The H-Block story*. Dublin: Ward River Press, 1980.

Curran, J. D. Deviant attitudes and personality of juvenile scheduled and juvenile delinquent offenders. Paper presented at Annual Conference of British Psychological Society, University of Aberdeen, April 1980.

Curran, J. D. Juvenile offending, civil disturbance and political terrorism—A psychological perspective. In L. McWhirter and K. Trew (Eds.), *The Northern Ireland conflict: Myth and reality. Social and political perspectives.* Ormskirk and California: G. W. & A. Hesketh, 1982.

Curran, J. D., Jardine, E. F., & Harbison, J. J. M. Factors associated with the development of deviant attitudes in Northern Ireland schoolboys. In J. Harbison and J. Harbison (Eds.), *A society under stress. Children and young people in Northern Ireland.* Somerset: Open Books, 1980.

Darby, J. Reform? In L. McWhirter and K. Trew (Eds.), *The Northern Ireland conflict: Myth and reality. Social and political perspectives.* Ormskirk and California: G. W. & A. Hesketh, 1982.

Darby, J., & Williamson, A. Violence, institutions and communities in Northern Ireland. In J. Darby and A. Williamson (Eds.), *Violence and the social services in Northern Ireland.* London: Heinemann, 1978.

Davis, E., & Sinott, R. *Attitudes in the Republic of Ireland relevant to the Northern Ireland problem.* Dublin: Economic and Social Research Institute, 1979.

de Mauser, L. *The history of childhood.* London: Souvenir Press, 1976.

Dillon, M., & Lehane, D. *Political murder in Northern Ireland.* Harmondsworth: Penguin, 1973.

Downing, T. (Ed.). *The troubles. The background to the question of Northern Ireland.* London: Thames Television Ltd. and Macdonald Futura Publishers Ltd., 1980.

Elliott, R., & Lockhart, W. H. Characteristics of scheduled offenders and juvenile delinquents. In J. Harbison and J. Harbison (Eds.), *A society under stress. Children and young people in Northern Ireland.* Somerset: Open Books, 1980.

Evason, E. *Poverty: The facts in Northern Ireland.* London: Child Poverty Action Group, 1976.

Evason, E. Myth and reality—The economy, social policy and social need. In L. McWhirter and K. Trew (Eds.), *The Northern Ireland conflict: Myth and reality. Social and political perspectives.* Ormskirk and California: G. W. & A. Hesketh, 1982.

Farrell, M. *Northern Ireland: The orange state.* London: Pluto Press, 1976.

Fraser, M. *Children in conflict.* London: Martin Secker & Warburg, 1973 (also Pelican Books, 1974, 1979).

Grünnewald, K. From the history of childhood: How aggression was built up. Paper presented at Rädda Barnen (Swedish Save the Children Fund) Seminar on Children in Conflict, Södertälje, Sweden, December 1981.

Harbison, J., & Harbison, J. (Eds.). *A society under stress. Children and young people in Northern Ireland.* Somerset: Open Books, 1980.

Hayes, M. The contribution of professionals to the easement of conflict. Paper presented to the Rädda Barnen (Swedish Save the Children Fund) Seminar on Children in Conflict, Södertälje, Sweden, December 1981.

Heskin, K. *Northern Ireland. A psychological analysis.* Dublin: Gill and Macmillan, 1980. a

Heskin, K. Children and young people in Northern Ireland: A research review. In J. Harbison and J. Harbison (Eds.), *A society under stress. Children and young people in Northern Ireland.* Somerset: Open Books, 1980. b

Heskin, K. Societal disintegration in Northern Ireland: Fact or fiction? *The Economic and Social Review,* 1981, *12*(2), 97-113.

Jardine, E., Curran, J. D., & Harbison, J. J. M. Young offenders and their offences: Some comparisons between Northern Ireland, England and Scotland. Paper presented to the Northern Ireland Regional Office, British Psychological Society Conference on Children and Young People in a Society Under Stress. Belfast, September 1978.

Johnson, P. *Ireland: Land of troubles.* London: Methuen, 1980.

Kee, R. *Ireland. A history.* London: Weidenfeld & Nicholson, 1980.

Lantz, G. Conflict solving through violence or non-violence. Paper presented at Rädda Barnen (Swedish Save The Children Fund) Seminar on Children in Conflict, Södertälje, Sweden, December 1981.

Lyons, H. A. Violence in Belfast—A review of the psychological effects. *Community Health,* 1973, *5*(3), 163-168.

Lyons, H. A. Health services. In J. Darby and A. Williamson (Eds.), *Violence and the social services in Northern Ireland.* London: Heinemann, 1978.

McCann, E. *War and an Irish town*. Harmondsworth: Penguin, 1974.

McCreary, A. *Profiles of hope*. Belfast and Ottawa: Christian Journals Limited, 1981.

McWhirter, E. P. Understanding of proportion as embodied in the concept of fullness. *Contemporary Educational Psychology*, 1978, *3*, 205-231.

McWhirter, E. P. The social work context. In J. Radford and D. Rose (Eds.), *The teaching of psychology. Method, content and context*. London: Wiley, 1980.

McWhirter, L. Segregated education and social conflict in Northern Ireland. Paper presented at conference of the Bush Program in Child Development and Social Policy on International Perspectives on Child Development and Social Policy, Toronto, August 15-16, 1981. a

McWhirter, L. Violence in Northern Ireland: Children's conceptions. Paper presented at 6th Biennial Conference of International Society for the Study of Behavioural Development, Ontario Institute for Studies in Education, Canada, August 1981. b

McWhirter, L. Awareness of conflict. In L. McWhirter and K. Trew (Eds.), *The Northern Ireland conflict: Myth and reality. Social and political perspectives*. Ormskirk and California: G. W. & A. Hesketh, 1982.

McWhirter, L., & Trew, K. Social awareness in Northern Ireland children. *Bulletin of British Psychological Society*, 1981, *34*, 308-311.

McWhirter, L., & Trew, K. Children in Northern Ireland: A lost generation? In E. J. Anthony (Ed.), *Children in turmoil—Tomorrow's parents. Vol. 7. Yearbook of the International Association for Child Psychiatry and Allied Professions*. Chichester: Wiley, 1982. a

McWhirter, L., & Trew, K. (Eds.) *The Northern Ireland conflict: Myth and reality. Social and political perspectives*. Ormskirk and California: G. W. & A. Hesketh, 1982.

McWhirter, L., Young, V., & Majury, J. Belfast children's awareness of violent death. *British Journal of Social Psychology*, forthcoming, 1982.

Magee, J. *Northern Ireland: Crisis and conflict*. London: Routledge & Kegan Paul, 1974.

Miller, L. Identity and violence. *Israel Annals of Psychiatry and Related Disciplines*, 1972, *10*, 71-77.

Moody, T. W. *The Ulster question 1603-1973*. Dublin: Mercier Press, 1974.

Moxon-Browne, E. Northern Ireland attitude survey: An initial report. Unpublished manuscript, Queen's University of Belfast, 1979.

Moxon-Brown, E. The water and the fish: Public opinion and the provisional IRA in Northern Ireland. In P. Wilkinson (Ed.), *British perspectives on terrorism*. London: George Allen & Unwin, 1981.

Murphy, D. *A place apart*. Middlesex: Penguin Books, 1978.

Murray, R. Patterns of violence. In L. McWhirter and K. Trew (Eds.), *The Northern Ireland conflict: Myth and reality. Social and political perspectives*. Ormskirk and California: G. W. & A. Hesketh, 1982. a

Murray, R. Political violence in Northern Ireland: 1969-1977. In F. W. Boal and J. N. H. Douglas (Eds.), *Integration and division. Geographic aspects of the Northern Ireland problem*. London: Academic Press, 1982. b

Nelson, S. D. Nature/nurture revisited II: Social, political and technological implications of biological approaches to human conflict. *Journal of Conflict Resolution*, 1975, *19*, 734-761.

O'Brien, C. C. *States of Ireland*. London: Hutchinson, 1972.

Opie, I., & Opie, P. *The lore and language of schoolchildren*. Oxford: Clarendon Press, 1959.

Ress, M. Terror in Ireland—and Britain's response. In P. Wilkinson (Ed.), *British perspectives on terrorism*. London: George Allen & Unwin, 1981.

Rose, R. *Governing without consensus: An Irish perspective*. London: Faber & Faber, 1971.

Rose, R. *Northern Ireland: A time of choice*. London: Macmillan, 1976.

Rosensweig, S. Outlines of a denotative definition of aggression. *Aggressive Behavior*, 1977, *3*, 379-383.

Schellenberg, J. A. Area variations of violence in Northern Ireland. *Sociological Focus*, 1977, *10*(1), 69-78.

Shaffer, D., Meyer-Bahlburg, H. E. L., & Stokman, C. L. J. The development of aggression. In M. Rutter (Ed.), *Scientific foundations of developmental psychiatry*. London: Heinemann, 1980.

Sterling, C. *The terror network*. London: Weidenfeld & Nicholson, 1981.

Stewart, A. T. Q. *The narrow ground: Aspects of Ulster 1609-1969*. London: Faber, 1977.

Taylor, P. *Beating the terrorists? Interrogation in Omagh, Gough and Castlereagh.* Harmondsworth: Penguin, 1980.

Trew, K., & McWhirter, L. Conflict in Northern Ireland: A research perspective. In P. Stringer (Ed.), *Confronting social issues.* Vol. 2. *European monographs in social psychology.* London: Academic Press, 1982.

Tugwell, M. Politics and propaganda of the provisional IRA. In P. Wilkinson (Ed.), *British perspectives on terrorism.* London: George Allen & Unwin, 1981.

White, B. The making of a paramilitary. *Belfast Telegraph,* November 13, 1981.

Whyte, J. Interpretations of the Northern Ireland problem: An appraisal. *Economic and Social Review,* 1978, *9*(4), 257-282.

Whyte, J. Why is the Northern Ireland problem so intractable? *Parliamentary Affairs,* 1981, *34*(4), 422-435.

Wilkinson, P. *Political terrorism.* London: Macmillan, 1974.

Wilkinson, P. *Terrorism and the liberal state.* London: Macmillan, 1977.

Wilkinson, P. (Ed.). *British perspectives on terrorism.* London: George Allen & Unwin, 1981.

17

Peru: A Functional Analysis of Aggression*

Jose Anicama

Aggression is a major and growing phenomenon in the world today. Its scope and impact demand continued effort at understanding its causes and gaining its control. As a contribution toward these goals, this chapter seeks to describe and analyze certain data relevant to individual and collective aggression in a country reflecting many underdeveloped characteristics.

The point of view assumed in this chapter derives from the learning theorists. Aggression is a response of high magnitude and specificity acquired by processes of discriminative stimulus control, modeling, and positive reinforcement; maintained and strengthened by a concurrent reinforcement program. This view, in general, emphasizes the role of environmental factors. In terms of this functional analysis learning perspective, Figure 17.1 summarizes the principal elements to be considered in the study of aggression.

Aggression can be expressed in different ways, and in individual and collective forms. In any event, however, aggression must be seen in the context of the specific social system in which it occurs. More strongly, we would hold that its present structural conditions determine the types of aggression that occur in a country. In Peru, the more frequent individual forms of aggression are: assault and juvenile delinquency; and, in its collective forms, students outbreaks or strikes, worker strikes, and terrorism. But there are other forms of aggression and violence, more subtle in some cases, which function as discriminative stimuli of instigation or precipitation, and which produce individual or collective responses of a higher magnitude (example: terrorism), we refer to economic and cultural aggression. These types of aggression in Peru will be considered below.

AGGRESSION IN ITS INDIVIDUAL FORM

The types of aggressive behavior in Peru with highest incidence are assault and robbery; the area in which these occur with greatest frequency is the capital city, Lima.

Table 17.1 describes the denunciations and arrests between 1972 and 1979. In this table,

*Dedicated to my father, J. Anicama, on his 61st anniversary, who taught me the value and importance of Social Justice. The author wants to express his appreciation to Cecilia Vilela, for her great help and commentaries; and to Mercedes Galvez, Rosa Vasquez, and Miriam Pando, who helped obtain information relevant to the contents of this chapter.

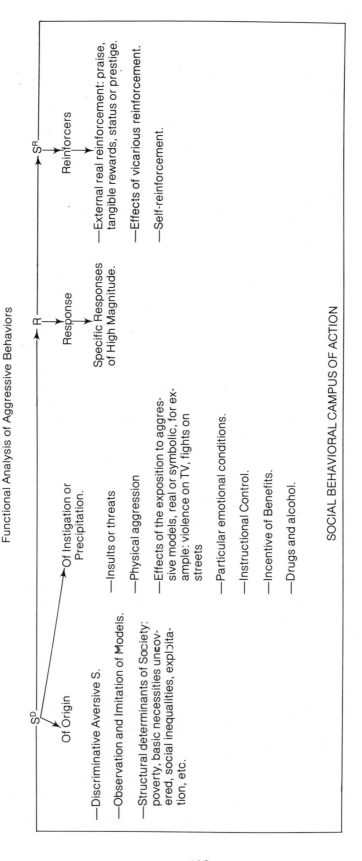

Functional Analysis of Aggressive Behaviors

S^D R S^R

Of Origin   Of Instigation or   Response   Reinforcers
       Precipitation.

—Discriminative Aversive S.

—Observation and Imitation of Models.

—Structural determinants of Society:
poverty, basic necessities uncovered, social inequalities, exploitation, etc.

—Insults or threats

—Physical aggression

—Effects of the exposition to aggressive models, real or symbolic, for example: violence on TV, fights on
streets

—Particular emotional conditions.

—Instructional Control.

—Incentive of Benefits.

—Drugs and alcohol.

Specific Responses
of High Magnitude.

—External real reinforcement: praise,
tangible rewards, status or prestige.

—Effects of vicarious reinforcement.

—Self-reinforcement.

SOCIAL BEHAVIORAL CAMPUS OF ACTION

Fig. 17.1. Scheme Describing Three Conditions for the Analysis of Aggressive Behaviors: Discriminative Conditions, Response Conditions, and Reinforcement conditions.

as in the others which follow, we use certain terms and categories in order to report delinquent actions (considered as aggressive behavior), as it is established in the Peruvian Penal Code. For example, the category "delicts" according to this code means: "the transgression of a fact considered as delict in the penal code, done as a punitive act." "Faults" means: "a minor transgression, without a punitive sanction, and that are not considered in the penal code as delict"; which in a major part of the cases receive only a severe admonition. Figure 17.2, describes graphically the data on denunciations during this same time period.

As can be seen from Table 17.1, the denunciations for "delicts" between 1972 and 1979 increased by 50 percent, "faults" only increased by 26 percent; but, if we compare 1976 and 1979, faults increased 60 percent. Arrests increased 19 percent for delicts and decreased 9 percent for faults, if we compare 1972 and 1979. It is important to say that 1978 and 1979 were years of great agitation, political and labor stress, in response to the difficult economic situation in Peru. While the population was growing by 22.45 percent, delicts grew almost 50 percent.

Table 17.2 shows with greater detail the number of denunciations which occurred between 1977 and 1979. An analysis of the data shows that denunciations for delicts and faults in 1977-1978 grew in incidence, especially in the categories of delicts against patrimony (robbery and assault). In the second place in incidence growth were the delicts against life, body, and health, and then delicts against good habits: sexual violation and corruption. In 1979, the situation was different, the major frequency of denunciations were for delicts against life, body, and health; in second place delicts against patrimony (robbery and assault), and in third place against good habits. It is important to emphasize that comparing the annual denunciations for homicide (in the category of delicts against life, body, and health), it decreased by 3 percent in 1978 compared with 1977, but in 1979 increased by 204 percent compared with 1978.

The specific behaviors of homicide, as a delict, decreased by 92 percent between 1977 and 1978; but increased by 7,800 percent from 1978 to 1979. Likewise, denunciations for "wounds," delicts for attack and physical aggression with or without weapons, increased in 1979 by 3,951 percent compared with 1978. In contrast, denunciations for specific behaviors of sexual violation and corruption decreased by 581 percent between 1977 and 1978, and 261 percent between 1977 and 1979; but increased between 1978 and 1979 by 88 percent. Comparing the global data of denunciations against patrimony (which includes robbery and assault), we observe an annual decrease of 426 percent comparing 1979 to 1977. But, as we

Table 17.1. Denunciations and Arrests for Delicts and Faults 1972-1979

YEARS	DENUNCIATIONS		ARRESTS	
	DELICTS	FAULTS	DELICTS	FAULTS
1972	55,930	208,696	40,522	188,783
1973	52,398	172,812	37,384	155,788
1974	60,915	194,257	44,143	172,433
1975	62,433	164,538	46,696	147,036
1976	64,340	164,412	45,503	141,258
1977	76,363	211,254	44,490	151,410
1978	71,662	277,183	56,721	193,088
1979	84,107	263,975	48,575	170,949

Source: Office of Planification-Civil Guard (Police) National Institute of Statistics-INE 1981.

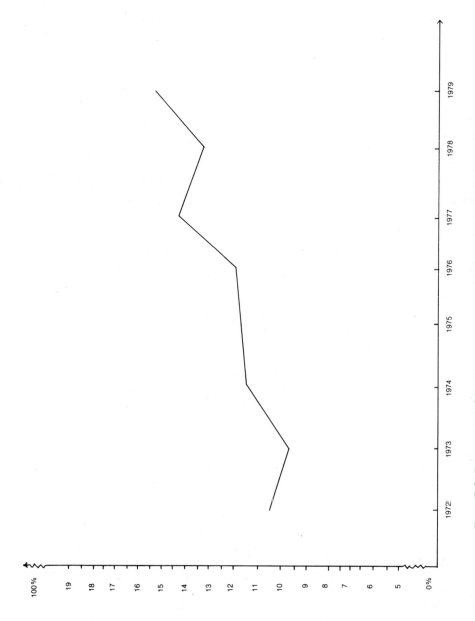

Fig. 7.2. Percentage of Dennunciations of Delicts Registered in 1972-1979

404

said before, delicts against life, body, and health increased. Denunciations against public security, usually expressed as a collective form of aggression, will be examined later in this
chapter.

Table 17.2 reports only global data concerning denunciations of "faults." It was not possible to obtain more information relevant to such events and, for this reason, we will not analyze
in detail such denunciations.

In Table 17.3, we present a descriptive analysis of the characteristics of people arrested for
"delicts and faults" between 1977 and 1979, according to their age, sex, and type of entrance. This table indicates that, in 1977, men over 18 years of age were the major target of arrests. They frequently were of primary entrance, i.e., this was their first delict or fault against
the law. In 1978, the overall picture of delicts remains the same. But, by doing comparisons
between one year and another, we find an increment in delicts by minors of 298 percent in
1978 over 1977. Minor women decreased in arrests by 53 percent comparing 1977 and
1978. In 1979, the situation is similar. Men over age 18, with primary entrance, are still the
major group of arrestees. The comparisons between years show a diminution of 9 percent in
the delicts of minors in 1977 compared with 1978; but arrests of women increased by 267 percent. For people over 18, the total number of arrests in 1979 was 20 percent less than in 1978;

Table 17.2. Denunciations for Delicts and Faults (1977–1979)

DESCRIPTION	1977		1978		1979	
	DELICTS	FAULTS	DELICTS	FAULTS	DELICTS	FAULTS
TOTAL	76,363	211,254	71,662	286,836	84,107	263,975
AGAINST LIFE, BODY, AND HEALTH	14,224	84,585	13,751	96,693	41,828	134,711
—Homicide	241		18		1,494	
—Abortion	58		16		490	
—Suicide Instigation	82		—		—	
—Wounds	4,971		614		24,876	
—Dispute	1,520		54		4,860	
—Leave a Person in Danger	—		6		216	
—Not Specified	7,352		13,043		9,892	
AGAINST GOOD HABITS	5,183	30,030	6,870	39,996	8,215	40,025
—Liberty and Sexual Honor	4,918		722		1,362	
—Corruption	265		3		37	
—Not Specified	—		6,145		6,816	
AGAINST FAMILY	291	—	721	—	961	—
—Substraction of Minors	—		12		561	
—Not Specified	291		709		400	
AGAINST LIBERTY	433		472		1,205	
—Kidnapping: Women and minors	—		—		84	
—Address Violation	58		—		467	
—Individual Freedom	375		472		—	
—Not Specified	—		—		654	

(continued)

Table 17.2. *Continued*

DESCRIPTION	1977		1978		1979	
	DELICTS	FAULTS	DELICTS	FAULTS	DELICTS	FAULTS
AGAINST PATRI-MONY	54,333	63,792	49,069	110,134	30,363	79,617
—Robbery and Assault	50,030		44,890		9,509	
—Illicit Appropriation	2,052		2,145		2,469	
—Swindle	1,126		711		987	
—Damages	1,125		1,322		1,022	
—Extortion	—		1		—	
—Not Specified	—		—		16,376	
AGAINST PUBLIC SECURITY	641	6,999	653	5,027	1,443	3,641
—Fire	55		80		157	
—Public Tranquility	—		130		754	
—Against Public Health	19		—		68	
—Not Specified	567		443		464	
OTHER DELICTS	1,248	25,848	107	25,388	92	5,981
—Against Public Faith	25		71		50	
—Against Public Authority	13		18		5	
—Against Popular Will	—		3		1	
—Against Justice Administration	79		4		34	
—Against Function Obligations	—		8		2	
—Against State and National Defense	—		3		—	
—Against Public Order	—	8,941	—	9,598	—	4,728
—Others	1,131		—		—	
MILITARY JUSTICE CODE	10		19		—	

Source: Office of Planification-Civil Guard Peru.

but, as was true for minors, arrests of women increased by 44 percent in comparison to 1978. In sum, Table 17.3 describes as initial characteristics of arrestees the following: they are predominantly male, over 18 years old, and this was their first arrest; however, in 1979, there was an increase in arrests of women.

Tables 17.4, 17.5, and 17.6 complete this description of delicts and faults in the 1977–1979 period, adding information about the marital, educational, and occupational status of offenders. Table 17.4 shows single persons as the ones who are arrested with a higher frequency for "delicts" (49 percent) and "faults" (35 percent) than any other marital status type. Table 17.5 describes the educational status of the arrested people. Most of those arrested during the time span examined have only a primary school education. In second place, we find people with less than a primary school education and, close behind, people with high school educations.

Table 17.3. Arrests for Delicts and Faults According to Age, Sex, and Type of Entrance

AGE, SEX, TYPE OF ENTRANCE	1977		1978		1979	
	DELICTS	FAULTS	DELICTS	FAULTS	DELICTS	FAULTS
TOTAL	44,490	151,410	56,724	193,844	48,575	170,949
BELOW 18 YEARS	4,080	18,796	16,241	85,004	14,852	62,906
—Men	3,519	15,819	14,556	73,672	12,788	52,762
Primary	2,724	12,717	11,311	59,802	9,887	42,366
Recidivism	795	3,102	3,245	13,870	2,901	10,396
—Women	561	2,977	1,685	11,332	2,064	10,144
Primary	472	2,189	1,416	8,107	1,571	7,633
Recidivism	89	788	269	3,225	493	2,511
MORE THAN 18 YEARS	40,410	132,614	40,483	108,844	33,723	108,043
—Men	35,909	115,715	37,559	92,077	29,510	94,649
Primary	26,169	99,006	31,784	78,152	24,595	80,496
Recidivism	6,740	16,709	5,775	13,925	4,915	14,153
—Women	4,501	16,899	2,924	16,767	4,213	13,394
Primary	3,709	13,682	2,265	13,188	3,513	2,838
Recidivism	792	3,217	659	3,579	700	10,556

Source: Office of Planification-Civil Guard Peru.

Table 17.4. Arrests for Delicts and Faults According to Marital Status (1977-1979)

STATUS	1977		1978		1979	
	DELICTS	FAULTS	DELICTS	FAULTS	DELICTS	FAULTS
TOTAL	44,490	151,410	58,724	193,088	53,575	170,949
Single	23,801	78,103	25,832	99,141	25,517	89,114
Married	14,339	56,182	19,037	72,436	17,090	65,809
Widower	1,397	5,319	5,507	8,694	2,467	6,727
Living Together	4,953	11,806	8,348	12,817	8,501	9,299

Source: Office of Planification-Civil Guard-Peru.

Table 17.5. Arrests for Delicts and Faults According to Educational Status (1977-1979)

INSTRUCTION	1977		1978		1979	
	DELICTS	FAULTS	DELICTS	FAULTS	DELICTS	FAULTS
TOTAL	44,490	151,410	56,718	193,088	48,575	220,943
Primary	26,633	88,794	28,620	107,646	26,846	97,160
High School	8,319	31,265	9,802	42,395	10,603	85,992
Superior	634	3,441	1,320	5,069	1,063	4,732
No Instruction	8,904	27,910	16,976	37,978	10,063	33,059

Source: Office of Planification-Civil Guard-Peru.

Table 17.6. Arrests for Delicts and Faults According to Occupational Status (1977-1979)

	1977		1978		1979	
OCCUPATION	DELICTS	FAULTS	DELICTS	FAULTS	DELICTS	FAULTS
TOTAL	44,495	151,410	56,724	193,088	48,575	170,949
With Occupation	14,958	83,854	20,442	99,714	18,731	82,966
Without Occupation	19,859	34,322	23,282	48,095	17,836	45,888
Fortuitous Works	9,678	33,234	13,000	45,279	12,008	42,095

Table 17.6 presents arrest data according to type of occupation. It shows that people without work have a higher frequency of "delicts"; but people with occupations have a higher frequency of actions against law of the "faults" type.

AGGRESSION BY ASSAULT

One of the individual forms of aggression with increasing incidence in the 1977-1979 period in Peru are assaults. One feels its seriousness dictates that it receive special attention in our presentation. Table 17.7 describes the characteristics of people arrested for assault, according to their age, sex, and type of entrance. Arrests for assaults increased by 34 percent from 1977 to 1979. Assailants were generally over 18 years of age, male, and first offenders.

Table 17.8 indicates that people arrested for assault have, principally, primary education; in second place we find those with high school education.

Table 17.9 describes the characteristics of those arrested according to their occupation.

Table 17.7. Arrests for Assaults According to Age, Sex and Type of Entrance (1977-1979)

AGE, SEX, TYPE OF ENTRANCE	1977	1978	1979
TOTAL	2,886	3,387	3,601
BELOW 18 YEARS OLD	254	501	402
—Men	234	474	369
Primary	171	311	227
Recividism	63	163	142
—Women	20	27	33
Primary	17	20	20
Recividism	3	7	13
MORE THAN 18 YEARS OLD	2,632	2,876	3,199
—Men	2,561	2,745	3,116
Primary	1,694	1,924	2,055
Recividism	867	821	1,061
—Women	71	131	83
Primary	57	90	38
Recividism	14	41	45

Source: Office of Planification-Civil Guard-Peru.

Table 17.8. Arrests for Assaults According to Educational Status
(1977-1979)

EDUCATION	1977	1978	1979
TOTAL	2,686	3,387	3,601
Primary	1,791	2,164	2,333
High School	559	680	759
Inferior	30	10	56
Without Instruction	306	533	453

Source: Office of Planification-Civil Guard-Peru.

People without occupation have a higher frequency of arrests; following this group, we find those with fortuitous work.

Table 17.10 shows the marital status of people arrested for assaults. The great majority are single; for example, in 1979, there were three times as many single as married assailants.

In short, people arrested for assaults are typically males, over 18, single, first offenders and unemployed.

COLLECTIVE AGGRESSION

The forms of collective aggression of greatest frequency are student and worker disorders and terrorism.

Student Violence

Students violence, including strikes, meetings, and marches of protest with street outbreaks and damage to property, which has motivated strong repressive actions from the police, has shown a substantial increase. However, it seems that this student agitation is periodical and is closely related with the defense of the autonomy for universities, budget changes, and also support to the popular replevin.

Labor Violence

Labor violence has been closely associated with demands for salary augmentation. Many forms have occurred—protest marches, strikes, sabotage to production, meetings, and so forth. In some cases, there are political goals to these actions, but almost always there is a ma-

Table 17.9. Arrests for Assaults According to Occupational Status
(1977-1979)

OCCUPATION	1977	1978	1979
TOTAL	2,686	3,387	3,601
With Occupation	654	492	470
Without Occupation	1,544	2,184	2,473
Fortuitous	488	711	658

Source: Office of Planification-Civil Guard-Peru.

**Table 17.10. Arrests for Assaults According to Marital Status
(1977-1979)**

STATUS	1977	1978	1979
TOTAL	2,686	3,387	3,601
Single	1,922	2,445	2,710
Married	504	648	666
Widower	216	237	51
Living together	44	57	174

Source: Office of Planification-Civil Guard-Peru.

jor focus upon economic control. Table 17.11 describes the frequency of labor strikes from syndicates and federations gathered in the four National Syndicate centers for Peruvian workers: CGTP or General Workers Center of Peru, Marxist orientation; CTP or Workers Center of Peru, left democratic; APRA (political party); CTRP or Workers Center from the Peruvian Revolution. Comparing the frequency of strikes in 1974 with 1979 we find a decrease of 9 percent. But, in an analysis of the internal events between 1974 and 1975, strikes increased by 59 percent. This year was very difficult in Peru, because a major financial crisis occurred, and the reaction of workers was severe, including economic demands of high magnitude. Political changes in the government and some economic improvements seem to explain why in the following years there appears a diminution in labor stress. If we compare 1975 with 1977, we find a decrease of strikes and labor conflicts by 74 percent. It has been impossible to obtain relevant data yet about 1980 and 1981, but the tendency for this aggression to decrease continues, as Table 17.11 and Figure 17.3 indicate.

Terrorism

Terrorism in Peru has been characterized by:

1. Organization of rural groups for specific objects of rural vigilance, as substitutes for policemen.
2. Organization and training of groups that seek a radical and violent change of society.
3. Organization of subversive and secret political movements.
4. Specific actions of terrorism:
   - Destruction of property: Roads, bridges, electric towers, water connection for the cities.
   - Destruction, even partially, of other elements of public and private activities: Government buildings, schools, private houses.
   - Violent assaults on banks.
   - Violence and torture in rural areas toward people.
   - Fights with government or local authorities, using weapons, dynamite, machine guns, etc.

Table 17.12 describes terrorists' transgressions registered in Peru between May 1980 and July 1981. On account of national security, we only could obtain overall numbers for 1981, because they are still being investigated; but we were able to obtain more information for the events of 1980. As table 17.12 shows, total terrorism transgressions were 288 in 1980; however, in the first seven months of 1981, the number of terrorists' transgressions was 332. This means that in seven months we had 15 percent more than in the whole year of 1980. An analysis of May 1980 with five transgressions vs. December 1980 with 80 transgressions, the increase is significant and dangerous. It is our impression that this increase may be associated with the high rate of inflation and related economic crises which occurred during that period. These data are graphically exhibited in figure 17.4.

SOCIAL SYSTEM AND AGGRESSIVE BEHAVIOR

It is our contention that certain structural conditions of Peruvian society provoke aggressive behaviors and violence. In 1981, the social economic crisis on Peru was quite serious. Dr. Javier Alva Orlandini, President of the Senate from the Congress of the Republic, in his inaugural lecture said:

> The salary for the public and private employees in the last year has decreased by 12%. The intern product, which we expect to increase by 6% during this year, is growing only by 3.5% . . . the

Table 17.11. Frequency of Strikes and Labor Conflicts Gathered in Workers Centers (Main Syndicates)

YEAR		TOTAL	
1974			
—CGTP	259 strikes		
—CTP	26 strikes		
—CTRP	18 strikes		
—CNT	6 strikes	309	18%
1975			
—CGTP	412 strikes		
—CTP	33 strikes		
—CTRP	39 strikes		
—CNT	8 strikes	492	30%
1976			
—CGTP	192 strikes		
—CTP	15 strikes		
—CTRP	14 strikes		
—CNT	8 strikes	229	14%
1977			
—CGTP	84 strikes		
—CTP	14 strikes		
—CTRP	19 strikes		
—CNT	—	117	7%
1978			
—CGTP	155 strikes		
—CTP	19 strikes		
—CTRP	25 strikes		
—CNT	—	199	12%
1979			
—CGTP	252 strikes		
—CTP	23 strikes		
—CTRP	7 strikes		
—CNT	—	282	17%
GENERAL TOTAL YEARS 1974-1979		1,628	98%

Source: Statistics Office. Investigation Police-Peru 1974-1979

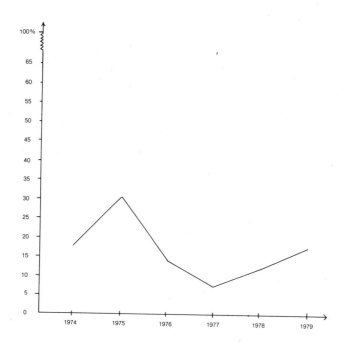

Fig. 17.3. Graphical Distribution of Percentages of Strikes in the Country between 1974 and 1979

Table 17.12. Terrorists' Transgressions Registered in Peru from May 14, 1980 to July 15, 1981

	YEAR 1980						YEAR 1981	
	TOTAL		DYNA-MITE	MOLO-TOV B.	IN-FLAM. INSTR.		TOTAL	
MONTH	N	%				MONTH	N	%
May	05	1.74%	01	02	02	January	56	16.87%
June	09	3.12%	02	03	04	February	20	6.02%
July	35	12.15%	21	11	03	March	46	13.85%
August	19	6.60%	08	07	04	April	99	29.82%
September	14	4.86%	07	06	01	May	93	28.01%
October	71	24.65%	37	27	07	June	13	3.91%
November	55	19.09%	29	24	02	July	05	1.51%
December	80	27.78%	44	28	08			
TOTAL	288	99.99%	149	108	31	TOTAL	332	99.99%
GENERAL TOTAL FROM 1980 to 1981:					620			

Source: Statistics Office. Investigation Police-Peru August 1981.

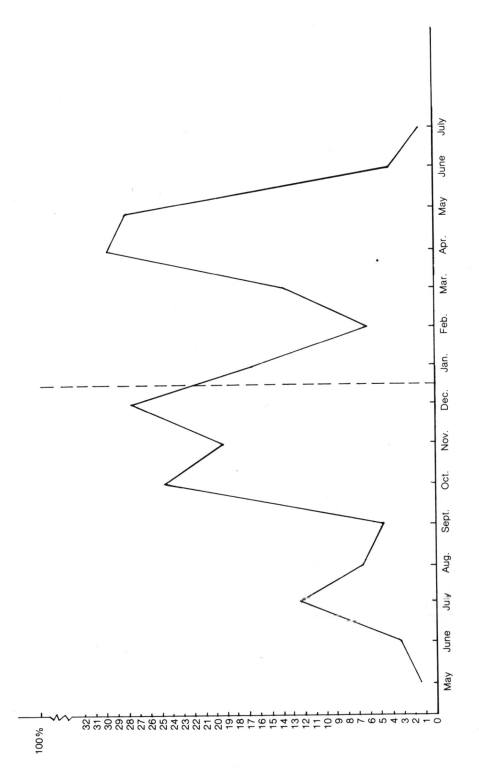

Fig. 17.4. Percentage of Terrorists' Transgressions Registered From May 14, 1980 to July 15, 1981, Peru.

413

International reserve of devices has decreased by 45%, the inflation rate in the last year, from July 80 to July 81 is 81%, and at this part of the year, inflation is already 39.5%. [*El Commercio*, July 27, 1981, p. 4]

Much the same conclusion can be drawn for earlier years in Peru. Aversive life conditions, frustration, poverty, and depressed environments do not satisfy the vital necessities as food. Need for justice and social equality appears to act as stimulus of instigation to aggression. As in our earlier functional analysis discussion, these conditions seem to be the independent variables which provoke, in one way or another, aggressive behavior. Tables 17.13 and 17.14 show dramatic data which describe the degree in which Peruvians succeeded or failed to provide for their basic necessities during 1971-1972. These tables are based on the ENCA Survey made by the Economic Council which found, besides other dramatic results, that 49.5 percent of Peruvian families had income levels below that necessary to satisfy their basic needs. As Couriel (1981) indicates:

> The magnitude of the phenomenon implicates that the problem is a consequence of the functioning of the economical, political and social model of Peru, in their various historical stages. [p. 55]

It is our impression that these survey results accurately reflect conditions in Peru today also. Satisfaction of basic needs, unemployment, underemployment, nutritional deficiency, weaknesses in the educational system, and inadequate shelter remain problems of considerable magnitude and a likely source of aggressive behavior. As table 17.15 indicates, a high and nondeclining birth rate combined with a low and declining death rate has further augmented these several social and demographically-associated stimuli to aggression. Further, it should be noted in future perspective what Wicht (1979) predicts that by the year 2000 Peru's current population of 17 million will have grown to almost 30 million.

PSYCHOLOGICAL REACTIONS TO WAR STRESS

Aggression and violence find their most intense and severe expression in warlike conflicts. War, as a collective action of governments and nations, has been present through almost all of human history. Peru, as a nation, has not escaped from such contingency, its history is also written

Table 17.13. Peru: Total Country, Indicators of the Degree in Which They Cover Basic Needs

1. Percentage of families who do not satisfy their Basic needs	49%
2. Percentage of families below the minimum salary changed into the minimum family income	51%
3. Percentage of families below the 90% of calories assigned 1971-1972	52%
4. Unemployment and underemployment rate	48%
5. Percentage of undernourished children, less than six years old, according to their weight 1971-1972	44%
6. Percentage of illiterate and semi-illiterated people of 15 years old or more, 1972	50%
7. Chance of life in the decade of the sixties	50.71 years.
8. Death rate in children less than 2 years old 1967-1968	169%
9. Death rate in children less than 1 year old	135%

Source: A. Couriel, "State, Development Strategic and Basic Needs in Peru," DESCO: Center of Studies and Development Promotion. Lima, 1981.

Table 17.14. Peru: Indicators Related to the Fulfillment of the Basic Needs.
Regional Differences. (percent)

	LIMA	COAST	SIERRA	SELVA	TOTAL PERU
1. Fulfillment of basic needs	28.5	33.7	63.0	56.9	49.5%
2. Extreme poverty	6.3	21.3	50.0	42.9	34.7%
3. Differences between families of the 30% with minor entrance, considering self-consumption. Rural Sierra = 1	5.4	3.5	1.2	1.5	1.5%
4. Underemployment rate	23.7	47.6	78.8	69.7	60.6%
5. Chance of life since birth (years)	54.8	53.5	46.6	52.5	50.7
6. Childhood death rate (0-2 years old)	100.0	154.0	209.0	160.0	169.0%
7. Percentage of children less than 6 years old with malnutrition according to their weight	19.0	35.0	56.0	63.0	44.0%
8. Percentage of houses without electric lighting system	25.9	56.2	89.1	88.6	69.6%
9. Percentage of houses without drinking water	39.4	71.8	92.4	92.6	77.5%
10. Percentage of houses without home devices	16.6	31.4	60.8	52.7	45.2%
11. Social Security*	26.8	65.2	86.2	87.6	64.1%
12. Differences between families of the 10% with major entrance. Rural Sierra = 1	2.1	1.4	1.2	1.6	1.8%

*Social Security: Percentage of workers and employees not registered in social security among the total occupied workers.
Source: A. Couriel, "State, Development Strategie and Basic Needs in Peru," DESCO: Center of Studies and Development Promotion. Lima, 1981.

Table 17.15. Birth and Death Rates in Peru

COMPARATIVE RATES/YEAR	1976	1979
Birth Rate	4.3	4.2
Death Rate	3.2	1.2
Demographic Growth Rate		2.9

Source: "Politics of Population in Peru Health Cabinet," Lima 1976. National Census ONEC 1972.

with war actions. Recently, in 1981, we had to face a serious conflict with a neighbor country, on account of territorial limits. After the bellicose actions had finished, the Peruvian citizens who were in the other country began to come back to Peru. A group of them, who had suffered bad treatment and torture, were sent to Cayetano Heredia General Hospital for their treatment and study. Our Clinical Psychology service examined these individuals for the psychological effects of aggressive acts. These individuals were subjected to:

- Application of electric current in various parts of the body, including genitals and anus.
- Wooden and firearms hits, all over the body.
- Being hung by a rope to the point of loss of consciousness.
- Partly drowned, introducing their heads into water tanks, while they were struck on the back, kidney, and sole of the feet with a butt of a firearm.
- Whipping on all parts of the body and trampling on the abdomen.
- Kicks in the abdomen after eating.
- In one case, partial hanging from the genitals.

Nonphysical, psychological, aggressive actions were also administered:

- Pseudo-executions and death stimulations. They were told that it was the hour for their death, they had a bandage placed on their eyes and stood up; their aggressors walked around the room and prepared their firearms, the order to shoot was given, the discharge was done to the air. Then they were taken back to their jail cells again.
- Threats of death against a relative or cellmate.
- Death simulations by execution of cellmates.
- Forced to pray out loud, insulted, or otherwise humiliated.

The results of the psychological tests administered to these persons yielded a consistent and major series of anxiety reactions: heightened fearfulness, severe depression, and a broad array of somatic complaints. Clearly, the citizens involved paid a heavy emotional and physical price as a consequence of their capture. Both the diverse forms of individual aggression examined earlier in this chapter and the treatment of war prisoners—as one Peruvian example of collective aggression—are dramatically expensive: socially, economically, and, especially, in terms of human suffering.

CONTROL OF AGGRESSION

Attempts have been made to control aggressive behavior in Peru by means of laws. Peruvian society has established a series of punishments and sanctions for those who perform criminal acts, especially for those classified as delict. The penal code describes punishments and sanctions for each of the forms of delicts which were described in table 17.2. These punishments range from simple preventive detention to life imprisonment. (In June 1980, the death penalty as a possible punishment was eliminated from the Peruvian penal code.) Under this penal code, various cases of execution by shooting occurred in 1978-1979, and in early 1980 for homicidal delinquents also. With these events, the delictive acts were reduced, as can be seen in table 17.2. But when the Constitution of 1979 came into effect in July 1980, the death penalty was abolished for delict acts, now it is only applied for high treason to the country.

It is evident that, on account of this major added liberty for delinquents, the denunciations about assaults, homicides, violent death of policemen, and terrorist acts increased between

1980 and July 1981. As there is no severe sanction, delinquents are committing more delict actions that are destroying more lives every day, of citizens and policemen. Today in Peru there is much discussion of the possibility of reintroducing severe penal measure. Concurrent with penal code revision, police forces have been progressively improving their equipment and personnel in order to improve their aggression control effectiveness.

Certain potential avenues of aggression control are used hardly at all in Peru. For example, essentially no scholarly research on aggression control methods, or other aspects of aggression, have been conducted in Peru. Radio and television could be used, for both aggression control and prevention purposes, but essentially have not in Peru. Some prevention potential, currently understaffed and underfunded, does exist, however. A brief, and since discontinued, educational campaign directed to children and their parents about safety and danger in the streets and at home seemed to represent a promising avenue for further work. Much the same encouraging view can be said for the Family Protection Institute pilot efforts at protecting and rehabilitating abandoned and delinquent children. And there are beginning efforts spotted throughout the Peruvian educational system, usually on sparse resources, to implement preventive and control efforts concerned with family violence and drug abuse. We are guardedly optimistic about the potential impact of such programs. Finally, we are somewhat less optimistic about the possible contribution of organized religion in Peru to the problem of aggression control. The country is predominantly Roman Catholic, and the influence of the church is perceived in many aspects, but when there are other types of social and economic problems which stimulate an aggressive response, neither self-control nor the influence of religious education can control it; it occurs as a social response to a complex and pressing society.

ALTERNATIVES TO AGGRESSION

In 1972, the Educational Reform Law was passed in Peru. This law mandates that the educational system seek to develop in its students a sense of justice, cooperation, awareness of the social environment, less competition and greater altruism, and related social goals. While this law is still in effect, and is reflected systemwide in courses, lectures, campus activities, special training programs for students and parents, and in other ways, it has yet to be formally evaluated for its effectiveness on aggression reduction in particular, or on the development of prosocial alternatives to aggression in general.

Another alternative source for the stimulation of prosocial behaviors in Peru is the family. Peru has been a very conservative country in its customs and social values. Traditionally, each family teaches its members the use of nonviolent methods, negotiation as a means of conflict resolution, models certain prosocial behavior patterns, stimulates communication between parents and children, and encourages self-control and other means to manage conflicts. Unfortunately, this practice has, in many instances, been discontinued, and much of this direct prosocial training happens only in some family groups. This happens because families face very serious social problems, so aversive and aggressive that a counteraggression appears as a way to stop abuse and violence from others.

Finally, I must say that I consider it would be possible to solve the problem of aggression and human violence if we were able to build a different world, one in which the aversive stimulation provided by social injustices would be eliminated, where the aggressive models used in different communication means would be replaced by cooperative and altruistic models, where damage to others' property or person would not have survival value due to changed contingencies of environmental reinforcement, where aggression would never function as a reinforcer, and where there would always be prosocial alternatives under a high rate of positive reinforcement. When we do all this, we will avoid aggression, individual and collective, and we would be building a better world, more civilized and human. Behavior, under these conditions of natural and positive reinforcement, is the best thing for human existence.

REFERENCES

Amat Y Leon, Carlos, et al. Structure and levels of family incomes in Peru. Economy and Financial Cabinet, General Direction of Financial Matters. Lima, MEF. 1978.

Bandura, A., & Walters, R. H. *Social learning and development of personality*. Madrid: Alianza Editorial, 1974.

CEPAL. A method to trace lines of poverty in Latin American countries. Santiago: CEPAL, 1977.

Couriel, A. State, development strategie and basic needs in Peru. DESCO: Center of Studies and Development Promotion. Lima: DESCO, 1981.

Dollard, J., Doob, L., Miller, N., Mowrer, O., & Sears, R. *Frustration and aggression*. New Haven: Yale University Press, 1939.

Economy and Finance Cabinet (MEF) & National Survey of Food Consumption (ENCA). Income levels in the Peruvian families. Lima: MEF & ENCA, 1975.

Economy and Finance Cabinet (MEF). Life levels. Analysis of the situation about nutrition in Peru. Lima: General Direction of Financial Matters, MEF, 1977.

Education Cabinet. Categorizing illiteracy. Lima: Sector Planning Office, ME, 1977.

El Comercio. Newspaper. Lima, July 27, 1981.

Freud, S. *A general introduction to psychoanalysis*. New York: Liveright, 1920.

Health Cabinet (MSP). Lineaments on politics of population in Peru. Lima: MSP, 1976.

Investigation Police of Peru: PIP, Statistic Office. Personal communication. Lima: PIP, August 1981.

Investigation Police of Peru: PIP, Statistics bulletins: PIP-DAC-II R-PIP. Lima: 1979, 1980, 1981.

Lorenz, K. *On aggression*. New York: Bantam, 1966.

National Office of Statistics and Census: ONEC. Census of population and development. Lima: ONEC, 1972.

National Office of Statistics and Census. ONEC. Growth perspective on Peruvian population 1960—2,000. Lima: Bulletin of Demographic Analysis No. 16, 1975.

National Office of Statistics and Census: ONEC. Death during the first years of life 1967-1968. Lima: Demographic Bulletin No. 1977.

Ribes, E. Some social consideration of aggression. In A. Bandura and E. Ribes (Eds.), *Behavior Modification: Analysis of aggression and delinquency*. Mexico: Ed. Trillas, 1975.

Skinner, B. F. *Science and human behavior*. New York: Macmillan, 1953.

Skinner, B. F. *Reinforcement contingencies*. Mexico: TRD. Ed. Trillas, 1979.

Ulrich, R. Understanding aggression. In A. Bandura and E. Ribes (Eds.), *Behavior modification: Analysis of aggression and delinquency*. Mexico: Ed. Trillas, 1975.

Vinod, T. The measurement of poverty across space: The case of Peru. Washington, D.C.: IBRD, 1977.

Wicht, J. The demographic situation of Peru. Documents: National Meeting on Population. Lima: AMI-DEP, June 1979.

Work Cabinet (MT). Occupational situation in Peru. Lima: General Direction of Employment, MT, 1972.

18

Turkey: Understanding and Altering Family and Political Violence

Guler Okman Fisek

INTRODUCTION

Writing about the place of aggression in contemporary Turkey is quite a difficult job for a number of reasons. One aspect of the problem is that little substantive research has been done on the topic, be it psychological, sociological, anthropological, or legal. A second problem has to do with the lack of reliable statistics on many forms of public aggression. In some ways, the most difficult problem is the fact that, until a few months ago, political aggression and violence was a gruesome fact of Turkish daily life. The very recency and complexity of this phenomenon makes it difficult to gather accurate data and make a dispassionate analysis.

Given these constraints, this chapter obviously suffers from certain limitations and is by no means an exhaustive treatment of the topic. It covers only those areas which appear to be particularly relevant to a discussion of aggression in Turkish culture. Accordingly, the chapter deals with four main forms of aggression: honor crimes, blood feuding, aggression in the family, and political violence. Discussion of these topics will be preceded by a description of Turkish society, family, and child-rearing practices in order to provide a framework within which to understand these phenomena. A discussion of various forms of aggression control will be followed by a final section on alternatives to aggression.

At this point, it may be helpful to present some examples of aggression as they might be reported in the Turkish news media:

- A woman is acquitted of killing her male neighbor who attempted to rape her; says she was defending her honor.
- A man shoots two men, he accuses them of having attempted to abduct his sister.
- A boy of 14 kills the man who had killed his father ten years ago; says his mother showed him his father's bloody shirt on each anniversary of the killing.
- A child playing with a gun accidentally kills his brother.
- Militant rightists gun down people sitting in a coffeehouse.
- Bodies of two murdered workers found in a ditch; leftist group claims responsibility.

Of the examples given above, the last two of collective aggression, would perhaps be more profitably analyzed from an economic and political perspective; but the first few examples have a definite place within the Turkish cultural context. Let us now look at the context within which they occur.

A BACKGROUND OF TURKISH CULTURE

The Cultural Context

As is true of many countries today, Turkish society is undergoing rapid social change from being a traditional, rural, agricultural, patriarchal society into an increasingly urbanized, industrial, modern, egalitarian society. However, since this change is not equally rapid in all areas of social functioning, especially in terms of values, many aspects of the culture can still be described as being somewhat traditional.

In terms of social relations within the culture, we can visualize the individual as being embedded in an ever widening network of close ties or series of ingroups, which define the social position of the person as well as protect him from the aggression of outsiders (Kâğitçibaşi, 1981; Stirling, 1965). In fact, in a system which is inefficient in providing institutional, social, and economic support structures, the kinship and other membership groups of the individual fulfill most supportive as well as controlling functions.

In rural areas, the network of relationships extends from the immediate relatives, to one's lineage group, to the section of the village one lives in and, finally, the whole village itself (Stirling, 1965). At each level, social relations are based on mutual responsibilities, rights, and duties to which one has to be loyal because one's membership within these groups confers identity and status upon him. Within these groups, factors such as one's age and sex, one's lineage, personal honor, wealth, learning, and urban contacts serve to define one's social status (Stirling, 1965), thus indicating a fairly differentiated hierarchy of status positions.

One outcome of such differentiation has to be an emphasis on authority; and, in fact, there is a high degree of respect for authority, whether it be specific, i.e., for elders; or general, i.e., toward any institutional authority (Kâğitçibaşi, 1970). However, this respect for authority needs to be distinguished from the authoritarian personality as identified in the West. Kâğitçibaşi (1970), in comparing authoritarian attitudes among Turks and Americans, found that the Turkish respect for authority reflected a normative social value, rather than a personality trait álá Adorno, Frenkel-Brunswick, Levinson, and Sanford (1950).

A second outcome of such structural differentiation is that an individual is quite clear as to his own and others' positions and role expectations within the group. However, in contrast to differentiated role expectations, the emotional relationships and individual psychological experiences of individuals may not be so clearly differentiated, since a strong emphasis on duty, loyalty, and interdependency would tend to function at the expense of individuality and autonomy (Fişek, 1982). In fact, lack of individuality and autonomy is an often cited observation of the rural individual (Geçtan, 1973; Öztürk, 1969).

As may perhaps be expected from relatively undifferentiated emotional relationships in which the boundaries of the self might be blurred, there exists a high level of mutual expectations and feeling reactions can be intense. Note that this state of affairs applies to relationships within the intimacy of a family, as well as in the larger groups, which may extend to cover a whole village composed of several hundred people. It is in this setting of widespread intimacy that people relate to each other, as often in fighting as in cooperating. As Stirling (1965) says "Even enemies . . . are intimate enemies [p. 30]". Thus, while people feel compelled to rely on each other for protection against the outside world, such reliance itself is bound to lead to occasional disappointment, disagreement, and conflict.

In urban areas, it would be impossible to maintain such widespread intimacy. However, it would appear that urban nuclear families from all socioeconomic levels are surprisingly successful in maintaining a similar supportive network of kinfolk, neighbors, and friends (Duben, 1982; Kongar, 1972). While status hierarchies are less explicit in the diversity of urban life, traditional norms and role expectations are still fairly functional (Kâğitçibaşi, 1981). Emotional relationships among individuals in larger groups may not be as immediate and intense, but there is still a certain lack of differentiation between self and others (Fişek, 1982). This issue of emotional relationships, of course, is especially relevant within the context of the family.

The Family

While young couples are increasingly in favor of choosing their own spouses, many marriages are still seen as a social and financial transaction between two families; and arranged marriages of some sort are quite common (Kâğitçibaşi, 1981).

The hierarchical ordering of the wider society is echoed in the nuclear family with the man as the highest authority, followed by the woman and children. Women's status is still quite low, despite many social changes and more egalitarian urban attitudes (Kandiyoti, 1974; Kiray, 1976; Köknel, 1970; Timur, 1972).

The status differentiation between husband and wife is reflected in a stereotypic definition of sex roles, and reinforced by the custom of physical and social segregation in daily activities (Kâğitçibaşi, 1981; Kandiyoti, 1977; Olson-Prather, 1976).

Husband-wife relations tend to revolve more around the economic survival and propagation aspects of family life than around emotional support and fulfillment (Fişek, 1982; Olson-Prather, 1976). There actually is not much communication in the traditional family, emotional or otherwise (Kâğitçibaşi, 1981; Kandiyoti, 1977). This is to be expected in a situation where the partners may not have chosen each other, live in partially separate worlds, and whose roles vis-a-vis each other are more or less prescribed for them.

Within this order, the husband carries on relations with the external world, protects his woman and children from external abuse, and the wife takes care of domestic production and child care. The husband has primary decision making power, extending from what to purchase for the home, to whom his wife can visit (Gökçe, 1976; Timur, 1972).

More modern, urban sectors show a trend toward status equalization (Kongar, 1972; Timur, 1972), but this is not always without its price in conflict. Families who have migrated to metropolitan areas recently and are faced with more modern sex role expectations, as well as reduced support from the environment, are especially vulnerable. The result is usually direct conflict between husband and wife (Sümer, 1969), high divorce rates (Levine, 1982), and occasionally violence (Özgür, 1980).

While children also have low status in the family, boys are definitely valued more than girls, since they are expected to carry on the family name and provide for the parents' future support and security. In fact, children tend to be valued more for such utilitarian reasons than as sources of psychological and emotional fulfillment (Kâğitçibaşi, 1981). However, there is evidence that more child-centered attitudes are increasing in metropolitan areas (LeCompte, LeCompte, & Özer, 1978; Okman, 1980).

The father tends to be remote from child care. However, there can be an overt relationship of affection and tolerance between father and daughter, while the father-son relationship is formal and authoritarian (Kandiyoti, 1977; Stirling, 1965). In contrast, the mother-son relationship is especially close (Kâğitçibaşi, 1981; Kiray, 1976; Öztürk, 1969). This closeness is to be expected, since the woman starts gaining status once she gives birth to a son, and looks to her children for emotional closeness, rather than her husband (Fişek, 1981).

Child-Rearing Practices

The relationship between parents and children is one of both love and control, in contrast to Western families in which a preponderance of control usually implies an insufficiency of love (Kâğitçibaşi, 1972). In this context, control does not mean harshness, but rather a restriction of autonomous action as seen in toilet training practices for example (Öztürk, 1969; Öztürk & Volkan, 1977).

Infants and toddlers are indulged and allowed to develop at their own pace. Discipline is spontaneous, relies more on external control than attempting to develop internal control and autonomy, and is more dependent on adult moods than on a systematic philosophy (Helling, 1966; Kâğitçibaşi, 1977). Common means of discipline are shaming, scaring through threats of castration, or calling upon supernatural beings and spanking (Le Compte, 1979; Öztürk, 1969; Sümer, 1969; Yörükoğlu, 1978.) However, children tend to be matter of fact in accepting these forms of discipline, since they do not feel personally rejected and receive enough love at other times. By and large, they are clear and secure with respect to their place in the network of intimate relationships surrounding them.

Sex role training starts early and is pursued unequivocally on stereotypic lines (Kâğitçibaşi, 1981). However, the expectation of obedience to authority applies to both sexes. Compliance, meekness, respect, and quietness are rewarded; and activity, curiosity, talk, and exploration are punished (Kâğitçibaşi, 1981; Öztürk, 1969; Stirling, 1965).

By elementary school age, indulgence is increasingly replaced by demands for conformity and competence (Öztürk & Volkan, 1977). The traditional comment from a father to a child's first teacher (or first master if the child was apprenticed) used to be "His meat is yours, his bones are mine," thereby, giving permission for strict discipline, including spanking. Spanking in schools is still practiced.

Most children would tend to accept this rather abrupt increase in adult aggression as the norm, rather than as a reflection of their own worth. They have learned that disobedience brings adult wrath upon their heads and accept this attitudinally (Savaşir & Savaşir, 1974). They also accept aggression among peers matter of factly, but reject the idea of aggression directed against adults or one's own self (Savaşir & Savaşir, 1974). Thus, it would appear that the forms of punishment used do not lead to internalization of controls but, rather, to a feeling of having paid one's dues appropriately and starting over with a clean slate every time.

Urban, middle-class families tend to favor a more democratic, egalitarian approach to discipline and an avoidance of physical punishment (Le Compte et al., 1978; Okman, 1980). However, it would appear that giving up spanking and other modes of harsh discipline is not necessarily accompanied by allowing children more autonomy, as would be expected from Western studies in which the two child-rearing attitudes have been found to covary (Okman, 1980). Instead, parents still seem to reinforce reliance on parental authority rather than on one's own resources.

THE PLACE OF AGGRESSION IN THE SOCIETY AND FAMILY

This section covers the implications of the Turkish social and family context and child-rearing practices for aggression. The forms of aggression specifically covered are honor crimes, blood feuding, violence in the family, and political aggression.

Three points of importance with respect to aggression stand out in the discussion of the social context. First, if a person's social identity is determined by his status within his group, he would be expected to be very quick to take offense at any attack on his status. He would feel compelled to retaliate somehow, no matter who the attacker is—an outsider or a fellow in-group member. Second, the lack of articulation and differentiation in the sphere of emotional relationships could easily lead to unfulfilled high expectations of one another, resulting in potentially highly charged confrontations which would have to be dealt with immediately. And third, the emphasis on authority, loyalty, and interdependence would tend to remove the locus of responsibility and control away from the individual on to the group. Thus, the individual could feel free to act spontaneously on his anger and not feel compelled to restrain himself, expecting restraints to come from outside. This last is indeed the case. It is a standard joke that, whenever a man gets angry at someone, he charges at his opponent yelling "Don't hold me back!" to those around him, who of course rush to do exactly that.

The above mentioned points are also relevant within the family context and create an atmosphere conducive to quick, unrestrained expression of anger. The other important factor which operates within the family has to do with the issues of status differences, especially between husband and wife. Since the man is the absolute authority in the family, he would be expected to feel entitled to and responsible for monitoring the behavior of his wife and children as he saw fit. Since cultural sanctions do not inhibit physical expression of anger, he could easily lean in that direction. The low status of women, coupled with the fact that rural girls are married off in their early teens, would tend to make wife beating seem not much different from child speaking, which is an accepted form of discipline.

While the author is not aware of statistics on wife beating, it would seem natural to expect that wife beating is most common among the lower socioeconomic groups. Consider a man whose sense of identity depends on status concerns, and yet he is at the bottom end of the social status hierarchy, thus being powerless and frustrated. One of the few avenues of self-enhancement and frustration release available to him would be to assert his power over those beneath him in the hierarchy, namely, his wife and children. Similarly, the low status woman may be all too ready to take out her frustrations on her children.

A more striking aspect of aggression in the family should be considered, namely, that of wife against husband. While considerations of status and the sex role definitions of women would tend to militate against such a possibility, there would seem to be enough frustration inherent in the woman's position to force her in that direction occasionally. Some empirical evidence—indicating that, when such aggression does occur, it tends to be violent—will be presented later.

The last topic to be covered in this section has to do with the role played by child-rearing practices in the manifestation of aggression. Most authors agree that the traditional child-rearing practices described earlier would foster the development of a passive, dependent, and somewhat physically undifferentiated person without a strong sense of autonomy and with a reliance on external sources of control and reinforcement (Geçtan, 1973; Helling, 1966; Kâğitçibaşi, 1981; Köknel, 1970; Öztürk, 1969). Such a person would be expected to be inhibited in expressing any assertive or aggressive feelings. However, we have seen from an analysis of the social and family context that the dynamics involved are conducive to the expression of open and spontaneous aggression under some circumstances. How, then, can we reconcile this apparent contrast between normative, social acceptance of aggression and the inhibitory trend of individual personality development?

The following represents one attempt. Öztürk and Volkan (1977) reason that the restrictive and controlling practices of early childhood training would lead to frustration and anger. However, since the overt expression of anger toward adults is forbidden, these feelings have to be repressed or suppressed. Interpreting this situation from a psychodynamic perspective, these authors conclude that an identification with the aggressor (in this case the authority figure) would have to occur. Thus, the individual's use of initiative and autonomy would be inhibited and only expressed through normatively accepted outlets, such as heroism and overvaluation of maleness and family honor.

There is plenty of evidence to support this notion. The Turkish male adolescent has, indeed, been found to be patriotic, politically aware, and respectful of his elders and authority in general (Kâğitçibaşi, 1972). And, although these topics will be covered in more detail later, we may mention here that masculinity, bravery, and being uncompromising in upholding one's honor are among the most, if not actually the most, important virtues a Turkish man can have (Ergil, 1980; Özgür, 1980; Tezcan, 1972).

Öztürk and Volkan (1977) also reason that early sex role training leads to an early and intense identification with the parent of the same sex, and an early adoption of adult roles and attitudes. One does not necessarily have to accept the psychodynamic flavor of these interpretations, but it is clear that the social environment of children, especially boys, provides definite opportunities for a modeling of the aggressive behaviors of adults.

In summary, the following pattern emerges with respect to the expression of aggression in Turkish society. The importance of status and fairly differentiated role expectations, the lack of differentiation in emotional relationships, and the emphasis on external loci of control serve to make the open expression of aggression acceptable. While child-rearing practices might be said to foster the development of an inhibited and constricted personality, identification with normative values related to masculinity would seem to allow giving vent to aggression in certain situations.

Let us now take a look at some of the situations in which aggression occurs.

Honor Crimes

As is true in most Mediterranean cultures (Lozios, 1978; Peristiany, 1965), personal honor (namus) is the most important virtue an individual, especially a man, can have. The concept subsumes different characteristics for men and women. For men it means being honest, loyal to one's family and kin, and keeping one's name, i.e., one's integrity, clean (Ergil, 1980). An important aspect of a man's honor has to do with his masculinity—qualities such as bravery, strength, unwillingness to compromise from one's beliefs, and favoring death over losing in a conflict (Ergil, 1980; Tezcan, 1972). For women, honor primarily means sexual innocence and purity, modesty, and shyness (Ergil, 1980).

One significant outcome of the emphasis on masculinity is a fondness for weapons, which are almost seen as an extension of one's self. In rural areas, most men, even boys, carry some sort of weapon all the time (Ergil, 1980; Stirling, 1965; Tezcan, 1972).

The most important operational implication of these characteristics is the idea that men show their honor through controlling and protecting the sexuality of their women, wives as well as other close female kin (Ergil, 1980; Kâğitçibaşi, 1981; Stirling, 1965; Tezcan, 1972). To the degree that the women of the family remain pure and modest, the man and the whole family have honor. And to the degree that the man is successful in monitoring his women and family and receiving social recognition for this, he earns social prestige (şeref).

Honor and social prestige are among the most important determiners of one's social status and identity (Stirling, 1965). Thus, threats to one's honor are threats to one's personhood and, as such, are not to be taken lightly. This means that immediate and definite reprisal is called for, which is violent, often to the point of homicide, and is consensually accepted (Ergil, 1980; Özgür, 1980; Tezcan, 1972).

The above statements cannot be said to apply to all of Turkish culture. While the concepts of honor and prestige are important overall, they are not so central a part of one's identity in all segments of the society. They are most relevant to the poorer, rural, or recently migrated urban segment. One can see the reason for this in these groups being more traditional and having fewer alternative means of competition for social prestige. Where money, learning, political power, and opportunities for initiative are relatively unavailable, one is left with one's integrity and strength as sources of feelings of self-worth and status (Ergil, 1980). The urban middle and upper classes are not so dependent on gaining self-esteem and status through personal honor since other means are available to them.

It was stated in the beginning of this chapter that accurate statistics were very difficult to obtain in this area. The following are sampling of figures from a variety of sources which may serve to give some idea of the state of affairs. Ergil (1980) searched through police records from 1970 to 1975 in the three largest cities of Turkey. He found that, of the 273 honor crimes committed during this time, 89 percent were committed by people of low socioeconomic status, of which 73 percent were male and 27 percent female. At the same time, Özgür (1980) found that, of an equal sample of male and female homicide offenders, only 22 percent of the men cited the honor motive, as opposed to 44 percent of the women. A survey of criminal youth found that honor crimes comprised 12.5 percent of the total number of crimes (Yavuzer, 1977).

Blood Feuds

Blood feuding refers to aggression (most often homicide) by members of one family toward members of another family for reasons of revenge, originating from a variety of initial causes and potentially lasting for decades. In fact, in the case of two rival groups within the same well known clan in southeastern Turkey, a feud has lasted for about 150 years and may erupt again (Tezcan, 1972). The main requirements regarding a blood feud are that revenge for the initial offense is a duty to be performed by the closest kin of the victim, sometimes even sons under legal age, and perpetrated upon the closest kin of the offender. The most common form of revenge is, of course, homicide, since the offense is seen as being major.

Tezcan (1972) points out that the localities in which blood feuds occur the most have not yet been sufficiently integrated culturally or economically with the larger population. He blames this lack of integration for the continuance of this old custom. The fact that blood feuding occurs mainly in the least developed and/or most remote areas of the country (northeast, east, and southeast) tends to support this claim. The groups living in these areas have to struggle against harsh geographic and climatic conditions, still live with a rather feudal organization, and derive little benefit from governmental services or protection.

Those who get involved in blood feuding cite two kinds of causes—economic and social (Tezcan, 1972). The economic causes have to do with scarcity of useful, and productive land and/or water, as the high number of land and border disputes and disputes over water and pasture rights indicates. The social causes are basically related to the causes given for crimes of honor, such as insults to one's honor, especially to one's women, kidnapping of girls of marriageable age to avoid paying bride price, etc. The custom of carrying weapons all the time and a lack of faith in governmental justice are also factors which facilitate taking the law into one's own hands.

Blood feuding is also a common tradition among other Mediterranean and Near Eastern cultures (Ergil, 1980; Stirling, 1965). However, Stirling (1965) found that the codes governing revenge taking are much less systematic and rigid in some parts of Turkey than in other countries of the area. He stated that it is possible that other realities, such as differences in power and status between the combatants, served to moderate the process. Thus, the economic realities of the situation may lead to feuding being practiced more among those equal in status—again, those who are relatively poorer—since richer and more powerful people may have alternative means of settling disputes.

Tezcan (1972), who has done the most comprehensive study of blood feuding to date, cites the following overall figures. In the period between 1957 and 1968, court cases involving murder in the whole country went from 4,995 to 11,683 per year. The number of murders due to blood feuding in 1957 were 14 and, with some fluctuation in the intervening years, 17 in 1968, that is .28 percent and .14 percent respectively. The figures appear to be rather low, indicating that this form of aggression is socially more troublesome in its violence and futility than in its commonness. However, these statistics cannot be said to be fully accurate, as people tend not to reveal feuding as the cause of their crime, since the sentence for murders of blood feuding is death (Tezcan, 1972). While Özgür (1980) found 6 percent of the men and 2 percent of the women admitted to blood feuding as the cause of the murder they committed, these figures are also low in the overall picture.

Aggression In The Family

The speculations made earlier with regard to aggression in the Turkish family indicated that a fairly differentiated set of role expectations coupled with undifferentiated emotional relationships is conducive to conflict over any perceived failure to fulfill those expectations. The status ordering within the family would seem to indicate that, most often, this anger and aggression would be directed from the husband to the wife and children and from the wife to the children. However, it was also stated that there could be striking incidents of aggression by women whose subjugation and desperation was extreme. Once again, rather than systematically collected statistics, there are scattered studies of this general topic. A review of some of these studies may provide us with an idea of the situation within the family.

In Ergil's (1980) investigation of honor murders cited earlier, the most common reason cited was domestic quarrels (25 percent), followed by "honor-wounding behavior by women" (22 percent). Many of the women convicts gave their specific reason as being beaten by their husbands or in-laws in front of the children and neighbors. It may bear repeating here that, by and large, these offenders were of a lower socioeconomic status.

An interesting point made by Ergil (1980) has to do with murder-suicide, which was found to be an overwhelmingly middle-class, middle-age male phenomenon. Of 28 murder-suicides, one was committed by a lower-class man and two by middle-class women. Ergil speculated that these men, who were already losing status due to increasing age, could not cope with slights to their self-esteem and impulsively resorted to violence. However, they could not face the consequent further losses they expected and opted out altogether.

Another example of aggression turned inward is Cürgen's (1969) survey of suicide attempters, which disclosed that the largest group (31 percent) reported family conflict as their reason. Within this group, husband-wife conflict came first (38 percent), with mother-daughter and mother-in-law-bride conflict following at 12 percent and 9 percent, respectively.

Özgür (1980) studied a sample of 100 male and female homicide offenders and also found that they tended to be low socioeconomic-status young people of rural origin. About 50 percent of these offenders had convicted relatives, 32 percent of them being immediate family members, with crimes against people being the most common. Özgür had the convicts rate various homicide motives as normative or nonnormative depending on their social acceptability. In this analysis, self-defense, honor, and property defense were rated as normative, while domestic quarrels, jealousy, blood feuds, and general aggressiveness were seen as nonnormative.

Somewhat to her surprise, Özgür found that women committed twice as many nonnormative murders as men. Primary among their motives were honor, general aggressiveness, and domestic quarrels (44, 24 and 14 percent respectively). Single women tended to commit murder to protect their honor, while married women murdered for the other motives. Men named self-defense as their most common motive, followed by honor and property defense (36, 22 and 20 percent respectively). The married women tended to kill family members, mainly husbands. Their crimes tended to be more violent, more often premeditated, and less often regretted than the crimes of the men. These women had been married quite young, between 11 and 15 years of age ("sold" in the words of some), and were quite unhappy with their lives. Özgür reflected that the female offenders' crimes seemed to represent a desperate revolt against their low status and misery.

This author could not find relevant statistics of aggression against children. Özgür's sample contains only one example of child murder by a woman, and there is no detailed information about this case. The description of child-rearing patterns indicates that mild forms of aggression, such as spanking, are rather matter of factly accepted. However, Olson (in press) states that child abuse in the technical sense of the term (e.g., battered children) is rare in Turkey, basing the statement on her anthropological observations. She argues that the existence of a supportive kinship network and the lack of high expectations of internal control from children would tend to mitigate against the kind of frustration which leads to child abuse in the West. However, while there is no data on the subject, she speculates that child brides, children in institutions, and rural children sent as servants to urban middle-class homes may suffer from aggression. The data from Ergil's (1980) and Özgür's (1980) studies indicates that, at least in the case of the brides, this may indeed be the case. Since status and a protective kinship network are so important in Turkish society, it would be natural to expect that any persons who are lacking in these two requirements would be common targets of aggression.

Political Aggression

An analysis of the political upheavals and violence which shook Turkey during recent years is in many ways beyond the scope of this chapter. The causes, manifestations, and extent of the phenomenon are so multifaceted and complex that a thorough analysis will probably be some time in coming. This section will only review some speculations and initial data on the topic.

Even a cursory look at Turkey's history indicates that the culture is no stranger to aggression in the form of wars. In fact, the time between the end of the nineteenth century and early 1920s could be said to be a period of almost constant war, including World War I and the War of Independence between 1919 and 1922. With the establishment of the republic in 1923, the country entered a period of peace which has lasted until today. Turkey managed to stay out of World War II and, while it sent troops to the Korean War, the country was (by and large) unaffected.

In the late 1950s, difficult economic conditions and political instability led to some student unrest, which was relatively mild from today's perspective. The fact that one student died in the confrontations with the police in 1960 led to widespread public outrage. The situation was controlled by a short-term miliary coup d'etat but, in the late 1960s, deteriorated again, leading to another intervention by the military in 1971.

Over the next few years, increased political instability, worsening economic conditions, the oil crisis, labor union unrest, unemployment, and possibly deliberate provocation led to a very serious left-right split in the country. The extreme left, which had no legitimate representation in parliament, fragmented into more than a dozen factions which fought each other, the rightists, and the government forces. The extreme right, which did have parliamentary representation, was spearheaded by a paramilitary band of youth that terrorized any group they branded as being leftist, political parties, university students and professors, union members, etc. A second right wing group with more religious overtones also did its share. An increasing inflow of smuggled arms that could not be checked by the government fueled this violence. By the end of the 1970s, political violence was claiming almost 30 lives a day. The situation showed every indication of continuing unabated in 1980 when, finally, the military stepped in for the third time on September 12, 1980. Since then, things have calmed down considerably, with fewer incidents. The events, however, are still fresh in people's minds, with nightly television reports of militant groups caught with their caches of arms and ammunition.

Since the incidents involved are so recent, detailed statistics are not available. However, a few figures may be enough to give an idea of the seriousness of the situation. Shortly after the military intervention, an official government statement indicated that, in the last two years, there had been 5,241 political killings and 14,152 woundings. A sampling of newspaper reports in February, March, and June 1980 revealed that the number of political murders in the country rose from 159 to 182 to 224 during these three months.

How is such a situation to be explained? In one of the few initial analyses of the subject, Ergil (1980) maintains that the basic cultural roots of the problem have to be sought in the same factors which lead to the existence of honor crimes and blood fuels. According to Ergil, most people in the country, especially in the large rural sector, are engaged in a constant struggle for survival and human dignity against a backdrop of poverty, scarce resources, and governmental ineffectiveness. This kind of situation breeds feelings of powerlessness, frustration, and alienation which can go only so long without an explosion. In the absence of other means of self-esteem, people cling to traditional and ultimately futile norms of masculinity and honor as the only sources of self-enhancement under their control and rely on weapons as a concrete symbol of these virtues. This combination of actual deprivation, lack of positive means of self-enhancement, frustration, and emphasis on masculinity occurs in a context where people in the same situation see each other as rivals and are only too ready to take sides in factionalism and competition.

The above description has been generally true of the Turkish peasant for a long time, but superimposed on this matrix is a more contemporary illness Ergil calls "social malaise" (1980, p. 53) and describes as follows. The socioeconomic structure of Turkish society is changing very rapidly, and new classes of people are being created (e.g., urban shanty town dwellers) that demand a larger share in political decision making. However, change does not necessarily mean development. That is, the demands created by change are not met with new educational, economic, or political structures that can answer these demands. This situation creates a lot of discomfort, especially in sectors with increased expectations but unchanged or even reduced opportunities. Poor urban youth is the main sector thus hit. The resultant feelings of insecurity, alienation, faithlessness, even despair have to find an outlet.

Political radicalism is a useful outlet in this situation, as it allows for a release of pent up frustration as well as giving people's lives meaning. Depending on his background, a frustrated young man can go one of two ways: either looking for a strong, confidence-inspiring authority to take over and make things right, who can be obeyed unequivocally (the solution of the extreme right), or to band together with his peers and shake the status quo through a revolution, in the hopes of a better social order, using violence if necessary (the solution of the violent extreme left factions). In either case, the alienated young man finds a meaning for his existence, a group to belong to, and something to hope for; in short, a sense of identity.

These speculations would seem to be supported by a survey done among 125 leftist and 162 rightist inmates, all male, in one of the prisons in Ankara, the capital city (Ergil, 1980). This is the only empirical investigation done on the topic to date. About 90 percent of the inmates were below the age of 30, about 80 percent below 25. At least 50 percent had been living in the poorer sections of cities but had rural roots. Again, about 50 percent of them were students, a lesser number workers. Those who had completed either their lycée (high school) or university education were fewer in number than those who had dropped out before receiving their diplomas. The fathers of about 73 percent had not finished middle school (junior high) and had a relatively low income. They came from large families with four or more children. More than 50 percent were married but continued to live with their parents. They reported that, with increasing age, they felt less and less need for consulting with others (e.g., parents, group leaders, peers) on issues they could not resolve by themselves.

Note that these figures apply to rightist and leftist alike; in fact, there was very little difference between the two groups. While the families of the rightists tended to be small shopkeepers, farmers, etc., those of the leftists tended to be workers, but this difference was not significant. Thus, the picture which emerges is a young man from the poor urban sector, who has not completed his education, who does not have economic independence even though he may be married. Thus, while he is not ignorant of the world around him, he has few means or opportunities to improve his life. This alienation might be said to be reflected in the fact that, while he seeks belongingness in a large group, he does not admit to needing others' support or guidance.

These preliminary results seem to indicate that the speculations presented earlier in this section do have some validity. Further, more intensive work should clarify the issue.

AGGRESSION CONTROLS

Since there is very little by way of research or empirical observation on the topic of aggression control in the Turkish literature, the following will be a mostly speculative analysis, based on the previous description of the culture.

One fact that emerges pretty clearly from the description of the culture is that aggression control, as most other forms of control, would have to be external rather than internal, in the form of guilt. The nature of intragroup and intrafamily relationships and the degree of other orientation and interdependency would seem to lead to an expectation of external control. External controls would seem to fall under a number of headings. Let us take each in turn.

Legal Controls

While the laws regarding aggression and violence are strict (e.g., death penalty for blood feud murders), they can not be said to be fully effective (Tezcan, 1972). There are a number of reasons for this: increasing difficulty of access to government forces in remote areas; coupled with this, a general distrust of central government among the peasantry, which has its roots in remote Ottoman history, and does nothing to foster a sense of participation in governmental processes; the fact that the courts are overburdened and that the bureaucratic processes move too slowly to satisfy one's need for immediate justice; and frequently politically motivated amnesties which reduce the deterrent effect that would ensue from an expectation of a long sentence in miserable prison conditions.

Religious Controls

Islam accepts the Old Testament ruling of "an eye for an eye" but emphasizes the preferability of forgiveness, or at least material restitution—financial or otherwise (Tezcan, 1972). Aggression in general is frowned upon, as seen in these proverbs: "where there is religion, there is no vengefulness," "when force enters by the door, religion goes out the chimney (Soykut,

1974)." However, religion in its daily application appears to be more a concrete set of rules about daily behavior than an abstract set of moral values, especially in rural areas (Kâğitçibaşi, 1981). As such, religious teachings appear to have been transformed to suit local convenience, through interaction with local customs (Stirling, 1965). An example is the belief in eastern Turkey that "he who takes revenge goes to paradise," although there is no such statement in Islamic teaching (Tezcan, 1972). Thus, the effectiveness of religious controls appears to be tempered by local customs.

Child-Rearing Practices

The earlier coverage of discipline indicates that the forms of discipline most commonly used in Turkey are not conducive to effective control of aggression, since they tend to reinforce an expectation of external control rather than the development of internal control. Thus, one would not expect feelings like guilt to be a potent factor in controlling aggression.

One possible result of such forms of discipline may be in fostering the development of a person who is fearful of the external consequences of aggression, even if he does not suffer much from external consequences and, thus, inhibits his aggression. An important factor here is status. A person rarely commits or condones direct aggression against someone who is superior to him in status, whether it be poor man to rich man in a village (Stirling, 1965), or child to adult in general (Savaşir & Savaşir, 1974). In fact, when aggression is directed against people of higher status, as from women to men, it tends to be under extreme duress and is violent and not regretted (Özgür, 1980).

Social Controls

If proverbs are a reflection of social mores, the folk wisdom in Turkey seems to find aggression a futile way of controlling events: "vengefulness is sickness," "don't dig a hole for another person, you will fall in it," "get up in anger, sit down in loss," "he who makes someone cry, can not laugh himself," "no good ever comes out of force" (Soykut, 1974). However, for each of these sayings, there appears to be another one indicating that force, violence, and anger are undeniable facts of life. Thus, one is left with a situation in which it is bad to aggress but it is hardly possible to avoid aggression (Stirling, 1965).

Given the intimacy of social relations and lack of psychological differentiation between self and others, the search for controls obviously and inevitably turns to one's immediate community. It is the duty of any and all bystanders to intervene in a fight, even at a risk to themselves (Stirling, 1965). This is true even with regard to domestic quarrels. Obviously, however, people do not see such intervention as necessarily a lasting deterrent, but as a way of averting immediate danger. Of course, the higher the status of the intervening individual, the more the likelihood of stopping aggression (Stirling, 1965; Tezcan, 1972).

A somewhat institutionalized form of such intervention is the use of reconciliation through the help of intermediaries. When people quarrel seriously or are involved in a feud, they do not "speak to each other," i.e., they break off social contact. It is then the job of intermediaries who have the trust of both sides to bring about a reconciliation. When the issue is as serious as a blood feud, the offending party usually makes restitution in the form of monetary or other material payment. Sometimes the reconciliation is reinforced by giving a girl in marriage to a member of the enemy clan, thus introducing kinship into the relationship (Tezcan, 1972).

As the culture becomes more modernized, urbanized, and middle class in its values, one would expect that more internally oriented control mechanisms will develop. The extent to which this expectation will be valid and the exact form such controls may take are issues to be determined by future investigations.

ALTERNATIVES TO AGGRESSION

Once again, the topic of prosocial alternatives to aggression is a topic on which there is very little written in the Turkish literature. This section will cover the areas of altruism, cooperation, and sharing, basing the discussion on the few bits of observation and research there are, in addition to speculations based on the earlier cultural description.

The same characteristic of the Turkish social group which is conducive to aggressive behavior would appear also to be conducive to altruistic behavior. Values such as loyalty, interdependence, face to face accountability, and lack of differentiation between self and significant others demands cooperation and mutual help as much as being a breeding ground for misunderstandings and flareups. In fact, in order to survive in a situation of scarce resources and economic difficulties, people need to cooperate with their fellow ingroup members as much as competing with outgroups. That the boundaries between these groups shift from nuclear families to whole lineage groups depending on the point of reference just complicates the matter in allowing aggression to coexist with altruism.

The hierarchic structure of the group confers certain responsibilities to people at each level. Islamic teaching clearly states that it is the duty of people who are well off to help those who are less fortunate. Altruism and cooperation are indeed a part of daily life. As mentioned earlier, it is the unquestioned duty of every bystander to intervene in a fight (Stirling, 1965). Family and kinship relations are based, to a large extent, on mutual assistance (Kongar, 1972). Duben (1981) stresses the "intimate reciprocities" among kinfolk in all levels of society. He points out that there is a lot of joint decision making, sharing of resources, and active mutual support to help fellow family members in various spheres, private and public. Mutual help does not stop at advice and moral support. Financial aid, from better off members of the extended family to those less successful without expectation of quick or exact repayment, is a common occurrence (Fişek, 1981; Kongar, 1972).

A common feature of Turkish business life is family firms, involving parents, siblings, cousins, and in-laws. More generally, the workers in many small factories and ateliers tend to be relatives or come from the same village or rural area as the owner. This behavior seems to reflect both a trust in the loyalty of one's fellow ingroup member and taking care of one's own people (Dubetsky, 1976).

In all these relationships, the assumption is that one need not expect immediate reciprocity, in an enduring relationship, everyone's turn to give and receive comes eventually. This assumption of altruistic obligation to one's own is so strong and beneficial that it transcends the boundaries of kinship. Duben (1981) states that a lot of interpersonal relationships are based on the assumption of a "kinship idiom," even where kinship does not exist, thus potentially accruing the benefits of kinship reciprocity. Even the closeness of ordinary friendship is compelling and enduring enough to lead to expectations of mutual altruism. This may be one way of explaining the widespread use of kinship terms among non-kin, even strangers on the street, with the use of such terms as aunt or uncle to an older woman or man.

One may even speculate that the nationalistic attitudes of most Turks (Kâğitçibaşi, 1970) derives in part from an extension of such a sense of obligation to one's group. In this context one is reminded of the pledge made by elementary school children " . . . to respect my elders, to protect those younger than I, to love my country and people more than my self . . . ". This sense is strong even among some violent radicals who however mistakenly believe they are fighting for their country.

In the only empirical investigation available on altruism, Imamoğlu (1979) found that adult Turkish respondents used the same dimensions as those found relevant in American research on the common sense psychology of altruism. However, there were a few additional dimensions that were also found relevant in the Turkish study. The dimensions relevant to both cultures had to do with the intent to help as a freely chosen act, without expectation of return or a sense of obligation, involving sacrifice if need be, and providing a meaningful benefit to the helpee. Those dimensions which had to be added as being relevant to Turkish culture were as follows: the helpee's feelings have to be taken into account and treated delicately; the help has to be kept secret, not talked about, and be of lasting meaningful benefit rather than being immediately useful; and the help has to be offered before it is asked for or offered by others. Thus, the implication is that one has to be very sensitive to other people's situations and be ready to offer help without any fanfare but with absolute modesty or matter of factness. This kind of awareness of others would most easily exist in a context of intimate and undifferentiated interpersonal relationships and, as such, would fit in with the previously described observations on altruism.

CONCLUSION

It may be helpful to restate here the thesis of this chapter as it emerged from the description and analysis of the culture, the family, and child-rearing practices. This thesis is twofold. First, the structure of both the society and the family is quite differentiated in terms of status positions and normative role expectations. Position within this structure gives one a sense of social identity and, as such, is important enough to be defended aggressively. Second, the dynamics of interpersonal and emotional relationships within these groups, as well as individual intrapsychic experience, are not so highly differentiated but, rather, boundaries separating self from others are somewhat blurred. The emphasis on loyalty and duty coupled with this relatively low degree of differentiation can often lead to situations of highly charged emotionality.

These two elements, namely, the importance of defending one's status and the possibility of frequent emotional confrontation are seen as being conducive to the emergence of aggressive behavior. However, the same pattern of relationships, in its emphasis on loyalty and interdependence, is seen as being conducive to altruism. While there is not a large body of research on either aggression or altruism in the Turkish literature, what evidence there is would seem to indicate that aggression and altruism do, indeed, coexist as two sides of the same coin.

However, there is one aspect of aggression which does not appear in the literature on altruism. Recurring throughout the discussion of the various forms of aggression, there are statements about the economic deprivation and political powerlessness of those groups who are most likely to resort to the major forms of aggression found typical of this culture. Honor crimes, blood feuds, family violence, and political violence all seem to be committed mostly by rural or recently urbanized people who are economically deprived, poorly educated, and poorly represented. They do not appear to have too many alternative ways of enhancing or maintaining their self esteem.

This fact leads one to speculate that, while psychological explanations of the manifestation of aggression in a given culture are important, they may need to be supplemented by a socioeconomic perspective for a more basic understanding of the problem and its solutions. The folk wisdom of the following proverb seems to hint at this issue in saying "the hungry dog can eat its own baby."

REFERENCES

Adorno, T. W., Frenkel-Brunswik, E., Levinson, D. J., & Sanford, R. N. *The authoritarian personality.* New York: Harper, 1950.

Duben, A. The significance of family and kinship in urban Turkey. In Ç. Kâğitçibaşi (Ed.), *Sex roles fami-*

ly and community in Turkey. 1982.

Dubetsky, A. Kinship, primordial ties and factory organization in Turkey: An anthropological view. *International Journal of Middle East Studies*, 1976, 7, 433-451.

Ergil, D. *Türkiye'de Terör ve Şiddet* (Terror and violence in Turkey). Ankara: Turhan Publ., 1980.

Fişek, G. O. Psychopathology and the Turkish family: A family systems theory analysis. In Ç. Kâğitçibaşi (Ed.), *Sex roles family and community in Turkey*, 1982.

Geçtan, E. Toplumumuz bireylerinde kimlik kavramlari ile ilgili sorunlar üzerinde bir tartişma (A debate on problems concerning identity concepts in the individuals of our society). *50. Yila Armağan*. Ankara: Eğitim Fakültesi Publ., 1973.

Gökçe, B. *Gecekondu Gençliği* (Gecekondu youth). Ankara, Hacettepe Universitesi Publ., C-15, 1976.

Gürgen, T. Y., Sosyal ve kültürel özelliklerin Türkiye'de intiharlar üzerine etkisi. (The influence of social and cultural characteristics on suicides in Turkey). *Neuro-Psychiatry Archives*, 1969, 6, 1.

Helling, G. A. *The Turkish village as a social system*. Unpublished monograph, Los Angeles, Calif.: Occidental College, 1966.

İmamoğlu, E. O. *Iyiliseverlik kavramina ilişkin yargi ve devranişlar* (Judgments and behaviors related to the concept of altruism). Ankara: Hacettepe Üniversitesi Publ., 1979.

Kâğitçibaşi, Ç. Social norms and authoritarianism: A comparison of Turkish and American adolescents. *Journal of Personality and Social Psychology*, 1970, *17*(3), 444-451.

Kâğitçibaşi, Ç. *Sosyal Değişmenin Psikolojik Boyutlari* (The psychological dimensions of social change). Ankara: Turkish Social Sciences Association Publ., 1972.

Kâğitçibaşi, C. *Cocugun Degeri: Türkiye'de Değerler ve Doğurganlik* (The value of children: Values and fertility in Turkey). Istanbul: Boğaziçi University Publ., 1981.

Kandiyoti, D. Some social-psychological dimensions of social change in a Turkish village. *The British Journal of Sociology*. 1974, *15*(1), 47-62.

Kandiyoti, D. Sex roles and social change: A comparative appraisal of Turkey's women. *Journal of Women in Culture and Society*. 1977, *3*, 57-73.

Kiray, M. Changing roles of mothers: Changing intra-family relations in a Turkish town. In J. Peristiany (Ed.), *Mediterranean family structure*. Cambridge: Cambridge University Press, 1976.

Köknel, Ö. *Türk Toplumunda Bugünün Gençliği* (Today's youth in Turkish society). Istanbul: Bozak Press, 1970.

Kongar, E. *İzmir'de Kentsel Aile* (The urban family in İzmir). Ankara: Turkish Social Sciences Association Publ., 1972.

Le Compte, G., Le Compte, A., & Özer S. Üç sosyo-ekonomik düzeyde Ankarali annelerin çocuk yetiştirme tutumlari: bir ölçek uyarlamasi (The child-rearing attitudes of mothers from three socioeconomic levels in Ankara: Adaption of an instrument). *Journal of Psychology*, 1978, *1*, 5-8.

Le Compte, G. Tükiye'de aile içi çocuk gelişimi ve eğitimi sistemi (Intrafamily child development and education system in Turkey). Unpublished project report, Istanbul: Boğaziçi University, 1979.

Levine, N. Social change and family crisis: The nature of Turkish divorce. In C. Kâğitçibaşi (Ed.), *Sex roles family and community in Turkey*, 1982.

Lozios, P. Violence and the family: Some Mediterranean examples. In J. P. Martin (Ed.), *Violence and the family*. New York: Wiley, 1978.

Okman, G. Bilişsel stilin etkenleri: ergenler üzerinde bir çalişma. (The factors influencing cognitive style: A study of adolescents). Unpublished monograph, Istanbul: Boğaziçi University, 1980.

Olson, E. A. Socio-economic and psychocultural contexts of child abuse and neglect in Turkey. In J. Korbin (Ed.), *Crosscultural perspectives on child abuse*. In press.

Olson-Prather, E. Family planning and husband-wife relationships in modern Turkey. Unpublished doctoral dissertation, University of California, Los Angeles, 1976.

Özgür, S. Social-psychological patterns in homicide: A comparison of male and female inmates. Unpublished masters thesis, Istanbul: Boğaziçi University, 1980.

Öztürk, M. O. Anadolu kişiliğinde özerklik ve girişme duygularinin kisitlanmasi (Inhibition of autonomy and initiative in the Anatolian personality). *Fifth National Neuro-Psychiatry Congress Reports*, 1969.

Öztürk, M. O., & Volkan, V. The theory and practice of psychiatry in Turkey. In C. L. Brown and N. Itzkowitz (Eds.), *Psychological dimensions of Near Eastern studies*. Princeton, N.J.: The Darwin Press, 1977.

Peristiany, J. G. *Honour and shame: The values of Mediterranean society.* London: Weidenfeld and Nicholson, 1965.

Savaşir, Y., & Savaşir, I. Orta Anadolunun iki uç kesimin çocuklarinda saldirgan davranişi ortaya çikaran durumlar ve bunlar hakkindaki tutum ve yorumlar (Situations eliciting aggressive behavior in children from two opposite cross sections of central Anatolia and attitudes and interpretations relating to these. *Tenth National Psychiatry and Neurological Sciences Congress Reports,* 1974.

Sokyut, I. H. *Türk atalar sözü hazinesi* (Treasury of Turkish proverbs). Istanbul: Ülker Publ., 1974.

Stirling, P. *Turkish village.* London: Weidenfeld and Nicholson, 1965.

Sümer, E. A. Değişen Türk kültürünün dinamik yönden analizi (The analysis of the changing Turkish culture from a dynamic viewpoint). *Fifth National Neuro-Psychiatry Congress Reports,* 1969.

Tezcan, M. *Kan gütme olaylari sosyolojisi* (The sociology of blood feuds). Ankara: Ankara University School of Education Publ., 24, 1972.

Timur, S. *Türkiye'de aile yapisi* (Family structure in Turkey)? Ankara: Hacettepe University Publ., 1972.

Yavuzer, H. Ankara, İzmir ve Elaziğ çocuk ceza ve islah evlerindeki suçlu çocuklarin zeka, yakin çevre ve kişilik özellikleri yönünden incelenmesi konusunda deneysel bir araştirma (An investigation of the intelligence, environmental and personality characteristics of child criminals in houses of correction and reform for youth in Ankara, İzmir and Elaziğ). Unpublished monograph, Istanbul University, 1977.

Yörükoğlu, A. *Çocuk ruh sağliği* (Child mental health). Ankara: Türkiye İş Bankasi Cultural Publ., 1978.

19

United States: Causes, Controls, and Alternatives to Aggression

Arnold P. Goldstein

INTRODUCTION

Most of the United States, most of the time, is nonaggressive. At any given moment, 99 percent of its population is *not* engaged in aggressive behavior. In recent decades, a wide array of social and legal changes have occurred in the United States, all directed at reducing or eliminating diverse forms of aggressive behavior and fostering prosocial alternatives thereto. These include greatly increased awareness on the part of legal authorities and greatly increased use of treatment on the part of the helping professions directed at reducing various forms of domestic violence, such as child abuse, spouse abuse, and sexual abuse. The penal system, while still among the most severe in the world in terms of both reliance on incarceration and length of sentence, appears in at least some jurisdictions to be moving slowly away from such overly punitive directions. Less arbitrariness and bias in sentencing, and especially increased use—particularly with juveniles—of an array of alternatives to incarceration are increasingly frequent goals and not infrequent realities. Demands for effective gun control legislation, while still only minimally successful, have greatly increased in volume and intensity. Efforts aimed at reducing collective aggression have taken many forms, especially humane and enlightened social legislation reflecting and respecting the rights and aspirations of minority groups, the elderly, and other special populations. It is not only laws which have become more humane, but also their enforcement as more and more American police departments have become highly professional, increasingly sophisticated in applying the findings and procedures of the behavioral sciences, and increasingly oriented toward the role of community service officer rather than only the apprehender of criminals. In parallel with these law enforcement trends, an American focus on prosocial behavior and its enhancement can also be clearly discerned in the emphasis on moral education, value clarification and character education in elementary and secondary schools, as well as in the substantial growth in U.S. universities of research and teaching dealing with altruism, empathy, cooperation, and helping, and with the development of other, prosocial behaviors. Consistent with the spirit of these trends, legislation to establish a National Peace Academy in being considered by the United States government. In a manner roughly analogous to America's military academies, one devoted to peace concerns would focus on the systematic study, teaching, and national dissemination of conflict reduction and conflict mediation information and techniques. All of these recent trends reflecting growing emphasis on the reduction of the antisocial and the promotion of the prosocial in American life are important and, hopefully, but a beginning.

Yet, all of this notwithstanding, aggression and the United States are long and intimate companions. Both historically and at the present time, individual and collective aggression are very substantial features of the American scene. In the present chapter, we will examine the roots of aggression in the United States; its current prevalence; its multiple forms, definitions, and causes; and contemporary theories of its origins. We will then turn to the diverse forms which efforts to reduce and control aggression have taken. Educational, criminological, and a number of other possible paths to aggression control will be examined. We will similarly focus on alternatives to aggression—their nature, enhancement, and future prospects. Here, we will emphasize the role that is and could be played in the American home, school, mass media, and by American behavioral science in understanding and promoting prosocial behavior.

An Historical Perspective

The United States was born in the crucible of individual and collective violence, a relationship which has persisted with but infrequent interruption for over two centuries. Its Revolutionary War lasted over seven years, and succeeded in its goal of a new and independent nation. It was also, as we shall see, but one of many examples of an instance in which aggression rewarded is aggression continued. The Revolutionary War, in particular, can be viewed appropriately as the beginning of America's long love affair with the gun, with the "right to bear arms"—over 100 *million* of which now exist in the United States. The new nation lay strung out along the Eastern coast of a 3,000 milewide, unexplored continent—a continent of buffalo and other game to kill, of native American Indians to displace, of a frontier to conquer.

American violence has taken many forms, almost all of which have involved citizen versus citizen aggression, rather than pitting citizens against the state. With the major exception of the Civil War, there are very few examples of insurrectional violence in U.S. history. Further, as Hofstadter and Wallace (1971) observe, it is also true of aggression in the United States, especially collective aggression, that until recent decades most of it was initiated by conservative forces.

> It has been unleashed against abolitionists, Catholics, radicals, workers and labor organizers, Negroes, Orientals, and other ethnic or racial or ideological minorities, and has been used ostensibly to protect the American, the Southern, the white Protestant, or simply the established middle-class way of life and morals. [p. 11]

Each era in U.S. history helped shape the particular forms of aggression that occurred. As the nation began moving westward in the late 1700s, frontier settlements and a frontier mentality prevailed. Independence, self-reliance, and impatience with the still poorly formulated civil and criminal laws of the nation were all characteristic. Justice was often "frontier justice," which meant "taking the law into one's own hands" by groups of local citizenry. Hanging for horse thievery, "riding undesirables out of town," and similar unorganized group aggressiveness may be viewed as the informal beginnings of what, especially immediately after the Civil War, became the vigilante movement. Frontier living, its purported glamor in the mass media notwithstanding, was often very difficult economically, giving rise not only to criminal gangs, bank robbers, counterfeiters, and other early crime in America, but also to aggressive behavior by many of its noncriminal, rural citizens. Shay's Rebellion in the State of Massachusetts (1786-1787), the Whiskey Rebellion in Pennsylvania (1794), and the series of similar incidents initiated by such groups as the Grangers, the Greenbackers, and the Farmer's Alliance are examples of the several economically-engendered agrarian uprisings characteristic of the day.

Beginning in the early 1800s, and peaking during 1830-1860, a major new feature was added to the American scene, and to aggression in the United States. This was a lengthy period of great immigration, as thousands and then millions of persons from diverse national, religious, and ethnic backgrounds migrated to the United States. The ingredients in this great, human melting pot often mixed poorly, and high levels of individual and collective aggression were the frequent result—particularly in America's cities.

The Civil War took place in the United States in 1861-1865, pitting Northerner against Southerner and, at times, neighbor against neighbor and even cousin against cousin in bitter, lethal conflict. Its price was high, and well beyond the actual war casualties (617,000 dead and 375,000 injured), for out of this war grew forces which engendered new and virulent forms of aggression throughout the country. During the postwar, reconstruction period, and stemming from war-related animosities, feuding, lynching, and high levels of vigilante activities occurred. The feud, primarily a phenomenon of the Southern mountain states, was a type of interfamily or interclan guerrilla warfare. Much more malignant in its effects was lynching. Here, unorganized, ephemeral mobs, in a deindividuated expression usually of anti-Black aggression, would capture and hang usually guiltless Black persons. It is the shame of America that 4,950 recorded lynchings occurred during the period 1882-1927, though it is happily the case that it has been an essentially nonexistent event in recent decades.

Vigilante aggression became more organized. Its targets included Blacks, but also many other (usually minority) groups. Among the 326 known vigilante groups recognized as having existed, perhaps the most infamous were the Ku Klux Klan, the Bald Knobbers, and the White Cappers. The cowboy gang, romanticized in book and movie, also became prominent during this post-Civil War period. Their specialties, train and bank robberies, while consistently portrayed as flamboyant derring-do by the media, were plain and simple acts of criminal violence.

The Industrial Revolution came to America's burgeoning cities during the late 1800s. It was progress, and brought with it hope, modernization, and economic growth. But not infrequently it also involved economic exploitation and management-labor violence. Strikes and boycotts grew to become riots, some of them among the bloodiest events in American history. The railroad strike in Pittsburgh in 1877, and the strife in the Pennsylvania coal fields around the Molly Magiure movement at about the same time are two prime examples. Industrial conflict continued at high levels as workers sought to unionize, and especially violent strikes occurred in the Colorado mining industry (1913-1914), and throughout the auto industry during the 1930s. During this extended period, there were 160 separate times in which state or federal troops were called out to intervene in industrial violence.

As others have found to be true in other nations, the level of individual and collective violence within the Unites States diminished considerably during the two world wars, and during the economic depression in the 1930s. Perhaps both events, war and depression, engender a sufficient sense of being joined against a common enemy, or at least of being caught in similar circumstances, that within-nation/outgroup hostility diminishes.

In the middle of the twentieth century, while labor violence, feuding, vigilante groups, lynching, and the aggression of the frontier West all became largely events of the past, America's affinity to violence continued in new forms. Crime, especially by juveniles, grew in both sheer amount and in its level of aggression. While conservative forces less frequently, or at least less obviously, initiated collective violence, radical forces took their place. In the 1960s, the United States was rocked time and again with student, racial, and antiwar riots, as well as a small number of terrorist events.

This litany of America's violent history would be much less than complete without mention of perhaps its saddest chapter. Starting in Tidewater, Virginia in 1607 and ending in 1890 in Wounded Knee, South Dakota, nearly 300 years of intermittent aggression was perpetrated against the American Indian. It is a history which can never be undone but, hopefully, is partially being redressed in the America of today.

This brief, historical overview of aggression in the United States must be kept in objective perspective. Not only is it a truism to note, as we did at the opening of this chapter, that most of the United States, most of the time, is nonaggressive, but we also concur with Hofstedter and Wallace (1971) who comment:

> Large-scale violence is so commonplace in the histories of societies that the American record, when put in a world-historical perspective, is not so remarkable as it first seems. What is impressive to one who begins to learn about American violence is its extraordinary frequency, its sheer commonplaceness in our history, its persistence into very recent and contemporary times, and its rather abrupt contrast with our pretentions to singular national virtue. What must also be observed about it, however, is the circumscribed character and the small scale of the typical violent incident. America has experienced one major internal war on an exceptionally costly scale. But its riots and massacres . . . do not otherwise loom inordinately large when projected against the long backdrop of history. [p. 7]

Current Trends

Our examination thus far of aggression in the United States has focused primarily upon collective aggression—riots, lynchings, vigilante violence, and aggression by other organized or informal groups of individuals. Individual aggression has been more difficult to capture in objective historical perspective for two reasons. First of all, the major means utilized in the United States for systematically recording and enumerating individual criminal acts, the Federal Bureau of Investigation's Uniform Crime Reports, was not begun until 1933. Thus, less systematic and comprehensive historical accounts must be relied upon for information regarding pre-1933 levels of criminal aggression in America. Secondly, certain forms of individual aggression, especially child and spouse abuse, were not a matter of general public concern and attention until the late 1960s. Such relative indifference has changed dramatically quite recently. Thus, we will be able in this section to provide considerable detail regarding the current levels and nature of individual aggression in the United States in its several forms.

We will not, however, have much to say about current levels and types of collective aggression. As was true for many nations during the 1960s, the United States was a place of considerable societal turmoil. But the ending of the military involvement in Viet Nam, somewhat lowered economic expectations following the decline of the Great Society era, the resignation of a president toward whom there existed great public hostility, as well as a number of other political, economic, and social changes in the United States appear to have greatly diminished the incidence of collective aggression. Labor and management bargain collectively and usually peacefully; collective agricultural unrest is quite rare, though not nonexistent; racial conflicts occasionally occur, but are now very infrequent; the Ku Klux Klan is still heard from, but rather weakly and unjoined by the remnants of any other vigilante-like groups; terrorism remains a concern, but has been a rare event in the 1970s and 1980s. Other forms of collective aggression have not emerged. Thus, at the level of the small or large group aggression in the United States at this period in time appears relatively minor and infrequent. Let us see if similarly hopeful conclusions are warranted vis a vis individual aggression.

The Federal Bureau of Investigation's Uniform Crime Report, derived from crime statistics voluntarily submitted by police departments across the United States, enumerates both the absolute number and relative rate (per 100,000 inhabitants) of major violent and property crimes in the United States. Violent crimes are defined to include murder, forcible rape, robbery, and aggravated assault. Property crimes include burglary, larceny-theft, and motor vehicle theft. Table 19.1, taken directly from the FBI Uniform Crime Report issued in 1979, presents this incidence information for the period 1960-1978.

The statistical levels and trends depicted in table 19.1 are, as may be suspected, the focus of a great deal of attention in the United States. These statistics often seem to lead to different interpretations and implications depending in large measure on whether one is a law enforcement official, a politician, a penologist, a political conservative, or a political liberal. The present author, in agreement with those of Davidson and Kushler (1981), Feldman (1977) and Neitzel (1979), generally sees crime in America as increasing in a consistent but moderate manner during the approximately fifteen year period, 1960-1975, and then essentially stabilizing in rate since that time. There are exceptions to this overall trend and, unfortunately, two such exceptions are particularly aggressive criminal acts—forcible rape and aggravated assault, both of whose rates have continued to increase.

Later in this chapter we will examine in detail an array of theoretical views purporting to explain the causes of crime and aggressive behavior in the United States. At this point, however, our understanding of table 19.1 will be enhanced if we point to one demographic fact which many authorities have suggested may account for a substantial portion of the major trends we have described. The 1960-1975 increase in violent crime and the stabilization of the crime rate since 1975 parallel directly the number of 14-24 year-old males in the United States. Persons in this age group account for a very high percent of the crime in America, but only a modest percent of the population. From 1960 to 1975, this age group increased by 63 percent. As the number of such persons began to stabilize in 1975, so did America's crime rate. Their decrease by 16 percent by 1990 vis a vis their 1975 level is likely, it has been suggested, to lead to corresponding decreases in the rates of violent crime. While this prognostication may be overly optimistic, since aggressive behavior clearly appears to be multiply determined, it is nevertheless an important, widely held, and hopeful view in the United States.

While *overall* crime rates indeed appear to have stabilized in America, we noted earlier that particularly violent crimes may well still be on the increase. In 1967, one in five robbery victims was physically injured during the commission of the robbery. In 1977, the comparable injury statistic was one in three. And the crimes committed by juveniles, however stabilized in rate they may be, also seem to be occurring at higher levels of aggressiveness. A recent U.S. Congressional report (Bayh, 1975) indicated that, in the three years between 1970 and 1973, in junior and senior high schools in the United States, homicides increased by 18.5 percent, rapes by 40.1 percent, assaults on students by 85.3 percent, assaults on teachers by 77.4 percent, and weapons confiscated by school authorities by 54.4 percent. In 1975, such secondary school youngsters, especially in urban secondary schools, committed 63,000 attacks on teachers, 270,000 school burglaries, and destroyed by vandalism $200 million worth of school property. In 1978, in the New York City schools, there were 1,856 assaults, 1,097 robberies, 310 suspicious fires, and 317 incidents involving weapons. In 1979, schools in the United States reported 20 million thefts, 400,000 acts of vandalism, 110,000 assaults on teachers. This litany of violent crimes by juveniles, though apparently not increasing in rate in recent years, is nevertheless dramatically high in an absolute sense, serious in a sociopsychological sense, and an urgent problem currently commanding considerable attention toward prevention and remediation in America.

A final set of observations regarding table 19.1 is worth making. To help place these American crime statistics in their most objective perspective, we wish to briefly highlight the alterna-

Table 19.1. Index of Crime, United States, 1960-1978

POPULATION	(1) TOTAL CRIME INDEX (2) + (3)	(2) VIOLENT CRIME (4) + (5) + (6) + (7)	(3) PROPERTY CRIME (8) + (9) + (10)	(4) MURDER AND NON-NEGLIGENT MAN-SLAUGHTER	(5) FORCIBLE RAPE	(6) ROBBERY	(7) AGGRA-VATED ASSAULT	(8) BURGLARY	(9) LARCENY-THEFT	(10) MOTOR VEHICLE THEFT
Number of offenses:										
1960— 179,323,175	3,363,700	286,900	3,076,800	9,060	17,130	107,570	153,140	906,600	1,543,100	327,100
1961— 182,002,000	3,466,800	287,800	3,179,000	8,690	17,160	106,400	155,560	943,800	1,500,300	334,000
1962— 185,771,000	3,729,500	209,860	3,420,600	8,480	17,490	110,580	163,310	988,300	2,075,800	365,600
1963— 188,483,000	4,084,400	315,230	3,769,200	8,590	17,590	116,180	172,880	1,079,800	2,282,000	401,900
1964— 191,111,000	4,537,100	362,210	4,174,800	9,310	21,350	130,500	201,500	1,205,800	2,497,800	471,200
1965— 193,526,000	4,710,800	385,260	4,325,500	9,010	23,330	138,340	213,680	1,274,700	2,555,600	495,200
1966— 195,576,000	5,102,000	427,840	4,761,100	10,980	25,730	157,590	283,530	1,401,500	2,803,300	559,300
1967— 197,457,000	5,888,100	497,290	5,370,800	12,170	27,580	202,400	255,190	1,622,200	3,001,000	637,600
1968— 199,399,000	6,680,300	501,980	6,088,300	13,730	31,580	262,180	284,510	1,847,600	3,450,700	781,000
1969— 201,385,000	7,410,900	661,870	6,749,000	14,760	31,170	298,850	311,090	1,981,900	3,888,600	878,500
1970— 203,235,298	8,098,000	738,820	7,359,200	16,000	37,990	349,860	334,970	2,205,000	4,225,800	928,400
1971— 206,212,000	8,588,200	815,500	7,771,700	17,780	42,260	387,700	368,700	2,399,300	4,424,200	948,200
1972— 208,230,000	8,248,800	834,900	7,413,900	18,670	46,850	376,290	393,090	2,375,500	4,151,200	882,200
1973— 209,851,000	8,718,100	875,910	7,842,200	19,640	51,400	384,220	420,650	2,565,500	4,347,900	928,800
1974— 211,392,000	10,253,400	974,720	9,278,700	20,710	55,400	442,400	456,210	3,039,200	5,262,500	977,100
1975— 213,124,000	11,256,600	1,026,280	10,230,300	20,510	56,090	464,970	484,710	3,252,100	5,977,700	1,000,500
1976— 214,659,000	11,304,800	968,580	10,318,200	18,780	56,730	420,210	490,850	3,089,800	6,270,800	957,600
1977— 216,332,000	10,935,800	1,009,500	9,926,300	19,120	63,020	404,850	522,510	3,052,200	5,905,700	968,400
1978— 218,059,000	11,141,300	1,061,830	10,079,500	19,560	67,130	417,040	558,100	3,104,500	5,983,400	991,600

Rate per 100,000 in-
habitants:

Year										
1960	1,875.8	160.0	1,715.8	5.1	0.5	60.0	85.4	505.6	1,027.8	182.4
1961	1,804.5	157.3	1,737.2	4.7	0.4	58.1	85.0	515.7	1,038.5	183.0
1962	2,007.6	161.4	1,846.2	4.6	9.4	59.5	87.9	532.0	1,117.4	196.8
1963	2,167.0	167.2	1,999.8	4.6	9.3	61.6	91.7	572.9	1,211.0	213.9
1964	2,373.7	189.5	2,184.2	4.9	11.2	68.0	105.4	630.9	1,306.8	246.5
1965	2,434.2	199.1	2,235.1	5.1	12.1	71.5	110.4	658.7	1,320.5	255.9
1966	2,654.7	218.8	2,435.9	5.6	13.2	80.6	119.4	716.6	1,433.4	286.0
1967	2,971.8	251.8	2,720.0	6.2	13.9	102.5	129.2	821.5	1,565.4	333.0
1968	3,350.2	296.9	3,053.3	6.9	15.8	131.5	142.7	926.6	1,735.1	391.7
1969	3,658.1	327.0	3,331.1	7.3	18.4	148.0	153.3	978.2	1,918.2	434.8
1970	3,560.9	361.7	3,599.1	7.8	18.6	171.7	163.6	1,078.4	2,065.5	455.3
1971	4,140.0	394.0	3,716.0	8.6	20.4	187.5	177.5	1,156.4	2,131.3	458.3
1972	3,937.3	398.9	3,538.9	8.9	22.4	180.3	187.3	1,133.9	1,980.4	421.6
1973	4,129.7	415.3	3,714.4	9.3	24.4	182.6	198.9	1,245.1	2,058.2	441.1
1974	4,821.4	458.8	4,362.6	9.7	26.1	208.8	214.2	1,429.0	2,473.0	160.6
1975	5,281.7	481.5	4,800.2	9.6	26.3	218.2	227.4	1,525.9	2,804.8	469.4
1976	5,266.4	459.6	4,806.8	8.8	26.4	195.8	228.7	1,439.4	2,921.3	446.1
1977	5,055.1	466.6	4,588.4	8.8	29.1	187.1	241.5	1,410.9	2,729.9	447.6
1978	5,109.3	486.9	4,622.4	9.0	30.8	191.3	255.9	1,423.7	2,743.9	454.7

Source: FBI, Uniform Crime Report, 1979.

441

tive suggestion that this table is an underestimation or an overestimation of the actual amounts and rates of violent and property crimes in the United States. Neitzel (1979) suggests it may be an underestimation and that, in fact, the actual levels of American crime may be as much as twice that indicated in the Uniform Crime Report. Some victims of crime, he suggests, do not believe that police can be helpful, and thus fail to report crimes perpetrated against them. Others do not want to take the time, or do not know how to report a crime, or fear reprisal if they do so—all of which leads to unknown, and perhaps substantial, levels of unreported crime. In addition, it must be noted that a small, but not insignificant number of American police departments suffer from inadequate and inconsistent record keeping, a further potential source of underestimated incidence levels.

But there exist considerations of equal plausibility and potency which may combine to yield reported crime levels and especially rates which spuriously overestimate the levels and rates of actual crime. Crime statistics are gathered by police departments across the country and reported to the FBI who, in turn, publish the Uniform Crime Report. The annual budgets of both the reporting departments and the FBI itself are directly affected by the level of crime reported, a storng and perhaps irresistible pressure at times to slant the levels or rates reported in an upward direction. Such pressures may also be reflected in the periodic campaign oratory of "law and order" politicians who seek votes from the electorate by assertively pointing to purported crime waves and the steps they would institute to end them. Crime levels and rates may also appear to be higher than they actually are because, for many police departments, reporting procedures have improved in contrast to past years. That is, the increasing professionalization of many American police departments in recent years has not only meant better handling of offenders, but also better record keeping and reporting about these offenders. As communities have come to recognize this increased level of professionalism, trust and respect for police has correspondingly grown, leading many citizens to be more willing to report crimes which previously had gone unreported. This phenomenon may be especially true in low income, previously distrustful segments of American communities, areas which are usually high in violent crime. Thus, we are suggesting, some unknown but not negligible portion of the increase in America's crime rates to its current levels may well be an artifactual consequent of more adequate reporting. Which of the two possibilities we have identified—underestimated or overestimated levels of actual crime—is in fact true is not discernible from available evidence at the present time.

In addition to absolute levels and relative rates, it will be useful in understanding aggression in the United States to note further characteristics of current crime trends. Violent crimes are, first of all, mostly a city phenomenon. The 26 U.S. cities with a population of 500,000 or more contribute half of America's crime, but only one-fifth of America's population. In these cities, the persons most likely to commit violent crimes are not only, as noted before, often in the 14-24-year-old age range, they are also likely to reside in poor housing, in the center of the city, have low income, an unstable employment pattern, little education, and, more generally, have little in the way of stable economic or familial resources to draw upon.

In the minds of many Americans in the early 1980s, the phrase "violent crime" not only conjures up images of a mugging or similar act on a dark city street by an aggressive adolescent, it also gives rise to images of a rather different type of aggressive act, a type only very recently labeled a "crime" in America and, in fact, a type of aggressive behavior only very recently arrived into public awareness in the United States. We refer to that cluster of behaviors we would collectively call domestic violence—child abuse, spouse abuse, and parent abuse. The American home is no stranger to physical aggression. A nationwide survey conducted in 1968 for the National Commission on the Causes and Prevention of Violence (Mulvilhill, Tumin & Curtis, 1969) revealed that 93 percent of the survey respondents reported being spanked as a child, 55 percent were slapped or kicked, 31 percent punched or beaten, 14 percent threatened or cut with a knife, and 12 percent threatened with a gun or actually shot at. Domestic violence is not only visited upon children, spouses, particularly wives, are also not infrequently the target of physical abuse. Strauss (1977) estimates that approximately 25 percent of American wives have been the target of physical aggression from their husbands, an estimate generally accepted as accurate (Rosenbaum, 1979). While such violence must be decried, current awareness of it, and the fact that in the eyes of most police departments and other legal authorities such behavior is increasingly considered criminal, represents marked progress away from the not-so-distant and generally accepted, if tacit, view in America that husbands had the right and even the responsibility to be physically abusive toward their wives when and if they deemed such behavior to be appropriate. The women's movement, as part of its "consciousness-raising activities," can fairly be given a substantial share of the credit for this major, if still developing, shift in American attitudes and law regarding spouse abuse.

The recent history of child abuse in the United States has followed a parallel path. As recently as the mid-1960s, the terms "child abuse" or "batter child syndrome" were not part of either public or professional awareness. Largely through the efforts of such persons as Gil (1970), Helfer and Kempe (1976), and Kempe, Silverman, Steele, Droegemueller and Silver (1962), a similar type of consciousness raising has occurred. America is now keenly aware of child abuse as a phenomenon, and has already taken significant legal and remedial steps toward its reduction. The level of child abuse has been estimated to vary from 40,000 to 2 million children abused annually. Thus, while a reliable incidence consensus is not yet available, the level is far from negligible in any event. But significant change is underway. Under the terms of recently enacted federal and state laws, professionals (e.g., physicians, nurses, teachers, psychologists) who work with children must, when suspecting the occurrence of child abuse, report their suspicions to the proper authorities for investigation. A network of child protective services and remedial agencies for the treatment of the abusing parents and the abused child are being developed or are now in place.

What may be said in summary of these current trends in America? Collective violence in its many forms does not currently loom large on the American scene. It has in the past, seemingly as a function of diverse economic and social forces which, at least at the present time, are relatively quiescent. Individual aggression is quite another matter. After an apparently steady increase for many years, the rates of most violent crimes—but clearly not all—seems to have stabilized at what some observers view at best as a moderately high absolute level, and others see as an acutely and distressingly high level. This plateau seems associated with a parallel plateau in the number of 14–24-year-olds, the high perpetrator age range. After many decades of its tacit toleration, domestic violence in America has become an overtly recognized phenomenon and a punishable crime. Child-beating and wife-beating still occur at what may fairly be described as alarmingly high levels, but an array of legal and remedial steps is under way.

THEORIES OF AGGRESSION

Thus far in this chapter, we have described an historical pattern of high levels of collective aggression in the United States, and a contemporaneous picture of high levels of individual aggression. In response to this long and disturbing history, there have been a great many theoretical efforts to better understand aggression, its roots, what maintains it, and how it may be reduced. These several efforts to understand and control aggression have come from an array of social and behavioral scientists, politicians, social philosophers, educators, the clergy, and numerous others. We wish in the present section of this chapter to highlight the major theories of aggression currently of significance in the United States, and have a word or two about their apparent validity.

Aggression as Instinct

Freud's early notions of a destructive urge or energy, the self-directed death instinct turned outward, as a basis for "explaining" and defining aggression was always a controversial and less than fully accepted part of psychoanalytic theory and has, for the most part, passed from the contemporary scientific scene in America, though there remains a small group of traditional psychoanalytic orientation still promulgating this earlier view. See, for example, Glover (1960), Storr (1960), and Zinberg and Fellman (1967).

However, the belief that aggression is best conceived in instinctual terms is still very much alive among the general public. In fact, it is easily the most popular American view of aggression. In the 1960s, three books championing the instinctive basis of aggression were published and widely received in the United States—Lorenz's *On Aggression* (1963), Ardrey's *The Territorial Imperative* (1966), and Morris' *The Naked Ape* (1967). Each espoused the view that aggression springs primarily from an innate fighting instinct. According to this view, aggressive energy, growing from this instinct, is spontaneously generated within the person in a continuous manner and at a constant rate. As time passes, aggressive energy is said to build up. The more of it that has accumulated, the weaker the stimulus necessary to set it off or release it into overt aggressive behavior. In fact, if enough time has passed since its last expression, overt aggression may occur spontaneously, with no apparent releasing stimuli. In this view, aggressive energy inexorably accumulates and inexorably must be expressed. The best one can hope for is its sublimated expression into channels which are not antisocial, the usual example suggested being competitive athletics.

Instinct theory—truly, more a blend of anecdote, analogical leaps, unsystematic journalism, and undefined concepts—is, nevertheless, seductively appealing. It is simple. It is irresponsible, in the sense that aggressive urges accumulate and must be expressed independent of the individual's choice. It is comprehensive, in that it can sweepingly "explain" diverse forms and rates of aggression when no other single cause, by itself, can do so. Yet, it is also wrong. To be sure, most contemporary scientific views of aggression do concur that one contributing factor is a genetic-physiological capacity to aggress. But to point to an unknown, and unknowable, accumulation of unseeable and unmeasurable energy as the basis for aggressive behavior is to use a mythology almost totally unsupported by, and in fact largely refuted by, scientific evidence. For example, the so-called cathartic expression of purported aggressive instinctual energy does not lead to reduced levels of overt aggression—as a "draining off" phenomenon would predict. In fact, the opposite effect is more likely to occur. Over aggression, under circumstances we will describe when we consider the social learning explanation of such behavior, usually leads to more, and not less, expression of subsequent overt aggression. The frequent failure of a cathartic effect is but one of many instances in which the predictions one might derive from instinct theory fail to accord with oft-replicated scientific findings regarding the expression of aggression.

Instinct theorists have, we believe, done a major disservice to efforts at advancing society's understanding and control of aggression. Their very popularity may appropriately be viewed as a major, unscientific detour diverting attention from where it belongs—the scientific study of aggression, its control, and the enhancement of its alternatives.

Aggression as Drive

As scientific interest in the purported instinctual basis of aggressive behavior waned in America, it was replaced by a focus upon the concept of drive. As we will see later in this chapter, belief in drive notions as the major motivators of overt aggression has itself waned in recent years, as social learning explanations have become most prominent in American thinking about aggression. But for over two decades, heaviest reliance in American scientific efforts to understand and control aggression was upon drive concepts. As Baron (1977) observes:

> The notion of spontaneously generated aggressive energy has been largely dismissed by the great majority of researchers in this field. The more general suggestion that aggression stems from an aggressive motive or drive (i.e., a heightened state of arousal that can be reduced through overt acts of aggression) has enjoyed a much more favorable reception. . . . Basically, such theories hold that human aggression stems mainly from the arousal of a drive to harm or injure others, which is itself elicited by various environmental conditions. [p. 21]

The major work responsible for initiating this viewpoint, and for shaping much of the drive-relevant research on aggression which was subsequently conducted, was *Frustration and Aggression,* by Dollard, Doob, Miller, Mowrer, and Sears (1939). Their basic initial thesis, which came to be known as the frustration-aggression hypothesis, held that (1) frustration always leads to some form of aggression, and (2) aggression always stems from frustration. Early research, however, revealed that "always" was too invariant a stance to assume and that frustration, at times, had nonaggressive consequences, and aggression also had nonfrustrating antecedents. The underlying drive notion was thus broadened (N.E. Miller, 1941) to reflect such findings. For example, the basic hypothesis was altered to read "Frustration produces instigations to a number of different types of responses, one of which is an instigation to aggression [p. 338]." It was in response to the same, broadened perspective on the consequences of frustration that such notions as the frustration-regression hypothesis (Barker, Dembo, & Lewin, 1941) and the frustration-fixation hypothesis (Maier, 1949) also appeared.

Other aspects of the theory sought to describe events likely to facilitate or inhibit the occurrence of frustration-induced aggression. The strength of the instigation to aggression, it was proposed, was a function of the importance of the frustrated goal response, the degree of frustration of this response, and the number of frustrated response sequences. As part of their effort to explain occasions in which frustration failed to instigate aggression, Dollard and his colleagues examined the role of inhibitory forces, especially punishment. Their view was that the likelihood that aggression would be inhibited varied directly with the amount of punishment anticipated. What, then, happens to the underlying drive to aggress? They proposed that either displacement occurs, in which aggression is overtly expressed toward persons less likely than the frustrator to be able or willing to punish the aggressor, or a process of catharsis occurs, in which other acts of aggression (even covert, indirect, or noninjurious) serve to lower the likelihood of overt aggression toward the frustrator.

The course of much of the research on the frustration-aggression hypothesis and its derivative propositions often proved not to be smooth. For example, while much was learned about frustration and about aggression, definitional problems persisted and the relationship of these two major variables suffered from a largely insoluble circularity. As Johnson (1972) notes, "The presence of frustration was taken to mean that subsequent behavior was likely to be aggressive, and the presence of aggression was used as evidence that the preceding experience had been frustrating [p. 133]." Leonard Berkowitz and Seymour Feshbach are two American psychologists whose long and distinguished contributions to our understanding of aggression have focused largely on drive theory, and both were active in efforts to revise and extend frustration-aggression thinking. Much of Berkowitz's (1962) work has elaborated the original notion along classical conditioning lines, suggesting for example that stimuli that are regularly associated with aggression instigation may gradually acquire the capacity to elicit aggressive actions from individuals who are previously provoked. Frustration, he proposes, induces an emotional state, anger, which by itself leads not to overt aggression but, instead, a readiness or set to respond aggressively. Actual overt aggression, Berkowitz proposes, will not occur unless suitable, aggression-relevant cues are present. These cues are usually stimuli (e.g., people, places, objects) associated with current or previous anger instigators.

Feshbach's (1970) contribution to this picture may in some ways be seen as transitional between the drive and social learning views of aggression. For example, he proposes that the likelihood that a given act of aggression would follow a given instance of frustration is importantly influenced by learning events, e.g., modeling and reinforcement. Feshbach has also taken drive theory in two additional, interesting directions. The first is to suggest, contrary to Berkowitz and most other drive theorists, that the infliction of injury is not really the major goal of most overt aggression; rather, the pain caused in the other person serves to restore or bolster the aggressor's self-esteem or sense of power. It would follow from such thinking that nonaggressive means for enhancing self-esteem should reduce aggressive drive, a process rather difficult to conceptualize in usual drive theory terms. Feshbach's second innovation, also somewhat lacking in its accounting of what happens to already-induced aggressive drive, is to suggest that aggression may often be reduced when the individual is able to redefine or reinterpret the stimuli to which he has begun to respond aggressively, thus truncating the likelihood of actual, overt, aggressive behavior. The seminal works of Berkowitz and Feshbach, so briefly sampled here, are but examples of the active theorizing and broad empirical effort drive theory has engendered in the United States. We also readily commend the reader to the writings of Buss (1961), Geen (1976) and Zillmann (1979).

Science advances slowly and incrementally by building upon earlier knowledge. The frustration-aggression hypothesis was truly a classic document. It took earlier Freudian notions and theoretically developed them in a manner which moved them away from their innate, instinctual base toward an environmental drive instigation of overt aggression. If the theory proved too simple, or otherwise inadequate to the task of explaining that very complex behavior called aggression, it was nevertheless a good theory in that it gave rise to the very research which some have used to revise and extend drive theory, others have interpreted to mean drive theory could and should be replaced by an approach purported to more adequately predict and explain aggression, i.e., social learning theory.

Aggression as Social Learning

As we have noted, both instinct and drive theories of aggression sought to understand, explain, and control aggression defined as behavior impelled by inner forces. But much of American psychology in recent decades shifted its concern largely away from such unobservable, purported inner determinants of behavior toward external influences on overt responses. In this era of the continued development and elaboration of learning theory, human behavior was studied extensively in terms of the stimuli which elicit it and the reinforcing consequences that maintain it. As Bandura (1973), perhaps America's leading social learning theorist, comments:

> Researchers repeatedly demonstrated that response patterns generally attributed to underlying forces could be induced, eliminated, and reinstated simply by varying external sources of influence. These impressive findings led many psychologists to the view that the causes of behavior are found not in the organism, but in environmental forces. [p. 8]

With specific regard to aggression, this extreme situational determinism perspective tended to reject any and all inner determinants of overt behavior. But, it appears, the pendulum had swung too far. Again, to quote Bandura (1973):

In a vigorous effort to avoid spurious inner causes, it neglected determinants of man's behavior arising from his cognitive functioning. . . . People can represent external influences symbolically and later use such representations to guide their actions; they can solve problems mentally without having to enact the various alternatives; and they can see the probable consequences of different actions and alter their behavior accordingly. [p. 42]

Yet it does appear to be the case that overt aggression can be predicted with much greater accuracy either from knowledge of such stimulus considerations as the social context (e.g., church, school, street corner), the potential target (e.g., peer, parent, priest), the person's role (e.g., salesman, policeman, soldier); or from such response considerations as the nature, intermittency, delay, or quantity of reward made available for behaving aggressively than from even in-depth assessment of the inner state of the individual involved. Stimulus-response considerations, therefore, do assume a highly significant role in social learning theory. But so, too, do inner cognitive determinants of overt behavior and, thus, as we shall see, much of Bandura's attention is devoted to symbolic, vicarious, representational, and related cognitive processes.

Social learning theory is not only a cognitive—stimulus-response—view of aggression, but of a wide variety of other behaviors as well. The processes responsible for the acquisition, instigation, and maintenance of aggression (Bandura, 1973) are, according to this view, essentially identical to the processes relevant to the learning, performance, and maintenance of most forms of overt behavior (Bandura, 1969). In table 19.2, we present a summary statement of the processes which, according to social learning theory, are responsible for the individual's *acquisition* or original learning of aggressive behaviors, the *instigation* of overt acts of aggression at any given point in time, and the *maintenance* of such behavior (Bandura, 1973, 1978; Feldman, 1977; Neitzel, 1979).

Acquisition. Social learning theory, reflecting its aspiration to comprehensiveness, acknowledges that an unknown and perhaps substantial contribution to the likelihood that a given individual possesses the potential to behave aggressively stems from neurophysiological characteristics. Genetic, hormonal, central nervous system, and the resultant physical characteristics of the individual, it is held, all influence his or her capacity or potential to aggress, as well as the likelihood that specific forms of aggression will, in fact, be learned.

Given the neurophysiological capacity to acquire and retain aggression in one's behavioral repertoire, Bandura suggests that such acquisition proceeds by means of either direct or vicarious experiences. In both instances, the role of reinforcement looms large. Overtly aggressive acts, occurring in the context of trial and error behavior or when under instructional control of others, are likely when reinforced to increase the probability that aggression will be learned or acquired by the individual. Bandura speaks of reinforced practice as a particularly consequential event in the learning of aggression via direct experiences—be it childhood pushing and shoving, adolescent fighting, or adult military combat.

But heaviest emphasis for the acquisition of aggression in social learning theory is placed upon vicarious processes. Such observational learning is held to emanate from three types of modeling influences—familial, subcultural, and symbolic. The physically abused child who, as a child, strikes out at peers and who, as an adult, batters his own child may in part be seen as having acquired such behaviors via observation of the abusive examples enacted by his own parents. Subcultural modeling influences on the acquisition of aggression are often exemplified by the behavior of adolescents in response to their observation of peer aggression, or the behavior of new soldiers successfully indoctrinated into combative behaviors. And vicarious symbolic modeling on television, in the papers, and in comic books, is also an apparently major source of learning of aggression in the United States. Crucial here is the fact that

Table 19.2. Social Learning Theory of Aggression

ACQUISITION	INSTIGATION	MAINTENANCE
I. *Neurophysiological* Genetic Hormonal C.N.S. (e.g., hypothalamus, limbic system) Physical characteristics	I. *Aversive* Frustration Adverse reductions in reinforcement Relative deprivation Unjustified hardships Verbal threats and insults Physical assaults	I. *Direct External Reinforcement* Tangible (material) Social (status, approval) Alleviation of aversiveness Expression of injury
II. *Observational Learning* Family influences (e.g., abuse) Subcultural influences (e.g., delinquency) Symbolic modeling (e.g., television)	II. *Modeling Influences* Disinhibitory-reduced restraints Facilitative Emotional arousal Stimulus-enhancing (attentional)	II. *Vicarious Reinforcement* Observed reward (Receipt-facilitation effect) Observed punishment (Escape-disinhibitory effect)
III. *Direct Experience* Combat Reinforced practice	III. *Incentive Inducements* Instrumental aggression Anticipated consequences IV. *Instructional Control* V. *Delusional Control* VI. *Environmental Control* Crowding Ambient temperature Noise Physical environment	III. *Neutralization of Self-Punishment* Moral justification Palliative comparison Euphemistic labeling Displacement of responsibility Diffusion of responsibility Dehumanization of victims Attribution of blame to victims Misrepresentation of consequences Graduated desensitization

such aggression usually "works." The aggressive model, be it parent, peer, or television character, is very often reinforced for behaving aggressively. Central to the observational learning process is that individuals tend to acquire those behaviors which they observe others enacting and being rewarded for. The likelihood of such acquisition of aggressive or other behaviors is enhanced by certain other characteristics of the model (e.g., perceived expertness; high status; same sex, age, and race as observer), of the behavior being modeled (e.g., its clarity, repetition, difficulty, detail, enactment by several models), and of the observer, i.e., the person viewing the model and learning from his (e.g., similarity to the model, friendliness toward the model, instructions to imitate and, most important, as noted above, reward for imitating).

Instigation. Once having learned how to aggress (and when, where, with whom, etc.), what determines whether the individual will in fact do so? According to social learning theory, the actual performance of aggressive behaviors is determined by several events.

Aversive Events. Aversive events may occur and serve as an evocation of aggression. Frustration is one such aversive instigator, as it is in drive theory. But, unlike its role in drive theory, it is both but one instigator among several, and a phenomenon recognized to have several generally equipotential consequents in addition to aggression, namely regression, withdrawal, dependency, psychosomatization, self-anesthetization with drugs and alcohol, and constructive problem solving. Adverse reductions in reinforcement are a second purported type of aversive instigation to aggression. Many commentators on collective aggression in the United States have pointed to this instigation, especially in the form of a perceived sense of deprivation relative to others or hardship perceived as unjustified—rather than deprivation or hardship in an absolute sense—as a major source of mob violence, riots, and the like. Verbal insults and physical assaults are additional, particularly potent, aversive instigators to aggression. Toch (1969) has shown that, at least among chronically assaultive persons, the types of insults most likely to evoke physically assaultive behavior include threats to reputation and manly status, and public humiliation. Physical assault as an aversive instigation to reciprocal behavior is most likely to occur when avoidance is difficult and the level of instigating assaultiveness is both high and frequent.

Modeling Influences. Just as modeling influences serve as a major means by which new patterns of aggression are acquired, so too can they function as significant instigators to overt aggressive behavior. If we observe another person (the model) behaving aggressively and not being punished for it, such observation can have a *disinhibitory effect*. Through a process akin to vicarious extinction of fear, such disinhibition can result in overt aggression by the observer. If the model not only goes unpunished but is rewarded by approval or by tangible means for the displayed aggression, a *response facilitation* effect may occur. The model's behavior, in this instance, functions as an external inducement to engage in matching or similar behavior. The sheer sight of others behaving aggressively may function as an instigation to similar behavior in yet another way. Viewing such behavior often engenders *emotional arousal* in the observer, and considerable empirical evidence exists that arousal facilitates the occurrence of aggressive behavior, especially in persons for whom such a response is well-practiced and readily available in their behavioral repertoires. Finally, Bandura (1978) also notes that modeling may influence the likelihood of aggression through its *stimulus enhancing* effects. The observer's attention, for example, may be directed by the model's behavior to particular implements and how they may be (aggressively) utilized.

Incentive Inducements. Feshbach (1970) and others have drawn the distinction between angry aggression and instrumental aggression. The goal of the former is to hurt another individual; the latter is an aggressive effort to obtain tangible or other rewards possessed by or otherwise at the disposal of the other. Incentive inducements to aggression relate to this second definition. As Bandura (1978) comments, "A great deal of human aggression . . . is prompted by anticipated positive consequences. Here the instigator is the pull of expected reward rather than the push of painful treatment [p. 46.]" Incentive inducements are clearly a major factor in many instances of individual and collective aggression. We will have more to say later in this chapter, when we consider the maintenance of aggressive behavior, about the types and conditions of reinforcement relevant to the instigation of such behavior. However, anticipating our later examination of aggression control in the United States, it is appropriate to point out here the perhaps obvious fact that aggression very often pays, that incentive or other-induced aggression often leads to the aggressor obtaining the sought-after incentive, and that therein lies one of if not the most fundamental obstacle to successful, widespread aggression control.

Instructional Control. Individuals may aggress against others because they are told to do so. Obedience is taught and differentially rewarded by family and school during childhood and adolescence, and by many social institutions during adulthood (e.g., at work, in military service, and so forth). Again, to quote Bandura (1973):

> Given that people will obey orders, legitimate authorities can successfully command aggression from others, especially if the actions are presented as justified and necessary and the enforcing agents possess strong coercive power. Indeed, as Snow (1961) has perceptively observed, "When you think of the long and gloomy history of man, you will find more hideous crimes committed in the name of obedience than have been committed in the name of rebellion." [p. 175]

Delusional Control. Bizarre beliefs, inner voices, paranoid suspiciousness, perceptions of divine messages, delusions of grandeur, or related psychopathological manifestations may all function as apparent instigators to aggression. The aggression may be justified in self-defensive terms, in messianic terms, as an expression of heroic responsibility, or on similar bases. While delusional control as an instigation to aggression is not to be minimized—at least some apparent instances of it (e.g., presidential assassinations) are major, far-reaching events—we suspect that the frequency of this form of instigation to aggression is greatly overestimated. The drama and publicity often associated with the relatively few actual instances of this type, the frequency with which it is appealed to as part of a legal defense of insanity in (also well-publicized) murder trials, and its appeal as an absolver of personal responsibility, all contribute to our sense of its overestimated frequency.

Environmental Control. As American psychology in recent years has become increasingly interested in the effects on behavior of external events, even going so far as "founding" the subfield of environmental psychology, the empirical examination of an array of external events as instigators to aggression has become a substantial investigative focus. Crowding, ambient temperature, noise, and several other characteristics of the physical, sensory, and psychological environment have been studied for their possible instigative potency. Evidence reveals that each may, but not necessarily does, function as an instigation to aggression. Whether aggressive behavior does, in fact, grow from crowded conditions, hot days and nights, high noise levels, or the like appears to be a somewhat complicated function of the physical intensity of these environmental qualities, their personological perception, the levels of emotional arousal they engender, their interaction, external constraints, and several other considerations.

Maintenance. As we noted in our introduction to social learning theory, and in our subsequent examination of its explanations of the acquisition and instigation of aggression, it is both a cognitive and a traditional S-R theory. This same dual focus is apparent in the social learning view of what sustains aggressive behavior once it is acquired and instigated. Bandura (1978) comments:

> As has been amply documented in psychological research, behavior is extensively controlled by its consequences. The principle applies equally to aggression. Aggressive modes of response, like other forms of social behavior, can be induced, eliminated, and reinstated when the effects they produce are altered. [p. 47]

Thus, whether aggressive behavior persists, disappears, or reappears is largely a matter of reinforcement. When aggression pays, it will tend to persist; when it goes unrewarded, it will tend to extinguish. This simple, and traditional, S-R notions as applied to aggression becomes a bit more complex in social learning theory, as the number and types of reinforcements held to thus influence the maintenance of aggression become elaborated.

Direct External Reinforcement. The persistence of aggressive behavior is directly influenced by the extrinsic rewards it elicits. Such rewards may be tangible (e.g., objects, money, tokens), social (e.g., status, approval, recognition), the alleviation of aversive treatment (e.g., pain reduction, other negative reinforcement), or, possibly, expressions of pain by the person against whom one is aggressing. These several classes of external reinforcement have been shown to have a maximal effect on the maintenance of aggression as a function of the same principles of reinforcement influencing any other behavior, i.e., latency, magnitude, quality, intermittency, and so forth.

Vicarious Reinforcement. Vicarious processes, central to the acquisition and instigation of aggression, are no less important in its maintenance. Observed consequences influence behavior in a manner quite similar to the effects of direct external reinforcement. The aggression-maintaining effects of observing others receive reward for aggressing comes about. Bandura (1978) suggests, via (1) its informational function, i.e., the event tells the observer what aggressive acts are likely to be rewarded under what circumstances; (2) its motivational function, i.e., the observer is encouraged by his observations to believe similar aggressiveness will yield similar rewards for himself; and (3) its disinhibitory effect, when the observer sees others escaping punishment for their aggressive behavior.

Self-Reinforcement. Social learning theory proposes that there are also self-produced consequences by which individuals reward or punish, and hence regulate, their own behaviors. With regard to aggression, most persons in the course of socialization learn by example or rules that aggressive behavior should be negatively sanctioned, and they do so themselves by what they say, do, or feel about themselves following their own aggressive behavior. Contrariwise, there also exist persons whose own criteria for dispensing self-reinforcement is such that overt aggression is a highly rewardable source of pride. They are prone to combativeness and derive enhanced feelings of self-worth from its success.

A number of other self-originated processes are suggested in social learning theory as factors which often function to maintain aggressive behavior. These are primarily neutralizations of self-punishment. They may take the several forms listed in table 19.2, each of which is a cognitive effort on the part of the aggressor to justify, excuse, ignore or otherwise avoid self-condemnation for aggression and its consequences.

Summary

Instinct, drive, and social learning are three diverse American approaches to understanding the origins and nature of aggressive behavior. The instinct view was, and remains, largely a detour away from an empirically based and societally useful comprehension of aggression and its control. Drive theory was also inadequate in many of its particulars, but served and continues to serve a major heuristic function via the research and theoretical efforts to which it has given rise. Social learning theory, in our view, represents the most theoretically sound, empirically supported, and pragmatically useful view of aggression available. As a good scientific stance should, it is a testable, logically consistent set of constructs of increasingly demonstrable validity.

CRIMINAL BEHAVIOR THEORIES

In addition to the three major theoretical perspectives on aggression we have now examined, there has long existed interest in systematic speculation, and investigation, regarding the causes and remediation of criminal behavior.

Physiological Theories

Physiological theories, while always present in one form or another, have never been popular for any sustained period in American thinking about crime. Hooton's (1939) early work on the purported physical and mental inferiority of criminals, Sheldon's (1949) well-publicized efforts to associate criminal behavior with body type, and more recent genetic investigation hypothesizing chromosomal aberration (i.e., Price & Whatmore, 1967; Rosenthal, 1970) as a basis for such behavior are three examples of how short-lived such biological and physiological speculation can be. Efforts such as these have consistently failed to find sustained empirical support; conclusions have grown from an inadequate data base and have been counfounded by psychological and cultural variables; and, unlike several of the theories we will examine shortly, the several physiological theories of criminal behavior have also consistently failed to yield useful public policy implications. Physiological theories also suffer from the same kind of one-dimensionality that characterizes a number of other approaches to understanding criminal behavior, each of which—in trying to supply the one-true-light—ignores the great likelihood that criminal behavior is multiple determined.

Psychological Theories

Psychological theories are a further example of the cost of wearing unidimensional theoretical blinders. Psychoanalytic speculation about criminal and related antisocial behavior has enjoyed a modicum of popularity in the United States, undeservedly in our view. Crime is viewed as a symptom of personality disturbance in which aggressive impulses are not restrained by internal impulse controls. The psychodynamic processes hypothesized to be responsible for such behavior include a need to be punished growing from Oedipal guilt, incomplete socialization stemming from maternal deprivation and thus a compensatory effort via the criminal behavior to obtain love and attention, and a defective superego which fails to hold id forces in sufficient check. The locus of criminality in this view is within the individual. Environmental, social, and cultural contributions are essentially ignored. This is but one of several reasons we concur with Davidson and Kushler (1981) who comment:

> This approach suffers from logical deficiencies, lacks a sound empirical base and is discrepant from patterns of actual criminal conduct. . . . Furthermore, in spite of its widespread utilization [in America], treatment programs based on psychoanalytic methods have been largely ineffective for both delinquent and adult offenders. [p. 9]

A second major U.S. example of a psychological theory of criminal behavior is the trait or type approach. As with psychoanalysis, the wellspring of criminality is seen as existing within the individual. The psychopath or the so-called antisocial personality are prime examples. Yet these terms, basically descriptions of repetitive criminality, tend to be imprecise, clearly are circular, apply at best to only a relatively small percent of those engaging in such behavior, and generally fail to lead to useful public policy implications. As with psychoanalytic thinking about criminal behavior, trait theories, which by definition place the locus of such behavior within the person, have some substantial continued credibility and popularity among the general American public, in spite of the serious conceptual weaknesses of these views and their consistent failure to lead to successful interventions. This phenomenon may well be yet another example of the American penchant to assign responsibility to the individual for his behavior, and assume he experiences free will in his ability to express or control it.

Control Theories

Both the physiological and psychological views of criminal behavior are examples of what has come to be known as control theories (Empey, 1978; Hirschi, 1969). Control theories assume that the proclivity to the antisocial lies within the individual, that society is essentially blameless, that morality is self-evident, and that the focus for intervention purposes must be upon the individual who is considered deviant and thus in need of assistance to control internal antisocial tendencies. Examples of such intervention might be a eugenics program for the genetic theorist, and certain penological classification and sentencing decisions by the trait theorist.

Sociological Theories

The control theories' perspective differs sharply from what have been termed cultural deviance theories, most of which grow from American sociology. These latter perspectives reject the notion that criminal deviance is, on one basis or another, an innate characteristic of the individual. Instead, they propose, such behavior is learned as an adaptation to real-world societal and cultural forces. There are two major examples of cultural deviance, sociological theories of criminal behavior.

Differential Association Theory. The differential association theory (Sutherland, 1947) holds that criminal behavior is learned behavior, and derives from interactions the individual has with small groups of intimates or peers who are engaged in such behaviors. Both general criminalistic attitudes and motivations, as well as specific antisocial behaviors are learned according to Sutherland. Such learning, he proposes, involves precisely the same mechanisms involved in learning any other type of behavior. The American practice of prohibiting individuals on probation or on parole from penal institutions from associating with known felons is one practical outgrowth of differential association theory. Community-based treatment programs, in which incarceration in penal institutions for certain convicted felons is avoided altogether, is a second differential association effort to minimize contact with sources of criminal learning. These are but two examples of the manner in which the impact of differential association theory remains significant in the United States at the present time.

Differential Opportunity Theory. Differential opportunity theory (Cloward & Ohlin, 1960) takes us yet a step further away from an individual locus of responsibility for so-called deviance, toward societal sources of criminal behavior. Cloward and Ohlin propose that criminal behavior grows from differential access to legitimate and illegitimate opportunities to reach both personal and social goals. When culturally approved means are blocked, illegitimate opportunities are sought and used. In their words:

> The disparity between what lower class youth are led to want and what is actually available to them is the source of the major problem. . . . Adolescents who form delinquent subcultures . . . have internalized an emphasis upon conventional goals, and unable to revise their aspirations downward, they experience immense frustration; the exploration of nonconformist alternatives may be the result. [p. 17]

Two close variants on this differential opportunity theme are (1) Cohen's (1966) reactance theory, in which antisocial behaviors occur among the same population as Cloward and Ohlin refer to, but following a repudiation of and not a subscription to middle class goals; and (2) the relative deprivation/unjustified hardship view of collective aggression espoused by Bandura (1973), which we examined in our earlier consideration of social learning theory. Differential opportunity theory has had, and continues to have, a significant impact upon social policy in the United States. Attempts to redress the imbalance of economic and social opportunity in America and more equitably and equally enhance its availability have taken a plethora of forms. Government-supported programs for expanded social services—job training, educational offerings, and a host of other activities—continues to be a major feature of contemporary American responses to criminal behavior by its citizens.

Sociopolitical Theories

Sociopolitical theories of criminal behavior place fullest emphasis upon forces lying outside the individual as responsible for, in their terms, "so-called" criminal behavior.

Social Labeling Theory. Social labeling theory (Becker, 1963; Lemert, 1967; Schur, 1969) is one major example. The differential association and differential opportunity views both concerned themselves with the person's reaction to social forces; the social labeling perspective focuses, instead, on society's reaction to the person. Stress is placed not upon the transgressive or aggressive behavior of the individual which brings him to the attention of legal authorities but, instead, upon society's reaction to this behavior. Deviance is seen not as a property inherent in any given behavior, but as a property conferred on behavior by societal representatives. The assignment of a label, e.g., "juvenile delinquent," is held by social labeling theorists to create an expectation in both others and the person himself regarding the latter's probable future deviance. Over time, this self-fulfilling prophecy quality of the label or stereotype functions to increase the actual occurrence of such behavior. The created role of "delinquent" or "criminal" enforces a progressive commitment to rule violation and deviation. While not seeking to explain the original infractionary or criminal behavior, social labeling theorists, therefore, believe that America's criminal justice system creates much of the very deviance it is mandated to correct, and that the further into this system an individual gets, the fuller and more tenacious are the effects of being labeled.

The recent movement in the United States to decriminalize certain activities (e.g., status offenses by juveniles, the increased use of diversion strategies which keep persons out of the criminal justice system altogether, or probationary tactics, which move them out of the system after adjudication but prior to incarceration) are all positive attempts to thwart the deviance-enhancing effects of social labeling.

Radical Theory. A more extreme sociopolitical theory of criminal behavior, one yet to have a significant policy-revision impact, is radical theory (Abadinsky, 1979), sometimes called by its proponents the new criminology (Meir, 1976). Going well beyond social labeling theory, this orientation focuses on the political meanings and motivations underlying society's definitions of crime and crime control. Crime, in their view, is a phenomenon largely created by those who possess wealth and power (by definition and as a function of America's social structure). America's laws are the laws of the ruling elite, used to subjugate the poor, minorities, and the powerless. The specific propositions (Quinney, 1974) which constitute radical theory further define its essence:

1. American society is based on an advanced capitalist economy.
2. The state is organized to serve the interests of the dominant economic class, the capitalist ruling class.
3. Criminal law is an instrument of the state and ruling class to maintain and perpetuate the existing social and economic order.
4. Crime control in capitalist society is accomplished through a variety of institutions and agencies established and administered by a governmental elite, representing ruling class interests, for the purpose of establishing domestic order.
5. The contradictions of advanced capitalism—the disjunction between existence and essence—require that the subordinate classes remain oppressed by whatever means necessary, especially through the coercion and violence of the legal system.
6. Only with the collapse of capitalist society and the creation of a new society, based on socialist principles, will there be a solution to the crime problem.

The radical theory of criminal behavior has to date rendered a limited, but not unimportant "consciousness-raising" service to American society. While the likelihood of implementation of the preferred solutions of radical theory does not seem to have increased appreciably, the United States (especially its social and behavioral scientists) does appear—perhaps in part because of radical theory—to be more aware of social conflict, instances of misuse of the criminal justice system, racism, exploitation, and related social ills relevant to criminal behavior.

Summary

The physiological and psychological theories we have examined looked to the individual perpetrator for explanations regarding criminal behavior—his genes, body type, unresolved Oedipal conflict, maternal deprivation, level of psychopathy, and so forth. Sociological theories looked more toward the individual's immediate environment—peers, job opportunities—and what was and was not learned in such environments. Sociopolitical thinking sought wider horizons, and tried to understand and explain criminal behavior in terms of society's reaction to persons labeled as criminals by society itself, or in the basic economic and social faults of the capitalist system. To varying degrees, each theory has had something worthwhile to offer in augmenting our understanding of criminal behavior. But all of these theories are essentially unidimensional. Aggressive and criminal behavior, we would hold, is multiple determined. To look to the person *or* to his immediate environment *or* to society at large as causatively both necessary and sufficient is to be theoretically narrow and parochial. The behavioral and social sciences must be used *in combination*, disciplinary lines must be crossed, criminal behavior must be viewed in multidimensional perspective.

Multidimensional Theories

Multidimensional theories of criminal behavior do exist. One is Bandura's (1973) social learning theory, which we have described in detail earlier. The second is Feldman's (1977) integrated learning theory—developed in Great Britain, but recently published in the United States and capturing increasing interest here. Both of these theoretical positions seek to explain criminal behavior as growing from a combination of biological-physiological, learning (from the immediate environment), and societal influences. For Bandura (see table 19.2), this multidimensional perspective is concretely reflected in attention to a neurophysiological substrate which provides the capacity to acquire aggressive behaviors; a direct and vicarious process which displays and rewards its acquisition, instigation, and maintenance; and both subcultural and symbolic experiences which make a similarly potent contribution to its learning, initiation, and sustained performance.

Feldman (1977), as noted, shares a related tripart orientation. Criminal behavior, he holds, is a joint function of individual predisposition, social learning, and social labeling. He suggests that the extroverted neurotic, who in Eysenckian (1970) terms displays high levels of conditionability on behaviors relevant to law breaking, is criminal behavior prone. Given this proclivity, the individual's likelihood of actually engaging in criminal behavior is increased if, in social learning theory terms, he is provided with appropriate models for such behavior, situational inducements for actually engaging in it, and direct reinforcement for having done so. The probable recurrence of such behavior, Feldman holds, is increased when and if its early occurrences result in social labeling of the individual as delinquent, criminal, or the like.

It is our view that multidimensional theoretical efforts most accurately reflect the nature of aggression and criminal behavior, and most heuristically will yield relevant empirical data helpful in furthering this understanding. The particular dimensions which constitute the two theories under consideration here may or may not prove to be sufficiently comprehensive or empirically adequate. But as a style of theorizing, a way of thinking about criminality and aggression, we strongly recommend this nonparochial, complex, integrating, multidimensional orientation. It is an orientation of marked and growing stature in American behavioral and social science thinking about aggression and criminality, and we think deservedly so.

CONTROLS AND ALTERNATIVES

We have examined the history of aggression in the United States, its current expression, and theoretical perspectives on its acquisition, instigation, and maintenance. In the remainder of this chapter, we wish to explore the more prosocial aspects of this domain by a consideration of aggression control and alternatives to aggression in the United States. We will seek to identify and evaluate what is occurring in America's criminal justice system; in its schools, agencies, and mass media; and among certain of its behavioral sciences to diminish current levels of aggression in the United States and to increase the frequency of nonaggressive, prosocial, alternative behaviors.

Criminal Justice

Penology. America's penal system is an enterprise of very considerable magnitude. As part of a criminal justice system which processes 2,500,000 offenders annually, America's 4,700 federal, state, and local prisons incarcerate 400,000 individuals, employ 200,000 individuals, and cost $4 billion per year to run. In the 200 years since America's founding, different philosophies have guided its penal system, with consequent major effects on its nature and concrete operations. Eighteenth century thinking centered upon ideas of *retribution*. Crimes, especially of violence, were sinful acts to be punished by often cruel, physical means. *Restraint and deterrence* as an alternative operating philosophy emerged in the early nineteenth century, largely through the efforts of what came to be known as the classical school of criminology. Rationality and hedonism were key concepts in this view. People were thought to carefully consider the advantages and disadvantages of any given behavior, and regulate their actions accordingly. As Davison and Kushler (1981) comment:

> Hence, the proper societal reaction [to crime] should be to administer "pain" to the offender in some specified amount such that individuals could take this measure of pain into acount in governing their actions. Imprisonment began its heightened popularity at this point, partly because it was viewed as more humane than earlier more grisly punishments and partly because it was a perfect vehicle for meting out specific lengths of punishment for specific crimes. . . . [p. 27]

Restraint and deterrence remain the guiding philosophy for much of what occurs in America's penal system, even though evidence is minimal at best that incarceration actually functions as a deterrent to recidivism. In addition to continued concern about its corrective effectiveness, at least with many types of offenders, and its often questionable humaness, incarceration is also expensive. Imprisonment costs approximately ten times as much per offender as does such a community alternative as probation. For these and related reasons, later nineteenth century penal thinking in America began to incorporate into its structure a *rehabilitation* philosophy. Its major concrete expressions have been probation, parole, and treatment.

Probation, the suspension of sentencing given the nonoccurrence of recidivistic behavior for a specified time period, is currently the judicial outcome for more than half of all adjudicated offenders in the United States. In particular, it tends to be utilized with most juveniles, first-time offenders, some types of misdemeanants, and many offenders who pose little hazard to community safety or order. Its rehabilitative qualities, when it works well, derive largely from the educational, vocational, and counseling programs conducted by community agencies to which the probationer is referred. When such services are not available, or when probation supervisor case loads grow too great—and the rehabilitative philosophy translates only to surveillance in the community—the outcome is often less good. Yet, evaluation evidence indicates that, even under these latter circumstances, the rate of recidivism is as low, or lower, than for persons who had been incarcerated.

Parole is the next most common form of community corrections in the United States. Parole is the selective and supervised relase of offenders who have been incarcerated and have served a portion of their sentence. Approximately 70 percent of inmates released from America's prisons are released on parole. Often operationalize in terms of time taken off from the original sentence for "good behavior" while serving the sentence, parole's rehabilitative thrust appears to be the pressure toward such noninfractionary behavior while incarcerated plus, perhaps, an earlier departure from the prison environment, often viewed in America as "seminaries for crime."

Psychological treatment became a prominent expression of the rehabilitation philosophy in many American prisons in the early and mid 1900s. Individual and group therapies, behavior modification programs of diverse types, and other clinical interventions became a significant penological component. Although as we shall see later in this chapter, such interventions can have a significant aggression control impact upon nonincarcerated persons, this does not seem to have happened, or perhaps even be possible, in a prison context. We tend to concur with Davidson and Kushler (1981) who observe, "What prison treatment does exist is liable to be primitive in nature and oriented more toward maintaining order within the institution than on true rehabilitation . . . [p. 57]." It is their position, as well as that of many others (e.g., Empey, 1978; Neitzel, 1979; Sommer, 1976) that a basic and unresolvable contradiction exists between a prison context—which can truly only incapacitate and restrain—and the very concept of rehabilitation. They would hold, and we agree, that rehabilitation, via a treatment route especially, can only very rarely occur in a prison setting. It is for this reason that, in the 1970s, there emerged in the United States a major variant of the rehabilitation strategy, a viewpoint that in some ways was a new perspective on criminal aggression control, namely *reintegration*.

Sharing some features with probation, especially community-based intervention, reintegration goes further to focus on prevention, on avoidance of social labeling effects, and on systemwide and not just individual change. Reintegration penal philosophy has been concretized via three specific strategies: deinstitutionalization, decriminalization, and diversion. Deinstitutionalization reflects the reintegrative belief that restoration of offenders will be maximized to the degree that institutional confinement is minimized. Furthermore, optimal correctional settings are similar in important respects to the societal context in which the eventual adjustment of the offender must occur. Deinstitutionalization in America has thus taken a variety of forms: graduated prison release, work release, educational release, furlough, discharge to a halfway house.

Decriminalization involves efforts to redefine societal response to certain behaviors so that they are no longer considered crimes, e.g., so-called victimless crimes, or behaviors by juveniles (i.e., status offenses). Diversion is quite literally an attempt to divert the individual away from and out of the criminal justice system. In successful diversion attempts, there is an early suspension of the arrest-arraignment-prosecution sequence and, as in probation, referral for community-based counseling and/or vocational assistance. (However, in contrast to diversion, probation involves referral for community services *after* conviction and consequent labeling.) At the present time in the United States, the reintegration philosophy is a major and growing component in penological thinking. Diversion, in particular, is heavily employed, a trend likely to accelerate in the years ahead.

Gun Control. Public opinion polls repeatedly indicate that a majority of Americans favor gun control legislation (Davidson & Kushler, 1981) and, in fact, there exist in the United States more than 20,000 federal, state, and local laws and regulations governing the use and ownership of firearms. But these laws have been accurately described as " . . . obsolete, unenforced, or unenforceable [Davidson & Kushler, 1981]," and pressure to emasculate their minimal effectiveness and thwart the passage and implementation of effective legislation continues in an unremitting manner. Perhaps just how little effective gun control there has been in the United States can be dramatically indicated simply by the fact that Americans now have in their private possession approximately 200 million guns. Since 1900, over 750,000 American civilians have been killed by privately owned guns. Each year, there are 200,000 gun related injuries and 20,000 gun related deaths: 3,000 by accident, 7,000 by homicide, 9,000 by suicide. Guns are involved in two out of every three murders in America, one-third of all robberies, and one-fifth of all aggravated assaults.

To us, these figures are indeed startling. It will help our understanding of aggression and aggression control in the United States if we briefly examine how this state of affairs came to be. During the early colonial period, several factors combined to make true the oft-stated observation that the United States was born with a gun. The multination struggle for control of North America physically introduced firearms to the continent. The need to hunt for food, for furs, or use weapons in the Indian conflicts which began during this period served to familiarize and universalize the usage of firearms throughout the population. And, as each of America's colonies was established, gun possession and usage became legitimatized as colonial militias consisting essentially of all adult male citizens were established.

In 1775-1781, the Revolutionary War took place, a landmark event in America's centuries-long love affair with the gun. Four hundred thousand victorious citizen-soldiers helped enshrine the right to bear arms in the United States' Constitution. The Constitution's second amendment states: "A well-regulated militia being necessary to the security of a free state, the right of the people to keep and bear arms shall not be infringed." This phrase has for 200 years been the center of contention, interpretation, misinterpretation and reinterpretation. Pro-firearms groups have leaned on it heavily as legitimization for private ownership of firearms. Gun control forces, in contrast, have viewed this amendment as providing sanction for corporate (e.g., militia) not individual possession of guns, and as in no way speaking against registration of same.

With firearms thus widely in use, widely admired, and—in the eyes of many—governmentally sanctioned, postrevolutionary America began moving West. This was America's frontier period. Guns were broadly used to hunt, attack, and protect. The Indian conflicts expanded. America's firearms industry took hold and grew rapidly. The romanticized traditions of gun-toting cowboys and the "Wild West" emerged and spread. Anti-gun voices were few and ineffectual.

America's Civil War (as all its wars) was a further major accelerant of gun use and popularity. As sheer reinforcement, it showed its participants (and others) that superiority of firepower indeed led to a victorious outcome. It increased the skill and familiarity with weapons of millions of men, accelerated the arms industry and, hence, the availability of firearms, and had significant anti-gun control postwar implications.

As will be recalled from our earlier discussion of the history of aggression in the United States, the post-Civil War era was a particularly turbulent time. Great urban upheaval occurred and, with these events as both precipitants and reactions, gun use increased. Thus, this was a time not only of increased "playful" use of weapons (widespread marksmanship contests, gun competitions, turkey shoots, etc.), but also a time of gun use in vigilante, riot, individual assault, and similar negative contexts.

The two world wars had, like the Civil War, a marked potentiating effect on gun manufacture, gun use, gun training, and gun adoration. To be sure, occasional legislation intervened, but only sporadically and weakly. Such legislative events have tended to occur in the United States following national traumas which involve firearms—presidential assassination, massive riots, and the like. Some of this legislation has effectively reduced a portion of the interstate and international traffic in certain types of guns, and related small bits of gun control progress can be discerned. But it is minimal progress at best. One hundred million guns are still loose in America! With regard to the firearms dimension of aggression control in the United States, we are at best very guardedly optimistic. We hope, but can only hope, that Kennett and Anderson (1975) are correct in their conclusion to their book, *The Gun in America*, when they state:

> But in the long run, time works against the gun. Increased social consciousness finds its excesses intolerable; whereas they were once accepted without thought. The era of thermonuclear war has made the citizen-soldier harder to defend. . . . Moreover, the police have come to regard the armed citizen more as a hazard than an ally. . . . In megalopolis the gun as necessity seems doomed; what can be salvaged of it as sport and diversion remains to be seen. In some attenuated form it will no doubt linger, the distinctive heritage of a nation that began with a shot heard "round the world." [pp. 255-256]

Police. The American police as a formal organization first became a reality in the early nineteenth century. It will be recalled that this was an era of rapid and major urbanization and industrialization in the United States. Millions of immigrants came to America during this period, largely to work in the factories of the northeast. The resultant overcrowding, unemployment, poverty, and social disorder called for stronger, more organized, and more efficient order maintenance and crime control than informally existed until then. Thus, early police departments were established in Philadelphia (1833), Boston (1838), New York (1844) and, by 1870, in all of America's major cities. Like its criminal justice companion, the penal system, policing grew over the ensuing 100 years to become a very substantial enterprise. By 1980, America employed approximately 500,000 police officers in 45,000 separate departments at a cost of three billion dollars per year.

During this century there has been not only growth, but also change. The early police department was not infrequently poorly trained, poorly managed, authoritarian, and sometimes corrupt. But in recent decades, a qualitatively different type of police department, and police officer, has gradually emerged in many, if not most, American towns and cities. He (and she) is an officer increasingly responsive to, and skilled in the face of the fact that literally 80 percent of police calls are for order maintenance and service activities, and only 20 percent (TV portrayals not withstanding) for criminal apprehension. He/she is increasingly humane and efficient in handling family disputes, the mentally disturbed, rape victims, and others in need of steady, professional, police response. So called "police science" in America is no longer only the study and improvement of weaponry and police tactics vis a vis criminal perpetrators. In what by now may well be the majority of American police departments, it is also serious concern with victimology, police-community relations, the causes of juvenile delinquency, due process of law, and a host of related domains combining to an increasingly professionalized, humane, efficient, and effective typical American police department.

Education

Our examination of aggression-relevant aspects of America's criminal justice system asked: How can criminal aggression be reduced, guns controlled, and police made more effective? These clearly are questions of aggression control. But throughout this chapter and this book the focus is upon cultural examples of two possible types of response to aggression: controls and alternatives. Not only must effort be expended to reduce, manage, deflect, eliminate, or otherwise control overt aggression; we believe societies must be equally concerned and active in fostering prosocial alternatives to such behavior. What can a given society and its institutions do to increase its levels of overt morality, altruism, empathy, cooperation, sharing, and the like? These are matters of aggression alternatives, one major source of which, in the United States, is teaching done by its formal and informal educational institutions.

Formal Education. Though family and church are the American institutions typically perceived as the primary sources for teaching morality and prosocial behaviors, the not inconsiderable levels of antisocial and aggressive behavior we have indicated to exist in America suggest that family and church may be necessary but clearly are not sufficient for these purposes for many persons. Parents and clergy are often either too weak as teachers, too unsystematic, too abstract, or simply bad behavioral models of the very behaviors they may verbally urge upon others. America's public education system was established in the midnineteenth century, and it was not long before such highly influential educators as Horace Mann and William T. Harris began to argue forcefully that moral education must be a significant component of what was taught in America's public schools. John Dewey had a particularly significant impact on this position. While many if not most of his contemporaries held firm to the position that school was a place for cognitive-intellectual and not moral learning, he championed the view that the two were inseparable. For him, morality involved the individual's ability to apply intellectual skills to social (especially problematic or conflictual) situations, and to behave in accordance with such reasoning (Dewey, 1909, 1916). The Character Education Movement (Chapman, 1977) of the 1920s also energetically put forth the view that moral instruction was a fundamental responsibility of public education—a sentiment echoed a number of times since then from several sources, including the National Education Association (Goble, 1973).

Many feel otherwise. A conservative, cognitive-intellectual-curriculum-only-stance exists, and in many instances, counterweighs the pro-moral education perspective. There have been, and remain, strong organizations in the United States that feel moral training is a family-church matter exclusively, and to do so in a school context is inappropriate indoctrination. This conservative view has been particularly popular in years of tight fiscal conditions. But whether waxing or waning, the forces favoring moral education in public school settings have always commanded at least some considerable attention, and do seem to constitute a viable force at the present time in the United States.

Moral education, broadly defined, consists of didactic and experiential activities and contents designed to enhance the prosocial quality of student thinking and behavior. The explicit educational goals of these activities have variously been termed values, humanism, character, morality, emotionality, and social awareness. The particular programs existing toward these ends are both many and varied. In addition to the three we will look at in a bit more detail— Character Education (American Institute for Character Education, 1974); Values Clarification (Raths, Harmon, & Simon, 1966); and Moral Education (Kohlberg, 1969, 1971, 1976)— there exist Ultimate Life Goals (Beck, 1971); the Learning to Care Program (McPhail, Ungoed-Thomas, & Chapman, 1975); Shaver's Public Issues Program (Newmann & Oliver, 1970); Moral Components (Wilson, 1972); the Classroom Meeting (Glasser, 1969); Identity Education (Weinstein & Fantini, 1970); Affective Education (J.P. Miller, 1976); Confluent Education (Castillo, 1974); and Human Relations Training in school contexts (Bradford, Gibb, & Benne, 1964).

Character Education, in its several contemporary forms—*The Good American Program* (Mayer, 1964); *Freedom's Code* (Hill, 1965); *As I Am, So is My Nation* (Trevitt, 1964) and, especially the *Character Education Curriculum* (American Institute for Character Education, 1974)—typically is used with lower, elementary grade children and employs a variety of didactic and participatory techniques—e.g., lecture, readings, group discussion, role play—to explicitly teach an array of character traits and standards of ethical conduct, such as generosity, honesty, courage, fairness, responsibility, and tolerance. Advocates of this approach to morality provide impressionistic evidence of its effectiveness; while educators and others opposed to its utilization in public schools object in particular to the manner in which Character Education programs appear to constitute an indoctrinational orientation to the teaching of specific values.

The Values Clarification (Raths, Harmon, & Simon, 1966) approach to teaching morality became popular in the United States in the mid 60s in part in response to this anti-indoctrination viewpoint. Values, they held, are not fixed, immutable, universal, nor is inculcation the appropriate means to their acquisition. Instead, in their view, values are relative to subgroups within society; to time, place, and circumstances; often conflict with one another; and, in any event, are a matter of personal discovery and choice, not external inculcation. Thus, rather than teaching a specific set of prosocial values, the Values Clarification approach seeks to teach youngsters how to develop and clarify their own values, i.e., the process of valuing. Specifically, teaching goals include how to choose values freely, how to choose from among alternatives, how to carefully weigh and consider alternative values, how to act upon one's value choices, and related valuing processes.

Values Clarification, therefore, proceeds not by (as in Character Education) teacher moralizing, sermonizing, advice-giving, or evaluating, but by what Raths, et al. (1966) call the value-clarifying response. Using an array of exercises, didactic and other discussion-generating activities and materials (see, for example, Simon, Howe, & Kirschenbaum, 1972), the teacher employing values clarification responds to students in ways that raise value questions in the student's mind, encourage him/her to examine value-relevant beliefs and actions, stimulate him/her to consider alternative values and their bases, and thus clarify his/her own values.

The Values Clarification approach has become a part of curricular activities in many elementary and secondary schools in the United States, and, it appears, will continue to have a substantial prosocial impact in the years ahead. Much the same hopeful conclusion may be drawn regarding the final approach to teaching aggression alternatives in public education that we wish to consider, Moral Education.

Though the Moral Education perspective has a number of proponents in America, Lawrence Kohlberg has been its most active theoretician and developer (e.g., Kohlberg, 1969, 1971, 1976). While concurring with the Values Clarification view that the teaching of particular values, as in Character Education, is indoctrination and to be avoided, Kohlberg also feels that major aspects of the Values Clarification stance favoring value relatively are erroneous. Instead, he holds, there is a basic consistency across people and across cultures in the stages through which people pass in their development of personal and social values, and, further, that certain of these stages of moral reasoning are better or more adequate than others. In his Piaget-like, cognitive-developmental stage theory of moral development, Kohlberg holds that the highest stage is the ideal end point of moral development, that movement across stages occurs in an invariant sequence, that each successive stage reflects an increasingly more integrated and effective mode of moral reasoning, and that the motivation for stage transition is cognitive conflict. The educational implication of this perspective is that moral education should take place by means of stimulating the development of increasingly more integrated and effective moral reasoning, i.e., facilitation through an invariant sequence toward the highest stage of moral development of which that individual is capable.

The specific stages of moral development in this view are:

I. *Preconventional Level.* The focus at this level is on the physical impact of behavior (punishment, reward) and the power of those who enunciate society's rules and regulations.
Stage 1. *Punishment and obedience orientation.* The physical consequences of an act, e.g., avoidance of punishment, determine its moral goodness or badness, regardless of the human value of such consequences.
Stage 2. *Instrumental relativist orientation.* Right action is that which satisfies one's own needs and occasionally the needs of others. This is a pragmatic, market place view of moral behavior.

II. *Conventional Level.* Maintaining the expectations of the individual's family, group, or nation is perceived as valuable in its own right, regardless of the immediate or obvious consequences of such behavior.
Stage 3. *Interpersonal concodrance; the "good-boy-nice-girl" orientation.* Good moral behavior is that which pleases or helps others and is approved by them. Emphasis is on conformity to stereotypical images of majority behavior.
Stage 4. *Law and order orientation.* Emphasis on respect for authority, adherence to fixed rules, and the maintenance of social order.

III. *Postconventional Level.* Morality is sought in values and principles that have validity apart from authority of those holding such values.

Stage 5. *Social-contract legalistic orientation.* Moral behavior is defined in terms of both individual rights and standards that have been examined and agreed upon by society at large. There is an emphasis on legal principle, but with consideration of the possibility of changing the law when rational considerations and social utility make such action appropriate.

Stage 6. *Universal ethical principle orientation.* Right is defined by the decision of conscience in accord with self-chosen ethical principles appealing to logical comprehensiveness, universality, and consistency.

We noted earlier Kohlberg's belief that motivation for stage transition is cognitive conflict. Consistent with this belief, the primary means utilized in the Moral Education approach for stimulating transition or movement as far along the six-stage sequence as the person is capable of moving is by the use of moral dilemmas. The presentation of a range of such dilemmas to groups of students whose members collectively show at least a one to two stage spread in their levels of moral development, and a free and open discussion of the dilemma, its alternative solutions, and the rationale for each alternative can engender precisely the intensity of cognitive conflict necessary to stimulate stage transition.

Lest the relevance of Moral Education and the enhanced levels of moral development it can promote be obscure as a prosocial alternative to aggression, it should be noted that, in the United States, according to Kohlberg (1976) and others (Fodor, 1972; Hudgins and Prentice, 1973), preconventional moral reasoning is characteristic of children under age 10, some adolescents, and the vast majority of juvenile delinquents and adult criminals. As we have noted elsewhere:

> These studies suggest that preconventional moral reasoning may well be a critical factor in consistent delinquent and criminal behavior. This should not be surprising since the preconventional individual, by definition, has not yet developed to the point where he/she can really understand, let alone consistently uphold, conventional societal rules, laws and expectations. [Edelman and Goldstein, 1980, p. 290]

Further, it should be noted that conventional moral reasoning (stages 3 and 4) is characteristic of the large majority of American adults and adolescents. Yet, is is postconventional moral reasoning which correlates most highly with such prosocial behaviors as nonviolence, altruism, resistance to cheating, and the like. It is clear, therefore, that Moral Education's already substantial inroad into American public education is to be greatly encouraged.

Interpersonal Skill Training. In the early 1970s in the United States, formal education's growing interest in values and morality combined with American Psychology's emphases on learning, behavior modification, and prevention to give rise to the Interpersonal Skill Training movement. Here, didactic techniques from the pedagogy of formal education, and behavior change techniques from the operant and social learning orientations to psychology are utilized to teach a wide array of prosocial behaviors to individuals chronically engaged in antisocial or asocial behaviors. For some, this skills training approach was viewed as a therapy, a psychoeducational therapy. For others, a sort of adult education program. Still others saw it as a type of either preventative or remedial intervention for a prosocial socialization process which had either failed to take place, or simply was late maturationally.

But, in any event, the relevance of the skills training movement to the aggression alternatives domain is substantial and explicit. In a great many of the twenty or so existing interpersonal skills training approaches, the target trainees are individuals frequently engaged in overt aggressive behaviors who are deficient in prosocial alternatives thereto. Some of the better established interpersonal skills training programs currently operative in America include Life Skills Education (Adkins, 1970); AWARE: Activities for Social Development (Elardo & Cooper, 1977); Couples Communication (Gottman, Motarius, Gonso, & Markham, 1977); Relationship Enhancement (Guerney, 1977); Teaching Conflict Resolutions (Hare, 1976); Social Skill Training (Hersen & Eisler, 1976); Personal Effectiveness (Liberman, King, De-Risi, & McCann, 1975); Interpersonal Skill Training (McFall, 1976); Directive Teaching (Stephens, 1976); and Structured Learning (Goldstein, 1973).

Structured learning, an interpersonal skills training approach developed by the present author and his colleagues (Goldstein, 1973; Goldstein, Sprafkin, Gershaw, & Klein, 1980) is particularly relevant to the training of aggression alternatives. Structured learning consists of the social learning techniques: modeling, role playing, performance feedback, and transfer training. In it, groups of skill-deficient individuals are exposed to live or audiovisual models enacting expert portrayals of skilled, prosocial behavior; given ample opportunity, guidance, and encouragement to systematically rehearse or role play the skilled behaviors displayed by the models; provided with approval, praise, tangible reward, or similar performance feedback as their role play enactments increasingly approximate those of the models; and engage in these and related procedures in such a manner that the likelihood will be enhanced that prosocial skills learned during the training will generalize or transfer and thus be available to the person to use in real-life, skill-relevant settings.

There have been many different applications of the structured learning approach to skills training, several of which entailed either chronically aggressive populations (e.g., juvenile delinquents, child abusing parents) or societal caretakers responsible for management of aggressive individuals (e.g., police teams detailed for management of family disputes and related domestic violence). In these and similar applications, structured learning has proven to be an effective method for training prosocial interpersonal skills, and for enhancing the transfer of such skill learning to community contexts. Skills taught have included negotiation, self-control, dealing with group pressure, understanding your feelings, expressing affection, responding to failure, dealing with an accusation, and, depending on the nature of the trainee, a prescriptive curriculum of as many as 50 other interpersonal skills concerned with social interaction, aggression alternatives, stress management, planning, and decision making.

As noted earlier, several interpersonal skills training approaches have emerged. They differ from one another somewhat, but often not greatly, in constituent techniques, skills taught, and trainee targets. But they combine to represent a healthy, empirically sound, still emergent, joint effort to promote prosocial learning in America by knowledge derived from the combined fields of education and psychology.

The interpersonal skill training programs we have enumerated and described are activities implemented in a number of America's schools, juvenile detention centers, mental hospitals and clinics, and related institutions. There is one interpersonal skill, however, which has become an unusually broad target of interest and training in the United States in the 1970s and early 1980s. Training to increase proficiency in it occurs not only in the formal institutions noted above, but also in the community colleges, adult education groups, special workshops, and via the popular press and related media. In fact, the sheer number of "how-to" books promoting enhanced proficiency in this skill, and the remarkable popularity of these books in contemporary America, is to us itself a sociological statement of the first magnitude. We refer to the skill, assertiveness—the firm, fair direct, overt, verbal, and other behavioral pursuit of one's rights. As described in such appropriately titled books as *Your Perfect Right* (Alberti & Emmons, 1974), *Pulling Your Own Strings* (Dyer, 1977), *Asserting Yourself* (Bower & Bower, 1979), *The New Assertive Woman* (Bloom, Coburn, & Pearlman, 1975), *Don't Say Yes When You Want to Say No* (Fensterheim & Baer, 1975), *I Can if I Want To* (Lazarus & Fay, 1975), and many others, America is being implored, encouraged, sanctioned, and trained to be less withdrawn and less aggressive but, instead, to seek out and express that ideal and idealized mid-point on a withdrawal-aggression continuum, namely, to be assertive. We are far from certain that America truly benefits from such training, nor do we know if the popularity of assertiveness training is but another "me generation" phenomenon. But that it is, in fact, a phenomenon of considerable substance in contemporary America there can be no doubt.

Assertion training aside, it is important to note that there are the substantial beginnings in America today of yet other types of interpersonal and related skill training with serious positive potential for teaching a wide array of persons important alternative responses to aggression. "Parent Effectiveness Training" (Gordon, 1970) is but one of several current attempts to take and enact the position that the behaviors which constitute effective child-rearing are definable and teachable. Reflecting this philosophy, a number of authorities and agencies in the United States are urging the enactment of legislation which would make systematic training in parenting skills available not only for special populations (e.g., abusive parents, pregnant teenagers), but for the adolescent and adult public at large. We applaud and in fact are a part of this effort, and hope it will come for further fruition.

Our final example of American skill training as an alternative to aggression is of a very different type. As we noted in some detail earlier in this chapter, one frequent though not invariant response to frustation is aggression. Constructive problem solving is one of several alternative responses. To the extent that effective problem solving can become a more dominant or frequent response to frustration, the need for overt aggression can diminish. With this position as our rationale, we would strongly encourage the development and utilization of problem solving skill training programs for this purpose. America's most prominent problem solving training programs have not been utilized in this fashion. Brainstorming (Osborn, 1953), Synectics (Gordon, 1961), and Creative Problem Solving (Parnes, 1967) have each been oriented toward the more impersonal problems of business or education. But recent pilot efforts to teach problem solving skills to impulsive children (Camp & Bash, 1975; Giebink, Stover, & Fahl, 1968), psychiatric patients (Coche & Flick, 1975), and interpersonally conflicted families (Bleckman, 1974) are encouraging of a perspective which holds that competence in such skills can indeed function as an important alternative to aggression. This perspective is encouraged further by the significant and extensive research and development program conducted by George Spivack and his co-workers during the past 15 years. Their "Interpersonal Cognitive Problem Solving Program" (Shure & Spivack, 1978; Spivack, Platt, & Shure, 1976; Spivack & Shure, 1974) is a systematic effort to teach preschool and in-school youngsters the skills: (1) alternative solution thinking, (2) consequential thinking, (3) causal thinking, (4) interpersonal sensitivity, (5) means-ends thinking, and (6) perspective taking—skills which combine to constitute their definition of effective problem solving. Their substantial, empirically sound evidence demonstrating that at several age levels, enhanced effectiveness in problem solving skills thus defined beneficially influences such criteria as adjustment, aggression, impulsivity, and inhibition is strong encouragement to us to champion further study and use of this approach in particular, and problem solving skill in general, as yet one further and important skill alternative to aggression.

Mass Media. America is not only taught, and learns, in the formal educational setting of its schools and the less formal contexts of its skill training groups and materials. Its most potent teaching, if sheer numbers be the guide, occurs via its mass media—newspapers, books, comic books, radio, and, in particular, television. In a landmark document, *Mass Media and Violence* (Baker & Ball, 1969) which was one of the almost dozen and a half volumes of the very important Report to the National Commission on the Causes and Prevention of Violence, the pervasiveness and potency of the mass media in American life was dramatically underscored:

In this country today there are 1,749 daily newspapers, 573 Sunday newspapers, 8,012 weekly newspapers, 652 magazines, 2,316 business and trade publications and innumerable school, labor union and other special publications. . . . There are 832 television stations . . . and 6,480 radio stations. Seventeen hundred and sixty-seven publishing houses produce 203,470,000 textbooks and 88,400,000 trade books a year. . . . There are 10,034 motion picture theaters and 3,685 drive-ins. . . . [p. 165]

While some of these absolute numbers have changed to a modest degree in the ensuing decade, the impact of America's mass media on the behavior of its citizens remains immense. One of its effects is to increase the level of violence in contemporary America. This assertion is still disputed in some quarters, but our reading of the combined evidence bearing upon the influence of television viewing (in particular, on overt aggression) leaves little room for doubt or equivocation. The very heavy, almost unremitting diet of violence on American television is a very substantial contributor to both the acquisition of aggressive behavior and the instigation of its actual enactment. The pernicious effects of television violence go further, and extend to the substantial decrease in sensitivity, concern, and revulsion to violence among the general viewing audience. Higher and higher levels of violence become more and more tolerable. These and still other of the aggression-enhancing and aggression-tolerating effects of American television have been documented in many sources; and, arguments of the television industry to the contrary notwithstanding, we believe that much of American television is appropriately viewed as pernicious and promotive of the worst in American behavior (Baker & Ball, 1969; Brown, 1976; Feshbach & Singer, 1971; Howitt & Cumberbatch, 1975; Lefkowitz, Eron, Walder, & Huessman, 1977; Liebert, Neale, & Davidson, 1973).

Yet it must be recalled that, in our earlier examination of social learning theory, we observed that the mechanisms responsible for the acquisition, instigation, and maintenance of aggressive, antisocial behavior—observational learning, direct reinforcement, incentive inducements, and so forth—were exactly the same mechanisms operative in the learning and performance of all other behaviors, including prosocial behaviors. An analogous cases can be made for the prosocial potency of American television (and the American mass media in general). Just as millions of advertising dollars can be spent, as they are, to write, produce, and enact attention-commanding "entertainment" depicting (and teaching) aggressive behaviors, the same dollars can utilize the same creativity and technology to interestingly and informatively depict and teach the prosocial. This message is far from new with us. Others have proclaimed it, and the television industry in the United States has, however faintly, begun to heed it. Both commercial and, especially, public-educational television in America have modestly but perceptibly begun to increase the prosocial among their offerings. At the preschool, in-school, adolescent, and adult levels, there now exist at least a few regular or special American television shows promoting cooperation, not selfishness; negotiation, not striking out; marital understanding, nor marital abuse; juvenile maturity, not juvenile delinquency. To be sure, these are still exceptions to the typically violent television fare in the United States. They are a feeble beginning, but a beginning they are. We are optimistic, and hope that U.S. television programming will continue, perhaps at an accelerated rate, toward teaching the prosocial, and not the antisocial, to its vast number of viewing pupils.

Psychological Contributions

American psychology has long had significant involvement not only in seeking to understand and theorize about the nature and causes of aggression, but also in enhancing its control and alternatives. Some of psychology's contribution to these domains we have already touched upon—moral education theory and research, the skills training movement, and much of the research on television and aggression. There are two further, and even more extensive ways in which the psychological enterprise in the United States has focused on aggression control and alternatives. Aggression control has been the remedial target of a wide array of psychological treatments; aggression alternatives have been the investigative targets of a wide array of psychological research. In this chapter's final section, we wish to examine these treatment and investigative contributions.

Psychological Treatment. From the 1920s through most of the 1950s in the United States, a psychodynamic orientation to the treatment of aggressive behavior prevailed, especially in the form of psychoanalytically-oriented casework (Redl & Wineman, 1952, 1957). As we noted in our mention of this approach as applied to incarcerated offenders, cumulative evaluation of its efficacy shows it wanting. At least in its application to aggressive adolescents, this orientation has consistently failed to be sufficiently responsive in both its theory and its therapeutic operations to a number of the real-world etiological bases for such behavior in this population. We refer here in particular to peer group pressure toward antisocial behavior, low income life circumstances, and pervasive deficiencies in prosocial skills. Awareness of the power of adolescent peer groups did, however, contribute importantly to the character of an alternative treatment approach to aggressive adolescents which emerged in the late 1950s and through the 1960s. Can we, the proponents of this approach asked, "capture" and utilize adolescent responsiveness to peer group pressure by seeking to develop and sustain a *prosocial* peer culture. This position was operationalized by such treatment programs as Guided Group Interaction (McCorkle, Elias, & Bixby, 1958; Richardson & Meyer, 1972), Positive Peer Culture (Vorrath & Bendtro, 1974), and several related efforts, e.g., the programs at Essexfields (Empey & Lubeck, 1971), Fricot Ranch (Jesness, 1965), Paso Robles School (Seckel, 1967); and Provo (Empey & Erickson, 1972). Most of these programs were not submitted to the scrutiny of empirical evaluation, but at least impressionistically and anecdotally, their prosocial impact on the participating aggressive adolescents appears not insubstantial.

In recent years in the United States, attempts to treat aggressive adolescents have shifted further away from either a correctional model (incarceration), medical model (psychodynamic casework), or a group dynamics model (Guided Group Interaction, Positive Peer Culture) to what has been termed a behavior deficiency model. As Bijou and Ribes-Inesta (1972) comment:

> Modern behavior theory suggests a behavior deficiency model of deviant behavior, where behavior problems . . . are viewed as deficiences in essential skills. These behavioral deficits are considered a result of inadequate histories of reinforcement and instruction, rather than as due to some hypothetical internal psychopathology. [p. 52]

Four types of treatment programs have emerged in the United States in the 1970s as expressions of this behavior deficiency model, all of which seek to utilize instructional and reinforcement interventions to explicitly promote prosocial behavior. These are (1) residential or group home programs usually relying rather heavily for their effectiveness on token economy and related procedures (Phillips, Wolf, Fixen, & Bailey, 1975); training parents as effective change agents for their own aggressive children (Patterson & Reid, 1973); the use of behavioral contracting (Burchard, Harig, Miller, & Amour, 1976; Stuart, 1971); and the interpersonal skill training described earlier in this chapter (Goldstein, et al., 1980). Unlike the approaches historically preceding it, treatment programs developed from the behavioral deficiency perspective have been systematically and rigorously evaluated, and generally found to yield reliable positive effects on the reduction of overt aggression and the enhancement of prosocial alternatives thereto. Their continued utilization for this purpose in America is occurring, and in our view is to be encouraged.

To a very substantial degree, the behavioral deficit perspective has also come to dominate treatment approaches concerned with adult aggression control and alternatives in the United States. At a popular or lay level, the skill training writings of George Bach (Bach & Goldberg, 1974; Bach & Wyden, 1968) on techniques for the constructive expression of aggression and "fair fighting" have attracted a widespread readership. In the relevant professional literature, a particularly wide array of behavioral interventions are being actively studied and clinically utilized for controls and alternatives purposes. We refer in particular to relaxation techniques (Filley, 1974; Goldstein, Monti, Sardino, & Green, 1977); communication skills training (Egan, 1976; Wahlroos, 1974); contracting (Dardig & Heward, 1976; DeRisi & Butz, 1975); and training in how to negotiate (Ilich, 1973; Karlins & Abelson, 1970). We view this empirically-based continuing emphasis on behavioral training very positively, are an active part of it, and wish to urge its further growth and evaluation as a major path for the treatment of aggression in the United States.

Psychological Research. The last 20 years have witnessed a dramatic increase in research on prosocial behavior by America's social and developmental psychologists. Altruism, empathy, cooperation, helping, and related domains have become the target of intensive and sustained theoretical attention and investigative inquiry. It is an active and vital scientific movement. Theoretical perspectives are contending—genetic, cognitive-developmental, social learning, distributive justice, and others. Unresolved theoretical issues are many and complex. What is the genetic contribution to altruistic capacity? How can the basic contradictions between altruism and the hedonistic requirements of reinforcement theory be resolved? How and why does empathy develop, and what is the role of vicarious processes in this development? The theoretical questions are many, the answers to date are few, but the field of inquiry is very active and answers will be forthcoming.

Research on prosocial alternatives to aggression to this point has been mostly parameter-identifying, rather than theory testing, a reflection of a field's need to establish a sense of its dimensions by accumulating a factual data base. What has been conducted, therefore, are primarily studies seeking to identify personality characteristics of prosocial persons, characteristics of situations in which prosocial behavior emerges or fails to emerge, and characteristics of persons who are likely to receive or be denied the prosocial efforts of others.

The search for personality characteristics of individuals likely to engage in prosocial behavior has not been an especially fruitful one. Some evidence exists of positive association between prosocial behavior and such person dimensions as social skill, extraversion, affiliativeness, age, dependency, stage of moral development, and internal control; and negative association with dominance, competitiveness, hostility. Perhaps most important from the person perspective is the person's motivational state vis a vis prosocial behavior. Does he want to help, share, cooperate? Staub (1978) proposes that, when prosocial motivation occurs, it is out of a desire for self-gain, adherence to internalized values or norms, or because of empathy with the person in distress. These findings and speculations are provocative, but constitute a scant data base as far as person characteristic antecedents of prosocial behavior are concerned. The Hartshorne and May studies of honesty in the 1920s (1928) demonstrated that, to a very large degree, prosocial behavior is situation-specific, and not an enduring characteristic of the person, necessarily enacted in all or most situations. Sixty years later, much the same conclusion may be drawn from contemporary research on several other forms of prosocial behavior. Person characteristics are not irrelevant, but of considerably greater importance seems to be characteristics of the situation in which prosocial behavior is possible. Altruistic, helping, and related prosocial behaviors are more likely to occur:

1. The less the ambiguity that help in fact is needed.
2. The greater the need for help.
3. The more clearly the responsibility for helping is focused on a particular person.
4. The greater the impact of instigating stimuli, e.g., closer in space, time, and exposure the expression of need is to the potential helper.
5. The less decision-making or initiative the potential helper must assume.
6. The lower the cost of helping—in time, effort, material goods, and risk to oneself.
7. The greater the social desirability of helping.
8. The existence of a relationship with the person in need.
9. When positive experiences and, hence, a favorable mood state have occurred just prior to the opportunity to help.
10. When the individual has been exposed to models displaying, and being rewarded for, the given prosocial behavior.
11. When the individual has been in the past, and expects on this occasion to be rewarded for engaging in the prosocial behavior.

Research on prosocial behavior has also identified a number of characteristics of persons in need which appear to influence the degree to which prosocial responses are elicited. For example, altruism is more likely to be forthcoming when, in the eyes of the potential helper, the helpee is perceived as dependent, a victim of circumstances, relatively unable to help himself, older, and/or similar to the helper on significant demographic or attitudinal dimensions.

Thus, as with aggression itself, the prediction and enhancement of prosocial behavior is complex and multifaceted. Situation and helper characteristics as well as helpee characteristics each contributes in varying degrees to the likelihood of a prosocial act. To what extent each does so, and to what extent yet other classes of determinants of such behavior exist and can be identified are among the several significant and challenging questions remaining to be answered in this research domain. We are confident that psychological research in the United States will continue, as before, to energetically and creatively seek to do so.

SUMMARY

We have examined the history of individual and collective aggression in the United States, its current levels, and an array of theories seeking to explain its acquisition, instigation, and maintenance. Aggression controls and alternatives were also our major focus, especially via America's criminal justice, educational, and psychological systems.

What can be said in overview of these materials? The nature of American society—its founding, composition, economic system, mythologies—has contributed to the not infrequent, if irregularly high, levels of aggressive behavior present over its 200 years history. At this particular point in time, the early 1980s, individual aggression is at a relatively high level, collective aggression is relatively low. Trends are somewhat difficult to predict, but there is at least some reason to believe, i.e., due to the declining number of 14-24 year olds, that individual aggression may in the near future decrease appreciably.

Our consideration of alternative theories of aggression and criminal behavior led us to conclude that the most heuristic and empirically supported approaches were those that viewed aggression and its control in multiple perspective. Both Bandura's Social Learning Theory and Feldman's Integrated Theory met this criterion, as each sought to predict the likelihood of aggressive behavior based jointly upon knowledge of the person, environmental characteristics of his situation, and societal response to the person. In our view, such comprehensive, multidimensional, theoretical thinking is a veridical reflection of the actual antecedents and consequents of aggression, and provides the optimal channels for further theorizing about its controls and alternatives.

Controls and alternatives to aggression in the United States take many forms, and we centered on three prominent examples. Some routes to controls and alternatives we are quite optimistic about. Penological reintegration, America's police departments, the efficacy of moral education and interpersonal skill training, and the vitality of psychological research on prosocial behavior are our main examples. Other channels, especially gun control legislation and the major thrust of the mass media, seem less likely, in the near future at least, to shift in substantial prosocial directions.

In all, we are moderately hopeful. The United States remains a place where aggression occurs far too much of the time. But maybe less so than earlier in its history And, we both hope and believe, it is becoming a nation whose greater awareness about aggression and whose enhanced means for controlling it and providing alternatives to it may make progressively less true in the years to come the now accepted truism that aggression is a major and significant component of life in the United States.

REFERENCES

Abadinsky, H. *Social service in criminal justice.* Englewood Cliffs, N.J.: Prentice-Hall, 1979.

Adkins, W. R. Life skills: Structured counseling for the disadvantaged. *Personnel and Guidance Journal,* 1970, *49,* 108–116.

Alberti, R. E., & Emmons, M. L. *Your perfect right: A guide to assertive behavior.* San Luis Obispo, Calif.: Impact Press, 1974.

American Institute for Character Education, *Living with me and others.* San Antonio, Texas, 1974.

Ardrey, R. *The territorial imperative.* New York: Atheneum, 1966.

Bach, G. R., & Goldberg, H. *Creative aggression.* New York: Doubleday, 1974.

Bach, G. R., & Wyden, P. *The intimate enemy.* New York: William Morrow, 1968.

Baker, R. K., & Ball, S. J. *Mass media and violence.* Vol. IX, National Commission on the Causes and Prevention of Violence. Washington, D.C.: U.S. Government Printing Office, 1969.

Bandura, A. *Principles of behavior modification.* New York: Holt, Rinehart & Winston, 1969.

Bandura, A. *Aggression: A social learning analysis.* Englewood Cliffs, N.J.: Prentice-Hall, 1973.

Bandura, A. Learning and behavioral theories of aggression. In I. L. Kutash, S. B. Kutash, & L. B. Schlesinger (Eds.), *Violence: Perspectives on murder and aggression.* San Francisco: Jossey-Bass, 1978.

Barker, R., Dembo, T., & Lewin, K. Frustration and regression. *University of Iowa Studies in Child Development,* 1941, *18,* Whole No. 386.

Baron, R. A. *Human aggression.* New York: Plenum Press, 1977.

Bayh, B. Our nation's schools—A report card. U.S. Senate. Washington, D.C.: U.S. Government Printing Office, 1975.

Beck, C. *Moral education in the schools: Some practical suggestions.* Toronto: Ontario Institute for Studies in Education, 1971.

Becker, H. S. *Outsiders: Studies in the sociology of deviance.* Glencoe, Ill.: Free Press, 1963.

Benson, H. *The relaxation response.* New York: Avon, 1975.

Berkowitz, L. *Aggression: A social psychological analysis.* New York: McGraw-Hill, 1962.

Bijou, S. W., & Ribes-Inesta, E. *Behavior modification: Issues and extensions.* New York: Academic Press, 1972.

Bleckman, E. A. The family contract game. *The Family Coordinator,* 1974, *23,* 269–281.

Bloom, L. Z., Coburn, K., & Pearlman, J. *The new assertive woman.* New York: Delacorte Press, 1975.

Bower, S. A., & Bower, G. H. *Asserting yourself.* Reading, Mass.: Addison-Wesley, 1979.

Bradford, L. P., Gibb, J. R., & Benne, K. R. *T-group theory and laboratory method.* New York: Wiley, 1964.

Brown, R. (Ed.) *Children and television.* Beverly Hills, Calif.: Sage Publications, 1976.

Burchard, J. D., Harig, P. T., Miller, R. B., & Amour, J. New strategies in community-based intervention. In E. Ribes-Inesta & A. Bandura (Eds.) *Analysis of delinquency and aggression.* Hillsdale, N.J.: Erlbaum, 1976. Pp. 95-122.

Buss, A. *The psychology of aggression.* New York: Wiley, 1961.

Camp, B. N., & Bash, M. A. *Think aloud program group manual.* Boulder, Colo.: University of Colorado Medical Center, 1975.

Castillo, G. *Left-handed teaching.* New York: Praeger, 1974.

Chapman, W. E. *Roots of character education..* Schenectady, N.Y.: Character Research Press, 1977.

Cloward, R. A., & Ohlin, L. E. *Delinquency and opportunity: A theory of delinquent gangs.* New York: Free Press, 1960.

Coche, E., & Flick, A. Problem solving training groups for hospitalized psychiatric patients. *Journal of Psychology,* 1975, *91,* 19-29.

Cohen, A. K. *Deviance and control.* Englewood Cliffs, N.J.: Prentice-Hall, 1966.

Dardig, J. C., & Heward, W. L. *Sign here: A contracting book for children and their parents.* Kalamazoo, Mich.: Behaviordelia, 1976.

Davidson, W. S., & Kushler, M. G. Organizational change. In A. P. Goldstein, E. Carr, W. S. Davidson, & P. Wehr (Eds.), *In response to aggression: Controls and alternatives.* New York: Pergamon Press, 1981.

DeRisi, W. J., & Butz, G. *Writing behavioral contracts.* Champaign, Ill.: Research Press, 1975.

Dewey, J. *Moral principles in education.* Boston: Houghton Mifflin, 1909.

Dewey, J. *Democracy and education.* New York: Macmillan, 1916.

Dollard, J., Doob, L. W., Miller, N. E., Mowrer, O. H., & Sears, R. R. *Frustration and aggression.* New Haven, Conn.: Yale University Press, 1939.

Dyer, W. *Pulling your own strings.* New York: Thomas Crowell, 1977.

Edelman, E., & Goldstein, A. P. Moral education. In A. P. Goldstein, E. Carr, W. S. Davidson, & P. Wehr (Eds.), *In response to aggression: Controls and alternatives.* New York: Pergamon Press, 1981.

Egan, C. *Interpersonal living.* Monterey, Calif.: Brooks/Cole, 1976.

Elardo, P., & Cooper, M. *AWARE: Activities for social development.* Reading, Mass.: Addison-Wesley, 1977.

Ellis, A., & Harper, R. A. *A new guide to rational living.* No. Hollywood, Calif.: Wilshire Book Co., 1976.

Empey, L. T. *American delinquency: Its meaning and construction.* Homewood, Ill.: Dorsey Press, 1978.

Empey, L. T., & Erickson, M. L. *The Provo experiment: Evaluating community control of delinquency.* Lexington, Mass.: Lexington Books, 1972.

Empey, L. T., & Lubeck, S. G. *The Silverlake experiment: Testing delinquency theory and community intervention.* Chicago: Aldine, 1971.

Eysenck, H. J. *Crime and personality.* London: Cranada Press, 1970.

Feldman, M. P. *Criminal behavior: A psychological analysis.* New York: John Wiley, 1977.

Fensterheim, H., & Baer, J. *Don't say yes when you want to say no.* New York: David McKay, 1975.

Feshbach, S. The function of aggression and the regulation of aggressive drive. *Psychological Review,* 1964, *71,* 247-272.

Feshbach, S. Aggression. In P. H. Mussen (Ed.), *Carmichael's manual of child psychology.* Vol. 2. New York: Wiley, 1970. Pp. 159-259.

Feshbach, S., & Singer, R. D. *Television and aggression.* San Francisco: Jossey-Bass, 1971.

Filley, A. C. *Interpersonal conflict resolution.* Glenview, Ill.: Scott, Foresman, 1974.

Fodor, E. Delinquency and susceptibility to social influence among adolescents as a function of level of moral development. *Journal of Social Psychology,* 1972, *86,* 257-260.

Geen, R. G., & O'Neal, E. C. (Eds.) *Perspectives on aggression.* New York: Academic Press, 1976.

Giebink, J. W., Stover, D. S., & Fahl, M. A. Teaching adaptive responses to frustration to emotionally disturbed boys. *Journal of Consulting and Clinical Psychology,* 1968, *32,* 366-368.

Gil, D. G. *Violence against children.* Cambridge, Mass.: Harvard University Press, 1970.

Glasser, W. *Schools without failure.* New York: Harper & Row, 1969.

Glover, E. *The roots of crime.* New York: International Universities Press, 1960.

Goble, F. *The case for character education.* Pasadena, Calif.: Thomas Jefferson Research Center, 1973.

Goldstein, A. P. *Structured learning therapy: Toward a psychotherapy for the poor.* New York: Academic Press, 1973.

Goldstein, A. P., Monti, P. J., Sardino, T. J., & Green, D. J. *Police crisis intervention.* New York: Pergamon Press, 1977.

Goldstein, A. P., Sprafkin, R. P., Gershaw, N. J., & Klein, P. *Skillstreaming the adolescent.* Champaign, Ill.: Research Press, 1980.

Gordon, T. *Parent effectiveness training.* New York: New American Library, 1970.

Gordon, W. J. *Synectics.* New York: Collier Books, 1961.

Gottman, J., Motarius, C., Gonso, J., & Markham, H. *A couple's guide to communication.* Champaign, Ill.: Research Press, 1977.

Guerney, B. G. Jr., *Relationship enhancement.* San Francisco: Jossey-Bass, 1977.

Hare, M. A. Teaching conflict resolution simulations. Presented at Eastern Psychological Association, Philadelphia, March 1976.

Hartshorne, H., & May, M. A. *Studies in the nature of character.* New York: Macmillan, 1928.

Helfer, R. E., & Kempe, C. H. *Child abuse and neglect.* Cambridge, Mass.: Ballinger, 1976.

Hersen, M., & Eisler, R. M. Social skills training. In W. E. Graighead, A. E. Kazdin, & M. J. Mahoney (Eds.), *Behavior modification: Principles, issues and applications.* Boston: Houghton Mifflin, 1976.

Hill, R. C. *Freedom's code: The historic American standards of character, conduct, and citizen responsibility.* San Antonio, Texas: The Children's Fund, 1965.

Hirschi, T. *Causes of delinquency.* Berkeley, Calif.: University of California Press, 1969.

Hofstadter, R., & Wallace, M. (Eds.) *American violence.* New York: Random House, 1971.

Hooton, E. A. *Crime and the man.* Cambridge, Mass.: Harvard University Press, 1939.

Howitt, D., & Cumberbatch, G. *Mass media violence and society.* New York: Wiley, 1975.

Hudgins, W., & Prentice, N. Moral judgments in delinquent and non-delinquent adolescents and their mothers. *Journal of Abnormal Psychology,* 1973, *82,* 145-152.

Ilich, J. *The art and skill of successful negotiation.* Englewood Cliffs, N.J.: Prentice-Hall, 1973.

Jesness, C. F. *The Fricot Ranch study.* Sacramento: California Department of Youth Authority, 1965.

Johnson, R. N. *Aggression in man and animals.* Philadelphia: W. B. Saunders, 1972.

Karlins, M., & Abelson, H. I. *Persuasion.* New York: Springer, 1970.

Kempe, C. H., Silverman, F. N., Steele, B. B., Droegemueller, W., & Silver, H. K. The battered child syndrome. *Journal of the American Medical Association,* 1962, *181,* 17-24.

Kennett, L., & Anderson, J. L. *The gun in America.* Westport, Conn.: Greenwood Press, 1975.

Kohlberg, L. Stage and sequence: The cognitive-developmental approach to socialization. In D. A. Goslin (Ed.), *Handbook of socialization theory and research.* Chicago: Rand McNally, 1969. Pp. 347-480.

Kohlberg, L. Stages of moral development as a basis for moral education. In C. M. Beck, B. S. Cirttenden, & E. V. Sullivan (Eds.), *Moral Education: Interdisciplinary approaches.* Toronto: University of Toronto Press, 1971. Pp. 23-92.

Kohlberg, L. Moral stages and moralization: The cognitive-developmental approach. In T. Lickona (Ed.), *Moral development and behavior.* New York: Holt, Rinehart & Winston, 1976. Pp. 31-53.

Lazarus, A. A., & Fay, A. *I Can if I Want To.* New York: William Morrow, 1975.

Lefkowitz, M. M., Eron, L. D., Walder, L. O., & Huessman, L. R. *Growing up to be violent.* New York: Pergamon Press, 1977.

Lemert, E. M. *Human deviance, social problems, and social control.* Englewood Cliffs, N.J.: Prentice-Hall, 1967.

Liberman, R. P., King, L. W., DeRisi, W. J., & McCann, M. *Personal effectiveness.* Champaign, Ill.: Research Press, 1975.

Liebert, R. M., Neale, J. M., & Davidson, E. S. *The early window: Effects of television on children and youth.* New York: Pergamon Press, 1973.

Lorenz, K. *On aggression.* New York: Harcourt, Brace & World, 1963.

McCorkle, L. W., Elias, A., & Buxby, F. L. *The Highfields story.* New York: Holt, Rinehart & Winston, 1958.

McFall, R. M. *Behavioral training: A skill acquisition approach to clinical problems.* Chicago: General Learning Press, 1976.

McPhail, P., Ungoed-Thomas, J. R., & Chapman, H. *Learning to care: Rationale and method of the lifeline program.* Niles, Ill.: Argus Communications, 1975.

Maier, N. R. F. *Frustration: The study of behavior without a goal.* New York: McGraw-Hill, 1949.

Mayer, H. C. *The good American program.* New York: American Viewpoint, 1964.

Meier, R. The new criminology: Continuity in criminological theory. *Journal of Criminal Law and Criminology,* 1976, *67,* 461-469.

Miller, J. P. *Humanizing the classroom: Models of teaching in affective education.* New York: Praeger, 1976.

Miller, N. E. The frustration-aggression hypothesis. *Psychological Review,* 1941, *48,* 337-342.

Morris, D. *The naked ape.* New York: McGraw-Hill, 1967.

Mulvihill, D. J., Tumin, M. M., & Curtis, L. A. *Crimes of violence.* Vol. 13. Report to the National Commission on the Causes and Prevention of Violence. Washington, D.C.: Government Printing Office, 1969.

Neitzel, M. T. *Crime and its modification.* New York: Pergamon Press, 1979.

Newman, F., & Oliver, D. *Clarifying public issues: An approach to teaching social studies.* Boston: Little, Brown, 1970.

Newton, G. D., & Zimring, F. E. *Firearms and violence in American life.* Vol. VII. Report to the National Commission on the Causes and Prevention of Violence. Washington, D.C.: U.S. Government Printing Office, 1970.

Novaco, N. W. *Anger control.* Lexington, Mass.: Lexington Books, 1975.

Osborn, A. F. *Applied imagination.* New York: Charles Scribner & Sons, 1953.

Parnes, S. J. *Creative behavior guidebook.* New York: Charles Scribner & Sons, 1967.

Patterson, G. R., & Gullion, M. E. *Living with children.* Champaign, Ill.: Research Press, 1974.

Patterson, G. R., & Reid, J. B. Intervention for families of aggressive boys: A replication study. *Behavior Research & Therapy,* 1973, *11,* 383-394.

Phillips, E. L., Wolf, M. M., Fixen, D. L., & Bailey, J. S. The Achievement Place model. In J. L. Khanna (Ed.), *New treatment approaches to juvenile delinquency.* Springfield, Ill.: Charles C Thomas, 1975.

Price, W. H., & Whatmore, P. B. Criminal behavior and the XYY male. *Nature,* 1967, *213.*

Quinney, R. *Critique of legal order: Crime control in capitalist society.* Boston: Little, Brown, 1974.

Raths, L. E., Harmin, M., & Simon, S. B. *Values and teaching: Working with values in the classroom.* Columbus, Ohio: Charles Merrill, 1966.

Redl, F., & Wineman, D. *Controls with within: Techniques for the treatment of the aggressive child.* Glencove, Ill.: Free Press, 1952.

Redl, F., & Wineman, D. *The aggressive child.* New York. Free Press, 1957.

Richardson, C., & Meyer, R. G. Techniques in guided group interaction programs. *Child Welfare,* 1972, *51,* 519-527.

Rosenbaum, A. Wife abuse: Characteristics of the participants and etiological considerations. Unpublished doctoral dissertation, SUNY at Stony Brook, 1979.

Rosenbaum, A., & O'Leary, K. D. Marital violence: Characteristics of abusive couples. *Journal of Consulting and Clinical Psychology,* 1981, *49,* 63-71.

Rosenthal, D. *Genetic theory and abnormal behavior.* New York: McGraw-Hill, 1970.

Schur, E. *Labeling deviant behavior: Its sociological implications.* New York: Random House, 1969.

Seckel, J. P. *The Freemont experiment: Assessment of residential treatment at youth authority reception center.* Sacramento: California Department of Youth Authority, 1967.

Sheldon, W. H. *Varieties of delinquent youth: An introduction to constitutional psychiatry.* New York: Harper & Brothers, 1949.

Shure, M. B., & Spivack, G. *Problem-solving techniques in childrearing.* San Francisco: Jossey-Bass, 1978.

Simon, S. B., Howe, L. W., & Kirschenbaum, H. *Values clarification: A handbook of practical strategies for teachers and students.* New York: Hart, 1972.

Sommer, R. *The end of imprisonment.* New York: Oxford University Press, 1976.

Spivack, G., Platt, J. J., & Shure, M. B. *The problem-solving approach to adjustment.* San Francisco: Jossey-Bass, 1976.

Spivack, G., & Shure, M. B. *Social adjustment of young children.* San Francisco: Jossey-Bass, 1974.

Staub, E. *Positive social behavior and morality.* New York: Academic Press, 1978.

Stephens, T. M. *Directive teaching of children with learning and behavioral handicaps.* Columbus, Ohio: Charles E. Merrill, 1976.

Storr, A. *Human aggression.* New York: Bantam, 1970.

Strauss, M. A. Wife beating: How common and why? *Victimology,* 1977-78, *2,* 443-458.

Stuart, R. B. Behavioral contracting within the families of delinquents. *Journal of Behavior Therapy and Experimental Psychiatry,* 1971, *2,* 1-11.

Sutherland, E. H. *Principles in criminology.* Philadelphia: Lippincott, 1947.

Toch, H. *Violent men.* Chicago: Aldine, 1969.

Trevitt, V. *The American heritage: Design for national character.* Santa Barbara, Calif.: McNally & Loftin, 1964.

Vorrath, H. H., & Bendtro, L. K. *Positive peer culture.* Chicago: Aldine, 1974.

Wahlroos, S. *Family communication.* New York: Macmillan, 1974.

Walker, C. E. *Learn to relax.* Englewood Cliffs, N.J.: Spectrum Books, 1975.

Weinstein, G., & Fantini, M. *Toward humanistic education: A curriculum of affect.* New York: Praeger, 1970.

Wilson, J. *Practical methods of moral education.* London: Heinemann Educational Books, 1972.

Zillmann, D. *Hostility and aggression.* Hillsdale, N.J.: Erlbaum, 1979.

Zinberg, N. E., & Fellman, G. A. Violence: Biological need and social control. *Social Forces,* 1967, 45, 533-541.

Afterword

We set out in this project to take a global perspective on human aggression. By this we meant two things—to examine aggression wherever in the world it occurs; and to view aggression as an array of behaviors that probably relate, in varying degrees, to a large number of factors—ecological, cultural, social, economic, physiological, and psychological—in complex interaction. To pursue this two-fold objective, we have sampled a number of contemporary societies, and have found that aggression is a matter of concern in all of them. At the same time, aggression was shown to vary in its forms and functions in ways that reflect the cultural context in which it is shaped, manifested, and controlled.

An overwhelming impression that one must gain from the bulk of accounts contained in this volume is that child-rearing antecedents must loom large in any framework that attempts to explain human aggressive behavior. It cannot be understood except as a complex product of the experiences that human beings have while growing up, wherever in the world they happen to be born.

This overarching generalization subsumes numerous others which may be derived from, and are consistent with, the pictures provided by the contributors to this volume. Among these, the following are among the most provocative.

1. Aggression is predominantly "masculine" behavior. Males tend to commit most of the aggressive acts described by our contributors. The availability of male role models and the behavior they display for emulation by their children is clearly implicated in the traits acquired by their children, particularly their sons. The nature of the relationships between the sexes during adulthood, which varies across societies, contributes, both positively and negatively, to the probability that aggression will be encouraged, emulated, and otherwise learned. In certain cases, a kind of compensatory machismo, of which displays of aggressive behavior will be a salient feature, will be alikely product of the way men relate to women and the way parents relate to their children.

2. The structure and function of societies matters greatly. The ability of "states" to provide for the needs of their citizens, to approach equity in the distribution of resources, to minimize stresses and frustrations, and to gain the respect and support of their citizenry affects the probability of both individual and collective aggression.

3. The role of certain forms of socially-sanctioned aggressive "outlets" such as body-contact athletic contests, e.g., soccer and rugby, may be, to the embarrassment of catharsis theory, to set the stage for and serve as a trigger for, non-socially-sanctioned violence. Similarly, postwar periods do not seem generally to be characterized by declines in internal violence.

4. The degree of cultural or ethnic homogeneity/heterogeneity of a society does not predict

very well the degree of aggression within the society. The nature of the culture(s) seems to be much more critical.

5. Punitiveness, either within families or in social institutions such as criminal justice systems, may very well enhance aggressive behavior. At least, the chapters contained in this volume provide no evidence that punitiveness reduces aggression.

6. For most of the societies described in the present volume, punishment of crime is more prevalent than efforts designed to prevent it. While a movement away from the death penalty and other extreme forms of punishment may be discerned and while efforts to control the availability of guns are underway in many countries, aggression control is still most often and most widely thought of in terms of after-the-fact reactions rather than prevention.

7. There is a disconcerting gap between the perceptions of the causes and consequent means of reducing aggression held by scholars and the citizenry of nearly all of the nations in which the scholars do their research. Popular beliefs about aggression are profoundly more pessimistic, in that they tend to treat aggression as inevitable and demanding punitiveness. Ironically, even if the scholars are right in their relative optimism, they will not be proven right until they somehow succeed in changing the perceptions of the public. For those public perceptions and beliefs necessarily contribute to self-fulfilling prophecies that will serve to maintain aggression at higher levels than would otherwise be the case.

These few generalizations, and several others that readers of this volume may glean for themselves from what they have read in it, do not comprise a complete answer to the question of why humans aggress in the ways and to the extent they do. To understand aggression and its antecedents, and to be in a position to prescribe programs and policies to reduce it, requires an ongoing research program to which, we hope, this volume can serve as both an introduction and an inspiration. The generalizations derivable from it we offer, then, not as answers but as hypotheses. We and the colleagues who joined us in the present effort will surely continue to search for hypotheses that are latent in our collective knowledge of aggression in the various societies in which we live. We invite our readers to do the same. And we trust that they and we will go forward with research on human aggression that is designed within a global framework, research that seeks details about the complex process whereby we humans, through our cultural creations, make subsequent generations in each of the ecocultural settings in which they will dwell, more or less aggressive than those of us who preceded them.

Author Index

Subject Index

Achievement orientation, 226
Action theory, 88, 91-93
Aggravated assault, 165-167
Aggression, acquisition, 447-449
  and age, 353-354
  and alcohol, 105-106, 336-337
  and authority, 354-355
  and childrearing, 338-339, 422
  and driving, 335-336
  and economic change, 105, 290
  and ethnicity, 179-183, 350-351
  and external conflict, 263
  and mass media, 465-466
  and modeling, 31
  and parental dominance, 194
  and personal myth, 344-345
  and psychoanalysis, 49-50
  and public abuse, 66-68
  and socialization, 315-316, 338-339
  and stress indicators, 266-267
  antecedants of, 186-191
  anthropological evidence, 5-21
  as instinct, 4-5
  causes of, 360-362
  childhood inculcation, 8-10
  collective, 68, 70, 238, 409-411
  control of, 100
  cosmic determinants, 241
  cross-cultural perspective, 1-43
  cultural context, 420-421
  cultural meaning, 263-264
  definition of, 22-23, 88, 287
  demographic factors, 314
  developmental aspects, 357-359
  development of, 222-226
  drive theory, 53, 91, 444-446
  ecological factors, 314-315
  economic antecedants, 411-414

economic causes, 428
effect on children, 386-392
employment factors, 316
environmental factors, 315-316
ethnographic evidence, 5-8
ethological approach, 50-51
familial antecedants, 315-316
family context, 421
functional analysis of, 401-402
gender-specific characteristics, 224-226
genetic influences, 61-62
geographic distribution, 380-384
habituation to, 386-392
hologeistic research, 7-8
ideological, 251-253
in children, 222-226
in China, 58-74
in Finland, 104-144
in France, 145-158
in Hawaii, 159-192
inhibition of, 62-64, 112
in Holland, 193-220
in Hungary, 221-236
in India, 237-260
in Israel, 261-286
in Italy, 287-312
in Japan, 313-324
in New Zealand, 325-347
in Nigeria, 348-366
in Northern Ireland, 367-400
in Peru, 401-418
in schools, 94-96
in sports, 332-333
instinct theory, 91, 444
instrumental, 92
instrumental use, 308
in the United States, 435-474
in Turkey, 418-434

About the Editors

Arnold P. Goldstein is Professor of Psychology and Director of the Center for Research on Aggression at Syracuse University. His research and writing have focused on seeking to understand and alter highly deviant behavior. This broad interest has been reflected in research on psychotherapy with resistive and chronic patients, behavior modification interventions with aggressive adolescents, and social skills training for child abusing and other antisocial individuals. His earlier books include *In Response to Aggression, Aggress-Less, Skillstreaming the Adolescent, School Violence, Hostage, Police Crisis Intervention, Psychological Skills Training,* and *Structured Learning Therapy.*

Marshall H. Segall is Professor of Social and Political Psychology in the Maxwell School at Syracuse University. His scholarly efforts have centered on the applications of psychology to the analysis of public policy alternatives in diverse societies. A cross-cultural psychologist, his current work emphasizes problems of economic and social development in sub-Saharan Africa. His earlier books include *Cross-Cultural Psychology: Human Behavior in Global Perspective, Human Behavior and Public Policy, Political Identity: A Case Study from Uganda,* and *The Influence of Culture on Visual Perception* (with D. T. Campbell and M. J. Herskovits).

Contributors

Henry I. Amatu
Alvan Ikoku College of Education
Owerri, Imo State
Nigeria

Jose Anicama
Department of Psychology
Universidad Peruana Cayetano Heredia
Lima, Peru

Ben Baarda
Department of Educational Psychology
State University of Utrecht
Utrecht, Holland

Benjamin Beit-Hallahmi
Department of Psychology
University of Haifa
Mount Carmel, Haifa
Israel

Agehananda Bharati
Department of Anthropology
Syracuse University
Syracuse, NY

Angela M. B. Biaggio
Universidade Federal do Rio Grande do Sul
Pós-Graduação em Educação
Porto Alegre, RS, Brazil

D. Caroline Blanchard
Bekesy Laboratory of Neurobiology
University of Hawaii
Honolulu, Hawaii

Robert J. Blanchard
Department of Psychology
University of Hawaii
Honolulu, Hawaii

Leonard Bloom
Department of Sociology
University of Calabar
Calabar, Nigeria

Michael H. Bond
Psychology Section
New Asia College
The Chinese University of Hong Kong
Shatin, N.T., Hong Kong

Dr. Francesco Bruno
Via dei Prati
Rome, Italy

Renaud DuLong
Centre d'Etude des Mouvements Sociaux
Paris, France

Franco Ferracuti
Facolta Di Medicina
Citta Universitaria
Roma, Italy

Guler Okman Fisek
Social Sciences Department
Bogazici University
Istanbul, Turkey

495

Arnold P. Goldstein
Department of Psychology and Center for
    Research on Aggression
Syracuse University
Syracuse, NY, U.S.A.

Susan B. Goldstein
Psychology Department and East-West
    Center
University of Hawaii
Honolulu, Hawaii

Jo Groebel
Institut für Psychologie der Rheinisch-
    Westfalischen
Technischen Hochschule
Aachen, West Germany

Toshio Ibaraki
College of Education
Saitama University
Saitama-ken, Japan

Simha F. Landau
Institute of Criminology
Hebrew University of Jerusalem
Jerusalem, Israel

Liz McWhirter
Department of Psychology
Queen's University of Belfast
Belfast, Northern Ireland

Lea Pulkkinen
Department of Psychology
University of Jyvaskyla
Jyvaskyla, Finland

Jenö Ranschburg
Department of Developmental Psychology
Institute for Psychology
Budapest, Hungary

James Ritchie
University of Waikato
Hamilton, New Zealand

Jane Ritchie
University of Waikato
Hamilton, New Zeland

Marshall H. Segall
Social and Political Psychology Program
    and Center for Research on Aggression
Syracuse University
Syracuse, NY
U.S.A.

Erwin Seydel
Department of Psychology
Technische Hogeschool Tivente
Enschede, Holland

Wang Sung-hsing
Anthropology Section
New Asia College
The Chinese University of Hong Kong
Shatin, N.T., Hong Kong

Oene Wiegman
Department of Psychology
Technische Hogeschool Tivente
Enschede, Holland

Pergamon General Psychology Series

Editors: Arnold P. Goldstein, Syracuse University
Leonard Krasner, SUNY at Stony Brook

DATE